Semantics

Semantics vs. Pragmatics

EDITED BY

Zoltán Gendler Szabó

CLARENDON PRESS • OXFORD

OXFORD
UNIVERSITY PRESS

Great Clarendon Street, Oxford OX2 6DP

Oxford University Press is a department of the University of Oxford.
It furthers the University's objective of excellence in research, scholarship,
and education by publishing worldwide in

Oxford New York

Auckland Cape Town Dar es Salaam Hong Kong Karachi
Kuala Lumpur Madrid Melbourne Mexico City Nairobi
New Delhi Shanghai Taipei Toronto

With offices in

Argentina Austria Brazil Chile Czech Republic France Greece
Guatemala Hungary Italy Japan South Korea Poland Portugal
Singapore Switzerland Thailand Turkey Ukraine Vietnam

Oxford is a registered trade mark of Oxford University Press
in the UK and in certain other countries

Published in the United States
by Oxford University Press Inc., New York

British Library Cataloguing in Publication Data

Data available

Library of Congress Cataloging in Publication Data

Data available

ISBN 0-19-925151-7
ISBN 0-19-925152-5 (pbk.)

1 2 3 4 5 6 7 8 9 10

Typeset by Newgen Imaging Systems (P) Ltd., Chennai, India
Printed in Great Britain
on acid-free paper by
Biddles Ltd, King's Lynn, Norfolk

ACKNOWLEDGEMENTS

I thank Oxford University Press for their assistance in bringing this volume to publication. In particular, I am grateful to Rebecca Bryant, Rupert Cousens, Peter Momtchiloff, and to two anonymous referees for their encouragement, help, and advice. Special thanks to Laurien Berkeley for her excellent copy-editing and for her supererogatory patience.

I am grateful to Allyson Mount for her precise and conscientious reading of all the final drafts including my Introduction, for her corrections, her clarificatory questions, and the excellent index she prepared for the volume. And, of course, to Tamar, who—as usual—helped me at every step.

Z. G. S.

CONTENTS

LIST OF CONTRIBUTORS

Kent Bach, San Francisco State University

Herman Cappelen, Vassar College

Michael Glanzberg, University of California, Davis

Jeffrey C. King, University of Southern California

Ernie Lepore, Rutgers University

Stephen Neale, Rutgers University

François Recanati, Centre National de la Recherche Scientifique, Paris

Nathan Salmon, University of California, Santa Barbara

Mandy Simons, Carnegie Mellon University

Scott Soames, University of Southern California

Robert J. Stainton, University of Western Ontario

Jason Stanley, Rutgers University

Zoltán Gendler Szabó, Cornell University

Introduction

According to the semiotic trichotomy proposed by Charles Morris in 1938, *syntax* is the study of "the formal relation of signs to one another", *semantics* is the study of "the relations of signs to objects to which the signs are applicable", and *pragmatics* is the study of "the relation of signs to interpreters".[1] Even today, this is roughly the way most philosophers and linguists conceive of the fundamental divisions within the domain of theoretical linguistics.[2] But there are dissenters: those who believe that the task of semantics does not extend beyond providing adequate translation manuals cannot accept this distinction between syntax and semantics, and those who subscribe to the view that the meaning of a linguistic expression is identical to its use must reject the proposed distinction between semantics and pragmatics.

Drawing the line between semantics and pragmatics is particularly problematic. Even if we reject the most radical versions of the use theory of meaning,[3] the question remains how the relation between linguistic expressions and the world can be studied in isolation from the way these expressions are employed in speech and writing. After all, a large part of what semantics is supposed to explain are judgments regarding the truth or falsity of certain sentences in certain actual or merely imagined circumstances—and these are hard to

---

[1] Charles Morris, *Foundations of a Theory of Signs* (Chicago: University of Chicago Press, 1938), 6. (Morris uses the now unusual term 'syntactics' for what has come to be called 'syntax'.)

[2] Of course, the definitions are supposed to be restricted to *linguistic* signs. Even so, Morris's definitions of syntax and pragmatics are rather broad: the former includes both phonology and morphology, the latter pretty much everything that is covered these days by psycho- and socio-linguistics.

[3] Radical versions of the use theory are hopeless. The meaning of an expression cannot be identified with its *actual* use (for there are many meaningful complex expressions which have never been used) or its *potential* use (for expressions could be used in ways that are incompatible with their actual meanings). Any sensible version of the use theory must identify meaning with certain *norms* of usage—the question is whether there is a non-circular way to specify *which* ones.

separate from judgments about the appropriateness or inappropriateness of certain uses of those sentences. For example, since the sentence 'I tried to drink my coffee' is decidedly inappropriate in describing a perfectly usual breakfast in which I easily downed two cups, the temptation is strong to say that the sentence cannot be true in that sort of situation, which in turn must be reflected somehow in the very meaning of the word 'try'.

Many have felt that such a temptation must be resisted, but the first systematic attempt to say why is due to Paul Grice. He recognized that what we need is "a theory which will enable one to distinguish between the case in which an utterance is inappropriate because it is false or fails to be true, or more generally fails to correspond with the world in some favored way, and the case in which it is inappropriate for reasons of a different kind".[4] The significance of such a theory goes well beyond linguistics or even philosophy of language. Contextualists about knowledge insist that ascriptions of knowledge vary in their truth-conditions depending on the contextual standard available at the time of the ascription; non-cognitivists believe that the expressive character of utterances of moral sentences guarantee that they cannot be true or false; nominalists attempt sophisticated explanations of how serious utterances of apparently true mathematical sentences can fail to be true. These proposals can only be properly evaluated if we have a principled and empirically well-grounded way to make distinctions among inappropriate utterances.

Grice does outline such a theory about linguistic communication but, strikingly, fails to be fully explicit about just how the theory is supposed to accomplish the task it is designed to achieve. Nonetheless, most commentators have assumed that the distinction between *what is said* and *what is implicated* is doing the trick. The distinction is made within what Grice called "the total signification of an utterance", which he equates with *what is meant* by the speaker.[5] A successful utterance

---

[4] Paul Grice, 'Prolegomena', in his *Studies in the Way of Words* (Cambridge, Mass.: Harvard University Press, 1989), 4. The idea that we need to catalogue carefully the different ways in which utterances can be inappropriate goes back to J. L. Austin; cf. *How to Do Things with Words* (Cambridge, Mass.: Harvard University Press, 1962), esp. lectures III and IV. Austin, however, was deeply suspicious of the possibility of a fully systematic theory about matters of language.

[5] Paul Grice, 'Further Notes on Logic and Conversation' and 'Utterer's Meaning, Sentence Meaning, and Word Meaning', in his *Studies in the Way of Words*, 41 and 118. The term is thus somewhat misleading: there is information to be extracted from an utterance that is not part of its total signification. When you hear me utter the words 'We have a nice day today', you can be quite certain that I am alive and awake, that I speak English, and if you are good at that sort of thing, you can even determine that I am not a native speaker. None of these were said or implicated in Grice's sense; I conveyed them without meaning to do so.

might be inappropriate because the speaker *said* something false—or because he *implicated* something false. Thus, an utterance of 'I tried to drink my coffee' in describing a perfectly usual breakfast is true but inappropriate because the speaker falsely implicated that he encountered some difficulty in imbibing. Semantics is concerned with what is said, pragmatics with what is implicated, and utterance interpretation—the process whereby the addressee ascertains what the speaker meant—has typically both a semantic and a pragmatic component. Call the view that draws the line between semantics and pragmatics this way the *traditional view*.

The traditional view is Gricean in its origin and motivation, but there are reasons to doubt that Grice himself held such a view. The least important reason is that he doesn't actually use the terms 'semantics' and 'pragmatics'. More significant is his commitment that there are components of the total signification of an utterance that are contributed by the conventional meanings of linguistic expressions but which nonetheless fail to belong to what is said. According to Grice, when the speaker combines two clauses with the words 'but' or 'therefore', instead of the word 'and', his choice does not affect what he said. Rather, he manages to conventionally implicate something—some sort of contrast in the case of 'but', or entailment in the case of 'therefore'. Since conventional implicature *is* a matter of linguistic meaning, it would be odd to say that Grice intended to exclude it from the scope of semantics. Finally, and even more significantly, the force of an utterance (the feature that distinguishes the case where 'Could you close the window?' is uttered as a question from the case where it is uttered as a request) is hard to locate in this picture. It cannot be part of what is said (it is part of *how* what is said is said) and it doesn't seem to be part of what is implicated (it isn't merely suggested or intimated). Nonetheless, force is part of what the speaker meant and it would be most unfair to assume that Grice intended to exclude it both from semantics and pragmatics.[6]

Whether or not Grice adopted it, the traditional view is still popular among philosophers. (Linguists tend to be more critical or at least more guarded in their approval.) Nonetheless, it may well be that some of the simplicity and intuitive appeal comes from a lack of clarity about what the view is actually committed to. Let me elaborate.

Consider a case when you are looking for the exit and in order to help you out I sincerely utter 'It's on the left'. There are two ways to think about what I meant

---

[6] Indeed, when he characterizes his wider program, he tends to restrict the scope of the distinction between what is said and what is implicated to "a large class of utterances" (ibid. 41) or "remarks" (ibid. 118), by which he presumably means assertions.

when I made my utterance. On the one hand, I certainly meant to bring about a certain effect—that you turn left and walk to the exit—and this was the reason I made the utterance. If you don't trust me and don't turn, there is a clear sense in which my utterance failed. But there is also another sense in which all I meant was to tell you that the exit is on the left, and in this I most likely succeeded even if I fail to get you to turn. Following Austin, we should distinguish between the *perlocutionary* and *illocutionary* acts involved in my utterance, and corresponding to these what I meant *by* the utterance (i.e. that you turn left and walk to the exit) and what I meant *in* making it (i.e. that the exit is on the left). Which one should we regard as the Gricean notion of what is meant, with respect to which the semantics–pragmatics distinction is to be drawn? If the aim of utterance interpretation is to make sense of the speaker's action in relation to the audience, we need to know what he meant by the utterance; if the aim is to state what the speaker did, irrespective of the addressee's reaction, we need to know what he meant in making it.[7]

Consider now the question of what I said when I uttered the sentence 'It's on the left' in the story described above. Again, there seem to be two ways to approach the question: their difference can be brought out by asking whether I said *what* it is that is on the left. In one sense I did not—I didn't have to, since in the context of my utterance it was clear that I am talking about the exit. In another sense I certainly did—I asserted that the exit is on the left. Again following Austin, we might want to distinguish between the *locutionary* act of saying (i.e. uttering certain meaningful words) from the *illocutionary* act of saying (i.e. performing a speech act in uttering those words). Corresponding to these two acts there are two notions of what is said—one that is neutral about what is said to be on the left in our case, and another that isn't. Which one is supposed

---

[7] This might make a big difference in the following sort of case, discussed by John Searle. An American soldier in the Second World War wishes to convince the Italians who have captured him that he is a German officer by uttering the only German sentence he knows: 'Kennst du das Land wo die Zitronen blühen?' Intuitively, Searle insists, the American did not mean that he was a German soldier. The moral for Searle is that in order for a speaker to mean something, he must intend that his primary intention to convey something be recognized *in virtue of the addressee's knowledge of the conventional meaning of the words he employed*; cf. John Searle, *Speech Acts* (Cambridge: Cambridge University Press, 1965), 49–50. But this revision has drastic consequences: it forecloses to possibility of a non-circular explanation of the emergence of conventional meaning from speaker meaning. One thing Grice *could* have responded to Searle is that although the soldier did not mean anything *in* making the utterance, he did mean something *by* making it and speaker meaning is a matter of the latter, not the former. But, as a matter of fact, he said something else instead; cf. Paul Grice, 'Utterer's Meaning and Intentions', 100–4.

to mark the scope of semantics? If semantics is supposed to be confined to what we know about linguistic expressions solely in virtue of being competent speakers of the language to which those expressions belong, its subject matter is what is said in the locutionary sense; if it is supposed to be fully explicit about how linguistic expressions relate to the world it deals with, its subject matter is what is said in the illocutionary sense.[8]

Drawing the distinctions between the locutionary and illocutionary senses of saying and between the illocutionary and perlocutionary senses of meaning may help to clarify the traditional view, but it is unlikely to preserve its intuitive appeal. Even if we take the ambiguities into account and we say that the semantics–pragmatics distinction is, for example, the distinction between what is said (illocutionary sense—in the cases traditionally focused upon: what is asserted) and what is meant (illocutionary sense—in the cases traditionally focused upon: what is communicated), the pretense of terminological innocence is gone. Asserting and communicating are not the notions of our "folk-theory" about talking—they are semi-technical terms waiting for further elaboration. Drawing the semantics–pragmatics boundary is not a matter of assigning a new label to a distinction we all make anyway in our ordinary thinking.[9]

---

[8] In discussing an utterance of 'He is in the grip of vice', Grice says that in order to fully specify what the speaker said we need to know *who* is said to be unable to rid himself of a bad character trait; cf. Paul Grice, 'Logic and Conversation' in his *Studies in the Way of Words*, 25. He would probably make an analogous commitment in the case of an utterance of 'It's on the left'. This probably settles that he did not construe 'what is said' along locutionary lines. It does not, however, settle whether he understood it in the illocutionary sense, or attached to it some vague intermediate sense. I am inclined to think that the latter is the case. Instead of asking whether I said *what* it is that is on the left, we might ask whether I said *which direction* the exit is. My utterance settles that question only if it is clear how the addressee is oriented in space. If Grice used 'what is said' in the illocutionary sense (in the sense of 'what is asserted') he would have to say that in order to know what is said by the speaker of an utterance of 'It's on the left' one must know the spatial orientation of the addressee. I doubt that Grice would have allowed this: he was firmly committed to the claim that what is said by the speaker of an utterance is tightly correlated with "the elements of [the sentence], their order, and their syntactic character"; cf. Paul Grice, 'Utterer's Meaning and Intentions', 87. If so, the only way to insist that the spatial orientation of the addressee is part of what is said would be to postulate some unpronounced element in the sentence that identifies it. Given Grice's general methodology, I think it unlikely that he would have been ready to do this. For further discussion of Grice's notion of 'what is said', see Kent Bach, 'You Don't Say', *Synthese*, 128 (2001), 15–44.

[9] The ways we *actually* use expressions like 'what she said' or 'what she meant' seem to be rather undisciplined. Standards of what counts as an adequate report of what a speaker said on an occasion (let alone what she meant) are subject to complicated and prima facie haphazard contextual changes; cf. Herman Cappelen and Ernie Lepore, 'On an Alleged Connection between Indirect Quotation and Semantic Theory', *Mind and Language*, 12 (1997), 278–96.

Once we see beyond the blanket terms 'what is said' and 'what is meant' it becomes obvious that there are a number of important distinctions that *could* be called the semantics–pragmatics divide. The best way to advance conceptual clarity and explanatory progress is perhaps not to focus on one or another of these distinctions prematurely, but to catalogue them so we can discuss their relations to one another. Only after we have explored the bordering region of semantics and pragmatics can we figure out which one of these (if any) divides the subject matter in a way that is both in harmony with current usage and makes best theoretical sense. Here are six reasonably clear theoretical divisions to be considered; there are probably more. (I restrict attention here to what is conveyed—intentionally or not—in assertions.)

(*a*) *Competence.* Typically, some but not all of what the speaker conveys could be grasped by any competent speaker without special knowledge.

(*b*) *Encoding.* Typically, some but not all of what the speaker conveys is encoded in the expression uttered.

(*c*) *Compositionality.* Typically, some but not all of what the speaker conveys is compositionally determined (by the syntax and the lexicon).

(*d*) *Rules.* Typically, some but not all of what the speaker conveys can be ascertained by following rules, as opposed to elaborate cognitive strategies.

(*e*) *Truth-conditionality.* Typically, some but not all of what the speaker conveys is truth-conditionally relevant.

(*f*) *Intention-independence.* Typically, some but not all of what the speaker conveys is independent of the speaker's specific intentions to talk about this or that.

It is not obvious that any two of these divisions coincide. Connotations (e.g. that 'dude' is informal and that 'Know you not the cause?' is archaic) are linguistically encoded, but knowledge of them is arguably not required for competence, so (*a*) and (*b*) come apart. We follow rules for interpreting intonation patterns but not all these rules are determined by the syntax and the lexicon, so (*c*) and (*d*) come apart. Disambiguation is clearly truth-conditionally relevant but it cannot be done without taking into account the intentions of the speaker, so (*e*) and (*f*) come apart. And so on—as far as I can tell—for any one of the remaining twelve pairs.

Where a piece of information conveyed in making an assertive utterance lies relative to these six distinctions is often hard to know. Is knowledge that 'John is a bachelor' entails 'John is unmarried' part of our linguistic competence or part of what we know about the world, i.e. knowledge of the nature of the properties of being a bachelor and being unmarried?[10] Is it linguistically encoded in 'Jack hates Jack' that in an utterance of such a sentence the names are presumed to refer to different people?[11] Is what someone asserts in uttering 'This leaf is green' compositionally determined, given that the truth of the assertion appears to depend on whether the speaker is sorting leaves for decoration or for the purposes of biological classification?[12] Is there a rule for assigning reference to occurrences of demonstratives, or is saying that they refer to what is being demonstrated (even if in fact there is no observable demonstration!) just a thinly veiled confession that there is *no* rule we could *follow*?[13] Is focus ever truth-conditionally irrelevant, given that 'John only introduced Bill to *Sue*' can be true even if 'John only introduced *Bill* to Sue' is false?[14] Is the reference of 'I' fixed independently of the specific intentions of the speaker, even in an utterance of a condemned prisoner of 'I am traditionally allowed to order whatever I want for my last meal'?[15]

All these questions lie at the border of semantics and pragmatics—in fact, they are often described as debates concerning the question whether a certain linguistic phenomenon is semantic or pragmatic in character. The fact that we do not have a robust and widely agreed upon explicit conception of what that distinction really amounts to does not make the debates futile: perhaps the participants share a tacit and fairly rich underlying conception of the distinction, a conception that has yet to be adequately articulated. Or, if this optimistic assumption proves illusory, perhaps there are a *few* such conceptions at play, some in some debates, and others in others. Either way, work needs to be done

[10] The standard answer is that this part of linguistic competence, but Fodor has long argued that the standard answer is wrong; cf. e.g. Jerry Fodor, *Concepts: Where Cognitive Science Went Wrong* (Oxford: Clarendon Press, 1998).

[11] Given that Chomsky's Principle A requires non-coindexing of the two names, the standard answer is 'yes'. For a dissent, see Stephen Levinson, *Presumptive Meanings* (Cambridge, Mass.: MIT Press, 2000).

[12] For an argument against compositionality using this example, cf. Charles Travis, 'On Constraints of Generality', *Proceedings of the Aristotelian Society*, new ser., 44 (1994), 165–88. For a reply, cf. Zoltán Gendler Szabó, 'Adjectives in Context', in I. Kenesei and R. M. Harnish (eds.), *Perspectives on Semantics, Pragmatics, and Discourse* (Amsterdam: John Benjamins, 2001), 119–46.

[13] The standard answer is, of course, that there is a rule we follow in fixing the referent of a demonstrative. For a negative view, see Dan Sperber and Deirdre Wilson, *Relevance: Communication and Cognition* (Cambridge, Mass.: Harvard University Press, 1986).

[14] Until Mats Rooth's dissertation 'Association with Focus' (University of Massachusetts, 1985) it was widely believed that focus is truth-conditionally inert (at least in English).

[15] Examples like this are discussed in detail in Geoffrey Nunberg, 'Indexicality and Deixis', *Linguistics and Philosophy*, 16 (1993), 1–43. The orthodox view that in any context of its utterance 'I' rigidly refers to the speaker comes from David Kaplan, 'Demonstratives: An Essay on the Semantics, Logic, Metaphysics, and Epistemology of Demonstratives and Other Indexicals', in J. Almog, J. Perry, and H. Wettstein (eds.), *Themes from Kaplan* (Oxford: Oxford University Press, 1989).

to bring the tacit conception(s) to the fore. The central aim of this volume is to contribute to a new debate about how this could be done.[16]

Some of the chapters in this volume defend a comprehensive view about the borderline between semantics and pragmatics while others look at phenomena that may fall on either side of this divide. In most cases these investigations go hand in hand: specific analyses of focus, presupposition, anaphora resolution, and the like may support or refute a general view about how to distinguish semantics from pragmatics, and the general view may in turn support or refute further specific analyses. In what follows, I provide a brief summary of the chapters.

Kent Bach has long argued for a conception of the semantics–pragmatics distinction that is Gricean in spirit, even though it abandons some of the key features of the traditional view. He agrees with Grice that the scope of the semantic is marked by what is said and that elements of what is said correspond tightly with elements of the linguistic expression that says it. (In fact, he construes the notion of what is said in a purely locutionary sense.) At the same time, he also thinks that what a typical declarative sentence says is not a complete proposition, and is consequently not even a candidate for being meant by the speaker. According to this picture, the gap between what is said and what is meant is a lot more glaring than it is for Grice, and this gap cannot be filled exclusively through implicature. Bach's chapter in this volume pulls together the main threads of this general view on linguistic communication, defending ten key theses. The underlying theme of his defense is that considerations that have moved him along with many other linguists and philosophers beyond the traditional view are insufficient to undermine the cogency of a clear semantics–pragmatics distinction. The thin, non-propositional semantic content he assigns to most declarative sentences may not be easily accessible to ordinary intuitions, and it may not be explicitly represented in the mind of the interpreter. Nonetheless, Bach argues, for both conceptual and empirical reasons we cannot abandon this notion.

The chapter by *Herman Cappelen* and *Ernie Lepore* is a defense of truth-conditional semantics against arguments from underdetermination. These arguments

---

[16] For other recent detailed discussions of different conceptions of the semantics–pragmatics distinction, see ch. 1 of Stephen Levinson, *Pragmatics* (Cambridge: Cambridge University Press, 1983), K. Turner (ed.), *The Semantics–Pragmatics Interface from Different Points of View* (Oxford: Elsevier Science, 1999), and Zoltán Gendler Szabó, 'The Distinction between Semantics and Pragmatics', in E. Lepore and B. Smith (eds.), *The Oxford Handbook of the Philosophy of Language* (Oxford: Oxford University Press, forthcoming).

charge that truth-clauses such as " 'Snow is white' is true in English iff snow is white" are insufficient to pin down semantic content. They are deemed insufficient either because they fail to answer certain crucial questions (e.g. whether snow is white even if much of it is blackened by mud) or because answers to such questions are not directed and restricted by linguistic meaning. Since the truth-conditions of (according to the radical view *all*, according to the moderate view *some*) disambiguated declarative sentences depend on these unruly contextual factors, semantic content is (in the radical version *never*, in the moderate version *rarely*) truth-conditional. Cappelen and Lepore start by arguing that the moderate version of this view collapses into the radical one: if the sorts of considerations listed in support of linguistically unconstrained context-dependence of truth-conditions work, they work for any declarative sentence. Against the radical view they point out that it fails to explain our disquotational intuitions: if the view is correct, truth-clauses for declarative sentences must be false or without truth-value, which is hard to believe. Against these sorts of considerations, Charles Travis, a defender of the radical view, has argued that utterances can *count as* true even if they are not, and that failure to make this distinction is what underlies disquotational intuitions. Cappelen and Lepore contend that such an appeal leads to inconsistencies in the radical view. The authors conclude their chapter by conceding one of the points proponents of the arguments from underdetermination insist upon: the disquotational truth-clause of declarative sentence often fails to fix what is said by utterances of that sentence. But according to them, this is not a semantically significant fact: precisely because it is extremely context-sensitive, the notion of what is said has, they insist, no place in semantics.

Philosophers often regard intuitions according to which there is a difference in meaning between 'John speaks Greek' and 'John speaks *Greek*' (uttered with pitch accent) as mistaken. Since the difference between the two sentences manifests itself only in speech, it is especially tempting to say that the distinction is pragmatic: the speaker of the second sentence implicates something not implicated by the speaker of the first (namely, that there is some other language that John might be expected to speak but in fact doesn't), but this is only a matter of what is meant, not a matter of what is said. However, associated with focus-sensitive operators (such as 'only' and adverbs of quantification) focus yields truth-conditional effects, and the phenomenon of focus-projection (among other things) strongly suggests that we need focus to be represented at the level of syntactic structure. A fairly standard reaction to these observations has been to stick with the usual pragmatic account of focus (according to which focused material is in some sense *new*, whereas the rest of the sentence represents information that is *given* in the context of utterance), combine this with a sophisticated semantics for focus-sensitive operators, and derive the truth-conditional effects accordingly. *Michael Glanzberg* argues that even if the resulting theory produces the right truth-conditions, the pragmatic component does a poor job in explaining question–answer congruence and is inadequate to handle (among other things) contrastive topics: we need a different pragmatic account of the *function* of focus. The theory Glanzberg favors is one according to which foci are discourse-structuring devices which impose a general felicity condition on sentences in which they occur by relating (in a complex way) a special semantic value they have to the topic of conversation at the time of utterance. Even though foci are syntactically marked context-sensitive elements in logical form, the pragmatic mechanisms through which they influence truth-conditions cannot be anything like the processes that fix demonstrative or indexical reference. This is exactly what makes focus of special interest for those who seek to understand the semantics–pragmatics distinction.

Jeffrey King and *Jason Stanley*'s chapter has a twofold aim. On the one hand they distinguish among three conceptions of the distinction between semantics and pragmatics—one according to which semantic content is independent of context, one according to which semantic content may depend on context (including aspects of the speaker's beliefs and intentions) as long as this dependence is constrained by linguistic meaning, and an intermediate one that recognizes linguistically constrained dependence of semantic content only on non-psychological facts—and they argue for the second conception. On the other hand, the authors present evidence that—given their way of drawing the line—there is a lot more to semantics than many have recently assumed. They argue that there is no need to succumb to *semantic skepticism*—according to which a level of content that is not pervaded by unconstrained contextual effects plays no role in language understanding—or to *semantic modesty*—according to which such a role is minimal. To illustrate this, King and Stanley look at particular examples from Robyn Carston and Stephen Levinson where context is supposed to intrude in semantic content. King and Stanley object to the examples by suggesting that they neglect the role of focus in interpretation. Once we recognize this, they contend, we can see that the relevant pragmatic effects arise from the interaction between the semantics for focus and the semantics of the indicative conditional (or some other modal expression whose semantic content includes a similarity relation among possible worlds), rather than from pragmatic intrusion.

One of the fundamental uses of the semantics–pragmatics distinction in philosophy of language has been to argue against wanton postulation of ambiguities—examples include Grice's arguments against the inclusive–exclusive ambiguity of 'or', Kripke's arguments against the referential–attributive ambiguity of 'the', and Ludlow and Neale's arguments against the specific–non-specific ambiguity of 'a(n)'. But there are cases where postulating ambiguity, even when there appears to be none, may be our best theoretical option. *Stephen Neale* argues that this is so when it comes to pronouns: the combined effect of aiming at simple and predictive syntactic constraints within a language (in this case, preserving the Binding Theory for the English possessive) and of trying to bring observations across languages within the scope of a single framework (in this case, explaining why Scandinavian languages distinguish lexically between reflexive and non-reflexive possessive pronouns) may convince us that, even if we set aside deictic uses, there are still two different pronouns pronounced as /hiz/ in English. The particular argument is embedded within a sketch of a view, according to which semantics never places more than non-deterministic constraints on the interpretation of pronouns. These constraints enter utterance interpretation indirectly: the reference of a pronoun uttered is fixed by the speaker's intentions, but in reasoning about what these intentions are the addressee presumes that they are sensible, which in turn brings in presumptions of conformity with syntactic and semantic rules. The considerations of the chapter are supposed to provide support for the general outlook (if not all the particular details) of Gareth Evans's theory of pronouns.

By contrast, *François Recanati's* chapter is an attack on the idea of ambiguity in pronouns in general, and on Evans's views in particular. Evans famously argued that we could unify anaphoric and bound uses: if anaphoric pronouns are represented in logical form by different occurrences of the same variable, applying standard semantics for the quantifiers gets the binding facts right. However, Evans also argued that the price of this unification is that we must regard free uses as fundamentally different: while free pronouns receive their value from context, the value of bound pronouns varies along with shifts in circumstances of evaluation. Recanati points out that Evans's argument rests on the assumption that pronouns are directly referential and claims that this cannot be the case in general. As Geoffrey Nunberg has argued, there are even deictic pronouns with descriptive content: 'He is usually Italian' uttered pointing at John Paul II can express a truth—the truth that in most relevant situations, the Pope in that situation is Italian—because the deictic 'he' in this case has the same content as the definite description 'the Pope'. If this is so, we should not expect that anaphoric pronouns are always directly referential either. Recanati suggests that anaphoric pronouns are descriptive and that their content can be given by an appeal to thematic roles. Although Recanati does not try to provide a systematic account of reflexives and Neale does not try to account for Nunberg-type deictic pronouns—and hence neither is explicitly concerned with the primary empirical motivation of the other—the juxtaposition of their chapters is particularly instructive in seeing how specific debates interact with the general disagreements about the scope of semantics and pragmatics.

Ever since the work of the later Wittgenstein, there has been a significant strand in philosophy of language which asserts the conceptual primacy of use over meaning. (Those who insist that meaning *is* use are generally reluctant to say use *is* meaning: rather, the view is that meaning can somehow be reduced to, derived from, or explained by use.) Theorists with this orientation—ones who subscribe to the *speech-act-centered conception of semantics*—focus on the illocutionary acts usually performed by speakers in uttering a sentence when investigating the semantic properties of that sentence. The result, *Nathan Salmon* argues, is a massive influx of pragmatic intuitions into semantic theorizing, which are often accommodated by introducing ambiguities that are otherwise theoretically unjustified. Attempts to assign semantic significance to Keith Donnellan's referential–attributive distinction through a postulation of ambiguity in the definite article are a case in point. Salmon suggests that we should embrace the alternative *expression-centered conception*, according to which semantic properties of linguistic expressions are not conceptually derivative of the speech acts performed by their utterers—they are intrinsic to the expressions themselves. The price of the clean semantics–pragmatics distinction is philosophical hardship: we no longer have the beginning of a story about where semantic properties come from. But if, as Salmon suggests, the first steps in this explanation go in the wrong direction anyway, this is certainly a price worth paying.

Presupposition is one of those linguistic phenomena that helped to clear away the fog surrounding the proper scope of a theory of meaning. Robert Stalnaker's early theory has helped many to see how phenomena that at first glance appear well within the bounds of a semantic theory may in fact arise from pragmatic factors. According to Stalnaker, presuppositions attach to utterances of sentences, rather than to sentences themselves, and they comprise the common ground of the conversation at the time of the utterance. *Mandy Simons's* chapter proposes an alternative pragmatic characterization of the phenomena. The core of the idea is that presuppositions of an utterance are what the hearer of the utterance must accept in order to find the utterance relevant. To make the notion of relevance more precise, she appeals to ideas of Dan Sperber and Deirdre Wilson. She argues that the relevance-theoretic approach to presupposition is as successful as the Stalnakerian picture in accommodating the fact that presuppositions are typically backgrounded, uncontroversial, defeasible, and come in varying strengths. And she suggests that the view fares better than its traditional rival in accounting for informative presuppositions (presuppositions that are *in fact* not common ground at the moment of utterance, although the speaker may act *as if* they were) and with dedicated presupposition triggers (lexical items whose sole function appears to be the triggering of a presupposition). The difficulties of the Stalnakerian view in these areas had been viewed by many as arguments against the pragmatic approach itself. (An old-fashioned Strawson-style semantic account faces much less severe difficulties here.) If Simons is right, the source of the difficulties is not in the pragmatic orientation itself, but in the particular pragmatic tools that were used to tackle these issues.

Scott Soames's chapter is an inquiry into the relation between semantic content (*what is said* in the locutionary sense) and assertoric content (*what is said* in the illocutionary sense). In *Beyond Rigidity*, Soames maintains that a fairly strong tie exists between these: although the proposition semantically expressed by a declarative sentence may fail to be the *only*, or even the *primary*, proposition asserted, it is nonetheless (setting aside cases on non-literal assertion and cases when the speech act performed is not assertion) always *one* of the asserted propositions. He now argues that this claim is too strong: there are declarative sentences involving negation or propositional attitude verbs besides proper names, where this principle is violated. For example, someone who sincerely utters 'Mary just learned that Peter Hempel is Carl Hempel' did not assert the false proposition that Mary just learned that Peter Hempel is Peter Hempel. The relationship between semantic and assertoric content is weak: the former is often a mere propositional skeleton providing the building blocks for assertions, and constraining how these blocks are assembled in normal contexts of use. Soames maintains that although the semantic contents of proper names are nothing but their referents, the semantic contents of sentences in which they occur contain slots associated with those referents, and at the level of what is asserted these slots can be filled by descriptive content obtained from the context of utterance.

Traditional neglect for the distinction between the locutionary and illocutionary notions of what is said is exacerbated by traditional assumptions about what we are entitled to neglect when we study linguistic expressions and their utterances. For example, we tend to bracket the observation that prima facie speakers can make assertions in uttering linguistic expressions that are less than complete sentences. *Robert Stainton* has long insisted that these appearances are not misleading and that properly appreciated they should move us far beyond the traditional view about the distinction between semantics and pragmatics. In his contribution Stainton responds to objections raised by Jason Stanley and Peter Ludlow against his ideas. Stanley has argued that the putative cases of non-sentential assertions do not form a unified set of phenomena: despite appearances some are not genuine (linguistic) assertions and some involve (through ellipsis or "shorthand") genuine sentences. Stainton argues that even if some of the examples can be handled in one of these ways, there are many others that cannot. Ludlow has claimed (using specific empirical considerations as well as general facts about the way certain contemporary syntactic theories work) that the sort of sub-sentential expressions Stainton thinks can be used to make assertions cannot even be interpreted outside the context of a sentence. After suggesting alternative explanations for the phenomena and recommending that we take certain aspects of contemporary syntax with a grain of salt, Stainton emphasizes that what is at stake is whether a strong version of Frege's context principle is sustainable. He thinks it is not, but in concluding the chapter he also calls attention to the fact that his views are nonetheless compatible with much more of the traditional view than it may appear at first.

1

Context *ex Machina*

Kent Bach

Once upon a time, it was assumed that speaking literally and directly is the norm and that speaking nonliterally or indirectly is the exception. The assumption was that normally what a speaker means can be read off the meaning of the sentence he utters, and that departures from this, if not uncommon, are at least easily distinguished from normal utterances and explainable along Gricean lines. The departures were thought to be limited to obvious cases like figurative speech and conversational implicature. However, people have come to appreciate that the meaning of a typical sentence, at least one we are at all likely to use, is impoverished, at least relative to what we are likely to mean in uttering it. In other words, what a speaker *normally* means in uttering a sentence, even without speaking figuratively or obliquely, is an enriched version of what could be predicted from the meaning of the sentence alone. This can be because the sentence expresses a "minimal" (or "skeletal") proposition or even because it fails to express a complete proposition at all.[1]

Indeed, it is now a platitude that linguistic meaning generally underdetermines speaker meaning. That is, generally what a speaker means in uttering a

---

Grateful thanks to Lenny Clapp, C. Bill Jones, John MacFarlane, Patrick Rysiew, Jenny Saul, and two anonymous readers for alert corrections and valuable suggestions, most of which I heeded.

[1] To keep matters relatively simple, I will generally limit the discussion to declarative sentences. These are the ones that are, or were, generally thought uncontroversially to express propositions. I will not worry about imperative, interrogative, and more marginal sorts of sentences. I will also assume, perhaps controversially, that declarative sentences are not marked for assertion (or for constative use, to borrow the generic term from speech act theory) in the way that imperative sentences are marked for directive use (for issuing orders, making requests, or giving advice) and interrogative sentences are marked for asking questions.

sentence, even if the sentence is devoid of ambiguity, vagueness, or indexicality, goes beyond what the sentence means. The question is what to make of this *Contextualist Platitude*, as I'll call it. It may be a truism, but does it require a radical revision of the older conception of the relation between what sentences mean and what speakers mean in uttering them? Does it lead to a major modification, or perhaps even outright rejection, of the semantic–pragmatic distinction? I think not. This platitude does not support the radical-sounding views that go by names like 'contextualism' and 'truth-conditional pragmatics'.

I have long accepted a certain picture, inspired partly by Austin and mostly by Grice, of what is involved in language and communication. In my judgment, this picture captures both the conventional and the rational (intentional and inferential) ingredients of communication. It provides a basis both for accepting the autonomy of linguistic semantics and for appreciating the complex, creative, and cooperative nature of what people do in speaking to and in understanding one another. It accentuates the importance of a number of fundamental distinctions, which often get blurred, confused, or even ignored. I will begin by sketching this picture of language and communication. Then, in its support, I will offer some simple arguments for ten points.[2]

The collective upshot of these arguments is that the older conception of the relation between what sentences mean and what speakers mean in uttering them is in better shape than has lately been supposed. Not only that, the semantic–pragmatic distinction holds up against the now widely recognized fact that what speakers mean generally goes beyond sentence meaning and does so in ways that not long ago were not even contemplated. I can sum up very simply the rationale behind my allegiance to this older conception. First, the Contextualist Platitude does not require a radical reconstrual of semantics, at least not if we take the meaning of a sentence to be determined compositionally by the meanings of its constituents in a way that is predictable from how its constituents fit together syntactically.[3] However, since for some sentences what is thus determined does not yield a complete proposition, it cannot be assumed

---

[2] The main elements of this intentional–inferential picture were presented in Bach and Harnish (1979) and are summarized in Bach (forthcoming). Various specific features of it are presented in my other papers listed in the References section and in the papers collected in the 'Semantics–Pragmatics Series', <http://online.sfsu.edu/~kbach>. At the expense of glossing over certain details, often important ones, here I will focus on the big picture.

[3] I am well aware that this is vague, but I want to put it in a theory-neutral way. Perhaps the semantics of a sentence is a projection of a particular level of its syntax, say its logical form as in Government and Binding Theory, or maybe there is no one level of syntactic structure that provides the entire input to semantics.

that the output of a semantic theory is a set of truth conditions for all the (declarative) sentences of the language. And there is no reason to assume that.[4]

Second, the Contextualist Platitude does not undermine the need for a purely semantic notion of saying and, correlatively, of what is said. We still need the distinction between saying something and meaning something, even if what is said, when not fully propositional, falls short of what a speaker *could* mean. So, for example, if the March Hare exclaimed, "I'm late, I'm late," but didn't add "for a very important date", he still would have said something, even though he didn't say what he was late for. He could be accurately reported as having said that he was late. Similarly, without the distinction between saying something and meaning something we would have to deny that speakers say anything at all when speaking figuratively. If a disorganized administrator says to his assistant "You are the CPU of this department", he really is saying that the assistant is the CPU of that department, even though computers, not departments, have CPUs.

Third, contemporary enthusiasts for contextualism trade on a number of ambiguities involving such terms as 'say', 'mean', 'refer', 'utterance', 'context', and 'interpretation' (see the Appendix for a list of these tricky terms and their dual uses). One especially pernicious ambiguity is displayed by the phrase 'utterance interpretation', which is often used by those who wish to replace sentence semantics with truth-conditional pragmatics. While using this phrase to mean the psychological process whereby listeners figure out what speakers are trying to communicate, some contextualists use it as if it meant something more abstract, something akin to semantic interpretation. That is, they treat utterance interpretation as if it were a mapping from syntactic structure to utterance contents, except that the mapping is sensitive to broadly contextual factors.[5] In so doing, they seem to think that an utterance (as opposed to a sentence) can express things independently of what the speaker means in making it, and to treat utterances almost as if they are agents.

The Picture: Language and Communication

For the sake of discussion, let's make the simplifying and rather artificial assumption that utterances are always utterances of complete, grammatical

---

[4] Many (declarative) sentences, though syntactically well-formed, are semantically incomplete, in that they do not express propositions at all, not even relative to a disambiguation and fixation of any references. See the last paragraph of point 1 below and also Bach (1994).

[5] I am unaware of any general account of what these factors are, although there are accounts of very special cases, such as indexicals and discourse anaphora.

sentences.[6] Then we can focus on sentences and utterances of them. In my view (see point 1), we should attribute semantic properties to sentences and pragmatic properties to utterances.[7] The reason for this is simple: taken as properties of sentences, semantic properties are on a par with syntactic and phonological properties—they are linguistic properties—whereas pragmatic properties belong to acts of uttering sentences in the course of communicating. This conception of the semantic–pragmatic distinction is inspired by, indeed is a generalization of, Grice's point that what a speaker implicates in saying what he says is carried not by what he says but by his saying it—and sometimes by his saying it in a certain way (1989: 39).[8] The speaker's act of uttering a sentence is what brings extralinguistic information into play.[9]

Then there is Austin's distinction between locutionary and illocutionary acts, between saying something and doing something in saying it. This distinction is easy to overlook. That is partly because the word 'say' plays a dual role as a locutionary verb and as an illocutionary one, roughly synonymous with

---

[6] This excludes the complications introduced by utterances of ungrammatical sentences and of mere phrases as well as by various sorts of speech disfluencies, such as breaking off sentences in midstream or punctuating them with 'um's, 'uh's, and 'ya know's. Also, I will be making the common simplifying assumption not only that sentences are the units of utterance (that what counts as one utterance is the utterance of one sentence) but that the units of communication are utterances of individual sentences. Though simplifying, this assumption does not imply that what speakers can communicate in uttering a sentence, or what their listeners take them to be communicating, does not depend on the previous discourse. Also, I will focus on spoken language, indeed face-to-face utterances at that. Presumably, though, the same basic principles that govern face-to-face communication govern other sorts of communication as well, even though in those cases the participants generally have less information to go on, about the communicative setting and about each other.

[7] I am supposing that utterances are acts of producing tokens of sentences. Uttered sentences have semantic properties; acts of uttering them do not (of course, speakers' communicative intentions have contents). As for tokens of uttered sentences, they have the semantic properties of the sentences of which they are tokens; they have no semantic properties of their own. Any seemingly semantic properties of tokens are really pragmatic properties of utterances. These depend entirely on the communicative intentions of speakers; semantic properties of sentences and their constituents do not.

[8] I should note that although I agree with Grice that what is said in uttering a sentence is closely correlated with the meanings of the sentence's constituent expressions and how they are put together syntactically, I do not accept his view that saying something entails meaning it. If one is not speaking literally, one is still saying something, even though one means something else. Also, Grice's conception of what is said did not countenance the case in which a sentence does not express, even relative to the context, a complete proposition. See Bach (1994: 141–4) for discussion of Grice's conception and my reasons for modifying it.

[9] I formulate, motivate, and defend my conception of the semantic–pragmatic distinction in Bach (1999).

'state' (or 'assert'). In the locutionary sense, one can say something without stating it (or performing any other illocutionary act whose content is what one says). One might not be stating anything, or one might be speaking figuratively and be stating something else, though not expressly. The illocutionary act a speaker performs in saying something depends on his communicative intention.[10] What he means in saying what he says (if he means anything at all) may be just what he says, what he says and more, or something else entirely. What he says provides the linguistic contribution to the audience's inference to his communicative intention. Communicative success requires uttering a sentence which, given the mutually salient information that comprises the extralinguistic cognitive context of utterance, makes the speaker's communicative intention evident and enables his audience to recognize it. The fulfillment of a communicative intention, unlike intentions of other sorts, consists in its recognition. Whereas you can't stand on your head by virtue of anyone's recognizing your intention to do so, you can succeed in communicating something if your listeners recognize your intention to communicate it.

Speakers and listeners rely on certain presumptions: speakers in order to make their communicative intentions evident and listeners in order to recognize those intentions. Although Grice appears to present his maxims as guidelines for how to communicate successfully, I think they are better construed as presumptions about speaker's intentions. The listener presumes, and the speaker expects him to presume, that the speaker is being cooperative and is speaking truthfully, informatively, relevantly, perspicuously, and otherwise appropriately. Because of their potential clashes, these maxims or presumptions should not be viewed as comprising a decision procedure. Rather, they provide different dimensions of considerations for the hearer to take into account in figuring out the speaker's communicative intention. They ground strategies for a speaker, on the basis of what he says and the fact that he says it, to make what he means evident to the hearer and for the hearer to figure out what the speaker means in saying what he says. Contrary to the popular misconception that these maxims or presumptions play a role only in implicature (and oblique and figurative speech generally), they are operative even when one means just what one says. However, if an utterance superficially appears not to conform to these

---

[10] Here I depart from Austin (1962), who assimilated all illocutionary acts to the regularized ones performed in special institutional or social settings, and follow Strawson (1964), who argued that most ordinary illocutionary acts are not conventional but communicative in character and succeed not by conformity to convention but, in Gricean fashion, by recognition of intention.

presumptions, the listener looks for a way of taking the utterance so that it does conform. He does so partly on the supposition that he is intended to do so. Communication is achieved when the audience understands the speaker in the sense of recognizing his communicative intention, partly on the basis of what he says, and partly on the basis, given the conversational presumptions, of the fact that he says it in that particular communicative context.

Here is a pair of simple examples. A surgeon says to his wife "I am going to cut the front lawn". For all that he says, he could mean that he will take a scalpel and use it to cut a number of blades of grass, but of course he does not mean that. His wife, relying on stereotypical knowledge of lawn mowing, presumes that if he did mean that, he would have said more (see point 6). So she rightly takes him to mean that he will cut the whole lawn with a lawnmower. Later he comes inside, hears the tea kettle screaming for a while, and finally goes into the kitchen. Surveying the damage, he finds his wife, tells her she forgot to turn off the stove, and adds "The tea kettle is completely black". For all that he says, he could mean that the tea kettle is black all over, rather than at least partly of some other color. But his wife takes him to mean that the tea kettle, which they mutually know to be made of aluminum, has been completely blackened as a result of the mishap in the kitchen. And presumably that's what he does mean. In both cases, she could not figure out what he meant unless she relied, at least implicitly, on the supposition that he intended her to figure it out, partly on the presumption that he was being relevantly informative. If he meant something less evident, he would have spelled it out. She is to presume, as Stephen Levinson puts it, that "what isn't said, isn't" and that "what is simply described is stereotypically exemplified" (2000: 31–2).

It is easy to exaggerate how well linguistic communication works. No doubt many failures of communication do not get noticed and, when they do, do not get mentioned. Still, in order for it to work as well as it does, we as speakers must be very good at selecting sentences whose utterance makes evident to our listeners what we mean, and as listeners we must be very good at figuring out what speakers mean in uttering them.[11] To the extent that we leave much of what we mean to

---

[11] Much attention has been paid to the processes involved in understanding utterances, but little has been paid to the production side, to how we manage to say what we say. Maybe this is because we don't really have a clue about how this process works, except in the simplest case, in which you utter a sentence whose semantic content is precisely what you are trying to convey, or, as it is casually said, you "put your thoughts into words". The thing is, though, we rarely do that. Psycholinguists who study language production generally assume, or at least pretend, that we generally do. Making this grossly simplifying assumption still leaves them with plenty to worry about. Even if speech were

inference, we rely on our listener's ability to figure out what we mean on the basis of what we say, given the circumstances in which we say it, the fact that we said that rather than something else, and the presumption that we said it with a recognizable intention. How we manage to make ourselves understood and how we manage to understand others are very complex processes which, like most cognitive processes, are far beyond the reach of contemporary psychology to explain. As theorists, the best we can do is speculate on some of the features of these processes, most notably what it takes to implement Grice's discovery that communication involves a distinctively reflexive intention (and its recognition). Specifically, the intention includes, as part of its content, that the audience recognize this very intention by taking into account the fact that they are intended to recognize it.

What is loosely called 'context' is the conversational setting broadly construed. It is the mutual cognitive context, or salient common ground. It includes the current state of the conversation (what has just been said, what has just been referred to, etc.), the physical setting (if the conversants are face to face), salient mutual knowledge between the conversants, and relevant broader common knowledge. As will be argued later (point 9), so-called context does not determine (in the sense of 'constitute'), but merely enables the hearer to determine (in the sense of 'ascertain'), what the speaker means. It can constrain what a hearer could *reasonably* take a speaker to mean in saying what he says, and it can constrain what the speaker could *reasonably* mean in saying what he says, but it is incapable of determining what the speaker actually does mean. That is a matter of the speaker's communicative intention, however reasonable or unreasonable it may be.

Simple Arguments for Ten Points

I will be offering some simple arguments for the following ten points:

1. Semantics concerns sentences, not utterances.
2. Saying something is one thing, stating or otherwise meaning it is another.

---

just a matter of putting a thought into words (perhaps by translating from the language of thought into a natural language), the task of explaining what is involved in speaking would still be daunting. When we have something to say, we need to come up with some linguistic means for saying it: a sentence. We need to recover lexical items and a syntactic form by which to say it, to know what sounds to produce, and to know how to produce them. These stages or levels of speech production are all areas of active psycholinguistic investigation (see Levelt 1989 for a comprehensive survey of the problems under study, and a well-developed approach to them). But the fact is that speaking is rarely a straightforward matter of putting a thought into words, however difficult even this is to explain.

3. Semantic content always underdetermines speaker meaning.
4. We generally don't make fully explicit what we mean, and what we don't is not part of what we say.
5. The semantic content of a (declarative) sentence cannot be equated with what it is normally used to assert.
6. Pragmatic regularities give rise to faulty "semantic" intuitions.
7. Focusing on sentences representative of those we use or might use is to commit a massive sampling error—even unusable sentences have semantic contents, however unintuitive.
8. What is said (in the locutionary sense) matters even though understanding an utterance often does not require entertaining or representing it.
9. Context does not literally determine what is said or what is meant.
10. Demonstratives and most indexicals do not refer as a function of context—they suffer from a character deficiency.

For some points there will be more than one argument. Indeed, under some there will be more than one point. And some of the arguments may not be entirely simple. So the title of this section is not to be taken quite literally.[12]

1. *Semantics concerns sentences, not utterances.*

According to the Contextualist Platitude, generally what a sentence means falls well short of what a speaker means in uttering it. Recognizing this platitude has led some implicitly to assume that semantics concerns utterances, not sentences, or even that there is no need for semantics at all (at least construed as that part of grammar that delivers sentence interpretations). The relevant task, it is thought, is to give a theory of something called "utterance interpretation", not quite psychological but not merely semantic. It is sometimes thought to concern the processes whereby hearers interpret utterances and sometimes to concern something more abstract, analogous to semantic interpretations of sentences but without having to be projections of syntactic structure. The picture of language and communication sketched above should suggest why, even though I accept the Contextualist Platitude, I am against the idea of utterance semantics, but there are direct arguments against it.

One such argument is due to David Kaplan, who stresses the importance of not confusing utterances with sentences-in-contexts. Focusing on the role of

---

[12] I have previously argued for some of the points I am defending now, but here I am offering simpler arguments for them. Points 2, 8, and 9 were defended in 'You Don't Say?' (2001*a*), points 3 and 4 in 'Speaking Loosely' (2001*b*), and point 6 in 'Seemingly Semantic Intuitions' (2002).

semantics in explaining entailment and formal validity, he points out obvious problems that arise, on an utterance semantics, due to utterances of sentences containing indexicals or demonstratives. For example, noting that "utterances take time, and [one speaker's] utterances of distinct sentences cannot be simultaneous" (1989*a*: 546), Kaplan argues that utterance semantics would get the wrong results. He proposes a somewhat idealized conception of context to make allowances for sentences that can be true but cannot be truly uttered ('I am not uttering a sentence'), sentences (or sequences of sentences making up an argument) that take so long to utter that their truth values can change during the course of the utterance, and sentences that are too long to utter at all. For different reasons, utterances of sentences like 'I know a little English' or 'I am alive' are likely to be true, even though their contents are not true in all contexts. For, as Kaplan points out, using 'I say nothing' to illustrate, "there are sentences which express a truth in certain contexts, but not if uttered" (1989*b*: 584). Similarly, utterances of sentences such as 'I don't know any English' and 'I am deceased' are likely to be false, even though these sentences can still express truths relative to some contexts. These facts can be explained only if semantic contents are assigned to sentences-in-contexts (where contexts here are construed more abstractly than as contexts in which sentences are actually uttered), not to utterances.

Kaplan's arguments are nice, but they exploit special features of particular sentences. There is a more general reason for rejecting utterance semantics. Consider that utterances are often nonliteral, in which case a speaker says one thing and means something else instead (also, many utterances are indirect—even if the speaker means what he says, he means something else as well). For example, one might say "I could eat a million of those chips" and mean something a bit more realistic. Now surely it is not the business of semantics to account for the contents of utterances that are not literal, since in such cases the speaker is trying to convey something that is not predictable from the meaning of the uttered sentence (or, if it is ambiguous, from its operative meaning). Obviously not just anything that a speaker means, no matter how far removed it is from what the sentence means, counts as semantic content, and the semantic content of the sentence is the same whether an utterance of it is literal or not. So semantic content is a property of the sentence, not the utterance. After all, the fact that the sentence is uttered is a pragmatic fact, not a semantic one.

Moreover, the only respect in which an utterance has content over and above that of the uttered sentence is as an intentional act performed by a speaker.[13] And in that respect, the content of an utterance is really the content of the speaker's communicative intention in making the utterance. In other words, the only relevant linguistic content is the semantic content of the sentence, and the only other relevant content is the content of the speaker's intention. Focusing on the normal case of successful communication, where the listener gets the speaker's communicative intention right, can make it seem as though an utterance has content in its own right, independently of that intention. But this is illusory, as is evident whenever communication fails. In that case, in which the speaker means one thing and his audience thinks he means something else, there is what the speaker means and what his listener takes him to mean, but there is no independent utterance content.

The claim that semantics concerns sentences, not utterances, is not undercut by the fact that many (declarative) sentences, though syntactically well-formed, are semantically incomplete, in that they do not express propositions at all, not even relative to a disambiguation and fixation of any references. Truth-conditional pragmaticists, especially relevance theorists (who imagine that virtually all sentences are semantically incomplete in this sense), are overly impressed by this fact. This fact exposes a tension between two traditional conceptions of sentence semantics—as giving truth conditions and as providing interpretations of logical forms. It used to be assumed that the two go together, at least in the case of declarative sentences. Every such sentence, it was thought, has a truth condition (at least relative to a context), and a semantic theory delivers the truth condition off the logical form of the sentence (assuming this is the level of syntactic representation that provides the input to semantics) as a function of the semantic values of the basic constituents of the sentence and their syntactic arrangement. However, since some, indeed a great many, sentences are semantically incomplete, the presumed confluence of the two conceptions breaks down—what the compositional semantics delivers often needs some sort of completion or augmentation before a truth condition (or something with a truth condition, i.e. a proposition) is yielded. But requiring a truth condition for every sentence conflicts with the other conception of semantics, on which the semantic content of a sentence is a projection of its syntax. In my view, we need to opt for this second conception. To do so is not to give up semantic compositionality but only to abandon the dogmatic assumption that every

---

[13] As explained in n. 7, I am taking utterances to be acts of uttering sentences, not the tokens of sentences thereby produced. Sentence tokens do not have semantic properties independently of the sentence types of which they are tokens.

(declarative) sentence has a truth condition (relative to a context).[14] Nor does it require, on the grounds that utterances of (declarative) sentences that do not have truth conditions do have truth conditions, changing the subject matter of semantics from sentences to utterances. We merely need to recognize that when speakers utter semantically incomplete sentences, they must mean something that includes an element that does not correspond to anything in the syntax of the sentence.

2. *Saying something is one thing, stating or otherwise meaning it is another.*

Austin's distinction between "locutionary" and "illocutionary" acts, between saying something and doing something in saying it, is commonly neglected these days. Perhaps that is because it is so easy to use 'say' interchangeably with 'state' (or 'assert'). But stating or asserting is a case of performing an illocutionary act, of meaning and trying to communicate something, and that goes beyond mere saying (in the locutionary sense).

Why is the locutionary notion of saying needed, along with the correlative, strictly semantic notion of what is said? It is needed to account for the each of the following cases, situations in which the speaker:

- says something but doesn't mean anything at all (by 'mean' here I mean 'intend to communicate');
- does not say what he intends to say, as in the misuse of a word or a slip of the tongue;
- means what he says and something else as well (cases of implicature and of indirect speech acts in general);
- (intentionally) says one thing and means something else instead (non-literal utterances).

So far as I know, no one who rejects a strictly semantic notion of what is said has addressed the question of what is said in each of these cases. In the first case, allowances have to be made for (the verbal side of) such activities as acting and translating. The need to provide for the second and third cases is obvious. As for

---

[14] Given the phenomenon of semantic incompleteness, it is not generally feasible to give the semantics of sentences, by means of T-sentences, in terms of truth conditions. For example, if 'Steel isn't strong enough' is semantically incomplete, then the T-sentence 'The sentence "Steel isn't strong enough" is true iff steel isn't strong enough' is semantically incomplete too. It is more feasible to specify the semantics of such a sentence in terms of its propositional content, whether or not complete. I call the contents of semantically incomplete sentences 'propositional radicals' (Bach 1994: 127), but sometimes they are called 'propositional matrices' or 'partial propositions'.

the last case, suppose someone speaks endearingly to his lover "You are the ketchup on my fries". Presumably he is not speaking literally (never mind the merits of his figure of speech). So whatever he means and thereby states (a matter of his communicative intention) is distinct from what he is saying. But this requires that he is saying something.[15]

3. *Semantic content always underdetermines speaker meaning.*

The Contextualist Platitude says that semantic content generally underdetermines speaker meaning. There are several obvious reasons for this. For one thing, the semantic content of many (declarative) sentences is not a complete proposition (something truth-evaluable). So if a speaker utters such a sentence and what he means must be a complete proposition, the semantic content of the sentence cannot comprise what he means. For another thing, in so far as much natural language is vague, then arguably, at least on the assumption that there are no vague propositions, there is no fact of the matter as to which proposition a given sentence expresses. Then, if what a speaker means in uttering a vague sentence is precise, the sentence's semantic content does not determine what he means.[16] A third reason why semantic content can underdetermine speaker meaning is that the speaker might not mean something determinately. A fourth reason is that even if the semantic content of the sentence a speaker utters is a complete and precise proposition, the speaker might mean something else or something more. He might not be speaking literally, and he might be speaking indirectly.

These are reasons why semantic content *often* underdetermines speaker meaning. But I am making a stronger claim: the semantic content of a sentence, even considered relative to a reading, a resolution of any vagueness, and a set of referents of context-sensitive elements, including indexicals and tense markers, *always* underdetermines what a speaker means in uttering it. Here's why. Even if

---

[15] There is a further reason for adopting a strictly semantic notion of what is said. As we will see in point 7 below, there are a great many sentences whose semantic contents are too bizarre for them ever to be uttered (what such a sentence means is not something a speaker would ever mean or could even say in order to mean something else). Nevertheless, if you uttered such a sentence, you would say something: whatever the semantics of that sentence predicts you'd say.

[16] On the other hand, if what a speaker means can be less than fully precise, it may be that the semantic content of the sentence he uses does comprise what he means. Here I am assuming a distinction between imprecision and indeterminacy—it can be determinate that the speaker means such-and-such even if the proposition that such-and-such is imprecise. Contrariwise, it could be indeterminate what a speaker means even if the plausible candidates for what he means are all perfectly precise propositions.

what a speaker means consists precisely in the semantic content of the sentence he utters and that content is precise, this fact is not determined by the semantic content of the sentence. The reason for this claim is very simple: no sentence has to be used in accordance with its semantic content. *Any* sentence can be used in a nonliteral or indirect way. A speaker can always mean something distinct from the semantic content of the sentence he is uttering. That he is attempting to communicate something, and what that is, is a matter of his communicative intention, if indeed he has one. If he is speaking literally and means precisely what his words mean, even that fact depends on his communicative intention.[17]

Also, what is said (in the locutionary sense) does not depend on the speaker's communicative intention. Although what a speaker chooses to say and how he chooses to say it (a certain sentence on a certain reading) depends on what he wishes to convey, what he says is compatible with any of the various communicative intentions that he might have in uttering it (if indeed he has any), regardless of how obscure that intention may be. So what he says cannot depend on what his communicative intention actually is.

4. *We generally don't make fully explicit what we mean, and what we don't is not part of what we say.*

We generally don't say what we mean, not because we're usually insincere but rather because we leave much of what we mean to inference. Even when we are using words or phrases literally, we generally do not use the entire sentence literally. That is, what the sentence means, and what we thereby say in uttering it, comprises merely a skeletal version of what we mean. For example, suppose a customer at a Taco Bell says "I want a taco". Presumably he means that he wants to be presented with, within a short time, a ready-to-eat, uncontaminated taco of a normal size. But obviously he doesn't say most of this, and the sentence he uses is not an elliptical version of some more elaborate sentence that spells these things out. This phenomenon is so pervasive that we tend not to notice it, not just when engaged in ordinary conversation but even when theorizing about language and communication.

To begin to appreciate this point, just glance at some examples of sentences taken out of context, in this case from newspaper articles or letters to the editor.

---

[17] This is why, contrary to a widespread misconception, Gricean maxims (or conversational presumptions, as I prefer to think of them) are operative *whenever* we use language to communicate. As mentioned earlier, they do not come into play only when a speaker seems to be implicating something, is performing an indirect speech act, or is not speaking literally—they always apply.

(1) It could have been worse.
(2) We regret any confusion.
(3) Water is a matter of public debate.
(4) The information really helped show us where there were holes in the system.
(5) San Francisco is less of a problem because we have more aggressive code enforcement.
(6) Requiring the use of barbless hooks, recycling fishing line, and posting signs in multiple languages that describe how to properly unhook birds would diminish the problem.

In each case, it should be obvious that something is missing in what is said, relative to what the writer meant, but what that is is not at all obvious.[18]

We generally don't make fully explicit what we mean in uttering a sentence, even when we're using the individual words in it literally. Then for every sentence we do utter, there is a more elaborate, qualified version we could utter that would make what we mean more explicit. However, these are not the sentences we do utter. Indeed, they are not ones we even think to utter. Surely we don't form a thought to express, think of an elaborate sentence to express it with, and then, in the interests of conversational efficiency, work out a stripped down version of the sentence to use instead. Whatever qualifications or disclaimers the writers of the above sentences may have intended, surely convoluted sentences expressing them didn't first come to their minds, only then to be edited.

5. *The semantic content of a (declarative) sentence cannot be equated with what it is normally used to assert.*

Offhand, one might think that for any sentence, the most likely use of that sentence is a literal one. However, this is not true of most sentences we use. Indeed, a great many sentences are very hard to use literally, even if one uses the individual words and phrases in them literally. Normal uses of the following sentences illustrate what I call *sentence nonliterality* (Bach 2001*b*). In each case, what a speaker is likely to assert includes the contents of the italicized parenthetical words, even though these are not parts of the sentences being uttered.

(7) Alice hasn't taken a bath *(today)*.
(8) Barry and Carrie went to Paris *(together)*.

---

[18] Note that to say that the utterance is taken out of context does not imply that context provides the missing elements. See point 9.

(9) The table *(in this room)* is covered with books.

(10) Fran will get George's job *(immediately)* after he retires.

(11) Eve had nothing *(suitable)* to wear.

Sentence nonliterality might seem paradoxical or at least puzzling, but it is not. It is entirely predictable, given the way in which the efficiencies of ordinary communication interact with linguistic meaning. Maybe there is a conversational presumption that sentences are used literally, but if so this is one presumption that is commonly overridden.

There is nothing particularly normal about speaking literally. Indeed, as point 4 suggested, most sentences that are used at all tend not to be used literally.[19] That is why it is naive to suppose that the semantic content of a declarative sentence (relative to a context) can be defined as what a speaker would normally assert in uttering the sentence. Indeed, to suppose that for most sentences a likely use of it is a literal one can, as we will see next, lead to erroneous semantic judgments (or so-called intuitions). Relying on such judgments implicitly assumes that if a sentence would normally be used in a certain way, that use is a literal use. In fact, it is to be expected that intuitions about what is said should be faulty, given our ability to say one thing and successfully convey something much richer and our correlative ability to recognize what others are doing when they are exercising that first ability. These abilities of ours are so fluent as to distort our reflective semantic judgments. What we think is expressed by a given sentence is colored by what we know a speaker is likely to mean in uttering it, especially if there is some one sort of context which we tend to imagine it being used in. To keep one's semantic judgments from being pragmatically contaminated, it is always a good idea to imagine a variety of contexts of use, even wildly improbable ones.

6. *Pragmatic regularities give rise to faulty "semantic" intuitions.*

Some philosophers think that explaining semantic intuitions is the job of semantics. One would have thought that its job is to explain semantic facts, for which intuitions are merely evidence. In my view, there is no particular reason to suppose that such intuitions are reliable and robust or, indeed, that they are responsive mainly to semantic and not to pragmatic facts. Moreover, there is no reason to suppose that such intuitions play a role in the process of communication.

---

[19]   A great many more sentences are not used at all, and most of those are not even feasible to use. See point 7.

Now according to the previous point, the semantic content of a (declarative) sentence is not to be identified with what it would normally be used to assert. Not only that, since our intuitions about the semantic contents of sentences tend to be geared to what they're used to assert, our intuitions are biased toward typical uses rather than literal uses.[20] To appreciate this reconsider the examples listed above and some variations on them.

(7a) Alice hasn't taken a bath.

(7b) Alice hasn't taken a bath *today*.

(7c) Alice hasn't taken a bath *since she found a dead rat in the tub*.

(8a) Barry and Carrie went to Paris.

(8b) Barry and Carrie went to Paris *together*.

(8c) Barry and Carrie *each* went to Paris *last summer*.

(9a) The table is covered with books.

(9b) The table *in this room* is covered with books.

(9c) The table *I finished painting five minutes ago* is covered with books.

(10a) Fran will get George's job after he retires.

(10b) Fran will get George's job *immediately* after he retires.

(10c) Fran will get George's job *but not for at least two years* after he retires.

(11a) Eve had nothing to wear.

(11b) Eve had nothing *suitable* to wear *to the opera*.

(11c) Eve had nothing *(at all)* to wear *when she finished skinny dipping*.

Regarding examples like these, it is often claimed that what a speaker says in uttering one of the (a) sentences is the same thing he would have said in uttering the corresponding (b) sentence. The only difference, it is suggested, is that the (b) sentence makes what is said more explicit.[21] However, it would seem that

---

[20] As the following examples illustrate, seemingly semantic intuitions tend to be responsive more to what is meant (or even implied) than to what is merely said. Interestingly, theorists who rely on such intuitions tend themselves to elide the distinction between what is meant and what is said. Part of the explanation for this tendency is that the sentences we utter tend to mean much less than what we mean in uttering them. The sentences we utter often express so-called "minimal" propositions rather than the richer propositions we mean in uttering them. However, theorists tend to let their conversational competence, which includes the ability to exploit various sorts of pragmatic regularities, get in the way of their professional judgment. They consider isolated sentences, implicitly assume typical contexts of utterance, imagine what utterances of them would likely be intended to convey, and attribute the result to the semantics of the sentence or to what it says. See Bach (2002) for further discussion.

[21] Some relevance theorists go so far as to claim that the (b) sentence gives the "explicit content" of the (a) sentence, even though an utterance of the (a) sentence is less explicit, relative to what the

to utter the (*a*) sentence is not to *say* something that would be said in an utterance of the corresponding (*b*) sentence. After all, even if a speaker meant what the (*b*) sentence expresses, he could have meant something else, such as what is expressed by the (*c*) sentence, in which case he would have *said* the same thing. No one would suggest that what the speaker would have *said* in that case is what the (*c*) sentence expresses. By parity of reasoning, there is no reason to suppose that if what the speaker meant is in fact what the (*b*) sentence expresses, this is what he said either.

People's intuitions about what sentences mean and what speakers say tend to be insensitive to the distinction between the semantic content of a sentence and what it is most likely to be used to convey. Intuitions are tainted also by the fact that when a sentence is considered in isolation, certain default assumptions are made about the circumstances of utterance. These assumptions depend on one's knowledge of the world and of people's typical communicative purposes. So we tend not to discriminate between the semantic content of a sentence and the likely force of uttering a sentence with that content. This is just what you'd expect if speakers typically don't make fully explicit what they mean and exploit the fact that it's obvious what they leave out.

We read things into the meaning of a sentence or into what a speaker says in uttering it that are really consequences of its being uttered under normal circumstances. Our seemingly semantic intuitions are responsive to *pragmatic regularities*. Pragmatic regularities include regularized uses of specific expressions and constructions that go beyond conventional meaning, as well as general patterns of efficient communication, which involve streamlining stratagems on the part of speakers and inferential heuristics on the part of listeners. These regularities are pragmatic because it is the speaker's act of uttering a given sentence, not the sentence itself, that carries the additional element of information.

That a speaker says what he says rather than something else can contribute to what a speaker is likely to be taken to mean. Indeed, that he says it one way, by using certain words rather than certain others, can also contribute to what he is likely to be taken to mean in using those words. But people's intuitions (even philosophers') about what is said tend to be insensitive to these subtleties. Even so, people's actual reasoning in the course of figuring out what speakers mean takes these considerations into account. So, for example, a listener supposes that:

- If the speaker could have made a stronger statement, he would have.

speaker means. Here they seem to overlook the obvious difference between something's being explicit and, as their term 'explicature' suggests, its being made explicit.

- If the speaker needed to have been more specific, he would have.
- If there was something special about the situation, the speaker would have mentioned it.

However, if what the speaker actually said is obviously not strong or specific enough but it is obvious how he could have explicitly made it stronger or more specific, he does not need to do so. It is presumed that additional information, were it mentioned, would have needed to be mentioned. In both reasoning generally and in rational communication in particular, we presume that things are not out of the ordinary unless there is reason to think that they are, and we presume that if there is such reason, this would occur to us (see Bach 1984). So, as Stephen Levinson puts it, "If [an] utterance is constructed using simple, brief, unmarked forms, this signals business as usual, that the described situation has the expected, stereotypical properties" (2000: 6). Otherwise, as he goes on to say, "If, in contrast, the utterance is constructed using marked, prolix, or unusual forms, this signals that the described situation is itself unusual or unexpected or has special properties."[22] Also, to make fully explicit what one means, when one could speak much more economically and exploit the default assumptions that in fact obtain in the circumstances in which one is speaking, would not only take an effort and be boring, it would be misleading.

So there is no need, at least not in general, to expect semantics to explain what people would normally mean in uttering a given sentence. One shouldn't let features of stereotypical utterance contexts get incorporated into the semantics of a sentence. Nor should the fact that the utterance of a given sentence is likely to have a certain intuitive content not obviously projectible from its form automatically elicit an explanation in terms of more subtle elements of form. Although there may be special cases that require semantic explanation, grounded in syntax or in lexical structure, these are only special cases. Generalizing from these cases leads to an overgeneration problem—more structure, hence more meaning or more meanings, than most sentences really

---

[22] Levinson identifies three presumptions, or "heuristics", that yield defeasible inferences as to a speaker's communicative intention (2000: 31–4):

> Q-heuristic: What isn't said, isn't.
> I-heuristic: What is simply described is stereotypically exemplified.
> R-heuristic: What's said in an abnormal way, isn't normal.

These are closely related, respectively, to Grice's (1989: 25–6) first maxim of quantity ("Make your contribution as informative as is required"), second maxim of quantity ("Do not make your contribution more informative than is required"), and maxim of manner ("Be perspicuous", and specifically to the submaxims "Avoid obscurity of expression" and "Avoid prolixity").

have. Similarly, there is no need for an expansive notion of what is said, on which what is said is not entirely predictable from the semantic content of the sentence.

7. *Focusing on sentences representative of those we use or might use is to commit a massive sampling error—even unusable sentences have semantic contents, however unintuitive.*

Most of the (English) sentences that philosophers and linguists use as examples (of course, linguists look at much wider and richer ranges of examples) presumably are representative of the vast variety of sentences that (English) speakers have used or might use (this ignores the fact that interest in particular linguistic phenomena often focuses attention on unrepresentative clumps of examples). However, sentences actually used or even potentially usable are not representative of (English) sentences in general. That is not just because most sentences are far too long to be used in real life. Most sentences, even ones of fairly modest length, express things that are too bizarre ever to say, much less mean (the really long ones express things that are just too complex to understand). Here are some random examples:

(12*a*) Three triangular raisins and an active, orbital clone brainwashed some unusually packaged concubines.

(12*b*) A ghastly horde of flunkies died in order to maim an erotic barn until forty-three rutabagas imploded.

(12*c*) Some refugees cashed in because a beef cake refused to protest against an overwhelmingly addictive searchlight.

(12*d*) Any support group can revolve unless the one and only blasphemous infrared asylum shoplifts with gusto.

(12*e*) Cyborgs blushed, as if your mom believed in ridiculously macrobiotic rainbows, while the plumb bobs rejoiced randomly.

To convince yourself that simply by concentrating on sentences people might actually use philosophers and linguists tend to commit a massive sampling error, visit a random sentence generator on the Internet. With its help you can find all the examples you want of sentences no one would ever have occasion to use, except perhaps under extremely bizarre circumstances.[23] Many of these,

---

[23] Alternatively, randomly pick sentences that you hear or read and in each one randomly substitute nouns for nouns, verbs for verbs, adjectives for adjectives, etc. Repeat as long as you want. If you think that some kinds of semantic anomaly yield ungrammaticality, try different random substitutions when need be until a grammatical sentence is yielded.

I bet, are sentences whose utterance most competent speakers would regard as utter nonsense, as not saying anything. Yet such sentences are perfectly meaningful (well, maybe 'perfectly' is a slight exaggeration) and are as much the business of semantics to reckon with as those that have a prayer of ever being uttered. They are perfectly typical sentences of English (or whatever the language in question), even if not typical of sentences we utter.

Why does this point matter? Because a great many claims that philosophers or linguists make about the semantics of sentences and about "what is said" by sentences (or by utterances of them) depends on ignoring such sentences. However, unusable sentences still mean something, and something would be said in uttering them, even though such sentences would never ever be used at all. Most sentences are unusable, and for them nothing counts as a normal use. That is enough to show (point 5) the error in supposing that what a sentence means, or its semantic content relative to a context of use, is what it would normally be used to assert. So we should not suppose that English grammar is so constrained that most meaningful, well-formed sentences express (have as their semantic contents) things we are ever likely to mean—or even say. The semantic contents of sentences that no one would ever have a use for are determined in just the same way as the semantic contents of other sentences, compositionally as a function of their constituents and their syntactic structure. For those sentences, we can't depend on our intuitions about what they mean or about what speakers would say or mean in uttering them. Their semantic contents are too bizarre to be at all intuitive.

8. *What is said (in the locutionary sense) matters even though understanding an utterance often does not require entertaining or representing it.*

Four reasons were given under point 2 above for the need for a strictly semantic notion of what is said. However, some have argued (neglecting such reasons) against the empirical relevance of a strictly semantic notion of what is said on the grounds that it plays no role in the psychology of utterance understanding.[24] Their argument comes down to this: people can usually figure out what a speaker says, in the looser, partly pragmatic sense of 'say', without having (first) to figure out what the speaker says in the strict semantic sense. However, as I have previously replied (Bach 2001a: 24–5), it is not obvious why facts about what the hearer does in order to understand what the speaker says should be relevant to what the speaker says in the first place. How could the fact (if it is

---

[24] See e.g. Recanati (1995, 2001); Carston (2002: 170–83).

a fact) that what is said sometimes doesn't get calculated (explicitly inferred) by the hearer show that it is a mere abstraction? Employing the semantic notion of what is said does not commit one to an account of the temporal order or other details of the process of understanding. This notion pertains to the character of the information available to the hearer in the process of identifying what the speaker is communicating, not to how that information is exploited. Even if what is said (strictly speaking) is not actually calculated, it can still play a role. Although a hearer might not explicitly represent what is said by the utterance of a sentence, hence not explicitly judge that it is not what is meant, still he would be making the *implicit* assumption that it is not what is meant. Implicit assumptions are an essential ingredient in default reasoning in general (Bach 1984) and in the process of understanding utterances in particular. Communicative reasoning, like default reasoning in general, is a case of jumping to conclusions without explicitly taking into account all alternatives or all relevant considerations. Even so, to be warranted such reasoning must be sensitive to relevant considerations and relevant alternatives. This means that such considerations can play a dispositional role even when they do not play an explicit role.

That's my previous, complicated reply to the argument that what is said, in any empirically legitimate sense, generally must be calculated by the hearer. Here is a simpler reply, a *reductio ad absurdum* based on recent work by the psycholinguist Raymond Gibbs (2002). Gibbs's work has shown, just as one would intuitively expect, that understanding of clearly figurative utterances can often be achieved without calculating what is said even in a loose sense. For example, listeners can figure out what a speaker means in uttering sentences like (13) and (14) without first calculating their literal meanings or figuring out what a speaker would mean if he used them literally:

(13) The best ladder to success is hard work.
(14) The economic downturn poured cold water over my ambitions.

If Gibbs is right, then the very argument designed to debunk a strictly semantic notion of what is said works just as well against the looser, allegedly more intuitive notion. In relying on the psychological fact that often the hearer need not calculate what is said in the strict semantic sense in order to understand what a speaker means, this argument would lead to the absurd conclusion that clearly figurative contents, when they are all that is calculated, count as what is said. So being the first proposition calculated by the listener is not a good test for being what is said by the speaker.

9. *Context does not literally determine what is said or what is meant.*

It is often casually remarked that what a speaker says or means in uttering a given sentence "depends on context", is "determined" or "provided" by context, or is otherwise a "matter of context". That's not literally true. Assume that by context we mean something like the mutually salient features of the conversational situation. Does context determine what the speaker says? Suppose he utters an ambiguous sentence, say "Gina wants to belong to a golf club". Presumably he is saying that Gina wants to belong to a group of golfers, but given the ambiguity of 'golf club', he could be saying, however bizarrely, that Gina wants to belong to a thing that is used to hit golf balls. Context doesn't literally determine that he does not.

And context doesn't constrain what a speaker actually means. It can constrain only what he can reasonably mean and reasonably be taken to mean. That is, it constrains what communicative intention he can have in uttering a given sentence and reasonably expect to get recognized. So suppose someone says "Harry has a happy face". Presumably what he means is something to the effect that Harry has a facial expression indicating that he's happy. Even so, he could mean, however strangely, that Harry's face is itself happy (as if faces can be in different moods on the sadness–happiness scale). Similarly, a speaker who says "Many investors lost every dollar", presumably means that many investors in some particular deal each lost every dollar that they respectively put into that deal, even though that goes well beyond the meaning of the sentence. But it is not literally context that determines that this is what the speaker means in uttering the sentence.

Breakfast Anyone?

To appreciate what context doesn't do, let's revisit a commonly discussed example and examine it more closely. The discussion will also revisit some earlier points about intuitions. This is relevant because it is often claimed that our intuitions correctly recognize the contribution of context to what is said.

(15) I haven't had breakfast.

The usual line on this example is that someone who utters it on a given day says that they haven't had breakfast *that day* and that this element of what is said is provided by context. If that were correct, then what one says in uttering (15) would be no different from what one would have said if one had uttered (15′) instead,

(15′) I haven't had breakfast today.

However, if you ask people if there's any difference between what is said when (15′) rather than (15) is uttered, many will say, yes, there is a difference: the speaker of (15) didn't *say* that he hadn't had breakfast that day. That's because he left this for inference (notice that this inference is much harder to make if (15) is uttered late in the day).

It might be replied that the speaker of (15) didn't *explicitly* say that he hadn't had breakfast *that day*. That is, he didn't spell out the relevant time period. But why suppose that this was *said* at all? Of course, it was what the speaker meant in saying what he said, but he just didn't quite say it and left it for his audience to figure out. Is that so hard to accept? Evidently.

All right. Then presumably someone who utters (16), the positive version of (15), on a particular day, says that they have had breakfast that day.

(16) I have had breakfast.

Well, then, compare what someone would say in uttering that with what they would say in uttering each of these sentences:

(17*a*) I have filed my tax returns.
(17*b*) I have eaten caviar.
(17*c*) I have had breakfast in bed.

In uttering (17*a*) a speaker wouldn't be saying that he has filed his tax returns that day. That year is more like it, but he is not *saying* that either. In uttering (17*b*), he wouldn't be saying that he has eaten caviar that day. Probably what he means is that he has eaten caviar before. And if he uttered (17*c*), surely he wouldn't be saying (or meaning) that he has had breakfast in bed that day. So context doesn't determine what he does mean.

Moreover, it is easy to imagine circumstances, however improbable, in which someone who utters (15) does not mean that he hasn't had breakfast that day. Here are a few such circumstances.

- The speaker works the graveyard shift and utters (15) to a co-worker shortly after midnight.
- It is common to have breakfast at work, even if one has already had it at home.
- People are permitted to have breakfast only one day each week.
- Having breakfast is illegal.

You can figure out for yourself what the speaker probably would mean in each of these situations. In none of them would someone who uttered (15) be saying, much less mean, that he hadn't had breakfast that day. So, it might be objected, the context makes the difference: someone who utters (15) in a *normal context* says that they haven't had breakfast *that day*. If they had uttered it in one of the other contexts, they would have said something else, and in each case the difference would be explained by the difference in context.

This context *ex machina* explanation is feeble. Context doesn't *determine* anything in these cases. Rather, it's the speaker's communicative intention that picks up the slack. But communicative intentions can affect only what is meant, not what is said. Communicative intentions cannot affect what is said in a given context, since one could say a certain thing in a given context and mean any one of a number of things in saying it. To be sure, maybe only one of those things is what one could reasonably mean in saying that, and only one of those things is what one could plausibly be taken to mean in saying that, but what one can reasonably mean or plausibly be taken to mean in saying something need not be what one actually said. And, as noted in Point 4 above, with many sentences what is said in uttering the sentence is something that one cannot reasonably mean or reasonably be taken to mean—in such cases it is very hard to mean that rather than some qualified version of what is said.

I neglected to mention why philosophers are inclined to insist that in uttering (15) a speaker says that he hasn't had breakfast that day, and not that he hasn't had breakfast, period. They are appalled at the alternative. Surely, they maintain, he didn't say that he hadn't *ever* had breakfast or that he hadn't *previously* had breakfast. But of course he didn't *say* either of those things (he didn't utter any such word). He *said* that he hadn't had breakfast, period. Objectors who complain that it is just counterintuitive to suppose that the speaker of (15) said that he hadn't had breakfast, period, support their complaint by arguing that my view makes the highly implausible assumption that a Gricean quality implicature is operative here. They suppose that I am committed to the claim that the listener has to infer that the speaker meant that he hadn't had breakfast that day (partly) from the fact that what he said was so glaringly false (surely he has had breakfast before). But this is not what I am assuming. The example is a case of conversational *impliciture*, not implicature (see Bach 1994), and what the speaker means is an expanded version of what he said, the proposition that is obtained from the explicit propositional content by including an additional element, in this case a restriction of the time period to the day of the utterance. What drives the inference is not the falsity of the explicit propositional content but its lack of relevant specificity. This is evident if we consider that the same thing occurs with the affirmative sentence 'I have had breakfast'. This sentence is obviously true rather than glaringly false, but what a speaker is likely to mean in uttering it is something more relevantly specific, that he has had breakfast that day.

10. *Demonstratives and most indexicals do not refer as a function of context—they suffer from a character deficiency.*

The reference of so-called pure indexicals, such as 'I' and 'today', is determined by their linguistic meanings as a function of specific contextual variables (this is context in the narrow, semantically relevant sense). However, the reference of other indexicals and of demonstratives is, as Perry puts it, "discretionary" rather than "automatic", and depends on the speaker's semantic intention, not just on "meaning and public contextual facts" (2001: 58–9). That is, the speaker's intention is not just another contextual variable, not just one more element of what Kaplan calls "character" (1989*a*: 505). The fact that the speaker's semantic intention determines the referent does not imply that the specification of the meaning of a discretionary indexical or a demonstrative contains a parameter for the speaker's intention. Rather, given the meaning of such an expression, in using it a speaker must have some intention in order to provide it with content relative to the context in which he is using it.

It is a separate question whether the audience can identify the referent (assuming the speaker is using the expression referentially). In order to ensure that, the speaker needs to take mutually salient contextual information into account in forming his intention. He must exploit such information in deciding what expression to use to refer to a certain individual. He would thereby intend his audience to rely on such information in order to identify that individual, and to take him as intending them to rely on it in so doing. In the course of forming an intention to refer to something and choosing a term to refer to it with, to make his intention evident a speaker exploits what is antecedently salient in the speech situation or else makes something salient by demonstrating it or with the words he uses (the gender of a pronoun, the nominal in a demonstrative phrase, or even the predicate in the sentence). The communicative context (context broadly construed) enables the audience to determine (in the sense of ascertain) what he is referring to, but it does not literally determine (in the sense of constitute) the reference. Of course, in order for his referential intention to be reasonable, he needs to utter something in that communicative context such that his audience, taking him to have such an intention and relying on contextual information that they can reasonably take him to intend them to rely on, can figure out what the intended reference is.

So neither sort of context, narrow or broad, determines the references of demonstratives and discretionary indexicals. Unlike pure indexicals, they do not refer as a function of the contextual variables, the narrow context, given by their meanings. Nor does the broad, communicative context determine the reference, in the sense of making it the case that the expression has a certain reference. That merely enables the audience to figure out the reference. So we might say that demonstratives and discretionary indexicals suffer from a *character deficiency*—they do not refer as a function of context. Accordingly, it is only in an attenuated sense that these expressions can be called "referring" expressions. Besides, they have clearly nonreferring uses, e.g. as proxies for definite descriptions and as something like bound variables.[25]

Some simple examples involving reference and anaphora will illustrate the role of speakers' intentions. Compare (18*a*) and (18*b*):

> (18*a*) A cop arrested a robber. He was wearing a badge.
> (18*b*) A cop arrested a robber. He was wearing a mask.

It is natural to suppose that in (18*a*) 'he' refers to the cop and in (18*b*) to the robber. It is natural all right, but not inevitable. The speaker of (18*a*) could be using 'he' to refer to the robber, and the speaker of (18*b*) could be using it to refer to the cop. Such speakers would probably not be understood correctly, at least not without enough stage setting to override commonsense knowledge about cops and robbers, but that would be a pragmatic mistake. Nevertheless, the fact that 'he' could be so used indicates that it is the speaker's semantic intention, not the context, which determines that in (18*a*) it refers to the cop and in (18*b*) to the robber. The same point applies to these examples with two anaphora:

> (19*a*) A cop arrested a robber. He took away his gun.
> (19*b*) A cop arrested a robber. He used his gun.
> (19*c*) A cop arrested a robber. He dropped his gun.
> (19*d*) A cop arrested a robber. He took away his gun and escaped.

In (19*a*) presumably 'he' would be used to refer to the cop and 'his' to the robber, whereas in (19*b*) both would be used to refer to the cop, in (19*c*) both would be used to refer to the robber, and in (19*d*) 'he' would be used to refer to the robber and 'his' to the cop. However, given the different uses of the pronouns in what is essentially the same linguistic environment, clearly it is the speaker's intention, not the context, that explains these differences in reference. It is a different, pragmatic matter how the audience resolves these anaphors and determines what they refer to. The broad, communicative context does not determine

---

[25] See Neale (1990, ch. 5). King (2001) shows likewise for complex demonstratives (demonstrative phrases of the form 'that F').

what these references are but merely provides the extralinguistic information that enables the audience to figure them out.

The Bottom Line

The ten points and the arguments for them presented here provide new support for the older picture of language and communication, and help sustain a fairly standard semantic–pragmatic distinction. The basic idea is very simple: what a speaker says (I don't mean the fact that he says it) depends on the semantic content of the sentence he utters and not on the communicative intention with which, or on the cognitive context in which, he utters it.

Context, like minoxodil and antioxidants, has limited benefits. Leaving aside the special case of pure indexicals, what varies from context to context (not to be confused with being determined by context) is what a speaker is likely to mean and could reasonably mean in uttering a given sentence. So consider these last examples:

(20*a*) I love you too.
(20*b*) Willie almost robbed a bank.
(20*c*) I feel like a burrito.

It is not hard to figure out that there are at least four different things that a speaker could mean in uttering each of them, but context is not what determines what that is. Rather, it helps the listener figure that out and it may constrain how the speaker can expect to be understood.

An utterance of a semantically incomplete sentence and a typical utterance of any sentence whose semantic content falls short of what a speaker is likely to mean in uttering it both involve conveying a proposition with constituents that are not articulated, but these are not part of the sentence's semantic content.[26] We need the level of locutionary act and, correlatively, a strict, semantic notion

---

[26] An unarticulated constituent does not correspond to anything in the syntax of the sentence but is nevertheless thought to be part of "what is expressed" by an utterance of the sentence. An alternative approach, which does not fall under the heading of "contextualism" or "truth-conditional pragmatics", is to posit hidden variables in the syntax, variables whose values are somehow "contextually provided". Although there are special cases, such as relative adjectives and nouns like 'local', 'foreign', 'neighbor', and 'disciple', for which this approach is plausible, freely positing hidden variables just to ensure that the semantic contents of sentences (relative to contexts) are complete propositions is unwarranted. And it is certainly not needed to account for the propositions that speakers are likely to convey.

of what is said, in order to account for (the content of) what a speaker does in uttering a sentence independently of whatever communicative intention (if any) he has in uttering it and regardless of how the content of that intention may depart from the semantic content of the sentence. Pragmatics contributes not to what is said, but only to the speaker's decision about what to say (in order to make evident what he means) and to the listener's identification of what the speaker means, given that the speaker said what he said.

The older picture of language and communication is compatible with the Contextualist Platitude, which says that the meanings of the sentences we use tend to be impoverished relative to what we mean in uttering them. That platitude does not support the radical-sounding views that go by names like 'contextualism' and 'truth-conditional pragmatics'. It should be recognized for what it is, a platitude.

APPENDIX: SOME DANGEROUS AMBIGUITIES

The following ambiguities (or perhaps polysemies) should be self-explanatory, especially given the picture presented above. The foregoing points and arguments should make clear why these ambiguities or polysemies are dangerous. In each case (except for 'semantic') the first use of the term is semantic in character and the second is pragmatic. The two should not be conflated.

semantic

- pertaining to or a matter of linguistic meaning
- pertaining to or a matter of truth conditions

reference

- by an expression to an object
- by a speaker with an expression to an object

meaning

- linguistic meaning: sense of an expression (word, phrase, or sentence)
- speaker's meaning: what a speaker means

speaker's meaning

- what a speaker means by a sentence (or phrase) when using it
- what a speaker means (tries to communicate) in uttering a sentence (or phrase)

utterance

- what is uttered
- act of uttering

utterance meaning

- meaning of an uttered sentence
- speaker's meaning in uttering a sentence

say

- perform a locutionary act
- state or assert, especially in using a declarative sentence without using any of its constituent expressions nonliterally

what is said

- the content of a locutionary act (or equivalently, the semantic content of sentence, relative to a context of utterance)
- the content of the assertion made in using a declarative sentence without using any of its constituent expressions nonliterally

context

- set of parameters whose values fix or delimit the semantic values of expressions with variable references
- set of salient mutual beliefs and presumptions among participants at a stage in a conversation

determine

- make the case (constitutive determination)
- ascertain (epistemic determination)

interpretation

- assignment of semantic values
- inference to speaker's communicative intention

demonstrative reference

- reference by a demonstrative
- speaker's reference by means of demonstrating

use (a term) to refer

- use a term that refers
- use a term and thereby refer

REFERENCES

Austin, J. L. (1962), *How to Do Things with Words* (Oxford: Oxford University Press).

Bach, Kent (1984), 'Default Reasoning: Jumping to Conclusions and Knowing when to Think Twice', *Pacific Philosophical Quarterly*, 65: 37–58.

—— (1994), 'Conversational Impliciture', *Mind and Language*, 9: 124–62.

—— (1999), 'The Semantics–Pragmatics Distinction: What It Is and Why It Matters', in Ken Turner (ed.), *The Semantics–Pragmatics Interface from Different Points of View* (Oxford: Elsevier), 65–84.

—— (2001*a*), 'You Don't Say?', *Synthese*, 128: 15–44.

—— (2001*b*), 'Speaking Loosely: Sentence Nonliterality', *Midwest Studies in Philosophy*, 25: *Figurative Language*, ed. P. French and H. Wettstein (Oxford: Blackwell), 249–63.

—— (2002), 'Seemingly Semantic Intuitions', in J. Campbell, M. O'Rourke, and D. Shier (eds.), *Meaning and Truth: Investigating Philosophical Semantics* (New York: Seven Bridges Press), 21–33.

—— (forthcoming), 'Speech Acts and Pragmatics', in M. Devitt and R. Hanley (eds.), *The Blackwell Guide to the Philosophy of Language* (Oxford: Blackwell).

—— and Robert M. Harnish (1979), *Linguistic Communication and Speech Acts* (Cambridge, Mass.: MIT Press).

Carston, Robyn (2002), *Thoughts and Utterances* (Oxford: Blackwell).

Gibbs, Raymond W., Jr. (2002), 'A New Look at Literal Meaning in Understanding What Is Said and Implicated', *Journal of Pragmatics*, 34: 457–86.

Grice, H. P. (1989), *Studies in the Way of Words* (Cambridge, Mass.: Harvard University Press).

Kaplan, David (1989*a*), 'Demonstratives', in J. Almog, J. Perry, and H. Wettstein (eds.), *Themes from Kaplan* (Oxford: Oxford University Press), 481–563.

—— (1989*b*), 'Afterthoughts', in J. Almog, J. Perry, and H. Wettstein (eds.), *Themes from Kaplan* (Oxford: Oxford University Press), 565–614.

King, Jeffrey C. (2001), *Complex Demonstratives: A Quantificational Account* (Cambridge, Mass.: MIT Press).

Levelt, Willem J. M. (1989), *Speaking: From Intention to Articulation* (Cambridge, Mass.: MIT Press).

Levinson, Stephen C. (2000), *Presumptive Meanings: The Theory of Generalized Conversational Implicature* (Cambridge, Mass.: MIT Press).

Neale, Stephen (1990), *Descriptions* (Cambridge, Mass.: MIT Press).

Perry, John (2001), *Reference and Reflexivity* (Stanford, Calif.: CSLI).

Recanati, François (1995), 'The Alleged Priority of Literal Interpretation', *Cognitive Science*, 19: 207–32.

—— (2001), 'What Is Said', *Synthese*, 128: 75–91.

Strawson, P. F. (1964), 'Intention and Convention in Speech Acts', *Philosophical Review*, 73: 439–60.

2

Radical and Moderate Pragmatics: Does Meaning Determine Truth Conditions?

Herman Cappelen and Ernie Lepore

> ... words are no good; ... words dont ever fit even what they are trying to say at.
>
> Addie Bundren, in William Faulkner's As I Lay Dying

1. Introduction

According to one conception of language, the meaning of a (indicative) sentence determines the conditions under which it is true, or determines what a speaker can say or express with that sentence. Anyone who understands (1) knows what it means and by virtue of knowing what it means knows that it is true just in case Rutgers University is in New Jersey; and knows that anyone who asserts (1) will have said or expressed that Rutgers University is in New Jersey.

Earlier versions of this chapter have been presented at various conferences and to various philosophy departments. We would like to thank the audiences of all these institutions for their helpful feedback, in particular, we would like to thank Jeff King, Kirk Ludwig, Mike Martin, Rob Stainton, Jason Stanley, Zoltan Szabó, Jessica Wilson, and especially Jerry Fodor and Charles Travis.

This chapter was completed in 2000. In other words, this chapter reflects our thinking about these issues from several years ago, and it does not fully or accurately reflect our current views. Our current views are laid out in our book *Insentive Semantics*. Rather than rewrite this chapter completely (which would be strange to do since there are published papers criticizing and referring to this version of it), we will leave it here as is. However, we recommend consulting our book for the complete truth about these issues.

(1) Rutgers University is in New Jersey.

Unlike (1),[1] sentences (2)–(3) include the context sensitive nouns 'that' and 'I' respectively, and so do not have truth conditions *tout court*.

(2) That's nice.
(3) I've eaten.

But the sort of context sensitivity exhibited in such sentences does not compromise the claim that meaning determines truth conditions, since recourse to context here is directed and restricted by conventional meaning alone. Anyone who understands sentence (2) knows that its utterances are true just in case whatever object is demonstrated in the context of utterance is nice; and he also knows that any utterance of (2) says of, or expresses about, whichever object is demonstrated that it's nice. (Similarly, anyone who understands (3) knows that any utterance of it is true just in case whoever utters it has eaten. And every utterance says of, or expresses about, the speaker that he or she has eaten.)

In sum, according to the thesis that meaning determines truth conditions, (indicative) sentences divide into two classes—those with truth conditions *tout court*, and those with truth conditions only relative to the semantic values of their context sensitive linguistic items being fixed in a context of utterance.[2]

A number of authors have challenged, in varying degrees of scope, this picture. At one extreme is what we shall dub 'Radical Pragmatics' (RP), the defining characteristic of which can be summarized as follows: Were you to take any English sentence S and

(*a*) specify the meaning (or semantic value) of every word in S (doing so in accordance with your favorite semantic theory);
(*b*) specify all the relevant compositional meanings rules for English (doing so in accordance with your favorite semantic theory);
(*c*) disambiguate every ambiguous expression in S; precisify every vague expression;
(*d*) fix the referents of every referring expression in S (including indexical ones, even those 'hidden' in logical form),

you would fail to provide (derive, or otherwise specify) any of (i)–(iii):

(i) the conditions under which S is true.
(ii) the proposition expressed by S.
(iii) what intuitively is (literally) said by S.

---

[1] For the purposes of this chapter we'll ignore considerations having to do with tense.

[2] We will need also to worry about ambiguity; take a sentence like 'Not all banks are banks'. Contingent on how one individuates words, this sentence may or may not be true. On one construal of word-individuation, this sentence requires a context in which to determine the extensions of its two occurrences of 'bank'.

According to RP, *sentences* neither have truth conditions, nor say nor express anything, even with (*a*)–(*d*) being settled. RP does not deny that speakers usually say and express something with their utterances, or that their utterances are sometimes true or false, and so have truth conditions. Rather RP charges that whatever truths or falsehoods are said or expressed are not determined by meaning and linguistically relevant contextual factors alone.[3]

Philosophers who explicitly endorse RP are John Searle and Charles Travis.

What words mean plays a role in fixing when they would be true; but not an exhaustive one. Meaning leaves room for variation in truth conditions from one speaking to another. (Travis 1996: 451)

. . . in general the meaning of a sentence only has application (it only, for example, determines a set of truth conditions) against a background of assumptions and practices that are not representable as a part of meaning. (Searle 1980: 221)

Both philosophers allude to Wittgenstein and Austin as their chief influences (Travis 1985: 187, 1996: 451; Searle 1980: 229).

A more Moderate Pragmatics (MP) holds that the meaning of only some (indicative) sentences for which (*a*)–(*d*) have been settled does not issue in (i)–(iii). According to MP, the truth conditions of many utterances go well beyond anything that semantics legitimately assigns to the sentences uttered. Many philosophers and linguists (Sperber and Wilson 1986; Perry 1986; Carston 1988; Crimmins 1992; Recanati 1993; Bach 1994; Schiffer 1995) endorse MP to some degree. Indeed, it's our impression that most people, wittingly or not, adhere to MP to some degree.[4]

Our polemical strategy here will be first to argue that MP is unstable. To wit, we will argue that there is no principled line to draw between MP and its fanatical cousin RP. So, if you inclined towards MP, you will inevitably wind up endorsing RP. We will also argue that neither RP nor MP has advanced sound arguments against the view that sentence meaning determines truth conditions.[5] And then we will argue that RP (and so MP) is internally inconsistent. Although our goals here are primarily negative, in the last part of this discussion we will speculate on alternative accounts of the data that have impressed

---

[3] Instead of assigning truth conditions to sentences, semantics for natural languages assigns something non-truth-evaluable: "fragmentary representations of thought" (Sperber and Wilson 1986: 193); "propositional radicals" (Bach 1994: 127).

[4] Indeed, there are passages in which it's difficult not to interpret some of these authors as witting proponents of RP.

[5] In this chapter we will concentrate on critical claim (i) of RP and not on claims (ii) and (iii); however, towards the end of our discussion we'll return to critical claim (iii), and, in effect, agree with RP—with this twist—we will deny its significance for truth conditional semantics.

Radical and Moderate Pragmatists in the first place, accounts which are consistent with the main thesis that meaning determines truth conditions.

A larger issue, one we have discussed elsewhere,[6] concerns the costs of insisting upon invoking context in determining truth conditions, when contextually sensitive items are neither linguistically represented nor syntactically motivated. We have argued (and maintain here as well) that these costs are unreasonably high, and so we adopt as a methodological policy not to permit context to collaborate with meaning in determining truth conditions unless morphology or syntax requires it.[7]

2. Incompleteness and Context Shifting

Proponents of RP tend to inundate their readers with lots of examples the upshot of which is supposed to be that you surrender to the claim that sentences lack truth conditions. As far as we can tell, all of their examples seem to be in the business of either advancing what we shall call an incompleteness charge or in establishing what we shall call a context-shifting claim. In this section we will look at each in turn.

Incompleteness

RP aims to establish that no meaning theory can determine truth conditions for, e.g., sentences (4) and (5) and, in particular, any theory which issues in, or entails, (4*) and (5*) fails to do so.

> (4) This kettle is black.
> (5) Smith weighs 80 kg.
> (4*) 'This kettle is black' is true iff the demonstrated kettle is black.
> (5*) 'Smith weighs 80 kg' is true iff Smith weighs 80 kg.

According to the incompleteness charge, (4*) fails to specify truth conditions for (4) *because* it fails to answer any of the following sorts of questions. (What follows are essentially quotations from Travis 1985: 197; similar ones can be found in Searle 1978: 208, 215; 1980: 224.) Would (4) be true of some demonstrated kettle if it is:

> (4a) made of normal aluminum but soot covered?
> (4b) made of normal aluminum but painted?

---

[6] See Lepore (2004) and Cappelen and Lepore (2002).

[7] Showing that RP and MP, and their collective arguments against truth conditional semantics, are flawed—we want to emphasize—is not a defense of truth conditional semantics directly, but it does fend off what has become a rather irksome opponent.

(4c) made of cast iron but glowing from heat?

(4d) enameled white on the outside but saturated in black light?

(4e) made of cast iron with a lot of brown grease stains on the outside?

Since (4*) doesn't tell us whether (4) is true when the demonstrated kettle is washed, black on its inside, black all the way through, painted, illuminated or not, etc., RP concludes that it fails to specify ('settle', 'decide', 'determine') conditions under which (4) is true.[8] Likewise, (5*) doesn't tell us whether (5) would be true were Smith to weigh:

(5a) 80 kg when stripped in the morning?

(5b) 80 kg when dressed normally after lunch?

(5c) 80 kg after being force fed 4 liters of water?

(5d) 80 kg four hours after having ingested a powerful diuretic?

(5e) 80 kg after lunch adorned in heavy outer clothing?

Since (5*) is mute on these (and endless related) questions, RP concludes that it fails to specify truth conditions for (5).

(4) and (5) are but two of the examples that RP advances; yet its intended scope is supposed to be limitless (see e.g. Travis 1996: 455; 1997a: 119; Searle 1978: 219; 1980: 227). *No sentence* has its truth conditions determined by linguistic meaning alone.

One rejoinder to incompleteness is to deny the data, and instead affirm, for example, that the truth conditions for sentences (4) and (5), as determined by their meanings, are not (4*) and (5*) but rather (4**) and (5**) (cf. e.g. Searle 1978: 212).

(4**) 'This kettle is black' is true iff the demonstrated kettle is black on its surface.

(5**) 'Smith weighs 80 kg' is true iff Smith weighs, naked, exactly 80 kg early in the morning before breakfast.

But (4**) and (5**) won't (and shouldn't) silence RP.

First, even with such qualifications implemented, indefinitely many other questions just like those in (4a)–(5e) remain unanswered. (4**), for example, fails to answer how much of its surface must be black for the surface to be black. Must it all be? Suppose it's chipped with white enamel underneath an otherwise black coat of paint. Is its surface still black? How chipped can a surface be before

---

[8] If we cannot specify the truth conditions for (4) and (5), Travis concludes that we cannot fully specify what's said by them nor can we specify which propositions they express. We'll put aside Travis's skepticism about what's said and the propositions expressed for the moment and focus on the truth conditional aspects of his discussion.

it is no longer black? Would it suffice for a surface to be black that it appear black to normal observers when illuminated? Must it be washed? Scrubbed? Similarly, (5**), for example, fails to tell us under what conditions an individual weighs exactly 80 kg in the morning before breakfast. Weighed where? On the moon? On earth? By which standard? Under which conditions?

In short, if it's the lack of answers to (4a)–(5e) that establishes (4*) and (5*) are incomplete, then there's no basis for saying that (4**) and (5**) specify truth conditions for (4) and (5) either.

A different sort of worry is that, even if we presume that (4**) and (5**) do succeed in attributing truth conditions to (4) and (5), we have been provided with no reason for deciding why they do. As we depart further and further from mere disquotation, and conditions become more and more specific, what is the principled basis for choosing among alternatives? What, for instance, is the principled basis for *not* including in (4**) the condition that the surface should be washed or scrubbed? Isn't it absurd to hypothesize that linguistic meaning should be expected to make these sorts of fine-grained discriminations?

Context Shifting

Incompleteness is supposed to establish that what determines the truth conditions for any given utterance is supposed to be a combination of what the uttered sentence means *and* a collection of various 'non-semantic' features surrounding its context of utterance (where 'non-semantic features' are those *not* employed in settling (a)–(d)).

But if we do assume that facts about context suffice to determine truth conditions for *utterances* of (4) and (5), why, then, can't we infer that they also determine truth conditions for (4) and (5) themselves? Simply take the truth conditions for utterances of (4) and (5) and posit them as the truth conditions for the sentences themselves. Here's where context shifting kicks in (see Travis 1985: 199–200; 1996: 454–5; Searle 1978: 212; 1980: 224–5).

RP proponents argue that in some scenarios an utterance of (5), for instance, with its meaning fixed, is true when conditions C obtain, while in another scenario C's obtaining would neither necessitate nor suffice for the truth of an utterance of (5). For example:

> *Scenario One*
> Smith has been dieting for the last eight weeks. He steps on the scale one morning, naked, before breakfast (but after having gone to the

bathroom), and it registers 80 kg. A friend at work who wants to let Smith's co-workers in on his achievement can use (5) to say something true. Notice it doesn't matter at all that Smith is, at that time, dressed, wearing a heavy overcoat, and has just consumed an enormous lunch.

Scenario Two
Smith is exactly as in Scenario 1. However, the speaker's circumstances (and purposes) have changed. At the time of this utterance of (5) (suppose the same time as in Scenario 1), Smith is about to enter an elevator with a capacity of no more than an extra 80 kg. An utterance of (5) in these circumstances could be both fatal and false. Note that what the scale registers when Smith is naked in the morning is in this context irrelevant.

So, two simultaneous utterances of the same sentence type with the same meaning, whose referring terms are assigned the same referents, are alleged to differ in their truth conditions due to 'non-semantic' differences surrounding their respective contexts of utterance. It is supposed to follow that truth conditions are generated in individual contexts of utterance, where the truth of an utterance depends on non-linguistic aspects like the non-linguistic interests of speakers, their shared non-linguistic background knowledge, etc. Since meaning is not in the business of tracking and revealing these sorts of interests and shared background information, it fails to determine these truth conditions.[9]

In summary, straightforward disquotational claims like (4*) and (5*) are alleged to be incomplete. And the articulation of truth conditions for a particular utterance of a sentence s cannot be converted into truth conditions for s itself since conditions that determine whether utterances of s are true can shift from context to context, and so singling out any one truth condition would fail to provide a sufficient condition for the truth of s.

RP claims that incompleteness and context shifting have nothing to do with ambiguity, vagueness, or ordinary linguistic ellipsis. Nor do they have anything to do with failing to locate and relativize (implicit or explicit) contextually sensitive items to a place, time, speaker, etc. (Searle 1980: 223). We will grant them all of this

---

[9] " . . . the notion of literal meaning of a sentence only has application relative to a set of background assumptions, and furthermore, these background assumptions are not and could not all be realized in the semantic structure of the sentence in the way that presuppositions and indexically dependent elements of the sentence's truth conditions are realized in the semantic structure of the sentence" (Searle 1978: 210).

for the purposes of our critical discussion.[10] Still, we believe that the phenomena that are invoked to establish incompleteness and context shifting are irrelevant to the concerns of semantics—we will argue as much below. However, RP, whatever its flaws, does exemplify one significant virtue, namely, it exposes the instability of MP.

3. Interlude: Moderate Pragmatics on Incompleteness and Context Shifting

MP, recall, contends that though the meanings of some sentences suffice to determine their truth conditions (relative to (a)–(d) being settled), the meanings of others do not. For these latter sentences only their individual utterances have truth conditions. Representative sample sentences include (6)–(9):

(6) Steel isn't strong enough.
(7) Tipper is ready.
(8) Peter's book is gray.
(9) It's raining.

Here are representative comments about these and like sentences:

though syntactically well-formed, [they] are semantically or conceptually incomplete, in the sense that something must be added for the sentence to express a complete and determinate proposition (something capable of being true or false). (Bach 1994: 127)

. . . the recovery of the proposition expressed by the utterance of a linguistic form has an even stronger degree of context-dependence than indexicality; some content supplied by the context received no direction at all from linguistic expressions . . . The logical form of the linguistic expression uttered is the semantic representation (or sense) assigned to it by the grammar and recovered in utterance interpretation by an automatic process of decoding. As we have seen, in a range of examples this logical form is frequently not fully propositional, and a hearer then has the task of completing it to recover the fully propositional form that the speaker intended to convey . . . There is always a linguistic contribution, but this contribution varies from near total determination [of what's said] to a very small role . . . (Carston 1988: 166–7)

---

[10] Indeed, in another paper, one of us argues that any effort to try to solve these sorts of worries by appeal to "hidden" indexicals at some level of linguistic analysis fails (Lepore 2004).

There is a widespread view that all the thoughts that a human might entertain and want to communicate could in principle be linguistically encoded. . . . What does it mean to say that every thought is expressible by some sentence? . . . If sentences do not encode thoughts, what do they encode? What are the meanings of sentences? Sentence meanings are sets of semantic representations, as many semantic representations as there are ways in which the sentence is ambiguous. Semantic representations are incomplete logical forms, i.e., at best fragmentary representations of thoughts. (Sperber and Wilson 1986: 191–3)

In order to assign a truth-value to my son's statement ('It's raining') . . . I needed a place. But no component of his statement stood for a place. . . . Palo Alto is a constituent of the content of my son's remark, which no component of his statement designated; it is an unarticulated constituent. (Perry 1986: 206)[11]

Proponents of MP infer that for utterances of sentences such as (6)–(9), through a non-linguistic process, e.g., of *free enrichment* (Recanati 1993, ch. 14), various conceptual materials ("background facts"; Perry 1986: 210) get added to their meanings and only then does it make sense to speak of truth conditions being determined.[12]

The reasoning that leads MP to conclude that the meanings of these sentences do not determine truth conditions for them seems to parallel RP, with respect to both incompleteness and context shifting.

With respect to incompleteness, alleged disquotational truth conditions such as (6*)–(9*),

(6*) 'Steel isn't strong enough' is true iff steel isn't strong enough,
(7*) 'Tipper is ready' is true iff Tipper is ready,
(8*) 'Peter's book is gray' is true iff Peter's book is gray,
(9*) 'It's raining' is true iff it's raining,

are deemed deficient because they fail to settle answers to crucial questions. (6*) fails to ascribe truth conditions to (6) because it doesn't answer questions such as 'Isn't strong enough for what?' (7*) fails to ascribe truth conditions to (7)

---

[11] Strictly speaking, (9) is treated differently from (6)–(8) by many authors in the literature, since (9) is thought to be able to express a proposition on its own in a way that the others cannot. Clearly, Perry is not thinking of (9) this way when he writes, "in order to assign a truth-value to my son's statement ('It's raining') . . . I needed a place".

[12] Not all of these authors agree about the status of these sentences. Some assimilate some of these examples to cases like (2) and (3), arguing, for example, that it's an integral part of the genitive that 'Peter's book' means 'the book that bears R to Peter', such that no definite content gets expressed unless R is given a semantic value.

because it doesn't tell us what Tipper is ready for. (8*) fails to ascribe truth conditions to (8) because it doesn't tell us what the relevant relationship is between Peter and the book. And (9*) fails to ascribe truth conditions to (9) because it doesn't tell us where it's raining. Had these sentences truth conditions, there would be answers to these questions forthcoming and these answers would supply part of these sentences' truth conditions.

With respect to context shifting, just as different utterances of (4) and (5) can, according to RP, be assigned distinct truth conditions, it's supposed to be obvious, according to MP, that different utterances of (6)–(9) can be assigned distinct truth conditions. So, although in some contexts, correct truth conditions for utterances of (6)–(9) are given by expansions (6b)–(9b) respectively (Bach 1994: 128 ff. Carston 1988: 167; Sperber and Wilson 1986: 188; Recanati 1993: 235; Perry 1986: 206; Crimmins 1992: 17),

(6b) Steel isn't strong enough to *support the roof*,
(7b) Tipper is ready *for the exam*,
(8b) The book *owned by* Peter is gray,
(9b) It's raining *in Palo Alto*,

in other contexts, (6) can be used to say that there's something else that steel isn't strong enough for; (7) can be used to say that Tipper is ready for something other than an exam; (8) can be used to say that the book chosen by Peter is gray; and (8) can be used to say it's raining somewhere other than the place of its use (Perry 1986: 209).

4. The Instability of Moderate Pragmatics

Something has gone wrong here. For why should we suppose that (6b*)–(9b*) succeed in specifying truth conditions for (6b)–(9b) if (6*)–(9*) fail to specify truth conditions for (6)–(9)?

(6b*) 'Steel isn't strong enough to support the roof' is true iff steel isn't strong enough to support the roof.
(7b*) 'Tipper is ready for the exam' is true iff Tipper is ready for the exam.
(8b*) 'The book owned by Peter is gray' is true iff the book owned by Peter is gray.
(9b*) 'It's raining in Palo Alto' is true iff it's raining in Palo Alto.

(6b*) fails to specify truth conditions for (6b) (we leave (7b*)–(9b*) as an exercise) because it doesn't settle for how long the support must last. Do a few seconds suffice? More than three days? Many years? Why mustn't (6b*) also settle whether (6b) is false if steel fails to support the roof when placed in temperatures over 390°? Then there is the question of why the amount of steel needed to support the roof mustn't be decided in order to settle whether (6b) is true. Would (6b) be false if one-tenth of a square inch of steel wouldn't suffice to support the roof?

Nothing in the meanings of the words in (6b) (or their composition) answers these questions, certainly nothing in (6b*). If the sort of reasons that led MP proponents to conclude that (6*) is incomplete are any good, why don't they extend to (6b*) as well? MP has provided us with no reason to believe that (6b*) gets it just right. If (6*) is incomplete because it doesn't answer the question 'Isn't strong enough for what?', then why isn't (6b*) also incomplete because it doesn't answer, *inter alia*, the question 'Isn't strong enough to support the roof for how long?'

So, if the reason why (6*)–(9*) are incomplete is because they fail to answer these kinds of 'would it be true if . . .'-questions, why should we hold that this alleged incompleteness is limited to some (more or less) circumscribed subset of English sentences? What RP proponents see clearly is that the same sorts of incompleteness can be found in any English sentence (as illustrated by (4)–(5) above). In other words, if (6)–(9) lack complete truth conditions, because it only makes sense to speak of their utterances as having truth conditions, why aren't all truth conditions generated in contexts of utterance (regardless of whether a sentence has context sensitive elements or not)?[13]

In sum, MP is unstable since no proponent of MP has provided a principled reason for how to stop expansions, e.g. at (6b)–(9b), and frankly, it's hard to see how such *non*-linguistic expansion should stop anywhere.[14]

5. Replies to Incompleteness and Context Shifting

Before turning to arguments directed against RP, we want to look more closely at its alleged skeptical consequences about meaning determining truth conditions.

---

[13] Recanati (1993: 260, 267) seems to be aware of this slippery slope but seems not to be aware of its implications for the more moderate position.

[14] And, indeed, this does seem like a no win situation for the MP, for to the extent that she can succeed in providing a principled delimitation of the mandatory parameters whose values must be settled before truth conditions can be assigned (or propositions expressed) she will have identified lexically semantically relevant argument structure, thus sustaining the traditional view that sentences, appropriately contextually relativized, have truth conditions after all.

We begin with a claim. Nothing that RP has so far argued shows, for example, that (5*) is not true.

(5*) 'Smith weighs 80 kg' is true iff Smith weighs 80 kg.

First, consider whether alleged context shifting shows that (5*) is not true. (5*) is not true just in case it is either false or lacks a truth value. With regard to falsity, context shifting doesn't show that for any utterance of (5*), its LHS and RHS can disagree in truth value. If Smith weighs 80 kg, (5) is true; and if he doesn't, (5) is false. Indeed, contrary to what was advertised, Scenarios 1 and 2 back up these intuitions. According to RP, in Scenario 1, (5) is true and in Scenario 2, (5) is false. Does this establish that (5*) is false? Well, what does Smith weigh in these two scenarios? Can Scenario 1 be accurately described as one in which Smith weighs 80 kg? The answer, it seems to us, is clearly 'yes'. Reread the description of Scenario 2. Does Smith weigh 80 kg in Scenario 2 (i.e. the scenario in which (5) is alleged to be false)? The answer, it seems to us, is exactly what (5*) predicts: No, he doesn't. If your intuition is that (5) is false, your intuition will also be that he doesn't weigh 80 kg. It's exceedingly hard for us to see how to pull these intuitions apart.[15]

Suppose the context shifting argument really worked. Then it should be possible to *explicitly* describe a scenario in which Smith doesn't weigh 80 kg, and still elicit the intuition that a literal utterance (in the context of this scenario) of (5) is true. If there are no such cases, context shifting fails to establish that (5*) is false. As far as we know, there are no such cases. We'll pursue this point further in the last part of the chapter.

Searle and Travis, as matter of fact, in their thought experiments, never actually say, for example, what Smith weighs or what color the kettle is. Maybe we should take the fact that they don't address these questions directly to indicate that they intend the main force of their arguments not to show (5*) is false but rather to show that it lacks a truth value altogether. But the charge of truth valuelessness is the force *not* of context shifting, but of incompleteness.

Can incompleteness establish a truth value gap for (5*)? In some places RP proponents get close to saying that unless the RHS of (5*) answers the sorts of questions they insist must be answered, it lacks a truth value, and if it does, so does (5*). If this is their claim, then it is urgent that they tell us why (5*) is supposed to

---

[15] We should emphasize that we are just going along with Travis's description of these examples (and the alleged intuitions) for the sake of argument. We wish to remain neutral about how these kinds of cases should be properly characterized.

settle answers to their questions. No semanticist ever said (5*) could (or should) answer these sorts of questions. We can only speculate on why anyone would think otherwise; so, in what follows we will present concerns that proponents of RP might have in mind in faulting truth conditional semantics, in particular, in faulting the likes of (5*).

An Epistemic Concern

Why think that the RHS of (5*) lacks a truth value? Here's an answer: Because it's impossible to *figure out* (or settle, or decide) the truth value of the RHS of (5*) without knowing more about the intentions of someone who uses it.[16] Without knowing answers to questions such as, 'Under what conditions should Smith be weighed?', we cannot figure out whether the conditions specified on the RHS of (5*) obtaining suffice to establish the truth of (5). But we cannot answer this and other questions unless we know why a speaker is interested in Smith's weight in the first place. When looking at the RHS of (5*) alone we're at a loss how to ascertain its truth value because we don't know what to look for. We require more non-linguistic contextual information.

Replies to the Epistemic Concern

Whether ordinary speakers are at a loss when looking at the RHS of (5*) is irrelevant to whether it lacks a truth value. Verificationism might explain why RP proponents hold that without answers to their questions there's a truth value gap. But they nowhere state that their arguments rest on verificationism. Of course, to be told that meaning doesn't determine truth conditions is a lot less exciting if we have to assume verificationism (especially since verificationism is false).

Second, what's really being asked for here? If what you need to know is whether to weigh Smith before or after breakfast to determine whether an utterance of (5) is true, why shouldn't you also need to know . . . [and now fill in innumerably many other possible questions; all the sorts of questions that Travis and Searle ask . . .]. But it's entirely unclear how any such inquiry could ever come to an end (as is suggested by both Searle 1980: 228 and Travis).

---

[16] "We know . . . what 'open' means and we know what 'mountain' means, but we don't know what 'open the mountain' means. If somebody orders me to open the mountains, I haven't the faintest idea what I am supposed to do" (Searle 1987: 147). We assume he would say the same about 'The mountain is open'. We don't know how to figure out whether it's true even though we know the meanings of each of its words, and how those meanings are put together.

As far as we can tell, on the most natural construal of 'completeness', every *specification* of conditions is open to an incompleteness charge (i.e. there's always some unanswered question of the form 'But would it be true if . . . ?'). Suppose, for the sake of argument, that this is so. Remember, proponents of RP hold that utterances can have truth conditions (and that we can recognize these conditions as obtaining). How else are they to explain that we recognize some utterances as being true? If so, then (on the assumption that completeness is unobtainable) incompleteness is not incompatible with having determinate truth conditions. But then the incompleteness objection to truth conditional semantics collapses. It becomes unclear why we can't just stop at (5*) and be done with it.

If, on the other hand, RP says that it is possible to specify a complete set of conditions, a set of conditions that somehow answers all questions of the form 'Would it be true if . . . ?', then we must be given an idea of what exactly would constitute this sort of completeness. Does it specify the possible 'truth makers' down to the smallest elementary particles? All the relevant laws of nature? In other words, an entire description of the universe (and, presumably, alternative universes)? If that's what completeness amounts to, then how can any utterance manage to be complete? We have no proof that such questions can't be answered, but absent a convincing story, we remain highly skeptical.

Context Dependency Concern

Maybe we're missing the point: maybe there's supposed to be the following intimate connection between context shifting and incompleteness. We are supposed to know from the context shifting claim that truth conditions change from context to context, so that the only way to know which truth conditions are expressed by the RHS of (5*) is to 'say more', i.e. provide answers to the relevant sorts of questions mentioned in backing up the incompleteness charge. What the correct answers are, of course, is contingent upon the particular details of the context of the utterance in question.

Reply to the Context Dependency Concern

This way of putting things mischaracterizes the scenarios used in trying to establish context shifting. None of these shows, so we have argued, that the truth conditions change from context to context. Every context in which an utterance of (5) is true is one in which Smith weighs 80 kg. We made this point above and will pursue it again at the end of our chapter.

We tentatively conclude, conditional on someone else coming up with a telling concern we've missed, that neither incompleteness nor context shifting establishes that RP is true.

6. Extension to Moderate Pragmatics

We have already urged that MP unavoidably slips into RP. However, it's useful to speak directly to these other cases. Not surprisingly, parallel reasoning establishes the same conclusion against attempts by proponents of MP to use incompleteness and context shifting to establish that (6*)–(9*) fail to specify truth conditions for (6)–(9). We'll use (8) to illustrate.

Any circumstances in which an utterance of (8) is true can be correctly described as circumstances in which Peter's book is gray. None can be described as ones in which Peter's book is not gray but in which (8) is true. So, everything we have said about (4) and (5) extends with equal force to (8).

Yet the incompleteness charge seems to many, we suppose, to be more powerful with respect to sentences like (8) than with respect to (4) and (5), and so we'll focus on it. Our claim is that whatever intuitions we harbor about (8*) being incomplete are irrelevant to truth conditional semantics.

If we are right that (8*) is not in the business of answering the sorts of questions proponents of MP raise about it, why might someone think otherwise? The concerns we discussed above all resurface here and our replies are as before. We'll revisit one old concern and discuss one new one.

Epistemic Concern Revisited

How, someone might wonder, can I figure out the truth value of the RHS of (8*) unless I'm told what the relevant–intended relation is between Peter and the relevant book? Is it authorship, possession, proximity, current choice, or what?

Reply to the Epistemic Concern

Our reply is twofold (you've seen both folds before). First, sentences like (8*) do (or at least certainly need) not specify verification conditions for their LHS, so the charge that they don't is irrelevant. This reply to the epistemic concern is fundamental.

Second, suppose we give you the following non-linguistically motivated 'expansion', 'enrichment', or 'completion' for a particular utterance of (8):

(8E) The book that Peter has authored is gray.

Does (8E) suffice to meet the epistemic concern? We've already shown that it doesn't. (8E) doesn't reveal *how* Peter must have authored the book. Would (8E) be true if he ghostwrote it for someone else (and this other person's name appears on its cover)? What if, what if, what if . . . In other words, if (8) isn't enough, we're not sure what it would be to satisfy the epistemic concern. Recall, we are *here* speaking on behalf of the MP, for whom completion is supposed to be possible. But if the demand is epistemological, until we are told why and how much, it's not clear there are any epistemologically satisfying completions, or at least it's not clear why it's permissible to stop with the likes of (8E). The proponent of MP seeks a middle ground where there just isn't one.[17]

Co-opting Charge

At this point proponents of RP and MP might with a certain irritation say that all of our responses to their concerns succeed only because we are smuggling their own position into our replies. They claim that (4)–(9) can only get completed (expanded, enriched, whatever) in contexts of utterance: only utterances produced by flesh and blood speakers have truth conditions. We, in our reply to context shifting, could be charged with exploiting this very aspect of their positions: In effect what we did is ask the reader to take a context of utterance C and suppose, for example, that (7) is true in C. Aren't we thereby merely pointing out that it would be true to describe context C by saying that *in it* Tipper is ready? But according to MP, (7) gets completed in C to something we might approximately describe with (7a). So, when we describe C, our utterance of (7*) (used in describing C) takes on the same completion, because our discussion of C has

---

[17] It is tempting to reply to this second concern that it all depends on context and speaker's intentions, that is, how much completion is required is determined in context. In some contexts (8E) is sufficient, and in other contexts it is not. In those contexts in which it is sufficient, the questions left unanswered can be settled any way we want, and it's irrelevant to the truth value of the sentences. In these contexts, the only thing that matters is whether the book that Peter has authored is gray. But this is clearly not a reply RP–MP can make. They were trying to show that there's something intrinsically wrong with (8*). That it simply doesn't specify truth conditions. On the current view, they are granting us that (8*) can specify 'complete' truth conditions.

rendered this completion contextually salient. So, proponents of MP would predict our response (and explain why we can give it).

Reply to the Co-opting Charge

This sort of reply has gotten the dialectic backwards. Recall that at this stage in the dialectic we are *not* trying to refute MP or RP. (We will do that in Section 7 below.) Instead, what we are trying to do is to show that none of the proposed data support either RP or MP. So, suppose, for the sake of argument, that RP and MP theorists can explain why any circumstance in which an utterance of (5) is true can be described as one in which Smith weighs 80 kg. Then so much the worse for their argument to the effect that truth conditions can change across contexts of utterance. It shows that even from the perspective of RP and MP, there's no consistent way to express the claim that the truth conditions change between contexts.

7. Refutation of Radical and Moderate Pragmatics

So far we've argued that incompleteness and context shifting fail to show that meaning doesn't determine truth conditions. None of this, however, establishes that meaning does determine truth conditions and we won't attempt to do that in this chapter. However, our reply to the context shifting argument, if correct, does provide a direct refutation of RP.

Recall that in response to context shifting we asked, how could any utterance of (5) be true unless Smith weighs 80 kg? If it cannot, it's hard to see what RP is complaining about. Travis has responded to a related concern:

What could make the given words 'The leaves are green' true, other than the presumed 'fact that the leaves are green,'[18] is the fact that the leaves counted as green on the occasion of that speaking. Since what sometimes counts as green may sometimes not be, there may still be something to make other words 'The leaves are green' false, namely that on the occasion of their speaking, those leaves (at that time) did not count as green. (Travis 1997b: 101–2; see also Travis 1996: 457)

This passage suggests the following response to our argument: an utterance of (5) can be true when Smith doesn't weigh 80 kg because he might count as

---

[18] We are no friends of facts, but we'll go along with this for purposes of discussion.

weighing 80 kg. Apparently, as Travis sees things, Smith can count as weighing 80 kg even if he doesn't weigh 80 kg.[19] This would establish that (5*) fails to specify correct truth conditions for (5). But Travis's (current) position is inconsistent with his own RP. We will show this with two different arguments.

First Inconsistency Charge[20]

What other than Smith weighing 80 kg can suffice for the truth of an utterance of (5)? Travis's answer: It suffices that Smith counts as weighing 80 kg (in a situation) and Smith can count as weighing 80 kg in some situation even though he doesn't weigh 80 kg. Notice that as soon as Travis provides this answer (more generally, any answer), he has in effect specified (generalized) truth conditions for (5). His position now seems to be that (5) is true in a context C just in case Smith counts in C as weighing 80 kg. Travis has provided no argument for thinking that this doesn't follow from the meaning of (5) alone. So, the correct T-sentence for (5), according to Travis, as determined by its meaning, is something like (5_{Travis}):

> (5_{Travis}) 'Smith weighs 80 kg' is true in a context C iff Smith counts in C as weighing 80 kg.

Notice that some version of (5_{Travis}) is available for whatever answer Travis or any other RP proponent provides to the question 'What can make an utterance of "Smith weighs 80 kg" true except Smith weighing 80 kg?' Travis's position is internally inconsistent. For as soon as he tells us what would suffice for the truth of (5) in a context C other than Smith weighing 80 kg (and he has to tell us that in order to answer our claim that nothing else would suffice), he has provided a (generalized) T-sentence.

This constitutes an objection to RP only if what fills in the RHS of (5_{Travis}) is determined by the meaning of the words (and their mode of combination). We don't see how a Radical Pragmatist could deny that the RHS of (5_{Travis}) is so determined. We are supposed to be able to figure out what the truth conditions of an utterance are from what sentence is uttered and the context. We don't go on nothing presumably, and different people figure out pretty much the same

---

[19] A natural extension would be that he thinks that an utterance of (5) can be false in a context C, when Smith does weigh 80 kg, as long as he doesn't count in C as weighing 80 kg.

[20] This inconsistency charge and the next are revised and elaborated in our forthcoming book *Insensitive Semantics*.

thing (that's why Travis can rely on our reaction to his examples). But if that's true, then there must be some sort of tacit rule guiding our interpretations. Something like: *Look for the relevant information (where this presumably has something to do with intentions and social practices) that actually determines the truth conditions.* If RP were right about the practice, this is a routine feature of interpretation of sentences, and everyone recognizes that everyone else follows the rule when we use sentences. Thus, that we follow these rules for looking for the relevant information looks like a convention associated with the use of sentences, and if we always (or almost always) use it, there's no reason not to say that it attaches to the use of the words as a matter of convention, and hence of their conventional meaning.

Second Inconsistency Charge[21]

The second inconsistency charge also arises from Travis's answer to the question 'What, other than Smith weighing 80 kg, could suffice for the truth of an utterance of (5)?' Note that Travis's answer itself is provided in a particular context. Since the answer as we encountered it occurs in a *Mind* article, we call this the Mind Context (MC, for short). According to Travis, the sentences in his paper have their truth conditions determined in MC. In particular, sentences containing the word 'green' in Travis's article must, according to RP, have the kind of context sensitive truth conditions RP claims all sentences have. So the truth conditions for

(10) What could make the given words 'The leaves are green' true, other than the presumed 'fact that the leaves are green,' is the fact that the leaves counted as green on the occasion of that speaking

are determined (in part) by what counts as green in MC, i.e. the semantic contribution of the expression 'green' as it occurs in an utterance of (10) in MC depends on what counts as green in MC. Let's say that something that counts as green in MC is Green$_{mc}$ But if so, (10) should be read as (10MC):

(10MC) What could make the given words 'The leaves are green' true, other than the presumed 'fact that the leaves are green,' is the fact that the leaves counted as green$_{mc}$ on the occasion of that speaking.

This, clearly, is not what Travis intends to say. He doesn't mean to suggest that the leaves counting as green$_{mc}$ is what would make an utterance of 'the leaves

---

[21] Some comments from Jessica Wilson helped us get clear on the issues in this section.

are green' true in contexts other than MC (and (10) is clearly about contexts other than MC). He seems to be trying to use 'green' as it occurs in (10) (note: at least the third occurrence of 'green' in (10), probably also the second occurrence) in a context insensitive way. According to Travis, such context insensitive uses are not possible. So (10) either says something false (i.e. that counting as green$_{mc}$ is what makes utterances of 'the leaves are green' true in contexts other than MC) or he uses the word 'green' in a way inconsistent with RP. (The same applies to our use of 'green' on the RHS of (5_{Travis})—and, for that matter, to our attempt to formulate this objection.)

8. A Simple, Underlying Argument?

It has been suggested to us by several philosophers (including Stephen Schiffer and Zoltán Szabó) that our discussion misses the 'fundamental' or 'underlying' argument or intuition in favor of RP–MP. To get at this intuition, go back to the context shifting argument. Why isn't its proper interpretation that since utterances of (9) have distinct truth values across scenarios, it can't be *sentence* (9) which has a truth value, and so it lacks truth conditions. On this interpretation, (9*) fails to ascribe truth conditions to (9), since it's everyone's intuition that at any given time not every utterance of (9) is true. Suppose, for example, on Tuesday 10 April 2001 you utter (9) while looking out of the window from your apartment in New York, watching rain fall gently from the sky, while I, at the exact same time, utter (9) looking out my window in New Jersey, mistaking droplets produced on my window from a sprinkler for raindrops. Isn't everyone's intuition that what you said is true and what I said is false? Yet according to (9*) the English sentence (9) is true just in case there is a raining event, and so we both said something true.

Properly understood, then, context shifting does not aim to show that truth conditions can shift from context to context, but rather that sentence types *cannot* be bearers of truth and falsity, only their utterances can. Your utterance of (9) is true because it is *about* a particular location, namely, New York, where it is raining; and mine is false, because it is about a different location, namely, New Jersey, where it is not raining. (9*) fails to capture these facts about our respective utterances.

We agree with Schiffer (and Perry and Crimmins) that when you produced your utterance of (9), you said something about New York and when I produced mine I said something about New Jersey. And indeed anyone who utters (9) in the contexts so described can be correctly reported as having said that it's raining in

New York and that it's raining in New Jersey respectively. Yet if the arguments of the last section are sound, we cannot appeal to RP–MP to explain these intuitions since these positions are internally inconsistent. So, how then are we to explain them? As far as we can tell, we have two choices remaining.

One strategy would be to treat (9) as more linguistically complex than it might seem. So, instead of treating (9*) as providing the correct interpretive truth conditions for (9), we might instead opt for (9′):

(9′) 'It's raining' is true relative to a place p iff it's raining at p.

The difference between (9*) and (9′) is that in effect (9′) treats (9) as harboring a context sensitive element whose semantic role is to pick out contextually salient places. Were one to adopt this strategy, one would have to show that positing this contextually sensitive indexical is motivated on syntactic or morphological grounds, and doing so doesn't raise more problems than it solves. Stanley (2000) has argued as such, by appeal to what he calls the binding criterion. He notes the grammaticality of (9^+):

(9^+) Wherever I go, it rains.

In this statement, the place where it rains can be understood to vary with the place introduced by the quantifier 'wherever I go'. On its most natural interpretation, (9^+) means 'For every location l such that I go to l, it rains in l'. For such binding to occur, Stanley argues, there must be a free variable l in (9). That variable can either be bound as in (9^+) or contextually given a value as in (9). If he's right, then the location contextually provided for rain is not unarticulated.

We will not have much to say about this strategy here. We are skeptical about the existence of such variables, and have argued as much elsewhere (see footnote 6 for references). Also, since we agreed for the purposes of this chapter not to pursue the suggestion that RP–MP could be countered by an appeal to further linguistic analysis, we want to entertain a second strategy. In what follows we will briefly and dogmatically present a framework within which intuitions about typical utterances of (9) can be accommodated without compromising a semantic theory according to which (9*) provides correct truth conditions for (9). We will then provide some motivation for this framework.

To begin with, we want to agree with RP–MP that the meaning of (9) (or any other sentence) need not determine *what's said* by utterances of (9) or what these utterances are *about*. To this extent, our position seems rather concessive, at least with respect to (iii) above in our original characterization of RP: for we are agreeing with RP–MP that the meaning of a sentence needn't determine what's said by its utterances.

Where we part company is with respect to the status of (i) above: we want to deny that there is any close relationship between correct reports of what others have said with their utterances of sentences and what the truth conditions of these utterances are. Accordingly, we don't think it follows from the fact that a particular utterance of (9) can say something about New York that (9*) fails to specify correct truth conditions for (9). Nor does it show that the meaning of (9) doesn't determine (9*) as its correct truth conditions.

To give a sense of why we believe this, we need to say a bit about what's said.

On What's Said

Briefly, here's how we see the relationship between sentences and their utterances: Sentences have truth conditions, as determined by their meaning. Utterances are used to make statements (i.e. to say things), ask questions, and perform other kinds of speech acts. Utterances typically (but not always) are of sentences, but what's said, what's asked, etc., by an utterance can depend not only on the truth conditions of the sentence uttered, but also upon a number of other 'non-semantic' features of the context of utterance. In short:

(a) The truth conditions of a sentence S need not correspond to what's said or stated by an utterance of S.

(b) What's said by an utterance of S can be true, even though the truth conditions for S aren't satisfied (and vice versa).

(c) What's said by an utterance of S can be 'about' something (e.g. New York City), even though the truth conditions for S make no reference (to that thing).

(d) Because of (a)–(c), intuitions about utterances of sentences can in no simple and direct way be used as guides to the truth conditions for those sentences.

Here we will briefly show how to support this general framework.

In Cappelen and Lepore (1997, 1998) we pointed out that reports of the form 'A said/asserted/stated that p' can be true even if A never uttered a sentence, appropriately contextualized, that is true just in case p. Since intuitions about what's said by an utterance are fixed by acceptable indirect reports, it follows that (a)–(d) are correct. We'll rehearse some data and arguments starting with rather obvious and trivial cases where there's a distinction between the truth conditions of the sentences uttered and what is said by that utterance. Consider sentence (11).

(11) Stephen lives in New York and Ernie in New Jersey,

Even if we assume that (11*) correctly specifies the truth conditions for (11),

(11*) 'Stephen lives in New York and Ernie in New Jersey' is true iff Stephen
      lives in New York and Ernie in New Jersey,

no one would deny that someone who utters (11) can be correctly reported as
having said that Stephen lives in New York.

Even if the truth conditions for (12) are (12*),

(12) John is a good friend
(12*) 'John is a good friend' is true iff John is a good friend,

if a speaker A utters (12) in a sarcastic tone of voice, it would typically *not* be correct to report A as having asserted, claimed, stated, or committed himself to
John being a good friend.[22] Everyone would, however, report A as having asserted/
claimed/stated and committed himself to John not being a good friend.

Summaries provide further support. Consider an utterance of (13) by O:

(13) Around 11 p.m. I put on a white shirt, a blue suit, darks socks, and my
      brown Bruno Magli shoes; I then got into a waiting limousine and
      drove off into heavy traffic to the airport, where I just made my
      midnight flight to Chicago.

We can all think of contexts in which (13r) would correctly and prudently
report an utterance of (13):

(13r) O said that he dressed around 11 p.m., went to the airport, and took the
      midnight flight to Chicago.

Yet no one thinks that (13r) specifies correct truth conditions for (13).

These cases are not peculiar; they are typical. (For further examples and critical discussion of these examples, we refer the reader to earlier work; see the list
of references.) Should we on the bases of these sorts of cases conclude that
sentence meaning does not determine truth conditions? It is true that what
these sorts of cases show is that what's said by an utterance, or what an utterance
is about, or even whether it is true or not, can be influenced by all sorts of
non-semantic aspects of the sentences being uttered. So, to that extent don't
these cases bear out the chief claims of RP (and MP)?

---

[22] In *Insensitive Semantics* we have more to say about sarcasm.

Take another case: Suppose that Professor Adams utters 'I failed no one'. He can be correctly reported to his student Mary as having said that he didn't fail her, and so what he can be reported as having said is about Mary, even though his original utterance made no reference to her. On the standard picture, a speaker says that *p* just in case he assertively utters a sentence that is true just in case *p*. Accordingly, a speaker's words make reference to an object or a domain just in case what he says with those words does as well. Therefore, on the standard picture, any true report of what's said with an utterance according to which a speaker makes reference to an object or a domain that neither he nor his words does must *misrepresent* what he said. However, what our examples establish is that determining what's said by an utterance often requires attending to *non-interpretive*, *non-semantic* considerations. When we try to represent or articulate what's said by an utterance we aim to characterize a speaker's act (that utterance). In so doing, our interests often are not in systematicity or generality, but rather our aim is to determine something about a particular act in a particular context C in order to pass it along onto to a particular audience situated in a (perhaps a very) different (sort of) context C*. In effect, our practice of indirectly reporting what's said treats it as a four-place relation between a sentence and a context of utterance and a reporting sentence and its context of utterance.

In determining what's said we obviously draw upon information about specific intentions, knowledge, and history of the speaker in C (and, not so obviously, we can also draw upon *like features of C**, the context in which we report what's said). Our reporting practices clarify that semantics should not a priori constrain what can and can't be said by an utterance. Competent speakers make such judgments all the time, often relying on information that exceeds anything about the meanings of the words used. This competence consists, in part, in a capacity to judge whether a report about what's said is accurate or misleading. There is no reason to believe that determining what's said will be simpler or more systematic than determining whether two items are similar.

What's the upshot for semantics? Not, we believe, what the proponents of RP (and MP) would have us believe. They would have us conclude that meaning doesn't determine truth conditions. But this inference is warranted only if we confuse aspects of our reporting practice with issues about the meanings of our words. For Schiffer *et al.*, since someone who utters (9) can say that it's raining in New York, how can a theory that insists upon (9*) as its full and explicit treatment of the semantics be correct? Our answer is that what's said isn't determined by meaning. Schiffer agrees, but on this basis he wants to junk truth conditional semantics since he presumes that if (9*) correctly specifies the truth conditions for (9), then every utterance of (9) is true as long as it's raining somewhere in the world at the time of utterance. However, his presumption reflects a misunderstanding about the relationship between semantics and what's said.

One of the ways in which our view can be implemented (and only one, since this requires substantial work in semantics to settle) is to say that (9) is true at a time t (to accommodate its tense) just in case there is a raining event at time t. So, whenever someone utters (9) at t what he is uttering is true (at t) just in case there is a raining event at t. Given this likelihood, almost every utterance of (9) is true at its time of utterance.[23] Still, when we ask whether what someone uttered is true, we might not be talking about whether the truth conditions for the sentence he uttered obtain or not. We might instead be asking about what he said with his utterance—something he did. And, so we have been arguing, what he said at time t may disagree in truth value with the very sentence he uttered at that time t. So, in effect, whether an utterance is true or not is ambiguous between whether the sentence uttered is true (which, according to us, is completely determined by what the sentence means together with facts about precipitation) and whether what was said by that utterance is true or not (which can be determined by non-linguistic, non-semantic considerations).

In many of the above cases, our interests in what was said went well beyond the meanings of the speaker's words (and the semantic values of the various expressions he used in his context of utterance). Once someone hears a sarcastic tone, his interests are likely to extend beyond what the words uttered mean. If one's interests are in particulars, he will try to turn a general claim like 'Everyone passed' into a specific one like 'Mary passed'. And so it goes.

We have suggested that there are two different ways in which a proponent of the view that meaning determines truth conditions might try to explain away some intuitions behind RP–MP. But still we can imagine someone saying that it ultimately comes down to whether one finds the frameworks we are working in more or less attractive than the one that proponents of RP–MP are working in. But, to repeat, if the arguments of the last section are sound, then RP–MP is internally inconsistent, and so it is not an option.

---

[23] Of course, one might argue that the range of the quantifier 'There is a raining event' is restricted in some way. We don't actually like this move, but recognize it as one way to render our position more palatable. Notice also that on our view a sentence like 'It's raining in Palo Alto' would mean that there is a raining event and it is occurring in Palo Alto, so there is no need to treat 'raining' as relational in this sentence.

Conclusion

We began by presenting what we have called the incompleteness charge and the context shifting claim, which taken together are supposed to establish RP. We then argued that there is no principled line to draw between RP and MP, so that if you are impressed by the sorts of considerations advanced in favor of MP, then you must embrace RP as well. We then proceeded to argue that neither separately nor taken together do incompleteness and context shifting establish that meaning doesn't determine truth conditions. We responded to the context shifting claim by noting that every context in which, for example, we thought an utterance of 'Smith weighs 80 kg' is true, we also thought that Smith weighed 80 kg, and vice versa. We responded to the incompleteness charge with a challenge: Why should we answer the questions that RP poses? We considered various concerns, and argued that none suffices to establish that sentence meaning fails to determine truth conditions. We then argued for two charges of inconsistency against RP. If right, not only does RP fail to establish that meaning doesn't determine truth conditions, but RP itself has provided no coherent alternative to the standard picture. In the end, we are left with a position, one we did not argue for here directly, that the effects of context on assigning truth conditions to an utterance are limited to fixing the values of context sensitive linguistic items, precisifying vague terms, and disambiguating ambiguous strings in the sentence uttered. In short, in determining truth conditions for utterances of sentences, context interacts with meaning only when triggered by the grammar of the sentence.

REFERENCES

Bach, Kent (1994), 'Conversational Impliciture', *Mind and Language*, 9/2: 124–62.

Cappelen, H., and E. Lepore (1997), 'On an Alleged Connection between Indirect Quotation and Semantic Theory', *Mind and Language*, 12: 278–96.

————— (1998), 'Reply to Richard and Reimer', *Mind and Language*, 13/4: 617–21.

————— (2002), 'Insensitive Quantifiers', in J. Campbell, M. O'Rourke, and D. Shier (eds.), *Meaning and Truth: Investigating Philosophical Semantics* (New York: Seven Bridges Press), 197–213.

————— (2004), *Insensitive Semantics: A Defense of Semantic Minimalism and Speech Act Pluralism* (Oxford Basil Blackwell).

Carston, R. (1988), 'Implicature, Explicature, and Truth-Theoretic Semantics', in R. Kempson (ed.), *Mental Representations: The Interface between Language and Reality* (Cambridge: Cambridge University Press), 155–81.

Crimmins, M. (1992), *Talk about Belief* (Cambridge, Mass: MIT Press).

Lepore, Ernie (2004), 'Is there a Problem with Incomplete Definite Descriptions', in M. Reimer and A. Bezuidenhout (eds.), *Descriptions and Beyond* (Oxford: Oxford University Press), 42–68.

Perry, John (1986), 'Thought without Representation', *Proceedings of the Aristotelian Society*, suppl. vol. 60: 263–83; repr. in his *The Problem of the Essential Indexical and Other Essays* (Oxford: Oxford University Press), 205–25.

Recanati, F. (1993), *Direct Reference* (Oxford: Basil Blackwell).

Schiffer, Stephen (1995), 'Descriptions, Indexicals and Belief Reports', *Mind*, 104: 107–31.

Searle, John (1978), 'Literal Meaning', *Erkenntnis*, 13: 207–24.

—— (1980), 'The Background of Meaning', in J. Searle, F. Kiefer, and M. Bierwisch (eds.), *Speech Act Theory and Pragmatics* (Dordrecht: Reidel), 221–32.

—— (1987), *Intentionality* (Cambridge: Cambridge University Press).

Sperber, D., and D. Wilson (1986), *Relevance* (Oxford: Basil Blackwell).

Stanley, J. (2000), 'Context and Logical Form', *Linguistics and Philosophy*, 23: 391–424.

Travis, Charles (1985), 'On What Is Strictly Speaking True', *Canadian Journal of Philosophy*, 15/2: 187–229.

—— (1996), 'Meaning's Role in Truth', *Mind*, 100: 451–66.

—— (1997a), 'Reply to Simmons', *Mind*, 106: 119–20.

—— (1997b), 'Pragmatics', in B. Hale and C. Wright (eds.), *A Companion to the Philosophy of Language* (Oxford: Basil Blackwell), 97–107.

3

Focus: A Case Study on the Semantics–Pragmatics Boundary

Michael Glanzberg

Focus is the term linguists use to describe a kind of *prominence* in a sentence, usually marked by stress on a particular word or phrase. For instance, *Greek* is focused in:

(1) He spoke GREEK.

Philosophers coming to language from the tradition of logical semantics have sometimes been inclined to discount this sort of phenomenon. It makes no difference to the truth conditions of this particular sentence, and may appear merely to be an aspect of the vocal realization of the sentence—of interest to phonologists, and perhaps to socio-linguists, but not of much importance to fundamental philosophical questions about semantics and pragmatics. This appearance is deceptive. In fact, as we will see below, focus is a locus of interaction between semantics and pragmatics. Understanding this innocent-looking phenomenon is important to understanding how semantics and pragmatics relate to one another.

Much of the recent philosophical debate over the semantics–pragmatics distinction has focused on the question of how much underlying syntactic structure is responsible for determining what is said by an utterance, and how much

This chapter grew out of a study of Elena Herburger's book *What Counts*. Its main ideas were presented as comments on that book at a semantics workshop at the Center for Cognitive Science of Rutgers University in September 2001. Thanks to the participants there, and especially Elena Herburger, for valuable discussion. Thanks also to Ernie Lepore and two anonymous referees for comments on earlier drafts.

what is said is determined by autonomous pragmatic processes such as 'free enrichment'. The debate has centered on a family of examples like:

(2*a*) I have had breakfast.
(2*b*) Ralph drinks.

These present cases in which what we intuitively see as the truth conditions of an utterance is determined by more than we see in the surface linguistic structure of the sentences, raising the question of whether the truth conditions are fixed by richer underlying syntactic structure or by purely pragmatic processes.[1]

One reason for studying focus is that it provides a very different set of examples. More so than the examples in (2), I believe, focus provides examples of how semantics and pragmatics *interact*. Understanding this interaction is a good way to come to understand the two sides of the semantics–pragmatics boundary. Indeed, it turns out that focus provides us with some very hard cases of semantic–pragmatic interaction. Studying hard cases cannot resolve all issues, and in this case, it will not resolve the debate over the nature of semantics and pragmatics. But hard cases do serve to set some parameters for theorizing. In this way, looking at focus will lead to several morals for the debate. Three seem to me to be especially important. First, the appearance that something is pragmatic can be deceptive. We will see good reason to take focus to be a semantic phenomenon, realized in logical form. But second, the fact that something is realized in a linguistic structure like logical form does not preclude its semantics triggering extremely complex pragmatic processes. For instance, a demonstrative, overtly present in the surface form of a sentence, triggers a pragmatic process of reference fixing. In the case of focus, I shall argue, a far more complex kind of pragmatic process is triggered: one of regulating the flow of information in a discourse.[2] As the reference-fixing process determines the value of a demonstrative, so the discourse-regulating process fixes the semantic contribution of focus. The semantic contribution of focus is thus heavily context-dependent. Finally, third, the kind of context dependence involved is different than the model of the demonstrative might lead us to expect. Though I take focus to be realized in logical form, its semantic contribution is not well characterized as simply the value of a parameter in logical form, and the pragmatic processes

---

[1] The former view is advocated by King and Stanley (Ch. 3 in this volume), Stanley (2000, 2002), and Stanley and Szabó (2000). The latter view is defended by a number of authors, including Bach (1994), Carston (1988, forthcoming), Recanati (1993), and Sperber and Wilson (1986). Of course, there are important theoretical difference between all of these authors.

[2] The phrase is borrowed from Kadmon (2001).

that affect its semantic contribution are not much like the processes that fix demonstrative or indexical reference.

These conclusions are not enough to resolve the debate over the semantics–pragmatics distinction. Both sides may take heart from some of them. But on balance, I am inclined to think they favor the side which sees what is said as determined primarily by linguistic structure, and the context dependence of elements in that structure. Focus shows us cases where unexpected structure can be found, which triggers processes which may well have looked purely pragmatic.

My discussion of focus is divided into six sections. In Section 1, I examine the pragmatic effects of focus, and sketch a simple pragmatic theory. In Section 2 I review arguments that focus has significant semantic effects, and must be marked in the appropriate syntactic structure. Then in Section 3 I outline a provisional approach to the semantics of focus, and show how it relates to the pragmatic theory of Section 1. In Section 4 I turn to arguments which show this pragmatic theory to be inadequate. These arguments indicate that a much richer pragmatic theory is needed, based on the structure of *discourse* and the pragmatic processes that regulate felicity in discourse. In Section 5 I investigate how such a theory might proceed (borrowing from work of Roberts 1996 and Büring 2003). I also consider what it tells us about the semantics of focus and how the semantics and pragmatics of focus interact. Finally, I conclude in Section 6 by returning to the general question of the semantics–pragmatics boundary.

1. A Purely Pragmatic Phenomenon?

Any utterance conveys a huge range of information, much of it well beyond what is *meant* by the utterance. Among the sources of extra information are features of the way the sentence is pronounced. For instance, the volume and tone of voice of the speaker will reveal a great deal about her to a sensitive hearer, much of which will be beyond what the speaker intends to convey in making the utterance.

One of the features of the way an utterance is pronounced that has been of great interest to linguists is that of *intonational prominence*. Any sentence will have some parts that are intonationally more prominent than others. For instance, consider:

(3) John kissed JANE.

The prominence of the last phrase *Jane* is indicated by capitals. This is what is sometimes called 'stress' or 'focal stress'. However, many phonologists insist on a difference between *stress*, pertaining to prominence in a rhythmic pattern, and *pitch accent* (or just *accent*) pertaining to prominence within an 'intonation contour' or 'tune'. One of the ways *Jane* is marked as prominent is by a high tone or pitch accent in the intonation contour of the sentence. For most of what follows, the phonology of how *Jane* is marked as prominent in (3) will not matter, and we can take a theoretically unreflective stance towards whatever the capitals indicate. However, at a couple of points we will have to distinguish different ways of marking, by different intonation contours, so I will follow those who talk about pitch accent rather than stress.[3]

Let us say that a constituent marked by pitch accent as prominent is *focused*. (Below, this definition will be refined somewhat, as we will come to see focus as a phenomenon which is normally realized by accent.) It is easy to observe that focus has some effect on the information conveyed in an utterance. But what is the effect? We will see several options. In this section I will restrict attention to purely pragmatic options. More semantically driven options will be addressed later.

1.1. The Pessimistic View

One natural idea is that focus is simply a way of highlighting some part of a sentence. It is a kind of phonological 'pointing'. What follows from this is only what may be rendered salient by such highlighting, but is otherwise unconstrained. This pessimistic view is nicely summed up by the title of Bolinger (1972), 'Accent is Predictable (if you're a Mind-Reader)'.[4]

The pessimistic view is too weak. The pragmatics of focus is more constrained than it allows. Consider a pair like:

(4*a*) John likes JANE.
(4*b*) JOHN likes Jane.

There is a uniform difference between these examples. In each, the focus indicates some kind of *contrast*. In (4*a*) it is indicated that John likes Jane, as opposed to, say, Sue or Mary. In (4*b*) it is indicated that it is John who likes Jane, as opposed to, say, Bill or Fred.[5]

---

[3] For some surveys of relevant aspects of phonology, see Kadmon (2001), Ladd (1996), and Pierrehumbert and Hirschberg (1990).

[4] Bolinger's real interest is in arguing that accent placement cannot be predicted by phonological rules.   [5] This aspect of focus is discussed in Dretske (1972).

In some cases, the indication of contrast can be central to the meaning of an utterance. A nice example is given by Francis Ford Coppola's film *The Conversation*. In it, a professional eavesdropper records someone saying to another:

(5) He'd kill us if he got the chance.

The eavesdropper is then faced with many worries about the safety of the people he spied upon. A plot twist leads to their committing a murder. Going back over the tape, the eavesdropper realizes the message is in fact:

(6) HE'd kill US if he got the chance.

Exactly what the contrast involved in focus is, and how it is determined, remains to be seen. But we can already observe that it is not merely a matter of unconstrained highlighting. We cannot hear the sentences in (4) any other way than indicating different contrasts. If the function of focus were mere highlighting, it should be possible to see the highlighting as not mattering, or indicating something having nothing to do with contrast. Moreover, the close relation of focus to what is meant by an utterance displayed in (6) is left unexplained by the pessimistic view.

It is worth pausing to note that in insisting that there is some more specific pragmatic effect of focus, I still allow that it may have further pragmatic effects of all sorts. For instance, it is known that focus often helps determine *scalar implicatures*. Consider two sentences:

(7a) I PASSED. (Focus on *passed*.)
(7b) I passed. (Focus on *I*.)

In many contexts, these sentences will trigger scalar implicatures, and what implicature is triggered will depend on the focus. (7a) is likely to trigger the implicature that I did not do any better than passing. (7b) is likely to trigger the implicature that other members of my study-group did not pass.

However, focus effects are not uniformly associated with scalar implicatures. In many contexts, any of (3), (4), and (6) may not display any scalar implicature of this sort at all. Furthermore, when we do see scalar implicatures, their cancellation does not void the pragmatic effects of focus. Consider:

(8) Well, I PASSED. That is what I really needed to stay in school. In fact, I think I probably did pretty well.

The implicature is explicitly canceled, but there remains some effect of contrast triggered by focus on *passed*.[6]

Finally, one more pragmatic aspect of focus, which will be crucial in what follows, highlights the constrained nature of focus. Focus helps determine *question-answer congruence*. Compare:

(9a) Who does John like?

    (i) John likes JANE.
    (ii) # JOHN likes Jane.

(9b) Who likes Jane?

    (i) JOHN likes Jane.
    (ii) # John likes JANE.

In each case, the answer to the question is infelicitous if the focus is in the wrong place.[7] These judgments are quite strong. It is not that the inappropriate answers are somehow less helpful—they are simply infelicitous.

I conclude that the pessimistic view under-appreciates the function of focus. Though it may be that phonological prominence can trigger a number of pragmatic effects, it has some that are regularly associated with it which are fundamental to interpreting an utterance. The appearance of contrast, felicity in question–answer congruence, and relevance to what is meant, all must be explained by any theory of focus, pragmatic or semantic.

1.2. An Initial Pragmatic Theory

The striking data of question–answer congruence, as well as of indications of contrast, suggest a more complete pragmatic account of focus. I shall sketch a version of this which seems to capture the nature of focus nicely in terms of familiar pragmatic ideas. This sort of theory is well known to require significant modification, but it is a good starting place.

Question–answer congruence examples like (9) invite an explanation in terms of the providing of information in a discourse. The question can be seen as a request for information, while the answer provides it. The felicity of an answer

---

[6] This example is from Rooth (1992), which works out the scale for (7b) in some detail. The example from *The Conversation* is mentioned in Rooth (1996a).

[7] I mark infelicity by '#'. Ungrammaticality, as usual, will be marked by '*'.

has something to do with whether or not it properly provides information that answers the question.

It has been a widespread idea to explain the effects of focus in terms of the distinction between *given* and *new* information. Very roughly, the focused constituent of a sentence marks the part of the sentence that provides new information; while the non-focused part provides given information. Question–answer congruence is the result of whether the new information answers the question asked.

To flesh out this approach, we need an analysis of the notions of given and new. This can be done in neo-Gricean terms. One of the core observations of pragmatics in the Gricean tradition is that utterances take place against a background of information, and of principles governing the exchange of information in discourse. What background information is relevant to a conversation? Ideally, that which is held in common among all participants in a conversation, and which all participants recognize to be held in common. This is what Stalnaker (1978) calls *common ground* and Schiffer (1972) calls *mutual knowledge*. We might take what is *given* at a particular point in a conversation to be what is common ground at that point. What is new is what is not given.

As Stalnaker (1978) stressed (building on work of Grice 1975), cooperative communication is sensitive to given and new information so understood. First of all, cooperative utterances must provide some new information. Moreover, in many cases, cooperative utterances rely upon given information to fix, for instance, the referents of indexicals and demonstratives. Thus, cooperative utterances must respect the status of given and new. It was suggested (e.g. by Clark and Haviland 1977) that, furthermore, cooperative utterances should mark what they take to be given and what they take to be new, in a way that itself will be common ground in the conversation. (This is what Clark and Haviland call the "given–new contract".[8]) The role of focus, this theory holds, is primarily to mark what is *new* in an utterance from what is given.

By marking constituents, focus partitions a sentence. Let us call the unfocused part of a sentence the *ground*. The pragmatic theory then proposes that there is a mapping between focus and new information, and between ground and given information. This should explain the phenomenon of question–answer congruence. Asking a question creates elements of common ground. A felicitous answer should add new information relevant to that background. It should also explain

---

[8] Clark and Haviland are more sensitive to speaker–hearer asymmetry than I have been. The contract requires speakers to mark as given what they think hearers already know.

the effects on interpretation we saw in (6). The significance of an utterance, irrespective of its truth conditions, is determined in part by what it takes to be common ground, and what information it adds to that ground. The effect of contrast noted in (4) remains a little more elusive on this theory. But there is a sense in which new information contrasts with given information, and that might be used to explain the contrast present in these examples. At least, for instance, (4a) contrasts *Jane* to *John*, in marking *Jane* as providing new information. (A more promising line is that the focus implicitly defines a contrast set. But this explanation will take us towards a theory of a very different sort, as we will see below in Section 5.)

There are a number of open questions about this sort of theory. One important one is how the mapping of parts of sentences to given and new information is to be achieved. In cases with focused noun phrases like (4), it is not clear how the focus corresponds to new information, nor how what is left of the sentence corresponds to given information.

One traditional answer to this question has been in terms of *focal presuppositions*. In a case like (4a), for instance, the informational correlates of the sentence appear to be something like:

(10) There is someone whom John likes, and it is JANE.

To specify this idea a little further, take the focal presupposition of a sentence to be the proposition resulting from replacing the focus of the sentence with a variable and existentially quantifying it. The focal presupposition is the given information. The new information is the proposition that the focus satisfies the ground. So we have:

(11) John likes JANE.

    (*a*) Focal presupposition: $\exists x \mathbf{likes}(\mathbf{n}, x)$.
    (*b*) New information: $\mathbf{likes}(\mathbf{n}, \mathbf{j})$.

The term 'focal presupposition' fits well with the pragmatic approach to presupposition of Stalnaker (1974). On that view, common ground or given information just is presupposition. So the theory tells us that among the presuppositions of a sentence is its focal presupposition. This presupposition characterizes the question to which the sentence is a felicitous answer.[9]

---

[9] This notion of focal presupposition is quite common. It is explicit in Chomsky (1971). It may be similar to the notion of *open proposition* used by Prince and her co-workers (e.g. Prince 1981a), though her view may be closer to that of Jackendoff (1972).

Appealing to focal presupposition is quite controversial, and I shall question it in Section 4. But without something like it, the notions of given and new information do not suffice. For instance, the status of the referent of a noun phrase as given or new does not explain the difference between focus and ground. As Reinhart (1981) notes:

(12a) Who did Felix praise?
(12b) Felix praised HIMSELF.

The referent of the focused constituent *himself* is already salient in the discourse, and so certainly counts as given rather than new. This is not peculiar to the reciprocal. We likewise have:

(13a) Who does Dick Cheney love?
(13b) Dick Cheney loves DICK CHENEY.

In each of (12) and (13) the referent of the focused noun phrase is already given. To get a mapping from focus to new and ground to given information, we need to make use of the sort of focal presupposition and new information structure sketched in (11). This makes the given information in (13) $\exists x \textbf{love}\,(\textbf{c}, x)$ and the new information $\textbf{love}\,(\textbf{c}, \textbf{c})$.[10]

Aside from the status of focal presupposition, another open question is how the partition of a sentence into focus and ground, which for all we have said so far is simply a matter of phonological prominence, gets associated with given and new information. Clark and Haviland (1977) propose a Gricean explanation, subsuming the focus–new/ground–given association under the maxim of manner. However, there is some reason to doubt that manner implicatures alone explain the association. In most cases, for instance, the maxims of manner involved are not violated when we see the effect of contrast, as in (4a). Indeed, we expect all sentences to contain some pitch accent, so we have no reason to think that the mere presence of a pitch accent (indicating focus) would be enough to trigger a manner

---

[10] There are a number of different notions of given and new information to be found in the literature, and discussions of focus have used several of them, as Prince (1981b) has discussed. For instance, the characterization of focus as what is new found in Halliday (1967) relies on the notion of what is given as linguistic material that is recoverable from previous discourse. In a theoretically quite different setting, a notion of givenness along similar lines is used in Schwarzschild (1999). Chafe (1976) goes out of his way to insist that the contrast involved in focus in not a matter of what he calls new information. But Chafe's notion of newness is one of psychological saliency, in the sense of being currently in consciousness.

implicature.[11] Moreover, manner implicatures should be cancellable, while many of the effects of focus we are trying to explain do not seem to be. We saw an example of this in (8). It is thus tempting to see the mapping of focus to new information as conventional.[12]

We now have an initial proposal for a purely pragmatic explanation of focus. It has some well-known problems, but it goes far enough to make the view that focus is a purely pragmatic phenomenon plausible. I shall now turn to some observations that support the opposing view, that focus is primarily a semantic phenomenon.

2. Semantic Aspects of Focus

Concentrating on examples like (4), it might be tempting to conclude the focus is entirely a pragmatic phenomenon. The neo-Gricean given–new analysis seems to support this conclusion. However, there are a number of well-documented *semantic* aspects of focus, and other grammatical aspects of it as well. I shall present a few of these here.[13]

2.1. Association with Focus

Among the more striking of the semantic effects of focus is its relation to so-called focusing operators, such as *only*. Following Rooth (1985), consider:

(14a) John only introduced Bill to SUE.

(14b) John only introduced BILL to Sue.

---

[11] As has often been noted, manner implicatures are triggered by suitably marked constructions. (See Horn 1989 and Levinson 2000 for further discussion.) That each sentence contains some pitch accent does not preclude an entire sentence being a focus. This is due to the phenomenon of focus projection, discussed in Section 2.2.

[12] A more recent, and much more phonologically nuanced, version of the idea that focus marks new information is given by Pierrehumbert and Hirschberg (1990). A relevance-based account is given by Sperber and Wilson (1986). They pick up on the idea that focus marks constituents as prominent, and explain the difference between focus and ground in terms of what they call the background and foreground implications, and their effects on relevance. Though some of the differences are significant, I believe this is a spelling out in relevance-theoretic terms of the same basic idea that drives the more classically Gricean picture I have been sketching here.

[13] The current discussion of focus tends to begin with Chomsky (1971) and Jackendoff (1972). Important later work on focus in generative grammar includes Rochemont (1986). Important earlier work comes from the Prague school (e.g. Daneš 1968; Firbas 1964).

Consider a circumstance where John introduced Bill to Sue and to Mary, and did no other introducing. In this case, (14a) is false, while (14b) is true.

Similar examples can be found with adverbs of quantification (also following Rooth 1985):

(15a) In St Petersburg, OFFICERS always escorted ballerinas.

(15b) In St Petersburg, officers always escorted BALLERINAS.

Finding a hapless officer escorting an opera singer falsifies (15b) but not (15a).

Other sorts of examples like this are easy to find, including modals and generics.[14] Picking up on terminology of Jackendoff (1972), Rooth (1985) dubs the phenomenon of truth-conditional effects of focus *association with focus*.

Association with focus shows that focus is in part a semantic phenomenon. First and foremost, it demonstrates *truth-conditional* effects of the placement of focus within a sentence. The effect, generally, is on the semantic structure of the sentence. In the adverbs of quantification cases, for instance, it is an effect on what constitutes the adverb's semantic *restrictor*. Something similar appears to be happening in the *only* examples as well. Furthermore, different placements of focus can generate *incompatible* truth conditions. This does not appear to be something readily accounted for by purely pragmatic means. First, without a focus, it is not clear if the restrictors on these sorts of operators or adverbs are well defined at all, making it unclear if there is any sense to be made of propositions for these cases in the absence of focus. Thus, it is hard to see how the effects of association with focus could be the results of Gricean implicatures.

Second, it seems doubtful that the kind of process of *free enrichment* discussed by relevance theorists (e.g. Carston 1988, forthcoming; Sperber and Wilson 1986; or related ideas of Bach 1994) can address this phenomenon. This is usually described as a *strengthening* of a fragmentary representation of a thought (an incomplete logical form), or of a proposition too weak to be pragmatically relevant. But the effect of association with focus is not simply to strengthen a proposition or a fragmentary logical form. This is shown by appeal to the incompatible truth conditions generated by different placements of focus. So, for instance, if we were to assume that a default, unenriched proposition corresponds to the right-most focus (not an unreasonable assumption, given

---

[14] Surveys of these phenomena can be found in Kadmon (2001), Rooth (1996a), and von Stechow (1991). A number of authors have taken up the idea that there is something in common across these examples, as each of them in some way involves restricted quantification (e.g. Hajičová *et al.* 1998; Krifka 1992; Partee 1991; von Fintel 1994).

the phonology of English), we find the focus assigned in (14*b*) not to be a strengthening of that proposition, but incompatible with it. Alternatively, if we were to start with a fragmentary logical form or representation corresponding to a sentence like (15) without any focus, it cannot be that both (15*a*) and (15*b*) result from enriching it by adding material. They cannot both be the result of enrichment, because each winds up with different material *already* present being mapped to the restrictor of the adverbial quantifier *always*. In cases like this, we get incompatible truth conditions from association with focus in part because focus does not merely add something to a logical form or a thought; rather, it induces a semantically significant *rearrangement* of the material we might have thought went into such a fragmentary logical form.[15]

This is not to deny that focus has pragmatic effects. Nor is it to deny that focus is heavily context-dependent. It is.[16] My point so far is only that association with focus appears to uncover a genuine semantic aspect of focus as well.

2.2. Grammar and Focus

In the last subsection I described the semantic phenomenon of association with focus, and argued that the sorts of pragmatic processes commonly appealed to are not able to explain it. I shall now pursue this point a little further. There are some good reasons, independent of the truth-conditional effects of association with focus, for seeing focus as represented in the underlying grammar of

[15] As I mentioned in n. 12, Sperber and Wilson (1986) propose a theory of focus in terms of foreground and background—in particular, in terms of a scale of foreground and background implications. To be clear, they do not claim that free enrichment or a similar process should explain focus. But like other purely pragmatic theories of the sort I discussed in Section 1, they do not take into account phenomena like association with focus at all. My suggestion here is that the only sort of mechanism they have at their disposal that might address this phenomenon is enrichment, but it is not able to do the job.

More generally, Sperber and Wilson's own proposals aside, the recent debate over semantics and pragmatics has concentrated on examples like (2), for which free enrichment or related mechanisms have been proposed. My point here is as much to draw attention to other sorts of examples, for which this mechanism is not well suited, as to criticize the concept of enrichment itself.

[16] I have discussed this at length in Glanzberg (2002). The arguments I have given here show that association with focus cannot be construed as a purely pragmatic phenomenon of a Gricean or relevance-theoretic sort. But they do not show the extent to which the semantics or the pragmatics of focus explain such phenomena as association with focus. We will return to this issue in Section 5. It has been discussed by a number of authors (e.g. Beaver *et al.* 2002; Partee 1999; Roberts 1996; Rooth 1992, 1996*b*).

sentences. Hence, there is even less motivation for seeking a purely pragmatic explanation of it.

First, some more on phonology. So far, we have taken focus to correspond to an accented constituent of a sentence. However, there is good reason to take focus to correspond to a feature represented in syntax, of which accenting is a phonological reflex. Question–answer congruence is sensitive to accent, but it is not sensitive to accent in an entirely straightforward way. Consider:

(16a) What did John do?
(16b) John drank BEER.

This is entirely felicitous. However, the question–answer congruence indicates that the focus is the verb phrase *drank beer*.

This is the phenomenon known as *focus projection*, in which an accent can indicate a larger phrase as focused. This requires that focus be marked in some other way than simply by the phonology. Cases like this point out that focus projection appears to be sensitive to *syntax*. (Generally, there is a preference for putting the accent on the internal argument of the phrase (*beer*) rather than the head (*drank*).) The precise story about how focus projects will not matter here. All that matters is that focus is more abstract than accent placement, and it must be represented somehow in a way that gives the semantics access to it. Conversely, it is often argued that phonological rules must have access to focus features. Focus must thus be marked in a way that is sensitive to syntax, and is an input to semantics and to phonology. In the traditional Government and Binding Theory, this lead to the conclusion that focus is a syntactic feature at the level of S-structure (minimalist versions will view the matter somewhat differently).[17]

Further evidence that focus is independent of its realization by pitch accent might be gleaned from the phenomenon of *second occurrence focus*. Partee (1991) gives the example:

(17a) Eva only gave xerox copies to the GRADUATE STUDENTS.
(17b) (No,) PETR only gave xerox copies to the graduate students.

The association of *only* with focus indicates that in (17b) *graduate students* is still in focus, even though it does not appear to carry an accent.

The conclusion that projection and second occurrence focus both indicate is that focus, as it appears in question–answer congruence and in

---

[17] There is not universal agreement on how focus projection works, or even whether it is an independent phenomenon. For discussion, see Kadmon (2001), Schwarzschild (1999), and Selkirk (1995).

association with focus, is a feature of constituents available for semantic interpretation (and maybe for other linguistic processes as well). We may assume it is a syntactic feature available at *logical form* (LF), which I take to be the syntactic input to semantic interpretation. We can thus assume we have available constituents marked with the feature $[\alpha]_F$. This feature is usually realized by pitch accent in English.[18] In fact, it is commonly held that focus is realized by a particular pitch accent: a high tone aligned to a stressed syllable, usually written H*.[19]

There appear to be roles for focus marking beyond the semantic effects of association with focus and the pragmatic effects surveyed in Section 1. For one, it appears that focus placement can affect grammaticality. Jackendoff (1972) noted:

(18*a*) John only gave his DAUGHTER a new bicycle.

(18*b*) *JOHN only gave his daughter a new bicycle.

The apparent generalization here is that *only* must have a focus within its scope.[20]

Another grammatical effect of focus is in ellipsis (Rooth 1992):

(19*a*) She beats ME more often than Sue (= than she beats Sue).

(19*b*) SHE beats me more often than Sue (= than Sue beats me).

---

[18] As I mention in n. 19, there may be other phonetic realizations of focus in English, though the issue is still controversial. Are there other syntactic or morphological realizations? Probably not in English (though the final word on this matter has certainly not been said). It is sometimes suggested that the cleft construction in English (e.g. *It is Bill who solved the problem*) is a syntactic realization of focus. However, it has been argued by number of authors (e.g. Kiss 1998; Roberts 1998; Rooth 1999) that the cleft construction has a distinct, stronger semantics than intonational focus, marked by pitch accent, in English. Clefts imply exhaustiveness (e.g. that no one other than Bill solved the problem), whereas focus does not. Furthermore, clefts carry genuine existential presuppositions, whereas focus does not, as I discuss in Section 4.1. (However, there are important interactions between clefts and focus, as has been discussed by Delin 1992 and Prince 1978.)

[19] An early explicit argument for positing a focus feature may be found in Jackendoff (1972). It is worth pausing to point out that a great deal of what is at issue here is highly controversial. I have already noted that how focus projects is still debated. Whether or not there is a second focus in (17*b*) is debated at well. Some authors (e.g. Vallduví and Zacharski 1994) challenge whether there is a focus at all (and claim that the restrictor effect is not a matter of focus). Beaver *et al.* (2002) and Rooth (1996*b*) argue that there is a marked focus, though with a phonetic realization distinct from the usual one. The idea that only the particular accent H* marks focus is quite common (e.g. Steedman 2000; Vallduví and Zacharski 1994), but has been challenged by Kanerva and Gabriele (1995).

[20] Of course, issues related to second occurrence focus, discussed above and in n. 19, complicate this generalization.

Consideration of other language may offer additional evidence of the grammatical realization of focus.[21]

These sorts of examples give us reason to think that the positing of an F feature at LF is not simply a matter of loading up LF to reflect everything that may look at first blush to be semantic. There are good reasons to see the feature there. Once it is there, we may use it to help explain the effects of focus, including the semantic effects of association with focus. (Hence, for instance, in examples like (14) the two focus placements (14a) and (14b) correspond to two distinct logical forms. They are 'two different sentences'.)

We may conclude that focus is a semantic matter in these (rather limited) respects: it is represented at LF, and focus features at LF have an effect on the truth conditions of sentences.

3. The Structure + Pragmatics Approach

We now have seen evidence that focus has semantic aspects as well as pragmatic ones. The question then becomes how these relate. One common idea is to make them substantially separate. Focus, the idea proposes, has structural reflexes which explain its semantic effects, but leave the pragmatic explanations we considered in Section 1 substantially intact.

I shall argue in Section 4 that this is not an adequate account of either the semantics or the pragmatics of focus, but it will be useful to consider what such a story would look like.

Much of the research on focus, especially that oriented towards solving the semantic problems of association with focus, has worked with the idea that focus induces a kind of structuring, either of the logical form of a sentence or of its propositional content.

Let us look again at the *only* case (14). The truth-conditional difference between (14a) and (14b) appears to be a difference in what *only* operates on.

---

[21] Vallduví and Engdahl (1996) offer an extensive cross-linguistic discussion of focus and related notions. These cross-linguistic comparisons are often quite delicate. To take one well-known example, it has been suggested by a number of authors (e.g. Kiss 1981; Szabolcsi 1981; Vallduví and Engdahl 1996) that Hungarian has a syntactically realized focus position. But it has also been argued (often by these very same authors) that the focus position in Hungarian differs in important respects from the focus marked by pitch accent in English (e.g. Kiss 1998; Roberts 1998; Szabolcsi 1981; Vallduví and Vilkuna 1998). In particular, as Kiss (1998) shows in some detail, the Hungarian position has a semantics closer to that of clefts in English (discussed in n. 18).

In (14a) the relevant property is that of being someone John introduced Bill to, and the claim is that the only such person is Sue. In contrast, in (14b) the relevant property is being someone whom John introduced to Sue, and the claim is that the only such person is Bill.

We can introduce some notation to mark these differences. I shall present this in terms of a *structured meaning* approach. Not much that I say will depend on whether we really make use of the apparatus of structured meaning, as opposed to any of the other ways we might mark the relevant structural differences. We can describe (14a) and (14b) as:

(14a') only $\langle \lambda x.\textbf{introduce}(\textbf{j}, \textbf{b}, x), \textbf{s} \rangle$
(14b') only $\langle \lambda x.\textbf{introduce}(\textbf{j}, x, \textbf{s}), \textbf{b} \rangle$

Only requires a semantics such that $\textbf{only}\langle \textbf{P}, \textbf{a}\rangle \leftrightarrow \textbf{P}(\textbf{a}) \wedge \forall x (\textbf{P}(x) \rightarrow x = \textbf{a})$. With this, the difference in structure indicated by the difference in focus explains why the two sentences have different truth conditions.

There are a number of questions about whether this sort of approach or another in its vein fully explains the semantic aspects of focus. For the moment, however, I want to consider what we would conclude if in fact it did explain all there is to explain about association with focus.[22]

One point to observe immediately is that it does not explain the pragmatic effects of focus at all. Neither the pragmatic indication of contrast nor question–answer congruence is explained by introducing F-marking or a semantic or syntactic partition of a sentence.

It is an appealing position that these can be explained independently of the semantic aspects of focus, by the pragmatic theory sketched in Section 1. If anything, the pragmatic theory will be strengthened, as the availability of F-marking should more accurately reflect the given–new correspondence required.

We have already, in Section 1, considered a mapping of focus to new information, and ground to given information. The structured proposition theory allows this mapping to be defined directly on structured propositions. Let's look again at (4a). This sentence maps to a structured proposition like:

(4a$'$) $\langle \lambda x.\textbf{likes}(\textbf{n}, x), \textbf{j} \rangle$

---

[22] Structured proposition theories like this are developed by Krifka (1991) and von Stechow (1991). There are other structure-based approaches, such as movement theories (see Kratzer 1991 for a survey), and a theory based on Davidsonian event quantification (Herburger 2000). I have not said anything about how the structured proposition approach derives these propositions from LFs. The view sketched in von Stechow (1991) relies on focus movement, while the one given in Krifka (1991) does not.

The given proposition—the focal presupposition—is simply the existential generalization of the first constituent: $\exists x \textbf{likes}(\textbf{n}, x)$. This expresses the basis of the contrast. The new information is the proposition resulting in applying the ground property to the focus: $\textbf{likes}(\textbf{n}, \textbf{j})$. More generally, when we have a structured proposition $\langle \textbf{P}, \textbf{a} \rangle$, the focal presupposition is $\exists x \textbf{P}(x)$ and the new proposition is $\textbf{P}(\textbf{a})$.[23]

If the pragmatic theory were good, this would appear to solve all our problems. Association with focus and related grammatical aspects of focus would be explained by the semantics, while the pragmatic aspects would be explained by the pragmatics. A nice division of labor. In the next section, however, I shall argue that the pragmatics are not well explained, and even the additional semantic structure does not indicate a good explanation of them. This will point towards a quite different treatment of both the semantic and pragmatic aspects of focus.

4. Problems for the Pragmatics

In this section I shall sketch a few problems for the pragmatic theory of Section 1. Many of these are well established in the literature. I shall then go on to suggest that, together, they call for far-reaching revision of the pragmatic story of Section 1.

We have already seen one problem for the pragmatic theory of Section 1. It has not offered a very good explanation of the effect of *contrast* observed in examples like (4). I asked there if the contrast between given and new would suffice to explain the effect. But it does not really look like it does. The effect in (4a) that John kissed Jane *as opposed to Sue or Mary* is not captured by the mere given–new contrast.

4.1. Focal Presuppositions?

There is another well-known family of problems. The focal presupposition around which the pragmatic theory was based in some cases appears to be too strong. Jackendoff (1972) famously considered:

(20) NOBODY likes Bill.

---

[23] Though she works with a different framework from structured propositions, the "quantifier structure and aboutness principle" of Herburger (2000) is a nice statement of this kind of idea.

This should not presuppose that someone likes Bill, as the Section 1 theory required.

Jackendoff proposed that the focal presupposition be weakened to the claim that the property $\lambda x.\textbf{ground}(x)$ is "well-defined in the present discourse" or "under discussion" (1972: 246). There has been a great deal of discussion of this over the years. It has been observed (e.g. Rooth 1999) that if the variable existentially bound in the focal presupposition of (20) is of quantifier-type, then the presupposition is trivial. On the other hand, Herburger (2000) argues that if we take Jackendoff's suggestion at face value, we lose the explanation of why simple examples like (3) with proper names do appear to carry existential presuppositions.

I want to side with Jackendoff and Rooth on this matter. Even in cases with proper names, presupposition is too strong. Recall, presupposition requires a proposition presupposed to be in the common ground. But less is required to license focus. Consider:

(21a) Did John kiss anyone?
(21b) John kissed JANE.

(22a) Suppose John kissed someone.
(22b) (Then) John must have kissed JANE.

These contrast with cases of *clefts*, which do appear to carry genuine existential presuppositions (cf. Rooth 1999):

(23a) Did John kiss anyone?
(23b) # It is Jane who John kissed.

It appears that the force of whatever goes with these cases is not quite presupposition, in the sense of taking to be part of the conversational common ground or background. It is enough that the material be part of a conversationally backgrounded *supposition*, of the sort that can be discharged or otherwise canceled later. This is not the way pragmatic presuppositions work. Jackendoff's idea of some property being 'under discussion' seems to capture reasonably well what happens with supposition, and so may be on the right track.

However, there are problems with this proposal as it stands. The talk of 'properties under discussion' is still just a metaphor—it does not really explain much. And more seriously, the pragmatic analysis we considered in Section 1 does not show us any way to flesh out the metaphor. The analysis of common ground or given information yielded the notion of presupposition. The dual of that is what is new. This apparatus does not suggest what it is to be under discussion, beyond what is common ground in a discourse, and so does not really help us to build a theory.

(I am not here arguing that the basic ideas of common ground and cooperative principles need to be abandoned—only that they do not explain what we need!)

4.2. Topics and Aboutness

We have thus seen that the pragmatic theory I sketched in Section 1 is not refined enough to explain the status of focus and ground. I shall now argue that in fact the situation is worse. The given–new division, even if we were to get the status of givenness right, is not enough to explain the question–answer congruence properties of focus.

The idea which is supposed to relate given–new to question–answer congruence is that what is given maps to the question—what we are talking about—while new maps to the answer—what we say about it. This is reflected in Jackendoff's idea that the focal presupposition is 'what is under discussion'. But I shall argue that the notion of 'aboutness' relevant to question–answer congruence is more fine-grained than this, and is not well captured by the binary given–new model.

To see that the notion of aboutness indicated by question–answer congruence is more fine-grained than the given–new or focus–ground division of Section 1, let us first consider (modifying Dahl 1974):

(24a) I wonder what people drink? What about John?
(24b) John drinks BEER.

There is a sense in which this utterance is about John. This sense is brought out by question–answer congruence, in:

(25) What about John?

    (a) As for John, he drinks BEER.
    (b) # As for what John drinks, it is BEER.

This already points to an aspect of question–answer congruence which the binary given–new distinction cannot explain. The infelicity of (25b) is not simply a matter of what is given, in the sense that corresponds to *ground* in a sentence. Rather, it is a matter of a further feature of the ground, which singles out the constituent *John* as the *topic*: what the sentence is about.

If this is right, we cannot identify the non-focused material in the sentence with what it is about, in whatever sense of 'aboutness' is captured by this sort of question–answer congruence test. Moreover, we need to capture this notion of aboutness to explain question–answer congruence. More generally, the idea that ground is mapped to what is 'under discussion' or 'what we are talking about' proves too loose to explain congruence. Hence, even if we resolve the question of focal presuppositions, we still do not have an explanation of congruence by appeal to the simple given–new distinction.

This sort of worry is driven home by the phenomenon of *contrastive topics*. In examples like (24), though we have a problem of how to characterize aboutness, it is plausible that what the utterance is about is closely related to the common ground. But with contrastive topics, this is not so. Krifka (1991) gives:

(26*a*) What did Bill's siblings do?
(26*b*) Bill's SISTER [kissed JOHN]$_F$.

The sentence is intuitively 'about' Bill's sister, as reflected by 'as for' congruence:

(27*a*) What did Bill's siblings do?
(27*b*) As for [Bill's SISTER], she [kissed JOHN]$_F$.

But note, nothing about Bill's sister needs to be in the common ground for this to be acceptable. She can be totally new to the conversation. Though she is an instance of Bill's siblings, it need not be common ground that Bill has a sister. Hence, the identification of ground with givenness is called into question again.

Another example of this phenomenon is given by Büring (1999):

(28*a*) What did the pop stars wear?
(28*b*) The FEMALE pop stars wore [CAFTANS]$_F$.

Again, the utterance seems to be about the female pop stars, and nothing in the common ground makes them under discussion per se. Again, though they are instances of the more general category pop star, this would be felicitous in the benighted context which does not presuppose any of them are female.

These examples raise a number of very subtle questions. According to the 'as for' congruence test, we find (26) to be about *Bill's sister*, and (28) to be about *the female pop stars*. It will be useful to mark the topic as detected by this test, by a feature T.[24] The topics in (26) and (28) carry some further implication of contrast, marked by the pitch accent on *sister* and on *female*. This is brought out by examples like:

(29*a*) What did the female pop stars wear?
(29*b*) # [The FEMALE pop stars]$_T$ wore [CAFTANS]$_F$.

---

[24] A battery of arguments for positing T-marking as well as F-marking are given by Vallduví (1990) and von Fintel (1994).

It appears that we have infelicity when we have an accented topic, and have the topic explicitly mentioned in the question. But this data is not robust. Jackendoff (1972) noted:

(30*a*) What about Fred? What did he eat?
(30*b*) [FRED]$_T$ ate [BEANS]$_F$.

Still, we seem to have:

(31*a*) What did Fred eat?
(31*b*) # [FRED]$_T$ ate [BEANS]$_F$.

I shall discuss in Section 5 an attempt by Büring (2003) to explain these cases. For now, we may still observe that a contrastive topic may depart from what is common ground or given, though we yet lack an explanation of how.

These sorts of cases are sometimes described as cases of 'focus in topic' (e.g. von Fintel 1994). In pragmatic terms, we seem to have a topic which invokes a contrast similar to that of focus. This makes the problem vivid. The original topic examples like (24) showed that ground—the complement of focus—does not correspond to aboutness in question–answer congruence. But the contrastive cases show more. In whatever sense in which *topics* map to what is given or common ground, we can still have within topics a contrast that our theory wants to explain as *new*. This requires that we have a status like 'new–given'. On the pragmatic model of given–new we have considered, based on common ground, this makes no sense. Something cannot be common ground and not common ground—it cannot be new and given.

The description as 'focus-in-topic' is vivid, but it misses an important point. Starting with Jackendoff (1972), it has been observed that examples like (28) are only felicitous if the accented part of the topic is given a particular pitch accent. On the felicitous reading of (28), *female* gets a kind of 'fall–rise' tune (usually written L + H*). This is different from the tune given to the focus *caftans*, which is accented by a simple high tone (usually written H*). Jackendoff dubbed the former the B-accent and the latter the A-accent. It appears to be the A-accent that marks focus, while the B-accent is specific to topics. Just as the A-accent marks focus, the B-accent marks a topic feature.[25] To indicate the

---

[25] The role of the B-accent is also discussed at length in Steedman (2000) and Vallduví and Zacharski (1994). Topic accenting is not nearly so thoroughly investigated as focus accenting, and there remain some difficult questions about the relation between the B-accent and the 'as for' congruence test.

difference, we may write a *C*-feature for what is marked by B-accent (*C* for contrast):

(32) [The [FEMALE]$_C$ pop stars]$_T$ wore [CAFTANS]$_F$.

Furthermore, observe that changing the accents in (28) generates infelicity:

(33*a*) What did the pop stars wear?
(33*b*) # The [FEMALE]$_F$ pop stars wore [CAFTANS]$_C$.

There is much more to say about topics. But this is enough to show that notions of question–answer congruence and of aboutness must take contrastive topics into account.[26]

The problem with contrastive topics is that they do not map onto given or presupposed information. Hence, the explanation of question–answer congruence by given–new information that was basic to the pragmatics of focus of Section 1 does not appear to be adequate. It might be replied that contrastive topics are simply cases of *accommodation*. The accent triggers an update of the common ground to include the needed 'given' information. But there are reasons to doubt this is right. In some cases, allowable contrastive topics are quite diverse, as in:

(34) Do you think Fritz would buy this suite?

(*a*) Well, [I]$_C$ certainly [WOULDN'T]$_F$.
(*b*) Well, [FRED ASTAIRE]$_C$ certainly [WOULDN'T]$_F$.

(The first case is from Büring 1999.) But there are limits on allowable contrastive topics. Compare:

(35*a*) What did the pop stars wear?
(35*b*) # [[BILL CLINTON]$_C$]$_T$ wore [a SUIT]$_F$.

---

[26] Much of the recent impetus for attention to notions of topic comes from Vallduví (1990). The general issue of topic and aboutness is much more messy than my observations about contrastive topics may make it seem. There are a number of different devices, over and above B-accenting, which are involved in marking phrases as topics. I used an *as for* construction above. Fronting constructions like topicalization and left dislocation also tend to mark topics. In some cases, there appear to be unmarked topics. How fronting constructions interact with accent is also a complex matter, as Prince (1981*a*, 1997) has stressed. Surveys of ideas about topic can be found in McNally (1998) and Vallduví (1990).

The problem here is that we have no trouble accommodating propositions about Bill Clinton into the common ground. But we still cannot have *Bill Clinton* as a contrastive topic.

We have seen that contrastive topics, as contrast-within-topic (focus within topic) configurations, challenge the given–new pragmatic account of focus. I believe we can see the same sort of problem in some focus-only cases, particularly those of *nested focus*. Sentences can contain multiple foci. This is brought out most clearly by the presence of focusing operators, as in Krifka (1991):

(36) John even$_1$ [only$_2$ [drank WATER]$_{F2}$]$_{F1}$.

(John is usually wild at parties, but at yesterday's party, not only was he restrained, he even only drank water.)

It is a virtue of the kind of rich semantic theory we are considering that it has little trouble handling nested foci. Propositional structure simply nests accordingly. The important parts of the semantic value of this sentence may look something like:

(37a) [drank water]$_F$: $\langle \lambda P(P), \lambda x \exists y (\mathbf{drank}(x, y) \wedge \mathbf{water}(y)) \rangle$ ($= \omega$)
(37b) [only [drank water]$_F$]$_F$: $\langle \lambda P(P), \mathbf{only}(\omega) \rangle$

Though solutions to the problems of the semantics of nested foci are ready to hand, the pragmatics is another matter. Just as contrastive topics seemed to call for a status of 'new–given', nested foci appear to call for a status of 'given–given'.

These cases are difficult in a number of ways. Though the presence of focusing operators makes clear that we can have nested foci when it comes to semantics, it is less clear what their pragmatic status is. It is unclear if we hear a 'nested contrast' in them. In a related matter, it is unclear if we can have nested focus without focusing operators. I am inclined to think we can. Consider:

(38a) (John rarely drinks at parties. But when he does, he usually drinks wine.) What did John do at the party?
(38b) John [DRANK [**WATER**]$_{F2}$]$_{F1}$.

I think this would be pronounced with higher prominence on *water*, but also high pitch accent on *drank*. I am inclined to think the foci are as marked, though as I said, it is not obvious, and the intonation could be taken simply to mark *drank water* with one focus.

Assuming there are nested foci here, we do not seem to have an explanation of the kind of 'contrast' that it presents. Our theory would require *drank* to map to given and to new, or *water* to map to a kind of 'double-given' status. As with contrastive topics, our pragmatics does not provide for this kind of status. As I said, the structured proposition semantics of association with focus has no problem with this sort of example, but the mapping from semantics to pragmatics fails to provide an adequate explanation of the pragmatic effects they generate.

Let me review where we have been. We have now seen that focus is a hot-spot in semantics–pragmatics interaction. How is this to be explained? We began by considering a relatively straightforward pragmatic account of focus. We then looked at semantic effects of focus, and considered a semantic theory able to explain them. We then set about considering how the semantics and pragmatics interact. It appeared there was a simple relation, leaving their functions autonomous but regularly mapped to each other.

In this section we have seen that the pragmatic theory with which we began will not suffice. That theory relied on the twofold distinction between common ground or given information and new information, and used it to explain such phenomena as question–answer congruence and contrast. But we have seen that none of these are really explained very well. More importantly, we have seen that question–answer congruence is a more complex phenomenon than the twofold distinction can address. The idea that what is given is 'what we are talking about', which is then answered by the focus, fails to take into account contrastive topics and the nesting of focus.[27]

---

[27] Many of these points apply to the theory of Sperber and Wilson (1986), discussed in nn. 12 and 15, as well. Particularly, like the neo-Gricean given–new theory, theirs does not offer a very robust explanation of the effect of contrast.

There are some points on which their theory might fare better. They might be able to explain some aspects of question–answer congruence (and might explain them better than the neo-Gricean theory), as there is a close relation between background implications and questions. This might provide resources for explaining the status of focal presupposition as well. Furthermore, as Sperber and Wilson point out, their theory indicates a *scale* for foreground and background, rather than a simple given–new distinction. This might provide some resources for explaining nested focus examples (if indeed they have nested pragmatic effects). As I have some reservations about the apparatus of relevance theory, I have some reservations about how successful these explanations might be; but full discussion of this would require a discussion of relevance theory which would take us far from focus, so I shall leave the matter unresolved. (As I mentioned in Section 2, phenomena like association with focus seem to undermine any purely pragmatic theory, neo-Gricean or relevance-theoretic.)

Even if Sperber and Wilson's theory can explain some aspects of question–answer congruence, I do not see how it can address the cases of contrastive topics I have discussed here. Contrastive topics do not involve a scale of more or less foreground (new) and background (given); rather, they involve the embedding of foreground *inside* background—they involve what would appear to be

The semantic component of the theory is not directly challenged by these problems. But the relation between semantics and pragmatics we examined in Section 3 is challenged. That relation embodied the mapping of focus to new, and ground to given. Though the semantic structures corresponding to focus and ground can nest, their pragmatic reflexes cannot. Without the mapping to pragmatics, we lose any explanation of, for example, question–answer congruence. Hence, though the structured meaning theory I sketched in Section 3 was never meant to be a theory of topics as well, it fails to be a sufficiently explanatory theory of focus.

In the next section I will investigate some ways of improving both the semantics and the pragmatics to provide a better semantics–pragmatics mapping. Indeed, the pragmatic problems we have seen in this section suggest a place to look for a better theory. The source of the problems seems to be the need for *iterated* discourse status, corresponding to categories like 'new–given' or 'new–new'. Such iterated structure, I noted, is not found in the pragmatics of common ground. But it is easy to observe in the structure of the discourses in which utterances appear. Questions and answers, for instance, can appear in nested structures. We will see in the next section that exploiting this gives us a more readily applicable account of the pragmatics, and the semantics, of focus.

5. A Discourse-Based Approach

Discourse clearly has complex structure. Most importantly to us, it has the kind of structure that allows for the nesting of notions like aboutness and new information. This is made more clear if we think about the role of question–answer structure in a discourse. We see, in many cases, a nested structure of questions and subquestions. For instance, a discourse might look like:

(39) How was dinner?

    (*a*) How was the food?
        Great.

'new–given'. I do not see how a scale of foreground and background can explain this. If anything, it would require inverting the scale, or mapping one end into the other.

The sort of pragmatic and semantic theory I think can explain this, to be discussed in Section 5, certainly invokes some ideas about strategies for answering questions which might be recast in relevance-theoretic terms. But as I shall discuss there, it is the way this account combines semantic and pragmatic aspects that I believe offers our primary moral for understanding the semantics–pragmatics boundary.

(b) How was the service?

(i.) Was the waiter attentive?
Yes.

(c) Was it easy to find the place?

This can be thought of as a tree-structure, in which dominating nodes are either a superquestion of a subquestion, or a question dominating an answer.

There are many constraints on what well-formed discourse must look like, and many of them are constraints on what moves in a tree of questions and answers may be like. Furthermore, we must observe that even discourses that are not explicitly in question–answer form have an implicit question–answer structures. Assertions in a discourse are made against the background of a *discourse topic*. The discourse topic may be taken to be the relevant question which is being answered. In some cases, this is marked explicitly by the asking of a question; while in some cases, it is fixed by other pragmatic mechanisms.[28]

5.1. Focus Effects

As we saw with the simpler pragmatic approach, the real complexity of discourse structure will only become crucial when we turn to examples like contrastive topics and nested foci. But let us start by seeing how appeal to the question–answer structure of a discourse explains the basic aspects of focus.

Following the tradition in intensional semantics (e.g. Groenendijk and Stokhof 1984; Hamblin 1973; Karttunen 1977), we may very roughly take the semantic value of a question to be the set of propositions that constitute answers to it. This is hardly to present a full-fledged semantics of questions, but it is enough to facilitate the comparison we need. Consider the question *Who does John like?* The semantic value of this will be the set $\{\textbf{likes}\,(\textbf{n},x)\,|\,x \in D_e\}$. (Actually, as usual, we should probably expect a contextual restriction on x. But for present purposes, we may suppress this.)

That there is some similarity between this value and the semantic of focus should be clear. Replacing with a variable the *wh*-word in the question (or, perhaps, deleting the *wh*-word and leaving the trace it binds), and replacing with

[28] For more on discourse topics and questions, see Glanzberg (2002), McNally (1998), van Kuppevelt (1995), Von Fintel (1994), as well as the works of Büring (1999, 2003) and Roberts (1996), which are central to my presentation here. A well-developed, DRT-based approach to questions and related issues of discourse structure is given by Asher and Lascarides (1998, 2003).

a variable the focused constituent in the answer, give the same structure: **likes**$(\mathbf{n}, x)$. The difference between the semantic value of the question $\{$**likes** $(\mathbf{n}, x) \mid x \in D_e\}$ and the ground constituent in the structured proposition $\lambda x.$**likes** $(\mathbf{n}, x)$ is then almost trivial. The latter is a function, the former is the range of values the function can take.

In frameworks not relying on structured propositions, the question value is the more useful construction. When derived from the declarative via its focused constituent, this set is usually known as the *alternative set* or *focus semantic value*. It was a fundamental observation of Rooth (1985) that these can be assigned compositionally, and that they provide an elegant solution to many of the problems of association with focus. For a sentence of the form $S(F)$ with focused constituent F, the focus semantic value $[[S(F)]]^f = \{S(x) \mid x \in D_F\}$ for appropriate type D_F.

To see how this explains question-answer congruence, compare:

(40a) Who does John like? Semantic value: $\{$**likes** $(\mathbf{n}, x) \mid x \in D_e\}$
(40b) John likes JANE. Alternative set: $\{$**likes** $(\mathbf{n}, x) \mid x \in D_e\}$

The two values are identical, and we have congruence. But consider:

(41a) Who does John like? Semantic value: $\{$**likes** $(\mathbf{n}, x) \mid x \in D_e\}$
(41b) #JOHN likes Jane. Alternative set: $\{$**likes** $(x, \mathbf{j}) \mid x \in D_e\}$

These are not matching, and we lack congruence.

So, we have an account of the role of focus in question–answer congruence. Focus determines a focus semantic value, and congruence is explained as identity between this value and the value of the question.

Other pragmatic effects of focus are explained by this view as well. Focal presuppositions, which seemed difficult on the previous approach, are simple here. With Jackendoff, we supposed the idea was that somehow the ground property $\lambda x.$**ground**(x) is 'under discussion'. We saw problems with how to understand this without making the presupposition existential, and I also complained that this is not really a theory, but just a metaphor. But both problems can be addressed in the current framework. The ground property, as we have seen, is more or less the alternative set of the sentence, which is the same as the semantic value of the question to which it is congruent. The idea of being 'under discussion' can then be glossed as being the question answered by a sentence, either as an explicit question or as an implicit discourse topic. Of course, a full theory here requires a more substantial theory of discourse topics. But this is enough to explain why we have more than a metaphor.

The appearance of 'contrast' is also nicely addressed by the question–answer congruence approach. The alternative set of a sentence (when appropriately contextually restricted) is exactly its set of contrasting values. In the original example (3), we noted that there appears to be a contrast in the sense that it says John kissed Jane, as opposed to Mary or Sue. This contrast is represented by an alternative set. Again, we see that a sentence is felicitous only if its alternative set is the value of the question it answers (either as an explicit question or as an implicit discourse topic). Hence, the range of contrasting options—the semantic value of the question—must be in the discourse for the sentence to be felicitous.

This is as much as we should want for the status of 'contrast'. In particular, we do not want contrast to imply uniqueness (unless the sentence contains *only*). We can have:

(42*a*) Who did John kiss?
(42*b*) John kissed JANE. In fact he also kissed SUE.

A felicitous sentence in effect asserts one of the members of its corresponding contrast class, but it does not assert that it is the unique element of that class to hold.

It thus appears that question–answer congruence, explained via alternative sets, gives us an elegant account of the pragmatic aspects of focus. We now must ask what the *semantics* of focus is, and how it maps to this pragmatics.

We still take it as established that focus is marked at LF. The important semantic construction is no longer a structured proposition, but an alternative set derived recursively from the focus-marked LF.[29] The mapping from semantics to pragmatics is given by a rule of felicity:

(43) A sentence is felicitous if the semantic value of its discourse topic (an explicit or implicit question) is identical to its alternative set.

(This will have to be modified to account for topics, as we will see below.)

What of the semantic effects of association with focus? There are two options for explaining them. One is to follow the original theory of Rooth (1985) and write alternative sets directly into the semantic of expressions like *only*. *John only introduced Bill to SUE* is true if and only if John introduced Bill to Sue, and this is the unique proposition in the alternative set $\{\mathbf{introduced}(\mathbf{j}, \mathbf{b}, x) \mid x \in D_e\}$.

This gets the semantics right. But more recent discussions of focus have suggested it is not a sufficient explanation. This theory simply posits a specific rule

---

[29] One of the original motivations for alternative semantics in Rooth (1985) was that it assigns semantic values to focus *in situ*, unlike movement theories.

for *only*, another for *even*, another for adverbs of quantification, etc.[30] A generalization seems to be in order. Focusing operators all appear to have a context-dependent restrictor. The alternative set provides the value for this restrictor. (More accurately, it constrains its value.) We then attempt to account for the value of the restrictor as a context-dependent domain restriction. Context sets its value.

How is this done? Roberts (1996) argues that the rule of question–answer congruence suffices (along with Gricean principles). If the restrictor is not set to the alternative set, we fail to get congruence with the appropriate implicit question.[31]

I shall not go into the details of Roberts's derivation. Rather, I shall pause to examine what the theory so far tells us about the semantics–pragmatics relation. As I mentioned, focus marking is present at LF. The main role of this feature of LF is to set up a felicity condition along the lines of (43). The felicity condition is given in terms of focus semantic values (alternative sets) derived compositionally. There may be other rules that make reference to these values, but if Roberts (1996) is right, the situation is rather that many lexical items have parameters whose values are set by Gricean processes triggered by the felicity condition.

In light of this, let us return to the debate over the semantics–pragmatics interface which I mentioned at the beginning of the chapter. In certain key respects, focus conforms to the pattern of pragmatic effects being driven by linguistic elements—elements of LF—as opposed to purely pragmatic processes like free enrichment. Focus is marked at LF; we saw independent reasons to hold that. And the pragmatic effects of focus are controlled by what appears at LF, in this case by way of focus semantic values. As with the paradigm of demonstratives, the semantic values derived from LF need to be supplemented by pragmatic processes. In the demonstrative case, the map from semantics to pragmatics is something like 'pragmatically determine the value of a variable at LF'. Here, the mapping is, rather, 'pragmatically determine felicity based on the focus

---

[30] An objection like this is raised in Rooth (1996a), but against the alternative semantics of Rooth (1985) and structured meaning theories of the sort we considered in Section 3.

[31] This is discussed further in Kadmon (2001). Rooth (1992) proposes a different explanation, based on a kind of anaphora on alternative sets. Rooth's theory is extended to cover some topic phenomena in von Fintel (1994). Space precludes a thorough comparison of this approach with Roberts's. They are in many ways in the same spirit. But it is worth noting that in its current form, Rooth and von Fintel's theories are not integrated into a theory of nested discourse structure, and so are not well suited to handle the sorts of pragmatic phenomena related to contrastive topics I have been concerned with here, without some significant modification.

semantic value derived from LF, the felicity rule (43), and other (Gricean?) pragmatic processes'. It is plausible that the felicity rule (43) itself follows from the Gricean cooperative principle, as it is an instance of relevance: make your utterance coordinate on the current discourse topic. We need the focus semantic value derived from LF to work this out, much as we usually need semantic information to determine if and how Gricean maxims are satisfied.

It thus appears that we have a linguistically controlled triggering of pragmatic processes, rather than anything like free enrichment. The same can be said of association with focus effects. If they are specifically encoded, this is obvious. But it remains so if they are encoded in LF as general domain restrictions, whose values are pragmatically set to associate with focus.

On the other hand, there are ways in which the picture deriving from Stanley (2000) may be too narrow to account for this. First of all, there is no reason I know of to think focus features behave like variables in LF. I know of no reason to think they are bindable, and there is generally reason to doubt that features marking constituents are bindable, unless the constituents themselves are. Focus can occur on too wide a range of constituents to make this likely. Focus is a genuine aspect of LF, and triggers an interaction with context, but not of the sort Stanley assumes. On the pragmatic side, though I argued that we may think of the felicity condition as falling under the Gricean cooperative principle, it should still be noted that (43) is not much like a rule for pragmatically fixing the value of a variable. Even if Gricean, felicity constraints seem to be fundamentally different in effect.

5.2. Topics Revisited

We now have an account of the basic semantic and pragmatic effects of focus. I have suggested it is in some ways more satisfying than the account I sketched in Section 3. But the primary reasons I offered for abandoning that account were the problems of contrastive topics and nested foci I presented in Section 4. We have yet to see how these might be handled by the current theory. At the same time, though we have made much of question–answer pairs, we have yet to exploit the nested structure of discourse topics I mentioned at the beginning of this section. It is this structure which enables us to handle the problem cases of topic and focus.

An account of question–answer congruence for contrastive topics in the Roberts-style framework I have sketched has been developed by Büring (2003). As contrastive topics are complex, so is his theory. I shall sketch enough of it to make good on my claim that the nesting of discourse topics can shed light on the pragmatics of contrastive topics. This should, I hope, justify my claim that the current framework offers a more complete pragmatic theory. I shall leave out as much detail as I can, and refer readers to Büring's own elegant presentation.

The basic idea is that contrastive topics invoke a more complicated felicity condition. Not only must a sentence with a contrastive topic be a congruent answer to the question which is its discourse topic; it must do so as part of a particular kind of *strategy* of investigation. A strategy, in this sense, is a pattern of questions and subquestions, organized to address some overarching question. Like a focus, a contrastive topic triggers a felicity condition, but this one makes more use of the complexity of discourse structure.

The patterns of felicity we saw above suggest what sort of strategy contrastive topics trigger. Examples like (26) and (28) suggest that a contrastive topic must narrow down the discourse topic. It should correspond to a subquestion, an answer to which at least partially answers a superquestion. The infelicity in (29) supports this. On the other hand, the contrast between (30) and (31) suggests that in some cases, when appropriate other options are available, a contrastive topic sentence may not have to narrow down a discourse topic. Furthermore, (34) and (35) suggest that in narrowing down a current discourse topic, attention needs to be paid to how this affects relevance for the rest of the discourse.

These observations suggest two conditions. First, if the topic is narrowed, the result must be part of a larger strategy for answering some prevailing superquestions. Moreover, the specific question the contrastive topic sentence answers, the implicitly or explicitly narrowed topic, must be part of a nontrivial range of subquestions which address the superquestion. Hence, we require either the narrowing of an explicit question, or the presence of other contrasting questions, as our examples suggested.

Let us look more closely at an example. Büring considers the familiar:

(44) $[FRED]_C$ ate $[the\ BEANS]_F$.

This appears appropriate to answer a general question:

(45a) Who ate what?
(45b) $[FRED]_C$ ate $[the\ BEANS]_F$.

On the other hand, suppressing the contrastive topic, the felicity conditions on focus appear to require a question–answer pair like:

(46a) What did Fred eat?
(46b) # $[FRED]_C$ ate $[the\ BEANS]_F$.

This, we have seen, is infelicitous. On the other hand, we have seen it becomes acceptable in:

(47a) Who ate what?
(47b) What did Fred eat? What did Mary eat? What did Jane eat? . . .
(47c) [FRED]$_C$ ate [the BEANS]$_F$.

The felicity of a contrastive topic sentence can be explained by the rule (43), so long as the question to which it is congruent is part of a sequence of subquestions which all address a standing superquestion.

This leads Büring to define a *strategy*. A strategy is a part of a discourse structure of questions and answers rooted at a question. It is a way of investigating the root question. A sentence *S* (really an utterance of *S*, in context) *indicates a strategy around S in a question–answer structure D* if there is a non-singleton set of questions Q' in *D* such that each $Q \in Q'$ either immediately dominates *S* or is a sister of the node that immediately dominates *S*, and each *Q* is congruent with *S*. We still need to define congruence for contrastive topic sentences. But the sense in which contrastive topics require appropriate strategies of questions and answers is given by a new felicity condition:

(48) A sentence *S* with a contrastive topic is felicitous if it indicates a strategy around *S*.

This is a supplement to (43), as we will see once we define congruence.

Congruence is defined in two steps, corresponding to the two levels in the strategy that makes *S* felicitous. Again, looking at our example define:

(49) $[\,[FRED]_C \text{ ate } [\text{the BEANS}]_F\,]^{tf} = \{\{\mathbf{ate}(x, y) \mid y \in D_e\}^f \mid x \in D_e\}^t$.

Each inner set is a corresponding focus semantic value (alternative set). These are indexed by topics, and correspond to the specific questions *What did Fred eat?*, *What did Mary eat?* . . . (I have put superscripts on the sets to make clear what they do—they play no theoretical role.) With this, we can fill in the notion of congruence involved in the felicity condition (48). It reduces to the same one we used for non-topic cases in (43). For each $Q \in Q'$, we require $Q \in [[S]]^{tf}$.

As I said, I shall leave the details to Büring (2003). But let me try to make the main idea clearer. By the time we get down to a specific question *Q*, we are looking for question–answer congruence basically as we explained it in the focus cases. Among the *Q*s will be the question *What did Fred eat?*, which is answered by *Fred ate the BEANS* (suppressing topic). The role of topic is to trigger the felicity condition (48), which requires that this question be part of a larger strategy, which has a superquestion *Who ate what?* and a non-singleton range of subquestions including this one, but also having others like *What did Mary eat?* The semantic side of this requirement is given by the value $[[S]]^{tf}$, which collects together the subquestions of this strategy.

In some cases, like (47), the strategy in which the contrastive topic figures is explicitly stated. In these, we see that there is an explicit question to which the non-topic-marked sentence is congruent, but also other questions. In most occurrences of contrastive topics, like (28), we do not see such an explicit question structure. This gives rise to the appearance that contrastive topics introduce new topics. They do so in the sense that to be felicitous, there must be an implicit strategy: an expanded tree of questions and answers, which contains the question–answer pair explicitly given. In many cases, the strategy will add a sequence of subquestions between the explicit question and its answer.

When I originally presented the problem of contrastive topics, I posed it as one about the pragmatic status of 'focus in topic' or 'new–given' information. We have now seen that contrastive topics really do make use of the nested structure of discourse topics in a discourse: the structure of explicit or implicit questions and their answers.

This is enough to shed light on the pragmatic status of contrastive topics. According to Büring's theory, a felicitous contrastive topic falls under a nested structure of a superquestion and a sequence of subquestions. Roughly, we can say that the contrastive topic marked material is 'given' relative to the appropriate subquestion. Suppressing topic marking, it is congruent in a way fixed only by focus-ground structure. But it is 'new' relative to the superquestion, in that the C-marked material indicates one of many partial answers to the superquestion. Hence, the nesting of sub- and superquestions indicates a nesting of 'focus in topic'. Indeed, Büring's analysis of contrastive topics indicates an even more refined status. In so far as a strategy for a contrastive topic requires multiple subquestions, we might be tempted to offer the gloss 'new–given–partial'. It is not vital to my claims here that the details of Büring's analysis prove accurate. Contrastive topics are not as well understood as we would like, and however appealing his analysis is, we should grant that the future may hold surprises. What is important is that it is based on nested discourse structure. It is that which allows us to explain the pragmatic status of contrastive topics, whether or not we have the details right.

To close this section, I shall return to the issue of nested focus I mentioned in Section 4. There I gave an example (38) which appeared to indicate pragmatic effects of nested foci. As I said there, I am uncertain what the right description of this case is. But on the assumption that there are such pragmatic effects, I shall offer some speculative remarks on how they might work. Above, I presented the sentence as answering the question *What did John do at the party?*, with the prior gloss that he rarely drinks, but when he does, he usually drinks wine.

Thinking about discourse structure, we might suppose the implicit question structure is more like:

(50) What did John do?

    (a) What did he drink?
       John [DRANK [**WATER**]$_{F2}$]$_{F1}$.

As with the topic cases, we can appeal to question structure to explain the appearance of 'new–new' status for the embedded focus. It is new—establishes congruence—relative to the lower question, while the wider focus does so for the higher question. 'New–new' is an answer to a question and a subquestion. Thus, as with topics, appeal to discourse structure can give us better versions of the pragmatic status of these cases.

This still leaves the rules for congruence in these cases unexplained. F_1 makes the answer congruous with the superquestion; while F_2 makes it congruous with the subquestion. Normally, we expect an answer to be congruous with the question immediately dominating it. We expect a felicitous answer to be about the *current* discourse topic. But that would indicate focus only on *water*. With the accents as I described above, this does not appear to be an option. There must be focus on the whole phrase *drank water*. Moreover, an answer to the subquestion, with focus on *water*, would entail an answer to the superquestion. So we do not need this odd accenting to keep relevance within the discourse as a whole.

To speculate. It may be that there is something else that needs to be done with the focus here. In particular, given the way I described the case, the wide focus triggers a *scalar implicature*. The context includes information about John's behavior patterns, which form a scale with not drinking anything at one end, then drinking wine, then drinking water. It may be that this provides a reason to place the accent on *drank*.

What does this say about the foci? It may be that in spite of the general rule that an answer is congruent with its immediately dominating question, this accent makes the answer congruent with both questions at once. It simultaneously but directly answers them both (rather than answering the superquestion via the subquestion). Does this mean the proper accents allow an answer to reach back and select prior questions? Or is this just an appearance generated by a scalar implicature? I am not sure.

6. Conclusion

What morals can we draw from focus for the nature of the semantics–pragmatics boundary? As I mentioned at the outset, it provides us with a very different set of examples than the sort I mentioned in (2). In those examples, the intuitive truth conditions and surface syntactic structures are relatively clear, and the issue becomes whether it is something linguistic—logical form—or something pragmatic—free enrichment—which mediates between the two. In contrast, focus presents us with cases where the relation between semantics and pragmatics must be more complex. First of all, it provides cases where what appears to be surface syntax is not a good guide to underlying linguistic form. This lesson has been learned before, but focus shows that what is on the surface but appears to be merely pragmatic can turn out to indicate underlying syntactic structure. Association with focus shows that this structure can be semantically significant. The first moral of focus is that the appearance of being merely pragmatic can drastically deceive.

Identifying a syntactic feature marking focus does not get us very far. We still need to explain its semantic and pragmatic effects. Here I think the differences with examples like those in (2) come to the forefront. These examples call for supplementation, which could be realized on the surface in a different sentence, as in *I have had breakfast* versus *I have had breakfast today*. If it is true that these examples already involve covert variables in LF, the pragmatics still simply provides values for these variables.

The semantics and pragmatics of focus do not work this way, as the dis-course-based view of Section 5 shows. The mapping between focus semantics and pragmatics is not one of filling in meaning. In particular, it is not simply a matter of setting a value for the *F*-feature. Rather, a much more complex process, in which semantics and pragmatics interact, is triggered. First, the focus feature is used to derive a focus semantic value (an alternative set $[[S(F)]]^f$, or $[[S(C, F)]]^{tf}$ if a contrastive topic is involved). This is basically a semantic process. The alternative set is then contextually restricted by the appropriate pragmatic process of domain restriction. This pragmatically restricted semantic value is then fed into a felicity condition (43, or if a contrastive topic is involved, 48). This condition regulates the discourse (and, I suggested, might itself follow from Gricean principles). It also triggers the pragmatic effects of question–answer congruence, contrast, and the appropriately weakened focal 'presupposition'. But at the same time, this pragmatic condition can *require* particular focus place-ment, so in a way, the pragmatics can trigger the semantics. Furthermore, with association with focus, we have the semantic values on which the felicity condition (43, 48) is based affecting the truth conditions of an utterance. If Roberts is right about association with focus, this is the result of the felicity condition pragmatically fixing the value of a restrictor to be the alternative set. If association with focus is more semantically encoded, it is the result of the semantics of expressions like *only* requiring access to alternative sets which determine felicity. Either way, focus reveals significant *interactions* between semantics and pragmatics, far more than we see in cases like (2).

As I said in Section 5, the semantics and pragmatics my discussion here has indicated seems to be in line with the view generally opposed to free enrichment, which insists on pragmatics always being mediated by logical form. Focus is marked at LF, and it appears to be a linguistic control on the pragmatic process to which it maps. But as I said there, the result is still quite a bit different from what the debate over (2) indicates. Focus does appear at LF, but not as a variable whose value is to be filled in by a pragmatic process. Rather, it is a trigger of an extremely rich discourse-based pragmatic process, which in turn interacts with the semantics of the sentence that triggered it. Focus shows the semantics–pragmatics boundary to be a complex and dynamic one.

REFERENCES

Asher, N., and A. Lascarides (1998), 'Questions in Dialogue', *Linguistics and Philosophy*, 21: 237–309.

—— (2003), *Logics of Conversation* (Cambridge: Cambridge University Press).

Bach, K. (1994), 'Conversational Impliciture', *Mind and Language*, 9: 124–62.

Beaver, D., B. Clark, E. Flemming, and M. Wolters (2002), 'Second Occurrence Focus is Prosodically Marked', MS.

Bolinger, D. (1972), 'Accent is Predictable (If You're a Mind-Reader)', *Language*, 48: 633–44.

Büring, D. (1999), 'Topic', in P. Bosch and R. van der Sandt (eds.), *Focus: Linguistic, Cognitive, and Computational Perspectives* (Cambridge: Cambridge University Press), 142–65.

—— (2003), 'On D-Trees, Beans, and B-Accents', *Linguistics and Philosophy*, 26: 511–45.

Carston, R. (1988), 'Implicature, Explicature, and Truth-Theoretic Semantics', in R. M. Kempson (ed.), *Mental Representation* (Cambridge: Cambridge University Press), 155–81.

—— (forthcoming), 'Explicature and Semantics', in S. Davis and B. Gillon (eds.), *Semantics: A Reader* (Oxford: Oxford University Press).

Chafe, W. L. (1976), 'Givenness, Contrastiveness, Definiteness, Subjects, Topics, and Point of View', in N. Li (ed.), *Subject and Topic* (New York: Academic Press), 25–55.

Chomsky, N. (1971), 'Deep Structure, Surface Structure, and Semantic Interpretation', in D. D. Steinberg and L. A. Jakobovits (eds.), *Semantics* (Cambridge: Cambridge University Press), 183–216.

Clark, H. H., and S. E. Haviland (1977), 'Comprehension and the Given-New Contract', in R. O. Freedle (ed.), *Discourse Production and Comprehension* (Norwood: Ablex), 1–40.

Dahl, Ö. (1974), 'Topic–Comment Structure Revisited', in Dahl (ed.), *Topic and Comment* (Hamburg: Helmut Buske), 1–24.

Daneš, F. (1968), 'Some Thoughts on the Semantic Structure of the Sentence', *Lingua*, 21: 55–69.

Delin, J. (1992), 'Properties of It-Cleft Presupposition', *Journal of Semantics*, 9: 289–306.

Dretske, F. (1972), 'Contrastive Statements', *Philosophical Review*, 81: 411–37.

Firbas, J. (1964), 'On Defining the Theme in Functional Sentence Analysis', *Travaux Linguistiques de Prague*, 1: 267–80.

Glanzberg, M. (2002), 'Context and Discourse', *Mind and Language*, 17: 333–75.

Grice, P. (1975), 'Logic and Conversation', in P. Cole and J. L. Morgan (eds.), *Speech Acts*, vol. 3 of Syntax and Semantics (New York: Academic Press), 41–58; repr. in Grice (1989: 22–40).

—— (1989), *Studies in the Way of Words* (Cambridge, Mass.: Harvard University Press).

Groenendijk, J., and M. Stokhof (1984), 'Studies in the Semantics of Questions and the Pragmatics of Answers', Ph.D. diss. (University of Amsterdam).

Hajičová, E., B. H. Partee, and P. Sgall (1998), *Topic–Focus Articulation, Tripartite Structures, and Semantic Content* (Dordrecht: Kluwer).

Halliday, M. A. K. (1967), 'Notes on Transitivity and Theme in English (Part 2)', *Journal of Linguistics*, 3: 199–244.

Hamblin, C. L. (1973), 'Questions in Montague English', *Foundations of Language*, 10: 41–53.

Herburger, E. (2000), *What Counts: Focus and Quantification* (Cambridge, Mass.: MIT Press).

Horn, L. R. (1989), *A Natural History of Negation* (Chicago: University of Chicago Press).

Jackendoff, R. S. (1972), *Semantic Interpretation in Generative Grammar* (Cambridge, Mass.: MIT Press).

Kadmon, N. (2001), *Formal Pragmatics* (Oxford: Basil Blackwell).

Kanerva, J. M., and L. A. Gabriele (1995), 'Intonation and Focus Layers', *Proceedings of the North East Linguistics Society*, 25: 335–46.

Karttunen, L. (1977), 'Syntax and Semantics of Questions', *Linguistics and Philosophy*, 1: 3–34.

Kiss, K. É. (1981), 'Structural Relations in Hungarian, a "Free" Word Order Language', *Linguistic Inquiry*, 12: 185–215.

—— (1998), 'Identificational Focus versus Information Focus', *Language*, 74: 245–73.

Kratzer, A. (1991), 'The Representation of Focus', in A. von Stechow and D. Wunderlich (eds.), *Semantics: An International Handbook of Contemporary Research* (Berlin: de Gruyter), 825–34.

Krifka, M. (1991), 'A Compositional Semantics for Multiple Focus Constructions', *Proceedings of Semantics and Linguistic Theory*, 1: 127–58.

—— (1992), 'A Framework For Focus-Sensitive Quantification', *Proceedings of Semantics and Linguistic Theory*, 2: 215–36.

Ladd, D. R. (1996), *Intonational Phonology* (Cambridge: Cambridge University Press).

Levinson, S. C. (2000), *Presumptive Meanings* (Cambridge, Mass.: MIT Press).

McNally, L. (1998), 'On Recent Formal Analyses Of Topic', in J. Ginzburg, Z. Khasidashvili, C. Vogel, J.-J. Lévy, and E. Vallduví (eds.), *The Tbilisi Symposium on Logic, Language and Computation* (Stanford, Calif.: CSLI) 147–60.

Partee, B. H. (1991), 'Topic, Focus and Quantification', *Proceedings of Semantics and Linguistic Theory*, 1: 159–87.

—— (1999), 'Focus, Quantification, and Semantics-Pragmatics Issues', in P. Bosch and R. van der Sandt (eds.), *Focus: Linguistic, Cognitive, and Computational Perspectives* (Cambridge: Cambridge University Press), 213–31.

Pierrehumbert, J., and J. Hirschberg (1990), 'The Meaning of Intonational Contours in the Interpretation of Discourse', in P. R. Cohen, J. Morgan, and M. E. Pollack (eds.), *Intentions in Communication* (Cambridge, Mass.: MIT Press), 271–311.

Prince, E. F. (1978), 'A Comparison of Wh-Clefts and It-Clefts in Discourse', *Language*, 54: 883–906.

—— (1981*a*), 'Topicalization, Focus-Movement, and Yiddish-Movement: A Pragmatic Differentiation', *Proceedings of the Berkeley Linguistics Society*, 7: 249–64.

—— (1981*b*), 'Toward a Taxonomy of Given-New Information', in P. Cole (ed.), *Radical Pragmatics* (New York: Academic Press), 223–55.

—— (1997), 'On the Functions of Left-Dislocation in English Discourse', in A. Kamio (ed.), *Directions in Functional Linguistics* (Amsterdam: John Benjamins), 117–44.

Recanati, F. (1993), *Direct Reference* (Oxford: Basil Blackwell).

Reinhart, T. (1981), 'Pragmatics and Linguistics: An Analysis of Sentence Topics', *Philosophica*, 27: 53–94.

Roberts, C. (1996), 'Information Structure in Discourse: Towards an Integrated Formal Theory of Pragmatics', *Ohio State University Working Papers in Linguistics*, 49: 91–136.

—— (1998), 'Focus, the Flow of Information, and Universal Grammar', in P. W. Culicover and L. McNally (eds.), *The Limits of Syntax*, vol. 29 of Syntax and Semantics (San Diego: Academic Press), 109–60.

Rochemont, M. S. (1986), *Focus in Generative Grammar* (Amsterdam: John Benjamins).

Rooth, M. (1985), 'Association with Focus', Ph.D. diss. (University of Massachusetts at Amherst).

—— (1992), 'A Theory of Focus Interpretation', *Natural Language Semantics*, 1: 75–116.

—— (1996*a*), 'Focus', in S. Lappin (ed.), *Handbook of Contemporary Semantic Theory* (Oxford: Basil Blackwell), 271–97.

—— (1996*b*), 'On the Interface Principles for Intonational Focus', *Proceedings of Semantics and Linguistic Theory*, 6: 202–26.

Rooth, M. (1999), 'Association with Focus or Association with Presupposition?', in P. Bosch and R. van der Sandt (eds.), *Focus: Linguistic, Cognitive, and Computational Perspectives* (Cambridge: Cambridge University Press), 232–44.

Schiffer, S. (1972), *Meaning* (Oxford: Clarendon Press).

Schwarzschild, R. (1999), 'GIVENness, AvoidF and Other Constraints on the Placement of Accent', *Natural Language Semantics*, 7: 141–77.

Selkirk, E. (1995), 'Sentence Prosody: Intonation, Stress, and Phrasing', in J. A. Goldsmith (ed.), *Handbook of Phonological Theory* (Oxford: Basil Blackwell), 550–69.

Sperber, D., and D. Wilson (1986), *Relevance* (Cambridge, Mass.: Harvard University Press).

Stalnaker, R. C. (1974), 'Pragmatic Presuppositions', in M. K. Munitz and P. K. Unger (eds.), *Semantics and Philosophy* (New York: New York University Press), 197–213; repr. in Stalnaker (1999: 47–62).

—— (1978), 'Assertion', in P. Cole (ed.), *Pragmatics*, vol. 9 of Syntax and Semantics (New York: Academic Press), 315–22; repr. in Stalnaker (1999: 78–95).

—— (1999), *Context and Content* (Oxford: Oxford University Press).

Stanley, J. (2000), 'Context and Logical Form', *Linguistics and Philosophy*, 23: 391–434.

—— (2002), 'Making It Articulated', *Mind and Language*, 17: 149–68.

—— and Z. G. Szabó (2000), 'On Quantifier Domain Restriction', *Mind and Language*, 15: 219–61.

Steedman, M. (2000), *The Syntactic Process* (Cambridge, Mass.: MIT Press).

Szabolcsi, A. (1981), 'The Semantics of Topic-Focus Articulation', in J. Groenendijk, T. Janssen, and M. Stokhof (eds.), *Formal Methods in the Study of Language (Part 2)* (Amsterdam: Mathematisch Centrum), 513–40.

Vallduví, E. (1990), *The Informational Component*, Ph.D. diss. (New York: Garland, 1992).

—— and E. Engdahl (1996), 'The Linguistic Realization of Information Packaging', *Linguistics*, 34: 459–519.

—— and M. Vilkuna (1998), 'On Rheme and Kontrast', in P. W. Culicover and L. McNally (eds.), *The Limits of Syntax*, vol. 29 of Syntax and Semantics (San Diego: Academic Press), 79–208.

—— and R. Zacharski (1994), 'Accenting Phenomena, Association with Focus, and the Recursiveness of Focus–Ground', *Proceedings of the Amsterdam Colloquium*, 9: 683–702.

van Kuppevelt, J. (1995), 'Discourse Structure, Topicality and Questioning', *Journal of Linguistics*, 31: 109–47.

von Fintel, K. (1994), 'Restrictions on Quantifier Domains', Ph.D. diss. (University of Massachusetts at Amherst).

von Stechow, A. (1991), 'Current Issues in the Theory of Focus', in A. von Stechow and D. Wunderlich (eds.), *Semantics: An International Handbook of Contemporary Research* (Berlin: de Gruyter), 804–25.

4

Semantics, Pragmatics, and the Role of Semantic Content

Jeffrey C. King and Jason Stanley

Followers of Wittgenstein allegedly once held that a meaningful claim to know that *p* could only be made if there was some doubt about the truth of *p*. The correct response to this thesis involved appealing to the distinction between the *semantic content* of a sentence and features attaching (merely) to its *use*. It is inappropriate to assert a knowledge-claim unless someone in the audience has doubt about what the speaker claims to know. But this fact has nothing to do with the semantic content of knowledge-ascriptions; it is entirely explicable by appeal to pragmatic facts about felicitous assertion (that is, a kind of use of a sentence).

According to the contextualist about knowledge, the (propositional) semantic content of knowledge-claims is sensitive to context. In a context in which skeptical possibilities are sufficiently salient, the word "know" expresses a relation that holds between persons and a highly restricted range of propositions. In a context in which skeptical possibilities are not salient, the word "know" expresses a different relation, one that a person can bear to a proposition even if she is in a fairly weak epistemic position with respect to it. In support of her position, the contextualist often points to the undisputed fact that speakers' willingness to make

We have given this paper at the Kentucky Language Association, the Universidad Nacional Autonóma de México, the Oxford Philosophical Society, and it was also discussed at the Bay Area Philosophy of Language Reading Group; thanks to participants at all of these events. Herman Cappelen, Robyn Carston, Maite Ezcurdia, Richard Heck, Ernie Lepore, and Rich Thomason deserve particularly special thanks. Kent Bach, Michaela Ippolito, Matthew Stone, Zoltán Gendler Szabó, and Brian Weatherson also helped with valuable suggestions. Thanks also to two anonymous referees for Oxford University Press.

knowledge-claims varies with context. Those who reject contextualism about knowledge typically try to give non-semantic accounts of variations in speaker hesitancy about knowledge-claims. In short, dissenters from contextualism try to argue that the facts that support contextualism are really facts about the *use* of knowledge-ascriptions, rather than their *semantic contents*.

In ethics, one version of internalism about reasons holds that someone understands a sentence containing genuinely normative vocabulary only if they are motivated in a certain way. That is, an internalist about moral reasons holds that being motivated is an essential part of the grasp of the semantic content of moral sentences. An internalist about reasons motivates her position in part by appealing to the fact that it is odd to utter an ethical sentence unless one has the relevant motivation. An externalist about reasons, by contrast, rejects the internalist thesis that being motivated is part of grasping the semantic content of moral sentences. An externalist seeks to explain the evidence about motivation by attributing it to facts (merely) about the proper *use* of ethical sentences, rather than the *semantic content* thereof.

These examples form but a representative few. Appealing to a distinction between the semantic content of a sentence and what a use of it only pragmatically conveys is simply a standard maneuver in debates across a wide range of disciplines in philosophy. The importance of the tactic is due to the nature of many philosophical claims. Typically, a philosopher who is discussing a certain discourse, whether it concerns knowledge or the good, makes claims about its content. Sometimes, there are features of the use of a word in that discourse that, if explained by reference to the content of the word, would threaten that philosopher's claims. In such a case, the philosopher who continues to advocate her claims has one of two options. First, she can reject the thesis that the ordinary word that purportedly expresses that content in fact expresses it (typically, this results in an error theory about ordinary discourse). Secondly, she can argue that the features in question are not explained by reference to the semantic content of that word, but are merely pragmatic facts about its use. In short, the distinction between *semantics* and *pragmatics* is fundamental to philosophical theorizing, because much philosophical theorizing takes the form of claims about the content of philosophically central discourse.

So, in a number of debates across, for example, metaphysics, epistemology, and ethics, one theorist's semantic content is another theorist's merely pragmatic effect. But a complicating factor in these debates is the lack of a clear and accepted criterion among philosophers of language and linguists for what counts as semantic versus what counts as pragmatic. That is, among philosophers of language, there is no stable agreement on the semantics–pragmatics distinction. Furthermore, even among those who agree on terminology, there is disagreement about the *scope* of semantic content. That is, it is a subject of much current debate how much of what is intuitively communicated is constituted by semantic content. Many philosophers of language have in recent years argued that sentences have only minimal, even non-propositional, semantic contents, much of their natural interpretation in a context being due to non-semantic effects (e.g. Bach 1994). Others in the philosophy of language and cognitive science community have gone further, to reject altogether any theoretical role for a semantic notion of what is said by a sentence. According to all of these theorists, instead of "truth-conditional semantics", we should be speaking, in the words of François Recanati, of "truth-conditional pragmatics" (Recanati 1993: 232 ff.).

Our first aim in this chapter is to provide a stable characterization of the distinction between semantics and pragmatics, one that theorists across a range of disciplines can exploit. This characterization will allow us to gain greater clarity about the debates concerning the scope of semantic content. Our second aim in this chapter is to argue that much more counts as genuinely semantic than skeptics about the scope of semantic content have maintained.

1. Three Conceptions of the Semantics–Pragmatics Distinction

Above, following tradition, we spoke of the distinction between semantics and pragmatics as a distinction between what words mean (semantics), on the one hand, and the *use* speakers make of words (pragmatics). However, this characterization is imprecise and unhelpful. For example, the case of indexical expressions, such as 'I' and 'today', shows that one word can have different denotations on different occasions of use. Nevertheless, each indexical word type has a univocal conventional meaning, that is, a meaning that does not vary from context to context. Since the referential content of a use of 'I' relative to a context of use seems to be a function of the conventional meaning of the word type 'I', it seems incorrect to relegate all facts about its content in a context to what speakers use 'I' to mean, rather than what the word means. But the initial vague characterization of the semantics–pragmatics distinction does not talk of word meaning relative to a context, and so gives us no handle on these facts. More precision is required.

Following Richard Heck (2001), let us call the conventional meaning of a lexical item *e* in a language L its *standing meaning*.[1] Some terms, such as the number determiners 'two' and 'three', or proper names such as 'Bill Clinton' and 'George Bush', seem to have a "stable" standing meaning, in the sense that users using such terms correctly (that is, in accord with their standard meanings), will always refer to the same object or property. Other terms, such as 'I', 'here', or 'this', have "unstable" standing meanings, such that, in different contexts, consistently with these standing meanings they can be used to refer to different objects. For example, the conventional meaning of 'I' in English does not vary across contexts; in every context, when used in accord with its standard meaning, the meaning of 'I' is (roughly) the same as 'the speaker in the context'. But in a context in which Bill Clinton is the speaker, Bill Clinton uses 'I' to refer to himself, when using 'I' in accord with its standing meaning. In contrast, Gray Davis uses 'I' in accord with its standing meaning to refer to himself, that is, Gray Davis. Loosely following recent terminology of John Perry, let us call the object or property that a user refers to in a context when successfully using a lexical item *e* (of a language L) in accord with its standing meaning in L the *referential content* of that term relative to that context.[2]

There is a bit of a terminological morass surrounding our distinction between "standing meaning" and "referential content". The term "referential" is most appropriate when used to discuss the content of *referential expressions*, expressions that can be used to refer, as opposed to merely denote, in the sense familiar from the work of Bertrand Russell. Such expressions, following tradition, are assumed to be singular terms, paradigmatically proper names such as 'Bill Clinton' and indexicals and demonstratives such as 'I' and 'this'. However, like Perry (2001: 79), we intend the expression "referential content" to have wider application than merely to referential expressions in contexts. Our distinction between standing meaning and referential content is meant to correlate with the distinction between, on the one hand, the context-invariant standing meaning of a term, and, on the other, the object, property, or function that the term has as its content in a context, which is potentially distinct from its standing meaning. As a consequence, the expression "referential content" may

---

[1] David Kaplan's (1989) technical reconstruction of standing meaning is what he calls character; John Perry's classic terminology is "role". Since we wish here to remain neutral about certain (albeit differing) theoretical commitments that, strictly speaking, Kaplan and Perry's terminology possesses, we adopt Heck's terminology for now.

[2] See ch. 5 of Perry (2001). We say "loosely", because Perry takes referential content to be a property of *utterances* of expressions. In contrast, we take referential content to be a property of an expression relative to a context.

need to have wider application than merely to the class of referential expressions. For there may be context-sensitive elements in the syntax of a sentence that are not referential expressions, as traditionally conceived (e.g. Heal 1997). If there are, we would need vocabulary to mark the distinction between standing meaning and content in a context for them as well. So, like Perry, we will speak of the referential content of an expression in a context in this broader sense.

The distinction between the non-relative notion of the standing meaning of a term and the relative notion of the referential content of a term relative to a context provides two general strategies for forging a distinction between semantics and pragmatics, and a third intermediate between them. We discuss each in turn.

According to the first strategy for making a distinction between semantics and pragmatics, the semantic interpretation of a complex expression *e* is the result of composing the standing meanings of the lexical items in *e* in accordance with the semantic composition rules corresponding to the syntactic structure of *e*. So, on this view, semantic properties are only properties of expression types; any property that an expression type has only relative to a context (or any property possessed only by expression tokens) is not semantic. The semantic content of the sentence 'I am tired' is the result of combining the standing meaning of 'I', the standing meaning of the copula (together perhaps with the present tense), and the standing meaning of 'tired'.[3]

Of course, relative to a particular context of use, speakers can use 'I' in accord with its standing meaning to refer to a particular person, namely the speaker of that context. But on this first conception of semantics, semantic properties do not accrue to expressions in context. The fact that in a particular context of use, 'I' has Bill Clinton as its referential content is a fact about the pragmatics of 'I', how it is used in a given context.

Propositions are the ultimate bearers of truth-values. This fact about the nature of propositions entails that the proposition expressed by 'I am a son of a president' varies from context to context. Relative to a context in which Bill Clinton is the speaker, the proposition expressed by 'I am a son of a president' is false, whereas relative to a context in which George Bush is the speaker, the proposition expressed is true. However, on this first way of thinking of semantics, no semantic value of an expression varies from context to context. Therefore, on this first way of distinguishing semantics from pragmatics, the *semantic* interpretation of 'I am a son of a president' is not a proposition.

[3] Of course, the syntactic structure of 'I am tired' is certainly considerably more complex than meets the eye, and presumably contains many non-obvious elements.

This conception of the semantics–pragmatics distinction is familiar from the work of Richard Montague. Montague suggests that the difference between semantics and pragmatics is that semantic values are not relativized to anything (or rather only to models or interpretations of the language), whereas pragmatic values are assigned relative to a context of use (as well as a model). Thus he writes: "It seemed to me desirable that pragmatics should at least initially follow the lead of semantics, which is primarily concerned with the notion of truth (in a model, or under an interpretation), and hence concern itself also with truth—but with respect to not only an interpretation but also a context of use" (Montague 1974: 96). Few linguists or philosophers now conceive of the distinction between semantics and pragmatics in this first way (though, as we emphasize in the next section, the reasons that justify abandoning it are subtle). According to a more contemporary conception of the semantics–pragmatics distinction, there are two levels of semantic value. The first is the non-relativized notion of the standing meaning of an expression. The second is the relativized notion of the referential content of an expression in a context.[4] On the most influential way of explaining the relation between these two levels of semantic value, the standing meaning of a lexical item determines a *function* that determines its referential content, given a context. Following the influential terminology of Kaplan (1989), the widely used name for this function is *character*; in what follows, when speaking of this formal explication of standing meaning, we adopt Kaplan's terminology. Most importantly, a complex expression relative to a context c has a referential content that is the result of combining the referential contents of its constituent terms relative to the context c in accord with the semantic composition rules corresponding to the syntactic structure of that expression. The result of this latter process is a genuine level of semantic value, which we shall call the *semantic content* of that complex expression relative to the context c.[5] The semantic content of a lexical item relative to a context c is, on this view, its referential content in that context.

---

[4] Some philosophers of language have advocated semantic theories that embrace more than two levels of semantic content. For example, Nathan Salmon (1986) holds that an adequate account of tensed discourse requires at least three levels of semantic value, and David Braun (1996) argues that an adequate treatment of demonstratives requires at least three levels of semantic value. However, for the sake of simplicity, we ignore in what follows the possibility that there are more than two levels of semantic value.

[5] There are basically two different styles of semantic theory. For the sake of simplicity, we take the content of an expression in a context to be a function from possible worlds to the appropriate type of extension; functions from possible worlds to truth-values we will call *propositions*. On a structured propositions semantics, however, semantic interpretation proceeds in two steps. First, an algorithm assigns structured propositions to sentences in contexts. Secondly, a definition of truth assigns truth-conditions to structured propositions. In what follows, we generally speak in the first style of semantics, but translate into the second in some instances.

On this second conception of the semantics–pragmatics distinction, the sentence 'I am a son of a president', relative to a context, has a propositional semantic content. If George is the speaker, and the time is t, the propositional content is that function that takes a possible situation s to the true if and only if George is a son of a president at t at s. On this conception of the semantics–pragmatics distinction, the pragmatic content is what the speaker communicates over and above the semantic content of the sentence he uttered.

So, for example, suppose George is asked whether he thinks he is going to be rich when he is older, to which he responds 'I am a son of a president'. The semantic content of George's sentence, relative to that context, is that he is a son of a president, which is the proposition that results from combining the referential contents, relative to that context, of the parts of the sentence. But by expressing this semantic content, he intends to flout Grice's maxim of relevance, thereby communicating the quite different proposition that it is quite likely that he will be rich, given his political connections. This proposition is communicated not by being semantically expressed by some sentence, but rather as a post-semantic result of the expression of a semantic value. Hence, it is part of the pragmatic content of the speech act, but not what is semantically expressed by the sentence in that context.

On this conception of the semantics–pragmatics distinction, the semantic contents of some terms depend upon non-linguistic context. Those who use "pragmatic" to refer to such contextual effects on linguistic interpretation may speak, somewhat paradoxically, of pragmatic effects on semantic content. But what this means is simply that some lexical items have different contents in different contexts. Non-linguistic facts about the context of use are relevant for fixing the referential content of some lexical items, such as pronouns and unpronounced free variables. But the nature of the lexical item dictates what non-linguistic facts are relevant, and constrains the nature of its referential content in a context. For example, if the lexical item is the English pronoun 'she', its standing meaning dictates that only certain sorts of intentions are relevant for fixing its referential content in a context, and constrains that content to be, for example, a salient female human (reference to boats, countries, etc., to one side). That is, speaker intentions are relevant to fixing the referential content of a lexical item in a context only when they are determined to be so by the standing meaning of a lexical item. So, the role played by speaker intentions in semantics remains significantly constrained, even on this conception of the semantics–pragmatics distinction, by the standing meanings of lexical items.

Employing this version of the semantics–pragmatics distinction, we can distinguish between two ways in which context determines what is communicated. The first way context may determine what is communicated is by affecting the semantic content, via resolution of the referential content of context-sensitive elements in the sentence uttered. This roughly corresponds to what Stanley and Szabó (2000: 228–9) and Perry (2001: 42 ff.) call the *semantic* role of context.[6] The second way is that context plays a role in determining what is communicated by the linguistic act over and above its semantic content. This is the genuinely pragmatic role of context (Stanley and Szabó 2000: 230–1).[7]

So, on this second conception of semantics, extra-linguistic context plays a role in determining the semantic content of certain expressions in context. Indeed, for many context-dependent expressions, certain kinds of intentions of speakers will likely be relevant for determining the semantic content of some expressions relative to a context. But this does not undermine the fact that these values are the semantic contents of the relevant expressions, given this semantics–pragmatics distinction. In accord with this, one can define two senses of "pragmatic effect", which we shall henceforth call "weak pragmatic effects" and "strong pragmatic effects". A weak pragmatic effect on what is communicated by an utterance is a case in which context (including speaker intentions) determines interpretation of a lexical item in accord with the standing meaning of that lexical item.[8] A strong pragmatic effect on what is communicated is a

---

[6] We say "roughly corresponds", since Stanley and Szabó make a point of not adopting the semantics–pragmatics distinction under discussion here (Stanley and Szabó 2000: 229–30). Rather, according to them, the semantic interpretation of an utterance is the proposition it expresses, whether or not all elements in the proposition expressed by the utterance are traceable to elements in the sentence uttered. So what Perry (2001: 44 ff.) calls the "content supplemental" role of context is, for Stanley and Szabó, a semantic role of context. We find this terminology disturbing, since it is unclear whether such a notion of the semantics–pragmatics distinction takes semantic content to be a property of expressions in contexts or utterances.

[7] Stanley and Szabó also discuss what they call the "grammatical role" of context in determining what was uttered, which corresponds directly to what Perry (2001: 40 ff.) calls the "pre-semantic" role of context. This is the role context plays in resolving ambiguity. Both Perry and Stanley and Szabó are too quick to lump these roles of context together. For the sense of "determine" here is quite distinct from the sense of "determine" we have exploited. Facts about context determine the semantic contents of contextually sensitive items, and the implicatures of the speech act. In contrast, facts about context do not determine which of two disambiguations a given utterance expresses; it is rather that hearers draw on context to figure out which unambiguous utterance was expressed.

[8] The purpose of the last proviso is to rule out deferred reference, cases such as 'The ham sandwich is getting irritated' (said by a waiter), as a weak pragmatic effect, since such cases are not ones in which context works to determine interpretation in accord with the standing meaning.

contextual effect on what is communicated that is not merely pragmatic in the weak sense.[9]

On the first conception of the semantics–pragmatics distinction we discussed, there are no pragmatic effects of context on semantic content, whether weak or strong. If there were, for example, a weak pragmatic effect on the semantic content of some expression, then its semantic content would have to be relativized to contexts, to incorporate this sensitivity. But there are no relativized semantic values on this first conception. On the second conception of the semantics–pragmatics distinction, the semantic content of a complex expression in a context is a function of, and only of, the referential contents of its constituents in that context, together with context-independent composition rules. A strong pragmatic effect on what is communicated is one in which context affects what is communicated, but not by affecting the referential contents of any lexical item in a sentence. So, by definition, there are no strong pragmatic effects on semantic content on the second conception of the semantics–pragmatics distinction.[10] However, unlike the first conception, all weak pragmatic effects of context are cases in which context has a semantic role. That is, all weak pragmatic effects are cases in which context affects semantic content.[11]

Some theorists, torn between the restrictiveness of the first conception and the perceived permissiveness of the second, choose to split the difference between these ways of approaching the semantics–pragmatics distinction. One way of adopting a semantics–pragmatics distinction intermediate between the first and second conceptions is to distinguish between different kinds of weak

[9] Resolving ambiguity is not a sense in which context "determines" what is communicated, and so counts as neither a strong nor a weak pragmatic effect on what is communicated.

[10] The Context Thesis of Zoltán Gendler Szabó is the principle that "The content of an expression depends on context only insofar as the contents of its constituents do" (Szabó 2001: 122). Szabó's Context Thesis, on the second conception, is a definitional truth about semantic content.

[11] One might worry that the second conception rules out strong pragmatic effects on semantic content only in spirit. For example, consider a purported strong pragmatic effect on what is communicated by a use of a sentence S. One could imagine transforming this into a weak pragmatic effect, by making some expression in S into an indexical. By this retranslation scheme, one could transform strong pragmatic effects into weak pragmatic effects. However, this maneuver is unpersuasive; the basic reply is that one cannot just *stipulate* that a word is context-sensitive. Given that context-sensitive expressions are typically identifiable, there is a high burden of proof on someone who wishes to maintain that a non-obviously context-dependent expression is in fact context-dependent (for discussion, see Stanley 2000: 430–1). Furthermore, there are tests to distinguish genuine indexical expressions from non-indexicals; for example, indexicals are invariant in interpretation under verb-phrase ellipsis, see Stanley (2003).

pragmatic effects. One can then use the resulting distinction to count some weak pragmatic effects as affecting semantic content, and others as not having effects on semantic content. Here is one way to motivate this position. As John Perry has emphasized, context-dependent expressions come in two classes.[12] First, there are what Perry calls "automatic" indexicals. Two examples of such indexicals, in English, are 'I' and 'tomorrow'. The referential content of these indexicals, in a context, is fixed independently of the beliefs or intentions of its user.[13] An occurrence of 'tomorrow' has, as its referential content, the day after the day it is used, independently of what the speaker intended it to refer to, or believed it referred to.[14] The vast majority of other context-sensitive expressions are what Perry calls "intentional". In the case of, for example, a use of 'that man', it is the speaker's intentions that help determine its referential content in a context.[15]

Given Perry's distinction between automatic and intentional context-sensitive expressions, one might adopt the following distinction between semantics and pragmatics. The semantic content of a sentence in a context is a function of (and only of) the referential contents of the automatic indexicals in the sentence relative to that context, together with the standing meanings of all other lexical items in the sentence, together with context-independent compo-sition rules. On this account, the semantic content of 'I am tired' differs from context to context, since 'I' is an automatic indexical. But the semantic content of 'that man is tired' does not differ from context to context, since 'that man' is an intentional context-sensitive expression, and so has its referential content in a context fixed by appeal to speaker intentions, which cannot, on this view, be relevant to the determination of semantic content.[16]

We have now discussed three different ways of drawing the distinction between semantics and pragmatics. We think the second of these three ways of

---

[12] See ch. 4 of Perry (2001). See also Perry (1997), which is a precursor.

[13] Except that, as Perry (2001: 596) points out, the user must intend the indexicals to be used in accord with their standard meaning.

[14] A *locus classicus* of this point, at least for 'I', is Wettstein (1984).

[15] As Ernie Lepore has pointed out to us, some philosophers, such as Chris Gauker, reject the existence of intentional indexicals. These philosophers are thoroughgoing contextualists; they hold that non-mental features of the context determine the value of all contextual parameters relevant for determining what is said (see Gauker 1997 for a good exemplar of this tradition). For a contextu-alist, the third conception of the semantics–pragmatics distinction collapses into the second.

[16] This third conception of the semantics–pragmatics distinction is, for example, clearly operat-ive in the work of Kent Bach; as he writes, "Contextual information in the narrow, semantic sense is limited to a short list of parameters associated with indexicals and tense, such as the identity of the speaker and hearer and the time of the utterance" (Bach 2002a: 285).

drawing the distinction is most plausible. There are powerful phenomenological considerations in its favor. Consider a sentence relative to a context. The result of composing the referential contents of its parts leads to a quite natural entity to take as its semantic content in that context, one that seems to play a fundamental role in interpretation, as the object of speech acts and attitudes. For example, the result of combining the referential contents of the parts of the sentence 'She is tired now', relative to a context in which the speaker intends to refer to Hannah and *t* is the time of utterance, is the proposition that Hannah is tired at *t*. This seems to be the object of propositional attitudes and what is understood in a successful case of communication. So, the entity that results from combining the referential contents of the parts of a sentence relative to a context in accord with composition rules seems to be one that plays a recognizably central role both in theorizing about linguistic interpretation, and in giving an adequate account of the semantic contents of some linguistic constructions.

But the main reason for favoring this second way of drawing the distinction between semantics and pragmatics is that there are difficulties facing the first and third ways of drawing the distinction between semantics and pragmatics, the resolution of which leads to the adoption of our favored conception. We devote the next two sections to a detailed discussion of these difficulties.

2. Semantic Content as Context–Independent Semantic Value

On the first way of drawing the semantics–pragmatics distinction, semantics is only concerned with assigning *un*relativized semantic values to sentences. Accordingly, any value assigned to a sentence that is relativized to a context, or point of evaluation, etc. (other than a model for the language) falls within the domain of pragmatics. We know of three ways such a view might be implemented. In this section we take each in turn and provide criticisms of them.

The first way of implementing the proposal is inspired by the work of Richard Montague. One assigns an unrelativized semantic value to expressions of the language (again, this semantic value may be relativized to a model or "possible interpretation" for the language, but it is not relativized to anything like contexts or points of evaluation; we will suppress this qualification henceforth). This value is a function from "points of reference" to appropriate extensions. Though the need for "double indexing" was recognized after the work of Montague on these topics, one can derive an updated version of Montague's approach by letting the points of reference be pairs of contexts and points of evaluation (we will not worry about precisely what elements comprise contexts and points of evaluation, except that contexts have as coordinates at least speakers, locations, times, and worlds, and points of evaluation have as coordinates at least worlds). Let us call functions from points of reference so understood to appropriate extensions *M-characters*. The M-character of a sentence, then, is a function from points of reference to truth-values. A sentence such as 'I am here now' has an M-character that maps a point of reference $<c,i>$ to True iff the speaker of c is in the location of c at the time of c in the world of i. Thus, if we require, as is usual, that the speaker of c be at the location of c at the time of c in the world of c, the sentence will be true at all $<c,i>$ where the world of i is the world of c.[17] On the current conception of the semantics–pragmatics distinction, since M-character is the only unrelativized value assigned to expressions, the assignment of M-character to sentences exhausts semantics.

Our objection to this view is essentially that of Stalnaker (1999*b*). M-characters map context–index pairs to truth-values. But then M-characters don't seem to be the kinds of things that are grasped in understanding sentences. Intuitively, it seems that in understanding a sentence, we combine the *referential contents* of the constituents of that sentence together according to its syntactic structure. Our understanding of a sentence in a context is due to a compositional procedure that calculates the content of the whole sentence from the referential contents of its parts. But on this conception of the semantics–pragmatics distinction, there is no room for a representation of this process, since sentences are not assigned referential contents in contexts at all. In short, this view does not assign *propositions* to sentences taken relative to contexts. But propositions are needed to be the things grasped in understanding sentences in contexts. M-characters are not suited to play this role; nor are they appropriate objects of the attitudes or entities on which natural language operators operate. Thus, we think Stalnaker gave the right reason for rejecting this way of implementing this conception of the semantics–pragmatics distinction.[18]

---

[17] This captures the idea that the sentence is "indexically valid", while avoiding the result that the sentence expresses a necessary truth with respect to a given context c, since it will be false for many pairs $<c,i>$ as i is varied; we suppress the relevant definitions of *indexically valid* and *expresses a necessary truth with respect to context c*.

[18] The focus of Stalnaker's criticism is that Montague's system does not allow for the representation of propositions as values. However, Stalnaker did not appear to conceive of this as a criticism of Montague's way of drawing the semantics–pragmatics distinction. In this sense, we are altering Stalnaker's criticism to fit our target.

On the other two ways of implementing the idea that semantics is distinguished from pragmatics by being concerned only with the assignment of non-relativized values to expression types, semantics consists of assigning to sentences entities that are, or determine, functions from contexts to contents or propositions (i.e. characters). On the first implementation, we assign to sentences (and complex expressions generally) *structured characters*. Assume that we assign to lexical items characters understood as functions from contexts to contents. The structured character of a complex expression is simply the concatenation of the characters of its lexical parts, where the characters are concatenated according to the syntactic structure of the complex expression. So for example, the structured character assigned to 'I am hungry now' would be something like $<I',H',n'>$, where I' is the character of 'I', H' is the character of 'hungry' and n' is the character of 'now'. This structured character, taken relative to the context c, yields the structured content or proposition $<I'(c), H'(c), n'(c)>$.

The first thing to note is that on this conception of semantics, there is no non-trivial *semantic* composition. For on this view, the *semantic* content of a sentence is its structured character (sentences only have structured contents or propositions relative to contexts; and so on the current way of understanding the distinction between semantics and pragmatics, these values that are relativized to contexts fall in the purview of pragmatics). But in deriving the structured character of a sentence like 'I am hungry now', one does not compose the characters in accord with the intuitively correct composition rules governing its syntactic structure. For example, one does not "saturate" the character of 'am hungry now' with the character of 'I' (or vice versa). As already mentioned, the character of 'I am hungry now' is rather a result of concatenating the characters of the elements of the sentence. So, the semantic content of a sentence is not really determined by composing the semantic contents of the parts via non-trivial composition rules given by the sentence's syntax. Instead, the semantic content of a sentence is determined by concatenating the semantic contents (i.e. characters) of the parts of the sentence. Eliminating non-trivial semantic composition, and in effect trivializing semantics, is an unattractive feature of this conception of the semantics–pragmatics distinction.

Our second concern about this way of understanding the semantics–pragmatics distinction is that we are skeptical about the utility of the sole semantics values, structured characters, allowed by such an approach. We see no use for these structured characters, and so do not see that a theory that employs them has any advantage over a theory that does not assign characters to complex expressions at all, but only assigns characters to syntactically simple expressions. If we are correct about this, then the current conception of the semantics–pragmatics distinction results in semantic values having no real use. Obviously, this would be a good reason to reject the current conception.

But are we correct in thinking that structured characters have no real use? David Braun (1994) has argued that we should accept a semantic theory that includes structured characters. Braun's primary argument involves complex demonstratives. Braun considers the following two complex demonstratives:

(1) that man
(2) that man who is either talking to Bush or not talking to Bush

Braun assumes that the content of a complex demonstrative in a context is its referent. (1) and (2) have the same content in every context (assuming we hold all contextual factors, including associated demonstrations, speaker intentions, etc., constant—see Braun 1994, n. 7). If we understand character functionally, as a function from context to content, (1) and (2) have the same character. But, Braun objects, (1) and (2) seem to differ in meaning. However, if we assign them only functional characters, we assign them no meanings on which they differ. Hence, Braun argues, we need to introduce structured characters, and assign different structured characters to (1) and (2). In this way, we can honor the intuition that (1) and (2) have different meanings.

Thus, Braun argues that, contrary to what we have claimed, there is an important use for structured characters. Before responding to Braun here, it is worth noting that he never actually gives an assignment of structured characters that assigns different structured characters to (1) and (2).[19] Given the incomplete nature of Braun's proposal with respect to (1) and (2), it is somewhat difficult to evaluate.

Overlooking this shortcoming, we have two responses to Braun's argument. First, even within the sort of framework Braun presupposes, on which the content or propositional contribution of a complex demonstrative in a context is its referent in that context (which we reject—see below), we are not convinced that honoring the pre-theoretical intuition that (1) and (2)

---

[19] See e.g. the first paragraph of his section 11—the problem is that he never assigns structured characters to complex nominals like 'man who is talking to Bush or not talking to Bush'.

have different meanings requires assigning them different structured characters. Even if the two phrases as a whole are assigned no characters (characters only being assigned to their syntactically simple parts) or only functional characters (so that (1) and (2) get assigned the same character), surely the fact that one phrase contains words with contents (or characters) that the other phrase does not contain would be enough to explain normal speakers' intuitions that the phrases differ in meaning in some way. Indeed, Braun seems to admit this himself when he writes: "We judge that (1) and (2) differ in meaning at least partly because they have different meaningful parts."[20] So even within a framework of the rough sort endorsed by Braun, Braun has failed to give good reasons for assigning structured characters to (1) and (2).

Secondly, there are accounts of complex demonstratives that explain Braun's data without any appeal to character. For example, consider the quantificational account of complex demonstratives recently defended in King (2001). On this account, (1) and (2) are contextually sensitive quantifiers. As such, the predicative material in them gets contributed to propositions expressed in contexts by sentences in which they occur. Thus, (1) and (2) used in the same context make different contributions to propositions expressed in those contexts by sentences in which they occur. Obviously, the fact that (1) and (2) in any context have different contents (i.e. make different contributions to propositions) should explain why we have the intuition that they differ in

---

[20] Braun (1994: 101). In a footnote to this remark, Braun says there are two other reasons for thinking that (1) and (2) differ in meaning. First, he says that to understand (2) one must grasp certain characters that one need not grasp to understand (1) (e.g. those of 'talking', etc.). Secondly, he claims that (1) and (2) would receive different translations into other languages. But none of this requires positing structured characters for (1) and (2) either. One could claim that understanding (1) and (2) requires grasping the characters of their lexically simple parts and how those parts are syntactically combined. This would mean that understanding (1) requires grasping characters that need not be grasped in understanding (2), even if we have assigned no character to (1) and (2) as whole phrases (or only a functional character). Further, one could claim that it is a constraint on translation that one translate a syntactically complex phrase of one language into a syntactically complex phrase of the other languages that has the same syntax and parts with the same meaning as the phrase being translated (at least, when this is possible). Again, this explains why (1) and (2) would be translated differently and does not require assigning structured characters to (1) and (2). Finally, Braun also argues that intuitive differences in the meanings of certain dthat terms in an extension of English containing dthat terms requires assigning them different structured characters. However, the response we give here to the comparable claim about English complex demonstratives carries over straightforwardly to the claim about dthat terms in an extension of English.

meaning. So King's account of complex demonstratives straightforwardly accounts for the intuition that (1) and (2) differ in meaning without positing structured characters.[21]

We conclude that Braun has given no compelling reason for positing structured characters. So we are left with the conclusion that on the way of distinguishing semantics from pragmatics we have been considering, where the sole job of semantics is to assign structured characters to complex expressions, the semantic values so assigned (structured characters) have no real function. Again, this is a significant problem for this approach.[22]

The final way to implement the view that semantics is distinguished from pragmatics in that the former is only concerned with assigning *unrelativized* semantic values to sentences (and complex expressions) is to take the job of semantics to be the assignment of *functional* characters to sentences (and complex expressions). On this way of proceeding, complex expressions are assigned as semantic values functions from contexts to appropriate contents. Further, the functional character assigned to a complex expression is compositionally determined from the functional characters of its simple parts and how they are syntactically combined.

To illustrate, consider the sentence 'I am here', and assume that as usual the characters of 'I' and 'here' are functions from contexts to the speakers of the contexts and the locations of the contexts, respectively. Loosely following Kaplan's notation, regiment 'I am here' as:

(3) Located (I, Here)

The character of 'Located' will be a (constant) function from contexts to a two-place relation between individuals and locations (since we want structured contents, relations should be understood as relations-in-intension). Write '$C(e)$' for the character of expression e. Then, suppressing considerable detail, the clause

---

[21] There are several other accounts of complex demonstratives that, like King's, account for the data discussed by Braun, without appealing to character. For example, according to Lepore and Ludwig (2000), complex demonstratives are similar to quantifier phrases in that the content of the nominal in a complex demonstrative affects the content of the whole sentence containing it. This theory, too, explains Braun's data without appeal to character. So too does the "appositive" account of complex demonstratives advanced by Joshua Dever (2001).

[22] One argument we know of that structured characters have some important role to play was given in Richard (1983). Richard argued that structured characters (which he calls *meanings*) have a role to play in the semantics of belief-ascriptions. We don't think such an account of the semantics of belief-ascriptions is promising, and Richard himself no longer endorses the position he defended in this paper (see Richard 1990: 122 n. 8).

assigning a character to (3) (assuming the characters of 'I' and 'Here' mentioned above) loosely runs as follows:

(4) C('Located(i,p)') for 'i' an individual term and 'p' a position term $= f$ such that for any context c, $f(c) = $ <C('Located')(c),<C('i')(c),C('p')(c)>>

So the character of (3) is a function f that maps a context c to the structured proposition <L,<s,o>>, where L is the relation that the character of 'Located' maps every context to, and s and o are the speaker and location of the context c, respectively. Note that we cannot complain here, as we did on the previous account, that there is no real compositional semantics. Here there is: the characters (semantic values) of parts of a sentence combine in accordance with the syntax of the sentence to give the characters (semantic values) of the whole.

So what is wrong with this view? Our first concern is that such an account intuitively assigns the wrong semantic significance to syntactic combination.[23] This fact is obscured somewhat by clause (4). For clause (4) leaves implicit the semantic significance that it accords to the syntactic concatenation of the elements of 'Located(i,p)'. So let us consider how the view would work with a simpler example. On this view, the significance of syntactically combining, for example, a name and a simple predicate, say 'Njeri runs', is not that of predicating a property of an object. For the compositional semantics for this sentence must combine the *character* of 'Njeri' with that of 'runs' to yield the semantic value (character) of the whole sentence. Thus the semantic significance of the syntactic concatenation here is that of a function that maps a pair of a function f from contexts to objects and a function g from contexts to properties to a function h that maps a context c to the pair <$f(c),g(c)$>. This seems grossly implausible as the meaning of the syntactic relation of predication.

Furthermore, it simply does not seem that in understanding such a sentence in a context, speakers employ this compositional semantics to determine a character for the sentence, and then apply it to the context yielding the relevant structured proposition. Intuitively, it seems rather that speakers evaluate in a context the characters of syntactically simple expressions in a sentence, and compositionally combine the resulting referential contents in grasping the proposition expressed by the sentence. Thus, the account seems to get the phenomenology of linguistic understanding wrong.

---

[23] The concern we develop here applies equally to the first way of implementing this conception of the semantics–pragmatics distinction.

However, the most important objection to this account is that (phenomenological considerations of the sort just raised aside) there seems to be no empirical difference between this account and one that assigns characters only to syntactically simple expressions. After all, the job of character is to give us content, and we can assign contents to complex expressions in contexts using only the characters of the parts, and combining the contents they determine in those contexts. Thus, imagine a theory that assigns no character to the sentence (3) as a whole, but assigns it a content in every context as follows:

(4′) The content of 'Located (i,p)' in any context c is $<C('Located')(c),<i^*,p^*>>$, where i^* is the content of 'i' in c and p^* is the content of 'p' in c.

(We presuppose a recursive assignment of referential contents in contexts to complex individual and position terms—in the general case 'i' and 'p' could be syntactically complex in 4′.) As did (4), (4′) assigns to the sentence (3) relative to a context c the content $<L,<s,o>>$, where L is the relation that the character of 'Located' maps every context to, and s and o are the speaker and location of the context c, respectively.

The point is that both a semantics that assigns characters to simple expressions and recursively assigns characters to complex expressions *and* a semantics that assigns characters to only simple expressions allow for an assignment of the same contents in contexts to simple and complex expressions. So unless the functional characters of complex expressions have some *additional* job to do, they are unnecessary. But there seems to be no such additional job. Thus, on the present proposal, the only semantic value that is assigned via semantic composition, i.e. the characters of complex expressions, have no purpose. We could just as well do everything we need to without them. So here again, the present conception of semantics makes semantics out to be something that assigns only values with no real use to complex expressions. This, we think, is sufficient to dismiss the account.

In this section we have discussed three different ways of implementing the first conception of the semantics–pragmatics distinction, which stipulates that semantic values must be context-independent. We have found difficulties with all three ways of implementing this approach. This suggests the need for some semantic values to be relativized to contexts. But this insight is consistent both with our favored way of drawing the semantics–pragmatics distinction, and with the third way of drawing the distinction, according to which only a highly restricted range of context-sensitive expressions count as having genuine context-relative semantic values. In the next section we turn to a criticism of this third way of drawing the semantics–pragmatics distinction.

3.   Semantic Content as Minimally Context-Dependent

On the first way of drawing the distinction between semantics and pragmatics, semantic content is context-independent semantic value. On our favored way of drawing the distinction between semantics and pragmatics, there is a level of semantic value, which we are calling semantic content, that is relativized to context. One and the same expression can have different semantic contents in different contexts. On this conception of semantics, relative to a context, every indexical and demonstrative element in a sentence has potentially different *semantic* contents in different contexts. For example, the semantic contents of both 'I' and 'she', relative to different contexts, may be different.

Some philosophers, however, hold that our favored conception of the semantics–pragmatics distinction allows context to affect semantic content to a greater degree than is plausible. We begin this section by discussing two worries that may motivate rejecting our favored conception in favor of the third, and more restrictive, conception of the semantics–pragmatics distinction discussed in the first section. We then turn to an extended discussion and critique of this third conception of the semantics–pragmatics distinction.

The first worry one might have with our favored conception of the semantics–pragmatics distinction that might move one towards the third conception of the semantics–pragmatics distinction is that it does not allow for a distinction between speaker meaning and semantic content. For example, there is a distinction between the semantic content of a sentence on an occasion, and what the speaker meant by uttering that sentence on that occasion. Suppose John is confronted by a nice man drinking water, who John falsely believes to be drinking a martini. John utters the sentence 'The man with the martini is nice'. The semantic content of John's sentence on that occasion concerns the property of being a man drinking a martini, rather than the man to whom he intends to refer. However, John's referential intentions concern the man he sees drinking water, so his speaker meaning is a proposition about that particular man. One might worry that by allowing speakers' referential intentions to affect semantic content, as one is likely to do in adopting this second conception of the semantics–pragmatics distinction, one blurs this important distinction.[24]

---

[24] We say "likely", because of Lepore's point, mentioned above, that one may adopt our preferred way of distinguishing semantics from pragmatics, but adopt a thoroughgoing anti-intentionalism about demonstratives and indexicals generally, of the variety favored by Chris Gauker. However, we

Restricting semantically relevant contextual effects to "automatic" indexicals, in Perry's sense, obviates this concern.

We are not persuaded by this concern. If speaker intentions are relevant for determining the semantic content of some indexical expressions, then there must be a principled distinction between the kinds of speaker intentions that are relevant to the fixation of semantic content and those that are not. It is important to be as clear as possible, in particular cases of context-sensitive expressions, which speaker intentions are semantically relevant, that is, relevant for the fixation of semantic content. However, we see no basis for skepticism about the possibility of distinguishing, in particular cases, those intentions that are semantically relevant from those that are not.[25]

A second concern one may have with our favored conception of the semantics–pragmatics distinction is that allowing context to affect semantic content always brings with it a cost in complexity and systematicity to the semantic theory. This is a rather imprecise concern, but nevertheless, we suspect, a quite influential one. The concern is that there is an inverse correlation between the amount of semantic context-sensitivity a semantic theory recognizes and the systematicity and simplicity of that semantic theory. This concern would lead one to adopt the third conception of the semantics–pragmatics distinction over our favored conception (and taken to its limit, the first conception over the third).

We suspect this concern reflects a long-standing prejudice from earlier debates in the philosophy of language. For example, consider the stalking horses of Grice's 'Logic and Conversation' (Grice 1989a). These philosophers (Grice's "informalists" and "formalists") held that the natural language counterparts of the logical expressions were so laden with context-dependency and vagueness in their use, that any "logic" of these natural language expressions would be "unsimplified, and so more or less unsystematic" (1989a: 24).[26] In contrast, Grice's favored

think it very likely that speaker intentions do play a role in determining the reference of many indexical expressions.

[25] For example, Jeffrey King, in his quantificational analysis of complex demonstratives, appeals to speaker intentions to fix the properties that saturate the argument places of the relation expressed by 'that'. King is quite explicit (King 2001: 28–31) about what sort of speaker intentions are relevant for the determination of content. Siegel (2002) supplies a particularly subtle discussion of the nature of those perceptual intentions that are relevant for reference fixing. Siegel's discussion makes significant progress towards a criterion to distinguish between those sorts of intentions that are relevant for reference fixation, and those that are not. (We should note a particular debt to Maite Ezcurdia for discussion of these issues; her work bears directly on drawing the required distinctions between semantically relevant and semantically irrelevant speaker intentions.)

[26] Although in Grice's writings these philosophers do not explicitly use the phrase "context-dependence" or "vagueness", this is one plausible reading of what is meant by "unsystematic".

approach is to provide pragmatic explanations of context-dependency, whenever possible, presumably leaving the semantics "simple" and "systematic".

We suspect that this dialectic has led philosophers of language, whether knowingly or not, to adopt the position that preserving the simplicity and systematicity of a semantic theory for a natural language somehow requires giving pragmatic (non-semantic) explanations of context-dependency whenever remotely possible. But to adopt this position is to accept the view that giving a context-dependent semantic treatment of a linguistic construction is tantamount to treating that construction as resistant to "systematic" semantic analysis. In the intervening decades between Grice's work and today, there have been analyses of a host of constructions (such as modals, indicative conditionals, quantifier phrases, and adjectival modification, to name but a few) that incorporate context-dependence into the semantics without compromising the systematicity of the semantic theory (in a sense, this was also the purpose of Montague's work on formal pragmatics). The view favored by Grice's opponents concerning the ramifications of semantic context-dependency looks therefore to have been superseded by later developments.

In fact, we believe an even stronger response is possible to the view that semantic context-dependency is correlated with less simple and more unsystematic semantic theorizing. For it can turn out that claiming that certain sorts of context-dependency are not semantic can result in a less simple and more inelegant semantic theory. This point is the basis of our criticism of the third way of distinguishing semantics from pragmatics. By relegating certain contextual effects to pragmatics, this third way of forging a distinction between semantics and pragmatics results in a more complex and inelegant semantic theory.

Recall that on this third conception of the semantics–pragmatics distinction, among context-sensitive expressions only the content of automatic indexicals affects semantic content (relative to a context). So, automatic indexicals are the only semantically context-dependent expressions, on this conception. Non-automatic context-sensitive expressions do not contribute their contents to the semantic content (relative to a context) of sentences containing them. So, the semantic content of the sentence 'I am human' is, relative to a context, the proposition, about the speaker of that context, that she is human. In contrast, the semantic content of the sentence 'She is human' is not the proposition, about the demonstrated woman, that she is human. The reason that the semantic content of 'She is human' is not the proposition about the demonstrated woman to the effect that she is human, on this third conception, is that the pronoun 'she' is not an automatic indexical, and so its content in a context does not contribute to the semantic content of sentences containing it.

The first point to note is that this third conception of the semantics–pragmatics distinction is quite similar to the first conception. For the list of automatic indexicals is highly restricted, confined to words such as 'I', 'today', and 'tomorrow'.[27] The vast majority of context-sensitive expressions are intentional. So semantic theories in accord with the first and third conceptions of the semantics–pragmatics distinction share considerable overlap in their assignment of semantic content. As a result, the third conception of the semantics–pragmatics distinction inherits many of the concerns facing the first. But there are additional problems with it besides.

On this third conception of the semantics–pragmatics distinction, the semantic content of 'I am human', relative to a context, is the proposition, concerning the speaker in the context, that she is human. But the semantic content of 'She is human', relative to a context, is not a proposition. The English pronoun 'she' perhaps does possess some context-independent meaning; the referential content of 'she' relative to a context must be female. So it seems one plausible semantic content for 'She is human', relative to a context, is the property of being a female human, a function from a possible situation to the set of women in that situation (or a "propositional radical" that determines such a function).

But this is, prima facie, a worrisome result. The sentences 'I am human' and 'She is human' differ only in that the first contains the first-person pronoun in subject position, and the second contains the third-person pronoun (and the concomitant facts about case). As far as their structural features are concerned, the sentences are identical. So the mapping rules from sentences to semantic contents should be the same. But the sentence 'I am human', relative to a context, is supposed to express a proposition, a function from possible situations to truth-values, while the sentence 'She is human', relative to a context, expresses a property, namely, the property of being a female human, a function of a very different sort. On this conception of the semantics–pragmatics distinction, if the subject term of a sentence is non-indexical, or an automatic indexical, then, roughly speaking, it contributes an object to the semantic content of that sentence relative to a context, but if it is a non-automatic indexical or demonstrative, then it contributes a property that is conjoined with the property expressed by the predicate of that sentence. It is not immediately clear how to derive these results in a non-ad hoc fashion.

---

[27]   As Robyn Carston (MS) has pointed out, even indexicals such as 'now' and 'here' are not really automatic, since speaker intentions determine the temporal scope of the referential content of 'now' relative to a context, and the spatial dimensions of 'here' relative to a context.

We have focused, for simplicity's sake, on very simple sentences in making this point. But it should be clear that the point generalizes to a host of different constructions. For example, according to this third conception of the semantics–pragmatics distinction, (5) and (6), despite sharing the same syntactic structure, have semantic contents of drastically different types:

(5) Every woman who met me yesterday is smart.
(6) Every woman who met her yesterday is smart.

(5), relative to a context, expresses a proposition. (6) does not express a proposition, even relative to a context, because it contains the non-automatic indexical 'her'. Even more problems are involved in constructing the semantic value of a sentence like 'That man in her car is wearing a hat', where the complex demonstrative 'that man in her car' involves a kind of double incompleteness. What kind of semantic values such sentences express, according to this third conception of the semantics–pragmatics distinction, and how to construct non-ad hoc semantic rules that assign these semantic contents to these sentences, is an interesting technical question.[28]

It is no doubt possible to write some kind of semantic algorithm to do the trick of assigning distinct types of semantic values to (5) and (6), relative to a context. However, making semantic content sensitive to the effects of context on the content of all context-sensitive lexical items, as on the second conception of the semantics–pragmatics distinction, results in simpler semantic theory. We can draw a moral here, one that tells against the view with which we began concerning the allegedly disruptive effects of contextual sensitivity on the systematicity of semantics. It can indeed turn out that allowing certain contextual effects to have semantic import allows one to give a simpler semantics than would be otherwise possible. Whether there is in the end a compelling "simpler semantics" argument against advocates of this third conception of the semantics–pragmatics distinction depends, of course, upon the details of an as yet non-existent semantic theory that is in accord with it.

---

[28] Thomas Hofweber has made the following suggestion to us. One could add, to each domain of type T, a set of "incomplete" entities of that type. So, in addition to complete properties, there would be incomplete properties, and in addition to complete propositions, there would be incomplete propositions. Composition rules could, for example, combine an incomplete object with a complete transitive verb meaning to yield an incomplete property. This move seems ad hoc to us. One wonders with what right one can classify an "incomplete X" as an X at all. Furthermore, one wonders how one would marry this semantics with the notion of "pragmatic enrichment". How would interpreters "add" on constituents to meanings, thus construed?

There is another set of worries that faces the advocate of this third conception of the semantics–pragmatics distinction who adopts the structured proposition conception of semantics. On this method of semantic interpretation, semantics takes place in two stages. First, there is an algorithm assigning structured propositions to sentences relative to a context. The resulting structured entity is a concatenation of the semantic contents of the elements of the sentence. The second stage of semantic interpretation involves giving a truth-definition for the resulting structured propositions. At this stage in the semantic process, the elements of the structured proposition are combined in accord with semantic composition rules.[29]

The advocate of this third conception of the semantics–pragmatics distinction might find this framework attractive. For example, she could argue that non-automatic indexicals contribute, say, an ordered pair of a property and an object representing a gap, such as the empty set, to the structured proposition expressed by sentences containing them.[30] The structured proposition

---

[29] Things are actually a bit more complicated than we make them out to be here. We talk here as though *no* significant composition of semantic contents of the elements of a sentence occurs in the mapping from sentence to proposition. This is true on the account of structured propositions sketched in King (1995: 6), on which the structures of propositions are identical to the structures of sentences expressing them (in a context). Thus, the semantic contents (in the context) of the lexical items in the sentence are not composed in any significant way in the mapping to the proposition: the proposition is literally the concatenation of these semantic contents, and is structurally identical to the sentence expressing it. By contrast, in the mapping from propositions to truth-values, there is significant composing of the constituents of the proposition (i.e. the semantic contents of the lexical items in the sentence expressing the proposition) to yield a truth-value. However, one might hold that in the mapping from sentence to proposition for example, a complex predicate contributes a property or a property and a time to the proposition (this view is suggested by clauses (22) and (28) of Salmon 1986: 145–6). On this view, the semantic contents of the lexical items in the predicate apparently *are* semantically composed to yield the property contributed by the predicate to the proposition (this would require a recursive assignment of properties to complex predicates, which Salmon does not actually provide—see again clause (28)). On this view, then, some significant semantic composition occurs in the mapping from sentence to proposition and the rest occurs in the mapping from proposition to truth-value. How much composition occurs in the first-stage mapping from sentence to proposition depends on how much of the sentence structure is "preserved" in the structure of the proposition. King (1995) argues that an account on which *no* significant composition occurs in the first-stage mapping is preferable. In any case, the more sentence structure is preserved in proposition structure, the less composition occurs in mapping from sentence to proposition, and the more occurs in the mapping from proposition to truth-value. The point remains that on any theory of structured propositions that preserves most of the structure of a sentence in the structure of the proposition, most of the significant composition of semantic contents occurs in the mapping from propositions to truth-values.

[30] Braun (1993), following a suggestion by Kaplan, advocates a gappy structured meanings account for the semantic content of sentences containing names without bearers.

assigned by the algorithm to a sentence is not a function of the composition rules corresponding to the syntactic structure of that sentence; the semantic values of the words in the sentence are simply concatenated in the structured meaning. So in the mapping to the structured proposition, one does not have to face the question of how to compose the semantic content of a non-automatic indexical with other elements. One could then argue that pragmatics intrudes before the truth-definition for structured propositions. In particular, pragmatics would intrude to assign values to the empty slots in the structured proposition.

On this picture, the semantic content of a sentence such as (6) would be a concatenation of properties and functions of various sorts, corresponding to the semantic values of the lexical items in (6). However, in the semantic content, corresponding to the place of the non-automatic indexical 'her' in (6), would be an object representing a gap and the property of being a woman. Pragmatics would then somehow replace this ordered pair by a contextually salient woman. Then, together with the semantic composition rules corresponding to the syntactic structure of the sentence, one could calculate the truth-conditions of the resulting proposition.

However, we believe that the picture that results amounts, if anything, to a rejection of a genuine distinction between semantics and pragmatics, rather than a novel way to draw one. On the structured propositions picture defended by King (1995: 6), Soames (1987), and others, semantic interpretation is a two-stage process. First, there is the assignment of a structured entity to a sentence relative to a context. Secondly, there is the definition of truth for that entity. On the picture we are now considering, pragmatics intrudes between the first stage of this process and the second. That is, pragmatic processes enter in to "fill in" the empty slots in the structured entity.[31]

We believe that no one who thinks that there is an interesting and important distinction between semantics and pragmatics should be content with the resulting picture of semantics and pragmatics. For the view amounts to a rejection of the possibility of a strictly compositional semantics for a language containing non-automatic indexicals. In mapping the sentence to the structured entity, one does not appeal to the composition rules corresponding to the syntactic structure within the sentence; one simply concatenates the semantic values of the individual terms in the sentence. The composition rules expressed

---

[31] Soames (Ch. 9 in this volume) develops a picture like this, albeit not one clearly motivated by the distinction between automatic and non-automatic indexicals.

by the syntactic structure of the sentence are relevant only for the definition of truth for the resulting structured entities. But pragmatic mechanisms intervene before the truth-definition, on this picture. That is, the gaps in the semantic contents are "filled" by enrichment before the definition of truth.

So, on this picture, composition rules do not just compose semantic values; they compose semantic and pragmatic values. Indeed, on this view, in interpreting most sentences, composition rules do not compose only semantic values. Significant composition of the elements of structured propositions is then, strictly speaking, part of pragmatics, not semantics. Perhaps one way of describing this is as a rejection of the possibility of a strictly compositional semantics for a natural language. There is only an attenuated sense in which one is preserving a significant role for semantic content on such a way of dividing the labor between semantics and pragmatics.

According to the first conception of the semantics–pragmatics distinction, the semantic content of an expression was its context-independent semantic value, and every other kind of content associated with the sentence was pragmatic in nature. On our favored conception of the semantics–pragmatics distinction, there are two levels of genuinely semantic content. On the first level are properties of individual words, rather than complex expressions. This is standing meaning, or character. On the second is semantic content, a property of expressions relative to contexts. The semantic content of any term relative to a context is the referential content in that context that is in accord with its standing meaning, and the semantic content of a complex expression is derived by combining the semantic contents of its parts in accord with the composition rules corresponding to its syntactic structure. On the third conception of the semantics–pragmatics distinction we have been discussing in this section, only some context-sensitive terms contributed their contents in a context to the semantic content, relative to that context, of more complex expressions containing them.

We know of no compelling arguments against our favored way of drawing the semantics–pragmatics distinction. In contrast, we have raised concerns with the two natural competing conceptions. Some of these concerns may be met by greater attention to the technical details of a semantic theory that respects, say, the third conception of the semantics–pragmatics distinction. But until such a theory is advanced, in the absence of any compelling objections against our own favored conception of the semantics–pragmatics distinction, it should clearly be the default conception of the relation between semantics and pragmatics.

On this conception, the effects of context on semantic interpretation are restricted to what we have called above "weak pragmatic effects". That is, context can only affect the semantic interpretation of an expression by being involved in the interpretation of some constituent of that expression. But semantic content is not limited to denotation assignment to "automatic" indexicals. The content of any syntactic constituent is relevant to the semantic content of expressions containing it. This is the picture of semantic content we will assume in the remainder of this chapter.

4. Skepticism and Modesty

Some disagreements in the philosophy of language concern the correct conception of the semantics–pragmatics distinction. No doubt some of these disagreements are terminological. But perhaps some are not. For example, in the last two sections we have suggested that there are some ways of drawing the distinction between semantics and pragmatics that face objections that our preferred conception does not. This suggests that there are some non-terminological issues involved in deciding what the "correct" distinction between semantics and pragmatics is. Be that as it may, once one fixes upon one way of drawing the distinction between semantics and pragmatics, many obviously non-terminological disputes arise.

We have settled upon one favored way to draw the semantics–pragmatics distinction. In this section we use this semantics–pragmatics distinction to describe three different views about the relative importance of the semantic content of a sentence, as we have characterized it. The disputes between these positions are definitely not terminological. In fact, they are largely empirical disputes, the resolution of which will require decades of cross-linguistic syntactic and semantic research, together with psychological studies. The different positions we describe correspond essentially to predictions about the ultimate outcome of these investigations.

The first position, and one which will centrally occupy us in the final section of this chapter, is what we may call *semantic skepticism* about what is said. Semantic skeptics hold that at no stage in linguistic interpretation does the semantic content of a sentence play a privileged role. For example, what is accessible in linguistic interpretation is a level of content that is thoroughly affected by strong pragmatic effects, in the sense discussed in the first section. Indeed, according to the semantic skeptic, there is no reason for an account of language understanding to grant the semantic content of a sentence, in the sense we have adopted, any important role. Every interesting level of content is affected by strong pragmatic effects.

According to the semantic skeptic, individual words have semantic content. However, there is no interesting notion of semantic content for sentences. The attitude of the semantic skeptic towards the semantic content of a sentence is therefore much like the attitude we adopted in the second section towards the character of a sentence. It is certainly an entity that one can define. But it lacks an interesting or central role in an account of any significant natural language phenomenon. Semantic skepticism has been one of the major positions among cognitive scientists for the last twenty years, thanks in large part to the influence of Relevance Theory, the theory of linguistic interpretation introduced and defended by Dan Sperber and Deirdre Wilson (1986). Its other prominent advocates include Robyn Carston, Stephen Levinson, and François Recanati, all of whom have been defending for years, on various grounds, the thesis that there is no interesting semantic notion of what is said by a sentence.[32]

The second position is what we call *semantic modesty* about what is said. In contrast to semantic skeptics, semantically modest theorists do believe that the semantic content of a sentence has a significant role to play in an account of linguistic understanding. Such theorists are loath to give up on a theoretically important notion of the semantic content of a sentence. However, they believe this role to be minimal. In particular, the semantically modest theorist agrees with the semantic skeptic that what is accessible to interpreters as the content of a speech act is thoroughly affected by strong pragmatic effects. Indeed, semantically modest theorists have produced some of the strongest arguments for this conclusion. However, the semantically modest theorist insists that the semantic content of a sentence still has a privileged role to play in an account of linguistic understanding. That is, the semantically modest theorist holds that there is an important notion of sentence content that is not sensitive to strong pragmatic effects.

---

[32] It is true that Sperber and Wilson (1986, ch. 4) do talk of "sentence meanings". However, for them, sentence meanings "do not encode thoughts"; they are rather "sets of semantic representations, as many semantic representations as there are ways in which the sentence is ambiguous" (p. 193). Semantic representations, in turn, are "incomplete logical forms" (ibid.). So, sentence "meanings" are in fact not semantic content at all—they are sets of expressions. What plays a theoretical role in Relevance Theory is not any notion of semantic content for a sentence, but rather the *syntax* of a sentence—its syntactic logical form. It is this that is subject to pragmatic enrichment, to obtain the representation of the thought. So, on Sperber and Wilson's theory, there is no role played at all by any notion of the *content* of a sentence, as opposed merely to its syntax.

Semantic modesty is a position that comes in degrees. On the one extreme, there are those who hold that most of our intuitions about what is said by a sentence in a context are affected by strong pragmatic effects. On the other end of the spectrum are theorists who hold that while generally intuitions about what is said by a sentence are reliable guides to semantic content, there is a restricted range of cases in which strong pragmatic effects may affect speaker intuitions about what they take to be the semantic content of a sentence. In what follows, we restrict the thesis of semantic modesty to the first extreme of this spectrum, since this is the position that has gained particular popularity among philosophers of language.

Three philosophers who have directly argued for an extreme version of semantic modesty are Kent Bach (1994, 2002*a*, *b*) and Herman Cappelen and Ernie Lepore (1997, 2002).[33] A different group of philosophers of language are led to embrace semantic modesty indirectly, by some of their antecedent semantic commitments concerning certain linguistic constructions. Most salient in this regard are the *neo-Russellians*. Neo-Russellians have a certain view about the semantic content of propositional attitude sentences. The neo-Russellian position is that the semantic content of a sentence such as 'John believes that Mark Twain was an author', relative to a context, is that John bears the belief relation to the singular proposition, concerning Mark Twain, that he was an author. According to the neo-Russellian, this is the very same semantic content, relative to the same context, as the sentence 'John believes that Samuel Clemens was an author'. However, neo-Russellians recognize that speakers intuitively believe that these sentences have different semantic contents, since speakers intuitively believe that their semantic contents can diverge in truth-value. So, neo-Russellians are committed to the view that there is a class of sentences with a semantic content that is relatively opaque to speaker intuitions. Neo-Russellians therefore find semantic modesty an immensely plausible position.[34]

---

[33] One difference between the version of semantic modesty advocated by Bach and the version advocated by Cappelen and Lepore is that (as we have discussed above) Bach thinks that the semantic content of a sentence relative to a context can be a non-propositional entity, whereas Cappelen and Lepore retain the thesis that it must be a proposition, or (in their Davidsonian framework) a truth-condition.

[34] Of course, one can imagine a neo-Russellian who rejects full-blown semantic modesty, and restricts her views about the inaccuracy of speaker intuitions about semantic content to propositional attitude ascriptions. Such a neo-Russellian is, we take it, a target of Saul (1997). In recent years neo-Russellians have exhibited an attraction to the more extreme forms of semantic modesty.

The main worry with semantic modesty is its tendency to collapse into semantic skepticism. Advocates of semantic modesty expend their greatest efforts arguing for an error theory about ordinary speaker intuitions about semantic content. That is, just like advocates of semantic skepticism, semantically modest theorists are most eager to establish that what ordinary speakers grasp in a speech act is not the semantic content of the sentence uttered relative to that context, but is instead thoroughly infected by strong pragmatic effects. But rarely do semantically modest theorists bother to explain what privileged role they believe semantic content in fact plays in language understanding. So it ends up being somewhat of a mystery what role these theorists believe semantic content has in an account of language understanding.

For example, one reason theorists have in producing semantic theories is to explain the systematicity and productivity of language understanding.[35] Given a finite vocabulary, and grasp of the composition rules expressed by syntactic structures, speakers have the ability to grasp the propositions expressed by an infinite number of sentences. If language users employ a compositional semantic theory in grasping the contents of speech acts, then one has a satisfactory explanation of the systematicity and productivity of a speaker's grasp of an infinite number of novel utterances. For then one can explain a language user's grasp of what is expressed by the utterance of a novel sentence by appealing to the fact that she grasps the words in the sentence and their modes of combination, together with whatever contextual information is required to interpret the context-sensitive elements in the sentence. Given compositionality, nothing else is required to explain her grasp of the proposition expressed, since what is expressed by the utterance is then a function of what she already grasps.

But it is difficult to see how the semantically modest theorist can appeal to this justification for taking the project of semantic theory seriously. For the semantically modest theorist holds that, in ever so many cases of successful communication, when someone utters a sentence, her interlocutor grasps a proposition that is not determined compositionally from the values of the elements in the sentence and their composition. Rather, tacit unsystematic pragmatic processes intervene. This is, after all, why competent hearers are so often wrong about semantic content, according to the semantically modest theorist. So the semantically modest theorist is committed to an alternative explanation of our grasp of an infinite number of novel utterances, one that does not proceed by attributing our competence to a simple, compositional mechanism.

---

[35] Thanks to Ernie Lepore for discussion that led to this point.

So it is hard to see how she could accept arguments for the necessity of semantic theory that proceed on the assumption that grasp of a compositional semantic theory is the only way to explain our ability to grasp an infinite number of novel utterances given finite means.

According to the semantically modest theorist, there is some role to be played by their minimal notion of the semantic content of a sentence, relative to a context. This role cannot be played by the semantic contents of words relative to a context, together with their syntactic structures. The difficulty of distinguishing between semantic skepticism and semantic modesty is that it is hard to see what explanatory role could be played by such a minimal notion of the semantic content of a sentence relative to a context, that could not also be played solely by appeal to the semantic contents of words (relative to contexts), together with the syntactic structure of sentences. But unless there is a genuine explanatory role that is played by the semantically modest theorist's notion of sentence content, relative to a context, semantic modesty dissolves into semantic skepticism.

A final worry about semantically modest theorists is that their views threaten to undermine the very data for semantic theories. As Stanley and Szabó note, "accounting for our ordinary judgments about the truth-conditions of various sentences is the central aim of semantics. Since these judgments are the data of semantic theorizing, we should be careful with proposals that suggest a radical revision of these judgments" (2000: 240). So, semantic modesty not only obscures the purpose of the semantic project, but also removes the central empirical data for its claims. For if, as semantic modesty has it, speaker judgments about truth-conditions are not reliable guides to the semantic content of sentences, it becomes unclear how to evaluate semantic proposals (cf. also DeRose 1995, sect. 16; 1999, sects. 9 and 10).

So, from our perspective, both semantic modesty and semantic skepticism pose similar threats. First, it is difficult to see what the purpose of semantic theory should be, on either view. For according to these views, what is intuitively said by an utterance of a sentence is not significantly constrained by the syntactic structure of that sentence, since the result of semantically interpreting the syntactic structure of a sentence relative to a context far underdetermines what is intuitively said by that utterance. Secondly, one may worry about the explanatory value of accounts of what is intuitively said by an utterance that appeal to pragmatic processes unconstrained by syntax. Given the degree to which pragmatic mechanisms can affect what is intuitively said on these views, the sense in which such theories make explanatory predictions about intuitive judgments is unclear. For example, one worry is that the unconstrained nature of such accounts leads to an unconstrained over-generation of predictions about what a sentence can be used to intuitively say, relative to a context (cf. Stanley 2002b: 161–7). In contrast, an account of what is intuitively said by a sentence relative to a context of the sort advocated here and in Stanley (2000), that appeals only to syntax, semantics, and weak pragmatic effects, does not involve appeal to mysterious unconstrained processes. So there needs to be a rather strong justification for the view of semantic skeptics and semantically modest theorists that what is intuitively said is not so constrained.

The kind of arguments such theorists advance all take the following form. First, they produce a linguistic construction L, uses of which speakers intuitively believe to have a certain interpretation I relative to a context c. Then, they argue that the interpretation I cannot plausibly be the semantic content of L in c, because I is not just the result of assignment of referential contents in c to the parts of L and composition. That is, proponents of semantic skepticism and modesty argue that the relevant interpretation is the result of strong pragmatic effects. If so, then speaker intuitions about semantic content are sensitive to strong pragmatic effects.

Opponents of such arguments have in recent years argued that the examples discussed by semantically skeptical and semantically modest theorists are insufficient to support their conclusions.[36] For example, Stanley and Szabó (2000) argue, as against advocates of semantic skepticism and semantic modesty, that our intuitions about what is said by quantified sentences track the semantic content of these sentences, and additional work extends these points to a number of different constructions that semantically skeptical and semantically modest theorists have taken to show that speaker intuitions about semantic content are not reliable.[37]

---

[36] See Stanley and Szabó (2000); Stanley (2000, 2002a, b); and Szabó (2001).

[37] The debate surrounding attitude-ascriptions is more complicated. One basic problem is that different parties in the debate do not share the same conception of semantic content. For example, Crimmins and Perry (1989) and Crimmins (1992) argue, apparently in response to the neo-Russellian, that modes of presentation affect the semantic content of propositional attitude ascriptions. But Crimmins and Perry have a different conception of semantic content from the average neo-Russellian. According to Crimmins and Perry, there are "unarticulated constituents" of the semantic content of some sentences (an unarticulated constituent of an utterance u, in the sense of Crimmins and Perry, is an element of the semantic content of u that is not the value of any element in the sentence uttered). Like us, most neo-Russellians accept a conception of semantic content according to which, by definition, there are no unarticulated constituents of semantic contents. So the substance of the debate between Crimmins and Perry, on the one hand, and neo-Russellians, on the other, concerns the right definition of semantics, rather than attitude constructions. Peter Ludlow (1995) has, however, argued quite directly for the syntactic representation of modes of presentation, which meets the neo-Russellian more squarely on her own ground.

In the next section we challenge one powerful argument in favor of semantic skepticism or modesty, one that has not yet received a response. Versions of the argument have been around for several decades. Perhaps the simplest form of the argument involves negated sentences such as:

(7a) John doesn't have three children, he has four.

(7b) I'm not happy, I'm ecstatic.

Assuming, as is usual, that "three" means at least three, in these cases, the negative element appears to negate not the semantic content of the sentence, but rather the semantic content together with its implicature. For example, a pragmatic (scalar) implicature of 'John has three children' is that John has no more than three children. Intuitively, what is negated in (7a) is the proposition that John has three children and no more than three. If so, then such cases are examples of strong pragmatic effects on the intuitive content of the speech act, and therefore support an error theory of speaker intuitions about semantic content, in the sense of "semantic content" we have adopted. Let us call this alleged kind of strong pragmatic effect, a "pragmatic intrusion".

There are problems with the pragmatic intrusion account of the examples in (7). Larry Horn has convincingly argued that the examples in (7) are instances of 'metalinguistic negation', where one is denying the appropriateness of an utterance, rather than its content, and even provides compelling phonetic diagnostics for such uses of 'not'. Horn's discussion undermines any clear argument from examples such as (7) to an error theory of speaker intuitions about semantic content. For example, it shows that it is wrong to characterize these cases as ones in which what is negated is semantic content somehow augmented with pragmatic implicatures. So defenders of pragmatic intrusion have wisely chosen not to stake their case on these uses of 'not'.

In recent years, however, increasingly more sophisticated arguments for pragmatic intrusion have made their way into the literature. For example, Robyn Carston (1988) has, with the use of these more sophisticated arguments, tried to provide evidence for the existence of the non-Gricean, relevance-theoretic pragmatic process of *explicature*. More recently Stephen Levinson has argued that the sorts of examples discussed by Carston support a related notion, what he calls *implicature intrusion*. Both explicature and implicature intrusion, if genuine, would entail the existence of strong pragmatic effects on the intuitive content of speech acts.

The debate between Carston and Levinson is important for pragmatics, but not for our purposes. Our expression "pragmatic intrusion" is intended to be neutral between notions such as that of the relevance-theoretic explicature, Recanati's free enrichment, and the more Gricean notion of implicature intrusion. If there is a significant range of cases of pragmatic intrusion, then that would provide strong support for the existence of strong pragmatic effects on what is intuitively said. In the next section, focusing on Carston and Levinson's arguments for pragmatic intrusion, we argue that the case for pragmatic intrusion is not compelling.

5. Pragmatic Intrusion

Levinson himself is admirably cautious about his arguments for pragmatic intrusions. As he notes, "There will always be doubts about whether a better semantic analysis of the relevant construction might not accommodate the apparent pragmatic intrusions in some other way" (Levinson 2000: 214). In this section we intend to substantiate Levinson's concern, by showing that the existence of pragmatic intrusion has yet to be substantiated. The arguments for it in the literature rest upon an inadequate grasp of the syntax and semantics of the particular constructions that appear to give rise to it.

The first case of pragmatic intrusion discussed by Levinson involves the comparative 'better than'. The first set of examples, discovered by Wilson (1975: 151), involve sentences like the following:

(8) Driving home and drinking three beers is better than drinking three beers and driving home.

As Wilson notes, it would seem that what is said by (8) is that it is better first to drive home, and then to drink three beers, than first to drink three beers, and then to drive home. If Grice is correct that 'and' does not have a temporal meaning, then the temporal information has to come from a pragmatic effect. But then what is said by (8) appears to be sensitive to the pragmatics of the use of the clauses flanking 'better than'. If so, then there are strong pragmatic effects on the intuitive contents of speech acts.

But as the discussion in and of Cohen (1971) makes clear, appealing to the data about the temporal nature of conjunction is complex. According to most twenty-first-century syntactic theories, each clause contains a tense phrase, the contents of which give information about the time that the proposition expressed by the clause concerns. So in a sentence such as 'John came in and sat down', there is a tense phrase associated with each verb in the underlying syntactic structure. Relative to a context, this conjunction expresses a proposition of the form 'John came in at time t and sat down at $t + n$'. As Levinson sums up the situation, for all the data shows, "Grice's position with respect to 'and' could be maintained, while the truth-conditional nature of the 'and then' inference could be attributed to the implicit indexical sequence of reference times in the two verbs" (Levinson 2000: 199).[38]

However, the conjuncts in (8), as Levinson notes, do not involve finite clauses, and hence have no obvious tense. Furthermore, (8) is a generic sentence, which adds an additional factor to the interpretation of the data. However, we think that the same response is available, despite these additional complexities. For many non-finite clauses do carry clear temporal information. For example, consider:

(9a) John will remember bringing the cake.
(9b) John remembered to bring the cake.

(9a) can express the proposition that John will remember bringing the cake *today*. (9b) can express the proposition that John remembered to bring the cake *today*. Such evidence suggests the existence of an indexical temporal element in the syntax of some gerunds and infinitives, which, relative to a context, can be assigned a contextually salient time or event.[39] Furthermore, the infinitives and gerunds in (9) can be modified by explicit temporal adverbs such as 'today' and 'tomorrow'. On virtually all contemporary accounts of the functioning of such adverbs, they modify the values of syntactically represented times or events.[40]

---

[38] The fact that the temporal element in the second conjunct is later than the temporal element in the first conjunct is due to a pragmatic maxim governing the description of events; as Partee (1984: 254) describes the condition, "there is a past reference time r-p specified at the start of the discourse, and . . . the introduction of new event sentences moves the reference time forward". We will argue that this is a pragmatic maxim that affects semantic content by influencing the semantic content of temporal elements in the syntax.

[39] We are in fact agnostic here as to the precise nature of the contextually sensitive temporal element here (though see King forthcoming). For example, in Higginbotham's (2002) account of sequence of tense, tenses express relations between events. On Higginbotham's account, times would not be the values of the syntactically represented context-sensitive elements.

[40] See Enc (1987: 652); King (forthcoming); Ogihara (1996: 41–9, 56–60). Parsons (1990, ch. 11) is another obvious example, though whether Parsons accepts the letter of this point depends upon the relation between his "subatomic" representations and syntax proper. Discourse Representation-Theoretic accounts of temporal adverbs also treat them as setting descriptive conditions on syntactically represented temporal elements, though in the case of such theories, they are represented syntactically only in the level of syntax called Discourse Representation Structure (see Partee 1984).

There is also additional clear syntactic evidence in favor of the existence of a temporal element in many infinitives and gerunds. For example, this element can interact with higher operators in variable-binding configurations, as in:

(10a) John asked to bring a cake many times.

(10b) John tried singing many times.

The sentences in (10) are ambiguous. On one reading of (10a), John asked something many times; on this reading, the temporal quantifier 'many times' binds a temporal element associated with the verb 'ask'. But on the second reading, John asked once, at some contextually salient past time, to bring a cake many times. On this reading, the temporal quantifier 'many times' binds a temporal element associated with the infinitive 'to bring a cake'.[41] Similarly, there is a reading of (10b) according to which John tried once in the past to sing many times. Such evidence provides support for the existence of a temporal element associated with many infinitives and gerunds (see Stanley 2000, 2002a, for discussion of this strategy).[42]

There is thus good evidence for a temporal element in the syntax of many non-finite clauses. (8) is a generic sentence, and so involves an unselective generic quantifier.[43] The temporal elements in the non-finite clauses in (8) are bound by this generic operator, yielding the interpretation in (11):

(11) Gen-x, y [Better-than(x driving home at y and x drinking three beers at $y+1$), (x drinking three beers at y and x driving home at $y+1$)].

(11) is the semantic content predicted by a standard theory of generics, coupled with a plausible hypothesis about the syntax of non-finite clauses. Thus, the right syntax and semantics for constructions such as (8) simply predicts they have the readings at issue. No appeal to effects of implicature on intuitive content are required in this explanation.

---

[41] It does not matter for our purposes whether this temporal element is in argument or adjunct position; we do not here commit ourselves on this matter. If the temporal element is an adjunct, perhaps its presence is optional.

[42] There is now a rather large and intricate literature in syntax on the question of tense in infinitives and gerunds, starting with Stowell (1982). Infinitives and gerunds that must inherit their tense properties from the matrix clause, and hence do not allow temporal modification, are usually not thought to contain a tense phrase (or to contain one that is deficient in its case-assigning properties). The gerunds in examples such as (8) are not contained in embedded clauses. However, they clearly can be modified by temporal adverbs such as 'today' and 'at nine o'clock'. Again, this alone suggests that they contain a temporal element.

[43] For unselective binders, see Lewis (1998) and Heim (1982, ch. 2). An unselective binder binds multiple variables in its scope.

Suppose a theorist is in the position of arguing that the semantic content of a certain construction must be augmented by pragmatic information to account for natural readings of that construction. To make out this claim, it is incumbent upon the theorist to provide a sketch of the correct syntax and semantics of the relevant construction. For it is only then that one can evaluate the claim that the syntax and semantics for the relevant construction does not by itself deliver the reading at issue. Far too often, those who advocate the thesis that a certain reading of a construction is due to pragmatics rather than semantics fail to live up to their obligation, and so make claims that are highly speculative and hence difficult to evaluate. Before we can evaluate the other alleged examples of pragmatic intrusion, we need to sketch a semantics for 'better than', with respect to which we can evaluate the claim that one cannot come up with a syntax and semantics that deliver the right readings.

For the sake of simplicity, we will treat only the 'better than' relation that relates propositions.[44] One natural proposal for the semantics for 'better than', as a relation between propositions, is as in (12):

(12) Better-than (p, q) if and only if the most similar p-worlds are preferable, in the contextually salient sense, to the most similar q-worlds.

There are two dimensions of contextual sensitivity required for this semantics. First, the relation of similarity between possible worlds that is relevant for the truth-conditions of a 'better than' sentence in a context is determined in part by facts about that discourse context. Secondly, the sense of preferability at issue is also a function of the discourse context.[45]

We do not mean to advocate this as a semantics for 'better than'; we find it unpleasantly skeletal. But, as we shall show, one can account for the other alleged examples of pragmatic intrusion without abandoning it. That is, as far as we have seen, the semantics just described can account for all of the data, without the existence of pragmatic intrusion. Or so we will argue.

Here are the first set of examples that appear to make Levinson's points, but do not involve apparent temporal readings of 'and':

(13a) Eating *some* of the cake is better than eating all of it.

---

[44] If 'better-than' expresses a relation between properties, then we can take 'Better-than (p, q)' to be true with respect to a situation if and only if the closest worlds in which p is instantiated are preferable, in the contextually salient sense, to the closest worlds in which q is instantiated.

[45] For example, in a context in which health is at issue, that John has spinach is preferable to that John has cake. But in a context in which pleasure is at issue, the opposite may be true.

(13*b*) Having a cookie *or* ice cream is better than having a cookie and ice cream.

(13*c*) Having *two* children is better than having three.

We are not certain whether 'better than', in the examples in (13), relates properties or propositions. But let us suppose that they relate propositions.[46] Given the semantics in (12), the examples in (13) all come out true and unproblematic on fairly plausible assumptions. For example, it is quite plausible that, in a given context of use in which the salient preferability relation is health, the most similar worlds in which (say) some cake-eating happens are ones in which some of the cake is eaten, rather than all of it. Similarly, it is plausible that the most similar worlds in which a cookie or ice cream is eaten are ones in which it is not the case that both are eaten. So, given plausible assumptions, these examples do not raise the specter of pragmatic intrusion.

But consider (14):

(14) Buying *some* of that cake is better than buying *all* of it.

Suppose, in the context in which (14) is uttered, the entire cake is on sale in the supermarket. There is no obvious way to purchase only some of it. In this context, the most similar worlds in which some of the cake is purchased are ones in which all of the cake is purchased. But then the semantic account given in (12) predicts that the truth of (14) requires such worlds to be preferable to themselves (in the contextually determined sense of 'preferable'). So (14) should seem radically false. But it seems that (14) can nevertheless be truly uttered.

As Levinson emphasizes, the phenomenon exhibited by (14) occurs with other determiners. For example, suppose that we live in a world in which 90 per cent of all childbirths give rise to triplets. It can nevertheless be true that:

(15) Having two children is better than having three children.

But, on the assumption that the semantic content of 'two' is 'at least two', the semantic clause in (12) appears to entail that (15) cannot be true in this situation. This is counter-intuitive.

---

[46] The sentences in (13) are generic sentences. Take (13*a*); it means something like 'Gen(*x*)(*x*'s eating some of the cake is better than *x*'s eating all of it)'. On this account, 'better than' relates the proposition expressed by the open sentence '*x* eating some of the cake' to the proposition expressed by the open sentence '*x* eating all of the cake', relative to the assignment function introduced by generic quantifier. So what one is comparing is propositions according to which one person ate some of the cake with propositions according to which that very person ate all of the cake.

There are three general strategies one can exploit in this situation. First, one can retain the semantic clause (12), and defend the thesis that (14) and (15) do not express true propositions relative to the envisaged situations. One might, for example, maintain that utterances of (14) and (15) communicate true propositions, despite the fact that the sentences in context express false ones.[47] Secondly, one can retain the semantic clause in (12), and argue that pragmatic processes affect the intuitive content. The third option is to reject (12), and seek an alternative semantic analysis of a comparative like 'better'.

Pragmatic intrusion approaches are versions of the second strategy, the one that Carston and Levinson adopt. In other words, they would retain the semantics in (12), and argue that the scalar implicature of 'some' "enriches" the semantic content of (14), and the scalar implicature of 'two' enriches the semantic content of (15).[48] On this account, there are strong pragmatic effects on the intuitive content of the utterance, which is the conclusion that Carston and Levinson wish to draw.

However, on both Carston's and Levinson's accounts, it is unclear how an implicature "enriches" semantic content. "Enrich" is certainly not a technical term; it is unclear what enriching a semantic content with an implicature is supposed to amount to in the end. In this respect, they have yet to provide an account of the phenomena. As we will now argue, closer attention to the way in which context affects these constructions reveals that only weak pragmatic effects are involved in the cases at hand. That is, we agree with Carston and Levinson that the second strategy is a promising one for accounting for the data. But the *way* in which pragmatics affects the intuitive content only involves a weak pragmatic effect of context on semantic content, that is, one triggered by the syntax and semantics.

There is a distinctive feature of the cases discussed by these authors, namely that they involve placing focal stress on the relevant expressions. Consider again:

(13a) Eating *some* of the cake is better than eating all of it.
(13b) Having a cookie *or* ice cream is better than having a cookie and ice cream.
(13c) Having *two* children is better than having three.

---

[47] See Levinson's discussions of the "Obstinate Theorist" in ch. 3 of Levinson (2000).

[48] In fact, surprisingly, Carston and Levinson do not provide a semantics for 'better than'. Nevertheless, their strategy is clearly to retain a relatively simple semantics for 'better than', and to account for the complexities pragmatically.

In each of these cases, one needs to place stress on the italicized expression to obtain the relevant reading.[49] The key to explaining the data lies in recognizing the effects of focal stress.

Giving focal stress to a word makes salient a contextually appropriate contrast class. So, for example, consider:

(16) John met *Bill*.

A speaker may utter (16), with focus on 'Bill', with the intention of asserting that John met Bill, as opposed to another contextually salient person or persons. One way of treating the phenomenon of focus is by saying that placing focus on a constituent gives rise to either the presupposition that the sentence-frame does not hold true of any of the contextually salient alternatives, or the implicature that it does not.[50] Suppose that Frank is the contextually salient person in the context of utterance of (16). Then, on this rough analysis, an utterance of (16) presupposes or implicates that it is not the case that John met Frank.

In the case of (16), a proper name is placed in focus. However, in the examples in (13), determiners ('some', 'two') and connectives ('or') are the expressions that are placed into focus. The same general analysis is applicable here, that focusing the expression gives rise to a presupposition or implicature that the sentence-frame is not true of contextually salient alternatives. However, in the case of these expressions, it is not as obvious to the untrained observer what the contextually salient alternatives in fact are.

In fact, determiners such as 'some', and connectives such as 'or', are conventionally associated with contextually salient alternatives, via the "scales" of scalar implicatures. For example, the scale for 'some' is <some, all>, and the scale for 'or' is <or, and>. These scales reflect an intuitive ordering of the "logical strength" of their members.

For example, placing focus on 'some' in (17) gives rise to the presupposition or the implicature that the sentence-frame that results from deleting the occurrence of 'some' is not true of the other element in the scale associated

---

[49] Levinson (2000: 400 n. 26) even explicitly suggests placing focal stress on words like 'some' in constructions like (13a) if one has trouble with the intuitions.

[50] We are neutral on whether focus gives rise to a presupposition or an implicature in what follows; as we discuss below, in either case, Carston and Levinson's examples only involve weak pragmatic effects. It is worth mentioning that some theorists (e.g. Glanzberg, Ch. 5 in this volume) hold that focus is syntactically represented. Since this position would stack the deck in favor of our position, we do not adopt it in what follows.

with 'some':

(17) *Some* bottles are on the table.

In other words, placing focus on 'some' in (17) gives rise to the presupposition or the implicature that the sentence-frame 'x bottles are on the table' is false as applied to the determiner meaning expressed by 'all'. Similarly, placing focal stress on 'or' in (18) gives rise to the presupposition or the implicature that the relevant sentence-frame is false for the function denoted by 'and':

(18) John can eat cake *or* John can eat cookies.

So, to sum up, focusing an element that is conventionally associated with a scale affects interpretation by giving rise to a presupposition or an implicature that the sentence-frame is false for the members of that scale that are of greater "strength".[51]

This fact has implications for the evaluation of complex constructions. For example, consider conditionals. On the standard Lewis analysis, a subjunctive conditional is true if and only if its consequent is true in the worlds most similar to the actual world in which its antecedent is true. So, the semantics of subjunctive conditionals, like the semantics of 'better than', involves reference to a similarity relation between worlds. Focusing an element can influence the selection of the similarity relation relevant to the truth-conditions of a particular subjunctive conditional.

Suppose that Frank met Sue at the airport, and invited her to our party, an invitation she declines. Hearing this, John utters:

(19) If *Paul* had met Sue at the airport, she would have accepted the invitation.

John's utterance is true if and only if the most similar worlds in which Paul had met Sue at the airport and Frank did not meet Sue at the airport are ones in which Sue accepted the invitation. This is so, even if the most likely way for Paul to meet Sue at the airport would be for Paul to go with Frank. Perhaps Paul cannot drive, so, in some more absolute sense, the most similar worlds to the actual world in which the antecedent is true are ones in which Frank and Paul had met Sue at the airport. But such worlds are irrelevant to evaluating the truth of (19) in the envisaged context. By placing focal stress on 'Paul' in uttering (19), John forces the selection of a similarity relation that is sensitive to the contrast class.[52]

---

[51] The connection between focus and scalar implicatures is well documented; see Rooth (1996: 274).

[52] Of course, this point holds for indicative conditionals as well. Suppose we don't know whether Frank or Paul picked up Sue at the airport, but we do know that if Frank was present, Sue would decline to go to any party. Someone then utters 'If *Paul* met Sue at the airport, she is at the party now'.

On one view of focus, focusing a constituent gives rise to a certain implicature or presupposition. If this view is correct, then this implicature or presupposition can affect the intuitive content of a subjunctive conditional. But this is not a strong pragmatic effect. Recall that on the conception of semantics we have adopted, speaker intentions, including those involved in implicatures, can affect semantic content, but only by affecting the choice of referential content in a context of some element in a sentence. In the case of focus and subjunctive conditionals, the way in which the implicature affects the semantic content of subjunctive conditionals fits this model.

We assume that the similarity relation relevant for the semantic content of subjunctive conditionals is traceable to the syntax of the conditional construction, perhaps to the words 'if' or 'then' themselves. So, the implicature that emerges by focusing a constituent affects the referential content of the element in the syntax of subjunctive conditionals that has, as its referential content relative to a context, a similarity relation. This is a weak pragmatic effect of context on what is communicated, rather than a strong pragmatic effect. Hence, even on the view that focus gives rise to an implicature, the fact that focus affects the intuitive content of subjunctive conditionals ends up as merely a weak pragmatic effect.

These facts are directly relevant to the facts cited by Levinson:

(20a) Eating *some* of the cake is better than eating all of it.
(20b) Having a cookie *or* ice cream is better than having a cookie and ice cream.

Focusing 'some' in (20a) gives rise to the presupposition or implicature that the sentence-frame 'eating x of the cake' is false of the other member of the scale associated with 'some', namely the determiner meaning of 'all'. This presupposition or implicature does affect the truth-conditions of (20a). But the way it affects the truth-conditions of (20a) is not by "enriching" the semantic content. One dimension of contextual sensitivity of 'better than' constructions, according to this semantics, is the relation of similarity between worlds. By focusing 'some' in (20a), one invokes a similarity relation according to which the most similar worlds in which some of the cake is eaten are not ones in which all of the cake is eaten. Similarly, by focusing 'or' in (20b), one forces a similarity relation in which the closest worlds in which a cookie or ice cream is had are ones in which it is not the case that a cookie and ice cream are had.

In other words, just as with subjunctive conditionals, by focusing the relevant words, one affects the choice of the similarity relation between worlds that is relevant for the truth-conditions of the 'better than' construction in that context. So, the truth-conditions of these constructions are affected by scalar facts, but independently of processes such as explicature or implicature "intrusion". Nor does the scalar information "enrich" the semantic content. Rather, the truth-conditions of 'better than' sentences are sensitive to the choice of a similarity relation between worlds, and focus affects the choice of the relation.

To show that the effect here is a weak pragmatic effect, we would have to demonstrate that the similarity relation is the value of some element in the syntax of comparative construction. We have not here provided an explicit syntax for comparatives, and so we cannot justify in detail the thesis that selection of a comparative relation is merely a weak pragmatic effect of context. However, we assume that it is likely that in the final implementation of the semantics in (12), one would trace the introduction of the similarity relation to some element in the expression 'better than'. If so, then it is possible to account for all of these alleged examples of pragmatic intrusion without accepting its existence. On the account we have given, one can easily explain the data within the semantics. For, assuming that the similarity relation is the value of some element in the comparative, the account just sketched exploits only weak pragmatic effects in deriving the relevant readings. This is an effect of context on semantic content, given the conception of semantics that we adopted in the first section.

The semantics given in (12) is no doubt oversimplified. And, as mentioned, we have not produced an analysis of the syntax of these constructions to justify our claim that the similarity relation is the value of some element in the syntactic structure of these constructions. Our point has merely been to show that it is not difficult to describe an account of the phenomena discussed by Carston and Levinson that does not invoke pragmatic intrusion, and indeed only makes appeal to weak pragmatic effects.[53]

Levinson's next set of examples involves indicative conditionals (see Carston 1988, sect. 7). Here are some of his examples:

(21a) If you ate *some* of the cookies and no one else ate any, then there must still be some left.

(21b) If the chair *sometimes* comes to department meetings that is not enough; he should always come.

---

[53] Levinson (2000: 201) also gives examples of what he claims are cases in which manner implicatures affect the intuitive content of sentences containing 'better than'. However, we find these examples straightforwardly unconvincing, and so do not discuss them here.

Levinson's point is that the intuitive content of (21a) is (22a), and the intuitive content of (21b) is (22b):

> (22a) If you ate some but not all of the cookies and no one else ate any, then there must still be some left.
>
> (22b) If the chair sometimes but not always comes to department meetings that is not enough; he should always come.

But if the intuitive content of the sentences in (21) is as given in (22), then it would seem that the implicatures of the antecedents affect the intuitive content of the sentences in (21).

However, Levinson is wrong to claim that these readings of the sentences in (21) are due to pragmatic intrusion. Rather, the readings in (22) of the sentences in (21) are genuinely semantic, due again to the focal stress placed on the words 'some' and 'sometimes'; Levinson's pervasive use of italics throughout his examples itself strongly suggests that this is how Levinson means them to be read (see again Levinson 2000: 400 n. 26). Without placing stress on 'some' in (21a), it is not naturally read as having the reading (22a). But this suggests that the relevant readings of the examples in (21) comes from the interaction between the semantics for focus and the semantics of the indicative conditional, rather than the purported phenomenon of pragmatic intrusion.

We assume a simple semantics for conditionals, where both indicative and subjunctive conditionals receive the same analysis in terms of possible worlds, the difference between them being due to the similarity relation relevant for their truth-conditions.[54] As Robert Stalnaker has argued, indicative conditionals normally exploit a similarity relation that counts only those non-actual worlds compatible with the mutually accepted background assumptions as similar worlds for purposes of semantic evaluation. In contrast, subjunctive conditionals involve a similarity relation that reaches outside the worlds compatible with the mutually accepted background assumptions. An indicative conditional is true if and only if the consequent is true in every one of the most relevantly similar worlds in which the antecedent is true. With Stalnaker, we assume that the actual world is always the most similar world, so that non-actual worlds are only relevant for the semantic evaluation of an indicative conditional when the antecedent is false (Stalnaker 1999c: 69). Finally, we again assume the syntax (and its semantics)

---

[54] Thanks to Brian Weatherson for discussion of the following treatment of conditionals.

of the conditional triggers a search for the contextually relevant similarity relation.[55]

Placing the above rough remarks about focus together with this straight-forward analysis of the indicative conditional, we may analyze Carston and Levinson's examples as follows. The focal stress on 'sometimes' and 'some' gives rise to a presupposition or implicature. For example, in (21a) the speaker intends to give rise to the presupposition or the implicature that not all of the cookies have been eaten by the hearer; this corresponds to the scalar implicature of 'some'. Similarly, in (21b) the speaker intends to give rise to the presupposition or the implicature that the chair does not always come to department meetings. So doing affects the choice of the contextually salient similarity relation for the sentences in (21). For example, in (21a), by focusing 'some', the speaker forces a similarity relation in which all the most similar (non-actual) worlds are ones in which the speaker did not eat all the cookies. This account directly yields the prediction that the conditionals in (21), with 'some' and 'sometimes' focused, have the truth-conditions given by the sentences in (22).

Let us go through this reasoning in detail with one example. Consider again:

(21a) If you ate *some* of the cookies and no one else ate any, then there must still be some left.

By focusing 'some', the speaker forces the selection of a similarity relation for the evaluation of (21a) according to which the most similar (non-actual) worlds are ones in which 'you ate x of the cookies' is false of the member of the scale associated with 'some', which is the determiner meaning of 'all'.[56] In other words, by focusing 'some', the speaker selects a similarity relation in which the most similar worlds do not include any worlds in which the addressee ate all the cookies. So, in the most similar worlds in the context set, it is not the case that the hearer ate all of the cookies. Applying the simple semantics for the indicative conditional to (21a) with this similarity relation, one then considers all of the most similar worlds in which the hearer ate some of the cookies and no one else ate any. Since all of these worlds are

---

[55] One difference between this treatment of indicative conditionals and Stalnaker's treatment is that we do not adopt Stalnaker's selection function, which singles out a unique closest world for the semantic evaluation of a conditional even when the antecedent is false. Fans of conditional excluded middle may retain Stalnaker's assumption if they like.

[56] Henceforth, we shall suppress "non-actual".

already worlds in which the hearer did not eat all of the cookies, the consequent is true in all such worlds.

It therefore falls out from an independently motivated account of focus, and an independently motivated account of indicative conditionals, that the sentences in (21) have the same truth-conditional effect as the sentences in (22). This effect is achieved without any appeal to pragmatic intrusion.[57] Of course, as with the discussion of 'better than', definitively establishing our case that these examples involve only weak pragmatic effects would require demonstrating conclusively that the similarity relation for indicative and subjunctive conditionals is the value of some element in their syntax (e.g. called upon by the lexical meaning of 'if'). We believe this to be plausible, but do not claim to have made the case for it here.

In the preceding discussion we have emphasized the role of *focus* in the evaluation of conditionals. In particular, we have shown that the "alternative set" for a focused element in a conditional may affect the semantic evaluation of that conditional, by affecting the choice of the similarity relation for that conditional. We take this to be an instance of the more general fact that the similarity relation for a conditional is affected by the assumptions made by conversational participants. As we discuss below, there are examples similar to the ones discussed by Carston and Levinson, in which no element is focused. Nevertheless, the same kind of response is available for such examples. For the general point is the familiar one that the similarity relation for indicative and subjunctive conditionals is determined as a function in part of the psychological states of the participants in conversational contexts. If there is an element in the syntax that is assigned a similarity relation, relative to a context, such examples are simply more evidence of weak pragmatic effects.

Levinson gives several other alleged examples of kinds of pragmatic intrusion in conditionals. The first kind of example is as in:

(23) If you have a baby and get married, then the baby is strictly speaking illegitimate. (Levinson 2000: 206 (25a))

Here Levinson again relies upon the thesis that the semantic content of a conjunctive sentence is not sensitive to temporal information. Given this

---

[57] If the effect of focus is to give rise to a presupposition, the account of the data in (21) is even smoother. For in this case, the focus-induced presuppositions will by definition be part of the context set for evaluation of the indicative conditional, and no appeal to a focus-induced shift of a similarity relation is needed.

assumption, the semantic content of the conjunct does not entail that the birth precedes the marriage. Then, the information that the first conjunct temporally precedes the second will have to be an implicature, one that furthermore enriches the semantic content of the conditional. However, we have already seen above that the assumption behind this argument, that the semantic content of a conjunctive sentence is not sensitive to temporal information, is incorrect. So these examples of Levinson (2000 (25a−d)) bear no additional comment.[58]

The rest of Levinson's examples also rely on controversial assumptions about what is and is not part of semantic content proper. For example, consider Levinson's example (26a) (2000: 206):

> (24) If Bill and Penny drive to Chicago, they can discuss sociolinguistics in the car for hours.

The antecedent of this conditional may have the intuitive content that Bill and Penny drive to Chicago together. Levinson assumes that the information that Bill and Penny are driving together to Chicago is not part of the semantic content, but rather is what he calls a 'together' implicature. However, most semanticists working on collective and distributive readings of verbs would certainly not treat this as a pragmatic implicature but rather as part of semantic content. For example, the semantic content of the antecedent of (24), on some theories, would be taken to be a proposition concerning a driving event with a plural agent.[59]

A further class of examples, again made salient by Robyn Carston (1988), involve causal relations. Consider:

> (25) Mr Jones has been insulted and he's going to resign. (Carston 1998)

This sentence is naturally understood as communicating that there is a causal connection between the fact that Jones was insulted and his resignation.

---

[58] Another group of Levinson's examples (2000: 207 (26c) and (26c′)) rely on the thesis that the semantic content of possessive constructions, such as 'Bill's book is good', is not sensitive to the contextually salient possession relation. This claim is not supported by the sort of detailed discussion of the syntax and semantics of possessive constructions that would be required to support it, and so is not worthy of lengthy consideration.

[59] An anonymous referee for this chapter commented that if the collective–distributive distinction is due to a genuine ambiguity that affects semantic interpretation, as we suggest here, this would have the false consequence that any utterance of the sentence 'If Bill and Penny drive to Chicago, Bill will get there first (as his car is the fastest)' would be semantically anomalous. But this objection is confused. If there is a genuine ambiguity between collective and distributive readings, then an utterance of the envisaged sentence would not be semantically anomalous, since the person who utters the sentence would intend the distributive reading of the antecedent of the conditional (according to which there are driving events with different agents).

However, it would not to be in the spirit of Grice's "modified Occam's Razor" to postulate a distinctive causal sense of 'and'.[60] After all, consider:

(26) John took out his key and opened the door.

A sentence such as (26) is naturally understood as communicating that John's door-opening was a result of the fact that John took out his key. If one postulated a distinctive sense of 'and' to account for the apparent causal reading of (25), one may have to postulate another distinctive sense of 'and' to account for the apparent resultative reading of (26). Such sense-multiplication is to be avoided if possible.

However, one can account for Carston's data without postulating distinctive causal or resultative senses of 'and'. As Jennifer Saul (2002) has suggested, there are general (and we think defeasible) pragmatic rules governing the order of listing of reported events (rules that can, as we have seen, affect the semantic evaluation of the temporal element associated with verbs). In particular, the maxim of manner requires speakers to "list events in the order in which they occurred, and to cite causes before effects" (Saul 2002: 362). As a result, unless they believe that the maxim of manner is being flouted, interpreters generally conclude from utterances of (25) that the first event causes the second, and in the case of (26), that the second is a result of the first.[61]

However, there is a more complex group of sentences, concerning which, contra Saul, no such account is plausible.[62] These cases involve conjunctions embedded inside conditionals, such as:

(27) If Hannah insulted Joe and Joe resigned, then Hannah is in trouble.

(27) seems to express the proposition that if Hannah insulted Joe and Joe resigned as a result of Hannah's insult, then Hannah is in trouble. Saul (2002: 363) claims that there is a "perfectly reasonable [Gricean] explanation" of these facts as well, one that "will precisely parallel" the explanation of

---

[60] This principle reads "Senses [of words] are not to be multiplied beyond necessity". For Grice's discussion of it, see Grice (1989b: 47 ff).

[61] Saul herself assimilates this phenomenon to *implicature*, stating that the speaker implicates that the second event is a cause or result of the first. We ourselves are agnostic as to whether this is best described as an implicature.

[62] We are particularly grateful to Robyn Carston for forcing us to treat this style of example in detail.

utterances of sentences such as (25) and (26). However, Saul overstates matters when she suggests that an explanation in terms of the maxim of manner of the intuitive truth-condition for utterances of (27) is "precisely parallel" to the explanation of utterances of sentences such as (25). There are significant differences between the two explanations, which make an explanation in terms of manner in the case of utterances of sentences such as (27) considerably less plausible.[63]

In the case of Saul's explanation of utterances of (25) and (26), the speaker expresses a true proposition, and, by saliently adhering to the maxim of manner, communicates a proposition that is informationally richer. It is perfectly plausible, in this case, to take the speaker as intending to express the true proposition that does not involve causal information, and thereby communicating an informationally richer proposition that does. However, the purportedly parallel account of utterances of (27) is different. In this case, speakers would typically express a false proposition not involving causal information, and thereby communicate a true proposition that does. Furthermore, in this latter case, it is not particularly plausible to suppose that speakers are aware of the false proposition they express in uttering (27).[64] These are significant differences between the two explanations.

Of course, speakers do sometimes knowingly express false propositions, and thereby communicate true ones. This is what happens, for example, in non-literal speech. But we are not considering cases of non-literal speech here; someone who assertively utters (27) does not intend to be speaking non-literally. There should be a strong presumption against treating speech that is intended literally (and used correctly) on the model of non-literal speech. In sum, the purported explanation for the intuitions in (27) has significant theoretical costs, ones that the explanation for the intuitions in (25) and (26) do not have. These

---

[63] Saul is aware of these differences (2002: 363). But she disagrees that they impinge on the plausibility of the explanation. It is also worth mentioning that the example Saul herself discusses is a case of apparently temporal 'and' embedded in the antecedent of a conditional. As we have made clear above, such temporal readings are generated *within* the semantics, though of course not by an alleged temporal reading of 'and'. There is no need for a post-semantic explanation of such cases.

[64] It is worth noting that the explanation here is even more extreme than pragmatic accounts of quantifier domain restriction. Defenders of such accounts can argue that the false proposition they claim to be expressed by someone who utters a sentence like 'Everyone is at the party' is easily accessible ('Do you really mean *everyone*?'). However, the false proposition supposedly expressed by (27), on this pragmatic account, is not so easily accessible. It is therefore harder to see how the speaker could intend to say it, or intend to make as if to say it.

costs should be unattractive whatever one's theoretical commitments. However, for those who reject semantic skepticism and semantic modesty, they are simply untenable.

Fortunately, however, there is no reason to give a non-semantic account of the intuitive readings of (27). The relevant reading of (27) is simply predicted by the semantics for indicative conditionals that we have endorsed. In a context in which the speaker has in mind a causal relationship between Hannah's insulting of Joe and Joe's resignation, all relevantly similar worlds in the speaker's context set in which Hannah insulted Joe and Joe resigned will *ipso facto* be ones in which Joe's resignation is due to Hannah's insult. The speaker's context set is what is epistemically open to her. This may include worlds in which the conjunction holds, and there is no causal relationship between the conjuncts. But given that it is salient that she has a causal relationship in mind, such worlds will not be the most relevantly similar worlds in the context set. So, if she has a causal relation in mind between the two events, that is just to say that the similarity relation for indicative conditionals will select those worlds in which there is a causal relationship between the conjuncts of the antecedent as the most similar worlds to the world of utterance in which the antecedent is true. So, the causal reading of (27) is predicted by the simple semantics for the indicative conditional that we have adopted above.

We have argued in this section that the examples of pragmatic intrusion given by Carston and Levinson are not convincing. The intuitions behind these examples can be accommodated within semantic interpretation, without requiring strong pragmatic effects to explain them. We think a general moral follows from this investigation. Before claiming that a set of intuitions cannot be due to semantic interpretation, theorists need to have investigated all of the semantic options. For, as Levinson admirably acknowledges, claims about what can only be derived pragmatically may very well be vitiated by subsequent syntactic and semantic investigation.

6. Conclusion

An important obligation of the philosophy of language is to provide a clear distinction between semantics and pragmatics. However, at the center of the philosophy of language and cognitive science there has been a sustained debate about the scope and interest of semantic content, with many theorists arguing that semantic content plays a marginal role in an explanation of linguistic behavior. These debates have been clouded by disagreement over the proper definitions of "semantic" and "pragmatic". Our intention in this chapter has been to provide a clear characterization of semantic content, and then use it to evaluate the debate about the scope and interest of semantic content.

As we have emphasized, these different positions on the scope of semantic content are, at this stage of research, merely educated guesses. Many philosophers and cognitive scientists maintain that, once syntactic and semantic inquiry are finished, it will turn out that the semantic content of a sentence relative to a context is not a good guide to what speakers typically use that sentence to communicate. This position has radical consequences for standard methodology in philosophy. If it is true, it is unclear, for example, whether any of the strategies canvassed at the beginning of this chapter are legitimate. In the final section we have addressed one of the strongest arguments in favor of skepticism about the scope of semantic content, and shown it to be unpersuasive. Our view is that, as yet, such skepticism remains unwarranted.

REFERENCES

Bach, Kent (1994), 'Conversational Impliciture', *Mind and Language*, 9: 124–62.

—— (2002*a*), 'Semantic, Pragmatic', in J. Campbell, M. O'Rourke, and D. Shier (eds.), *Meaning and Truth: Investigations in Philosophical Semantics* (New York: Seven Bridges Press), 284–92.

—— (2002*b*), 'Seemingly Semantic Intuitions', in J. Campbell, M. O'Rourke, and D. Shier (eds.), *Meaning and Truth: Investigations in Philosophical Semantics* (New York: Seven Bridges Press), 21–33.

Braun, David (1993), 'Empty Names', *Noûs*, 27 4: 449–69.

—— (1994), 'Structured Characters and Complex Demonstratives', *Philosophical Studies*: 74: 193–21.

—— (1996), 'Demonstratives and their Linguistic Meanings', *Noûs*, 30 2: 145–73.

Cappelen, Herman, and Ernie Lepore (1997), 'On an Alleged Connection between Indirect Speech and the Theory of Meaning', *Mind and Language*, 12 3 and 4: 278–96.

—— (2002), 'Insensitive Quantifiers', in J. Campbell, M. O'Rourke, and D. Shier (eds.), *Meaning and Truth: Investigations in Philosophical Semantics* (New York: Seven Bridges Press), 197–213.

Carston, Robyn (1988), 'Implicature, Explicature, and Truth-Theoretic Semantics', in R. Kempson (ed.), *Mental Representations: The Interface between Language and Reality* (Cambridge: Cambridge University Press), 155–81.

—— (MS), 'Linguistic Underdeterminacy and Pragmatic Enrichment'.

Cohen, L. J. (1971), 'Some Remarks on Grice's Views about the Logical Particles of Natural Language' in Y. Bar-Hillel (ed.), *Pragmatics of Natural Language* (Dordrecht: Reidel), 50–68.

Crimmins, Mark (1992), *Talk about Beliefs* (Cambridge, Mass.: MIT Press).

—— and John Perry (1989), 'The Prince and the Phonebook: Reporting Puzzling Beliefs' *Journal of Philosophy*, 86/12: 685–711.

DeRose, Keith (1995), 'Solving the Skeptical Problem', *Philosophical Review*, 104: 1–52.

—— (1999), 'Contextualism: An Explanation and Defense', in John Greco and Ernie Sosa (eds.), *The Blackwell Guide to Epistemology* (Oxford: Basil Blackwell), 187–205.

Dever, Joshua (2001), 'Complex Demonstratives', *Linguistics and Philosophy*, 24 3: 271–330.

Enc, Murvet (1987), 'Anchoring Conditions for Tense', *Linguistic Inquiry*, 18: 633–57.

Gauker, Christopher (1997), 'Domain of Discourse', *Mind*, 106: 1–32.

Grice, Paul (1989a), 'Logic and Conversation', in Grice, *Studies in the Way of Words* (Cambridge, Mass.: Harvard University Press), 22–40.

—— (1989b), 'Further Notes on Logic and Conversation', in Grice, *Studies in the Way of Words* (Cambridge, Mass.: Harvard University Press), 41–57.

Heal, Jane (1997), 'Indexical Predicates and their Uses', *Mind*, 106: 619–40.

Heck, Richard (2001), 'Do Demonstratives have Senses?', *Philosophers' Imprint*, 2 2: 1–33.

Heim, Irene (1982), The Semantics of Definite and Indefinite Noun Phrases, Ph.D. diss. (University of Massachusetts).

Higginbotham, James (2002), 'Why is Sequence of Tense Obligatory?', in G. Preyer and G. Peter (eds.), *Logical Form and Language* (Oxford: Oxford University Press), 207–27.

Kaplan, David (1989), 'Demonstratives', in Perry Almog and H. Wettstein (eds.), *Themes from Kaplan* (Oxford: Oxford University Press), 481–564.

King, Jeffrey (1995), 'Structured Propositions and Complex Predicates', *Noûs*, 29 4: 516–35.

—— (2001), *Complex Demonstratives: A Quantificational Account* (Cambridge, Mass.: MIT Press).

—— (forthcoming), 'Tense, Modality, and Semantic Value', *Philosophical Perspectives*.

Lepore, Ernie, and Kirk Ludwig (2000), 'The Semantics and Pragmatics of Complex Demonstratives', *Mind*, 109: 199–240.

Levinson, Stephen (2000), *Presumptive Meanings: The Theory of Generalized Conversational Implicatures*, (Cambridge, Mass.: MIT Press).

Lewis, David (1998), 'Adverbs of Quantification', in Lewis, *Papers in Philosophical Logic* (Cambridge: Cambridge University Press), 5–20.

Ludlow, Peter (1995), 'Logical Form and the Hidden Indexical Theory: A Reply to Schiffer', *Journal of Philosophy*, 92: 102–7.

Montague, Richard (1974), 'Pragmatics', in R. Thomason (ed.), *Formal Philosophy* (New Haven: Yale University Press), 95–118.

Ogihara, Toshiyuki (1996), *Tense, Attitudes, and Scope* (Dordrecht: Kluwer).

Parsons, Terence (1990), *Events in the Semantics of English: A Study in Sub-atomic Semantics* (Cambridge, Mass.: MIT Press).

Partee, Barbara (1984), 'Nominal and Temporal Anaphora', *Linguistics and Philosophy*, 7: 243–86.

Perry, John (1997), 'Indexicals and Demonstratives', in Robert Hale and Crispin Wright (eds.), in *A Companion to the Philosophy of Language* (Oxford: Basil Blackwell), 586–612.

—— (2001), *Reference and Reflexivity* (Stanford: CSLI).

Recanati, F. (1993), *Direct Reference* (Oxford: Basil Blackwell).

Richard, Mark (1983), 'Direct Reference and Ascriptions of Belief', *Journal of Philosophical Logic*, 12: 425–52.

—— (1990), *Propositional Attitudes: An Essay on Thoughts and How We Ascribe Them* (Cambridge: Cambridge University Press).

Rooth, Mats (1994), 'Focus', in Shalom Lappin (ed.), *The Handbook of Contemporary Semantics* (Oxford: Basil Blackwell), 271–97.

Salmon, Nathan (1986), *Frege's Puzzle* (Cambridge, Mass.: MIT Press).

Saul, Jennifer (1997), 'Substitution and Simple Sentences', *Analysis*, 57 2: 102–8.

—— (2002), 'What Is Said and Psychological Reality: Grice's Project and Relevance Theorists' Criticisms', *Linguistics and Philosophy*, 25: 347–72.

Siegel, Susanna (2002), 'Perception and Linguistic Demonstration', *Philosophers' Imprint*, 2 1: 1–21.

Soames, Scott (1987), 'Direct Reference, Propositional Attitudes and Semantic Content', *Philosophical Topics*. 15: 47–87.

Sperber, D., and D. Wilson (1986), *Relevance* (Cambridge, Mass.: Harvard University Press).

Stalnaker, Robert (1999a), *Context and Content* (Oxford: Oxford University Press).

—— (1999b), 'Pragmatics', in Stalnaker (1999a: 31–46).

—— (1999c), 'Indicative Conditionals', in Stalnaker (1999a: 63–77).

Stanley, Jason (2000), 'Context and Logical Form', *Linguistics and Philosophy*, 23 4: 391–434.

—— (2002a), 'Nominal Restriction', in G. Preyer and G. Peter (eds.), *Logical Form and Language* (Oxford: Oxford University Press), 365–88.

—— (2002b), 'Making it Articulated', *Mind and Language*, 17 1 and 2: 149–68.

—— (2003), 'Context, Interest-Relativity, and the Sorites', *Analysis* 63 4: 269–80.

—— and Zoltán Gendler Szabó (2000), 'On Quantifier Domain Restriction', *Mind and Language*, 15 2 and 3: 219–61.

Stowell, Tim (1982), 'The Tense of Infinitives', *Linguistic Inquiry*, 13: 561–70.

Szabó, Zoltán Gendler (2001), 'Adjectives in Context', in I. Kenesei and R. M. Harnish (eds.), *Perspectives on Semantics, Pragmatics and Discourse* (Amsterdam: John Benjamins), 119–46.

Wettstein, Howard (1984), 'How to Bridge the Gap between Meaning and Reference', *Synthese*, 58: 63–84.

Wilson, Deirdre (1975), *Presuppositions and Non-Truth-Conditional Semantics* (London: Academic Press).

5

Pragmatism and Binding

Stephen Neale

1. Introduction

Names, descriptions, and demonstratives raise well-known logical, ontological, and epistemological problems. Perhaps less well known, among philosophers at least, are the ways in which some of these problems not only recur with pronouns but also cross-cut further problems exposed by the study in generative linguistics of morpho-syntactic constraints on interpretation. These problems will be my primary concern here, but I want to address them within a general picture of interpretation that is required if wires are not to be crossed. That picture will be sketched in Sections 3 and 4; subsequent sections will focus on pronouns and binding, drawing heavily on what has preceded.

It will be obvious to linguists that this chapter is written by a philosopher, albeit one very sympathetic to the generative enterprise as articulated over the years by Noam Chomsky. Chomsky's ideas permeate both the syntactic and philosophical theses pushed here. As I was completing the chapter I was introduced to several works in linguistics I wish I had seen earlier, in particular Bresnan (2001), Elbourne (2001, 2002), Jacobson (1999), Kayne (2002), Keenan (2002), Reuland (2001a,b), Reuland and Sigurjónsdóttir (1997), Safir (forthcoming), and Szabolcsi (2003). I gesture towards some of these in various footnotes. (Very likely I would have gone about certain matters a little differently if I had come across these works earlier; and I am not convinced some of the discussion could not be more usefully formulated within variable-free systems). I thank the members of the New York University Linguistics Department for inviting me to present this work at their colloquium series—discussion (then and subsequently) with Mark Baltin, Paul Elbourne, Richard Kayne, Paul Postal, Michal Starke, and Anna Szabolcsi was most helpful. I also thank José Luis Bermúdez, Robert Fiengo, James Higginbotham, Paul Horwich, Mikael Karlsson, Richard Larson, Colin McGinn, Eric Reuland, Ken Safir, Stephen Schiffer, Barry Smith, Matthew Whelpton, Deirdre Wilson, and Höskuldur Þráinsson for their advice and suggestions, and Erlendur Jónsson, Hörður

Interpreting an utterance or inscription involves substantially more than identifying and interpreting the individual words uttered and grasping their syntactic arrangement. Probably there isn't much it *doesn't* involve, and it is hardly surprising that we have not yet succeeded in producing a theory of interpretation with much empirical clout. There have been successes in some of the *sub*theories—phonology and syntax, for example. But there is widespread suspicion that producing an overarching theory of interpretation will require nothing short of a complete theory of mind.[1] Paul Grice once summed up the situation rather well to me. Compare the following 'maxims':

(1) Put the subject first; put the object after the verb.

(2) Be relevant; be informative.

We appear to have improved upon (1):

$$S \rightarrow NP\ VP$$
$$VP \rightarrow V\ NP.$$

But, said Grice, we haven't got the foggiest how to improve upon (2).

It is not just in the realm of implied meaning (or implicature, to borrow Grice's term of art) that interpretation may seem wide open. Identifying who someone intends by 'John' or 'that man' or 'he', or 'his', for example, is not simply a matter of linguistic decoding; it involves the exercise of seemingly inferential abilities, and to this extent quite general concerns about interpretation impinge upon the identification of what a speaker is *saying* as well as what he is implying.

Where pronouns are concerned, traditional grammars suggest something like the following picture. Demonstrative pronouns ('this', 'that') are used to refer to things that are *salient* (or being made so by their users). Personal pronouns are used to refer to persons: first-person pronouns ('I', 'me', 'my', 'mine', 'myself') are used to refer to oneself; second-person pronouns ('you' etc.) are used to refer to one's audience; and third-person pronouns ('he', 'she', 'it', etc.) are used in place of 'fuller' phrases ('Plato', 'Athens', 'the current budget

Sveinsson, Hrafn Ásgeirsson, Jón Ólafsson, Ólafur Páll Jónsson, Mikael Karlsson, Ósk Sturlusdóttir, Sigrún Svavarsdóttir, Ragga Guðmundsdóttir, and Þórdís Helgasdóttir for help with some of the Icelandic examples. I gratefully acknowledge the generous support of Rutgers University, the University of Iceland, the Georg Brandes School, Institute for Nordic Philology, and the John Simon Guggenheim Foundation.

[1] See e.g. Chomsky (2000), Davidson (1986), and Fodor (1983, 2001). For assessment, see Carston (2002).

deficit') to refer to persons, places, or things speakers could have referred to using those fuller phrases. The personal pronouns also have possessive ('his') and reflexive ('himself') forms; the third-person has an interrogative/relative ('who') form; and some differ in form according as they are subjects ('I', 'he', 'who') or objects ('me', 'him', 'whom'). Possessives indicate possession (construed broadly), reflexives signal anaphoric connections to expressions (of the same number and gender) in the immediate environment, and the interrogative/relative form is used in asking questions ('who owns a donkey?') and in forming relative clauses ('every man who owns a donkey').

While there is much sense in this traditional taxonomy it is at best a first step in coming to terms with matters of interpretation familiar to philosophers and linguists who have wrestled with opacity, deixis, scope, variable-binding, and (my personal *bête noire*) co-reference. Although many philosophers share with linguists the desire to understand how pronouns fit into a general account of the workings of natural language, much of the interest in pronouns in philosophy is driven by the shenanigans these devices get up to in indexical inferences, modal statements, and propositional attitude ascriptions, and in talk of scepticism, self-knowledge, substitutivity, existence and identity, including personal identity—'Hesperus is Phosphorus, but John does not think *it* is', 'I thought your yacht was longer than *it* is'; 'every barber thought *his* reflection was of someone other than *him*'; 'Hob thinks a witch killed Nob's cow, and Bob thinks *she* blighted his mare'; 'if a man is born at the rising of the Dog-Star, *he* shall not die at sea'; 'most men who have only one donkey take good care of *it*'; 'every pilot who shot at *it* hit the MiG that was chasing *him*', '*I* will be buried tomorrow if, and only if, my body is buried tomorrow, yet *I* will be held in great esteem by my colleagues tomorrow even if my body is not.'

Largely under Chomsky's tutelage, the accomplishments of empirical linguistics in the investigation of syntactic constraints on interpretation are impressive—despite many unsolved problems and despite the fact that every proposed theory of practically every phenomenon of significance appears to be frustrated by all sorts of counterexamples. If there is one overarching problem that has plagued the study of pronouns it is this: from the perspectives of syntax and interpretation, all sorts of superficial generalizations and distinctions can be made, but it is unclear which are of theoretical significance and which are mere distractions; and equally it is unclear which of a number of competing unifications and classifications will pay theoretical dividends and which are ultimately dead ends. As a result, all sorts of problematic assumptions and misleading locutions are apt to burrow their way into the work of even the most philosophically attuned linguists, as well as into the work of the most linguistically attuned of those philosophers mad enough to get involved. Probably anyone bothering to read this chapter knows, or has known, a philosophically attuned linguist or a linguistically attuned philosopher. But I fear interaction has not been as good as it should have been, and the fact remains that getting a philosopher to give up a day's sailing on the Hudson to discuss long-distance reflexives in Icelandic, infinitival clauses, subject-orientation, and the Binding Theory is like trying to get a linguist to give up a day's sailing off Cape Cod to discuss privileged access, speaker's intentions, and epistemic asymmetry. And this is a crying shame, because on all of these issues, it seems to me, philosophers and linguists have an awful lot to gain from working together, making some of their work on these topics more accessible to the other party, and critiquing one another's works in helpful ways.[2]

It is in this spirit that the present chapter is written. It's hardly cutting-edge syntax or formal semantics, and it's hardly cutting-edge moral psychology or philosophy of mind. But it is a serious attempt to respond to pressures exerted by all four, rather than cutting-edge talking-down-to-philosophers-and-linguists-at-the-same-time. We are lacking some common solid ground, it seems to me, a place where linguists and philosophers can meet to address issues of mutual concern using words like 'pronoun', 'anaphor', 'binding', 'scope', 'syntactic', 'semantic', 'pragmatic', 'co-referential' 'interpretive', 'ambiguity', 'context', and 'identity' without driving one another to drink. Syntactic and interpretive notions are sometimes conflated in the literature, as are importantly distinct interpretive notions. And spells cast by false or insignificant generalizations only add to our woes. Some effort is required to tease apart things that have been run together and to recombine key elements in ways that make the issues sufficiently transparent and render the central theoretical posits truly explanatory, but I intend the whole of this chapter to be accessible to both linguists and philosophers, so members of one tribe may find themselves cruising through one section while members of the other are busy making extensive notes. This is unavoidable, I think, and I ask for readers' forbearance.

2. Pronouns as Variables

For many years philosophical and logical interest in pronouns centred on distinguishing their use as something akin to the *bound variables* of quantification theory,

---

[2] Matters are complicated by (i) the quite unwarranted hostility of many philosophers to Chomsky's talk of 'knowledge' of language, and (ii) the rightly sceptical position many linguists

their *deictic* (or *demonstrative*) use to refer to salient individuals ('*he* looks happy'), and their use as devices that obviated repetition ('if John does not hurry, he will miss the train').[3] The dictum 'to be is to be the value of a bound variable' probably does not hold as much sway as it did when Quine first pressed it, but the quantifier–variable combination is still part of philosophy's lingua franca. When we introduce variables in introductory logic classes we sometimes get the ball rolling by saying they are the formal counterparts of third-person pronouns. The following semester we teach the philosophy of language, and if third-person pronouns come up in discussions of reference we begin with the statement that they are the natural language counterparts of variables in logic (raising a few eyebrows among those in the back row). The matter of the precise relationship between pronouns and variables is one among many that come up in the study of *anaphora* (from the Greek, 'carry back'), construed as the study of *interpretive dependencies*, the study of the ways in which the interpretations of occurrences of certain expressions, particularly third-person pronouns, are tied to the interpretations of occurrences of other expressions. For several reasons, the relationship is nowhere near as straightforward as many philosophers supposed initially.

(i) Unlike variables in logic, natural language pronouns are typically marked for such things as *gender*, *number*, and *case*: 'she' is nominative, feminine, and singular; 'them' is accusative and plural. And it is a matter of some debate whether such features impinge upon the truth or falsity of what people say when they utter sentences containing them. Some pronouns are also singled out as *reflexive*, and it is a matter of debate whether occurrences of 'he', 'him', 'his', and 'himself' impinge upon truth conditions in the same way.

(ii) Unlike variables in logic, natural language pronouns appear to bifurcate in respect of *locality* conditions on binding.[4] For example, 'him' *cannot* function as a variable bound by 'every man' in (1), whereas the so-called reflexive 'himself' *must* so function in (2):

(1) every man loves him
(2) every man loves himself.

That is, (1) *cannot*, but (2) *must*, be understood as expressing what (2′) expresses:[5]

(2′) [*every x: man x*] *x loves x.*

take towards some philosophers' talk of 'reference' which appears to have dragged in its wake an unwarranted scepticism about the notion of *speaker's* reference.

³ Quine (1960); Geach (1962).   ⁴ Chomsky (1981, 1986, 1995).

⁵ Throughout, the formalism of a system of restricted quantification RQ will be assumed in illuminating the 'logical forms' of sentences. Assuming a Tarskian account of quantification, the

This interpretive contrast appears to involve *locality*: the non-reflexive 'him' is *too close* (in some sense to be elucidated) to 'every man' in (1), but not in (3), for example:

(3) every man loves the woman who married him.

And the reflexive 'himself' is *too far* from 'every man' in (4):

(4) every man loves the woman who married himself.

So, where (3) *can* be used to express what (4') expresses, (4) *cannot*:

(4') [*every x: man x*] x *loves the woman who married* x.[6]

Since there is no condition on variables in first-order logic corresponding to this locality difference, its existence in natural language is something that needs to be described exactly and explained. For it *appears* that natural language is making things more complicated than it might.

(iii) Wherever we find a pronoun bound by a quantifier, we can replace the quantifier by a name (or some other singular term). For example, we get the following quantified-singular pair:

(5) every man loves himself
(5') John loves himself.

The naive answer to the question of how the pronoun functions in the singular case (5') is that it is co-referential with 'John', that it is a special type of referring expression whose reference is determined by some other expression. On such an account, pronouns may function in a way that variables in logic do not. If we are wedded to a choice between treating the pronoun in (5') as a variable or treating it as a constant, it would seem we will have to go with the latter. And

---

relevant axiom may take the form of (i):

(i) [*every* $x_k:\phi(x_k)$]$\psi(x_k)$ is true of a sequence *s* (of objects) iff $\psi(x_k)$ is true of every sequence that $\phi(x_k)$ is true of differing from *s* at most in the *k*-th position.

[6] If definite descriptions are quantifier expressions, we can get a little closer to the logical form of (4) with something like (i) (reflecting Geach's 1972 *Latin prose theory* of relative clauses):

(i) [*every x: man x*] [*the y: woman y* • *y married x*] x *loves y*.

If, as Quine (1960) and Evans (1977) suggest, relative pronouns are devices of abstraction, we get still closer with something like (ii), where *who z* functions as an abstraction operator (see n. 9):

(ii) [*every x: man x*] [*the y: woman y* • *y*(*who z: z married x*)] x *loves y*.

For immediate purposes, such a level of detail is not necessary.

this might lead to the idea that 'himself' is a device for avoiding repetition, that an underlying form 'John loves John' surfaces as (5′) in ordinary English.[7]

But are we not missing something on such an analysis? Surely our capacity to understand sentences like (5′) is connected in some important way to our capacity to understand sentences like (5).[8] Indeed, there is a strong intuition that 'himself' functions *identically* in (5) and (5′), that a single closed predicate 'loves himself'—$\lambda x(x \, loves \, x)$—occurs in both sentences and functions identically, that (5) and (5′) are both used to make claims involving the following condition:[9]

(5″) $x \, loves \, x$.

(5) is used to say that this condition is true of every man, and (5′) is used to say that it is true of John. Isn't it this that explains the validity and immediacy of the following inference?

(6) every man loves himself; John is a man; so John loves himself.

So if 'himself' is really functioning as a bound variable in the quantified case (5)—no other theory seems to be lurking in the wings—shouldn't we at least countenance the idea that it also functions in this way, rather than as a device of co-reference, in the singular case (5′)? And if that is right, in order to preserve as much strict compositionality as possible, shouldn't we see all predicates as ultimately devices of abstraction, 'snores' expressing $\lambda x(x \, snores)$, 'loves' expressing $\lambda y(\lambda x(x \, loves \, y))$, and so on? We cannot be sure there is not a genuine *ambiguity* between a bound variable reading of 'himself' and a co-referential reading, one that is truth-conditionally inert in (5′) but not in more interesting examples such as those involving verbs of propositional attitude. But we have to start somewhere, let us assume until further notice that we have only one anaphoric reading of (5′) to deal with: 'himself' is bound by 'John' in (5′) in whatever way it is bound by 'every man' in (5), details to be provided.[10]

[7] In the context of generative grammar, Langacker (1966), Lees and Klima (1963), Postal (1966), and Ross (1967).   [8] Evans (1980); Higginbotham (1980, 1983a).

[9] Geach (1962, 1972); Heim (1982/1988); Heim and Kratzer (1998); Kamp (1981/1984); Partee (1975); Reinhart (1983); Salmon (1986, 1992); Soames (1990, 1994); Wiggins (1976). λ is the *lambda* (or *abstraction*) operator. On the usage adopted here, λx (x snores) and $\lambda x(x \, loves \, x)$ are one-place predicates. Thus *John* ($\lambda x(x \, loves \, x)$) is a sentence.

[10] I say I am going to start here, but I am also going to *finish* more or less here. The combined force of points made by Castañeda (1966, 1967, 1968), Geach (1962), Heim and Kratzer (1998), Partee (1975), Reinhart and Reuland (1993), Reuland (2001a, b), Salmon (1986, 1992), and Soames (1990, 1994) seems to me to undermine beyond the point of possible repair any unitary de jure co-reference account of anaphora such as the one offered by Evans (1977, 1980), and any 'pragmatic' account of the phenomena, such as those proposed by Lasnik (1976) and K. Bach (1987, 1994). Some of these points will emerge as we proceed.

(iv) It is evident that variable-binding cannot supply everything we need. Take (7) and (7′):

(7) every man loves his wife
(7′) John loves his wife

On one use of 'his' it is a device of anaphora, bound by 'every man' in (7), and by 'John' in (7′), the respective sentences used to make claims involving the following condition:

(7″) x loves x's wife.[11]

(7) is used to say the condition is true of every man, and (7′) to say it is true of John, the common predication being $\lambda x(x$ loves x's wife). In line with what was said about reflexives, let us call this the *bound* use of 'his'.

On a second use of 'his', it is *free*: it is used to make independent, indexical reference to some particular male. Suppose we have been talking about Paul, who is known to be married to a woman who is utterly captivating. We might use 'his' in (7) and (7′) to refer to Paul, to make claims involving not condition (7″) but condition (7‴):

(7‴) x loves Paul's wife.

If we insist on stating everything in terms of variables, then we can say that on this use of 'his' it functions as a *free* variable, an expression to which some specific value must be assigned for interpretation to take place.

A question now arises concerning the precise relationship between these two uses of 'his'. One might rest content with an ambiguity story and cite in its defence the fact that translating (7) and (7′) into some languages requires making a choice between two quite distinct pronouns depending upon whether the bound or indexical reading of the English 'his' is intended.[12] Alternatively, one might eschew the aforementioned ambiguity theory and seek some form of *unification*, taking the

---

[11] Again, I suppress some logical structure. If possessives like 'his wife', 'John's wife', and 'that man's wife' are definite descriptions, the condition given in (7″) might be specified more fully using (i):

(i) [the y: y wife x] x loves y.

I will offer something more appealing later.

[12] In Icelandic, for example, a possessive pronoun agreeing in gender (feminine) and case (accusative) with the noun for 'wife' is used for the bound reading:

(i) [sérhver maður]/[Jón elskar konuna sína
[every man]/John loves wife-DEF POSS-FEM-ACC
[every man]/John loves his (bound) wife.

model of bound and free occurrences of variables at face value: a variable must be assigned a value somehow, and this means assigning it a single value directly or allowing its value to vary systematically with the value of some other expression.

(v) Closely related to the matter of ambiguity is the matter of the interpretation of expressions pared down by rule-governed ellipsis.[13] We need to explain the contrast between (8) and (9), for example:

(8) John loves himself. So does Paul.
(9) John loves his wife. So does Paul.

There is a single reading of (8). But there are two quite distinct readings of (9), one upon which Paul is being said to satisfy (9′), another on which he is being said to satisfy (9″):

(9′) *x loves x's wife*
(9″) *x loves John's wife.*

This might suggest we need to distinguish a reading of (9) upon which 'his' is bound by 'John' and another upon which it is an indexical used to refer to John, the same person 'John' is being used to refer to. This would comport with the idea that the elliptical structure is understood as 'so does Paul love his wife' with 'his' preserving its interpretation either as a variable to be bound by the subject expression or as an indexical used to refer to John. It would also explain why (8) has only one reading: reflexives permit only bound readings.[14]

(The letter ð (*eð*, 'eth') is pronounced like 'th' in English 'the'.) But if the English 'his' is understood as an indexical it must be translated using a simple genitive *hans* here, which occurs in the masculine and enters into no agreement relations whatsoever with *konuna* ('wife'):

(ii) [*sérhver maður*]/*Jón elskar konuna hans*
    [every man]/John loves wife-DEF his-MASC-GEN
    [every man]/John loves his (free) wife.

The question would now arise whether there are languages that distinguish bound and indexical uses of 'he' and 'him', which Icelandic does not. I should stress that matters are more complex in Icelandic than this note might suggest. In order to add a modicum of breadth to the discussion and motivate certain avenues of research, later in the chapter I shall make frequent comparisons between English and Icelandic drawing upon published work by generative linguists (see below for references) and investigations I have undertaken myself over the past few years with the help of various Icelandic philosophers and friends.

[13] Heim and Kratzer (1998); May (2002); Partee (1975); Sag (1976); Williams (1977).

[14] This proposal and the common predication in singular and quantified pairs seems to explain the fact that we understand and immediately see the validity of things like (i):

(i) Every man loves himself. Since John is a man, it follows that John loves himself.

   And since Paul is a man, it follows that he does too.

But might the second reading of (9) not be the product of a *referentially depend-ent* use of 'his'? The idea would be that on this second reading 'his' is not bound by 'John' in the first clause of (9″) but is rather co-referential with 'John' by virtue of being referentially dependent upon it. On such an account, the ellip-ted structure is understood as 'so does Paul love his wife' with 'his' preserving its interpretation as referring to whoever 'John' refers to.

(vi) A pronoun may be used in such a way that it seems to be interpreted neither as a variable bound by some antecedent phrase nor as an indexical.[15] That is, anaphoric dependencies seem to exist that do not involve binding. Consider (10) and (10′):

> (10) Just one man ate haggis. He was ill afterwards.
> (10′) John ate haggis. He was ill afterwards.

Treating 'he' as a variable bound by 'just one man' in (10) yields the wrong result:

> (11) [*just one x: man x*] (*x ate haggis · x was ill afterwards*).

(11) can be true if two men ate haggis but only one of them was ill afterwards, i.e. its truth is consistent with the *falsity* of the first conjunct of (10).[16] Thus (11) appears to capture the meaning not of (10), but of (11′):

> (11′) Just one man ate haggis and was ill afterwards.

So we are still without an account of the pronoun in (10). However, the fact that (10) and the ungainly (10″) below appear to be equivalent suggests there is something to be gained by exploring the view that the pronoun in the former functions as a disguised definite description:[17]

> (10″) Just one man ate haggis. The man who ate haggis was ill afterwards.

But the desire to preserve a uniform treatment of pronouns as variables might suggest exploring a rather different idea: that the occurrence of 'he' in (10) is a variable bound by *something other than* 'just one man', something not revealed until we have an account of the underlying *logical form* of the sentence and a general theory of the *pragmatics of discourse*.[18]

---

[15] Cooper (1979); Evans (1977); Heim (1982/1988); Kamp (1981/1984); Partee (1972).
[16] Evans (1977).
[17] Cooper (1979); Davies (1981); Elbourne (2001, 2002); Evans (1977, 1980); Neale (1990, 1994).
[18] Heim (1982/1988); Kamp (1981/1984).

Now what of the singular case (10′)? If the quantifier 'just one man' cannot bind the pronoun 'he' in (10), there is no good reason to think 'John' can in (10′). We would appear to have three options for dealing with the pronoun in (10′); we could view it (i) as an indexical being used to refer to John, this being licensed in some way by John's salience; (ii) as a pronoun of laziness, interpreted as if it were just another occurrence of 'John'; (iii) as a device of co-reference—the difference between positions (ii) and (iii) would need to be articulated clearly.

The issue raised by the pronoun in (10) recurs with more interesting examples. Consider the so-called 'donkey' sentence (12):

(12) every man who bought just one donkey paid cash for it.

If the quantifier 'just one donkey' is to bind 'it' it will have to be given large scope:

(13) [*just one y: donkey y*] [*every x: man x · x bought y*] x *paid cash for y*.

But again this yields the wrong result. The fact that (12) appears to be equivalent to the ungainly (12′) below suggests there is something to be gained by exploring the view that the pronoun in (12) functions as a disguised definite description:[19]

(12′) every man who bought just one donkey paid cash for the donkey he bought.

On such an account, the description the donkey pronoun 'it' abbreviates itself contains a pronoun 'he' bound by the subject expression 'every man who bought a donkey'. While this is certainly unproblematic as far as (12′) is concerned, it raises questions about the nature of the mechanisms involved in interpreting a pronoun that appears to be anaphoric but not bound by the expression upon which it appears to be anaphoric, and this might suggest sweeping up all anaphoric pronouns within a theory of the pragmatics of discourse.[20] Alternatively, it might suggest sweeping them up with a description-based approach.[21]

With these logical issues in mind, let us now turn to the general interpretive framework within which they should be soluble.

3. Linguistic Pragmatism

Let us call a theory that aims to explain how hearers manage to identify what speakers are seeking to communicate a *theory of utterance interpretation*, or a *theory of*

---

[19] See n. 17.   [20] Heim (1982/1988); Kamp (1981/1984).   [21] Elbourne (2001, 2002).

interpretation for short. To say that we are interested in providing a theory of interpretation is not to say we are prejudicing the issue against communication that does not involve speech or writing. It might simply turn out—it surely will—that a theory of interpretation will make reference to cognitive capacities involved in interpreting non-linguistic acts of communication, indeed non-linguistic acts more generally.[22]

The project of explaining interpretation has many components and involves people from several fields. Philosophers have two roles, one in the boardroom, the other on the shop floor, as it were. First, they will attempt to articulate clearly the nature of the project (distinguishing it carefully from various other projects with which it might be confused), distinguish clearly the various sub-projects, and distinguish and analyse the central concepts or at least the relations between them (for example, meaning, saying, implying, referring, and intending). At the same time, they will attempt to work alongside linguists whose expertise involves explaining how individual words are assembled into sentences and the extent to which communicatively relevant features of the sentences we use to say things depend upon features of the words out of which they are assembled and the mode of assembly itself; and alongside psychologists who can tell philosophers and linguists about cognition, in particular about the way we integrate information from different sources and channels in the process of identifying what someone is trying to communicate.

Before getting down to pronouns per se, I want to sketch the general picture within which I think we should be operating. With distinct nods to the American Pragmatists, to Wittgenstein, Sellars, and Quine, to Perry, and to Sperber and Wilson, I call the general outlook I have on the matter of interpretation, *linguistic pragmatism* (or *pragmatism* for short). It is an outlook that can be held by philosophers, linguists, psychologists, and no doubt others—no diplomas are checked at the door—who take themselves to be involved in the project of constructing a general theory of (utterance) interpretation, construed as an empirical theory and, as such, a contribution to cognitive psychology. It might be seen as a collection of theses that can emerge *only* in the context of attempting to articulate the outlines of such a theory, theses whose truth may well have repercussions elsewhere but which are not themselves motivated by the desire to bolster this or that philosophical or political doctrine even if distinctions inherent in certain theses emerged from reflections on the language used in stating philosophical problems and positions. (The pragmatist outlook may well be implicated in

---

[22] See Grice (1989); Sperber and Wilson (1986, 1995); Carston (2002).

various works of a 'contextualist' nature, but I am anxious to distance my own views from extant contextualist proposals in epistemology, metaphysics, ethics, and political philosophy, many of which seem to me rather suspect.)

Some of the central tenets of linguistic pragmatism were accepted by a number of British philosophers in the 1950s, particularly Austin, Strawson, and (contrary to the claims of some pragmatists) Grice.[23] But it was not until the late 1970s, by which time the Language of Thought hypothesis articulated by Fodor, the Chomskyan idea of LF (Logical Form) as a level of linguistic representation, and important distinctions made by Grice and Searle had truly sunk in, that the conceptual resources were generally available to articulate the outlook clearly and in a form that made it relevant to more formal studies of language that were by that time blossoming in linguistics and philosophy departments in the United States. To the best of my knowledge, it was not until the work of Sperber and Wilson began to appear in print in the early 1980s that pragmatists made sustained efforts to render explicit the basic tenets of their work. Indeed, without Sperber and Wilson's work, and the work of Chomsky, Fodor, Grice, and Searle upon which it drew, philosophy and linguistics might still lack the distinctions and resources needed to say anything more substantive than the ramblings about 'contextual meanings' and 'relative meanings' that issue periodically from the darker areas of philosophy and linguistics departments (not to mention departments or 'programmes' housing people unaccountably known as 'theorists' or 'philosophers').

It would be a mistake, I think, to attempt a *definition* of linguistic pragmatism as it is essentially an outlook that engenders a very practical approach to interpretation. I cannot go into the sort of detail I go into in *Linguistic Pragmatism* here, so I have produced twenty-four labelled points (without much in the way of argument) to give the general flavour of pragmatism as I think it should be developed. Some of the points are quite general or intuitive, others are very specific or

---

[23] A somewhat simplistic picture of the relationship between the focus on 'ordinary' language and the use of 'ideal' or 'formal' languages appears to be accepted by many linguists and even some philosophers. The received view in linguistics appears to be that for some years there was a major philosophical conflict (between 'formalists' and 'informalists') which Grice somehow dissipated by distinguishing what a speaker said from what he 'conversationally implicated'. (The picture is perhaps fostered by a naive reading of the opening paragraphs of Grice's 'Logic and Conversation' (1975a) and by Strawson's (1969) bizarre claims about a 'Homeric struggle' in his inaugural lecture 'Meaning and Truth'.) Some of the people in the grip of this picture have been led to conclude that Grice was not actually a pragmatist. I know from conversations with him (a) that he saw the problem of providing an accurate account of what the speaker says when using an incomplete description as providing powerful *evidence* for pragmatism, and (b) that he never intended to be seen as denying pragmatism.

theory-laden. Some are less central than others and could be withdrawn without upsetting the whole too much, but I am strongly inclined to go along with the whole lot, and there is no doubt that many gain strength through association with others. A few are held by some philosophers and linguists I would call anti-pragmatists; several are rejected by some with pragmatist outlooks; and a few are conspicuous here by their absence elsewhere in the literature.[24]

1. *Cooperation.* Typically speakers (writers) want to be understood, and hearers (readers) seek to understand. To this extent they are involved in a cooperative exercise. *Ceteris paribus*, both parties tacitly assume they are using words with shared meanings, combining these words in accordance with a shared syntax, and operating in accordance with shared and very general, rational principles of *interpretation.*

2. *Meaning.* A theory of interpretation should explain how hearers (and readers) manage to integrate linguistic and non-linguistic information to identify what a speaker (or writer) *meant* on a given occasion by uttering (or inscribing) a linguistic expression X.[25] Valuable information can be gleaned from examining situations in which we report on speech acts using sentences of the form

by uttering (or writing) X, A meant that *p*

where the reporter is using the expression replacing 'A' to pick out an agent and the expression replacing 'X' to pick out a linguistic expression, and where the

[24] Putting aside differences of terminology and philosophical temperament, as well as apparent disagreements about particular analyses, I am inclined to view all of the following as operating in a broadly pragmatist spirit—although my own brand of linguistic pragmatism is, I suspect, rather too ascetic, inferential, beholden to ordinary language strictures, and driven by underlying concerns about practicality and the concepts of society and regulation for many of them: Austin (1962); Barwise and Perry (1983); Bezuidenhout (1997); S. Blackburn (1984); W. Blackburn (1988); Blakemore (1987); Carston (1988, 1993, 2002); Chomsky (1977, 1986, 1995, 2000, 2002); Crimmins (1992); Crimmins and Perry (1989); Evans (1982, 1985); Fodor (1987, 2001); Grayling (1995); Grice (1989); Heal (1997); Neale (1990, 1993); Papafragou (1998, 2000); Perry (1986, 2000, 2001); Quine (1940, 1960); Recanati (1987, 1989, 1993, 2001); Rouchota (1992); Searle (1969, 1979, 1980); Sellars (1954); Sperber and Wilson (1986, 1995); and Strawson (1950, 1952). I suspect pragmatism is also taken for granted by many others who take truth to be a property of what a speaker says or expresses by uttering a sentence X on a specific occasion, and not of what X itself says or expresses relative to a context. I shall point to or draw liberally from the work of these pragmatists as I go. By saying I am a pragmatist, I do not mean to be saying that I endorse the details of Recanati's (1989, 1993) or Rouchota's (1992) or Sperber and Wilson's (1986, 1995) or Bezuidenhout's (1997) or Carston's (2002) pragmatic analyses of definite descriptions and the attributive–referential distinction, all of which I find problematic. I propose an account that should be attractive not only to them but to Russellians and ambiguity theorists alike in Neale (2004).

[25] Linguistic pragmatism does not necessarily assume there is much chance of ever producing an empirically interesting theory of interpretation. At least two pragmatists, Chomsky (2000) and

expression replacing 'p' is a declarative sentence. Examples:

> by uttering 'I'm tired', John meant that he was tired
> by uttering 'I'm tired', John meant that he wanted us to leave.

We should be suspicious of locutions of the form 'X means that *p*', where the expression replacing 'X' is being used to pick out a sentence (e.g. 'the sentence "snow is white" means that snow is white').

3. *Explanation.* To interpret is to provide an *explanation*, and the concept of interpretation makes no sense in the absence of a *problem* to be solved. We reflexively generate *hypotheses* about the things we perceive. Nowhere is this more in evidence than when we perceive one another's *actions*. We act out of *reasons*. To interpret an action is to form a hypothesis about the *intentions* behind it, the intentions that *explain* it. Interpreting a speech act is a special case of this. The use of language is one form of rational activity, and the principles at work in the interpretation of linguistic behaviour are intimately related to those at work in interpreting intentional *non*-linguistic behaviour. What makes interpreting a speech act special is that a proprietary body of information, knowledge of language, is accessed immediately in the interpretation process. The hearer's or reader's goal is to identify what the speaker or writer meant. When this has been done, the interpretive problem has been solved.[26]

4. *Asymmetry.* The epistemic situations of the speaker and hearer are fundamentally asymmetric: the speaker *knows* what he means whereas the hearer has to *work it out*. If you want to find out whether I'm hungry (or in pain) you will have to watch me, see what I do, or ask me. *I* don't have to do that. I have 'privileged access' to that information.[27] Similarly if you want to know whether I am

---

Fodor (1983, 1987, 2001), have argued that asking for a theory of interpretation is tantamount to asking for a 'theory of everything', a complete cognitive psychology, because virtually anything can impinge upon the holistic process of interpretation. For more optimistic pragmatist outlooks, see Sperber and Wilson (1986/1995) and Carston (2002). The present chapter assumes neither outlook, but it brings into sharp relief the need for a clear picture of what the more tractable subtheories of a theory of interpretation are supposed to do and how they must come together.

[26] I mean this to apply equally to interpretations in literary theory. The idea of textual interpretation makes no sense if there is no problem (about, for example, a word or phrase, a character, a plot, a work, or even a whole genre) to which an interpretation constitutes a possible solution. It is embarrassing that some 'theorists' who also call themselves 'philosophers' are unable to see this.

[27] There are philosophers concerned to deny this idea today, but no coherent case has been made (indeed could be made) for a total failure of asymmetry. The idea of 'privileged access' to a state is often introduced with the idea of 'incorrigibility' (the idea that I cannot be mistaken about whether I am in the state in question). While the case for denying this might be more promising, the fact that

worried about missing my flight, where on an aeroplane I prefer to sit, or whether I think Norway is a member of the European Union. And similarly where we have speech. Unlike you, I have privileged access to what I mean when I utter X on a given occasion. We can characterize a typical speech situation as follows. Person A intends to communicate something to some other person B. He selects a form of words X that he thinks will, in the circumstances, get across his point (and, perhaps, also get it across in some particular way or other. A knows what he means by uttering 'That's his bank', for example. He knows *which thing* he meant by 'that', *who* and *what relation* he meant by 'his' and *what* he meant by 'bank'.

B's situation is quite different: B is trying to work out what A meant and he must use anything he can get his hands on to get the job done since he has no direct access to A's communicative intentions. The words A uses constitute partial evidence for what A meant. Other evidence may come from the physical environment, from B's take on the conversation up to that point (if any), from B's beliefs about A, and a whole lot more besides. The epistemic asymmetry of speaker and hearer underscores (i) the need to separate the *metaphysical* question concerning what *determines* (or fixes) what A means and the *epistemological* question concerning what is used by others to *identify* what A means, and (ii) the need to scrutinize simplistic appeals to *contexts, maxims of conversation, salience*, and *pragmatic factors*, which are frequently (and mistakenly) introduced together with *intentions* in contemporary discussions as if these things conspire to bridge certain interpretive gaps. Scanning the context of utterance for salient objects and bringing to bear pragmatic principles (e.g. Grice's conversational maxims) is not going to provide A with any information that will help him identify what he meant. From A's perspective, context and pragmatic principles have already fulfilled their roles: A's perception of the context—whatever a context turns out to be—his perception of B's perception of the context, the assumption that B is operating in accordance with the same pragmatic principles as A, and A's estimation of B's ability to work things out (and probably a whole lot more besides) have already impinged upon whatever processes led A to use the particular form of words he used with the intentions with which he used them.

5. *Reciprocity.* Despite the epistemic asymmetry, the perspectives of A and B are not independent. The asymmetry is *reciprocal* or *complementary* as in adjoining

---

incorrigibility is at least *arguable* (and has been argued) in the first-person case, and is not in the least arguable (and has not been argued except, perhaps, by the deluded) in the third-person case, is enough to distinguish the cases here.

pieces of a jigsaw puzzle. In producing his utterance, A relies on what he takes to be B's capacity to identify what he intends to convey; B assumes that A is so relying. And, possibly, so on. The ways in which A and B operate form a *dovetail joint* and are *mutually sustaining*. And to this extent, there is simply no possibility of making sense of B's capacity to interpret A without making sense of A's capacity to exploit that capacity, and vice versa. So the project of constructing a theory of interpretation may be approached from either of two complementary perspectives, and an adequate answer must make sense of both.

6. *Intention*. What A *meant* by uttering X on a particular occasion is determined by, and only by, certain very specific *interpreter-directed intentions* A had in uttering X. The precise content of a psychological state such as a belief or intention may be determined, in part, by something external to A and beyond A's control ('externalism'). Furthermore, the formation of genuine intentions is severely constrained by beliefs. I cannot intend to become a prime number, intend to digest my food through my lungs on alternate Tuesdays, or swim from New York to Sydney because (roughly) I cannot intend *what I believe to be impossible*. (There is no need to get into the exact force of the modal or the exact formulation of the constraint here. It is enough to recognize, as Grice 1971 does, that it is severe.) If, as Grice suggests, what A meant by uttering X on a given occasion is determined by certain interpreter-directed intentions, then assuming he is being cooperative A cannot mean that *p* by uttering some sentence X if he believes it is impossible for his audience B (or at least any rational, reasonably well-informed interpreter in B's shoes) to construe him as meaning that *p*. Among the things constraining A's communicative intentions are A's beliefs about the world, his (tacit) beliefs about the sorts of interpretive principles B will be employing, and his (tacit) estimation of B's capacity to work certain things out (the list is not meant to be anywhere near exhaustive). So without some stage-setting A cannot mean that Jones is no good at philosophy by producing the sentence 'Jones has excellent handwriting and is always punctual', for example, or by reproducing the mating call of some exotic bird.

7. *Factorization*. What A meant by uttering X may be factored into what A *said* (or *asked*) by uttering X and what A only *implied*.[28] Thus, again following Grice, what A said and what A implied are determined by, and only by, certain very specific

---

[28] In my view it is vital to distinguish between (roughly) (i) what A implied *by uttering* X, and (ii) what A implied *by saying what he said*. This distinction seems to me to get to the heart of Grice's distinction between conventional and conversational implicature, and to provide the framework within which to solve problems concerning the former (cf. Frege's notion of tone or colouring), non-detachability, dictiveness and formality, and central vs. non-central speech acts.

interpreter-directed intentions A had in uttering X.[29] Nonetheless, although it would be perverse to insist upon a distinction between what A meant and what A *intended* to mean (and for good reason if Grice is right), a distinction between what A said and what A intended to say is not one obviously lacking a point. In the first instance, we should separate (i) *what A intended to say by uttering X on a given occasion*, and (ii) *what a rational, reasonably well-informed interpreter in B's shoes would think A intended to say by uttering X on that occasion* (which is not to say there are not problems with the idea of *a rational, reasonably well-informed interpreter in B's shoes*). In cases where (i) = (ii), we can talk freely about *what the speaker said*. In cases where (i) ≠ (ii), certainly we *could* argue about which of (i) or (ii) or some third thing has the 'right' to be called *what is said*, but what would be the point? First, what third thing distinct from (i) and (ii) could be of any significance to a theory of interpretation? There is simply no role for a transcendent notion of what is said upon which (i) and (ii) converge when all goes well. It is the *coincidence itself* of (i) and (ii) that constitutes success, and it is the *potential* for such coincidence, independently of some third thing, that *gives sense* to the very idea of saying. (Contrary to linguistic appearances the concept of *intending* to say is, in fact, more basic than the seemingly simpler concept of saying.) Second, why is a choice between (i) and (ii) needed in cases where (i) ≠ (ii)? Conceptually they are distinct, and both are needed in a theory of interpretation. When all goes well, they coincide, and it's just too bad they don't always do so. There is no philosophical pay-off in

---

[29] This factorization is the arithmetical lynchpin of Grice's framework. Its existence, however, in Grice's work has been denied by Saul (2002*a, b*), based on some spectacular oversights and unfettered extrapolations from one or two sentences in Grice's published corpus. According to Saul, "Grice's characterizations of speaker meaning and conversational implicature are cast in very different terms—the former completely in terms of speaker intentions and the latter incorporating a good deal about the audience. As a result, the notions do not fit neatly into the simple picture I was taught: there are many things that which speakers mean that they neither say nor implicate. . . . For Grice, what speakers say and what speakers implicate is not simply a matter of what they intend." (2002*a*: 229). Here, Saul has missed the centrality to Grice's programme of the following: (i) the *cooperative nature* of (at least certain typical) talk exchanges and its rational underpinnings; (ii) the *epistemic asymmetry* of speaker and hearer that forces upon us different locations when discussing the two perspectives; (iii) the *reciprocal* or *dovetailed nature* of these perspectives, (iv) the fact that the intentions Grice is concerned with are *audience-directed* and intended to be recognised, and (v) the fact that intentions are *constrained by beliefs* and that speaker intentions in particular are constrained by the speaker's beliefs about the *audience* towards whom the intentions are directed. In consequence, Saul's claims about saying and implicating, and her grumbles about the standard reading of Grice she was taught are baseless. For a detailed textual examination, see *Linguistic Pragmatism*, where Saul's criticisms of Wilson and Sperber (1981), Sperber and Wilson (1986) and Carston (2002) are shown to be spurious.

On a related note, if what A said is determined by, and only by, certain very specific *interpreter-directed intentions* A had in uttering X, then at least some contemporary talk of 'contexts' 'fixing' or 'determining' aspects of what A said—for example, the references of indexical expressions—must involve some form of confusion. See below.

bestowing the honorific 'what was said' on one rather than the other when they diverge. (Everything I have just said about saying carries over mutatis mutandis to implying and referring.)

Among the things that constrain the formation of A's *saying-intentions* are A's beliefs (including beliefs about his audience), his knowledge of the meanings of the words he is using, and his (tacit) knowledge of the syntax of the language he is using. Thus A cannot (intend to) say that snow is white by uttering the sentence 'grass is green'. And he cannot (intend to) say that John asked his brother to shave him by uttering 'John asked his brother to shave himself'. More generally, he cannot (intend to) say that *p* by uttering X if he believes it is impossible for his audience B (or at least any rational, reasonably well-informed interpreter in B's shoes) to construe him as intending to say that *p*.

8. *Speakers.* Saying and implying are things *people* do. Following ordinary usage, *the speaker* is taken to be the understood subject, so to speak, of the verbs 'say' and 'imply' the verbs in talk about 'what is said' and 'what is implied'. (Similarly, with verbs such as 'communicate', 'convey', and 'get across'.) We should be initially suspicious of talk about what *uses of sentences* say (imply, communicate, etc.) and talk about what *sentences-relative-to-contexts* say (imply, communicate, etc.), unless such talk is taken to be straightforwardly translatable into talk about things that speakers are doing. And we should deplore the unannounced slipping and sliding back and forth between different subjects of 'say' ('imply', 'communicate', etc.). At the same time, we should be open to the idea that new, *technical* uses of the verbs 'say' ('imply', 'communicate', etc.) may need to be defined, or at least developed, in the course of our inquiries, such uses earning their keep because of ineliminable theoretical work they do.

9. *Truth.* What A says and implies are the sorts of things that are true or false. (Perhaps A may say things that are neither true nor false, but it might prove useful to start out sceptical about this.) It does not follow that when A utters a sentence he says only one thing or that he implies only one thing. Nor does this talk of truth mean that in order to produce a theory of interpretation we shall have to construct a theory that recursively assigns *truth conditions* to sentences relativized to contexts of utterance (a *semantic* theory, in *one* sense of 'semantic'), or construct a theory that assigns things in the world to linguistic expressions relativized to contexts of utterance (a theory of *reference*, in *one* sense of 'reference').

10. *Judgement.* Our intuitive judgements about what A meant, said, and implied, and judgements about whether what A said was true or false in specified situations constitute the primary data for a theory of interpretation, the data it is the theory's business to explain. (Since *no one* has intuitive judgements about *what*

is said by a sentence X relative to a context C or about the *semantic content* of X relative to C (these being philosophers' notions), several distinct mistakes would be involved in the claim that linguistic pragmatism aims to show that our intuitive judgements about what a speaker said may be 'unreliable guides to semantic content'. If talk of the 'semantic content' of a sentence X relative to a context C is just a snazzy way of talking about what the speaker said by uttering X on a particular occasion—the occasion that C is being used to partially model—then of course we can accept its empirical significance. If it is not, then its empirical significance must be justified in some other way, from *within* the theory of interpretation by reference to some empirical role it is required to play in an explanation of what a speaker says and implies by uttering X on a given occasion, in much the same way that notions such as binding and scope are motivated from within.

11. *Reference.* Saying typically involves *referring* and *saying of*. That is, saying something typically involves *referring to* something and *saying* something *of* it. Saying that London is pretty, for example, involves referring to London and saying of it that it is pretty. One way of doing this is to use 'London' to refer to London and 'is pretty' to say of it that it is pretty. Following ordinary usage, the *speaker* is taken as the understood subject, so to speak, of 'refer to' and 'say of'. Initially, we should deplore the unannounced slipping and sliding back and forth between different subjects of 'refer to' and 'say of', and we should be suspicious of talk about what *uses of words* refer to and say of things, and of talk about what *words-relative-to-contexts* refer to and say of things—unless such talk is taken to be straightforwardly translatable into talk about things that speakers are doing. But we should be open to the idea that new, *technical* uses of 'refer to' and 'say of' may emerge in the course of our inquiries. Who or what A is referring to by uttering some expression X is determined by A's *referential intentions* in uttering X. (Talk of 'contexts' 'fixing' or 'determining' the references of expressions—for example, the references of indexical expressions—must involve some form of confusion.)

Nonetheless, a distinction between what A referred to and what A *intended* to refer to is not one obviously lacking a point. So, in the first instance we should separate (i) *who or what A intended to refer to by an expression X on a given occasion*, and (ii) *who or what a rational, reasonably well-informed interpreter in B's shoes thinks A intended to refer to by X on that occasion*. In cases where (i) = (ii), we can talk freely about *what the speaker referred to*. (In cases where (i) ≠ (ii), we *could* argue about which of (i) or (ii) or some third thing has the 'right' to be called *the person or thing referred to*, but what would be the point? First, what third thing distinct from (i) and (ii) could be of any significance to a theory of interpretation? There is simply no role for a transcendent notion of what was referred to upon which (i) and (ii) converge when all goes well. Referring is like saying and implying: it is the coincidence itself of (i) and (ii) that constitutes success, and it is the *potential* for such coincidence, independently of some third thing, that gives sense to the very idea of referring. (Contrary to linguistic appearances the concept of intending to refer to X is, in fact, more basic than the seemingly simpler concept of referring to X.) Second, why is a choice between (i) and (ii) even needed in cases where (i) ≠ (ii)? Conceptually they are distinct, and they are both needed in a theory of interpretation. When all goes well, they coincide, and it's just too bad they don't always do so. Surely there is no philosophical pay-off in bestowing the honorific 'what was referred to' on one rather than the other when they diverge.) Referential intentions are constrained by belief and knowledge. Assuming he is being cooperative, A cannot (intend to) refer to some particular person α by uttering some expression X on a given occasion if he believes it is impossible for his audience B (or at least any rational, reasonably well-informed interpreter in B's shoes) to construe him as referring to α.[30] Among the things that constrain the formation of A's referential intentions are A's knowledge of the meanings of the referring expressions he is using and his (tacit) knowledge of the syntax of the language he is using (which may bear on the matter of co-reference or binding where pronouns are concerned).[31]

12. *Aphonicity.* It is now time to get more theoretical. A distinction between PF ('Phonetic Form') and LF ('Logical Form') in something like Chomsky's sense, is almost certain to play a key role in a theory of interpretation, where a sentence's PF is (roughly) a representation that expresses its phonology, and its LF a representation that expresses *all* syntactic properties relevant to interpretation.[32] This distinction brings with it the possibility of revealing in the LF of a sentence X syntactic objects that have no counterparts in X's PF. Such aphonic (phonologically null) expressions are as much in need of interpretation when X is uttered as any other elements in X's LF. (If a sentence's LF expresses *only* syntactic properties relevant to interpretation, as current theory dictates, this becomes a matter of definition.)

13. *Indexicality.* Identifying the LF of a sentence X does not constitute identifying what A says on a given occasion by uttering X. For one thing, X's LF may contain an indexical expression like 'I' or 'he' or 'that'. So identifying X's LF still

---

[30] I mention *cooperation* because in certain circumstances one may seek to disguise one's intended referent from others, for example in cryptic poetry, diary entries, or dramatic irony. In such cases, there is either no intended audience distinct from oneself or some individual distinct from oneself with whom one is engaged but with whom one is being less than fully cooperative in the sense discussed earlier. The issues here are intimately connected to Grice's (1989) discussions of communicative intentions in the absence of an audience and to the issue of whether one's future self constitutes an audience.

[31] As it turns out, I think there are no syntactic constraints on co-reference or referential dependence, only on binding. See below.   [32] See Chomsky (1986, 1995, 2000).

leaves B some interpretive work to do, work that will involve accessing and integrating all sorts of information not carried or revealed by the LF itself.[33]

14. *Anchoring*. Idealization and abstraction from the details of particular speech situations or contexts are unavoidable if work is to proceed. To this extent, we may temporarily avail ourselves of the formal 'indices' or 'contexts' of indexical logics in order to anchor or co-anchor the interpretations of indexical or anaphoric expressions that are not of primary concern at a certain point of investigation. We should not take formal indices themselves particularly seriously, however. They are useful transitory tools, methodological or heuristic devices, not serious posits in a theory of utterance interpretation.

15. *Mongrels*. Since LFs may contain aphonics and may contain indexicals, we should be open to the possibility that they may contain aphonic indexicals. (At the same time, we should no more take seriously the idea that pairing a formal 'context' with an aphonic indexical in a sentence X *eo ipso* solves a genuine problem about the *interpretation* of an utterance of X than we should take seriously the idea that pairing a formal 'context' with a *phonic* indexical does so.) Aphonic indexicals are not the only possible mongrels. Since LFs may contain aphonics and may contain bindable variables, we should be open to the possibility that they may contain aphonic bindable variables. (Compare 'everyone wants John to leave' and 'everyone wants to leave'. Perhaps the subject of 'to leave' in the latter is an aphonic variable bound by 'everyone'. Certainly it is not an aphonic copy of 'everyone'.) And why not aphonic, indexical, bindable variables?

16. *Isomorphism*. It is at least methodologically useful to say that identifying what a speaker said by uttering a sentence X on a given occasion involves 'entertaining' a sentence of Mentalese; or that it involves 'entertaining' a structured proposition. (Perhaps entertaining a sentence of Mentalese ultimately amounts to entertaining a structured proposition because it involves entertaining a representation whose role in our mental life can be explained only in terms of it having a certain 'content' that a structured proposition supplies. Who knows?) With Sperber and Wilson, let us work for the moment with Mentalese. Since LFs are not full-blown representations of Mentalese (and so do not express propositions), but only 'blueprints', 'schemas', 'skeletons', or 'templates' for such, in

[33] This does not mean that the pragmatist cannot, for certain expository or investigative purposes, operate *as if* a description of a sentence's LF gives us a descriptions of what A said *relative to certain heuristic stipulations*. Formal 'contexts' or 'indices' are used in logic to anchor or co-anchor indexical elements in order to cancel or pair their effects across similar structures. Without commitment to the view that formal contexts play any sort of role in a theory of interpretation, the linguistic pragmatist may sometimes borrow this technique in order that a particular investigation may focus on particular non-indexical properties of LFs that are relevant to a theory of utterance interpretation.

advance of serious empirical investigation we cannot rule out the possibility of a *failure of isomorphism* in the mapping between the LF of a sentence X and a Mentalese representation the entertaining of which constitutes understanding what A said by uttering X on a particular occasion (or in the mapping between X's LF and a structured proposition, the entertaining of which constitutes understanding what A said by uttering X on a particular occasion). That is, we cannot rule out atoms of the Mentalese representation (or atoms of the structured proposition) to which no element of X's LF corresponds. (A might utter the sentence 'The embassy is closed' on a particular occasion and B may be required to entertain the Mentalese sentence all too conveniently rendered as THE US EMBASSY IN LONDON IS CLOSED in order to grasp what A said.[34] A may utter 'the ham sandwich wants extra pickles', and B may be required to entertain the Mentalese sentence THE MAN WHO JUST ORDERED A HAM SANDWICH WANTS EXTRA PICKLES. A may utter 'the hostages landed back on American soil today' and B may be required to entertain the Mentalese sentence THE FORMER AMERICAN HOSTAGES AT THE US EMBASSY IN TEHRAN LANDED BACK ON AMERICAN SOIL TODAY. It would seem that A may even utter less than a whole sentence—for example, 'no thank you' or 'a cappuccino, please'—and thereby say something.)

We cannot rule out the possibility, however, that future work in syntax will indicate that we are closer to isomorphism than superficial appearances suggest, for all sorts of aphonics in LF may be revealed. Presumably, Mentalese representations will have to contain elements that function as (or at least do the work done by) bound variables, so we may well have to consider the possibility that interpreting a particular utterance of a sentence X may involve entertaining a Mentalese representation that contains a mental variable with no counterpart in X's LF. On the other hand, syntactic evidence might be found for the existence of an aphonic variable in X's LF. We cannot dogmatically assume that there *must* be isomorphism, and we should recoil from the unargued goal of attaining isomorphism by freely adding aphonics to LFs as if adorning some garish Christmas tree with a new light wherever it seems too dark. (We shouldn't get hooked on aphonics.)

17. *Ellipsis.* Corresponding to the sentence–utterance distinction impressed upon us so forcefully by Austin, Grice, and Strawson, we must take seriously two important and distinct uses of the words 'ellipsis' and 'elliptical'. The first is a strict linguistic (or grammatical) notion found in talk of elliptical *sentences* in generative linguistics, a notion sometimes called *deletion* and which involves erasing

---

[34] If you know English and your shift key works, Mentalese is a cinch (Mentalease?). Structured-Propositionese is a little harder: you need good angled brackets.

elements in the generation of PF representations.[35] Linguistic ellipsis concerns the superficial incompleteness of *structures*, and as such is subject to a stringent condition on the constancy of form and interpretation that has been investigated by linguists under the rubric of *recoverability*. (A can use the sentence 'I can tango but Mary can't' to say that he can tango but Mary can't *tango*, but not to say that he can tango but Mary can't *sing*. This is because it is elliptical for the complete sentence 'I can tango but Mary can't tango'.) The second notion of ellipsis is a pragmatic (or speech act) notion, found in talk of elliptical *utterances* of (elliptical on non-elliptical) sentences.[36] Pragmatic ellipsis concerns the incompleteness of *interpretations*, and as such is governed only by general pragmatic principles of interpretation. (A can use the sentence 'I'm going to a party at the embassy' to say that he's going to a party at the British embassy in Athens, for example, or to say that he's going to a party at the US embassy in London because there is no particular complete sentence that the sentence A uttered is an incomplete or elliptical version of.) We must accept that people often speak elliptically without much (if any) conscious effort and that hearers interpret elliptical utterances without much (if any) conscious effort. In such situations typically the speaker and hearer can both readily expand upon the sentence uttered in such a way that explains the ellipsis. Many distinct expansions may be perfectly acceptable, what is said being (to a lesser degree than what is implied) somewhat indeterminate.

18. *Competence.* Three major components of a theory of interpretation are a *syntactic theory*, a *semantic theory*, and a *pragmatic theory*. Certain preconceptions about the labels 'syntactic', 'semantic', and 'pragmatic' need to be put to one side if the pragmatist position is to be understood, for these words are used in very precise ways. (Self-serving edicts from those who claim to have isolated the 'correct' way of making the semantics–pragmatics distinction or the 'correct' uses of the terms 'semantics' and 'pragmatics' should be ignored.) A *syntactic* theory for a person A who speaks a language L is an abstract description of A's syntactic *competence* (in Chomsky's sense), A's tacit knowledge of the syntax of L. This only becomes interesting when we are clear about what counts as a syntactic fact or phenomenon. Are binding and scope syntactic phenomena? A *semantic theory* is an abstract description of A's semantic *competence*, his knowledge, tacit or otherwise, of the semantics of L. This only becomes interesting when we are clear about what counts as a semantic fact or phenomenon. Are binding and scope semantic

---

[35] See e.g. Sag (1976); Williams (1977); Heim and Kratzer (1998); May (2002). The last of these provides a particularly clear and user-friendly discussion of linguistic ellipsis. The grammatical notion clearly has its roots in talk of ellipsis and elision in some traditional grammars.

[36] See e.g. Quine (1940); Sellars (1954); K. Bach (1981); Salmon (1982); Neale (1990).

phenomena? Binding shows that a sharp division between syntax and semantics is illusory (which is why Chomsky is prepared to use the label 'syntactic' in connection with much of what many philosophers and linguists label 'semantic'). Drawing a sharp line between semantics and pragmatics is straightforward. A *pragmatic theory* transcends individual speakers and particular languages. It is an abstract description of the mechanisms that make it possible for interpreters to identify what a speaker means by uttering a sentence (or sentence fragment) X on a given occasion given (at most) what a semantic theory has to say about X. As such, a pragmatic theory is a description of an intentional and richly inferential system, our common pragmatic *competence*. There is no assumption here, nor is there any antecedent reason to suspect, that the semantics–pragmatics distinction just drawn will be coordinate with the saying–implying distinction.

19. *Semantics*. Words and the ways in which they can be combined have properties that enter into an explanation of why speakers use the particular combinations they do, and why hearers interpret in the ways they do. The two most obvious properties are the *meanings* of words and *syntax*. *Qua* description of semantic competence, a semantic theory for a language will explain how the syntactic structure of a sentence (or sentence fragment) X and the meanings of the individual words in X conspire to constrain what speakers can *say* using X. Flushing out the modal: a semantic theory for a language L will provide, for each sentence X of L, a *blueprint* for (a *template*, a *schematic* or *skeletal* representation of) what someone will be taken to be saying when using X to say something. The blueprint associated with X is its *semantics*, and the set of such blueprints, one for every sentence of a language L, is the *semantics* for L. (The study of these blueprints is also called *semantics*. The study of the role of word meanings is called *lexical* semantics; the study of the role of syntax is called *compositional* semantics.) Semantic competence comprises at least (i) knowledge of the meanings of individual words and (ii) knowledge of syntax (syntactic competence). It is a matter of debate whether it involves more. On the one hand, if A claims not to understand a sentence X, then it would seem that either the meaning of some word in X eludes him or else some aspect of X's structure (ultimately X's LF) does. On the other, having a model aeroplane kit, a foolproof set of instructions, excellent glue, plenty of space, good lighting, and the fingers of a heart surgeon is not the same thing as having the model aeroplane (that's why they write 'kit' on the box). Settling this debate involves settling (among other things) what syntactic competence amounts to and how bad the model aeroplane analogy is. (Certainly knowledge (in the requisite sense) of syntax does not amount to the propositional representation of a set of syntactic rules.)

20. *Pragmatics.* Whereas each language (perhaps even each idiolect) has its own syntax and its own semantics—which is not to say that vital syntactic and (hence) semantic properties are not shared across languages as a result of our common biological endowment—there is, so to speak, only *one* pragmatics. *Qua* description of our shared pragmatic competence, a pragmatic theory will explain how interpreters identify what a speaker means by uttering a sentence (or sentence fragment) X on a given occasion given (at most) what a semantic theory has to say about X.

The semantics–pragmatics distinction, thus construed, is not coordinate with the saying–implying distinction. What A means by uttering X on a given occasion comprises what A *said* and what A *implied*. So a pragmatic theory will explain how interpreters identify what A said and implied by uttering X on that occasion given (at most) what a semantic theory has to say about X. If a *pragmatic* theory explained only how interpreters identify what A *implied* given (at most) what the speaker *said* as 'input', a gaping hole in our taxonomy of *theories* would appear. A *semantic* theory specifies the constraints that word meanings and syntax place on what A can *say* by uttering X, a blueprint for X. What would we call a theory that explains how interpreters identify what A *said* on that occasion? Not a *semantic* theory, for that specifies only a blueprint for what *A said*, i.e. the *sort of thing* he said. Clearly, a pragmatic theory has *two* roles in a theory of interpretation. Even if an utterance of a sentence X always wore on its sleeve an unambiguous representation of its syntactic structure with no ambiguous elements, a semantic theory could still fail to identify fully what A said by uttering X on a particular occasion. For one thing, X may contain 'he', 'this', 'here', or 'John', in which case the interpreter needs to identify who or what A is referring to.[37] Since

---

[37] My wording should make it clear that I am putting aside, for now, the fact, stressed by many pragmatists, that a pragmatic theory may have to be invoked in order to identify what *sentence* A uttered because of ambiguities at PF. Among the things a hearer or reader has to do in order to identify what A is saying on a given occasion is to identify which *words* A is using. /Bank/ is the superficial form of either a single, ambiguous word of English or else of two distinct unambiguous words, and I do not want one's position on this matter to impinge upon one's understanding of the Insufficiency Thesis (see point 21). (If /bank/ is the superficial form of a single, ambiguous word, then identifying what A is saying when he utters 'I'm going to the bank' involves identifying which *meaning* A has in mind for /bank/; if /bank/ is the superficial form of two distinct, unambiguous words then identifying what A is saying when he utters /I'm going to the bank/ involves identifying which of the two *words* A is using. The latter view seems more useful in theorizing about language. 'Word' and 'sentence' are quasi-technical terms, there are no ambiguous words or sentences, and (following Chomsky) every sentence comprises a superficial form PF and an underlying form LF, the former being what is relevant to speech perception, the latter what is relevant to speech comprehension. When I wish to talk explicitly about an expression's PF or about the sound common to two expressions, and when I wish to avoid commitment one way or the other as to whether I am talking about one expression or two, I shall borrow the old slash notation of phonology

these words are not ambiguous in the way /pen/ or /bank/ are said to be, and since each is not merely the unambiguous surface form of a context-insensitive definite description, something other than a semantic theory must be invoked.[38]

The slack is taken up by a *pragmatic* theory: identifying what A said involves the exercise of cognitive capacities that integrate the semantic information carried by the sentence uttered and all sorts of 'pragmatic' or 'contextual' information including, but not limited to, information obtained by perception from the physical environment, information about the interpretation of prior utterances in the conversation (if any), information in memory, and information about how people typically behave, particularly in communicative exchanges. That is, identifying what A said involves processing not only the semantic information encoded in a sentence's form, but accessing and processing information that must be picked up by listening, watching, remembering, hypothesizing, and inferring, essentially the capacities exercised in identifying what A *implied*. To this

(but with standard orthography rather than a phonological representation enclosed, as in /bank/) to individuate coarsely in terms of phonological properties. (On one use, then, /bank/ is what Perry 1998 calls a *vocable*.) Thus I sometimes use /he/, /him/, and /his/ because it is arguable that each corresponds to two distinct words in English, one that is bound and another that is not, an idea that appears to gain some plausibility when we consider scandinavian languages where something close to the distinction appears to be lexicalized. Similarly, I sometimes use /the/ so as not prejudge the issue on the matter of a purported ambiguity in the definite article(s). Of course if /he/ and /the/ really are ambiguous, the ambiguity in question will have to be more systematic than the sort found with /pen/ or /bank/. It is easy enough to cause trouble for my use of the slash notation. Almost certainly we want to distinguish the phonologically identical but orthographically distinct 'so', 'sew', and 'sow^a' (as in *seeds*), distinguish the orthographically identical but phonologically distinct 'sow^a' (as in *seeds*) and 'sow^b' (as in *pig*), and distinguish the phonologically and orthographically identical 'pen^a' (as in *writing instrument*) and 'pen^b' (as in *enclosure*); but probably we shall not need not bother distinguishing the (merely) orthographically distinct 'judgment' and 'judgement' or the (merely) phonologically distinct 'cóntroversy' and 'contróversy'. (Actually, I'm not so sure I should have said that: perhaps there are worries here not entirely unconnected to those Kripke 1979 brings up in connection with 'Paderewski'.) So when I want to individuate coarsely in terms of (roughly) phonology, I use the slash notation. Thus /pen/ and /sew/ (and, unfortunately, /sow^a/ and /sow^b/). If a single word can have two distinct orthographies ('judgment' and 'judgement') and a single word can have two distinct phonologies ('cóntroversy' and 'contróversy'), should we explore the idea that a single word can have two distinct orthographies *and* two distinct phonologies? Or should we say that something is a single word only if it is grounded in a single phonology or a single orthography? Or should some intermediate position be explored that invokes etymology or the relative similarity of distinct orthographies and phonologies, a position according to which /doctor/ and /physician/ would be too far apart to qualify, orthographically, phonologically, and etymologically? (Notice how the notation just exploded.) Many Greek villages or islands still have two names, and the reason we talk this way is because the names seem too far apart to count as a single name (e.g. 'Thíra' and 'Santoríni'). But what about 'Aperáthou' and 'Apeíranthos'?

[38] Three points must be separated here: (i) failure of lexical ambiguity, (ii) context sensitivity, and (iii) rigidity.

extent, then, identifying what is said is a *pragmatic* as well as a semantic matter. It involves *pragmatic inference* as well as *linguistic decoding*. Identifying what a speaker *implied* is something explained by a pragmatic theory, typically taking into account what A *said*; but identifying what the speaker *said* is also something explained by a pragmatic theory, taking into account (in a big way, to be sure) a sentence's blueprint, which is explained by a semantic theory. Underpinning the difference between identifying what A said and what he implied is a distinction in the type of typical *input*: to identify what A *said* on given occasion by uttering X the pragmatic system typically takes as its primary input what the speaker said. This leaves many questions open: (1) To what extent is pragmatic processing deductive? (2) To what extent does it take place unconsciously? (3) What sorts of things affect its speed? (4) To what extent is it task-specific or modular?

21. *Underdetermination.* It is now possible to bring together several points. The role of a pragmatic theory in identifying what A said by uttering X on a given occasion is not restricted to identifying who or what A is referring to by any referential expressions in X. Saying involves referring and predicating; and just as identifying what A is up with any referential devices in X involves more than consulting a mental lexicon, so does identifying what he is upto with any predicative devices in X. It may, for example, require the 'saturation' of an 'implicit argument' as in 'it's raining' or 'I've finished'. (Some implicit arguments may be mandated by syntax as well as semantics.) Or it may require 'enriching' a predicate in some way that is reasonably obvious and presumably acceptable to A. The sentence 'every woman has a job' might be used to say that every woman in Flint has a job, or that every woman in Woodside has a job, etc.

It will pay to separate and rejoin two points here, one epistemological, the other metaphysical, both intimately connected to the points made earlier about *Asymmetry* and *Reciprocity*. The epistemological point concerns *insufficiency*, the metaphysical point *underdetermination*. From the hearer's perspective, we can talk first about the fact that knowledge of the syntax of X and knowledge of the meanings of all the words in X do not suffice for identifying what A is saying by uttering X (even where the superficial form evinces no lexical or structural ambiguity). At most they yield a blueprint. Now we can bring in A himself. What A says is wholly determined by certain specific intentions he had in speaking, intentions massively constrained by his knowledge of syntax and word meaning (and a whole lot more). A tacitly knows that B's knowledge of word meaning and syntax will not suffice to furnish B with a complete account of what he has said. We can now introduce some theoretical shorthand to obviate the need to keep talking about speakers' and hearers' knowledge, tacit or otherwise. Let us say that syntax and word meaning together *underdetermine* what is said (all the time remembering this is shorthand). But we are not yet where we need to be. The first thesis we need is this:

(IT) *The Insufficiency Thesis.* Identifying what a speaker or writer, A, is *saying* by uttering an unambiguous, declarative sentence X on a given occasion goes well beyond recovering X's underlying syntax, knowing the meanings of all of the words in X, and identifying who or what A is referring to by any referential expressions in X.

This goes beyond the insufficiency just mentioned because it entails that even when B has identified who A is referring to by any referential expressions in X (/John/, /he/, /here/, /that/, /I/, /you/, and so on), B still doesn't have everything he needs to identify what A said. A tacitly knows that B's knowledge of word meaning, knowledge of syntax, *and* knowledge of who or what A is referring to by any referring expressions in X will not suffice to furnish B with a complete account of what he has said. Corresponding to this we can formulate the shorthand we really want:

(UT) *The Underdetermination Thesis.* What A *says* by uttering an unambiguous, declarative sentence X on a given occasion is underdetermined by X's syntax, the meanings of the words (and any other morphemes) in X (and the meanings, if any, of prosodic features of X), and the assignment of references to any referring expressions in X.[39]

---

[39] The Underdetermination Thesis is regularly stressed by linguistic pragmatists, and some view it as a cornerstone of the general outlook. This use of 'underdetermination' is found in the work of Sperber and Wilson (1986, 1995) and borrowed by many of those they have influenced, including Bezuidenhout, Blakemore, Carston, Papafragou, Recanati, Rouchota, and me (*Descriptions*, 1990: 105 n. 16; 114 n. 46; 116 n. 54). In the language of Perry (1986, 2000, 2001), talk of underdetermination is roughly equivalent to talk of constituents of propositions expressed that are 'unarticulated', i.e. constituents corresponding to no constituents of the sentence uttered. (As Perry sometimes puts it, we don't always articulate things when it's clear from context what they are.) I don't know why underdetermination is rejected so vehemently by some philosophers of language, but I have a suspicion two related factors may be implicated, both involving fear and philosophical temperament. The first is a simple unwillingness to concede apparently hard-earned territory, a reluctance to accept that some of the traditional problems involved in so-called 'compositional semantics' are actually the products of specious questions in the philosophy of *language* with genuine and important counterparts in the philosophy of *mind*, mostly about *inference* and *the composition of thought* (a reluctance to accept that as far as natural language is concerned, trying to build pure *content* is as futile as trying to build pure *character*). The reluctance, it seems to me, amounts to little more than obstinacy or fear of a philosophical pink slip. The second fear might be viewed as an extension of the first: the fear that if there is not at least one component (what is said) of what a speaker means that can be nailed down precisely and completely without taking into account too many 'pragmatic considerations', then systematic semantics as typically understood is doomed, and with it any chance of producing a serious theory of language. This fear seems to me entirely unwarranted. Natural

As far as constructing and evaluating a theory of interpretation are concerned, we must make sure we separate talk of (a) the *interpretive target* (stipulated in advance by the theorist in particular cases on the basis of intuitive judgement, modulo reflective equilibrium with the best theory up to that point), and talk of (b) the *knowledge and mechanisms* in play (under investigation and hypothesized by the theorist). And in talk of knowledge and mechanisms we must be careful to separate (i) the role of syntax; (ii) the role of word meaning; and (iii) the actual pragmatic mechanisms.

An interpretive target is a characterization of what our intuitive judgements reveal the speaker to have said and which an adequate theory of interpretation should deliver. It is common to specify interpretive targets using more language: By uttering 'she has a job' A is saying that Margaret Thatcher has a job; by uttering 'every woman has a job' A is saying that every woman living in Woodside has a job. There is, of course, something a bit funny about this, for surely we can now ask for a characterization of *what the theorist said* when he uttered the sentence 'By uttering "every woman has a job", A is saying that every woman living in Woodside has a job'. Nonetheless, this is what we do, and when pressed often we wheel out some set theory: By uttering 'every woman has a job', A is saying something that is true if at the time of utterance *t*, the intersection of the set of things that are women at *t* and the set of things living in Woodside at *t* is a subset of the set of things that have jobs at *t*. While this may provide us with the conditions under which what A said is true, it falls short of specifying *what* A said for familiar reasons. (First, A is sure to deny it. Second, surely A would have said something different had he uttered 'every woman has a job and $19^2 = 361$'.) So when pressed again we wheel out something like a *situation* or a *structured proposition*.

Where *knowledge* of syntax, word meaning, and the theory of blueprints are concerned, there is much work to be done by philosophers of language and linguists together. As far as *mechanisms* are concerned, we are squarely in the realm of psychology, and some philosophers of language and linguists may well opt out here. The psychological part of the overall project may certainly be informed by philosophical reflections, such as Grice's, on the nature of rational, purposive behaviour, but ultimately it is a wholly empirical enterprise the aim of which is to identify the cognitive mechanisms whereby the hearer effects the relevant identifications on a given occasion.

language semantics may not be quite as straightforward or far-reaching as many have thought, but there is plenty of systematic semantics for all of us (and more) to do for longer than we will ever have to do it.

22. *Indeterminacy*. What a speaker says and implies may be indeterminate in at least the following sense: in any vocabulary in which what someone says or implies can be usefully specified, there will be alternative and strictly distinct specifications between which no principled choice can be made. We should not worry that indeterminacy of this sort presents problems for particular semantic proposals. (For example, we should not regard traditional accounts of descriptions as damaged in any way by the indeterminacy attaching to intuitive 'completions' of those that are said to be 'incomplete' relative to particular occasions of utterance.)

23. *Convergence*. A univocal saying–implying distinction is *empirical, ordinary,* and *beneficial (practical)*. The distinction is empirical in so far as it assumes that, typically, representations corresponding to what A said and implied are the outputs of cognitive mechanisms involved in the interpretation process. It corresponds to something entrenched in ordinary talk (despite the fact that we may disagree in particular cases). And it underpins the very idea of codifying principles meant to regulate societies and the behaviour of their members (e.g. laws, contracts, and commitments) by virtue of being a distinction one side of which (saying) is about as *objective* as anything can be, a fact itself guaranteed by the empirical and ordinary nature of the distinction. (To say this is not to say there cannot be disputes about what was said, changes of opinion after discussion of problematic cases, or specialists (or at least professionals) in societies to whom tough cases are referred when the issue needs forcing. Rather it is to say that there is enough overlap in judgement to render regulation, commitment, and so on meaningful notions.)

24. *Formalism*. Advances in our thinking about language have come out of developments in logic and formal philosophy, particularly by way of the construction and use of various types of broadly mathematical theories, systems, or analyses—the predicate calculus, model theory, modal logics, set theory, recursion theory, and generalized quantifier theory to name the most obvious. But it does not follow that associating utterances with models, possible worlds, structured propositions, indices, functions, or even favoured formalisms *eo ipso* constitutes part of a theory of utterance interpretation. Rigorous formalism almost certainly has its place in articulating certain parts of a theory of interpretation; but a favoured mathematical idea and an associated formalism must not so dominate our inquiry that the questions motivating it in the first place become obscured or transmogrified to the point of demanding purely technical answers. We should strive to use our formalisms judiciously, sparingly, only where they were needed to effect a useful idealization or abstraction, forestall a

potential ambiguity, capture a generalization, facilitate a transition, or usefully abbreviate something. Appeals to, say, higher-order functions or set-theoretic entities (and the use of corresponding notations) are ultimately dispensable in the theory of interpretation, sets and functions being no more than occasional, transitory tools of no intrinsic interest outside mathematics proper and the philosophy thereof. Such entities are not the objects of semantic investigation themselves, and it should not be a goal of any branch of philosophy to drag them into investigations whenever the opportunity presents itself.

4. Pronouns and Anchors

Following Grice, let us talk about what a speaker A *means* on a given occasion by uttering some sentence X, factoring this into what A *says* and what he (merely) *implies*. As Grice notes, *identifying* what the speaker is saying is not simply a matter of identifying X and recovering its linguistic meaning (blueprint), if only because of the existence of pronouns. Unlike some of his critics, Grice is careful not to run together epistemological and metaphysical points here, despite their evident interconnectedness. The important metaphysical question is: what *determines* what a speaker said on a given occasion? And the Gricean answer is: certain specific *intentions* he had in producing his utterance, intentions that are severely constrained by his beliefs about the meanings of the words he uses, about his audience, about the context, about the topic of conversation, and probably a whole lot more.[40] The important epistemological question is: what knowledge or information does a hearer use in *identifying* what the speaker said? And the Gricean answer is: knowledge of the linguistic meaning of the sentence uttered, pragmatic knowledge about the way rational, cooperative beings operate, knowledge about the speaker, knowledge of context, and just about anything else he can get his hands on. Let us take a concrete example. If I say something by uttering a sentence X that contains the personal pronoun 'he' and the demonstrative 'this', then (in the simplest case, at any rate) my referential intentions determine who I mean by 'he' and what I meant by 'this'. (Similarly, my lexical intentions determine what I meant by /bank/ if X contains one of the words we write that way.) Your job as hearer is to identify what I meant by uttering X, and very likely you will not succeed unless you identify who I meant by 'he' and what I meant by 'this'. (Similarly, what I meant by /bank/.)

---

[40] See Grice (1989).

Sperber and Wilson (1986, 1995) point out that pronouns are just the beginning: quite generally, what a speaker says is underdetermined by the meaning of the sentence uttered, even relative to reference assignment. Now one can perfectly consistently accept Sperber and Wilson's underdetermination thesis without rushing to embrace the details of their Relevance Theory, as Récanati (1987, 1989, 1993, 2001) does and as I do in *Descriptions* (1990: 105 n. 16; 114 n. 46). For that theory is meant to provide an account of the mechanics of utterance interpretation, of the richly inferential processes providing the basis of an empirically satisfying account of how interpreters (i) identify which sentence a speaker has produced on a given occasion in cases where identification of phonological form fails to yield a unique result; (ii) identify what the speaker *said* by uttering X on a given occasion in cases where identification of the meaning of X falls short; and (iii) identify what the speaker implied by uttering X on that occasion. Relevance Theory goes well beyond the thesis that the meaning of a sentence X may underdetermine what a speaker says by uttering it on a given occasion and well beyond the vague Gricean idea that quite general principles governing the way we reason about the behaviour of others lie at the heart of an explanation of how we communicate.

In principle just about any information could be relevant or brought to bear on interpretation, and one of the main problems involved in constructing a pragmatic theory is explaining how the information that actually *is* brought to bear is delimited.[41] The second problem concerns *how* it is brought to bear. Linguistic pragmatism finds little sense in the idea that two quite distinct sets of information-gathering and inferential mechanisms are at work when a hearer tries to identify what a speaker means, one set that works on sentence meanings and yields what the speaker said, and another set that works on what the speaker said and yields what he meant but did not say (i.e. what he implied).

It is odd that some philosophers write as if (or even claim that) two quite distinct sets of cognitive mechanisms must be at work. I detect two related ideas lurking behind this assumption: (i) something to do with 'simplicity' (or 'degree of difficulty') or 'systematicity' (or 'range of possibilities'); (ii) the influence of 'indexical logics'.

(i) While it is true that identifying who or what a speaker intends to be referring to on a given occasion by some particular referring expression X

---

[41] There is a division here between the optimists and the pessimists. Unlike Sperber and Wilson, Blakemore (1987), Carston (2002), and other Relevance Theorists, Fodor (1983, 2001), Chomsky (2000), and Davidson (1986) suspect that producing an overarching theory of interpretation will require nothing short of a complete theory of mind. I'm not sure where Perry lies on this scale. For discussion, see Carston (2002).

is constrained by the linguistic conventions governing the use of X, this does not necessarily make matters particularly straightforward or reduce the number of hypotheses that could, in principle, be investigated and assessed. Consider the interpretation of an utterance of the pronoun 'it'. As Sperber and Wilson (1986: 187) note, all that the linguistic conventions governing the pronoun 'it' insist upon, in any context, is that the object should be non-human, giving every hearer in every context an indefinitely large choice of possible referents. And surely the same general considerations about, say, relevance, truthfulness, informativeness, or whatever, that are invoked in identifying what a speaker is implying on a given occasion will be invoked in identifying who or what a speaker is referring to by 'it' on a given occasion.

The point can also be made in connection with an incomplete description like 'the table' or some other incomplete quantifier expression like 'every man' or 'no one'. It is sometimes said that identifying what A says by uttering a sentence containing such an expression involves either (*a*) coming up with an appropriate domain of quantification *implicit* in the utterance (the 'implicit' approach), or (*b*) coming up with an appropriately 'richer' nominal A could have used to make his meaning more *explicit* (the 'explicit' approach).[42] Whatever the final merits of such suggestions, one thing is quite clear: the same general considerations about, say, relevance, truthfulness, informativeness, or whatever, that are invoked in identifying what a speaker is implying on a given occasion will have to be invoked in identifying an appropriate domain or an appropriate completing expression.[43]

(ii) Many philosophers write as if (or even argue that) understanding what a speaker A said on a given occasion by uttering a sentence X with its conventional meaning is a matter determined by the meaning of that sentence and a 'context', in a sense of this frequently invoked word that is meant to make it more than simply a label for whatever it is that 'bridges the gap' between the meaning of X and what A said by uttering X on that occasion. For example, it is frequently claimed that all

---

[42] For detailed discussion, see Neale (forthcoming *a*).

[43] Postulating an aphonic indexical, *domain* variable in underlying syntax makes no more of a contribution to explaining *how* hearers interpret utterances than does postulating an aphonic indexical *assertion* variable in underlying syntax (or an aphonic indexical *irony* variable). That is, the interpretive task facing the hearer is made no easier by the existence of an aphonic contextual variable, even when, as in the case of the supposed assertion or irony variables, there are just two possible values to choose from. And of course, giving phonetic form to such operators—'asserting-or-not, it's Tuesday' or 'being-ironical-or-not, it's a lovely day'—doesn't help the hearer either. However, if it can be demonstrated that such variables are bindable, then their existence might, be justified though far from required on minimalist assumptions. (On the purported bindability of domain variables, see Stanley and Szabó 2000 and Stanley 2000, 2002.)

one needs to bridge the gap is some sort of formal object, an 'index' or 'context' in the form of an ordered *n*-tuple that secures the references of a few annoying 'indexical' pronouns ('I', 'you', and 'he', for example) and one or two other 'indexical' words that have a somewhat pronominal nature ('here' and 'now', for example).[44]

This idea is rightly spurned by Sperber and Wilson (in *Relevance*), by Evans (in *The Varieties of Reference* and *Collected Papers*) and by Chomsky (in *Reflections on Language* and practically every book or article he has written in which the interpretation of pronouns is discussed). For there is an implicit recognition in these works, and in many others that bear their influence, that while formal contexts may have a useful *methodological* role from time to time, they are strictly irrelevant to a proper theory of utterance interpretation.

For various semantic and syntactic purposes, it is often desirable—if not mandatory—to abstract or idealize away from facts to do with particular speech situations—'pragmatic' or 'contextual' factors, as they are sometimes called—in order to get on with a particular piece of work. And as long as caution is exercised there is no harm in this. For example, *with certain restricted purposes in mind*—and without any sort of absurd commitment to the idea that such entities play a role in utterance interpretation—formal 'indices' can be introduced to serve as 'contexts' with which sentences can be paired in order to 'anchor' or 'co-anchor' the interpretations of certain indexical expressions. The usual idea is to treat such expressions as indexicals construed as free variables and treat indices as sequences or functions that assign these variables values. Famously, this idea has been used to capture model-theoretically the validity of inferences whose premises and conclusions are stated using indexical sentences:[45]

A: If the next left is not Bank Street, that man gave you the wrong directions.
B: It's not Bank Street; so he gave me the wrong directions.[46]

[44] The word 'indexical' is itself part if the problem, suggesting as it does that interpreting such devices involves merely looking something up in an 'index'. People can be more influenced by labels than they sometimes realize.

[45] See e.g. Kaplan (1989); Lewis (1972); Montague (1974). A lot in this area turns on one's conception of logic, and my wording evinces a particular stance, though not one I want to insist on: logical relations hold among what is expressed by sentences not among sentences themselves. (Various issues about the notion of formal validity and inference rule must be faced (but usually are not) by people who hold this view of logic.) The point I am making in the text is not dependent upon this stance. Cf. discussions of the difference between the logical form of a proposition and the logical form of a particular sentence used to express that proposition.

[46] A related point might be made in connection with anaphora:

Every man loves his mother
John is a man
———————————
John loves his mother.

It is paramount in such work to keep things tightly under control in the following sense: the logician wants a mechanism that can (*a*) scan a set of sentences for occurrences of symbols on some pre-existing list of devices that do not carry their values with them, then (*b*) use an index to assign a value to each occurrence of such a symbol. If this goes well, logical deductions can proceed (assuming a semantics for items of a pre-selected 'logical' vocabulary of course). If there is still slippage after the index has made its assignments, on standard assumptions there is only one solution: posit further indexical symbols in the sentences involved, symbols which are invisible in surface syntax yet revealed by an analysis of their 'logical forms', then try again.[47]

In the philosophy of language, indices have a methodological role for they can be used to anchor or co-anchor indexical and anaphoric expressions and so allow work to proceed more easily on *other* expressions and on what people say (and imply for that matter) by uttering them on given occasions.[48] However, there is an idea that has emerged from work on indexical logics for which we can have little sympathy. This is the idea that sentence meanings and contexts can be paired to provide something of *empirical* significance: what a *sentence X says relative to a context C.*[49] We must not lose sight of certain facts. First, as far as utterance interpretation is concerned, such 'contexts' are strictly irrelevant. Utterances do not come with

---

[47] It is, perhaps, tacit recognition of this fact that has led some philosophers to conclude that there is no hope of producing a theory of *utterance interpretation* without positing all sorts of aphonic, indexical elements in the underlying syntax of natural language sentences. We may use anything we like to throw light on the syntax of natural language, but we must never lose sight of the fact that discerning the syntactic structures of our sentences is an empirical exercise. Certainly the idea of aphonic elements in syntax is not objectionable in itself. On the assumption that syntax relates sound and meaning, we must certainly allow for the possibility of elements that have sound but no meaning ('it' in 'it's raining'?), or meaning but no sound (the understood subject of 'leave' in 'Tom wants to leave'?). And there can be little doubt today that great advances in our understanding of syntax have been made by those such as Chomsky who have not shied away from aphonic items in syntax and argued for their existence and explanatory value. But we cannot simply *assume* that whenever we encounter some feature of what is said that does not appear to correspond to any element or feature of the sentence uttered it follows that there is some element in underlying syntax waiting to be exposed.

[48] See Neale (1990, ch. 3), for example.

[49] I am putting aside here some very real concerns about talk of *sentences* saying things relative to contexts. I am sceptical about the value or relevance of the use of the verb 'say' assumed in this way of talking to the project of constructing a theory of utterance interpretation, unless it is understood as a stylistic variant of talk of *speakers* saying things by uttering sentences on given occasions. Judgements about what a *speaker* said, and about whether what he said was true or false in specified situations, constitute the primary data for a theory of interpretation, the data it is the business of such a theory to explain. What a speaker *says* and what he *implies* (e.g. conversationally implicates) on a given occasion are the things that together constitute what the speaker *means*, and a theory of interpretation is meant to explain the role of linguistic meaning and inference in the hearer's identification of what the

such devices attached that anchor or co-anchor indexical, demonstrative, or anaphoric pronouns. The hearer has plenty of *pragmatic* work to do, much of it rightly called inferential, albeit inferential in a way that is steered by the meanings of individual words. A few passages from Evans (1982, 1985) summarize the situation well:

All that the conventions governing the referring expression 'he' insist upon, in any given context, is that the object referred to should be male. (1982: 312)

There is no linguistic rule which determines that a 'he' or a 'that man' refers to x rather than y in the vicinity, or that it refers to someone who has just left rather than someone who has been recently mentioned. (1985: 230–1).

'This' and 'that' are even less specific, contributing merely the vaguest suggestion of a contrast between nearer and further (in some generalised sense) . . . [*Footnote*: Often the *predicate* does more to narrow down the range of possible interpretations of the referring expression than does the referring expression itself . . .]. (1982: 312)

Let me take another example: the expression 'you': If a speaker addresses a remark to someone, saying, 'You are a crook', it is surely clear that an identification is called for on the part of the audience: in order to understand the remark, it is not enough to know that there is one, and only one, person whom the speaker is addressing, and that the speaker is saying of that person that he is a crook . . . a quite specific *kind* of identification is called for; the person addressed has not understood the remark unless he realizes that the speaker is saying that *he* is a crook. . . . understanding the remark requires the hearer to know *of* an individual that he is being addressed. (1982: 314)

Nothing about the meaning of the word 'you' tells you that you are being addressed.[50]

---

speaker meant. No one has intuitions about *what is said by a sentence X relative to a context C* or about the truth or falsity of X relative to C unless this is just a formal way of talking about what the speaker said by uttering X on a particular occasion—the occasion that C is being used to partially model or approximate. If such talk is straightforwardly transposable into talk about what the speaker said, then we can accept its empirical significance. If it is not so transposable, then its empirical significance must be justified in some other way, from *within* the theory of interpretation by reference to some empirical role it is required to play in an explanation of what a speaker says and implies by uttering X on a given occasion, in much the same way that notions such as LF, scope, and binding are motivated from within. If some such motivation is forthcoming, we should be only too happy to listen. I suspect it will not be forthcoming because the notion of what a *sentence says* relative to a context is going to be too thin and overly detached from speakers' communicative intentions to carry any empirical weight. Nonetheless, I adopt a wait-and-see approach. We are involved in an empirical enterprise after all.

[50] As soon as we introduce anaphoric pronouns—those that are linked in some interpretive fashion to other expressions (their 'antecedents')—matters become more complicated. The reflexive 'himself' *must be* so linked; the non-reflexives 'he', 'him', and 'his' *can be* so linked (under certain conditions). Very roughly, reflexives cannot be 'too far away' from their antecedents, and non-reflexives cannot be 'too

Quite generally, there is something artificial about construing the meanings of (e.g.) 'I', 'we', 'you', 'he', 'she', 'it', 'they', 'this', 'that', 'these', 'those', 'here', 'now', 'there', 'then', 'today', 'yesterday', and 'tomorrow' as functions from contexts to references. The meanings of these devices, as Evans (1982, 1985), and Sperber and Wilson (1986) stress, are just *constraints* on references, more precisely constraints on the referential intentions with which the devices can be used. I am mystified why much mainstream philosophy of language misses this. We need to distinguish two ideas about formal contexts, one sensible, the other silly. The silly idea is that utterances come with pre-packaged 'contexts' that provide values for indexical expressions. The sensible idea is what I call *methodological anchoring (anchoring* for short). For various pragmatic, semantic, and syntactic purposes, it is often helpful, perhaps even mandatory, for a theorist to abstract from various 'contextual effects' or 'pragmatic factors' in order to get on with a piece of work, and so it is sometimes useful to use an 'index' as a way of anchoring the interpretations of indexical expressions that are not, at that moment, the objects of primary concern, *even though the theorist knows the interpretation of these indexicals is not as straightforward as invoking an index might suggest.* If one is working on definite descriptions, for example, one might want to prescind, as much as possible, from the effects of, say, indexical pronouns occurring inside nominals; and if one is working on 'and', for example, one might want to prescind, as much as possible, from the effects of, say, indexical pronouns occurring inside conjuncts:[51]

(1) *he* drove home and *he* drank those six beers *you* bought *him*
(2) *he* drank those six beers *you* bought *him* and *he* drove home.

To this end, we might use an index to anchor or co-anchor these expressions, to keep their special features and the complexities they introduce out of the picture as it were.[52]

close' to them, putting the two in virtual complementary distribution as far as interpretive dependence is concerned, as suggested by Chomsky's (1981, 1986) Binding Theory. See below.

[51] The following examples are due to Deirdre Wilson.

[52] Carston (1988, 1993, 2002) implicitly anchors in her examinations of 'pragmatic enrichments' in connection with utterances of conjunctions (indeed, it is what she implicitly does throughout). Similarly, Evans implicitly anchors in *The Varieties of Reference* (and elsewhere), Sperber and Wilson do it throughout *Relevance* (and elsewhere), and I do it explicitly in ch. 3 of *Descriptions* in connection with the effects of indexicals appearing in definite descriptions such as the following:

(i) the first person *I* saw this morning
(ii) *my* mother
(iii) the *present* king of France
(iv) the girl who made *this*.

A certain amount of care is needed in the use of the word 'semantic' when indices are used to anchor (or co-anchor) indexical expressions. To the extent that we are investigating the conventions governing a word whose role cannot be set out clearly without taking into account the conventions governing other expression(s) with which it combines to form larger expressions, we may find it convenient to talk about the (derived) conventions governing the larger phrases with respect to a particular index. For example, if the semantics of 'the' is being investigated, it may be useful, even mandatory, to anchor indexicals so that *other* contextual effects may be monitored. And although we may want to talk about the 'linguistic meaning' of, the 'semantics' of, or the 'conventions governing' an indexical or any other expression, we may also wish to talk about its 'semantic value' relative to a particular index, the object conveniently assigned to it by an index in order that work on pressing matters is not held up needlessly.[53] There is no harm in such talk as long as everyone is clear about what is going on. 'Semantic values' in this sense are just *stipulated interpretations*, and the anchoring it involves is quite consistent with the idea that the interpretation of indexical expressions is basically a pragmatic matter only steered by semantic constraints.

Although I have not seen the point discussed explicitly in the literature, I get the impression some 'anti-pragmatist' sentiment may have as its underlying source the worry that it involves self-suspension, a willingness to abstract from contextual effects in ways that are self-defeating or paradoxical. In reality, the situation is not that different from Neurath's. The pragmatist certainly has to tread carefully, all the while monitoring for and then abstracting from aspects of what is said that are not fixed by syntax and word meaning, and as a matter of working practice, subtle and silent measures are usually taken to prevent things from becoming unmanageable, measures that certainly narrow the pragmatist's options on the vexed matter of the relation between linguistic structure and the structure of thought.[54] Pragmatist abstractions from context are always going to be juggling acts, the artistry of which is rather like that involved in solving for several variables at once while looking for an unknown number of others that are not yet in the equation and cannot be located without extremely good approximate values for those that are. On the basis of perceived use, intuition, discussions with friends, books we have read, and who knows what else, we isolate what we take to be the 'linguistic

Chomsky also does something analogous to anchoring in every work in which he discusses pronouns. (I say 'analogous' because of Chomsky's concerns about reference.)

[53] This convenience is employed time and again in *Descriptions*.

[54] If there is a worry about pragmatism, it surely resides here and not in minutiae like relativization (implicit binding).

meaning' or 'semantics' of an expression α—its invariant role in determining what someone says by uttering sentences containing it—not unreasonably confident that certain things speakers mean when they use α in their speech and writing are explicable in very general terms as things they only imply, and are not of a gravity sufficient to make us question the meaning we think we have isolated. Holding the meaning of α constant, we go on to investigate and isolate the meaning of β and find we can make some headway by appealing to 'facts' about the meaning of α. And so on, until we get further up the alphabet and find our best attempts at meaning isolation force us seriously to question whether we were really right about all of α, β, γ, etc., and to re-examine our methods of abstraction and idealization, which may have led us to oversimplify in ways we now worry about. Certainly it takes some skill to keep all of the balls in the air in a stable configuration.

5. Pronouns and Anaphora

I have been struck, when discussing or lecturing on linguistic pragmatism, how often people assume it implies, or at least strongly suggests, a 'pragmatic' theory of pronouns along the lines of those recommended by Chomsky (1976), Lasnik (1976), or K. Bach (1987, 1994).[55] According to such theories, the third-person pronouns in the following sentences are interpreted in a uniform manner:

(1) He's up early
(2) Mary loves him
(3) John's wife loves him
(4) John loves his wife
(5) Mary thinks John loves his wife
(6) John thinks his wife loves him.

They all function as referring expressions, it is claimed. In each case the speaker is free to choose any male he likes. Even John. No special *co-referential* or otherwise *anaphoric* use of 'he' or 'him' or 'his' is exemplified by any of these sentences. Co-reference is a 'pragmatic' matter. John is just one of the legitimate referents for an indexical use of, say, 'his' in (4). And in such cases 'his' and 'John' are co-referential. No rule of grammar is involved, and to that extent the phenomenon of co-reference is not illuminated by talk of *anaphora*, construed as a grammatical notion.

---

[55] This label is employed by Evans (1980) and K. Bach (1987, 1994).

At first blush, the pragmatic theory of pronouns is economical, relying, as it does, on a single reading of, say, 'his'. It is, however, forced to posit a second, *bound* reading of pronouns, to be employed when they are hooked up to quantified expressions, and heroic efforts would be needed to reduce binding to indexicality. More importantly, the pragmatic theory just makes the wrong empirical predictions in very many cases and is, in any case, unilluminating of the way pronouns are used.[56] At the heart of the right theory, I maintain, is the thesis that every pronoun *seemingly* anaphoric on a name α (or any other referring expression) is either (i) *bound* by α (in the usual semantic sense) or else (ii) an occurrence of an indexical that is merely co-referential with α. It will take some time to work up to the sort of general theory I think will be satisfactory, but it will help to see where I am going if I state three of the main theses immediately.

1. *Binding*. The pronouns in (4)–(6) *do* admit of readings upon which they are anaphoric on 'John'; and on those readings they are *not* co-referential with 'John' but *bound* by it in precisely the same way they are bound by 'every man' on the analogous readings of (4′)–(6′):[57]

(4′) every man loves his wife
(5′) Mary thinks every man loves his wife
(6′) every man thinks his wife loves him.

More generally, if a pronoun β is genuinely anaphoric on an expression α, that is because α binds β. It is important to appreciate that although the analysis of (4) according to which 'his' is bound by 'John' is equivalent to an analysis according to which 'his' is de jure co-referential with 'John', this is merely an artefact of the example. The corresponding analyses are not equivalent for sentences (5) and (6).[58]

2. *Co-reference*. From the fact that anaphora always involves binding, it follows that co-reference plays no role whatsoever in a theory of pronominal anaphora. Anaphora involves only binding. Reference and co-reference are pragmatic notions (as the 'pragmatic' theory says). Speakers use names, demonstratives, descriptions, and pronouns to refer to people, places, and things. Furthermore, sometimes they use such expressions, particularly pronouns, to refer to things

---

[56] On this matter, I find myself largely in agreement with points made by Evans (1977, 1980), Geach (1962), Partee (1975), Sag (1976), Soames (1989, 1990, 1994), and Williams (1977).

[57] The proposal is essentially Geach's (1962).

[58] Partee (1975); Soames (1990, 1994). I am not here concerned with the de dicto readings of (5) and (6), the truth of which do not require anyone to actually have a wife.

they have already referred to. In such cases we get co-reference. We can call this 'pragmatic anaphora' or 'discourse anaphora' or 'unbound anaphora' if we like; but let us not confuse the notion with linguistic, i.e. bound, anaphora.[59]

3. *Determiners*. Following Postal (1966) and others, third-person pronouns are definite determiners. We must be careful, then, to distinguish the determiner $[_{D}he]$ from the full determiner phrase $[_{DP}[_{D}he][_{NP}e]]$, where the NP e is aphonic. The entire DP is in effect a definite description, hence a quantificational expression.

In the next few sections I am going to abstract from speakers' intentions in order that we may focus on constraints on the interpretation of pronouns imposed by grammar. When the time is right, the picture of pronouns that develops will be set in a broader pragmatist picture.

6. Pronouns in Generative Grammar

One weakness in early work on pronouns undertaken by philosophers was inherited from the dominant 'descriptive' picture of reference that would be overturned in the early 1970s.[60] Another stemmed from failures to appreciate ways in which grammatical structure constrains scope possibilities and thereby bound variable readings of pronouns. By contrast, the principal weakness in early work undertaken by linguists stemmed primarily from failures to appreciate logical, semantic, and epistemic distinctions that seemed self-evident to philosophers weaned on a common fare of logical puzzles and truth definitions for formal languages. The situation in both disciplines improved dramatically in the 1970s and 1980s as a result of fertile interaction;[61] and a better understanding

---

[59] If this is right, the labels 'anaphora' and 'anaphoric pronoun' are ill-chosen, and we would be better off just talking about *binding* and *bound pronouns*. In *The New Shorter Oxford English Dictionary* we find the following under anaphora: '*Rhet.* The repetition of the same word or phrase in several successive clauses . . . *Ling.* The use of an expression which refers to or stands for an earlier word or group of words.' In *Webster's* we find this: '*Rhet.* repetition of a word or words at the beginning of two or more successive verses, clauses, or sentences . . . *Gram.* the use of a word as a regular grammatical substitute for a preceding word or group of words.' (*Webster's* goes on to give us an example: 'as the use of *it* and *do* in *I know it and he does too.*') As far as pronouns are concerned, perhaps 'anaphora' would be more properly applied where we have what Geach (1972) calls *pronouns of laziness*. Be that as it may, the word is used widely in linguistics and philosophy and there is no turning back the clock.

[60] Kripke (1980); Kaplan (1989).

[61] Chomsky (1981); Cooper (1979); Evans (1977, 1980, 1982); Harman (1972); Heim (1982, 1988); Higginbotham (1980, 1983a); Kamp (1981/1984); Karttunen (1976); Keenan (1971); Lakoff (1972); Lasnik (1976); Lewis (1975); McCawley (1976); May (1977); Partee (1972); Reinhart (1976, 1978); Sag (1976); Wasow (1972); Williams (1977).

emerged of the ways in which the interpretation of pronouns reflects general organizing principles of grammar.[62] Work from that period is still at the centre of much current research, although grammatical theory underwent one of its periodic 'perspective' changes in the 1990s, the implications of which are still being examined in connection with what is known as the Binding Theory.[63] A potted history of how pronouns have been regarded by generative linguists will help frame the issues we need to address.

One of the central ideas in generative linguistics in the 1960s was a distinction between a sentence's *surface* structure and its *deep* structure.[64] Deep structures were generated by context-free phrase structure rules such as

$$S \rightarrow NP + VP$$
$$VP \rightarrow V + NP.$$

Transformational rules would then map deep structures into surface structures by processes that might delete, add, reorder, or substitute constituents.[65] For example, a surface structure of roughly the form of (1) might be derived by a *pas-sivization* transformation from something of roughly the form of (1′):

(1) Mary was kissed by John
(1′) John kissed Mary.

The surface structure (2) might be derived from the deep structure (2′):

(2) John wishes to leave
(2′) John$_1$ wishes John$_1$ to leave

by a *deletion* transformation on the basis of an *identity* in the latter, the presence of two distinct occurrences of the same noun phrase 'John', marked in some way in grammar as co-referential, perhaps using integers as indices.[66] That identity

---

[62] Chomsky (1981); Higginbotham (1980). [63] Chomsky (1995, 2000); Reuland (2001a, b).
[64] Chomsky (1964, 1965).

[65] Strictly, deletions and additions suffice to produce reorderings and substitutions, but it was easier to work with more complex transformations.

[66] Chomsky (1965); Postal (1966). The non-synonymy of (2) and (2′), and related pairs, was not appreciated by linguists at the time. Consider,

(i) Mary thinks John wishes to leave.

For an utterance of this to be true Mary must believe that John satisfies *x wants x to leave*. It is not enough that Mary believe he satisfies *x wants John to leave*. Furthermore, any adequate account of the original sentence (2) must reflect the fact that an utterance of it cannot be true unless (roughly) John conceives of the experiencer of his wish and the agent of the wished-for event (or at least the

of form was required seemed clear from the fact that the deletion transformation could not apply to, say, 'John wants Mary to leave'; that identity of interpretation was required seemed evident from the fact that (2) cannot be used to say that John Lennon wants John Wayne to leave.[67]

It seemed natural within this framework to explore the idea that anaphoric pronouns were the superficial manifestations of fuller noun phrases, derived by a *pronominalization* and *reflexivization* transformations.[68] The surface structures (3) and (4) (on their anaphoric readings), for example, were taken by some linguists to be derived transformationally from the deep structures (3′) and (4′), respectively (on the basis of noun phrase identity in those deep structures):

(3) John$_1$ thinks he$_1$ is the best person for the job

(3′) John$_1$ thinks John$_1$ is the best person for the job

(4) John$_1$ loves his$_1$ wife

(4′) John$_1$ loves John$_1$'s wife.

---

agent of an event of the wished-for type) as identical. (Stephen Schiffer has suggested to me that this is too strong and over-intellectualizes what is involved. I think he may be right, but there is an itch here that needs scratching.) This is not so for every utterance of (2′). On a closely related note, consider the non-synonymy of (ii) and (ii′), discussed in detail by Fodor (1975: 133–41):

(ii) Only Churchill remembers giving the speech about blood, sweat, toil, and tears.

(ii″) Only Churchill remembers Churchill giving the speech about blood, sweat, toil, and tears.

Contemporary syntactic theory maintains that in both (i) and (ii) the embedded clause, infinitival in (i), gerundive in (ii), has as its subject an aphonic pronoun PRO. The contrast between (ii) and (ii′), as well as that between (2) and (2′) in the text, shows that the interpretive properties of PRO must differ from those of names. Moreover, the contrast between (ii) and (ii″) shows that the interpretation of PRO must differ from those of reflexive pronouns:

(ii‴) Only Churchill remembers himself giving the speech about blood, sweat, toil, and tears.

Any adequate account of (ii) must reflect the fact that an utterance of it cannot be true unless (roughly) Churchill conceives of the experiencer of the memory and the agent of the remembered event as identical. (Again, Schiffer's worries loom large.) For extensive discussions of these and related issues, see Castañeda (1966, 1967, 1968), Chierchia (1990), Fodor (1975), Higginbotham (1990), Lewis (1979), Partee (1975), Perry (1979, 2000), Salmon (1986, 1992), and Soames (1990, 1994). The combined force of these works establishes two incontrovertible results. First, not all pronouns are the product of transformations; second, anaphora cannot be reduced to de jure co-reference. These results will loom large in what is to come, but the reader is asked to bracket them for the purposes of following the potted history in this section.

[67] Chomsky (1965); Postal (1966).

[68] Langacker (1966); Lees and Klima (1963); Postal (1966); Ross (1967).

It was soon clear, however, that pronominalization could not provide an explanation of *all* anaphoric pronouns.[69] First, anaphora on quantified phrases was a problem. Transformational rules were supposed to be meaning-preserving.[70] Thus (5) (on its anaphoric reading) could not be derived from (5'), as they clearly differ in meaning:

(5) [every man]$_1$ loves his wife

(5') [every man]$_1$ loves [every man]$_1$'s wife.

Second, infinite regresses were discovered in so-called 'crossing co-reference' or 'Bach–Peters' structures like (6):[71]

(6) [the pilot who shot at it$_2$]$_1$ hit [the MiG that was chasing him$_1$]$_2$.

(6) contains two anaphoric pronouns, 'it' and 'he', each of which appears to be anaphoric on an expression containing the other. If these pronouns are the products of pronominalizing 'the MiG that was chasing him' and 'the pilot who shot at it' respectively, then (6) derives from (6'):

(6') [the pilot who shot at [the MiG that was chasing him$_1$]$_2$]$_1$ hit [the MiG that was chasing [the pilot who shot at it$_2$]$_1$]$_2$.

But (6') contains occurrences of 'him' and 'it' that need to be derived. If they are derived by pronominalization too, obviously we have an infinite regress on our hands.

In the light of the considerations just adduced and others, by the mid-1970s it was generally accepted that at least some anaphoric pronouns were 'base-generated', i.e. present at deep structure rather than derived by a pronominal-ization transformation. Around the same time, the idea that there might be general constraints (or conditions) restricting the nature of transformations was being explored.[72] Soon enough, pronominalization was abandoned in favour of the idea that all pronouns were base-generated.[73] And soon enough, the original idea that anaphoric relations were marked in syntax was itself called into question: the reading of a sentence upon which a (non-reflexive) pronoun β is seemingly anaphoric on some expression α is nothing more, it was

---

[69] Bach (1970); Fodor (1975); Helke (1971); Jacobson (1977); Jackendoff (1972); Karttunen (1969, 1976); Lasnik (1976); McCawley (1976); Partee (1975); Wasow (1972). That pronouns anaphoric on quantified phrases could not be interpreted as repetitions of their antecedents was already recognized by Geach (1962).   [70] Katz and Postal (1964); Chomsky (1964, 1965).

[71] Bach (1970).   [72] Ross (1967); Chomsky (1973).

[73] Jackendoff (1972); Wasow (1972).

suggested, than a reading upon which nothing in the grammar *precludes* α and β from being co-referential.[74] The interesting task was seen to be that of specifying precisely the syntactic conditions that precluded co-reference in examples such as those marked with an asterisk below:

(7) John₁ thought he₁ would win

(8) * he₁ thought John₁ would win

(9) his₁ mother thought John₁ would win

(10) although he₁ was tired, John₁ could not sleep

(11) *Mary told him₁ about John₁

(12) *Mary told John₁ about him₁.

However, by 1980 the wisdom of giving up the idea that anaphoric relations were marked in syntax was being called into question by at least philosophers working on syntax and semantics.[75] To talk of conditions on *co-reference*, it was pointed out, was to talk of conditions on a *symmetric* relation. But the anaphoric relations at issue are inherently *asymmetric*. Talk of de facto co-reference, and even talk of intentional co-reference, needed to be replaced, it was argued, by talk of *referential dependence*, a species of de jure co-reference. Co-reference is *not* actually precluded in the examples marked with asterisks above; what is precluded is *referential dependence*.

It is my belief that all talk of de jure co-reference and referential dependence is ultimately misplaced in a theory of anaphora. In accordance with where we began in our discussion of pronouns, let us say that what is precluded in the relevant examples above is *binding*, leaving it open for now whether binding is a primitive notion, as many people believe, or one that can be analysed in terms of some form of de jure co-reference as, for example, Evans (1977, 1980) holds. Thus I shall talk of both quantifiers and names binding pronouns, deferring until later precisely how a unified theory is to be elaborated.

7. 'Binding' and 'Scope'

One of the main aims of generative grammar, according to Chomsky, is to render explicit and systematic what the native speaker–hearer implicitly knows about the structure of his or her language simply in virtue of *being* a native

---

[74] Lasnik (1976); Chomsky (1976); Reinhart (1976).   [75] Evans (1977, 1980); Higginbotham (1980).

speaker–hearer, and thereby to shed light on the nature of the human language faculty. We acquire language because we have a *language faculty*, a component of our shared biological endowment that unfolds in accordance with a pre-set programme under the triggering and shaping effect of linguistic experience. While the final state may differ across individuals—particularly in so far as their exposure is to different speaker–hearers in different communities—the shaping effect of experience is quite limited. And it is this limited variation alone that leads us to talk informally about people being speakers of 'different languages'.[76] Although the study of conditions (or constraints) on rules of grammar had begun in the 1960s, it was not until the early 1980s that the emphasis in generative linguistics shifted dramatically from rules for generating (and interpreting) particular linguistic structures to constraints on possible structures and their interpretations.[77] Diverse linguistic phenomena, seemingly governed by intricate rules that differed from language to language, were now viewed as consequences of the interaction of general principles of the human language faculty, principles that were meant to be invariant across typologically distinct languages, superficial differences between particular languages reflecting only the setting of different values to each of a batch of structural parameters as part of the process of language acquisition, and the peripheral effects of relatively unimportant, learned idiosyncrasies. The interpretation of pronouns was prominent in this work because of the importance within the emerging theory of a subtheory that concerned itself with the *binding* of one expression by another.[78]

The conception of binding involved in the Binding Theory is often said to be *syntactic*. But it would be quite incorrect to say it is *purely* syntactic (except on a very broad and ultimately unhelpful use of 'syntactic') because it has a clear interpretive dimension. (The nature of this interpretation, via the notion of abstraction, will be examined later.) The usual Binding Theory definition of binding might be put as follows:

α binds β iff   (i) α and β are *co-indexed*, and
          (ii) β is within the *scope* of α.

Of course, much turns on what is meant by 'scope' here. If the word merely labels a precise relation that holds between points of a tree, then it is easy to see why this definition of binding is called syntactic: whether or not α binds β in a

---

[76] For a highly readable and comprehensive account of Chomsky's work, its implications, and the evolution of the core grammatical ideas, see Smith (1999).   [77] Chomsky (1977, 1981).
[78] Chomsky (1981, 1986).

sentence $S(\alpha,\beta)$ is something that can be determined by simply consulting $S(\alpha,\beta)$'s syntactic structure, i.e. its LF, assuming minimalism. Nonetheless, we must not overlook the fact that our hypothesis about $S(\alpha,\beta)$'s LF was formed partly on the basis of judgements of an *interpretive* nature; for a sentence's LF, as Chomsky has consistently maintained, incorporates 'whatever features of sentence structure (i) enter into the semantic interpretation of sentences and (ii) are strictly determined by properties of sentence grammar'.

Let us take scope first. In the first-order predicate calculus, a variable β may be bound by a quantifier α (in a formula X) only if β resides in *the smallest sentence (open or closed) (in X) that contains* α. Following Russell, this is precisely what we mean when we say that a variable may be bound by a quantifier only if it lies within the quantifier's *scope*. The only non-atomic expressions in the calculus are whole sentences (open or closed) and the only expressions whose scopes we care about are the sentence operators $(\forall x), (x), \sim, \bullet, \vee, \supset$, and $\equiv$. So we say, with seeming generality, that an expression β is within the scope of an expression α iff β resides in the smallest *sentence* containing α. In short:

> For any *sentence operator* α, α's scope $=$ the smallest *sentence* properly containing α.[79]

The temptation to simplify and fully generalize is hard to resist:

> For any *expression* α, α's scope $=$ the smallest *constituent* properly containing α.[80]

---

[79] In the terminology of syntactic theory, β's being within the scope of α amounts to α's *commanding* β in Langacker's (1966) sense: α commands β iff the minimal S node dominating α also dominates β.

[80] In the terminology of syntactic theory again, β's being within the scope of α now amounts to α's *c-commanding* β in Reinhart's (1976, 1978) sense: α *c-commands* β iff the first branching node (of whatever category) dominating α also dominates β. (α and β are assumed to be non-overlapping.) The route to c-command in linguistics was tortuous. In effect, *c-command* superseded Lasnik's (1976) less general notion of *kommand*: α kommands β iff the minimal cyclical node (S or NP) dominating α also dominates β. (NP in Lasnik's definition corresponds to what we call DP today.) *Kommand* itself was meant to supersede Langacker's (1966) still less general notion of *command*: α commands β iff the minimal S node dominating α also dominates β. The route through command and kommand to c-command is somewhat surprising given that the last is the simplest and most general. As Evans (1977) notes, what amounts to a c-command account of scope was in fact employed back in 1964 by Klima, who was investigating the scope of negation and *wh*-phrases. Klima offers a conditional not a biconditional: 'A constituent . . . is "in construction with" another if the former is dominated by (that is, occurs somewhere lower down the branch of) the first branching node . . . that dominates the latter' (1964: 297). Evans puts Klima's notion to use in straightforwardly characterizing when a pronoun is within the scope of (and hence bindable by) a quantifier expression. See also Wasow (1972); Wexler *et al.* (1974); Culicover (1976).

Not only does this generalization appear right for natural language, minimalist assumptions appear to explain *why*: it is *beautifully idiotic*. Why is it that (1) below is perfectly acceptable, while (2) is not?

(1) John told Paul's mother a lot about himself
(2) *John's mother told Paul's mother a lot about himself.

That is, what prevents 'himself' being bound by 'John' in (2)? The lay answer is that 'John' is not the *subject* of (2), 'John's mother' is.[81] However, while there are, in fact, languages in which a reflexive must be bound by a subject expression (e.g. German and Icelandic), English appears not to be such a language, witness (3):

(3) John^1 told Paul^2 a lot about himself$_{1/2}$.

Here, 'himself' can be bound by 'John' or 'Paul' (I indicate binding possibilities by placing a numerical superscript on the binder and a corresponding subscript on the bound).[82] Although the lay answer to our question appears to be technically incorrect, it is *right in spirit*. The *subject* of a sentence S is the DP that combines with a VP to form S (the DP 'immediately dominated' by the S node). This simple fact gives us *everything we need* to understand scope. We can characterize scope 'inclusively' (in the manner familiar to philosophers and logicians), or 'exclusively' (in a manner more familiar to linguists):[83]

> If α and β merge to form $\{\alpha\,\beta\}$, then $\{\alpha\,\beta\}$ = the scope of α = the scope of β. ('My sister and I form my scope.')
> If α and β merge to form $\{\alpha\,\beta\}$, then α = the scope of β, and β = the scope of α. ('My sister is my scope').

I say this is 'beautifully idiotic' because *scope is something you get when you merge expressions*. And from a combinatorial or computational point of view, this makes the notion virtually trivial, something that arises as a matter of virtual conceptual necessity once we accept the possibility (as we must) of expressions merging to form larger expressions.[84] It is a good methodological assumption to view

---

[81] Since mothers are female, there is no acceptable reading of (2). By contrast, brothers are male, so there is an acceptable reading of (i), despite the fact that 'himself' still cannot be bound by 'John':

(i) John's brother told Paul's mother a lot about himself.

[82] In Icelandic, the two readings of (3) are captured using two different pronouns. See below.

[83] The *inclusive–exclusive* terminology was suggested to me by James McCawley. The word 'merge' is used in an intuitive sense here, but it is meant to foreshadow talk in the next section of its use within Chomsky's (1995) minimalist framework.

ourselves as computational idiots, as beings who require the representations over which computations are defined to be as simple as possible. It is hard to imagine anything more in line with the idiot assumption than scope.[85]

It is now easy to see what is going on in (1)–(3). In (1), 'himself' lies within the scope of 'John' but not within the scope of 'Paul'; in (2) it lies within the scope of neither; and in (3) it lies within the scopes of both.

We turn now to *indexing*. To say that α and β are *co-indexed* is to say something of syntactic import that may or may not have interpretive consequences, depending upon how indexing is elaborated. Let us suppose each DP is assigned some index, which we might indicate with a subscript.[86] What prevents co-indexing being of 'merely syntactic' interest (if this even makes sense) is its *interpretation*. The whole point of indices would disappear if co-indexing were not meant to indicate something of *interpretive* significance. When 'himself' takes the same index as 'John' in (3) we think of the two expressions as linked for purposes of interpretation. One option is to say that the linking involves *co-reference*, the reflexive being *referentially dependent* upon the name. But let us continue with the idea that the linking actually involves *binding* in the sense familiar from quantification theory, with the aim of providing a uniform treatment of (3) and (3')

(3') [every bishop]^1 told [some prince]^2 a lot about himself$_{1/2}$.

When 'himself' takes the same index as 'John' in (3), it is being used to say something that is true iff the following condition is true of (is satisfied by) some person John:[87]

(4) *x told Paul a lot about x.*

---

[84] So why 'branching nodes' in Reinhart's original definition of c-command? Because she and others wanted to allow for the possibility of *non*-branching nodes, i.e. nodes that immediately dominate a single node. If we wanted to allow for the possibility of non-branching nodes, we could make the obvious adjustments. If a good case can be made that all non-terminal nodes are branching—perhaps even binary-branching, as seems very plausible to some linguists—then reference to non-uniqueness and branching nodes could be dropped. On my understanding of the minimalist programme, the idea of a non-branching node makes no sense.

[85] On this matter, I take myself to be largely in agreement with Reinhart (1983, 2000) and Reuland (2001*b*).

[86] As Chomsky (1995) points out, such a use of indices is not obviously consistent with his minimalist assumptions.

[87] To say this does not preclude the possibility that in more interesting cases these two characterizations come apart.

When 'himself' takes the same index as 'Paul', it is being use to say something that is true iff the following condition is true of (is satisfied by) some person Paul:

(4′) *John told x a lot about x.*

If we did not have distinct interpretations in mind, we could never have even reached the point of bringing indices into the picture. And to this extent it would be misleading to say that binding and co-indexing are *purely syntactic* notions. It is quite clear that the principal phenomenon we are investigating is an *interpretive* one with a *syntactic* dimension. (*Any discussion* of the syntactic conditions governing anaphora is up to its neck in matters of *interpretation*, for tautologically that is *precisely* what the facts that are being accounted for involve.) And to this extent talk of the syntactic conception of binding being a *purely syntactic* notion, and talk of facts about binding being *purely syntactic*, can be taken with a large grain of salt.

8. The Binding Theory

Chomsky's Binding Theory comprises three 'locality' principles meant to characterize the syntactic constraints on the interpretation of pronouns. It aims to capture the fact that (A) a reflexive pronoun (e.g. 'himself') must not be 'too far' from its binder; that (B) a non-reflexive (e.g. 'him') must not be 'too close'; and that (C) a name (broadly construed) must not have a binder at all.

In the 1980s and 1990s great effort was expended on defining 'too far' and 'too close' in connection with binding. To a first, rough approximation—revisions will appear later—the first of the three principles that make up the Binding Theory, Principle A, requires that the antecedent α of a reflexive pronoun β lie in β's own clause (i.e. within the smallest clause containing β):

> *Principle A.* A reflexive is to be interpreted as bound by an expression in its own clause.

Consider (1) and (2) (asterisks before subscripts signal impossible bindings):

(1) $[_S$ John^1 says that $[_S$ [no barber]^2 shaves himself $_{*1/2}]]$
(2) $[_S$ John^1 says that $[_S$ Paul^1 shaves himself $_{*1/2}]]$.

The reflexive 'himself' in utterances of these sentences is bound by the subject of the embedded clause—'no barber' in (1), and 'Paul' in (2)—not by the subject of the larger clause ('John', in both examples). It is common in linguistics to say that pronouns satisfying Principle A are 'locally bound.'[88] (It is also common to avoid calling them 'pronouns' and call them 'anaphors', but I eschew the former stricture here.)

By contrast, the non-reflexive 'him' in utterances of $(1')$ and $(2')$ below *cannot* be bound by the subject of the embedded clause, but *may* be bound by the subject of the larger clause:

$(1')$ $[_S \text{John}^1 \text{ says that } [_S [\text{no barber}]^2 \text{ shaves him}_{1/*2}]]$

$(2')$ $[_S \text{John}^1 \text{ says that } [_S \text{Paul}^2 \text{ shaves him}_{1/*2}]]$.

These data are in accordance with the second principle of the Binding Theory:

> *Principle B.* A non-reflexive is not to be interpreted as bound by an expression in its own clause.[89]

---

[88] It is not difficult to find apparent violations of Principle A once we turn to other languages. In the Icelandic (i), for example, either *Jón* or *Páll* may bind the reflexive *sig*:

(i) *Jón¹ segir að [Páll² raki sig₁/₂]*
John says that Paul shaves-SUBJ self-ACC
('John¹ says that Paul² shaves him₁/himself₂').

The interesting question here is whether this and related cases (in Chinese, for example) undermine the core concepts of the Binding Theory, merely push in the direction of explicable revisions, or indicate a lexical division between two different types of reflexive, only one of which satisfies Principle A. (The general issue is discussed in a way that philosophers will find highly congenial by Baker 2001.) The matter is complicated by various factors. First, the Icelandic violation is not possible when the clause containing *sig* is *indicative*—it must be subjunctive, as in (i), or infinitival as in (ii) (where PRO is the aphonic subject of the embedded infinitival clause):

(ii) *[Jón¹ taldi Pál² á [PRO₂ aðraka sig₁/₂]]*
John persuaded Paul-ACC shave-INF self-ACC]
('John¹ persuaded Paul² [PRO₂ to shave him₁/himself₂]').

(I have skated over certain matters here that are discussed later.) Second, Icelandic reflexives are subject-oriented, by which is meant that they may be bound only by subject expressions. (There are interesting exceptions, however.) Third, only the monomorphemic reflexive *sig* and its case variants (*sér* (DAT), *sín* (GEN)) engage in Principle A violations of this sort. The corresponding complex reflexives (*sjálfan sig, sjálfum sér, sjálfs sín*) are locally bound. Fourth, some verbs (e.g. *raka sig* ('shave oneself'), appear to be intrinsically reflexive and to resist complex reflexives. This collection of characteristics is not uncommon for long-distance reflexives across languages and certainly makes one wonder whether there are not simply two types of reflexive pronoun in natural languages; see Baker (2001), Cole *et al.* (2001), Pica (1987, 1991). Icelandic pronouns have been investigated in detail by Bresnan (2001), Maling (1984, 1986), Reuland (2001a), Reuland and Sigurjónsdóttir (1997), Sells (1987), Sigurðsson (1990), Sigurjónsdóttir (1992), Þráinsson (1976, 1990, 1991), and others.

[89] There are certain predicates that may require (or at least strongly favour) a particular non-reflexive bound pronoun as an argument. Higginbotham (1980) gives an example similar to (i):

(i) John brought a date with him.

The origins of Principle B are in Chomsky's (1976) rule of non-co-reference.

The third and final principle concerns names (broadly speaking):

> *Principle C.* A name is not to be interpreted as bound.

Thus, an utterance of (3) may not be understood in such a way that 'Tully' is bound by either 'Cicero' or 'a barber':

(3) [$_S$ Cicero^1 says that [$_S$ [a barber]^2 shaves Tully$_{*1/*2}$]].

To say this is not to say that 'Cicero; and 'Tully' may not be de facto co-referential.[90] It is just to say that 'Tully' cannot be bound by 'Cicero'. On the assumption that the concept of binding involves interpretive as well as syntactic notions, it is unclear why the issue of binding a name should come up in the first place, and this might cast doubt on the need for Principle C.[91]

Despite all manner of counterexamples, the Binding Theory still holds centre stage in discussions of pronouns and anaphora—although syntactic theory itself has hardly stood still—a fixed point from which to explore. Providing a clear and precise specification of the (seemingly) complementary distribution of reflexives and non-reflexives with respect to their binding possibilities, one that holds across a multitude of languages would be a phenomenal accomplishment, of course. But even if a version of the Binding Theory were to emerge that everyone found acceptable, it might still fall well short of where Chomsky wants us to be, for what he wants (and surely we should agree with him here) is not just a *description* of the facts, but an *explanation* of *why* the Binding Theory holds. The theory would certainly not be 'necessary' in any sense of this word usually employed by philosophers; but this does not mean it may not be 'conceptually' or 'empirically' necessary in Chomsky's (1995, 2002) sense: if a grammar is the optimal solution to the problem of relating form and meaning for a system as expressively rich as the ones we do, as a matter of empirical fact, possess, it may turn out that the interpretive difference between 'himself' and 'him' (or, rather more plausibly, between two more general classes of expressions) is pretty much unavoidable. As Chomsky might put it, it is a matter of 'virtual conceptual necessity'.[92] Since there is no condition on variables in first-order logic corresponding to the locality difference described by the Binding Theory,

---

[90] Evans (1980).

[91] The origins of Principle C are in Lasnik's (1976) rule of non-co-reference, and as such it appears to be a hangover from a time when linguistics ran together the symmetric notion of de facto co-reference and the asymmetric notion of referential dependence. See Evans (1977, 1980).

[92] See Reuland (2001*b*).

its existence in natural language is something that needs an empirical explanation, as it *appears* natural language is making things more complicated than it might.[93]

One terminological point can be made immediately. The word 'pronoun' tends to be used in a special technical way by Chomsky and many other linguists so as to exclude what we have been calling 'reflexive pronouns'.[94] Along with reciprocals ('each other'), reflexives fall under the label 'anaphor' for Chomsky. Principle A is meant to govern the interpretation of 'anaphors', so a more general formulation would contain 'anaphor' where we put 'reflexive pronoun' earlier. The non-reflexive 'him', by contrast, is a 'pronoun' (or 'pronominal') for Chomsky. Since Principle B of the Binding Theory is meant to govern the interpretation of 'pronouns', a proper formulation would contain just 'pronoun' where we put 'non-reflexive pronoun'. This usage will not be adopted here for two reasons. First, we want to ensure continuity with the philosophy literature (and, indeed, a good portion of the linguistics literature, where there is frequent talk of 'unbound anaphora'), so we shall continue to use 'pronoun' in the broad way, distinguishing reflexive and non-reflexive forms. Second, it is perfectly consistent with Chomsky's thinking that his anaphor–pronoun distinction— an anaphor being an expression that falls under Principle A, and a pronoun one that falls under Principle B—is at best a taxonomic artefact, one that may be useful in our standard bootstrapping practice, but one that finds no place in a final theory.[95]

9. 'Pragmatic' and 'Ambiguous'

Before looking more closely at binding, I want to embed the picture that is developing within the broader pragmatist picture of interpretation with which I began. Evans (1982: 309) rightly stresses there is 'no infallible linguistic guide' to determining when understanding what someone is saying on a given occasion requires grasping a thought about a particular individual, for 'most expressions which are conventionally apt for such a use also have other uses'. In this connection, he immediately cites pronouns, on the grounds that they may be used to make independent reference to individuals (rather like demonstratives) or as

---

[93] My own suspicion about the source of the locality bifurcation enshrined in Principles A and B has to do with the concept of predication.   [94] Chomsky (1981, 1986, 1995).

[95] Reuland (2001a, b).

the natural language counterparts of bound variables. When philosophers and linguists discuss expressions with more than one use, the adjectives 'ambiguous' and 'pragmatic' are soon in the air. Where pronouns are concerned, we might easily fall into using these words in a number of ways that, although related, are not identical, and we must take care not to cross wires.[96] One very common use of 'pragmatic' is pointed out by Evans (1980). If A utters

(1) *He*'s up early,

referring to a man who is walking by, or

(2) I'm glad *he*'s left,

referring to a man who has just left, the references of (A's utterances of) the third-person pronouns are determined by 'what may loosely be called "pragmatic" factors' (1980/1985: 216) and not by 'reference to *the rules of the language*' (1980/1985: 230). What Evans means here is that neither the meaning of the word 'he' nor any rule of sentence grammar (nor the combination) determines who the pronouns in (1) and (2) are being used to refer to in the situations sketched:

All that the conventions governing the referring expression 'he' insist upon, in any given context, is that the object referred to should be male. (1982: 312)

There is no linguistic rule which determines that a 'he' or a 'that man' refers to *x* rather than *y* in the vicinity, or that it refers to someone who has just left rather than someone who has been recently mentioned. (1980/1985: 230–1)

In the language of the early part of this chapter, who A is referring to by 'he' in the imagined utterances of (1) or (2) is determined by A's referential intentions. And these intentions are constrained by the (known) conventions governing the referring use of 'he' as well as all the other sorts of things discussed earlier. As soon as we introduce anaphoric pronouns matters become more complicated, but not unmanageably so. In accordance with Principle A of the Binding Theory, the reflexive 'himself' *must be* bound. In accordance with Principle B, the non-reflexives 'he', 'him', and 'his' *can be* bound. As stated, the principles put

---

[96] Every now and then one comes across a self-serving edict on the 'correct' or 'best' uses of 'semantic' and 'pragmatic'. But these words have been used in so many related ways in the philosophy of language and linguistics that any detailed attempt to explore, separate, and legislate is pointless and perverse. The best one can hope for is consistency in one's own usage—if not across an entire body of work at least within some useful portion—with occasional pointers that serve to differentiate one's usage from others with which it might be confused.

reflexive and non-reflexives in complementary distribution as far as binding possibilities are concerned.

Consider:

(3) John[1] told Paul's[2] wife a lot about himself$_{1/*2}$.

It would be a mistake to say the speaker had a choice here about which expression he intends to be understood as binding 'himself'. Among other things, what the conventions governing the use of 'himself' seem to insist upon, in any given context, is that it be bound by a masculine DP that stands to it in a configuration satisfying Principle A. (To be sure, this is not how an ordinary speaker would put things, but I take that to be irrelevant.) Principle A, once formulated to linguists' satisfaction, precludes 'Paul' from playing that role.

It is not difficult, however, to construct from (3) a case in which Principle A does not force a unique result. Compare (3) with (4), where 'himself' may be bound by either 'John' or 'Paul':

(4) John[1] told Paul[2] a lot about himself$_{1/2}$.

And this fact might occasion another use of the word 'pragmatic'. If it is false that the reflexive's binder is uniquely fixed by 'reference to *the rules of the language*', it might be suggested, surely we need *some* help from 'what may loosely be called "pragmatic" factors'.[97] But we must be careful here. Earlier I stressed the asymmetric, indeed dovetailed, epistemic positions of the speaker and the hearer, and I separated, and then reconnected, the roles of the rules of the language and the roles of the speaker's intentions in theoretical talk about *what determines what a speaker is saying* and about *what determines who or what a speaker is referring to*. If we are not careful to bear all this in mind we will find ourselves with a classic case of two wrongs engendering the illusion of no wrong whatsoever, for the contrast

---

[97] The ambiguity in (4) is not mirrored in all languages. In Icelandic, for example, only an expression in subject position may bind a reflexive:

(i) *Jón[1] sagði Páli[2] frá (sjálfum) sér$_{1/*2}$*
John told Paul-DAT about (EMPH) self-DAT
('John[1] told Paul[2] about himself$_{1/*2}$').

(The simplex reflexive in Icelandic inflects for case, but not for number or gender: *sig* (ACC), *sér* (DAT), *sín* (GEN); there is no nominative form. In (i) it is assigned dative case by the preposition *frá*.) To produce an Icelandic sentence equivalent to the reading of (4) upon which 'his' is bound by 'Paul', one would have to use a non-reflexive pronoun—one might even use the equivalent of 'him Paul'. The matter is rather more complicated than I am making out, however, for reasons that will emerge.

between (3) and (4) brings out rather nicely a pair of quite distinct confusions which, like many other pairs, may manage to avoid detection for a good while by effectively drawing attention away from one another, screening one another off, as it were.

To cement ideas, I want to examine a simple example in some detail. Early one evening I uttered the following sentence to someone who had just arrived in Reykjavik and called me on the telephone:

(5) He is going to collect you at seven o'clock, then come over here for me.

Let us assume, for simplicity, that there is no interesting lexical or structural ambiguity we need to examine in connection with (5). The sentence itself does not reveal fully what I intended to say because (for starters) it doesn't tell you who I meant by the pronoun 'he'; nor, contrary to the way some philosophers seem to write on this topic, does it tell you who I meant by 'you', 'here', or even 'me'.

Evans's (1982) discussion is helpful here (see esp. 9.2, pp. 309–20). On his account, the conventions governing a referring expression α, as uttered on a particular occasion, associate with α a property which an individual must satisfy if it is to be the referent of 'a fully conventional use' of α, on that occasion. For example, the utterance of 'I' or 'me', on a given occasion, is associated with the property of *being the person making the utterance*; and the utterance of 'you', on a given occasion, with the property of *being the person being addressed in that utterance* (1982: 311). The conventions governing 'he' and 'this' and 'that' are much less discriminating, Evans notes. And, this fact, he rightly says, 'precludes any simple functional definition of the notion of 'a referring expression in an utterance' as the expression which indicates which object the speaker is talking about' (1982: 312 n. 9). In many cases, he notes, the *predicate* used may do more for the hearer 'to narrow down the range of interpretations of the referring expression than does the referring expression itself' (ibid.).

Four notions are frequently invoked at this point in discussions: (i) *context of utterance*, (ii) *salience*, (iii) *Gricean or other pragmatic principles*, and (iv) *speaker's intentions*. And unfortunately they are often introduced as components of a single entity, as if they somehow conspire to 'bridge the gap' between the meaning of a sentence and what a speaker says on a given occasion by uttering that sentence. As we saw earlier, category mistakes will be our reward if we fail to separate the perspectives of speaker and hearer, but if the earlier discussion is respected, we shall have no trouble.

What is it *I know* about my utterance, beyond knowing the meaning of the sentence I used (or at least the meanings of its words and their syntactic arrangement), that makes it the case that *I know* what I intended to say? Answer: *I know* to whom I intended to refer by 'he' (Mike), 'you' (Don), and 'me' (Stephen), and I know what I intended to refer to by 'here' (my apartment). I intended to say to Don that Mike was going to collect him at seven o'clock (that same evening), then come over to my apartment to collect me.

But *how* do I know to whom or to what I intended to refer by 'he', 'you', 'me', and 'here'? Answer: I have privileged access to my referential intentions. They were, in fact, perfectly *respectable* referential intentions in the circumstances because I could reasonably expect Don to recognize that I intended to refer to Mike, Don, myself, and my apartment, respectively. (The situation would not have been dramatically different if I had used 'Mike' instead of 'he'.)

I was directly aware of my communicative intentions. I know who or what I intended to refer to by 'he', 'you', 'me', and 'here', and what I meant quite generally. Scanning the environment is not going to provide me with any information that can help me identify what I meant, though of course my awareness of the immediate environment or context *constrains* the referential and more generally communicative intentions I can reasonably have given my choice of words. The formation of genuine intentions is severely constrained by belief, and a speaker's referential intentions are no exception, being constrained by knowledge of word meaning and syntax, tacit beliefs about who was speaking, who was being addressed, who was salient in the conversational context, and much more besides. But nothing like a 'dynamic salience metric' or a formal 'context' or 'index' 'fixed' or 'determined' who and what I intended to refer to in the example just given; for, tautologically, *that* was determined by *my referential intentions*, and it is these intentions it is the task of the hearer to identify.[98]

To understand the nature of the constraints on the formation of referential intentions, let us switch quickly to the perspective of the hearer. Don heard me utter (5). What did *he need to know* about my utterance, beyond knowing the meaning of the sentence I uttered (or at least the meanings of its words and their syntactic arrangement), in order to identify what I intended to say? Answer: he needed to establish whom I intended to refer to by 'he' (Mike), 'you' (Don), and 'me' (Stephen), and where I was referring to by 'here' (my apartment). And since Don had no direct access to my referential intentions, he had to establish these things *in some other way*.

Let us begin with 'he'. We no more need to say that 'he' is ambiguous in order to make sense of 'he' being used with the intention to refer to different

---

[98] As pointed out earlier (n. 30) in certain circumstances one may seek to disguise one's intended referent.

individuals on different occasions than we need to say that 'I' is ambiguous. When I uttered 'he' as part of my utterance of (5), I intended to refer to Mike. And this referential intention was implicated in a *communicative* intention I had: to convey to Don that Mike was going to collect him at seven o'clock (that same evening), then come over to my apartment for me. In fact, I intended Don to understand me as *saying* that Mike was going to collect him at seven o'clock, then come over to my apartment for me. And I could not reasonably be credited with such an intention if I thought it unlikely that Don would understand me as intending to say that. Why was I prepared to put so much faith in a use of the word 'he'? Because (i) I know it is part of what one knows when one knows the meaning of the word 'he' that it is to be used to refer to a male, (ii) I know Don speaks English, (iii) I tacitly take Don to be operating in accordance with shared general pragmatic principles, and (iv) Don had just asked me a question about Mike—something like 'I can't get through to Mike. What's the plan for tonight? Is he picking us up?'—making Mike, whom we both know to be male, an object of conversation (salient). So I used the pronoun 'he' intending to refer to Mike and expecting Don to *recognize* this. Exactly *how* this happens is something a cognitive theory of utterance interpretation (such as Relevance Theory) must tell us. And although we do not yet have a complete story about the cognitive processes involved, we do seem to have a plausible philosophical account of *what* happens, in the sense of what the net result is. That's what our *judgements* tell us.

Neither context nor salience nor pragmatic principles nor word meaning nor syntax 'fixed' or 'determined' who I intended to refer to by 'he', for tautologically that was determined by *my referential intention* in using it. Which is not to say that context, salience, pragmatic principles, word meaning, and syntax played no role. They played two dovetailed, mutually sustaining roles. They were things that *Don used* (in different ways to be sure) in identifying my referential intention. But they were also things that *I used* because my beliefs (tacit or otherwise) about context, salience, pragmatic principles, word meaning, and syntax are things that bear on the formation of referential intentions.

We must distinguish, then, (a) *what determines who I intended to refer to* by 'he' and (b) *what Don uses in identifying who I intended to refer to* by it. There is only misery in store for those who would confuse these notions. Don used the meaning of the word 'he', its syntactic position, and information about the context of utterance to identify my referential intention.[99] And my referential intention was

---

[99] If I had said 'He told Mike to pick you up . . .' the position of 'he' would have steered Don away from interpreting me as referring to Mike by 'he' (assuming only one person named 'Mike' is

constrained by the position and meaning of the word 'he', which I tacitly assumed Don also knew, by my tacit beliefs about who was salient and about the pragmatic principles we both employ, and so in sum by my estimation of Don's ability to recognize that, in this particular context, I would be intending to refer to Mike.[100]

So our respective perspectives on the exchange are not independent. In producing my utterance, I relied on what I took to be Don's capacity to identify what I intended to convey, an intention partly shaped by my estimation of that capacity. And Don assumed that I was so relying. And, possibly, so on. In short, the ways in which Don and I were operating were dovetailed and mutually sustaining, and this is quite general, cases of breakdown only reinforcing the point.

If we think about this a little more, we see it has little to do with pronouns or indexical expressions per se. Suppose I utter a sentence X that no one has ever uttered before, a sentence whose words are all individually unambiguous and free of contextual variability (perhaps there is no such sentence, in which case my point is already made). And suppose that these features of X ensure that wherever and whenever anyone utters X he or she will always be saying that p and so always be taken to be saying that p by any rational person who hears the utterance correctly, though I, the speaker, have never reflected on this fact. There is still something I intend to be taken as *saying* when I utter X, and I reasonably expect that I will be so taken. My hearer does not have direct access to this communicative intention and is, as ever, in the position of having to identify it on the basis of my utterance and information obtained from context. I expect him to succeed because I assume he knows the meanings of the words

relevant to the exchange). Indeed, given the question Don asked, he would have struggled to come up with a sensible interpretation.

[100] Whenever the notion of intention is introduced, there are philosophers who immediately bring up error. What if the person the speaker intends to refer to by 'he' is female? What if the intention turns out to involve no one at all? What if the person A intends to refer to by 'Smith' is not Smith but Jones? What if there is no object that A intends to refer to by 'that' because he has been fooled by a reflection or is hallucinating? What if A meant to utter the word 'brother' rather than 'father' but misfired? It is here that disputes may arise, among ordinary speakers and philosophers alike. And it would seem that as far as a philosophical theory of interpretation is concerned, we will have to see where theoretical developments take us. My own strong inclination is to say that such problem cases illustrate conflicts *among intentions* not a problem with the intentional story per se. Certainly we should not construct our theories primarily with a view to producing clear results in cases where things go wrong and where we ourselves are not clear. As Chomsky, Davidson, and Grice have stressed, in their own ways, let us not lose sight of the many cases in which things go right, the cases that motivated our inquiries in the first place. As far as the present chapter is concerned, nothing of consequence to my main point turns on cases of error.

in X and their syntactic arrangement and can hear me clearly and exploit contextual information, and so on. It just so happens that, by hypothesis, in this particular case no *additional* information that may be extracted from context will have any impact whatsoever on the hearer's task. If the case is implausible, so much the better for my point.

The situation with respect to my uses of 'you', 'here', and 'me' in my utterance of (5) differs only in the nature of the constraints the meanings of these words impose on viable referential intentions. My knowledge of the meanings of 'you', 'here', and 'me' involves knowing that they constrain my referential intentions to be directed towards (roughly) my audience, my location, and myself, respectively, giving me considerably less leeway than with the third-person 'he'. When I uttered 'you', 'here', and 'me' in uttering (5), I exploited the fact that Don knew the meanings of these words and would, in consequence, take my referential intentions to be directed towards him, my location, and myself, respectively.

Again, it is important to see that context does not *determine* who I am referring to by 'you', 'here', and 'me'. My intentions determine these things, but the intentions I may have are constrained by my beliefs about the context of utterance, about what I know about the meanings of 'you', 'here', and 'me', about what I assume Don knows about them, and so on. The context of utterance is important not because it determines who I am referring to but because it serves up a body of information used by Don to identify who I am referring to, a body of information I, the speaker, tacitly assumed he would draw upon.

Let us now return to (4):

(4) John^1 told Paul^2 a lot about himself$_{1/2}$.

Imagine the simplest case. The speaker, A, is fully aware that the rules of the language require him to use 'himself' in his utterance of (4) in such a way that it is bound by either 'John' or 'Paul'. And imagine that A has operated in accordance with these rules and that his hearer, B, knows he has (let's say A even *tells* him as much). B is still not home yet. It is here that 'context', 'intentions', 'salience', 'pragmatic principles', and so on are usually brought into the picture, and it is important to get the picture right. Let us suppose that A uttered 'himself' intending it to be understood as bound by 'John', the latter used to refer to, say, John Lennon. A intended to say something about John Lennon, namely that he satisfied the condition

(6) *x told Paul a lot about x*

(or that the predicate (λx (x *told Paul a lot about* x)) applied to him). In order to do this, A selected (4). Why such confidence in the reflexive pronoun? Because A knows, and assumes B knows, that the rules of language require 'himself' to be bound by 'John' or 'Paul' when uttering this particular sentence. And given what A and B have just been talking about—the way John Lennon has been telling people about himself today, let us suppose—A is quite justified in supposing B will interpret 'himself' as bound by 'John'. In summary, A has a *binding* intention.[101] For simplicity, let us say that a binding intention is a special form of referential intention (without committing ourselves to the position that ultimately binding must be (or is best) explained in terms of co-reference (a position which seems to me false).

The question of what determines the interpretation of 'himself' in an utterance of (4) is one that resists certain simplistic answers found in the literature—'syntax', 'context', 'salience', 'pragmatic principles'. If there is a short answer at all it is 'the speaker's intentions'. But the formation of particular intentions is severely constrained because of A's tacit understanding of such things as syntax and pragmatic principles, and his beliefs (tacit or otherwise) about who or what is salient. Given A's knowledge of the way ordinary middle-sized objects behave, he cannot sensibly intend to jump over the Empire State Building; and given his knowledge of the rules of the language, he cannot sensibly intend to use 'himself' in (4) in such a way that it is bound by neither 'John' nor 'Paul'. In the envisaged scenario, A assumes that the famous pragmatic factors will lead B to plump for 'John'.

From the perspective of the hearer, simplistic answers will not do either. B seeks to interpret A's remark and will fail unless he identifies which name A intends to be understood as binding 'himself'. He has no direct access to A's binding intentions, but there are lots of things he can get his hands on, as well as an important fact entailed by the rules of the language: on the assumption that A has not misspoken, 'himself' must be bound by either 'John' or 'Paul'. So grammar narrows down the options to two, and the famous pragmatic factors enable B to narrow these down to one.[102]

---

[101] If the position, to be adopted later, that the binding of a pronoun β by an expression α amounts to the merging of α with a λ-predicate whose operator binds β, formally spelling out what goes on when 'Paul' is meant to be binding 'himself' in (4) is a little tricky, perhaps indicating why there is a tendency to subject-orientation of reflexives in many languages. This matter is discussed later in connection with the existence of locality constraints.

[102] I am not articulating a psychological theory of what is taking place in the heads of A and B, of course, but rather giving a philosophical reconstruction of what a psychological theory must explain, in much the same way as Grice does in his philosophical psychology.

At the beginning of this chapter I said that a major problem that has plagued the study of pronouns is that all kinds of superficial generalizations and distinctions can be made, that it is difficult to establish which are of theoretical significance and which are mere distractions, and just as difficult to establish which of various competing classifications and unifications are going to pay theoretical dividends and which are ultimately going to lead to dead ends. This is particularly true when we examine disputes about ambiguity. Here there is no quick way to tell when we are onto something of deep theoretical significance, or even when there is a genuine dispute in any given case: all we can do is attempt to construct a general theory of pronouns (as part of an overall theory of interpretation) and see where we find the most useful unifications and bifurcations, not just within a language but also across languages—at least if we are serious about explaining linguistic structures in terms of general principles of the language faculty and thereby shedding light on the logical problem of language acquisition.

In order not to prejudge too many issues, let us continue using the phonologists' old slash notation when talking about the superficial form of a string of words. Consider

(7) /every man loves his wife/.

(7) contains what is often called the possessive or genitive pronoun /his/, and thereby the possessive or genitive description /his wife/.[103] It is frequently said that (7) is ambiguous, because /his/ admits of two quite distinct uses, one on which it is bound by 'every man', another on which it is used to make independent, indexical reference to some salient male.[104] If this description of the situation is accurate, then one of the tasks facing a hearer, B, when presented with an utterance of (7), is to identify whether the speaker, A, is using /his/ in the

---

[103] As far as English is concerned, it appears not to matter whether we draw a distinction between the possessive and the genitive. This is not true for all languages, however. See the discussion of Icelandic below.

[104] I should stress that there exist theories according to which there is no ambiguity or dual use of the sort I have just described, at least in cases in which the pronoun has a singular antecedent such as (i):

(i) John loves his mother.

Lasnik (1976), for example, and following him K. Bach (1987) argue that the occurrence of 'his' in (i) refers to some salient male. On this account, the two uses of 'his' have posited correspond to the choice of different salient male, in one case someone already mentioned in the sentence, in the other someone not so mentioned. This theory is thoroughly undermined by points made by Evans (1980) and Soames (1990).

indexical or bound way. And even if the distinction between these two uses of /his/ is encoded *grammatically* there is still nothing in *the superficial form* (7) to indicate which use A intends; so B must use *non-linguistic* information to establish how A is using /his/. And in *this* respect, interpreting an utterance of (1) is a *pragmatic* matter, on one perfectly useful and sensible use of the adjective 'pragmatic'. Nothing changes if we take these two uses of /his/ to correspond, strictly speaking, to the use of *two distinct words* pronounced /his/.[105]

That said, B's knowledge of word meaning and syntax *do* tell him something important about any utterance of (7), though B may not have reflected consciously on this: that A may be using /his/ in one of two distinct ways, that two different *types* of interpretation may be associated with utterances of (1). It is surely part of what B knows by virtue of knowing English that A may legitimately intend /his/ to be read as making independent reference to some particular individual or as bound by 'every man'. This is *not* a pragmatic matter. B knows this fact about (7) without appealing to any non-linguistic information. It is a *linguistic* fact—a syntactico-semantic fact—that these two uses of (7) are possible.

10. Minimalism, LF, and Binding

In the 1990s syntactic theory evolved considerably in the light of *minimalist assumptions*, the net effect of which was to restrict the posits of grammatical theory—whether categories, processes, constraints, or levels of representation—to those that are conceptually necessary or empirically unavoidable.[106] A motif that runs through this work is an argument from 'virtual conceptual necessity': complexity and stipulation are to be avoided as, all else being equal, language will employ only those devices needed to link sound and meaning. On the assumption that there is a component of the mind–brain dedicated to language, the human language faculty, one consequence of the minimalist outlook is that

---

[105] Analogy: interpreting utterances of /John is at the bank/ and /visiting professors can be a nuisance/. (But see below.) The possessive /his/ brings up an orthogonal interpretive problem: the nature of the intended relation. There are many possibilities for, say, /his horse/, which is why I used the nominal /wife/ in the example above. (Actually, all sorts of possibilities are possible for /his wife/, but you probably didn't realize that when you first looked at (7).) Why didn't I use /he/ or /him/ to circumvent distracting side issues about possession? Because using /his/ enables me to make an important point I cannot make using the others. See the discussion of Icelandic below.

[106] Chomsky (1995, 2002).

all properties of sentences relevant to sound and meaning—and this includes *binding* properties—should be derivable from quite general considerations about the way the language faculty must engage with two other cognitive systems, one dealing with the articulation of sounds and their perception (henceforth *the sound system*), the other trading in intentional–conceptual representations (henceforth *the intentional system*). A particular language can be seen as an instantiation of the language faculty (with certain options specified), something that can provide 'instructions' to be interpreted by the sound system, on the one hand, and the intentional system, on the other. More specifically, a language is a computational system that generates pairs $\langle \pi, \lambda \rangle$ of representations, where π is a PF (or 'Phonetic Form') to be read by the sound system, and λ an LF (or 'Logical Form') to be read by the intentional system. (Where early generative grammar distinguished the Deep Structure and Surface Structure of a sentence, and later versions distinguished its D-Structure, S-Structure, PF, and LF, minimalism allows for just PF and LF.)

For convenience we can identify a sentence with a pair $\langle \pi, \lambda \rangle$. For Chomsky, the basic idea behind the concept of LF representations has remained robust since its inception: An LF incorporates 'whatever features of sentence structure (1) enter into the semantic interpretation of sentences and (2) are strictly determined by properties of sentence grammar' (Chomsky 1976: 305). The only difference today is what is meant by 'strictly determined by properties of sentence grammar'. With the emergence of the minimalist outlook, this phrase may be usefully understood as 'strictly determined by the exigencies of connecting sound and meaning'.

As Chomsky has stressed for a quarter of a century, LFs are not full-fledged *intentional* representations, not as rich in content as those involved in beliefs, intentions, or expectations, not objects with truth conditions (or the analogues thereof), inferential roles, and so on. LFs are simply the grammar's contribution to the generation of such representations by the intentional system—which receives inputs from various cognitive faculties. To get the flavour of this idea it is helpful to think of the intentional system as trading in representations something like the sentences of the 'language of thought' in Fodor's (1975, 1983) sense, a modality-neutral symbolic system of representation in which thought takes place and into whose sentences utterances of natural language sentences must be mapped if understanding is to take place. LFs exhaust the grammar's contributions to this system; an LF is not an interpreted object with an intentional content: it is simply a syntactic representation, determined by sentence grammar, of those features of grammatical structure that enter into the interpretation of utterances of that sentence (for example, relations of scope and binding). Not only do LFs fail, for example, to specify references for referentially independent occurrences of pronouns, they fall short of being full-blown intentional representations in all sorts of other ways.[107]

Reference to the theory of phrase structure is virtually eliminated in the minimalist framework, there being no phrase structure rules in the traditional sense and, strictly speaking, no constituent structure to a PF representation. Again we can borrow the old /slash/ notation from phonology when talking about PFs, but with standard orthography rather than phonological symbols inside the slashes, thus individuating coarsely in terms of phonological properties:

(1) /John said he was at the bank/
(2) /every man loves his mother/.

We can still allow ourselves the convenience of using a phrase structure tree or a labelled bracketing to explicate superficial structure, so to speak, even if what we write down is strictly a hybrid of PF and LF. In contemporary syntactic theory, expressions such as 'some man', 'a man', 'the man', 'every man', and so on

---

[107] See Chomsky (1975, 1976, 1986, 1995, 2002), Sperber and Wilson (1986, 1995), and Carston (2002). In a Davidsonian spirit, Higginbotham and May (1981), Higginbotham (1980, 1983a,b), Larson and Segal (1995), Ludlow (1989), Neale (1994), and others have treated LFs as objects which (relative to assignments of values to referential elements, some of which may be of an indexical nature) have recursively specifiable truth conditions, an idea Chomsky rejects. There is, I think, *something* of real importance in the alternative conception of LF that needs to be superimposed upon the official Chomskyan conception to give it bite, but it is difficult to make this precise. In trying to effect the superimposition, my own earlier discussions of LF evince deeply worrying ambiguities. In *Descriptions* (1990) the discussion is very Chomskyan: I treat LFs as no more than syntactic objects encoding those aspects of syntax relevant to interpretation, and I am careful to distinguish LFs themselves from the formulae in a system of restricted quantification I use to represent the truth conditions of utterances of sentences, formulae that could depart significantly in structure from the LFs of the sentences uttered (for example, in the discussions of perceptual reports, incomplete descriptions, and descriptive pronouns). Various people tried to convince me I needed to embrace, or at least move closer to, the truth-evaluable conception of LFs, but the interpretation of *utterances* containing incomplete descriptions and other underspecified DPs, as well as the interpretation of D-type pronouns, held me back as it seemed, and still seems, preposterous to treat LFs as containing all sorts of unrecoverable *predicative* material not present in surface syntax. At the same time, it has always seemed to me that if the Chomskyan LF of a sentence X is meant to lay bare the contribution made to the process of *interpretation* by X's syntax, it must provide genuine constraints on what someone uttering X can be *saying*, something for which the alternative truth-conditional conception is tailor-made. In 'Logical Form and LF' (1994), I attempted a reconciliation of sorts—originally with Larson—by abstracting as much as possible from *pragmatically* determined aspects of the truth conditions of utterances. The attempt was ultimately unsuccessful, I think, because I strayed so far from the Chomskyan conception of LF.

are usually called DPs (determiner phrases) to reflect the idea that they are projected from the Ds (determiners) 'some', 'a', 'the', 'every', and so on (rather than from the N (noun) 'man' as earlier theory suggested).[108] On this usage, which we shall follow, the label NP is reserved for the nominal expression, simple or complex, with which the determiner merges to form a DP, as in the following tree and labelled bracketing:[109]

(3)

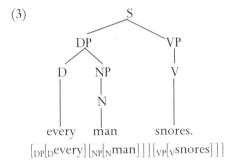

$$[_{DP}[_D every][_{NP}[_N man]]][_{VP}[_V snores]]]$$

The LF corresponding to the PF (3) will look something like (3′):[110]

(3′)

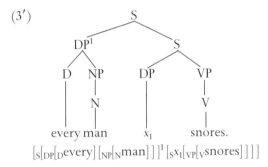

$$[_S[_{DP}[_D every][_{NP}[_N man]]]^1[_S x_1[_{VP}[_V snores]]]]]$$

In (3′) the quantifier expression 'every man' has been extracted—indeed forced by general principles of morphosyntax—from its original position (discernible in the *mélange* (3)) and has merged with the original S node to form another. From this 'new' position it binds the variable x that has been left as a sort of 'trace' in its 'original' position, that position being within the scope of its new position. The numerical *sub*script on x indicates that it is to be interpreted as bound

---

[108] For discussion, see Abney (1987); Cardinaletti (1994); Cardinaletti and Starke (1999); Chomsky (1995); Elbourne (2001, 2002); Szabolcsi (1994). In the elementary exposition of DPs that follows, I simplify dramatically as certain ongoing debates in linguistics about the details are not crucial to the philosophical issues of concern here.

[109] Prior to the work of Abney (1987), what are called DPs today were usually called NPs to reflect the idea that they were projections of Ns.

[110] Higginbotham (1980, 1983a); Higginbotham and May (1981); May (1977, 1985).

by the quantifier expression 'every man', which bears the same index as *super-script*.[111] This talk of variables and binding amounts to a description of an important part of the *interpretive* information carried by (3), precisely the sort of thing Chomsky ascribes to LFs. Variables are expressions *interpreted* in a certain way.

One question that will have to be addressed is whether quantifier expressions are the *only* DPs that are raised at LF in this way or whether the phenomenon is fully general, involving names, pronouns, and possessives, for example (DPs whose structures we will look at shortly):[112]

(4) $[_S[_{DP}John]^1[_S[_{DP}Ann]^2[_S x_1[_{VP}loves x_2]]]]$

(5) $[_S[_{DP}he]^1[_S[_{DP}Ann]^2[_S x_1[_{VP}loves x_2]]]]$

(6) $[_S[_{DP}John]^1[[_{DP}his_1 wife]^2[_S x_1[_{VP}loves x_2]]]]$.

It is at least clear from (6) that if the possessive description 'his wife' is raised, then 'John' will have to be raised too if it is to bind 'his'.

When the Binding Theory was first formulated, a sentence was not factored into just its PF and LF. D-Structure and S-Structure were grammatical levels bona fide and so it was possible to debate where the Binding Theory had to apply. Some advocated LF, others S-Structure; some suggested it must apply at both levels, others at at least one; and examples were even found that suggested D-Structure might be the appropriate level. Within a minimalist framework such debate is impossible. The Binding Theory can be only a set of constraints imposed by virtually unavoidable facts about an interpretive system, a set of principles operative at the interface of the language faculty and the system of conceptual–intentional representations, i.e. it holds at LF. (It should be noted, however, that Chomsky himself has suggested the Binding Theory disappears under minimalist assumptions. I remain unconvinced.)

11. Pronouns as Determiners

A proposal from 1960s linguistics that has been resuscitated to great effect recently is Postal's idea that pronouns are determiners.[113] While this idea might seem odd at first, reflection reveals it to be rather intuitive and well-motivated.

---

[111] Using only subscripts to co-index would obscure the fact that binding is an asymmetric relation. I am deliberately simplifying here. For example, I have ignored the fact that the superscripted index on the DP 'every man' has been projected upwards from the index on D 'every'.

[112] If, as seems plausible, possessives are definite descriptions, and definite descriptions are quantifier expressions, then we already have our answer in one case.

[113] Postal (1966); Stockwell *et al.* (1973); Abney (1987); Elbourne (2001, 2002).

Traditional grammars distinguish sharply between the possessive (or genitive) determiners in (1) and their absolute possessive (or genitive) counterparts in (1′):

(1) *our/your/his/her/John's/their* car is the one on the left

(1′) *ours/yours/his/hers/John's/theirs* is the one on the left.

In many cases it is as if the characteristically genitive 's' falls away when the determiner occurs with no overt NP.[114] Indeed generative linguistics suggests a single possessive determiner the superficial form of which depends upon whether it occurs with a *phonic* (phonologically non-null) or *aphonic* (phonologically null) NP complement:[115]

(2) $[_{DP}[_{D}\text{his}][_{NP}[_{N}\text{car}]]]$ is the one on the left

(2′) $[_{DP}[_{D}\text{his}][_{NP}e]]$ is the one on the left.

---

[114] Irregularities: 'his' and 'whose' remain as they are; 'mine' and 'thine' typically become 'my' and 'thy' in modern speech.

[115] The postulation of expressions that are aphonic despite having syntactic roles and semantic properties is surely no more or less problematic than the postulation of expressions that are semantically empty despite having syntactic roles and phonological properties ('it' in 'it's raining', for example). The idea of an expression that is phonetically *and* semantically empty is harder to gets one's mind around, and on the interpretation of Chomsky's present framework I endorse—syntax is whatever it is that relates PF and LF—the possibility of such an expression is straightforwardly excluded. The discovery or postulation of *any* expression constitutes a contribution to syntax and its existence is justified only if it is doing something at LF or PF. Consequently, the discovery or postulation of an *aphonic* expression must be justified by its role at LF. To this extent, it will contribute in one way to the project of producing a theory of utterance interpretation. The point should not be exaggerated, however. Discovering or postulating occurrences of a bound, aphonic expression *e* has very clear consequences for a theory of interpretation: an expression has been discovered or posited that is understood as a bound variable, effectively answering all questions about its interpretation on a given occasion. Contrast this with the discovery or postulation of an aphonic, *indexical* expression, one every bit as flexible in its interpretation as the overt expressions 'this' or 'that' or 'he' (when used to make independent reference). The interpretation of an utterance of a sentence containing an occurrence of an aphonic indexical is always going to be a full-fledged *pragmatic*, i.e. inferential, matter, the semantics of the aphonic expression itself placing only non-deterministic constraints on interpretation.

By contrast with pronouns, proper names might be viewed as Ns, serving as NPs, serving as full DPs by virtue of merging (in English) with aphonic Ds:

(i) $[_{DP}[_{D}e][_{NP}\text{John}]]$.

(In many languages (e.g. ancient and modern Greek) names appear regularly with the definite article. In certain contexts names may occur with the definite article and other determiners in English: 'That John Smith is not the John Smith I was talking about'). Perhaps we find NPs with aphonic Ds elsewhere:

(ii) $[_{DP}[_{D}e][_{NP}\text{whales}]]$ are $[_{DP}[_{D}e][_{NP}\text{mammals}]]$.

$[_{NP}[_{N}car]]$ is phonic, $[_{NP}[_{N}e]]$ is aphonic. Let us distinguish, then, *absolute* ('his', 'hers') and *reliant* ('his', 'her') occurrences of determiners according as they occur with aphonic or phonic NP complements.[116]

There are two ways to think about the aphonic $[_{NP}e]$ serving as the complement of a possessive determiner. (i) It might be construed as the result of a process of *NP-deletion* at PF.[117] With (3) and (3′), this seems fine:

(3) John prefers my painting to $[_{DP}[_{D}hers][_{NP}e]]$

(3′) John prefers my painting to $[_{DP}[_{D}her][_{NP}[_{N}painting]]]$.

But if (2) and (2′) derive from a single LF, we lose the recoverability of deletion.[118] (ii) Alternatively, $[_{NP}e]$ might be construed as an NP that itself appears in the LF of (2′) and as such is in need of pragmatic interpretation just like an occurrence of a pronoun.

Possessives are not the only determiners that have both reliant and absolute occurrences:

(4) *many* (people) applied but *few* (people/of them) were suitably qualified

(5) *both* (senators) spoke in favour but *neither* (senator/of them) was convincing

(6) *some* (guests) arrived late but *some/others/most* (guests/of them) did not

(7) *only two* (guards) fell asleep but *all three* (guards/of them) will have to be fired

(8) *that* (piece) is geometric; *this* (piece) is Mycenaean.

The following examples reveal another type of aphonic expression, this time a whole DP:

(iii) John promised Ann to sing

(iv) John asked Ann to sing.

Traditional grammars talk about the 'understood subject' of the verb 'sing' in such examples: in (iii) it is 'John', in (iv) it is 'Ann'. In syntactic theory this is captured by a difference in the status of an aphonic element (usually called PRO) occupying the subject position of the embedded infinitival clause:

(iii′) $[_{S}John^{1}$ promised Ann $[_{S}e_{1}$ to sing]]

(iv′) $[_{S}John$ asked Ann$^{2}[_{S}e_{2}$ to sing]].

In (iii′) the interpretation of *e* is required (by the syntax and the meaning of the verb 'promise') to proceed by way of the interpretation of the subject expression 'John' ('promise' is a *subject*-control verb). In (iv′), by contrast, the interpretation of *e* is required (by the syntax and semantics of the verb 'ask') to proceed via the interpretation of the object expression 'Ann' ('ask' is an *object*-control verb (in this construction)).

---

[116] One matter that needs to be taken up later is whether *all* occurrences of, say, /his/ have the same syntactic structure. If one ends up distinguishing bound and indexical uses of /his/, there is always the possibility that they are distinguished in virtue of syntactic structure.

[117] Elbourne (2001, 2002).

[118] It is arguable that (3)/(3′) does not satisfy it either, at least if 'painting' is stressed (see Neale 2004).

The determiners 'no', 'a', 'the', and 'every' seem always to be reliant:

(9) no/a/the/every guard fell asleep.
(9′) *no/*a/*the/*every fell asleep.

But we must not overlook the possibility, found with possessives, of morphological variation depending upon the phonicity of the complement.[119] For example, it is plausible that 'none' is the absolute form of the reliant 'no', and that 'one' is the absolute form of the reliant 'a' (as well as of the reliant 'one'):

(10) many people had dessert but *none* (of them) ordered coffee
(11) many people had dessert; indeed *one* (of them) had two portions.

Is there an absolute form of 'the'? The hypothesis at hand is that there is, and that it comes in three gender variants: 'he', 'she', and 'it'.[120] Third-person pronouns, on this hypothesis, are actually forms of the definite article taking aphonic complements:

(12) $[_{DP}[_{D}the][_{NP}[_{N}president]]]$ is asleep
(13) $[_{DP}[_{D}he][_{NP}e]]$ is asleep
(14) Don't wake $[_{DP}[_{D}him][_{NP}e]]$.

In the first instance, the reflexive 'himself' might be viewed as a fusion of the determiner 'him' (or, perhaps more plausibly (see below), the possessive determiner 'his') and the nominal 'self':

(16) every man loves $[_{DP}[_{D}him][_{NP}self]]$.

If this is adequate, and if we wish to retain the idea that reflexives and some occurrences of third-person pronouns are understood as bound, it might look as though we will have to say that some occurrences of *determiners* are bound variables. But we can obtain the desired result with something interestingly weaker: a purportedly bound occurrence of a third-person pronoun is just the head of a DP that *contains* a bound variable. Take a bound occurrence of 'he' in a sentence such as (17):

(17) [every man]^1 thinks that he$_1$ snores.

---

[119] Elbourne (2001, 2002).

[120] Postal (1966); Stockwell *et al.* (1973); Elbourne (2001, 2002). When I was a graduate student my adviser, John Perry, used to joke that I took every noun phrase to be a definite description until proven otherwise. If I had known about Postal's thesis in the 1980s, I would almost certainly have attempted to see it as the basis of a theory of descriptive anaphora of the sort sketched in chs. 5 and 6 of *Descriptions*.

On the hypothesis we are considering, the occurrence of 'he' in (17) has the form $[_{DP}[he][_{NP}e]]$. Our task is to make sense of the idea that this DP contains (or is at least interpreted *as if* it contains) a variable bound by 'every man'. Suppose we add to our formal language RQ a new quantificational determiner *he*. And suppose, mirroring the pronominal hypothesis we are considering, that *he* is a special form of *the* (forget about gender for a moment). Then the following trivial modification of the familiar Russellian axiom for *the* is what we want for *he*:

(HE) $[he\ x_k: \phi;]\psi$; is true of a sequence s iff ψ is true of every sequence that ϕ is true of differing from s at most in the k-th position, and there is exactly one such sequence.

(If we want gender to affect truth conditions, we just insist that ϕ contain *male x* as a conjunct.) The truth conditions of (17), on one of its readings, are captured by *either* of the following sentences of RQ:

(18) $[every\ x_1: man\ x_1]\,(x_1\ thinks\ that\ ([he\ x_2: x_2 = x_1]\,(x_2\ snores)))$

(18′) $[every\ x_1: man\ x_1]\,(x_1\ thinks\ that\ ([he\ x_2: man\ x_2 \cdot x_2 = x_1]\,(x_2\ snores)))$.

If we see $[_{NP}e]$ as the product of NP-deletion, then we will see (17) as derived from something like (17′):

(17′) [every man] realizes that [he man] snores.

And on such account, there is a natural inclination to use (18′) in characterizing the logical form of (17). By contrast, if we see $[_{NP}e]$ as base-generated, so to speak, then (18) seems more natural. Either way, the unrestricted quantifier *he* binds the occurrence(s) of x_2 in the open sentence with which it combines to form a restricted quantifier; and either way the restricted quantifier—$[he\ x_2: x_2 = x_1]$ in (18), $[he\ x_2: man\ x_2 \cdot x_2 = x_1]$ in (18′)—binds the occurrence of x_2 in x_2 *snores*; so either way, we get a variable inside the matrix of a restricted quantifier that the other restricted quantifier $[every\ x_1: man\ x_1]$ binds.

We need to tie all this up with the English syntax of course; and in order to keep our options open, we need to do it for both (17) and (17′). If the structure of the DP 'he' in (17) is $[_{DP}[he\ [_{NP}e]]]$, we get what we want if this DP is understood as equivalent to $[he\ x_2: x_2 = x_1]$ in (18), which we get if the D 'he'—which is only *part of the DP* 'he'—is understood as equivalent to the RQ determiner *he x_2* and if the NP $[_{NP}e]$ is understood as equivalent to the RQ formula $x_2 = x_1$. The morpho-syntax of English will, in fact, insist upon the complement of 'he' always being $[_{NP}e]$.[121] So we might schematically specify the semantics of $[_{NP}e]$ as given by $x_k = x_j$ (for $j \neq k$) when such a device functions as the complement of the determiner 'he' (thus the aphonic NP in $[_{DP}[_D he][_{NP}e]]$ has a definite semantic role here—made transparent by (18)—which would justify its existence in a minimalist framework). When we have a suitably placed co-indexed binder as in (17), we have what will amount to a *bound* occurrence of 'he'. If there is no such binder, we have what amounts to a *free* occurrence of 'he', used to make indexical reference to some individual.[122]

Talk of *bound* pronouns is still perfectly intelligible on this account. The D 'he' is not bound; indeed it is a binder. And the DP 'he' is not *wholly bound* the way a bound variable is; rather it is just *bound-into*. The subscript on 'he' in (17) must now be understood as indicating that $[_{DP}[_D he][_{NP}e]]$ is *bound-into* rather than wholly bound.

Two questions of largely notational import now arise: (i) Where should we place the subscript '1' in the spelled-out DP? (ii) Will we ever need a subscript '2' corresponding to the '2' in the RQ rendering (18)?

(18) $[every\ x_1: man\ x_1]\ (x_1\ realizes\ that\ ([he\ x_2: x_2 = x_1]\ (x_2\ snores)))$.

In order to have something fixed, let us adopt the conventions implicit in (17″) if we are asked to set everything out in gory detail:

(17″) $[_{DP}\ every^1\ [_{NP}[_N man]]]^1$ realizes that $[_{DP}[_D he^2]\ [_{NP}e]_1]^2$ snores.

The index '1' is placed on the empty NP (or at least on its node); and just as the index '1' on the D 'every' projects to the DP 'every man' it heads, so the index '2' on the D 'he' projects to the DP 'he' it heads.

On this account, the RQ sentences (19′) and (16′) might explicate the logical forms of (19) (on one of its readings) and (16), respectively:

(19) every man thinks Mary loves him
(19′) $[every\ x_1: man\ x_1]\ (x_1\ thinks\ that\ ([him\ x_2: x_2 = x_1]\ (Mary\ loves\ x_2)))$
(16) every man loves himself
(16′) $[every\ x_1: man\ x_1]\ ([him\ x_2: x_2 = x_1]\ (x_1\ loves\ x_2))$.

(The axiom (HIM) for the RQ determiner *him* is just (HE) with $[he\ x_k: \phi]$ replaced by $[him\ x_k: \phi]$.)

---

[121] Examples like 'he, Chomsky, thinks that . . .' are epenthetic, hence irrelevant.
[122] Of course, we will need the usual constraints on indexing to prevent a DP binding into a pronoun that is meant to be free, as in (i):

(i) [every man]^1 thinks he [free] likes him$_1$.

We can probably improve upon $(16')$ once we have dealt with the possessive 'his'. There is a long tradition in philosophy of treating possessive DPs as definite descriptions, motivated in part by the apparent equivalence of 'Smith's murderer' and 'the murderer of Smith', and so on.[123] So, in the first instance we might explicate the logical form of (20), on its bound reading, by treating it as a superficial variant of (21), the logical form of which we can sketch using $(21')$:

(20) every man loves his wife

(21) every man loves the wife of him

$(21')$ $[every\ x_1: man\ x_1]\ ([the\ x_2: x_2\ wife\ x_1]\ (x_1\ loves\ x_2))$.

Now $(21')$ is only a sketch because it contains a (mere) variable corresponding to the occurrence of the DP 'him' in (21), a view we have already gone beyond. What we really need is $(21'')$:

$(21')$ $[every\ x_1: man\ x_1]\ ([the\ x_2: [him\ x_3: x_3 = x_1]\ (x_2\ wife\ x_3)]\ (x_1\ loves\ x_2))$.

Now what of (20) itself? A desire for a sentence of RQ more closely resembling the English sentence whose semantic structure it is meant to explicate might lead one to add another determiner, *his*, to RQ:

$(20')$ $[every\ x_1: man\ x_1]\ ([his\ x_2: x_2\ wife\ x_1]\ (x_1\ loves\ x_2))$.

The relevant axiom will be an interesting modification of the one for *he*, to be given in a moment. To bring out another feature of possessives, let us switch examples. Consider a particular utterance of (22):

(22) $[every\ man]^1$ groomed his$_1$ horse.

The DP 'his horse' might be understood as (e.g.) 'the horse he owned' or 'the horse he rode' or 'the horse he trained'. In RQ we might represent the DP as $[his\ x_k: horse\ x_k \cdot R(x_k, x_j)]$ where R is *owned* or *rode* or *trained*, as the case may be.[124] The following axiom would appear to yield what we want:

[123] Russell (1905); Kripke (1977); Higginbotham (1983a); Neale (1990). It is arguable that some possessives are better seen as *indefinite* descriptions ('John sprained his ankle', 'my cousin is visiting'). This matter is skirted here. In some cases the possessive must cede to the form beginning with 'the'. Thus we say 'the weight of this' not 'this's weight' (despite the acceptability of both 'the weight of this man' and 'this man's weight'. This appears to lend support to the view that the demonstrative pronouns 'this' and 'that' are just occurrences of the demonstrative determiners 'this' and 'that'.

[124] No specific relation is encoded by the possessive marker per se (Sperber and Wilson 1986). At most it signals that some relation or other is to be inferred, a relation that may differ from utterance to utterance. Sometimes the relation a speaker intends can be inferred from a relation inherent in the meaning of the noun: 'wife', 'mother', 'murderer', 'teacher', and 'mayor', for example, bring

(HIS) $[his\ x_k\colon \phi]\psi$ is true of a sequence s iff ψ is true of every sequence that $\phi \bullet R(x_k, x_j)$ is true of differing from s at most in the k-th position, and there is exactly one such sequence.

Of course this does not actually throw any light on the syntactic relation (if there is one) between the English sentences (20) and (21).[125]

Finally, the reflexive 'himself'. We might see this as the result of combining a pronominal determiner with 'self', construed as a genuine nominal like 'wife'.[126] If the determiner in question is just a phonetic variant of 'his', we can think of 'himself' as a possessive just like 'his wife' and use (16″) rather than (16′) to explicate the logical form of (16):

(16) every man loves himself
(16′) $[every\ x_1\colon man\ x_1]\,([him\ x_2\colon x_2 = x_1]\,(x_1\ loves\ x_2)\,)$

with them relations to things or places (but see below). But many nouns forming the complements of possessive determiners do not bring with them such relations ('donkey', 'man', 'table'); and while a default ownership relation may be understood in many cases, it is easy enough to find cases in which ownership is not the intended relation. I may use 'my horse', 'his horse', and 'Smith's horse' to describe the horses Smith and I have staked money on in the Cheltenham Gold Cup; or to describe the horses Smith and I were riding one afternoon; and it would be a stretch to say I am thereby using possessives non-literally. Furthermore, even in cases where the noun in use brings a particular relation along with it, that relation may not be the one of paramount importance to understanding what the speaker is saying. At a school sports day Smith and I may decide to bet on the outcome of the teachers' three-legged race or the mothers' egg-and-spoon race; at a prison sports day we might bet on the outcome of the cat-burglars' high-jump or the murderers' 100 metres. In recounting the day's results I may use 'Smith's murderer', 'my murderer', 'his mother', 'my teacher', and so on quite felicitously to talk about the contestants we have bet on. (Does this mean I can use 'my mother is not my mother' without contradiction? Yes. Similarly, someone whose birth mother is not his familial mother or legal mother. Of course we might be asked to expand on our respective remarks.)

[125] The LF of (20) may well be close to the LF of (21). The following is notoriously ambiguous:

(i) this is John's former house.

It may be used to say (a) that this house was formerly John's or (b) that this former house is John's (after an earthquake, for example). Larson and Cho (1999) suggest that this is the product of a scope ambiguity, roughly between (ii) and (iii):

(ii) this is the former [house of John]
(iii) this is the [former house] of John.

Working out the details seems to require seeing the PF (i) as corresponding to two distinct LFs, roughly those corresponding to the PFs (ii) and (iii).

[126] On the creation of English reflexives, see Keenan (2002) and references therein. In languages other than English not just analogues of 'self', but names of various body parts, are used in creating reflexives.

(16″) $[every\ x_1:\ man\ x_1]\ ([his\ x_2:\ x_2\ self\ x_1]\ (x_1\ loves\ x_2)\ ).$

On this account, no new axiom is needed as 'himself' is just a special case of 'his NP' where the relation R is identity.[127] Alternatively we could introduce a new determiner *himself* whose complement is always understood as an identity:

(16‴) $[every\ x_1:\ man\ x_1]\ ([himself\ x_2:\ x_1 = x_2]\ (x_1\ loves\ x_2)\ ).$

The axiom (HIMSELF) for *himself* will involve a trivial modification of (HIM). (Of course, it does not provide an explanation of what is *special* about reflexives; that is something we still need to provide.)

The upshot of all this is that even if pronouns are determiners, as much current linguistic theory suggests, there is no barrier to making sense of the idea that some occurrences (indeed, all occurrences of reflexive pronouns, for reasons that ought to emerge) are *bound*. To say that an occurrence of, say, 'him' is bound by a quantifier α is to say that the determiner 'him' is the head of a DP $[_{DP}[_D him]\ [_{NP}e]\ ]$ whose aphonic complement is understood as containing a variable bound by α.

One problem people have worried about in connection with binding in syntactic theory has been silently solved. Contrast the following:

(23) $[every\ man]^1$ realizes that $[some\ man]^2$ loves himself.$_{*1/2}$
(24) $[every\ man]^1$ realizes that he^2 loves himself.$_{*1/2}$

In (23), only 'some man' can bind himself, as predicted by Principle A of the Binding Theory. Similarly, only 'he' can bind 'himself' in (24). But surely 'every man' can bind 'he' in (24), just as it can in (25):

(25) $[every\ man]^1$ realizes that he$_1$ loves Mary.

So in (24) we need 'every man' to bind 'he', and 'he' in turn to bind 'himself'. If 'he' were a mere variable a *transitive* conception of binding might be required, the semantics of which might involve some rather fancy footwork. But on the proposal sketched here, what is needed drops out automatically, with Principles A and B respected. *Qua binder* the DP 'he' bears a superscript; *qua* device that is *bound-into*, its NP bears a subscript:

(23′) $[every\ man]^1$ realizes that $[_{DP}he\ [_{NP}e]_1]^2$ loves himself.$_{*1/2}$

---

[127] In examples like (i) and (ii), discussed by Jackendoff (1992) and Nunberg (1997), R would be some other relation only *involving* identity:

(i) At Madame Tussaud's, Bill Clinton took a photograph of himself.
(ii) Yeats hated hearing himself read in an English accent.

We can usefully abbreviate this:

(23″) [every man]^1 realizes that he$_1{}^2$ loves himself.$_{1/2}$.

Putting everything together, the sentence comes out as equivalent to the following, confirming that the Binding Theory has not been violated:

(24) $[\textit{every } x_1\colon \textit{man } x_1]\,(x_1 \textit{ realizes that } ([\textit{he } x_2\colon x_2 = x_1]\,([\textit{his } x_3\colon x_3 \textit{ self } x_2]\,(x_2 \textit{ loves } x_3))))$.

   A final word about the free or indexical use of pronouns before we move on. There is no obvious reason to think they differ syntactically from those that are bound (in English, at any rate). Either way, the general form is $[_{DP}[\text{he } [_{NP}e]]]$. But what of the interpretation of an indexical occurrence? Since the D 'he' is not indexical on the current proposal, the indexicality of the DP 'he' must lie in $[_{NP}e]$. The right thing to say is that whereas a bound use of 'he' is understood as $[\textit{he } x_j\colon x_j = x_k]$ with x_k bound by some other DP, on an indexical use it is understood as $[\textit{he } x_j\colon x_j = x_k]$ with x_k free to refer indexically. Thus what amounts to a unitary theory.

   Now we need to unify names and quantifiers in their binding of pronouns.

12. Unification: Farewell to Co-reference

We have been working on the assumption that an anaphoric pronoun is one occurring within the scope of some other expression α that binds it, even when α is a name (or some other singular term). But, famously, many linguists and philosophers have assumed that when α is a name, the pronoun functions as a device of *co-reference*. In (1), for example, it is sometimes suggested that if /John/ is the antecedent of /his/, the two expressions are co-referential:

(1) John^1 loves his$_1$ wife.

While this may be a harmless assumption for many philosophical purposes, we cannot afford to be so incautious or incurious if we are in the business of providing a comprehensive theory of pronouns and anaphora. One reasonable desideratum is a uniform account of how /his/ (and derivatively /his wife/ and /loves his wife/) function in (1) and (2):

(2) [every man]^1 loves his$_1$ wife.

And it is not immediately obvious how a co-reference account of /his/ in (1) and a bound variable account of /his/ in (2) can constitute a unified account.

Evans's co-reference rule is straightforward: a pronoun β anaphoric on a singular term α refers to whatever α refers to.[128] This ensures that on the reading of (1) that interests us, the reference of 'his' is identical to the reference of 'John', and that an utterance of the whole sentence is true if and only if John loves John's wife. What of (2), the quantified counterpart of (1)? Evans opts for a 'Fregean' interpretation of quantifiers. The rule for 'every ϕ' is straightforward (if unfamiliar to those weaned on Tarski). An utterance of sentence (2) is true if and only if 'x loves his wife' is true of every man; and 'x loves his wife' is true of an arbitrarily selected man m if and only if, taking α as a name of m, the sentence 'α loves his wife' is true. If the language happens to contain no name of m, then we consider a minimal *extension* of the language that *does* contain a name for m; that is, we add to our language a *new* name to use when referring to m.[129] Once the rule for 'every ϕ' has been applied, Evans's co-reference rule is applied, and we obtain the result that 'α loves his wife' is true if and only if the referent of α loves the wife of the referent of α, i.e. if and only if m loves m's wife. Since m was chosen arbitrarily, this means an utterance of (2) is true if and only if for every man x, x loves x's wife.[130]

But there is a problem here, one Evans appears to recognize but whose severity he appears to underestimate. Versions of the problem have been raised by Castañeda (1966), Partee (1975), and Soames (1989, 1990, 1994). Consider the following quantified-singular pair:

(3) Mary thinks that John[1] loves his$_1$ wife
(4) Mary thinks that [every man][1] loves his$_1$ wife.

The bound variable treatment of the pronoun in (4) delivers (4')—with an eye to readability, henceforth I shall often use x, y, and z, in place of x_1, x_2, and x_3, where possible:

(4')　*Mary thinks that ([every x: man x] (x loves x's wife)).*

---

[128] Evans himself does not actually require that β be within the scope of α—he wants his co-reference rule to operate quite generally.

[129] There is no assumption here that there is some extension of the language that contains a name of *every* man, only an assumption that for every man there is some extension of the language that contains a name of him.

[130] See Evans (1980/1985: 227–8). As Soames (1989) points out, Evans assumes that all singular terms in natural language are rigid. This is a view Evans (1982) defends. It is, of course, an empirical thesis about natural language that singular terms are rigid. The fact that one can construct formal languages that contain non-rigid singular terms or design non-rigid singular terms to be added to theoretical fragments of natural language is neither here nor there.

This captures the fact that (4) is true (on one of its readings) iff Mary thinks that every man is an own-wife's lover. Of course (4′) is actually quite schematic as we are treating 'his' as a determiner. (4″) is closer to what we want:

(4″) *Mary thinks that* ([*every x: man x*] ([*his y: y wife x*] (*x loves y*))).

The analogous reading of (3) is true iff Mary thinks that John is an own-wife's lover, but that reading is *not* captured by saying that 'John' and 'his' are co-referential.[131] For on such an account an utterance of (3) could be true if Mary believes that John loves the wife of some man she sees but does not realize is John.[132] So even if 'his' can be used as a device of de jure co-reference—which has not yet been established—we still appear to need to take into account its use as a device that can be bound by names. We are left with three remaining questions, then: (i) Can we provide a plausible unification in the reverse direction? (ii) If so, can we do it without treating names as quantifiers; and (iii) Can we then dispense altogether with appeals to a use of 'his' as a device of de jure co-reference?

(i) In order to explain what is going on in (3), we seem to need the *abstraction* introduced by the quantification in (4′). That is, we appear to need a formula in which the name 'John' binds a variable. Schematically, (3′), with more detail (3″):

(3′) *Mary thinks that* ([*John x*] (*x loves x's wife*))
(3″) *Mary thinks that* ([*John x*] ([*his y: y wife x*] (*x loves y*))).

This suggests we unify the treatment of pronouns bound by quantifiers and those bound by names by treating names as quantifiers.[133] (If one is already convinced that proper names are generalized quantifiers, or that they are disguised Russellian descriptions—then one is already persuaded. But if one has reasons for thinking names are *not* quantifiers, other possibilities will have to be explored.)

For simplicity, let us go back to example (1), the logical form of which, on the present account, may be sketched using (1′):

(1′) [*John x*] ([*his y: y wife x*] (*x loves y*)).

[131] Soames (1990, 1994); Reinhart and Reuland (1993); Heim and Kratzer (1998). The problem is replicated for other de jure co-reference accounts of pronouns bound by names as well as for the 'pragmatic' co-reference accounts of Lasnik (1976) and Bach (1987).

[132] Various assumptions are made here, some of which may be non-trivial. See Soames (1990, 1994).   [133] On names as quantifiers, Montague (1973), Barwise and Cooper (1981).

In a Tarskian vein, the following axiom would appear to suffice for a quantifier *John*:

(JOHN) $[John]_k\psi$ is true of a sequence s iff ψ is true of every sequence with John in the k-th place differing from s at most in what it assigns to x_k and there is exactly one such sequence.[134]

We appear now to have a complete theory of bound pronouns, one according to which quantifiers, names, and pronouns can all bind pronouns, indeed one which makes semantic sense of the seemingly transitive binding in a sentence like (5) and at the same time respects the Binding Theory:

(5) John says that he loves his wife
(5′) $[John\ x]\,(x\ says\ that\,([he\ y: y = x]\,([his\ z: z\ wife\ y]\,(y\ loves\ z))))$.

(ii) If one is determined to resist the idea that names are quantifiers, all is not lost. For there are reasons for thinking that the relevant abstraction emerges in another way. On an account of predication that has much to commend it independently, an intransitive V, say 'snores', amounts to a one-place predicate '$\lambda x(x\ snores)$' which exhausts the VP.[135] An intransitive verb, say 'loves', amounts to a two-place predicate $\lambda y(\lambda x(x\ loves\ y))$. On such an account, α's binding β amounts to α's merging with a λ-predicate whose operator binds β.[136] Schematic logical forms of (1) and (2) are given by (1″) and (2″):

(1) John loves his wife
(1″) $John(\lambda x(x\ loves\ x's\ wife)\,)$
(2) every man loves his wife
(2″) $[every\ y: man\ y]\,(y(\lambda x(x\ loves\ x's\ wife))\,)$.

Spelling out the finessed 'his' we get (1‴) and (2‴):

---

[134] If Montague's approach is taken, the quantifier would be regarded as standing for a higher-order property: 'every man' would stand for that property true of just those properties every man has; 'John' would stand for that property true of just those properties John has.

[135] One reason for espousing this approach to predication is that it appears to explain what is going on in sentences containing conjoined VPs without seeing such sentences as sentence conjunctions. For example, (i) is understood as (ii):

(i) John snores and sleepwalks
(ii) $John(\lambda x\,(x\ snores \bullet x\ sleepwalks))$.

To better mirror English surface forms, here and throughout I put the lambda predicate after the term it applies to.

[136] Heim and Kratzer (1998); Reuland (2001*a*, *b*); Reinhart (2000); Salmon (1986, 1992); Soames (1990, 1994).

(1‴) *John*(λx([*his z: z wife x*] (*x loves z*))

(2‴) [*every y: man y*] (*y*(λx([*his z: z wife x*](*x loves z*)))).

We now seem to be in a position to say something about locality. The VPs 'loves him' and 'loves himself' are both formed by merging the verb 'loves' with a DP. On the assumption that economy drives languages to contain devices whose job is to register mandatory binding, there will surely be pressure on such devices to be locally bound. The V 'loves' is understood as '(λy(λx(*x loves y*)))', and it is implicitly asking the DP with which it combines to form a VP how *y* stands with respect to *x*. The reflexive replies, '*y* = *x*', thus terminating discussion—the question cannot arise again for *that* reflexive later in the building process—meaning that the reflexive is locally bound. (In an alternative framework the reflexive might be understood as λPλxPxx.) By contrast, the non-reflexive 'him' replies, '*y* ≠ *x*', leaving the matter open.

On this view, 'himself' might be seen as the reflexive form of the accusative 'him'. The absence of a reflexive form of the nominative 'he' would now be explained: the subject of S is outside the scope of the λ-operator introducing the VP of S. This leaves us with /his/, about which I shall have much to say later—to foreshadow, it is the surface form of distinct reflexive and non-reflexive pronouns.

Relatedly, we must now take on the matter of subject-orientation. In many languages, reflexives can be bound only by subject expressions. This is exactly as one would expect on the current proposal. But of course English is not such a language as we saw earlier with (6), which contrasts in this respect with the Icelandic (6′):

(6) John[1] told Paul[2] a lot about himself$_{1/2}$

(6′) *Jón*[1] *sagði Páli*[2] *frá (sjálfum) sér*$_{1/*2}$.

Let us hold off on this matter until we have more data to work with.[137]

(iii) Can we now dispense with talk of de jure co-reference in an account of pronominal anaphora? Examples like (7) might suggest not:

(7) John loves his wife. Yesterday I saw him buying her roses again. He spends a lot of money on flowers. His wife is very lucky.

---

[137] Corresponding to the simplex reflexives *sig* (ACC), *sér* (DAT), and *sín* (GEN) are complex counterparts *sjálfan sig*, *sjálfum sér*, and *sjálfs sín*, hence the parenthetical *sjálfum* in (6). Simplex reflexives get up to tricks their well-behaved complex counterparts do not (see below). This is also the case in many other languages—and not just the Scandinavian or even Germanic languages—and it is widely held that this is directly connected to the fact that the simplex reflexives have fewer 'φ features', which include things like person, number, and gender, which at least in principle could make them less restrictive in application. Contrast English 'himself', which can only be used of males, and Icelandic *sig*, which is not so restricted.

On the proposed unification we have no account of the apparently cross-sentential, unbound anaphora exemplified here. We can say that the first occurrence of /his/ is bound by 'John'; but then we appear to be stuck. The occurrences of /him/ and /he/, and the second occurrence of /his/, are not within the scope of 'John' so they are not bound; yet they can certainly be used to refer to John. But does this mean they are *anaphoric* on 'John' in any sense relevant to grammatical theory? Is there anything problematic involved in saying (following Kripke and Lewis in one context, and Lasnik and Bach in another) that John has been raised to sufficient salience by the use of 'John' in the first sentence of (6), that he is a reasonable target for indexical uses of /he/, /him/, and /his/ in the subsequent sentences? If not, then it seems we have not yet found a good reason for thinking that co-reference plays a role in a theory of anaphora.

But are we absolutely certain we can dispense with the notion of de jure co-reference in cases of *c-command* anaphora? Here matters are tricky, as we can see by looking at an example of linguistic ellipsis. The literature on this form of ellipsis is vast and consensus is not easy to find, but traditionally linguistic ellipsis is subject to a stringent parallelism condition on form and interpretation.[138] 'A constituent may be deleted at PF only if it is a copy of another constituent at LF,' as Heim and Kratzer (1998: 250) put it, moreover a copy *interpreted in the same way*. We may as well call this *recoverability* as it is basically today's analogue of what used to be known as the *recoverability of deletion* (see Chomsky 1964), itself basically a consequence of Katz and Postal's (1964) hypothesis that transformational rules do not affect meaning.[139] Compare (8) and (9):

(8) John loves himself, and Paul does too

(9) John loves his wife, and Paul does too.

---

[138] For recent, user-friendly discussions of linguistic ellipsis, see Heim and Kratzer (1998) and May (2002).

[139] As Heim and Kratzer note, 'A main insight of work on ellipsis in the 1970s was that the relevant level had to be one which was fully disambiguated with respect to interpretation' (1998: 250). As K. Bach (1981), Larson and Segal (1995), and Ostertag (1999) have warned, it is important to distinguish two quite different uses of the words 'ellipsis' and 'elliptical' in the philosophy of language. The first, a *pragmatic* notion, is found in explicit talk of elliptical *uses* or elliptical *utterances* of sentences, by Quine (1940), Sellars (1954), Kripke (1977), K. Bach (1981), Neale (1990), and others in their respective appraisals of Russell (1905). The second, a *grammatical* notion, is found in explicit talk of elliptical *sentences* by Strawson (1954) and Stanley (2002), which corresponds to linguistic ellipsis in generative linguistics. There can be only embarrassment in store today for those who run the two together. It is somewhat surprising that Strawson (1954), who in 1950 impressed upon us so forcefully the distinction between *sentences* and *utterances of sentences* in his critique of Russell, misses it completely in his critique of Sellars's (1954) defence of Russell, despite the fact that Sellars himself

There is a single reading of (8). But there are two quite distinct readings of (9):

(9′) *Paul*(λx([*his z: z wife-of x*](*x loves z*)))
(9″) *Paul*(λx([*his z: z wife-of John*](*x loves z*))).

The former is usually called the *sloppy* reading, the latter the *strict* reading. The sloppy reading is readily explained on the assumption that 'his' is bound by 'John' in the first clause of (8). On that assumption, the first clause predicates λx([*his z: z wife-of x*](*x loves z*)) of John, the second predicates it of Paul.[140]

But what about the strict reading? There would appear to be two ways to go here. The first involves abandoning the dream of dispensing with de jure co-reference altogether in a final theory of anaphora: 'John loves his wife' is ambiguous between two distinct anaphoric readings, one on which 'John' binds 'his', yielding the sloppy reading of (9) as before, the other on which 'his' is a device of de jure co-reference, referentially dependent upon 'John', yielding the strict reading. However, this proposal might be thought to be undermined by the absence of a strict reading of (8), which demonstrates that 'John loves himself' has only a bound reading (if 'himself' could be used as a device of de jure co-reference, referentially dependent upon 'John', a strict reading of (8) should be available). On the other hand, the contrast might be construed as merely illustrating an important difference between reflexives and non-reflexives: the former permit only bound readings.

The alternative proposal involves saying there is only one anaphoric use of 'his', the bound use, and then explicating the strict reading of (9) in terms of an *indexical* use of 'his', one upon which it is used to refer to John, who has been made salient by the use of 'John' (thus taking a leaf out of Lasnik's book). This seems to me the correct analysis, but it raises an interesting issue. Principle B prevents 'him' from being *bound* by 'John' in (10):

(10) John loves him.

(i) respects the sentence–utterance distinction, (ii) consistently talks of elliptical *utterances*, and (iii) makes it very clear this is what he is talking about in connection with utterances of descriptions. As a result, Strawson's objections, parroted by Stanley (2002), are stillborn. For detailed textual analysis and a discussion of the issues, see Neale (2004).

[140] Keenan (1971); Sag (1976); Williams (1977); Heim and Kratzer (1998); Reinhart (1983); Grodzinsky and Reinhart (1993). The common predication in singular and quantified pairs seems to explain the fact that we understand and immediately see the validity of the sloppy (i):

(i) Every Englishman loves his wife, but John doesn't, so John can't be English.

That is, Principle B prevents (10) from being read as (10′):

(10′) *John* ($\lambda x(x\ loves\ x)$).

But aren't we now forced to posit a principle that prevents a speaker from using 'him' indexically in an utterance of (10) to refer to John, to block the reading whose truth conditions we might represent using (10″)?

(10″) *John* ($\lambda x(x\ loves\ John)$).

This is far from obvious. First, I might utter (10) while pointing at a man I do *not* take to be John but *do* take to be someone John loves, unaware that it is actually John. At most it would seem we need a principle that prevents a speaker from using 'him' indexically in (10) to refer to someone he takes to be the referent of his use of 'John'. But even this seems too strong. Suppose you and I are sitting at a sidewalk café discussing John. You say to me, 'He loves no one'. I am about to reply, 'Untrue. John loves himself', when I notice John across the street and instead utter, 'Untrue. John loves him', pointing at John, knowing that you will recognize him immediately.[141]

On this account, only indexical readings of the pronouns are possible in (11)–(13), as they do not lie within the scope of 'John':

(11) /his wife loves John/
(12) /the woman he married loves John/
(13) /the woman who married him loves John/.

This seems to me a good result. First, only indexical readings of the pronouns are available in the quantified counterparts of (11)–(13):

(11′) /his wife loves every man/
(12′) /the woman he married loves every man/
(13′) /the woman who married him loves every man/.

If we are serious about giving a unified account of what is going on in quantified-singular pairs like (1) and (2), we should be just as serious about giving a unified

---

[141] Reinhart (1983, 2000), Grodzinsky and Reinhart (1993), Reinhart and Reuland (1993), and Reuland (2001*b*) have explored various formulations of some sort of interpretive condition on (roughly) intrasentential co-reference. The underlying thought is if a given message can be conveyed by two LFs differing only in whether a particular pronoun β is construed as bound by α or as co-referential with α, the former is to be strongly preferred. An alternative has been explored by Heim (1993).

account of what is going on in the quantified-singular pairs $(11')-(11)$, $(12')-(12)$, and $(13)-(13')$.

For each of $(11)-(13)$ there is certainly a reading upon which the pronoun and 'John' are co-referential. But that is no threat to the theory at hand: the occurrences of /his/, /he/, and /him/ in $(10)-(12)$ can be used indexically to refer to whoever 'John' is being used to refer to, John being as salient as any other potential target of an indexical occurrence of a masculine pronoun (at least by the time the name 'John' is uttered). With utterances of the quantified examples, by contrast, there is no corresponding individual to target (i.e. no individual who is also the intended referent of the relevant DP, which is quantificational).[142]

---

[142] Do we have here the germ of an argument for a semantically distinct referential reading of definite descriptions? Larson and Segal (1995) appear to think so. Here is a version of the argument they mount, cast in the terminology of the present chapter. Consider the following:

   (i) /his wife loves the man I talked to/
   (ii) /the woman he married loves the man I talked to/
   (iii) /the woman who married him loves the man I talked to/.

Binding is out of the question—witness $(11')-(13')$. But seemingly contrary to expectations, these examples pattern with the *singular* examples $(11)-(13)$, not with the quantified examples $(11')-(13')$, in admitting of readings upon which the direct object and the pronoun buried in the subject DP seem to co-refer. How is this to be explained? Answer: the pronoun must be functioning as a referring expression that inherits its referent from the direct object, just as in $(11)-(13)$ where the direct object is a referring expression. But in that case the descriptions in $(i)-(iii)$ must also be functioning as referring expressions.

This argument is essentially a syntactically elaborate version of the Argument from Anaphora presented by Strawson (1952) for a referential reading of descriptions, and as such appears to fall short of its target for reasons given by Ludlow and Neale (1991) and Neale (1990) using an observation made by Kripke (1977) and Lewis (1979). Using a description referentially—no one doubts referential *usage*, only its semantic significance—can make a particular individual salient (just as using a name can), rendering that individual a natural target for an occurrence of a pronoun used freely. The Russellian does not deny that the pronouns in $(i)-(iii)$ may be used to refer to the same individual the speaker is referring to using the descriptions; at the same time, he agrees with the syntactician that these pronouns are *not bound by* those descriptions. There is no contradiction here, indeed no tension whatsoever. If the antecedent description is used *non*-referentially, as it might be in a particular of, say,

   (iv) his prime minister walks behind the monarch,

plausibly it is descriptive (see below). That we might be on the right track seems to be supported by the following contrast:

   (v) his wife loves a man I was just talking to
   (vi) his wife loves a man.

It is easier to use the richer 'a man I was just talking to' referentially here than it is to use 'a man' so.

If this general framework is right, we need to be careful with our words again, particularly 'pragmatic'. Identifying whether A is using /his/ in the bound or in the indexical way *is* a pragmatic matter: although B's knowledge of word meaning and syntax tell B that A must be using /his/ in either the bound or indexical way, it does not provide B with enough information to establish *which one* A *intends* on any particular occasion. At the same time, *if* A is using /his/ in the bound way, then the pronoun's interpretation *is fixed relative to that use*: if B happens to know that A is using /his/ in the bound way—suppose, for the sake of argument, that A reveals this to B—there is no *further* pragmatic work for B to do with respect to /his/: its interpretation is now secured. By contrast, *if* A is avowedly using /his/ in the indexical way, there is still some pragmatic work for B to do: B needs to establish whether A is using /his/ to refer to, say, John, or Paul, or George, or Ringo.

All of this serves to indicate once again that we must pause to reflect when we come across claims that the interpretation of pronouns, or of certain pronouns, or of certain occurrences of pronouns is a 'pragmatic' matter. All sorts of claims, some correct, others false or misguided, may lurk beneath the surface of such loose remarks.

Does the fact that /his/ admits of distinct bound and indexical uses mean that it is *ambiguous*, and that (1) and (2) are correspondingly ambiguous?[143] The fear of being assailed for postulating ambiguities has driven philosophers to heroic lengths in preserving unitary semantic analyses.[144] But ambiguity is a tricky notion: some forms (by whatever fancy name) are seemingly less expensive than others; some may result in theoretical simplification elsewhere; and some may make more sense if seen from the perspective of more than one language, as we shall see.

13. Bound and Free

Suppose we were to find languages in which there is no unique translation of either (1) or (2) because quite unrelated pronouns—rather than mere

---

[143] The question is somewhat reminiscent of the question whether /the/ is ambiguous because definite descriptions have distinct attributive and referential uses. My own view is that /the/ is not ambiguous (at least not in a way that the attributive–referential distinction brings out).

[144] Classic cases of this involve the interpretation of /the/, /a/, /and/, /or/, /if/, /because/, /know/, and /see/.

morphological variants—were used depending upon whether a bound or indexical use of /his/ is intended:

(1) /John loves his wife/
(2) /every man loves his wife/.

And suppose these languages contained only one translation of (3), containing the indexical pronoun where English has 'his':

(3) /his wife loves John/.

A native English speaker might say that these languages make a pointless lexical distinction. But a native speaker of a Scandinavian language (Danish, Faroese, Icelandic, Norwegian, or Swedish), in which there appears to be a *lexical* distinction between genitive and possessive pronouns (the latter being reflexive), might say that the English /his/ is ambiguous, albeit in a systematic way. Translating (1) or (2) into Icelandic, for example, requires fixing whether or not /his/ is bound by the subject expression:

(1′) *Jón¹ elskar konuna sína₁*
John loves wife-the self's-FEM + ACC + SG
('John¹ loves his₁ wife').
(2′) [*sérhver maður*]¹ *elskar konuna sína₁*
every man loves wife-the self's-FEM + ACC + SG
('[every man]¹ loves his₁ wife').

The word *sína* is a reflexive possessive (or possessive reflexive), feminine, accusative, and singular to agree with *konuna*, the noun it qualifies (which is why I have rendered it as *self's*, rather than *his*).[145]

---

[145] The Icelandic definite article typically takes the form of a suffix added to the noun (its origins in a free-standing definite article which is rarely encountered in ordinary talk today). Without the suffix the noun is typically understood as indefinite. So, for example, in the nominative (used primarily for the subject of a verb) the feminine noun *kona* ('woman' or 'wife') becomes *konan* ('the woman' or 'the wife') when definite. In the accusative (used primarily for the direct object of a verb but also with some prepositions) *konu* becomes *konuna* when made definite, as in the example discussed above. Apart from certain standardized exceptions, the counterparts of English possessive descriptions are formed using the definite rather than the indefinite form of the noun. There are two main types of exception. The first is where the noun to which the possessive is attached expresses a close family relation, with the notable exception of *kona* (which can translate 'woman' as well as 'wife'). The second will be explained once the difference between possessive and genitive pronouns in Icelandic has been set out.

But if the English pronoun is understood indexically, indicated here with a subscripted arrow, (1) and (2) must be translated as follows:[146]

(1″) *Jón elskar konuna hans*
John loves wife-the he-($\text{MASC}+\text{GEN}+\text{SG}$).
('John loves his ↓ wife').

(2″) *sérhver maður elskar konuna hans*
every man loves wife-the he-($\text{MASC}+\text{GEN}+\text{SG}$).
('every man loves his ↓ wife').

Here *hans* is the simple genitive, which (unlike *sína*) occurs in the masculine and enters into no agreement relations whatsoever with *konuna*.[147] The important *interpretive* point is that *sína* is always bound and hence always within the scope of its antecedent.[148]

On the assumption that anaphoric readings are marked *syntactically*, what exactly do we say about the English (1) and (2)? Given the data from Icelandic,

---

[146] The arrow notation is borrowed from Evans (1980), but it may be viewed here as a formal non-numerical subscript the presence of which blocks assignment of a numerical subscript.

[147] The genitive is also used with proper names (and with common nouns) to indicate possession. Thus the accusative form of 'John's wife' will be *konu Jóns*—that is, unlike in cases involving posses-sive pronouns (*konuna sína*) and cases involving genitive pronouns (*konuna hans*), in cases involving gen-itive names (*konu Jóns*), the suffix for the definite article is *not* added to the noun; thus the second type of exception mentioned a moment ago.

[148] Linguists who have investigated Icelandic often point to special contexts in which a simple reflexive may appear despite lying strictly outside the scope of its purported antecedent. (See e.g. Maling 1984, Þráinsson 1991, Reuland and Sigurjónsdóttir 1997.) (i) might be used to make the point:

(i) [$_{DP}$*trú Jóns*[1]] *viraðist vera Þú elski sig*$_1$/*konuna sína*$_1$
[$_{DP}$belief John's] seems be that you love-SUBJ self/wife-the self's
('John's[1] belief seems to be that you love him$_1$/his$_1$ wife').

The following features appear to be crucial to these examples: (*a*) the subject expression must express something like a perspective or centre of consciousness of the individual referred to by *Jón*; (*b*) the verb must be in the subjunctive. In a switch to my perspective all is lost:

(ii) [$_{DP}$*trú Jóns*[1]] *fær mig til aðhalda Þú elskir sig*$_{*1}$ *konuna sína*$_{*1}$*sig*$_{*1}$
[$_{DP}$belief John's] leads me to think that you love-SUBJ self-the self's
('John'[1]'s belief leads me to think that you love him$_{*1}$/his$_{*1}$ wife').

Such facts suggest to some linguists that these reflexives are *logophors* rather than *anaphors*. A pronoun β is *logophoric* if (i) some antecedent expression α has been used to refer to some individual x, and (ii) β is now used to refer to x from x's own perspective. (The perspective manifests itself in the stretch of discourse containing α and β—for example, the speaker or writer might be reporting or more

one might consider associating two distinct LFs with each, one in which /his/ is a bound pronoun (subscripted with a numeral) and one in which it is an indexical:

(4) $[_S[_{DP}\text{every man}]^1 [_S e_1^1 \text{ loves his}_1 \text{ wife}]]$

(5) $[_S[_{DP} \text{every man}]^1 [_S e_1 \text{ loves his }_\downarrow \text{ wife}]].$

But on the proposal outlined earlier, once these LFs are specified more precisely it is tempting to say that 'his' is unambiguous: it is an unambiguous D, part of DP, part of the NP of which needs a value, and that value can be fixed through binding or, if unbound, indexically:

(4′) $[_S[_{DP}\text{every man}]^1 [_S[_{DP}\text{his}^2 [_{NP}\text{wife } e_1]]^2 [_S e_1 \text{ loves } e_2]]]$

(5′) $[_S[_{DP}\text{every man}]^1 [_S[_{DP}\text{his}^2 [_{NP}\text{wife } e_\downarrow]]^2 [_S e_1 \text{ loves } e_2]]].$

14. Pragmatic Anaphora?

There is no shortage of English sentences in which a pronoun β appears to be anaphoric on an expression α (singular or quantified) yet does not lie within α's scope and hence cannot, on our assumptions, be bound by α. Let us use

generally representing x's speech, thoughts, feelings, or perceptions.) (Logophors were brought to the attention of linguists by Hagège 1974, to whom the term appears to be due, and Clements 1975 in their investigations of certain African languages.) In connection with Icelandic the logophor hypothesis is the hypothesis that in certain subjunctive constructions that crucially involve something like the perspective of some individual, a simple reflexive need not occur within the scope of its antecedent. Indeed it is arguable that such a reflexive may have *no overt antecedent whatsoever*, as in the following example discussed by Sigurðsson (1990):

(iii) *María var alltaf svo andstyggileg*
Mary was always so nasty
Þegar Ólafur kæmi segði hún sér áreiðanlega að fara . . .
When Olaf would come-SUBJ, she would certainly tell self to leave
[self ≠ Olaf, but the person whose perspective or thought is being represented].

On the other hand, the contrast between (i) and (ii) may bear some similarity to the contrast in English between the near c-command cases (iv) and (v):

(iv) [Bush's opinion] is that pictures of himself in uniform all over town will capture votes

(v) [Bush^1's campaign] requires pictures of himself in uniform to be put up all over town.

(iv) is certainly more acceptable than (v) to my ear (in my dialect 'him' must replace 'himself' in both, but (iv) seems more forgivable). For interesting recent discussion of the issues here, see Reuland (2001a).

subscripts in parentheses if the (purportedly) anaphoric connection is not one of binding:

(1) John^1 is cleaning the house. His$_{(1)}$ wife returns today
(2) If John^1 is late, Mary will be upset with him$_{(1)}$.

It would seem sufficient to say that the use of the name 'John' in utterances of (1) and (2) renders some individual salient enough to be a natural target for indexical uses of the pronouns 'his' and 'him'. If we insist on using the words 'anaphora' and 'anaphoric' here, let us preface them with a qualifier like 'seeming' or 'unbound' or 'discourse' or 'pragmatic'. (The Icelandic translations of (1) and (2) comport with this idea, requiring unbound *hans* for /his/, and unbound *hann* for /him/, respectively.) Continuing with Postal's idea that 'his wife' and 'him' are descriptions, the idea would be that $[_{DP}$him $[_{NP}e]]$ in (2), for example, is understood as $[him\ x_1: x_1 = x_2]$ with x_2 free to refer indexically to John.

What about cases in which a pronoun is seemingly anaphoric on a quantified DP outside whose scope it lies, for example (3) and (4)?

(3) John bought [only one donkey]^1 and Paul vaccinated it$_{(1)}$
(4) If John buys [just one donkey]^1 then he pays cash for it$_{(1)}$.

As Evans (1977) points out, construing the pronouns in these examples as variables bound by the quantified DPs upon which they appear to be anaphoric, by giving the quantifiers large scope, yields the wrong results. Someone who utters (3), for example, would not be claiming that only one donkey satisfies *John bought x and Paul vaccinated x*. For that claim is consistent with John buying two donkeys, while the claim made by uttering the original conjunction in (3) is not.

If genuine grammatical anaphora involves binding, what are we to say about these discourse pronouns? We have construed a pronoun seemingly anaphoric on, but not bound by, a *name* as an indexical co-referential with the name. What is the analogue of this where the seeming antecedent is a quantified DP? A number of philosophers and linguists have argued that the pronouns in question *go proxy for descriptions* and hence are themselves quantified DPs (assuming Russell's Theory of Descriptions) just like their purported antecedents.[149] On such an account, the occurrence of the pronoun 'it' is understood as if it were an

---

[149] Cooper (1979); Davies (1981); Ludlow and Neale (1991); Neale (1990, 1994, 2004). In a different vein, see also Elbourne (2001, 2002). Such theories have their origins in Evans's (1977) theory of E-type pronouns, which several of the aforementioned people, as well as Soames (1989), see as both confused and empirically flawed. According to Evans, the pronouns in (3) and (4)—and, indeed, all others apparently anaphoric on quantified expressions that do not bind them—form a natural group in *having their references fixed rigidly by descriptions*, singular or plural as the case may be. In (3), for

occurrence of the description 'the donkey John bought'; in (2) it is understood as if it were an occurrence of 'the donkey John buys'. Let us call pronouns that go proxy for descriptions in this way *D-type* pronouns. Since descriptions may enter into scope relations with other expressions, the so-called D-type proposal can explain certain ambiguities. For example, (5) appears to have two readings according as /he/, understood as going proxy for 'the man who assaulted the queen last night', is read with small or large scope in the second sentence:[150]

> (5) A man assaulted the queen last night. The police think he's an escaped convict.

The D-type proposal appears to be successful with examples like (6) and (7) involving what is known variously as 'relativization', 'covariation', or 'implicit binding':

> (6) every villager owns [a donkey]^1 and feeds it$_{(1)}$ at night
> (7) every villager who bought [a donkey]^1 vaccinated it$_{(1)}$.

The pronoun /it/ is naturally understood as going proxy for the description /the donkey he bought/, read with smaller scope than the subject quantifier, capturing the implicit binding of the pronoun /he/ in the description for which 'it' goes

---

example, /it/ has its reference fixed by 'the donkey John bought'; and in (4), /it/ has its reference fixed by 'the donkey John buys'. (On Evans's account, the larger group to which E-type pronouns belongs also includes descriptive names such as 'Julius', introduced by a description such as 'the man who invented the zip'. See Evans (1982, 1985) for discussion.

[150] This ambiguity seems beyond the reach of Evans's E-type theory. In the same vein, consider (i):

> (i) [Mary^1 wants [$_s$PRO^1 to marry [a wealthy man]^2]]. He$_{(2)}$ must be a millionaire.

The first sentence in (i) may be read *de dicto* (as the Russellian would put it, the scope of 'a wealthy man' may be small, just the embedded sentence). Moreover, the pronoun 'he' in the second clause can be discourse-anaphoric on 'a wealthy man'. But as Karttunen (1976) notes, on this *de dicto* reading the modal expression 'must' must be present for the discourse anaphora to work. Compare (i) with (ii):

> (ii) [Mary^1 wants [$_s$PRO$_1$ to marry [a wealthy man]^2]]. He$_{(2)}$'s a millionaire.

In (ii) it is not possible to get the *de dicto* reading for the antecedent clause if 'he' is discourse-anaphoric on 'a wealthy man'. The contrast between (i) and (ii) is explicable on the assumption that 'he' is interpreted as if it were the description 'the man Mary marries', which may take small scope with respect to the modal 'must' in (i) (an infelicitous existence implication results if it is interpreted with large scope). In (ii) on the other hand, since there is no modal operator with respect to which the pronoun can be understood with small scope, the sentence has no felicitous reading when the antecedent clause is read *de dicto*.

proxy.[151] Obviously the D-type proposal harmonizes with the general idea that third-person pronouns are descriptions. There is no explicit commitment in the proposal itself, however, to the view that whereas the PFs of (6) and (7) contain 'it' their LFs contain the fleshed-out definite description 'the donkey he owns'; but that is certainly one option that might be explored.[152]

With the distinction between bound and 'pragmatic' anaphora in mind, let us reflect for a moment on the nature of the distinction between, on the one hand 'his$_k$' and the Icelandic *sína* (etc.), and on the other 'his $_\downarrow$' and the Icelandic *hans*. A donkey sentence containing a relative clause can be used as a diagnostic:

(8) [every man who has [a son]^2]^1 admires his$_{1/(2)}$ wife.

The important feature of (8) is that /his/ is *within* the scope of the subject DP /every man who has a son/ but *outside* the scope of the DP /a son/. When /his/ is

---

[151] On Evans's E-type account, /it/ has its reference fixed in (6) and (7) by the description /the donkey he owns/, the interpretation of 'he' covarying with objects that 'villager' is true of in (6) and objects that 'villager who bought a donkey' is true of in (6). So although the pronouns in (6) and (7) are not themselves bound, interpreting them does involve recognizing implicit binding because the interpretation of /he/ in the description that fixes the referent of /it/ must covary with other items. The word 'implicit' is vital here, for Evans makes no claim about the existence of a variable in the underlying syntactic structures of (6) or (7) that is bound by the subject quantifier. Certain contortions are required to make Evans's theory fly here because, to speak very loosely, the description that fixes the reference of the pronoun must be interpreted as within the scope of the subject quantifier in order to get the required variation, and this seems initially strange given that Evans claims E-type pronouns are rigid referring expressions. Soames (1989) notes that when Evans's formalism is examined, E-type pronouns are effectively equivalent to descriptions with largest scope. On the basis of examples like (6) and (7) Evans ends up making the confused claim that the use of a *binary* quantification $[theX](\phi (x) ; \psi (x))$ to represent 'the ϕ is ψ' is compatible with Russell's claim that descriptions are incomplete symbols whereas the use of a unary restricted quantification $[theX: \phi (x)]\psi (x)$ is not. See the appendix to Neale (2001) for discussion.

[152] Stanley and Szabó (2000) and Stanley (2000) assume that implicit binding always requires an actual variable at LF, even if aphonic. Oddly, they do not mention Evans's (1977) implicit binding or the implicit binding in description-proxy variants of Evans's account such as those by Davies (1981), Neale (1990), and Ludlow and Neale (1991), mentioned below, all of which are careful not to say they are postulating a variable at LF that the subject quantifier binds. See Elbourne (2001, 2002) for a discussion of the virtues of having descriptive material in the LF. If one holds the truth-evaluable conception of LFs, then perhaps one would need something like this (although there is a healthy and growing literature on both variable-free logics and variable-free semantics for natural language). There is also no commitment in the D-type proposal to the view that the description for which a particular D-type pronoun goes proxy can be extracted by some automatic procedure from the immediate linguistic context. It does seem clear, however, that there is a default procedure or heuristic that yields extremely good results in very many cases. For discussion, see Neale (1990, ch. 5).

anaphoric on the subject DP it is bound; but when it is seemingly anaphoric on
/ a son/ it is unbound (plausibly going proxy for the relativized description 'his
son's'). Since Icelandic reflexives (possessive or otherwise) are always bound—as
already noted there are seemingly logophoric examples that add complications—it is not surprising that the translation of (8) depends upon whether
/his/ is to be read as bound by /every man who has a son/ or as an unbound
pronoun seemingly anaphoric on /a son/:

(8′) [*sérhver maður sem á son*]^1 *elskar konuna sína*$_1$
     every man who has son loves wife-the self's-FEM+ACC+SG
     ('[every man who has [a son]^2]^1 loves his$_{1/*2}$ wife')

(8″) [*sérhver maður sem á son*] *elskar konuna hans*$_{(2)}$
     every man who has son loves wife-the his-MASC+GEN+SG
     ('[every man who has [a son]^2] loves his$_{(2)}$ wife').

On the bound, reading, /his wife/ will be rendered as *konuna sína*; on the unbound
('donkey') reading it will be rendered as *konuna hans*.[153]

---

[153] It should be noted that an alternative explanation of the data could be provided. Icelandic
possessive reflexive pronouns are like non-possessive reflexives in being subject-oriented:

(i) *Jón*^{1} *sagði Páli*^{2} *frá konunni sinni*$_{1/*2}$
     John told Paul-DAT about wife-the-DAT self's-DAT
     ('John told Paul^2 about his$_{1/*2}$ wife').

(ii) *Jón*^{1} *gaf Páli*^{2} *mynd af konunni sinni*$_{1/*2}$
     John gave Paul-DAT picture of wife-the self's-DAT
     ('John^1 gave Paul^2 a picture of his$_{1/*2}$ wife').

And as with non-possessives, the slack is taken up by non-reflexive counterparts (here the genitives)
thereby giving rise to apparent Principle B violations:

(iii) *Jón sagði Páli*^{2} *frá konunni hans*$_2$
     John told Paul-DAT about wife-the-DAT his
     ('John told Paul^2 about his$_2$ wife').

(iv) *Jón gaf Páli*^{2} *mynd af konunni hans*$_2$
     John gave Paul-DAT picture of wife-the-DAT his
     ('John gave Paul^2 a picture of his$_2$ wife')

In (iii) and (iv) *hans* is bound by *Páll*. This demonstrates a point that will be useful in a moment: it is a
mistake to think the distinction between reflexive possessives and genitives corresponds exactly to a
distinction between bound and unbound. It corresponds, rather, to a distinction between reflexive
(hence bound) and non-reflexive (whether bound or free). See below. (It should not be overlooked
that issues about the syntax of double object constructions arise in connection with (i)–(iv).)

The situation is parallel when we have a name inside the relative clause:[154]

(9) [everyone who knows John]^2]^1 pities his$_{1/(2)}$ wife.

(9′) [allir sem þekkja Jón]^1 vorkenna konunni sinni$_1$
everyone who knows John pities wife-the self's-FEM+DAT+SG
('[everyone who knows John]^1 pities his$_1$ wife').

(9″) [allir sem þekkja Jón^2] vorkenna konunni hans$_{(2)}$
everyone who knows John^2 pities wife-the his-(MASC+GEN+SG)
('[everyone who knows John]^1 pities his$_{(2)}$ wife').[155]

Given the distinction between, on the one hand, (8′) and (9′), and on the other, (8″) and (9″), and assuming a plausible syntax of sentences in which 'only' modifies a name, we should expect to see the same distinction in translations of (10):[156]

(10) [$_S$[$_{DP}$only [$_{NP}$John]^2]^1 loves his$_{1/(2)}$ wife].

Here, /his/ is within the scope of 'only John' but not within the scope of 'John'. Where /his/ is bound by the DP /only John/, (10) is used to say that John is the only one who satisfies *x loves x's wife*. Where it is used simply to refer indexically to

---

[154] The verb *vorkennir* ('pity') in (9′) and (9″) assigns the dative case to *konunni* ('wife'), which is why the reflexive possessive pronoun appears in the dative, feminine, singular form *sinni* there. (Unlike the simple reflexive *sig*, which inflects for case only, the possessive reflexive inflects fully to match its noun.) The prepositions *af* and *frá* also assign dative case in examples that will appear later.

[155] It has been suggested to me more than once that the distinction might not involve the structural notion I have been focusing on but a desire to avoid ambiguity. This is easily disproved. First, consider the following case where there *is* ambiguity, just as in English (I here assume a standard Quine–Evans account of relative pronouns):

(i) Jón^1 vorkenninr [manninum sem^2 elskar konuna sína$_{1/2}$]
('John^1 pities the man who^2 loves his$_{1/2}$ wife').

Second, consider the following cases where there is no relevant ambiguity (assuming no same-sex marriages):

(ii) *Jón^1 er farinn. María er að hugga konuna sína$_1$
('John^1 has left. Mary is comforting his$_{(1)}$ wife').

(iii) *ef Jón^1 fer þá mun María hugga konuna sína$_1$
('if John^1 leaves, then Mary will comfort his$_{(1)}$ wife').

If *sína* is replaced by *hans* in (i) and (ii), all is fine.

[156] That things should turn out this way was pointed out to me by James Higginbotham.

John it is used to say that John is the only one who satisfies *x loves John's wife*. In Icelandic the distinction is indeed reflected in the use of the bound *sína* and the unbound *hans*:

(10′) [*aðeins Jón*]¹ *elskar konuna sína₁*
      only John loves wife-the self's-FEM+ACC+SG
      ('[only John]¹ loves his₁ wife').

(10″) [*aðeins Jón²*] *elskar konuna hans₍₂₎*
      only John loves wife-the his-MASC+GEN+SG
      ('[only John²] loves his₍₂₎ wife').

As certain double genitives are permitted in Icelandic, however, *konuna hans Jóns* (roughly equivalent to 'his, Jóhn's, wife', but not felt to be epenthetic) would almost always be used instead of the simple *konuna hans* in (10″) in order to make one's meaning clearer (this being something of a national obsession).

As one might now expect, the only Icelandic translation of (11) is (11′) because the pronoun is not within the scope of the name:

(11) his wife loves John
(11′) *konan hans elskar Jón.*

As in English, intended co-reference is not excluded, but *konan hans* would almost always cede to *konan hans Jóns* in actual speech if co-reference were intended.

Using the distinction between bound and discourse pronouns, we can explain facets of an old chestnut mentioned earlier (for details, see Jacobson 1977 and Neale 1990):

(12) [the pilot who shot at it₍₂₎]¹ hit [the MiG that was chasing him₁]².

If the subject DP has larger scope in (12), 'him' is bound and 'it' is a D-type pronoun understood as 'the MiG that was chasing him'. Suppressing some details (in particular, the structure of 'him'), (12) will be read as follows:

(12′) [*the x: pilot x* • [*the y: MiG y* • *y chased x*](*x shot at y*)]
      ([*the y: MiG y* • *y chased x*](*x hit y*)).

(If the object DP has larger scope the situation is reversed: 'it' is bound and 'him' is D-type, understood as 'the pilot who shot at it'.) Similarly, in (13) 'it' will be a D-type pronoun understood as 'his paycheck':

(13) [the man who gave [his paycheck]² to his wife]¹ was wiser than
      [the one who gave it₍₂₎ to his₁ mistress].

$(13')$ $[the\ x:\ man\ x \bullet [his\ y:\ y\ paycheck\ x]([his\ z:\ z\ wife\ x](x\ gave\ y\ to\ z)]$
$([the\ w:\ man\ w \bullet [his\ y:\ y\ paycheck\ w]([his\ z:\ z\ mistress\ w](w\ gave\ y\ to\ z)]$
$(x\ was\ wiser\ than\ w)\ )$.

As noted earlier earlier, the English sentence (14) is ambiguous according as 'his' is understood as used to make independent reference to John (the strict reading) or as bound by 'John' (the sloppy reading):

(14) John loves his wife, but Paul does not.

The bound–sloppy reading is captured by (15) in Icelandic:

(15) *Jón elskar konuna sína en ekki Páll.*
John loves wife-the *self's* but not Paul
('John[1] loves his[1] wife but Paul does not').

To capture the strict reading, however, something like the following must be used:

(16) *Jón elskar konuna sína en Páll elskar hana ekki.*
John loves wife-the *self's* but Paul loves her-ACC not
('John[1] loves his[1] wife but Paul does not love her').

That is, the reading cannot be captured naturally using a VP elliptical sentence.

Two other English examples mentioned earlier raise similar issues. Reasonable Icelandic renderings of (17) and (18) are $(17')$ and $(18')$, respectively, which seem to involve not VP ellipsis but something more akin to what is usually called *VP anaphora*, making use of a pronominal expression (*það*, 'it'):

(17) if every man loves his wife then clearly John does
$(17')$ *ef sérhver maður elskar konuna sína, þá gerir Jón það augljóslega líka*
(18) every Englishman loves his wife, but John doesn't, so John can't be English
$(18')$ *sérhver Englendingur elskar konuna sína, en Jón gerir það ekki,*
svo Jón getur ekki verið Englendingur.

15. The Binding Theory Revisited

The precise statement of the Binding Theory has exercised linguists for nearly a quarter of a century. I stated a simple version earlier (the subscripts indicate this is our first attempt):

Principle A_1: A reflexive is to be interpreted as bound in its own clause.

Principle B₁: A non-reflexive is not to be interpreted as bound in its own clause.

Principle C₁: A name is not to be interpreted as bound.

This statement served us reasonably well, but it is now time to look at certain problems and potential revisions.

The examples in the previous section do not constitute a knock-down case for scope being the sole structural relation necessary to isolate occurrences of the possessive reflexive in Icelandic. In the English (1) and (2), either 'John' or 'Paul' may bind the relevant pronoun:

(1) John^1 told Paul^2 about himself$_{1/2}$
(2) John^1 told Paul^2 about his$_{1/2}$ wife.

This fact is not mirrored in Icelandic, where reflexives are *subject-oriented*. Only the subject expression *Jón* may bind the simple reflexive *sér* in (1′) and the reflexive possessive *sinni* in (2′):

(1′) *Jón^1 sagði Páli^2 frá (sjálfum) sér$_{1/*2}$*
     John told Paul-DAT about (EMPH) self-DAT
     ('John^1 told Paul^2 about himself$_{1/*2}$').

(2′) *Jón^1 sagði Páli^2 frá konunni sinni$_{1/*2}$*
     John told Paul-DAT about wife-the-DAT self's-FEM + DAT + SG
     ('John^1 told Paul^2 about his$_{1/*2}$ wife').

This contrast between English and Icelandic needs to be explained, and it is *not* explained by the Binding Theory. Similarly the contrast between English (3) and Icelandic (3′):

(3) [$_S$John^1 [$_{VP}$gave Paul^2 [$_{DP}$a photograph of himself$_{1/2}$]]
(3′) *Jón^1 gaf Páli^2 ljósmynd af (sjálfum) sér$_{1/*2}$*
     John gave Paul-DAT photograph of (EMPH) self-DAT
     ('John^1 gave Paul^2 a photograph of himself$_{1/*2}$').[157]

---

[157] (3) and (3′) involve double object constructions *seemingly* of the form [$_{VP}$V DP DP]. The first DP is called the *indirect* object, and the second the *direct* object. In Icelandic different verbs may assign different cases to their objects; for example *gefa* ('give') assigns dative case to its indirect object, *Páli* in (3′), and accusative case to its direct object, *ljósmynd*. There are two worrying features about the structure [$_{VP}$V DP DP]: (*a*) it involves ternary rather than binary branching of the VP node, and (*b*)

If one wanted to refer back to the referent of *Páli* here one would be forced to use the non-reflexive *honum (sjálfum)* in (3′). *Mutatis mutandis*, with 'his wife' in place of 'himself' in (3), and *konunni sinni* in place of *sig* in (3′). If one wanted to refer back to the referent of *Páli* this time one would be forced to use the non-reflexive *konunni honum*.[158]

As far as English is concerned, the interesting contrast is between (3) and (4):

(4) John^1 gave [$_{DP}$Paul^3's father]^2 [$_{DP}$a picture of himself$_{1/2/*3}$].

'Paul' in (3) and 'Paul's father' in (4) both contain 'himself' within their scopes, and each occurs in the reflexive's immediate clause, so Principle A explains why they are potential binders. By contrast, the reflexive is not within the scope of 'Paul' in (4), so Principle A explains why 'Paul' is *not* a potential binder here.

Following the discussion earlier, we can say that (i) it is a syntactico-semantic fact, known by A and B if they are speakers of English, that either 'John' or 'Paul' may bind the pronouns in (1) and (2); and (ii) since B's knowledge of word meaning and syntax do not provide him with enough information to nail down fully which name A intends to be understood as binding /himself/ or /his/ when he utters (1) or (2), B must use *non-linguistic* information to discern that intention. In this respect, interpreting /himself/ or /his/ on any particular occasion in which (1) or (2) is uttered is a *pragmatic* matter (constrained by syntax, of course). Furthermore, (i′) it is a syntactico-semantic fact, known by A and B if they are speakers of Icelandic, that only *Jón* may bind *sér* and *sinni* in (1′) and (2′); and (ii′) since B's knowledge of word meaning and syntax *do* provide him with enough

---

the indirect and direct objects lie within one another's scopes. There are reasons for thinking both of these are problematic and that the syntax of the double object construction is not [$_{VP}$V DP DP] at all. On the sort of analysis proposed by Larson (1988), for example, (3) and (3′) have structures more like (i) and (i′):

(i) John [$_{VP}$gave^i [$_{VP}$[$_{DP}$ Paul]^2 [e_i [$_{DP}$a photograph of himself$_{1/2}$]]]].
(i′) Jón^1 [$_{VP}$gaf^i [$_{VP}$[$_{DP}$ Páli]^2 [e_i [$_{DP}$ljósmynd af (sjálfum) sér$_{1/*2}$]]]].

In these structures e_i is an aphonic interpreted via the verb (*gave/gaf*), within whose scope it lies, and which I have adorned with an alphabetically identically superscript. On Larson's account, we can think of double object verbs as effectively factored into two components (one within the scope of the other). The net result of this analysis is that the direct object is now within the scope of the indirect object, a structural asymmetry that appears to have considerable explanatory value, particularly where binding is concerned. Making the point more firmly requires examining inverted double object constructions and the niceties of Icelandic case; this is not the place for such excursions. I refer the reader to Larson (1988).

[158] The pronoun *hann* (NOM ACC), *honum* (DAT), *hans* (GEN) is a genuine masculine with constant gender inflection.

information to establish which name *A* intends to be understood as binding *sér* and *sinni* when he utters (1') or (2'), *B* does *not* need non-linguistic information to discern that intention. And in this respect, interpreting *sér* and *sinni* on any particular occasion in which (1') or (2') is uttered is *not at all* a pragmatic matter.

The notion of *subject* will have to be broadened if the claim that Icelandic reflexives are subject-oriented is to be maintained. Principle A makes correct predictions in cases like the following, where the reflexive and its binder are constituents of a subject DP:

(5) [$_{DP}$Paul^1's photograph of himself$_1$] won first prize.
(5') [$_{DP}$*ljósmynd Páls^1 af sjálfum sér$_1$*] *vann fyrstu verðlaun.*

Notice *Páls* is not the subject of (5'), yet it still binds *sér*. The explanation for this may well lie in an observation made by Chomsky (1973): from a structural point of view, the possessive determiner 'Paul's' (*Páls*) stands to the entire possessive DP 'Paul's photograph of himself' (*ljósmynd Páls af sjálfum sér*) as a subject DP stands to the whole sentence:

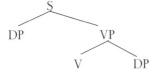

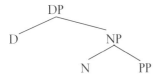

As Chomsky sometimes puts the point, the possessive determiner seems to act as the *subject* of the possessive DP. This idea will assume some importance later.

The fact that reflexives in many languages are subject-oriented is taken by some linguists to be tightly connected to seeming violations of Principle A of the Binding Theory.[159] Let us note first that the following is not a counterexample to Principle A:

(6) John^1 promised Paul to shave himself$_1$.

---

[159] Chomsky (1986); Pica (1991).

On pretty standard syntactic assumptions, (6) has the following structure,

(6′) John^1 promised Paul $[_S e$ to shave himself]

where, e is an aphonic element serving as the subject of the infinitive infinitival clause $[_S e$ to shave himself], which is the reflexive's immediate clause.[160] Moreover, this occurrence of e must be bound by 'John', a fact dictated by the syntax and meaning of 'promise', a so-called subject-control or subject-binding verb (e is bound by the verb's subject). Hence e bears as subscript the same numeral 'John' bears as superscript. Additionally, e binds 'himself', which is why it bears as superscript the same numeral 'himself' bears as subscript. In accordance with what has preceded, (6′) must be shorthand for something more like (6″):[161]

(6″) John^1 promised Paul $[_S [_{DP}[_D e]^2[_{NP} e_1]]^2$ to shave himself$_2$].

$[_D e]^2$ is the aphonic version of the D 'he', and $[_{DP}[_D e]^2[_{NP} e_1]]^2$ is the aphonic version of the whole DP 'he', understood as $[he\ x_2: x_2 = x_1]$. On fairly standard assumptions, the aphonic version of the pronoun is required because (i) the verb occurs in the infinitive, (ii) only finite verbs assign case, and (iii) without case a DP may not occur in phonic form.[162]

---

[160] In syntactic theory this type of phonetically null pronoun is often called PRO (see Chomsky 1981, 1986). I eschew talk of PRO (and also *trace*) here, as the differences between types of aphonic DPs are not germane to my main points. It should be stressed, however, that PRO may well have interpretive properties not shared by other pronouns. One difference comes out in comparing the following sentences, due to Grice (1971) (Grice did not use PRO of course):

   (i) I remember PRO biting my nurse
   (ii) I remember my biting my nurse
   (iii) I remember I bit my nurse.

In order for A to say something true using (i), A must remember performing—not just remember the performance of—a particular nurse-biting. While (ii) and (iii) may certainly be used to say as much, such readings are not forced upon them. The issues here bristle with complexities raised by Castañeda (1966, 1967, 1968), Chierchia (1990), Higginbotham (1990), Lewis (1979), Perry (1979, 2000), and others.

[161] For simplicity I work with an annotated surface form rather than the LF as the main point can be made without setting out the LF.

[162] On 'promise' and other control verbs, see Larson (1991). Also, contrast the following, with clausal adjuncts:

   (i) John^1 learned karate^2 $[_S [_{DP}[_D e]^3[_{NP} e_1]]^3$ to protect himself$_3$]
   (ii) John^1 hired bodyguards^2 $[_S [_{DP}[_D e]^3[_{NP} e_2]]^3$ to protect him$_1$].

Aphonic subjects are not always subject-controlled: 'persuade', for example, is an object-controlled verb which dictates that the structure of (7) is something like (7′):

(7) John persuaded Paul[1] to shave himself[1]

(7′) John persuaded Paul[1] $[_S[_{DP}[_D e]^2[_{NP}e_1]]^2$ to shave himself[2]].

Again Principle A is observed. But this type of construction leads us straight into an apparent problem posed by Icelandic. In (8), either *Jón* or *Pál* may bind *sig*:

(8′) $[Jón^1\ taldi\ Pál^2\ á\ [_S[_{DP}[_D e]^3[_{NP}e_2]]^3\ að\ raka\ sig_{1/3}]]$
John persuaded Paul-ACC $[_S$ x to shave-INF self-ACC]
('John[1] persuaded Paul[2] $[_S[_{DP}[_D e]^3[_{NP}e_2]]^3$ to shave him[1]/himself[3]').

That is, the grammar of Icelandic appears to allow the binding of *sig* by something outside its immediate clause (if non-indicative), something that Principle A prohibits. We have here what linguists often call *long-distance* reflexivization.[163] We find the same situation in (9) (the subjunctive is vital):

(9) $[_S Jón^1\ segir\ að\ [_S Páll^2\ raki\ sig_{1/2}]]$
John says that Paul shaves-SUBJ self-ACC
('John[1] says that Paul[2] shaves him[1]/himself[2]').

The simplest structural account of the connection between the subject-orientation of Icelandic reflexives and their 'long-distance' binding possibilities appears to be wrong: reflexives of both the simplex form (*sig, sér, sín*) and the morphologically complex form (*sjálfan sig, sjálfum sér, sjálfs sín*) are subject-oriented, but only simplex reflexives give rise to seeming violations of Principle A.[164]

---

[163] The label is misleading. Distance per se is not the issue, witness the distance between 'John' and 'himself' in (i):

(i) John bought a poster of a photo of a sketch of a statue of himself.

The issue is really about the possibility of binding reflexives (and only morphologically simple reflexives at that) across certain boundaries. Interest in the Binding Theory in connection with Icelandic and 'long-distance' phenomena developed largely as a result of a paper by Maling (1984) and then a collection of papers edited by Koster and Reuland (1991), especially the paper by Þráinsson (1991). For earlier discussion, see Þráinsson (1976). For more recent discussion, see Reuland and Sigurjónsdóttir (1997), and the collection edited by Cole *et al.* (2001) especially the paper by Reuland (2001a). I ride roughshod over many points of detail here. Reading Reuland's papers (after completing the bulk of the present chapter) has made me see various possibilities not reflected here.

[164] There is no hope of sorting out long-distance reflexives here. Complexities involving the proper domain of binding, subject-orientation, intrinsic reflexivity, feature assignment, feature

Simplifying somewhat, I want now to set out, in a way that philosophers should find immediately accessible, the sorts of problems the Binding Theory as we have stated it must overcome, and run quickly through a series of revisions that have been, or might be, contemplated.

One of the most interesting types of problem arises in connection with *representational* nouns like 'representation', 'picture', 'portrait', 'sketch', 'watercolour', 'photograph', 'image', 'statue', 'sculpture', 'bust', 'bronze', 'rendering', 'recording', or 'description'.[165] Linguists usually call the DPs in which such a noun is the principal noun *picture DPs*. It was noted above that our original Binding Theory correctly predicted the legitimacy of the binding relation in a sentence like (5)–(5'):

(5) $[_{DP}[_{D}Paul^1's]$ [picture of himself$_1$]] won first prize

(5') $[_{DP}mynd[_{D}Páls^1]$ af sjálfum sér$_1$] vann fyrstu verðlaun.

When picture DPs occur in non-subject positions, we encounter problems, however. The unacceptability of one reading of (9) appears to show that a revision of Principle A$_1$ is required:

(9) $[_{S}John^1 [_{VP}bought [_{DP}[_{D}Paul^{2}'s][_{NP}picture of himself._{1/2}]]]]$.

The problem is that although 'John' is a constituent of the smallest sentence containing 'himself' (which lies within its scope), something stops it binding it.

Is it the DP boundary? An obvious first shot at revision would have it that S and DP form a unified category for purposes of binding, that a reflexive must be interpreted as bound by an expression in the smallest S or DP containing it— not the smallest S or the smallest DP containing it, but the smaller of the two. With future revisions in mind, let $[S(\beta)]$ be the smallest S properly containing β,

---

movement, LF movement, VP ellipsis, double object verbs, factivity, logophoricity, simplicity, and acquisition make the topic daunting. See the interconnected works of Grodzinsky and Reinhart (1993), Reinhart (1983, 2000), Reinhart and Reuland (1993), Reuland (2001a, b), Reuland and Sigurjónsdóttir (1997), and Sigurjónsdóttir (1992), which are chock-a-block with interesting ideas, but hard going in places for philosophers. To give a taste (in condensed and simplified form and running a few things together) drawing upon the idea that interpreting a pronoun via binding *as a matter of syntax* is 'easier' (in some robust cognitive sense) than interpreting it as merely co-referential with some other expression or as referring to some salient entity, and the idea that the more impoverished the descriptive content of a pronoun (compare *sig* with 'himself') the more in need it is of a discourse-central referent, the suggestion is made that a simplex anaphor like *sig* can be interpreted as an independent pronoun with a highly restricted usage.

[165] I suppose one could always cry 'Logophors!' here; but let's see how far we can get without doing so.

let $[DP(\beta)]$ be the smallest such DP, and let $[S/DP(\beta)]$ be the smaller of $[S(\beta)]$ and $[DP(\beta)]$. Our second attempt at Principle A is this:

Principle A_2. A reflexive, β, is to be interpreted as bound within $[S/DP(\beta)]$.[166]

Counterexamples to Principle A_2 are readily produced by replacing the possessive determiner 'Paul's' by a simple determiner:

(10) $[_S John^1 [_{VP} bought [_{DP}[_D a/this/that][picture of himself_1]]]]$.[167]

The contrast between (9) and (10) now has to be explained. It might be thought that in (9) 'Paul' must be the binder because it is the *nearer* of two c-commanding DPs in $[S(\beta)]$ bearing the right number and gender. But (11) and (12) are just as bad as (9) on the relevant indexings:

(11) $[_S John^1 [_{VP} bought [_{DP}[_D my/your][picture of himself_{*1}]]]]$
(12) $[_S John^1 [_{VP} bought [_{DP}[_D the museum's][picture of himself_{*1}]]]]$.

So an intervening, c-commanding DP of the right number and gender appears not to be *necessary* to block the binding of 'himself' by 'John' in the structures we are considering; *any* intervening DP will do the trick. And the presence of an intervening, c-commanding DP is not sufficient in *other* structures—at least not in English—witness (13) and (14):

(13) $[_S John^1 [_{VP} told me/Paul^2 about himself_{1/2}]]$
(14) $[_S John^1 [_{VP} gave me/Paul^2 [_{DP}[_D a][_{NP} picture of himself_{1/2}]]]]$.

This suggests the contrast between, on the one hand, (9), (11), and (12), and on the other, (10) must have *something* to do with the presence in each of the former of a *possessive* DP, one whose determiner is essentially a genitive DP ('John's', 'that man's', 'every man's') occupying the blank position of the schematic DP

(15) $[_{DP} \underline{\quad} [picture of himself]]$.

A straightforward modification suggests itself. Let $[S(DP > \beta)]$ be the smallest S containing β and a c-commanding DP. Now $[S/DP(DP > \beta)]$ will be the smaller

---

[166] Given the hypothesis that pronouns are determiners we need to be careful how we interpret Principle A_2 so as not to render it trivially false. If 'himself' has the structure $[_{DP} him [_{NP} self]]$ understood as $[him \, x_2 : x_2 = x_1]$ in 'John loves himself' the bound element (corresponding to x_1) is really contained in the NP, in which case 'John' does not lie in $[S/DP(\beta)]$ if β is construed as the bound element. But on the determiner hypothesis facts about the bound *element* are not what we are interested in, of course, when we contemplate the Binding Theory. We are interested in facts about the DP 'himself', i.e. we are talking about $[S/DP(\beta)]$ where β is the DP 'himself'.

[167] Who says you can't bind into a complex demonstrative?

of $[S(DP>\beta)]$ and $[DP(DP>\beta)]$. We can try again to formulate a successful Principle A:

> *Principle A₃.* A reflexive, β, is to be interpreted as bound within $[S/DP(DP>\beta)]$.

The examples we have looked at so far are now accounted for. Principle A_3 also makes the correct predictions in embedded picture constructions, which demonstrate that the absolute distance between 'John' and 'himself' is immaterial; it is simply the presence of a possessive determiner that blocks binding:

(16) John^1 bought [$_{DP}$a photograph of [$_{DP}$a sketch of [$_{DP}$a bust of himself$_1$]]]

(17) John^1 bought [$_{DP}$Mary's/Paul^2's/my photograph of [$_{DP}$a sketch of [$_{DP}$a bust of himself$_{*1/2}$]]]

(18) John^1 bought [$_{DP}$a photograph of [$_{DP}$Mary's/Paul^2's/my sketch of [$_{DP}$a bust of himself$_{*1/2}$]]]

(19) John^1 bought [$_{DP}$a photograph of [a sketch of [$_{DP}$Mary'/Paul^2's/my bust of himself$_{*1/2}$]]].

Here is a problem case, however:

(20) John^1 bought [$_{DP}$a photograph of [$_{DP}$Paul^2 and himself$_{1/2}$].

In (20) the DP 'Paul' is a constituent of $[DP(\beta)]$, and of $[S/DP(DP>\beta)]$ (i.e. of 'Paul and himself'). So (i) why can't 'Paul' bind 'himself' here? and (ii) why is 'John' a legitimate binder of 'himself'?

(i) To answer the first question, it might be suggested that 'Paul' cannot bind 'himself' in (20) because 'himself' c-commands 'John' (just as 'John' c-commands 'himself', 'DP and DP' being structurally symmetric).[168] Alternatively, it might be suggested that 'Paul' *can* bind 'himself' in (20), the reading being merely unlikely except, perhaps, in Jackendoff-type cases of what we might call *waxwork* anaphora. Imagine a photograph of Paul McCartney standing next to a waxwork dummy of himself in Madame Tussaud's; if John Lennon bought the photograph we might use (20) to report the facts. This is not really the right venue for discussing the complexities of such examples, or those that raise related issues, such as the following, due to Nunberg (1977):

(21) Yeats hated hearing himself read in an English accent.

(ii) If the second response to question (i) is accepted, no answer to the question why 'John' is a legitimate binder of 'himself' seems possible. But the first

---

[168] Those who look affectionately upon co-reference versions of Principle C might be attracted to this way of proceeding.

response might open up an avenue: A binder α of β must meet a morphological condition and a structural condition. The morphological condition amounts to α's agreeing in number and gender with β. We have been assuming that the structural condition amounts to α's c-commanding β; but perhaps this is not quite enough: perhaps we need to add that β must not c-command α; and if this is right, we might then invoke the concept not of a DP being a potential binder *simpliciter* (which involves morphology as well as position) but the concept of a DP being a potential binder structurally speaking, i.e. the concept of a DP occupying a position from which it can bind some expression β. In short, we replace 'DP>β' in Principle A$_3$ by 'DP$\gg$$\beta$' interpreted as 'DP that c-commands but is not c-commanded by β' in order to get closer to the truth of the matter:

Principle A$_4$ A reflexive, β, is to be interpreted as bound by an expression within $[S/DP(DP\gg\beta)]$.

But here's another problem:

(22) *John^1 believes that $[_S[_{DP}$a picture of himself$_1]$ is on display
(22') *Jón^1 telur að $[_S[_{DP}$mynd af sjálfum sér$_1]$ sé á syningu
John believes that picture of EMPH-self is-SUBJ on display.[169]

Principle A$_4$ does not block this. So what is it about (22)–(22') that makes it unacceptable on the indicated indexing? Surely it is the S boundary. It looks as

---

[169] Some speakers claim to find the English (22) acceptable. To my ear it is awful. It must not be confused with the acceptable infinitival form (i) and its acceptable Icelandic translation (i'):

(i) John^1 believes $[_S[_{DP}$a picture of himself$_1]$ to be on display]
(i') Jón^1 telur $[_S[_{DP}$mynd af sjálfun sér$_1]$ vera á syningu].

Following Postal (1974), it is not implausible to suppose that (i) and (i') involve what he calls 'raising to object'. The subjects of the embedded infinitival claused are 'raised' to become the objects of the main verb. This might be viewed as triggered by the inability of the infinitival to assign case. That the expressions alleged to be raised are really the objects of the main verb is strongly suggested by the assignment of accusative case to pronouns occupying the same positions:

(ii) John^1 believes himself$_1$ to be intelligent
(iii) John believes him ↓ to be intelligent.

When a tensed verb is used, the pronoun appears in the nominative, as a normal subject:

(iv) John^1 believes he$_{1/↓}$ is intelligent.

Presumably the subject of the embedded clauses in (i) (and in the Icelandic (i')) is an aphonic non-reflexive pronoun bound by the raised DP. And certainly it can itself bind:

(v) John believes himself to have harmed himself.

though β's binder must lie inside [S(β)], so we seem to need the following revision:

> *Principle A₅.* A reflexive, β, is to be interpreted as bound within both [S(β)] and [S/DP(DP≫β)].

In effect, this amounts to the following:

> *Principle A₆.* a reflexive, β, is to be interpreted as bound within the smaller of [S(β)] and [DP(DP≫β)].

Probably a little work will reveal a problem for Principle A₅. But the *real* problem with where we're going is this: Principle A (and thereby, presumably Principle B) is just getting too messy and complicated to have any real appeal or explanatory value. Our original division between devices satisfying Principle A and those satisfying Principle B dropped out as a trivial consequence of composition, of *merging*. But now we seem to have something considerably more complicated, and it is tempting to think we need to change tack, to see the data as flowing from a simpler Binding Theory together with orthogonal conditions on interpretation.

There are all sorts of ways of proceeding here, and I will mention just one that seems to me not obviously devoid of merit. What feature do S and DP share that might bring them together in a statement of the Binding Theory? Frege thought he saw a connection: Ss and DPs (at least the simplest DPs, names) are both types of *referring* expression. They are Frege's *atoms*, his *building blocks*, the syntactic and semantic categories from which all others are derived. (Names

---

The binding details are not importantly different from those in (vi):

(vi) John believes he has harmed himself.

Certainly (v) is less appealing than (vi), but that may be because of the repeated 'himself' in the former. Chomsky (1973) once suggested explaining examples like (ii) in terms of what he called the Tensed Sentence Condition (TSC), which required a reflexive's binder to be in the smallest *tensed* clause containing the reflexive. But now the mater of the unacceptability of (vii) would be unexplained:

(vii) John¹ believes [ₛme to love himself₁].

Chomsky (1973) suggested explaining it in terms of what he called the Specified Subject Condition (SSC), which required there to be no intervening subject between the binder and the bound. The occurrence of 'me' in (vii) was such a subject and hence blocked the binding of 'himself' by 'John'. If the raising idea just mentioned in the main text is incorrect, then perhaps Principles A and B will have to incorporate the restrictions imposed by the TSC and SSC. With respect to the latter, see the discussion of examples (2) and (2′) in the main text.

and sentences are saturated, they refer to *objects*; predicates are unsaturated, they stand for *concepts*.)

Suppose we follow Frege in viewing DP and S as primitive: a VP is whatever combines with a DP to form an S. We can at least then say that the Binding Principles we have considered make reference to no *defined* categories. The most serious complications we have seen were induced by genitive determiners formed from expressions of the right syntactic category to engage in binding themselves, expressions that seem to *draw attention to themselves* as potential binders in much the same way as subjects of sentences do. The reason a *subject* does this is obvious. A subject is one *half* of a sentence: it merges with a VP to yield a complete S, and this makes the whole S its scope. This makes subject DPs quite different from object DPs. And of course we have seen that in some languages *only subject* DPs may bind reflexives.[170]

Chomsky (1970, 1973) suggested that genitive DPs as well as Ss may be viewed as having subjects. And later, when exploring refinements of the Binding Theory, Chomsky (1986) suggested that statements of Principle A might have to make reference to subjects in this sense. On such an account, 'Paul' will be the *subject* of the DP 'Paul's photograph of himself'. If the subject of DP hypothesis were wrong, Icelandic, being subject-oriented in respect of reflexive-binding, should not permit what English allows in (2):

(2) $[_S \text{John}^1 [_{VP}\text{bought} [_{DP}[_D\text{Paul}^2\text{'s}] [_{NP}\text{picture of himself.}_{1/2}]]]]$.

But as we saw earlier, *it does* permit it:

(2′) *Jón keypti* $[_{DP}\text{mynd} [_D\text{Páls}^2] af (sjálfum) sér_{1/2}]$
John bought picture Paul-GEN of (emph-DAT) self-DAT
('John¹ bought Paul²'s picture of himself$_{1/2}$').

It's as if *Páls* is acting as the subject of the object DP. So let us try another tack. Where XP is any category, we might consider the following revision:

Principle A$_7$. A reflexive, β, is to be interpreted as bound by a DP within $[\text{XP}(\text{SUBJECT}, β)]$.

---

[170] English is not such a language, and to that extent it appears more permissive. On the other hand it does not permit the long-distance binding of simplex reflexives we find in, say, German or Icelandic. Perhaps there is *only so much reflexivization* a language can tolerate. Or, more accurately, only so many *roles* for reflexive forms before we lose any meaningful distinction between local and non-local binders. Having reflexives as victims of *both* non-subject binding and long-distance binding in the same system just put too much pressure on it. Or, if a logophoric account of apparently

What's nice about this conceptually—forget any coverage problems for a minute—is that it seems to get us back where we started: *merging is what creates scope*. The primary role that DP plays in creating a sentence—merging with VP—is a role it replicates in the creation of further DPs: it merges with NP in the same way it merges with VP, except it does so in its possessive form and functions syntactically as a D. The act of merging creates a subject's scope, and a reflexive within its scope is *bindable*, thus closing off the binding question.

16. Ambiguity Revisited

The Binding Theory is meant to explain among other things the seemingly complementary distribution of reflexives and non-reflexives in respect of binding possibilities and requirements. Where Principle A requires a reflexive (more generally an 'anaphor') to have a binder inside some local domain (to be specified), Principle B requires a non-reflexive (more generally a pronominal) *not* to have a binder in the same domain.

Despite evident problems, the theory seems to go some way towards explaining a wealth of data about the behaviour of reflexive and non-reflexive pronouns across languages. If, as we have been assuming, 'he', 'him', 'his wife', and 'himself' have the same general syntactic structure, $[_{DP}DET[_{NP}N]]$, examples (1) and (2) illustrate a simple dilemma:

(1) John^1 loves his$_1$ wife
(2) John^1 says that Paul loves his$_1$ wife.

Since we are ignoring the DP boundaries on the target DPs themselves, sentence (1) appears to show that 'his$_k$' (or at least 'his NP') behaves like the reflexive 'himself$_k$', and unlike the non-reflexives 'he$_k$' and 'him$_k$': it is bound by something in $[S/DP(\beta)]$ (assume, for the sake of argument, this is the local domain). So either 'his$_k$' is a reflexive and falls under Principle A, or else it is not a reflexive and Principle B needs to be modified. But sentence (2) appears to show that 'his$_k$' behaves like the *non*-reflexives 'he$_k$' and 'him$_k$', and unlike the reflexive 'himself$_k$': it is *not* bound by something in $[S/DP(\beta)]$; it is bound by 'John'. (Moreover, an occurrence of 'his$_k$' could be bound by 'Paul' in the same environment.) So

long-distance binding is plausible, having reflexives as victims of *both* non-subject binding and rampant logophoric usage may just put too much pressure on the system. It's as if reflexive forms are being asked to do not inconsistent jobs but *too many jobs at once*—and something has to give.

either 'his$_k$' is a non-reflexive and falls under Principle B, or else 'his$_k$' is a reflexive and Principle A needs to be modified.

One way out of this dilemma would be to say that we have misunderstood the nature of possessive DPs, that 'his' does not stand to its phonic NP as 'he' and 'him' do to their aphonic NPs. Aphonicity itself cannot be the key, however, because the absolute possessive DP 'his' can be used wherever 'his wife' can be used, for example in (1) and (2) above. Sorting this out would require having a well-thought-out account of the structure of possessive DPs, and that I do not have. So let me pursue another idea.

By way of softening up the ground, notice the dilemma recurs with coordinated DPs:

(3) John^1 took photos of his$_1$ wife and himself$_1$ on the yacht
(4) John^1 knows that Paul took photos of his$_1$ wife and him$_1$ on the yacht.

If (3) is grammatical, it would seem 'his$_k$' and 'himself$_k$' must fall under the same principle of the Binding Theory. If (4) is grammatical, so must 'his$_k$' and 'him$_k$'; but how can this be if 'himself$_k$' and 'him$_k$' fall under different principles and are in complementary distribution for binding purposes?

The solution I will sketch sees a distinction between two distinct pronouns /his$_k$/, a reflexive that occurs in (1) and (3), and a non-reflexive that occurs in (2) and (4). Icelandic, as we have seen, makes a *lexical* distinction along what seem like these lines:

(5a) *Jón^1 elskar konuna sína$_1$*
(5b) *Jón elskar konuna hans.*

In (5a), *sína* is a reflexive possessive that has to be understood as bound by *Jón* to satisfy Principle A. In (5b), by contrast, *hans* is a genitive pronoun that *cannot* be understood as bound by *Jón* (it occurs in the masculine to indicate the gender of its referent). It is a non-reflexive pronoun satisfying Principle B. I want now to look at English through Icelandic eyes, as it were.

If our aim is uncover very general principles of the language faculty that help explain language acquisition and data across distinct languages, we should at least consider the possibility of a cross-linguistic distinction between reflexive and non-reflexive possessives. For it might turn out that the best overall theory of pronouns posits the existence of precisely such a distinction in English, /his$_k$/ being the superficial manifestation of *two* distinct bound possessives, one reflexive, the other non-reflexive, which we can represent as '$_+$$_rhis_k$' *and* '$_-$$_rhis_k$' respectively (the former functioning as what could easily have materialized as the non-existent form 'himself's').[171] On such an account, we would find the former in (6) and the latter in (7):

(6) John knows that [$_S$ Paul^2 loves $_{+r}$his$_2$ wife]

(7) John^1 knows that [$_S$ Paul loves $_{-r}$his$_1$ wife].

Initially this might seem extravagant. But notice that we may need a reflexive possessive 'their' in (8a) to explain the fact that it appears in the same syntactic position as the reciprocal in (8b):

(8a) [the senators]^1 love their$_1$ secretaries

(8b) [the senators]^1 love each other$_1$'s secretaries.

In the first instance, we would need to distinguish two sentences, (9a) and (9b) below:

(9a) John^1 loves $_{+r}$his$_1$ wife

(9b) John loves his$_\downarrow$ wife.

(9a) contains an occurrence of the bound reflexive possessive '$_{+r}$his$_k$' (corresponding to the occurrence of *sína* in the Icelandic (8a)) while (9b) contains an occurrence of the independent possessive 'his$_\downarrow$' (corresponding to the occurrence of *hans* in the Icelandic (8b)).

Now comes the more interesting part. (10) also has two translations in Icelandic:

(10) John knows that Paul loves his wife.

And in (11a) *sína* can only be understood as bound by *Páll*:

(11a) *Jón^1 veit að Páll^2 elskar konuna sína*$_{*1/2}$

John knows that Paul loves wife-the self's

('John^1 knows that Paul^2 loves his$_{*1/2}$ wife').

---

[171] The possessive form 'his own' is sometimes said to be the English reflexive possessive, but this does not appear to be correct, witness the following old favourite (given to me by Stanley Peters) in which 'his own' does not have a c-commanding antecedent:

(i) The judge doesn't believe him. His own lawyer doesn't believe him.

(11*b*) *Jón¹ veit að Páll elskar konuna hans₁*
  John knows that Paul loves wife-the his
  ('John¹ knows that Paul² loves his$_{1/*2}$ wife').[172]

Now (10) and (11) are more interesting than their predecessors. Earlier it was convenient to think of the distinction between *sína* and using *hans* as corresponding to a distinction between 'his$_k$' and 'his$_↓$'. As far as simple examples like (5) and (9) were concerned, we made no serious error in seeing things that way. But (10) and (11) demonstrate that this is not actually the right way to think about the difference between *sína* and *hans*. It corresponds not to a difference between bound and unbound but to a distinction between reflexive (hence bound) and non-reflexive (whether bound or free). For if *sína* is used as in (11*a*), it *must* be read as bound by *Páll*. If one wants a pronoun bound by *Jón* in this structure, one must use (11*b*) just as one must if one wants an indexical pronoun. So the right distinction in Icelandic appears to be between a reflexive possessive (*sína*) and a non-reflexive possessive (*hans*). The former must be bound; the latter may, but need not, be.

All of this suggests the following mapping between English and Icelandic for a possessive pronoun (applying to a male, but attached to a feminine noun in the accusative):

Possessive				
Bound		Unbound		
Reflexive	Non-reflexive			
$_{+r}$his$_k$	$_{-r}$his$_k$	his$_↓$	English	
sína$_k$	hans$_k$	hans$_↓$	Icelandic	

---

[172] The verb *vita* ('know') is factive so we find an indicative embedded clause after *veit*. If a non-factive verb such as *segja* ('say') is used the embedded clause may be subjunctive and *Jón* may indeed bind *sína* (just as it may bind *sig* in relevantly parallel environments):

(i) *Jón¹ segir að Páll² elski konuna sína₁/₂*
  John says that Paul loves-SUBJ wife-the self's
  ('John¹ says Paul² loves his$_{1/2}$ wife').

   Replacing *sína* in (i) by the non-reflexive genitive pronoun *hans* produces a reading in which some third party is the expected referent. However, although *hans* cannot be construed as bound by *Jón* in this variant, it can be understood as used indexically to refer to John, used in (perhaps) an awkward way of resolving an ambiguity by 'brute force' as it were. (I owe this wording to Ólafur Páll Jónsson.)

Or, if we prefer to focus on reflexivity rather than binding:

	Possessive			
Reflexive	Non-reflexive			
	Bound	Unbound		
$_{+r}his_k$	$_{-r}his_k$	$his_\downarrow$	English
$sína_k$	$hans_k$	$hans_\downarrow$	Icelandic

So with an eye to generality, perhaps we should say that both languages contain *three* distinct pronouns here. In English all three coincide phonetically, but in Icelandic only two do.[173] It would be interesting to know whether there are languages in which only the counterparts of '$_{+r}his_k$' and '$_{-r}his_k$' coincide phonetically—I doubt there are languages in which only the counterparts of '$_{+r}his_k$' and '$his_\downarrow$' coincide—and languages in which all three are phonetically distinct.

On this model, we can see the two bound possessive's '$_{+r}his_k$' and '$_{-r}his_k$' at work in (13a) and (13b), respectively:

(13a) John knows that [$_S$ Paul^2 loves $_{+r}his_2$ wife]

(13b) John^1 knows that [$_S$ Paul loves $_{-r}his_1$ wife].

In (13a) the pronoun is bound from within [DP/S(β)]; in (13b), by contrast, the pronoun is *not* bound from within [DP/S(β)]. Given that '$_{+r}his_k$' is a reflexive and '$_{-r}his_k$' a non-reflexive, this is as it should be—at least if the Binding Theory is on the right track. Both of these must be distinguished, of course, from (13c):

(13c) John knows that [$_S$ Paul loves $his_\downarrow$ wife].

---

[173] Things go in the other direction too. The third-person contrast between the reflexive *sig* and the non-reflexive *hann* is absent in the first and second persons: *mig* is used for *myself* and *me*, and *þig* for *yourself* and *you* (in the accusative):

(i) *þú rakar þig*
('you shave yourself')

(ii) *Jón rakar þig*
('John shaves you').

Grammar books often say that Icelandic *lacks* first- and second-person reflexives, that the first- and second-person personal pronouns are used *instead*. This is not a helpful way of describing matters. For one thing, it would mean that Icelandic first- and second-person pronouns trivially violate Principle B: (i) contains a non-reflexive that is bound by something in its immediate clause (*þú*). A better characterization is this: in the first and second person, reflexive and non-reflexive pronouns share the same form. That is, Icelandic contains two pronouns *þig*, one of which is reflexive, the other of which is not.

Similarly, we ought really to go back to (11*b*) and break it down in (11*b*) and (11*c*):

(11b) *Jón¹ veit að* [_S_ *Páll² elskar konuna hans*₁/*₂]

(11c) *Jón¹ veit að* [_S_ *Páll² elskar konuna hans*↓].

One down side of the proposal is economic: we have postulated a lexico-syntactic ambiguity, in the form of two homophonic bound English possessive pronouns '₊ʳhis$_k$' and '₋ʳhis$_k$'. But upon reflection the price does not seem exorbitant. The fact that 'himself₁' and 'his₁ wife' may be conjoined to form a DP as in

(14) [every candidate]¹ introduced his₁ wife and himself₁ to the governor

seems to show that there must be a possessive /his/ with the same binding properties as the reflexive 'himself'; and the fact that /he₁/ and /his₁ wife/ may be conjoined to form a DP as in

(15) [every candidate]¹ told the governor that he₁ and his₁ wife were happily married

seems to show that there must be a possessive /his/ with the same binding properties as the non-reflexive /he/. But we know that /he₁/ and /himself₁/ cannot be conjoined in this way because each has the mirror image of the other's binding properties, as enshrined in usual formulations of Principles A and B.

All of the suggestions about pronouns and binding I have sketched here are based on a few ideas from generative grammar, the philosophy of language, and philosophical logic that seem to intersect in interesting ways, and on a simple and preliminary comparison of third-person pronouns in English and language that is importantly similar but interestingly different. Very likely, once these suggestions are examined by linguists who can bring into the picture more languages, more complex examples, and more powerful machinery, they will require all sorts of revisions or scrapping altogether. The idea that natural languages contain two very different forms of reflexives may have much going for it, members of one type (call it the *sig*-type) being monomorphemic, subject-oriented, not subject to Principle A, and logophorically licensed, members of the other type (call it *himself*-type) being morphologically complex, not subject-oriented, locally bound, and not logophorically licensed. And if so, the facts about English possessives may find a much better explanation when all is revealed. One of the joys of grammatical theorizing is that every known theory or claim of genuine interest is frustrated by countless counterexamples that immediately suggest different claims, and one's pleasure often derives from the process of bringing disparate things together or pursuing seemingly batty ideas. Which just reinforces my main point: there is clearly much to be gained by linguists and philosophers working together in this area.

REFERENCES

Abney, S. (1987), 'The English Noun Phrase in its Sentential Aspect', Ph.D. diss. (Massachusetts Institute of Technology).

Austin, J. L. (1962), *How to do Things with Words* (Oxford: Clarendon Press).

Bach, E. (1970), 'Problominalization', *Linguistic Inquiry*, 1: 121–2.

Bach, K. (1981), 'Referential/Attributive', *Synthese*, 49: 219–44.

—— (1987), *Thought and Reference* (Oxford: Clarendon Press).

—— (1994), *Thought and Reference*, 2nd edn. (Oxford: Oxford University Press).

Baker, M. (2001), The Atoms of Language (Oxford: Oxford University Press).

Barwise, J., and R. Cooper (1981), 'Generalized Quantifiers and Natural Language', *Linguistics and Philosophy*, 4: 159–219.

—— and J. Perry (1983), *Situations and Attitudes* (Cambridge, Mass.: MIT Press).

Bezuidenhout, A. (1997), 'Pragmatics, Semantic Underdetermination and the Referential/Attributive Distinction', *Mind*, 106: 375–409.

Blackburn, S. (1984), *Spreading the Word: Groundings in the Philosophy of Language* (Oxford: Clarendon Press).

Blackburn, W. (1988), 'Wettstein on Definite Descriptions,' *Philosophical Studies*, 53: 263–78.

Blakemore, D. (1987), *Semantic Constraints on Relevance* (Oxford: Blackwell).

Bresnan, J. (2001), *Lexical-Functional Syntax* (Oxford: Blackwell).

Cardinaletti, A. (1994), 'On the Internal Structure of Pronominal DPs', *Linguistic Review*, 11: 195–219.

—— and M. Starke (1999), 'The Typology of Structural Deficiency: A Case Study of the Three Classes of Pronouns', in H. van Riemsdijk (ed.), *Clitics in the Languages of Europe* (Berlin: Mouton), 145–233.

Carston, R. (1988), 'Implicature, Explicature and Truth-Theoretic Semantics' in R. Kempson (ed.), *Mental Representations: The Interface Between Language and Reality* (Cambridge: Cambridge University Press), 155–82.

—— (1993), 'Conjunction, Explanation and Relevance', *Lingua*, 90: 27–48.

—— (2002), *Thoughts and Utterances* (Oxford: Blackwell).

Castañeda, H.-N. (1966), 'He*: A Study in the Logic of Self-Consciousness', *Ratio*, 8: 130–57.

—— (1967), 'Indicators and Quasi-Indicators', *American Philosophical Quarterly*, 4: 85–100.

—— (1968), 'On the Logic of Attributions of Self-Knowledge to Others', *Journal of Philosophy*, 65: 439–56.

Chierchia, Gennaro (1990), 'Anaphora and Attitudes de Se', in R. Bartsch *et al.* (eds.), *Language in Action.* (Dordrecht: Foris), 1–31.

Chomsky, N. (1964), *Current Issues in Linguistic Theory* (The Hague: Mouton).

—— (1965), *Aspects of the Theory of Syntax* (Cambridge, Mass.: MIT Press)

—— (1970), 'Remarks on Nominalization', in R. Jacobs and P. Rosenbaum (eds.), *Readings in English Transformational Grammar* (Waltham, Mass.: Ginn), 184–221; repr. in D. Davidson and G. Harman (eds.), *The Logic of Grammar* (Encino, Calif.: Dickenson, 1975), 262–89.

—— (1973), 'Conditions on Transformations', in S. Anderson and P. Kiparsky (eds.), *A Festschrift for Morris Halle* (New York: Holt, Rinehart & Winston), 232–86.

—— (1975), *Reflections on Language* (New York: Pantheon).

—— (1976), 'Conditions on Rules of Grammar', *Linguistic Analysis*, 2: 303–51.

—— (1977), 'On WH-movement', in P. Culicover, T. Wasow, and A. Akmajian (eds.), *Formal Syntax* (New York: Academic Press), 71–132.

—— (1980), *Rules and Representations* (New York: Columbia University Press).

—— (1981), *Lectures on Government and Binding* (Dordrecht: Foris).

—— (1986), *Knowledge of Language: its Nature, Origin, and Use* (New York: Praeger).

—— (1995), *The Minimalist Program* (Cambridge, Mass.: MIT Press).

—— (2000), *New Horizons in the Study of Language and Mind* (Cambridge: Cambridge University Press).

—— (2002), *On Nature and Language* (Cambridge: Cambridge University Press).

Clements, G. N. (1975), 'The Logophoric Pronoun in Ewe', *Journal of West African Languages*, 10: 141–77.

Cole, P., G. Hermon, and C.-T. J. Huang (eds.) (2001), *Syntax and Semantics, 33: Long-Distance Reflexives* (San Diego, CA: Academic Press).

Cooper, R. (1979), 'The Interpretation of Pronouns' in F. Heny and H. Schnelle (eds.), *Syntax and Semantics, 10: Selections from the Third Gröningen Round Table* (New York: Academic Press), 61–92.

Crimmins, M. (1992), *Talk About Belief* (Cambridge, Mass.: MIT Press).

—— and J. Perry (1989), 'The Prince and the Phone Booth: Reporting Puzzling Beliefs', *Journal of Philosophy*, 86: 685–711.

Culicover, P. (1976), 'A Constraint on Co-referentiality', *Foundations of Language*, 14: 109–18.

Davidson D. (1986), 'A Nice Derangement of Epitaphs', in E. Lepore (ed.), *Truth and Interpretation: Perspectives on the Philosophy of Donald Davidson* (Oxford: Basil Blackwell), 433–46.

Davies, M. (1981), *Meaning, Quantification, Necessity* (London: Routledge & Kegan Paul).

Elbourne, P. (2001), 'E-Type Anaphora as NP-Deletion', *Natural Language Semantics*, 9: 241–88.

—— (2002), 'Situations and Individuals', Ph.D. diss. (Massachusetts Institute of Technology).

Evans, G. (1977), 'Pronouns, Quantifiers and Relative Clauses (I)', *Canadian Journal of Philosophy*, 7: 467–536; repr. in Evans (1985: 76–152).

—— (1980), 'Pronouns', *Linguistic Inquiry*, 11: 337–62. repr. in Evans (1985: 214–48).

—— (1982), *The Varieties of Reference* (Oxford: Clarendon Press).

—— (1985), *Collected Papers* (Oxford: Clarendon Press).

Fiengo, R., and R. May (1994), *Indices and Identity* (Cambridge, Mass.: MIT Press).

Fodor, J. A. (1975), *The Language of Thought* (New York: Crowell).

—— (1983), *The Modularity of Mind* (Cambridge, Mass.: MIT Press).

—— (1987), *Psychosemantics: The Problem of Meaning in the Philosophy of Mind* (Cambridge, Mass.: MIT Press).

—— (2001), 'Language, Thought, and Compositionality', *Mind and Language*, 16: 1–15.

Geach, P. T. (1962), *Reference and Generality* (Ithaca, NY: Cornell University Press).

Geach, P. T. (1972), *Logic Matters* (Oxford: Basil Blackwell).

Grayling, A. (1995), 'Perfect Speaker Theory', in J. Hill *et al.*, *Reference and Meaning,* suppl. to Filosofia.

Grice, H. P. (1957), 'Meaning', *Philosophical Review*, 66: 377–88.

—— (1961), 'The Causal Theory of Perception', *Proceedings of the Aristotelian Society*, suppl. vol. 35: 121–52.

—— (1971), 'Intention and Uncertainty', *Proceedings of the British Academy*, 263–79.

—— (1975a), 'Logic and Conversation', in P. Cole and J. Morgan (eds.), *Syntax and Semantics, vol. 3: Speech Acts* (New York: Academic Press), 41–58; repr. in Grice (1989).

—— (1975b), 'Method in Philosophical Psychology: From the Banal to the Bizarre', *Proceedings and Addresses of the American Philosophical Association*, 23–53.

—— (1989), *Studies in the Ways of Words* (Cambridge, Mass: Harvard University Press).

Grodzinsky, Y, and T. Reinhart (1993), 'The Innateness of Binding and Coreference', *Linguistic Inquiry*, 24: 69–101.

Hagège, C. (1974), 'Les Pronoms Logophoriques', *Bulletin de la Société de Linguistique de Paris,* 69: 287–310.

Harman, G. (1972), 'Deep Structure as Logical Form', in D. Davidson and G. Harman (eds.), *semantics of Natural Language* (Dordrecht: Reidel), 25–47.

Heal, J. (1997), 'Indexical Predicates and Their Uses', *Mind*, 106: 619–40.

Heim, I. (1982/1988), 'The Semantics of Definite and Indefinite Noun Phrases', Ph.D. diss. (University of Massachusetts, Amherst, 1982); pub. as *The Semantics of Definite and Indefinite Noun Phrases* (New York: Garland).

—— (1990), 'E-Type Pronouns and Donkey Anaphors', Linguistics and Philosophy, 13: 137–78.

—— (1993), 'Anaphora and Semantic Interpretation: A Reinterpretation of Reinhart's Approach', in *MIT Working Papers in Linguistics*, 25: 205–46.

—— and A. Kratzer, (1998), *Semantics in Generative Grammar.* (Oxford: Basil Blackwell).

Helke, M. (1971), 'The Grammar of English Reflexives', Ph.D. diss. (Massachusetts Institute of Technology).

Higginbotham, J. (1980), 'Pronouns and Bound Variables', *Linguistic Inquiry*, 11: 679–708.

—— (1983a), 'Logical Form, Binding, and Nominals', *Linguistic Inquiry,* 14: 395–420.

—— (1983b), 'The Logic of Perceptual Reports: An Extensional Alternative to Situation Semantics', *Journal of Philosophy,* 80: 100–27.

—— (1990), 'Reference and Control', in R. Larson, S. Iatridou, U. Lahiri, and J. Higginbotham (eds.), *Control and Grammar* (Dordrecht: Kluwer), 79–108.

—— and R. May (1981), 'Questions, Quantifiers, and Crossing', *Linguistic Review,* 1: 41–80.

Huang, C.-T. (1995), 'Logical Form', in G. Webelhuth (ed.), *Government and Binding Theory and the Minimalist Program* (Oxford: Basil Blackwell), 125–75.

Jacobson, P. (1977), 'The Syntax of Crossing Coreference Sentences.' Ph.D. diss. (University of California, Berkeley).

—— (1999), 'Towards a Variable-Free Semantics', *Linguistics and Philosophy*, 22: 117–84.

—— (2000), 'Paycheck Pronouns, Bach-Peters Sentences, and Variable-Free Semantics', *Natural Language Semantics*, 8: 77–155.

Jackendoff, R. (1972), *Semantic Interpretation in Generative Grammar* (Cambridge, Mass.: MIT Press).

—— (1992), 'Madame Tussaud Meets the Binding Theory'. *Natural Language and Linguistic Theory*, 10: 1–31.

Kamp, H. (1984), 'A Theory of Truth and Semantic Interpretation', in J. Groenendijk *et al.* (eds.), *Truth, Interpretation, and Information* (Dordrecht: Foris), 1–43.

Kaplan, D. (1989), 'Demonstratives' and 'Afterthoughts', in J. Almog, J. Perry, and H. Wettstein (eds.), *Themes from Kaplan* (New York: Oxford University Press), 481–614.

Karttunen, L. (1969), 'Pronouns and Variables', in R. Binnick *et al.* (eds.), *Papers from the Fifth Regional Meeting of the of the Chicago Linguistic Society* (Chicago: University of Chicago Press), 108–15.

—— (1976), 'Discourse Referents', in J. McCawley (ed.), *Syntax and Semantics, Vol. 7: Notes from the Linguistic Underground* (New York: Academic Press), 363–85.

Katz, J., and P. Postal (1964), *An Integrated Theory of Linguistic Descriptions* (Cambridge, Mass.: MIT Press).

Kayne, R. (2002), 'Pronouns and their Antecedents', in S. Epstein and T. Seely (eds.), *Derivation and Explanation in the Minimalist Program* (Oxford: Basil Blackwell), 133–66.

Keenan, E. L. (1971), 'Names, Quantifiers, and the Sloppy Identity Problem', *Papers in Linguistics* 4/2: 1–22.

—— (2002), 'Explaining the Creation of Reflexive Pronouns in English', in D. Minkova and R. Stockwell (eds.), *Studies in the History of English: A Millenial Perspective* (The Hague: Mouton de Gruyter), 325–55.

Klima, E. (1964), 'Negation in English', in J. Fodor and J. Katz (eds.), *The Structure of Language* (Englewood Cliffs, NJ: Prentice Hall), 246–323.

Koster, J. and E. Reuland (eds.) (1991), *Long-Distance Anaphora* (Cambridge: Cambridge University Press).

Kripke, S. A. (1977), 'Speaker Reference and Semantic Reference', in P. A. French, T. E. Uehling, Jr., and H. K. Wettstein (eds.), *Contemporary Perspectives in the Philosophy of Language* (Minneapolis: University of Minnesota Press), 6–27.

—— (1979), 'A Puzzle about Belief', in A. Margalit (ed.), *Meaning and Use* (Dordrecht: Reidel), 239–83.

—— (1980), *Naming and Necessity* (Cambridge, Mass.: Harvard University Press).

Lakoff, G. (1972), 'Linguistics and Natural Logic', in D. Davidson and G. Harman (eds.), *Semantics of Natural Language* (Dordrecht: Reidel), 545–665.

Langacker, R. (1966), 'On Pronominalization and the Chain of Commmand', in D. Reibel and S. Schane (eds.), *Modern Studies in English* (Englewood Cliffs, NJ: Prentice-Hall), 160–86.

Larson, R. (1988), 'On the Double Object Construction', *Linguistic Inquiry*, 19: 335–91.

—— (1991), 'Promise and the Theory of Control', *Linguistic Inquiry*, 22: 103–39.

—— and S. Cho (1999), 'Temporal Adjectives and the Structure of Possessive DPs', in S. Bird *et al.* (eds.), *Proceedings of WCCFL 18* (Somervill, Mass.: Cascadilla Press), 299–311.

—— and Segal, G. (1995), *Knowledge of Meaning: An Introduction to Semantic Theory* (Cambridge, Mass.: MIT Press).

Lasnik, H. (1976), 'Remarks on Coreference', *Linguistic Analysis*, 2: 1–22.

—— (1989), *Essays on Anaphora* (Dordrecht: Kluwer).

Lees, R. and E. Klima (1963), 'Rule for English Pronominalization', *Language*, 39: 17–28; repr. in D. A. Reibel and S. A. Schane (eds.), *Modern Studies in English: Readings in Transformational Grammar* (Englewood Cliffs, NJ: Prentice-Hall, 1969), 145–59.

Lewis, D. (1972), 'General Semantics', in D. Davidson and G. Harman (eds.), *Semantics of Natural Language* (Dordrecht: Reidel), 169–218.

—— (1975), 'Adverbs of Quantification', in E. L. Keenan (ed.), *Formal Semantics of Natural Language* (Cambridge: Cambridge University Press), 3–15.

—— (1979), 'Scorekeeping in a Language Game', *Journal of Philosophical Logic*, 8: 339–59.

Ludlow, P. (1989), 'Implicit Comparison Classes', *Linguistics and Philosophy* 12, 519–33.

—— and S. Neale (1991), 'Indefinite Descriptions: In Defence of Russell', *Linguistics and Philosophy*, 14/2 (1991), 171–202; repr. in P. Ludlow (ed.), *Readings in the Philosophy of Language* (Cambridge, Mass.: MIT Press, 1997), 523–55.

McCawley, J. (1976), *Grammar and Meaning* (New York: Academic Press).

Maling, J. (1984), 'Non-Clause Bounded Reflexives in Modern Icelandic', *Linguistics and Philosophy*, 7: 211–41.

May, R. (1977), 'The Grammar of Quantification', Ph.D. diss. (Massachusetts Institute of Technology).

—— (1985), *Logical Form: Its Structure and Derivation* (Cambridge, Mass.: MIT Press).

—— (2002), 'Ellipsis', *Macmillan Encyclopaedia of Cognitive Science* (London: Macmillan), 1094–1102.

Montague, R. (1973), 'The Proper Treatment of Quantification in Ordinary English', in R. Thomason (ed.), *Formal Philosophy: Selected Papers of Richard Montague* (New Haven: Yale University Press, 1974), 247–70.

—— (1974), *Formal Philosophy: Selected Papers of Richard Montague*, ed. R. Thomason (New Haven: Yale University Press).

Neale, S. (1990), *Descriptions* (Cambridge, Mass.: MIT Press).

—— (1993), 'Grammatical Form, Logical Form, and Incomplete Symbols', in A. D. Irvine and G. A. Wedeking (eds.), *Russell and Analytic Philosophy* (Toronto: University of

Toronto Press), 97–139; repr. in G. Ostertag (ed.), *Definite Descriptions: A Reader* (Cambridge, Mass.: MIT Press, 1998), 79–121.

—— (1994), 'Logical Form and LF', in Otero, C. (ed.), *Noam Chomsky: Critical Assessments* (London: Routledge), 788–838.

—— (2001), *Facing Facts* (Oxford: Clarendon Press).

—— (2004), 'This, That and the Other', in A. Bezuidenhout and M. Reimer (eds.), *Descriptions and Beyond* (Oxford: Oxford University Press), 68–181.

—— (forthcoming *a*), *Descriptions*, expanded edn. (Oxford: Clarendon Press).

—— (forthcoming *b*), *Linguistic Pragmatism* (Oxford: Clarendon Press).

—— (forthcoming *c*), *Pronouns* (Oxford: Clarendon Press).

Nunberg, G. (1977), 'The Pragmatics of Reference', Ph.D. diss. (City University of New York).

Ostertag, G. (1999), 'A Scorekeeping Error', *Philosophical Studies*, 96: 123–46.

Papafragou, A. (1998), 'Modality and Semantic Underdeterminacy', in V. Rouchota and A. Jucker (eds.), *Current Issues in Relevance Theory* (Amsterdam: John Benjamins), 237–70.

—— (2000), *Modality: Issues in the Semantic-Pragmatics Interface* (Oxford: Elsevier Science).

Partee, B. (1972), 'Opacity, Coreference and Pronouns', in D. Davidson and G. Harman (eds.), *Semantics of Natural Language* (Dordrecht: Reidel), 415–41.

—— (1975), 'Deletion and variable binding', in E. Keenan (ed.), *Formal Semantics of Natural Languages* (Cambridge: Cambridge University Press), 16–34.

—— (1989), 'Binding Implicit Variables in Quantified Contexts', in *Proceedings of the Chicago Linguistics Society*, 25 (Chicago: University of Chicago Press), 342–65.

Perry, J. (1979), 'The Essential Indexical', *Noûs*, 13: 13–21.

—— (1986), 'Thought Without Representation', *Proceedings of the Aristotelian Society*, Supp. Vol., 60: 137–51.

—— (2000), *The Problem of the Essential Indexical and Other Essays*, expanded edn. (Stanford: CSLI Publications).

—— (2001) *Reference and Reflexivity* (Stanford: CSLI Publications).

Pica, P. (1987), 'On the Nature of the Reflexivization Cycle', *North East Linguistic Society*, 17/2: 483–99.

—— (1991), 'On the Interaction between Antecedent-Government and Binding: The Case of Long-Distance Reflexivization', in J. Koster and E. Reuland (eds.), *Long-Distance Anaphora* (Cambridge: Cambridge University Press), 119–35.

Postal, P. (1966), 'On So-called Pronouns in English', in F. Dineen (ed.), *Report on the Seventeenth Annual Round Table meeting in Washington on Linguistics and Language Studies* (Washington: Georgetown University Press), 177–206; repr. in D. A. Reibel and S. A. Schane (eds.), *Modern Studies in English: Readings in Transformational Grammar* (Englewood Cliffs, NJ: Prentice-Hall, 1969), 201–24.

—— (1974), *On Raising* (Cambridge, Mass.: MIT Press).

Quine, W. V. O. (1940), *Mathematical Logic* (Cambridge, Mass.: Harvard University Press).

—— (1960), *Word and Object* (Cambridge, Mass.: MIT Press).

Recanati, F. (1987), 'Contextual Dependence and Definite Descriptions', *Proceedings of the Aristotelian Society*, 87: 57–73.

Recanati, F. (1989), 'Referential/Attributive: A Contextualist Proposal', *Philosophical Studies*, 56: 217–49.

—— (1993), *Direct Reference: From Language to Thought* (Oxford: Basil Blackwell).

—— (2001), 'What is Said', *Synthese*, 128: 75–91.

Reinhart, T. (1976), '*The Syntactic Domain of Anaphora*', Ph.D. diss. (Massachusetts Institute of Technology).

—— (1978), 'Syntactic Domains for Semantic Rules', in F. Guenthner and S. J. Schmidt (eds.), *Formal Semantics and Pragmatics for Natural Languages* (Dordrecht: Reidel), 107–30.

—— (1983), *Anaphora and Semantic Interpretation* (London: Croom Helm).

—— (2000), 'Strategies of Anaphora Resolution', in H. Bennis *et al.* (eds.), *Interface Strategies* (Amsterdam: Royal Academy of Arts and Sciences), 295–325.

—— and E. Reuland (1993), 'Reflexivity', *Linguistic Inquiry*, 24: 657–720.

Reuland, E. (2001*a*), 'Anaphors, Logophors and Binding', in P. Cole, G. Hermon, and C.-T. J. Huang (eds.), *Syntax and Semantics, 33: Long-Distance Reflexives* (San Diego: Academic Press), 343–70.

—— (2001*b*), 'Primitives of Binding', *Linguistic Inquiry*, 32: 439–92.

—— and Sigurjónsdóttir, S. (1997), 'Long Distance "Binding" in Icelandic: Syntax or Discourse', in H. J. Bennis, P. Pica, and J. Rooryck (eds.), *Atomism and Binding* (Dordrecht: Foris), 323–41.

Ross, J. R. (1967), '*Constraints on Variables in Syntax*', Ph.D. diss. (Massachusetts Institute of Technology).

Rouchota, V. (1992), 'On the Referential/Attributive Distinction', *Lingua*, 87: 137–67.

—— (1994), 'On Indefinite Descriptions', *Journal of Linguistics*, 30: 441–75.

Russell, B. (1905), 'On Denoting', *Mind*, 14: 479–93; repr. in R. C. Marsh (ed.), *Logic and Knowledge* (London: George Allen & Unwin, 1956), 41–56.

Safir, K. (forthcoming), *The Syntax of Anaphora* (Oxford: Oxford University Press).

Sag, I. (1976), '*Deletion and Logical Form*', Ph.D. diss. (Massachusetts Institute of Technology).

Salmon, N. (1982), 'Assertion and Incomplete Definite Descriptions', *Philosophical Studies*, 42: 37–45.

—— (1986), 'Reflexivity', *Notre Dame Journal of Formal Logic*, 27: 401–29.

—— (1992), 'Reflections of Reflexivity', *Linguistics and Philosophy*, 15: 53–63.

Saul, J. (2002*a*), 'Speaker Meaning, What is Said, and What is Implicated'. *Noûs* 36, 228–48.

—— (2002*b*), 'What is Said and Psychological Reality: Grice's Project and Relevance Theorists' Criticisms.' *Linguistics and Philosophy*, 25, 347–72.

Searle, J. (1969), *Speech Acts* (Cambridge: Cambridge University Press).

—— (1979), *Expression and Meaning* (Cambridge: Cambridge University Press).

—— (1980), 'The Background of Meaning', in J. R. Searle, F. Kiefer, and M. Bierwisch (eds.), *Speech Act Theory and Pragmatics* (Dordrecht: Reidel).

Sellars, W. (1954), 'Presupposing', *Philosophical Review*, 63: 197–215.

Sells, P. (1987), 'Aspects of Logophoricity', *Linguistic Inquiry*, 18: 445–79.

Sigurðsson, H. A. (1990), 'Long Distance Reflexives and Moods in Icelandic', in J. Maling and A. Zaenen (eds.), *Modern Icelandic Syntax* (New York: Academic Press), 309–46.

Sigurjónsdóttir, S. (1992), 'Binding in Icelandic: Evidence from Language Acquisition', Ph.D. diss. (University of California, Los Angeles).

Smith, N. V. (1999), *Chomsky: Ideas and Ideals* (Cambridge; Cambridge University Press.)

Soames, S. (1989), Review of Gareth Evans, *Collected Papers, Journal of Philosophy,* 89: 141–56.

—— (1990), 'Pronouns and Propositional Attitudes', *Proceedings of the Aristotelian Society,* 191–212.

—— (1994), 'Attitudes and Anaphora', *Philosophical Perspectives,* 9: 251–72.

Sperber, D., and D. Wilson (1986), *Relevance: Communication and Cognition* (Oxford: Basil Blackwell).

—— (1995), *Relevance: Communication and Cognition,* 2nd edn. (Oxford: Basil Blackwell).

Stanley, J. (2000), 'Context and Logical Form', *Linguistics and Philosophy,* 23: 391–434.

—— (2002), 'Making it Articulated', *Mind and Language,* 17: 149–68,

—— and Z. Szabó, (2000), 'On Quantifier Domain Restriction', *Mind and Language,* 15: 219–61.

Stockwell, R., P. Schachter, and B. Partee (1973), *The Major Syntactic Structures of English* (New York: Holt, Rinehart & Winston).

Strawson, P. F. (1950), 'On Referring', *Mind,* 59: 320–44.

—— (1952), *Introduction to Logical Theory* (London: Methuen).

—— (1954), 'Reply to Mr Sellars', *Philosophical Review,* 63: 216–31.

Szabolcsi, A. (1994), 'The Noun Phrase', in F. Kiefer and K. Kiss (eds.), *Syntax and Semantics 27: The Syntactic Structure of Hungarian.* (New York: Academic Press), 179–275.

—— (2003), 'Binding on the Fly: Cross-sentential Anaphora in Variable-free Semantics', in Kruijff and T. Oehrle (eds.), *Resource-Sensitivity in Binding and Anaphora* (Dordrecht: Kluwer), 215–29.

Wasow, T. (1972), 'Anaphoric Relations in English', Ph.D. diss. (Massachusetts Institute of Technology); repr. as *Anaphora in Generative Grammar* (Ghent: E. Story-Scientia, 1979).

Wexler, K., Culicover, P. and H. Hamburger (1974), *Learning Theoretic Foundations of Linguistic Universals,* Social Science Working Papers, 60 (Irvine: University of California Press).

Wiggins, D. (1976), 'Identity, Necessity, and Physicalism', in S. Körner (ed.), *Philosophy of Logic* (Berkeley: University of California Press), 159–82.

Williams, E. (1977), 'Discourse and Logical Form', *Linguistic Inquiry,* 8: 101–39.

Þráinsson, H. (1976), 'Reflexives and Subjunctives in Icelandic', *Proceedings of the North East Linguistics Society,* 6 (Amherst: University of Massachusetts Press) 225–39.

—— (1990), 'A Semantic Reflexive in Icelandic', in J. Maling and A. Zaenen (eds.), *Modern Icelandic Syntax* (New York: Academic Press), 289–307.

—— (1991), 'Long-Distance Reflexives and the Typology of NPs', in J. Koster and E. Reuland (eds.), *Long-Distance Anaphora* (Cambridge: Cambridge University Press), 49–75.

6

Deixis and Anaphora

François Recanati

1. Towards Unification

Uses of Pronouns

It is well known that pronouns have a number of distinct uses, which fall under three major headings: free uses, bound uses, and anaphoric uses. Consider the sentence

(1) John loves his mother.

The possessive pronoun 'his' can refer back to John (anaphoric use), or to some other person who turns out to be salient in the conversational context (free use). As a result, (1) says either that John loves his own mother, or that he loves that person's mother. We get a bound use if we embed the sentence in a quantificational context, as in

(2) Every boy is such that John loves his mother.

This sentence is susceptible to both of the uses mentioned above: 'his mother' can still refer to John's own mother, or to the mother of someone else who turns out to be salient in the conversational context. But the most likely understanding

I wish to thank Eros Corazza, Philippe Schlenker, Zoltán Gendler Szabó, and two anonymous reviewers for their comments on a first draft of this chapter. Thanks also to European Science Foundation EUROCORES Programme 'The Origin of Man, Language and Languages' for supporting this work.

of the pronoun in (2) corresponds to a third type of use, in which the mother at stake is not a single individual but, for every boy, the mother of that boy. This is the bound use, characterized by the fact that the value of the pronoun varies with the individuals introduced by the quantifier.[1] The bound use is similar to the anaphoric use, since in both cases there is a linguistic expression ('John' or 'every boy') which intuitively serves as 'antecedent' for the pronoun. When the antecedent is a quantifier, however, the pronoun is not assigned a definite value but a course of values.

The three types of use can be represented by indexing the pronoun and its possible antecedents. In bound uses, the pronoun will be co-indexed with an antecedent quantifier; in anaphoric uses, it will be co-indexed with a referring expression; in the absence of co-indexing, the pronoun will be understood as 'free'. The three readings for (2) can be spelled out as follows:

Bound use
Every boy$_{(i)}$ is such that John$_{(j)}$ loves his$_{(i)}$ mother.

Anaphoric use
Every boy$_{(i)}$ is such that John$_{(j)}$ loves his$_{(j)}$ mother.

Free use
Every boy$_{(i)}$ is such that John$_{(j)}$ loves his$_{(k)}$ mother.

Of course, not every pronominal expression tolerates the three uses. For example, the first person pronoun 'I' is always free: except perhaps in a few exceptional cases, its referent comes from the context. At the opposite end of the spectrum, reflexive (and logophoric) pronouns are often described as not tolerating free uses. Still, it is unlikely that the pronouns which allow for the three types of use are merely ambiguous: the phenomenon is too systematic to count as a crude ambiguity. There obviously is something common to the different uses—something which we must attempt to capture within a unified framework.

Anaphoric and Bound Uses

The first thing we notice when we attempt to unify the various uses is that pronouns are like variables in logic. Variables are not ambiguous, yet they have two uses: they can be bound by quantifiers, or they can remain free, depending on the syntactic environment in which they occur. With pronouns the situation is

---

[1] What I am calling the 'quantifier' here is the quantified noun phrase 'every boy', not the quantificational determiner 'every'.

similar. A pronoun can be bound by a quantifier or it can be contextually assigned a value. Such a contextual assignment is what I call a 'free' use for a pronoun. (Many speak of a deictic use, but that is a bit too specific, as we shall see.)

What about anaphoric uses? Can they be assimilated to either free uses or bound uses? They obviously have a lot in common with bound uses. First, as we have seen, there are pronouns which tolerate only free uses, and there are pronouns which do not tolerate free uses. The former tolerate neither bound nor anaphoric uses, while the latter tolerate both. This suggests that bound and anaphoric uses fall into the same category. Second, anaphoric and bound uses have this in common, that in both cases the pronoun depends, for its interpretation, upon an antecedent (singular term or quantifier). Free uses, on the other hand, are characterized by the lack of a linguistic antecedent.

Can we go further and provide a unified description of anaphoric and bound uses? Such unification can proceed in two directions, one of which seems to me more promising than the other. We may construe anaphoric uses as a special case of bound use, or bound uses as a special case of anaphoric use. I will refer to the first, less promising strategy as the 'binding strategy', and to the other one as the 'anaphoric strategy'. The anaphoric strategy will be introduced in the next subsection.

The most straightforward way of implementing the binding strategy proceeds by extending the notion of a quantifier so as to encompass singular terms as well (along the lines of generalized-quantifier theory).[2] On that view the anaphoric reading is the special case of bound use in which the pronoun is bound by a singular term. Alternatively, we may extend to anaphoric pronouns in general the treatment of reflexive pronouns as pronouns bound by an abstraction operator. Just as the sentence 'John loves himself' is analysed by means of a formula such as

$$\lambda x\,[x\,\text{loves}\,x]\,(\text{John}),$$

we may analyse the anaphoric pronoun 'his' as bound in 'John loves his mother', along the lines of

$$\lambda x\,[x\,\text{loves}\,x\text{'s mother}]\,(\text{John}).$$

Here 'John' may be construed as a genuine singular term, denoting an individual, rather than as a quantifier, denoting a function from properties to truth-values. Still, the pronoun 'his' is bound (by the lambda-operator).

---

[2] See e.g. Keenan and Westertahl (1997) on 'Montagovian individuals' as the interpretation of proper nouns, personal pronouns, and demonstratives.

Whichever option we choose, the attempt to reduce anaphoric uses to bound uses faces a fatal objection. Sometimes the singular term from which a pronoun inherits its reference cannot be taken to include the pronoun in its syntactic scope. Thus the pronoun and its antecedent may occur in different sentences, or the antecedent may be too deeply embedded to take scope over the pronoun. Now, whether or not we treat the singular term itself as a quantifier, it must take scope over the pronoun if the latter is to be treated as bound. It follows that the binding strategy fails: not all anaphoric uses can be treated as cases in which the pronoun is bound (Heim and Kratzer 1998: 241–2).

The Anaphoric Strategy

According to Frege and Russell, a quantificational statement such as 'Something grows' is not on a par with the sort of statement one makes when one uses a singular term. A ground-level statement such as 'John grows' tells us something directly about an object, namely, the object which the singular term stands for (John). A quantified statement such as 'Something grows' is a *higher-level* statement. It tells us that the statement-schema 'x grows' is "sometimes true" (Russell), i.e. that at least one instance of that schema, obtainable by replacing the variable by a singular term referring to an object, is a true ground-level statement. In Frege's terms, just as the ground-level statement 'John grows' is about John, the higher-level statement 'Something grows' is about the property which the ground-level statement ascribes to John: it tells us that that property—the property of growing—is instantiated.

To be sure, it is possible to devise a quantifier which will mimic the singular term 'John'. Let us write it 'John*'. The higher-level statement 'John* grows' tells us that the schema 'x grows' results in a true statement when the variable is replaced by a name for John. While 'John' denotes an individual object, namely John himself, 'John*' denotes a function from properties or sets of objects to truth-values, namely that function which, for any given set of objects or property, yields truth iff John belongs to that set or possesses that property. Obviously, 'John*' can substitute for 'John' everywhere *salva veritate*. But the fact that we can use 'John*' to mimic the ground-level name 'John' (and, perhaps, stand for it in our formal reconstruction of natural language) does not suppress the difference between ground-level statements and higher-level statements. It is from the cognitive point of view that that difference matters. We can easily imagine organisms endowed with the ability to make ground-level statements in the absence of any mastery of the higher-level apparatus; but it is not so easy to imagine the opposite situation, because higher-level talk presupposes ground-level talk. If we are to make sense of higher-level statements like 'Every man is F', we must first understand ground-level statements such as 'This man is F'.

Let us apply this idea to the issue at hand. Following Evans (1977), let us assume that, if we are to make sense of higher-level statements like 'Every man loves his mother', we must first understand ground-level statements such as 'John loves his mother'. The former tells us that for every man y, the schema 'x loves his mother', of which the latter is an instance, results in a true statement if we replace the variable by a name for y. Now, how are we to understand the schema itself? To do so we must fix the interpretation of 'his mother'. If we give the pronoun the free interpretation, the schema will be equivalent to 'x loves z's mother' and the higher-level statement will say that for every man y, 'x loves z's mother' is true if we replace 'x' by a name for y. If we give the pronoun the anaphoric interpretation, the schema will be equivalent to 'x loves x's mother' and the higher-level statement will say that for every man y, 'x loves x's mother' is true if we replace 'x' (on its two occurrences) by a name for y. This reading corresponds to the 'bound' interpretation of the pronoun. In this way we achieve an understanding of bound uses in terms of anaphoric uses, rather than the other way round. Anaphora is seen as a ground-level phenomenon, operative in sentences such as 'John loves his mother'. If, in such a sentence, we abstract the complex predicate '( )$_i$ loves his$_i$ mother' and use it to form a higher-level statement by combining it with a quantifier, the anaphoric pronoun is automatically bound by the quantifier in the resulting quantified statement. Bound uses of pronouns turn out to be a reflection, at the higher level, of the ground-level phenomenon of anaphora (Evans 1977).

Anaphoric Uses as Free Uses

Let us admit that bound uses are best analysed in terms of anaphoric uses (rather than the other way round). To complete the analysis, we must clarify the relation between anaphoric uses and free uses. Here also there are two possible—but, this time, complementary—directions of analysis: we may treat anaphora as a variety of free use, or free uses as varieties of anaphora.

It is natural to consider anaphora as a variety of free use, because we independently need a distinction between various sorts of free use. I said that a free use of a pronoun refers to an object salient in the conversational context. In a first type of case the referent of the pronoun is given and perceptually accessible in the situation of utterance. This type of case is the deictic use: some object is perceptually available to the participants, and the speaker refers to it while, possibly, pointing to it in order to draw the hearer's attention to it. (If the object by itself is sufficiently salient, no pointing is necessary.) In a second type of case, the referent is not given in the situation of utterance and it cannot be pointed to. But it is cognitively accessible because the speech participants 'have it in mind', that is, are thinking about it or about matters with which it is closely associated in their memory or 'mental encyclopaedia'.[3]

From such uses to anaphoric uses there is but a short step. If the conversation is about a certain object, the participants have that object in mind—simply because they are talking about it and, perforce, have been thinking about it in virtue of processing a piece of discourse about that object. A person may be cognitively salient because she has been mentioned in the discourse, just as she can be salient because, say, we are driving past the place where she lives. We end up with three basic forms, or sources, of salience: perceptual salience, discursive salience, and associative salience, corresponding to three varieties of free use. Deictic uses exploit perceptual salience; anaphoric uses exploit discursive salience; and uses of the third type (associative uses, as I will call them) exploit associative salience.

The prototype of a free use of a pronoun is generally considered to be the deictic use, where the referent is perceptually salient (see e.g. Clark 1992: 47; Bühler 1934, pt. II). The other forms of salience are seen as ersatz forms: the object is not really given, but we do 'as if' it was given (and use a demonstrative form) because it is given 'in imagination' or 'in thought'. Free uses that are not deictic are therefore treated as etiolated or secondary deictic uses. But there is another way to look at the relation between the various forms of free use. We may consider the *anaphoric* use as prototypical, because it transparently reveals a central feature of the free use of pronouns.

Free Uses as Anaphoric Uses

The central feature of free uses which makes them all anaphoric in a certain sense is not specific to pronouns: it is a property of singular terms in general. According to Strawson, who initiated this line of research and whose views have

---

[3] Geoff Nunberg gives the following example: we are walking through Versailles, and you say

Gee, he certainly spared no expense.

The obvious reference here is Louis XIV, Nunberg says. Even though Louis XIV is not physically present, and cannot be demonstrated, he is "salient in the consciousness of the conversational participants" (Nunberg 1992: 294).

been very influential (see e.g. Evans 1982; Heim 1988), the use of a definite singular term presupposes "resources of identifying knowledge antecedently in possession of the audience" (Strawson 1961: 60). As he puts it,

In any communication situation a hearer (an audience) is antecedently equipped with a certain amount of knowledge, with certain presumptions, with a certain range of possible current perception. There are within the scope of his knowledge or present perception objects which he is able in one way or another to distinguish for himself. (Strawson 1961: 59)

Understanding a singular term consists in linking up that singular term with the relevant stretch of identifying knowledge about a particular object. Following a well-established tradition I call such a stretch of identifying knowledge a 'mental file'. According to Strawson, a use of a singular term invokes a mental file in the mind of the interpreter, and is successful only if the interpreter actually connects the singular term with such a mental file, that is, only if

the singular term used establishes for the hearer an identity, and the right identity, between the thought of *what-is-being-spoken-of-by-the-speaker* and the thought of some object *already within the reach of the hearer's own knowledge, experience, or perception*, some object, that is, which the hearer could, in one way or another, pick out or identify for himself, from his own resources. (Strawson 1961: 63)

In this framework, the different sources of salience I mentioned above (perceptual, discursive, and associative salience) correspond to different bodies of identifying knowledge exploited by the speaker. Anaphora turns out to be a special case: the case where the resources brought to bear on the interpretation of a referential utterance consist of 'information imparted by earlier sentences in the same conversation'.[4] Yet there is a sense in which that case is prototypical and captures what is common to all cases. In all cases, indeed, *the task of the interpreter is to find a suitable antecedent for the singular term* (a suitable mental file). In anaphoric uses the antecedent is located in the previous discourse, or rather, in the mental representation resulting from the hearer's processing of the previous discourse. But in deictic cases also an antecedent mental file is invoked, corresponding to the hearer's perception of the referent. And the same thing holds for associative uses.

---

[4] "There are . . . many different types of resource upon which a speaker may draw or rely . . . He may draw upon what the [hearer] can be presumed to be in a position then and there to see or otherwise perceive for himself. He may rely upon information imparted by earlier sentences in the same conversation. He may rely upon information in the hearer's possession which is not derived from either of these sources" (Strawson 1961: 63).

This unification of free uses under the general heading of anaphora is quite apparent in Discourse Representation Theory. Kamp uses Discourse Representation Structures (DRSs) to stand for the mental representations formed in the process of interpreting a discourse, and shows how such representations get incremented as the discourse unfolds (see e.g. Kamp and Reyle 1993). In this theoretical endeavour, anaphoric relations play a crucial role. But the DRSs have been exploited also to represent all the information in the hearer's possession, including perceptual information, in so far as it is relevant to speech understanding. It is widely assumed that perceptual information can be used to enter a 'discourse referent', just as discourse information can. A deictic use of a pronoun can therefore be considered as anaphoric on such a 'perceptual' discourse referent. In Heim's framework that is explicit—all definite NPs are said to be anaphoric.[5]

The notion of cognitive 'salience' can now be cashed out in terms of the degree of activation, or accessibility, of the antecedent mental file. Among singular terms, some demand that the mental file they connect with be highly accessible. There is a difference, in this regard, between pronouns, demonstrative phrases like 'that man', definite descriptions ('the man'), and proper names. Unstressed pronouns presuppose the highest degree of salience or accessibility. The referents of pronouns, according to Chafe (1974), must be in the hearer's consciousness at the time they are referred to. If the referent is not salient enough (if the relevant file is not currently active) it is preferable to use another type of expression. (See Ariel 2001 for an overview of 'accessibility theory'.)

Deixis and Anaphora: Perspectives for Empirical Research

The unification of the various types of free use, including the anaphoric use (in the strict sense), opens up an interesting field of investigation. In particular, it invites a comparative study of the tracking abilities involved in deixis and anaphora.

In so far as demonstratives secure their reference via perception, we need an account of how perception itself can provide the appropriate grounding for deictic reference. As Austen Clark pointed out, such an account is bound to locate a primitive form of demonstrative reference in sensory processes

[5] This treatment, Kadmon points out, "is quite compatible with deictic uses of definites. Given that on Heim's approach the file is a representation of the common ground (and not merely of information expressed by preceding utterances), the antecedent discourse referent of a given definite NP need not be triggered by linguistic text" (Kadmon 2001: 78).

themselves (Clark 2000). There is, indeed, a growing body of evidence showing that something like demonstrative reference takes place in vision. Preconceptual 'object-files' or referential 'indices' are used to track visual objects and gather information concerning them (Treisman and Gelade 1980; Treisman 1988; Pylyshyn 1989, 2000; Leslie *et al.* 1998). Thus Pylyshyn holds that "we have a mechanism that allows preconceptual tracking of a primitive perceptual individuality"; a mechanism that "is able to individuate and keep track of about five visual objects and does so without using an encoding of any of their visual properties" (Pylyshyn 2001: 143).

One obvious question that arises in this area concerns the generality of the indexing mechanism studied by Pylyshyn and others. Is it restricted to vision, or is the same (or the same sort of) indexing system involved also in, say, auditory perception? Pylyshyn himself asks that question, but there is another one, more relevant to our present purposes. Is this mechanism restricted to perception, and to deixis in so far as it is based on perception, or can we go as far as to imagine that a similar indexing system may be at work in discourse processing, enabling us to keep track of about five objects simultaneously at the highest level of accessibility? (Think of what happens when we process a piece of discourse like: 'Yesterday, my brother talked to the policeman about the burglar we saw. *He* told *him he* thought *he* had escaped, but the policeman would not believe *him*, arguing that someone was awake, and *he* would have seen the burglar if *he* had left.')

Those issues are worth pursuing empirically, but only if we accept that there is a unified field of investigation involving both deixis and anaphora. Now this age-old assumption has been questioned, and the quest for unification criticized as illusory. According to Gareth Evans (1980), whose argument I will discuss in the second part of this chapter, any unified treatment of deictic uses and anaphoric uses is doomed to failure. If anaphoric uses are like deictic uses, that is, if they are free uses, then, he says, the referent of an anaphoric pronoun will be determined on a pragmatic basis, by appealing to considerations pertaining to contextual salience, etc. This is indeed what has been claimed by defenders of the 'pragmatic theory' of anaphora, such as Lasnik and Chomsky. Evans argues that any such theory has unacceptable consequences, however.

2. Evans's Argument against Unification

The Structure of Evans's Argument

Evans's argument proceeds in two steps. First, he attempts to show that the three uses of pronouns cannot be unified. We are faced with a dilemma, he says. Either we account for the connection between bound uses and anaphoric uses (by appealing to the 'anaphoric strategy'), and that forces us to give up the connection between free uses and anaphoric uses; or we maintain that connection, and we no longer understand that between bound uses and anaphoric uses. The second (and less explicit) step in Evans's argument consists in providing a reason for choosing the first horn of the dilemma. He argues that the connection between bound uses and anaphoric uses is too fundamental to be given up. The same thing cannot be said of the connection between free uses (e.g. deictic uses) and anaphoric uses. Since nothing essential hinges on that connection, it can be dismissed if necessary.

In what follows, I will be concerned only with the first step of Evans's argument. I do not accept the dilemma—I think we *can* unify the three uses of pronouns. More specifically, I reject the idea that, if we account for the connection between anaphoric uses and bound uses, we are no longer in a position to maintain the link between anaphoric and free uses. I will argue that we can preserve that link, appearances notwithstanding.

The Dilemma

According to Evans, we must account for the fact that bound uses of pronouns occur in quantified statements (e.g. 'Every man loves his mother') only if anaphoric uses of the same pronouns occur in the same argument-places in the corresponding substitution instances (e.g. 'John loves his mother'). That, he says, can hardly be a coincidence. To account for that fact, we must acknowledge the dependency of bound uses upon anaphoric uses. Evans makes that dependency explicit as follows. To understand 'Every man loves his mother' (on the bound reading of the pronoun), two conditions must be satisfied:

(i) we must understand substitution instances of the form 'β loves his mother', where 'β' names a man and 'his' is given the *anaphoric* reading;
(ii) we must understand the quantified statement as saying that such a ground-level statement is true whichever man we take 'β' to refer to.

In other words, we need a general understanding of anaphora in ground-level sentences, and a general understanding of (universal) quantification, but that is all we need. Bound uses of pronouns turn out to be nothing but a higher-level reflection of the ground-level phenomenon of anaphora.

On this analysis, the pronoun does not refer in the quantified statement, since it is bound by the quantifier; but in each substitution instance the pronoun refers: it inherits the reference of its antecedent (that's what makes it anaphoric).[6] Now we can state Evans's objection to the pragmatic theory of anaphora. To treat an anaphoric use as a *free* use is to treat its reference as determined on a pragmatic basis, by appealing to considerations pertaining to contextual salience. This theory, however, cannot apply to the anaphoric pronouns that feature in the substitution instances. *Which* contextual factors could possibly influence the reference of a pronoun in a substitution instance? The substitution instances are not real statements: they come into the picture only in the semantic evaluation of the quantified statements, but from a pragmatic standpoint they do not exist: there is, for them, no context of utterance, since they are not uttered. The only context available is the context in which the quantified statement is uttered, but, at that level, no act of reference takes place: reference there is only at the level of substitution instances.

If we want to maintain that anaphoric uses are free uses, Evans concludes, we must give up the analysis of bound uses as involving anaphoric uses at the level of substitution instances; for no 'free' use can be found at that level. If we insist on maintaining the suggested analysis for bound pronouns, then we must give up the view that anaphoric uses are free uses. That's the dilemma. As I pointed out, Evans chooses to give up the connection between anaphoric uses and free uses. He construes anaphoric uses of pronouns (and other expressions) as referential uses characterized by the fact that the reference of the expression is not determined by contextual factors such as salience, but by a *linguistic rule*—the rule of anaphora. That rule applies whenever a singular-term position p_i in a ground-level sentence is 'chained to' another singular-term position p_j elsewhere in the sentence.[7] The rule says that the singular term at p_i refers to whatever the singular term at p_j refers to. In virtue of the rule, an anaphoric pronoun inherits the reference of its antecedent, quite independently of any consideration of salience. Nothing prevents such a rule from applying to anaphoric pronouns in substitution instances.

---

[6] On Evans's approach, in contrast to Geach's, the non-referential character of bound pronouns is compatible with the referential character of the anaphoric pronoun in the corresponding substitution instances. See Evans (1977).

[7] Evans explicitly considers the possibility that chaining may take place cross-sententially: "It requires only a trivial modification of the grammar to allow the chaining of singular term positions to singular terms which occur in other sentences [even if they are uttered by different people]. No modification of the referential semantics is required at all, once we allow the units processed by our semantic theory to be chunks of dialogue, not just single sentences" (Evans 1977: 102).

Higher-Level Demonstratives

The difficulty which Evans raises for the pragmatic theory of anaphora can be summed up as follows. When I say 'Every man loves his mother' in a context C, there is no salient man *in C* to whom I refer by means of the pronoun. The pronoun 'his', in that bound use, is *not* referential: it is a stand-in for anaphoric pronouns at the level of substitution instances. At the level of substitution instances, the pronoun refers, but the referent which it acquires in a particular substitution instance is not available in the context in which the quantified statement is made. Since that is the only context available, Evans concludes that the reference of the pronoun is not provided by context but via a linguistic rule.

To dispose of Evans's argument, my strategy will be to look at a similar example involving a *deictic* use. Deictic uses of pronouns are the most uncontroversial case of free use. If the problematic phenomenon can be reproduced with deictic uses, then it cannot be used to show that anaphoric uses are not free uses. Or so I will argue.

Consider the following example, due to Geoff Nunberg. Gesturing towards John Paul II as he delivers a speech with a Polish accent (shortly after his election), I say:

(3) He is usually an Italian, but this time they thought it wise to elect a Pole.

The pronoun 'he' here is deictic: what I am pointing to in the situation of utterance (namely, the pope) plays a crucial role in determining the semantic value of the pronoun. Yet the pronoun is not referential: I am not saying that John Paul II is usually an Italian, but, rather, that *the pope* is usually an Italian. This is equivalent to saying that for most situations of a certain type, the person who is pope in that situation is an Italian.

Were we to evaluate the first conjunct of (3), we would have to look down to the level of substitution instances and, for every relevant situation, evaluate the statement 'he is an Italian', where 'he' refers to the person filling the role of pope in that situation. This is formally similar to the case discussed by Evans. If Evans's argument goes through, it should go through in this case as well. With respect to (3), indeed, Evans might say the following. In the context C' in which the quantified statement 'He is usually an Italian' is made, only John Paul II is given. The popes of which *being an Italian* can be truly predicated only come into the picture when we consider the situations quantified over by 'usually', that is, they come into the picture and become available for reference only at the level of substitution instances. But those situations of evaluation in which we find referents for the pronoun are not contexts of utterance for either the quantified statement or the substitution instances. The former is uttered in a different situation (the actual situation in which the pope is Polish) while the latter are not uttered at all. Hence the reference of the pronoun 'he' in the substitution instances 'He is an Italian' cannot be determined by context: it must be determined by a linguistic rule.

I shall start by criticizing the Evans-inspired argument as applied to the deictic case. This will enable me to expose a flaw in Evans's original argument, and to present an alternative picture of the relations between context, content, and reference in the relevant examples.

Rebutting the Evans-Inspired Argument

As applied to the deictic case, the Evans-inspired argument rests on a confusion. What characterizes deictic uses of pronouns is the fact that the *semantic contribution* (the 'content') of the pronoun on such a use is determined by the speaker's intentions as externalized through his or her pointing gestures (Kaplan 1989*b*). That contribution typically is an individual to which the pronoun refers, *but it need not be*. What makes the demonstrative pronoun 'he' in (3) nonreferential is precisely the fact that its semantic contribution, though determined by the speaker's pointing gesture, is not an individual but a *role*, namely, the role of pope which the demonstrated individual happens to instantiate. Exactly the same semantic contribution would be made if we replaced the pronoun by the definite description 'the pope';[8] but while the role in question is linguistically encoded by the description 'the pope', its being contributed by the pronoun in (3) is determined by the speaker's intention as revealed by his pointing gesture. The semantic contribution of the demonstrative pronoun in (3) is therefore as much determined by context as it would be if the pronoun had been used to refer to John Paul II and say something about him (rather than about the role which he instantiates). Hence there is no reason to deny that the use of the pronoun in (3) is a free use—indeed a deictic use.

What about substitution instances? The pronoun in (3) is admittedly nonreferential, but in substitution instances it refers, according to Evans, and its

---

[8] I assume that a definite description 'the F' contributes a role, which can be formally represented as a partial function from situations to individuals. The value of the role is the object (if any) which possesses the property F in the relevant situation. If, in a given situation, no object, or more than one object, possesses the property, the function is undefined for that situation. When referentially used, descriptions arguably contribute the value of the role (Fauconnier 1985).

reference cannot be determined by context. Does it not follow that, in substitution instances at least, the pronoun cannot be free, let alone deictic?

Here again, I think there is a confusion. In evaluating the first conjunct of (3), we proceed as follows. We consider all the situations in the relevant domain, and with respect to each of them we evaluate 'He is an Italian', where 'he' contributes the role THE_POPE. To do so we evaluate the role THE_POPE in each situation s and check whether the resulting value is an Italian (in s). If the answer is yes in most situations, we evaluate the quantified statement as true. Speaking like Evans, we may say that the pronoun acquires a 'reference' (or, better, an extension) at the level of substitution instances. The reference in question is the value of THE_POPE in the situation relevant to the substitution instance at stake. Let us focus on a particular substitution instance, A, and call 'Oscar' the reference of the pronoun in the situation s_1 relevant to A. What determines that Oscar is the reference? Is it a linguistic rule? No. The reference of the pronoun with respect to A is determined by two facts: (i) the fact that the pronoun contributes the role THE_POPE, and (ii) the fact that THE_POPE (s_1) = Oscar. The first fact is determined by context and speaker's intentions, as we have seen. It is determined by the context in which *the quantified statement* is made. (That's the only context available.) The second fact is determined by features of the situation of evaluation.

To sum up, the pronoun in (3) is used deictically, even though its semantic content is general (a role) rather than singular (an individual). It is a free use, because the semantic contribution of the pronoun is determined by contextual factors such as the speaker's intention. Since the statement is quantificational rather than referential, evaluating it requires evaluating substitution instances, and that involves evaluating the role THE_POPE in various situations. If we adopt Evans's way of talking, we may say that the values of the role in the situations in question are what the pronoun 'refers to' in the substitution instances. But then we must acknowledge that the 'reference' of the pronoun in a given substitution instance is determined, quite normally, by the semantic *content* of the pronoun (together with facts about the situation of evaluation), which semantic content itself is determined by the context of the quantified statement. And the fact that the content of the pronoun is determined by context is sufficient to justify classifying the pronoun as 'free', even though the reference of the pronoun is not (directly) determined by context.

The Flaw in Evans's Argument

To clarify the discussion, let me introduce a handful of notions, borrowed from the theory of direct reference (Kaplan 1989*a*; Recanati 1993). A (disambiguated) expression is *context-sensitive* or *context-dependent* if and only if its semantic content depends upon, and varies with, contextual factors such as the speaker's intention, etc. Indexical expressions and free uses of pronouns are context-sensitive in this sense. The *semantic content* of an expression is that property of it which (i) must be grasped by whoever fully understands the expression, and (ii) determines the expression's extension. It can be represented as a (possibly partial, and possibly constant) function from circumstances of evaluation to extensions. The *extension* of a prima facie singular term (name, pronoun, definite description, etc.) is an individual object—the reference of the term. A prima facie singular term is *directly referential* (or 'referential', for short) iff its content directly fixes its extension (its reference), prior to the encounter with the circumstance of evaluation. Thus we may take the content of a proper name to be the individual it refers to, or at least to determine it directly, in such a way that the reference relation is 'rigid' and independent of the circumstance of evaluation. Among definite singular terms, some are directly referential in this sense, while others are not. Thus definite descriptions, on certain uses at least, nonrigidly refer to whatever happens to satisfy the condition encoded by the description. The semantic content of the description is a role (a partial function from situations to individuals), but that role does not directly determine the reference of the description: the reference of the description (the value of the function) systematically depends upon the circumstance of evaluation (the argument of the function) and may shift accordingly.

So far, so good. Now I take Evans's argument to go through only if we assume that the expressions at issue (anaphoric pronouns in substitution instances such as 'β loves his mother') are directly referential. Whenever the content of an expression *is* its reference (or fixes it directly), the definition of context-sensitivity I gave above entails that, if the expression is context-sensitive (i.e. if its content is determined by context), then its *reference* is determined by context. It follows that, if the reference of the expression is *not* determined by context, then its content is not determined by context either and the expression cannot count as 'free'. *Evans precisely argues from the fact that the reference of certain anaphoric pronouns is not determined by context to the conclusion that those pronouns cannot be counted as free.* But that transition is truth-preserving only if the expressions at issue are directly referential. If they are not, the conclusion does not follow. Let me illustrate this by considering the case of a definite description.

Take the description 'the US President in 2023'. Let's assume that Woody Allen will be the US President in 2023. Then Woody Allen is the reference of the description. Does the reference of the description, in such a case, depend upon the context of utterance, as the reference of an indexical does? Certainly not. The reference depends upon (i) the content of the description, namely the role US_PRESIDENT_IN_2023, and (ii) the circumstance of evaluation (namely, the US situation in 2023). Now consider a variant of the example: the description 'the next US President'. Here also the reference is fixed by (i) the content of the description and (ii) the circumstance of evaluation. It is not assigned directly in the context of utterance. But in the new variant the context plays a role in determining the *content* of the description (because of the indexical 'next'): depending on when the description is uttered it will contribute different roles, e.g. US_PRESIDENT_IN_2005 or US_PRESIDENT_IN_2023. When the role which is the description's content depends upon the context in this fashion (instead of being encoded in a context-independent manner), the description can be said to be context-sensitive even though the reference of the description is not assigned directly in the context of utterance but is determined by contingent features of the situation of evaluation.

What I have just said is enough to show that Evans's reasoning is faulty. There are cases in which the content of an expression is determined in part by contextual factors, even though the reference of the expression is determined only by circumstantial factors. Hence it will not do to argue from the fact that the reference is not assigned in context to the conclusion that the expression is not context-sensitive or (in the case of pronouns) that it is not 'free': that piece of reasoning is acceptable only if we assume that the expression at issue (the pronoun) is directly referential, in such a way that its content can't be fixed by context without its reference also being fixed by context. In other words, *Evans's argument goes through only if we rule out a descriptive analysis of the pronoun's content.*

Such a descriptive analysis is precisely what I have provided in the deictic case. In (3), I claimed, the pronoun contributes a role, and its content is the same as that of the description 'the pope'. If that's right, and if the same thing holds when we move to the level of substitution instances, then *the fact that the reference of the pronoun in substitution instances is not determined by context in no way shows that the pronoun itself is not free.* Similarly, I think we should not rule out the following option: perhaps the pronoun 'his' in examples like 'Every man loves his mother' contributes a role, and perhaps the situation is not fundamentally different when, in the course of evaluating the statement, we move to the level of substitution instances. Let's assume that is the case. Then from the fact that the reference of the pronoun in substitution instances is not determined by context, it does not follow that the pronoun is not free. Evans's argument simply begs the question by assuming a referential analysis of anaphoric pronouns—an analysis which is not forced upon us simply in virtue of the fact that we want to analyse bound uses in terms of anaphoric uses.

3. Outline of a Unified Theory

Index vs. Content, 1: Deixis

If what I have said is correct, there can be deixis without reference. In (3) the pronoun is admittedly not referential: it does not refer to an individual person like John Paul II or anyone else. John Paul II is demonstrated, but he is not referred to. (If he were, the statement would say that John Paul II is usually an Italian.) Still, the pronoun is used deictically. What is distinctive of deixis is not the fact that the semantic contribution of the pronoun (its content) is an individual singled out in the situation of utterance, but rather the fact that its semantic contribution is determined via its relation to something which is singled out in the context of utterance (Nunberg 1993).

Following Nunberg, let us distinguish two steps in the interpretation of an indexical expression. The first step is the identification of the *index*, i.e. an aspect of the situation of utterance to which the expression draws the hearer's attention and in terms of which he or she can identify the expression's content. In the case of the first-person pronouns 'I' and 'we' the index is *the speaker*—the person making the utterance. In the case of indexicals like 'now', 'today', 'tomorrow', etc., the index is the *time of utterance*. In the case of demonstratives the index may be taken to be *a place indicated by the speaker* using his pointing finger, the direction of his gaze, or any other means. (Here I depart from Nunberg, who thinks the index of a demonstrative is the demonstrated object.)

The second step in the interpretation is the identification of the expression's content (its reference, in standard cases) in terms of the index. In the case of 'I' the reference happens to be identical to the index, but that is a special case. The reference of 'we' is *a group containing* the index; the semantic value of 'today', similarly, is a day including the index, etc.

What about demonstratives? I said that a demonstrative indexes a position in physical space—the position indicated by the pointing gesture. In some cases that position can be the semantic content of the demonstrative expression ('look *there*'), but in most cases the reference or semantic content will be something other than the position—for example, an object found at that position ('look at *that*).[9] Even in such cases the position is primary, for the reference is identified in relation to it. Given this primacy of places in demonstrative reference, 'that man' can be analysed as something like *the man who is there*, where 'there' indexes a place, and the whole phrase refers to the man at that place (Lyons 1975: 68).

A deictic pronoun can also contribute a property or a role, rather than an individual. Example (3) is a case in point. The pronoun remains deictic because it indexes a place in the situation of utterance and contributes something which bears a certain relation to that place (namely the role of pope, which is instantiated at that very place by John Paul II).

I suggest that we apply the same sort of analysis to anaphoric and bound uses of pronouns. Anaphoric pronouns, I will argue, have an essential feature in common with deictic pronouns: in both cases, the pronoun indexes something, and its semantic contribution is determined in relation to the index.

Index vs. Content, 2: Anaphora

What anaphoric pronouns index is not a position in physical space (like demonstratives) but a position in linguistic space, namely an *argument position*.

An argument position is a position in the grammatical structure of a sentence where an argument role is articulated. For example, in the sentence

(4) Bill gave the book to Mary

there are three argument positions:

( )$_i$ gave ( )$_j$ to ( )$_k$.

They articulate three roles constitutive of the action (or event) of giving: the role of giver, the role of gift, and the role of recipient. These thematic roles can be construed as relations between the action described by the sentence and the entities which participate in the action. Following Davidson, Parsons, Higginbotham, and others, we may construe (4) as positing the existence of a giving event e to which Bill, the book, and Mary respectively stand in the relations corresponding to the three roles.

---

[9] According to Nunberg, deictic expressions such as 'here' and 'there', 'this' and 'that', lexically encode two sorts of information: deictic information pertaining to the index and classificatory information pertaining to the reference. The former is conveyed via features like *proximal* and *distal* in terms of which 'here' contrasts with 'there', 'this' with 'that', and 'these' with 'those'. The latter information is conveyed via features like gender, number, and animacy and also by explicit or implicit sortals. As to the relation between index and reference, it is contextually determined (rather than lexically encoded, as in the case of pure indexicals like 'tomorrow').

A number of problems arise in the theory of thematic roles. For example, it's still an open question whether thematic roles are universal across types of action, or specific to them. Do we need a specific role of 'giver', or can we manage with the general role of 'agent', as applied to various types of action (givings, walkings, etc.)? I cannot even begin to address such issues here. On the other hand, there are two guiding principles of the theory that I would like to mention, as they are directly relevant to the points I want to make:

Principle 1. In conjunction with the lexical semantics of the verb, the grammatical positions occupied by noun phrases uniquely determine the thematic roles associated with those noun phrases.

Principle 2. A given thematic role can be articulated only once in a simple sentence. (Fillmore 1968: 21)

In virtue of Principle 1 (to be qualified later), the argument position which an anaphoric pronoun indexes uniquely determines a thematic role. The role may therefore be considered as part of what is indexed. Going further, we may be tempted to say that what an anaphoric pronoun indexes is less the position than *the thematic role articulated at that position*. But nothing much hinges on the precise choice of index (argument position or thematic role), in so far as the position uniquely determines the thematic role. Hence, for the time being at least, we can indifferently talk of the position or the role as being indexed.

In virtue of Principle 2, there can be at most one entity filling a given thematic role in the (minimal) event described by a simple ground-level sentence.[10] The entity in question may be plural: it may be, for example, a group of people. But whichever entity it is, that entity is the only filler of the role. The reason for that is the following. An entity x fills a given role r in the minimal event e described by a ground-level sentence S only if S ascribes x to r as its value. Now S ascribes x to r as its value only if x is referred to by some expression occupying a position articulating r in S. By Principle 2, at most one position can articulate r in S. It follows that there can be at most one entity filling role r in e, namely the reference of the term occurring at the unique position articulating r in S. Thematic roles can therefore be represented not merely as relations between the actions (events, situations) described by the simple ground-level sentences and the entities

---

[10] The minimal event described by a ground-level sentence is an event type fitting the description provided by the sentence, such that no proper part of that event itself fits that description. See Heim (1990: 146). By 'the event (situation, etc.) described by a ground-level sentence', I will always mean the minimal event (situation, etc.) described by that sentence.

which participate in them, but as *functions* taking those actions as arguments and those entities as values.[11]

Armed with those principles, let us consider the issue of semantic content. What is the semantic content of an anaphoric pronoun? Typically it will be the *value* of the indexed role, when that role is fed as argument the action described by the antecedent sentence.[12] The value in question is the referent of the term occupying the indexed position. Thus imagine that (4) is followed by an utterance of

(5) He hopes she will appreciate it.

The three pronouns may be interpreted as indexing the three argument positions distinguished earlier in sentence (4), as follows:

he$_i$ hopes she$_k$ will appreciate it$_j$.

Those positions uniquely determine three thematic roles in the action e_1 described by (4), namely that of giver, that of recipient, and that of gift. The semantic value of 'he' in (5) will therefore be GIVER $(e_1) =$ Bill, that of 'she' will be RECIPIENT $(e_1) =$ Mary, and that of 'it' will be GIFT $(e_1) =$ the book.[13]

In this way anaphoric pronouns inherit the reference of their antecedents, yet they do not do so in virtue of a brute 'rule of anaphora', but in virtue of being a variety of indexical expressions which (i) index an argument position and (ii) contribute the value of the thematic role articulated at that position.[14]

---

[11] Notationally, I will distinguish between the two construals by using small letters for roles-as-relations and capital letters for roles-as-functions. Thus EXPERIENCER $(e) = \iota x$: Experiencer(x, e).

[12] By 'antecedent sentence', I mean the sentence in which the indexed position is found. (This may be the same sentence as that in which the anaphoric pronoun occurs.) For the time being I assume that the antecedent sentence is a ground-level sentence. Cases in which the indexed position is occupied by a quantifier rather than by a referential expression will be dealt with in the next section.

[13] The event variable 'e_1' is free here, in contrast to the event variable 'e' that is bound by an existential event quantifier in the logical form of both sentence (4) and sentence (5). Sentence (5) says that there is an eventuality e, such that e is a state of hope, and the experiencer of e is the value of the role GIVER in event e_1 (where e_1 is the minimal event described by (4)), and so on and so forth.

[14] An anonymous reader had trouble with "the suggestion that identification of the thematic role is instrumental in a crucial way in the identification of the reference". "Surely", he or she says, "it is the classification information (as defined in note 9) together with general knowledge about presents being the kind of things that are appreciated 'in virtue of which' we are able to give the pronouns in (5) an antecedent or reference, downstream in the discourse to (4)." I agree, but this is consistent with what I say. I claim that, to understand an anaphoric expression, one has to identify its index (the relevant argument position or role). This is consistent with the fact that, to identify the relevant index, one often relies on the sort of information the reader mentions. (Similar considerations apply to demonstratives.)

Index vs. Content, 3: Bound Pronouns

When the indexed position is occupied by a quantifier rather than a referential expression, the semantic content of the pronoun cannot be the value of the role articulated at the indexed position, since the antecedent sentence does not ascribe a particular value to that role (but only a course of values). I assume that, in such a case, the semantic content of the pronoun is the role itself. The pronoun is therefore equivalent to a definite description, as in Evans's theory of E-type anaphora. Thus I distinguish two varieties of anaphora: *referential anaphora*, where the semantic content of the anaphoric pronoun is the value of the indexed role (i.e. where the pronoun inherits the reference of its antecedent); and *descriptive anaphora*, where the content of the anaphoric pronoun is the role itself. E-type anaphora is a special case of descriptive anaphora (see next section).

Bound uses of pronouns are another special case of descriptive anaphora, characterized by the fact that the pronoun is in the scope of the quantifier that occupies the indexed position. Consider, for example, sentence (6):

(6) Every man$_i$ loves his$_i$ mother.

The pronoun 'his' is not referential here: it does not inherit the reference of its antecedent, since its antecedent is not referential. Still it is anaphoric. What makes the pronoun anaphoric is the fact that *it indexes an argument-position in the sentence*, namely, the position occupied by 'every man' in surface structure. In a ground-level statement such as 'John loves his mother' the pronoun does the same thing: it indexes the argument-position occupied by the subject of the verb. The difference is that in the ground-level statement the argument-position is filled by a referential term, in such a way that the anaphoric pronoun can inherit its reference. In the higher-level statement the argument-position is occupied by a quantifier, so that the semantic content of the anaphoric pronoun can only be the role articulated at the indexed position. This is an instance of descriptive anaphora.

The role which is the content of the anaphoric pronoun in (6) is the role articulated at the indexed position. Since the indexed position corresponds to the subject of the verb 'love', the articulated role is that of LOVER, i.e. the experiencer in the *love*-relation. Sentence (6) says that for every man x, there is a state of love of which x is the experiencer (the LOVER) and the theme of which (the LOVER) is the mother of the experiencer, i.e. the mother of x. Using definite descriptions and a standard event semantics, we can represent the logical form of (6) as follows:

(6/D) [Every x: man x][∃e] (State_of_love (e) & Experiencer (x, e)
       & Theme (ιz: Mother of (z, ιy: Experiencer(y, e)), e)).

In evaluating (6), we have to look down to substitution instances of the form 'β loves his mother', where 'β' names a man. What is the content of the pronoun in such a substitution instance? There are two possible options here. What has been said about ordinary instances of anaphora such as 'John loves his mother' suggests that, with respect to a situation in which a particular man β fills the role of lover, the anaphoric pronoun refers to that very man. If that is so, then the semantic content of the pronoun in substitution instances is the value of the role, even though the semantic content of the pronoun in the quantified statement is the role. To justify this shift in semantic content from the quantified statement to its substitution instances we might say that the semantic content of an anaphoric pronoun is *always* the value of the role it indexes, *unless* no such value is available. In quantified statements evaluation of the role is not directly possible and has to wait until substitution instances are brought into the picture. But in the substitution instances, as in ordinary anaphoric utterances, evaluation of the role is possible.

But why should we accept the invoked principle, to the effect that the content of an anaphoric pronoun *must* be the value of the indexed role, whenever such a value is accessible? Is this not too rigid? Whoever is impressed by the analogy between anaphoric uses and free uses will be prepared to acknowledge the fact that the semantic content of an anaphoric pronoun, like that of a deictic pronoun, is very much up to the speaker. Thus I take it that, when the indexed position is occupied by a referential expression, *the semantic content of an anaphoric pronoun may be either the value of the indexed role, or the role itself.* This is hidden by the fact that the two readings of 'John loves his mother'—the reading in which the content of the anaphoric pronoun is the role of LOVER, and the reading in which the content of the pronoun is the value of that role—are truth-conditionally indistinguishable in simple sentences. But we can reveal the ambiguity by using VP ellipsis:

(7) John, loves his, mother, and Paul does too.

On the role reading, that means that Paul too loves his (own) mother. On the value reading, that means that Paul too loves John's mother.

When the anaphoric pronoun indexes a position occupied by a quantifier, as in (6), there is no choice: the value reading is ruled out, as the role cannot be directly evaluated (since the antecedent sentence does not ascribe a specific value to the role). Note that the same thing seems to happen in syntactic contexts in which the reflexive would be used: 'John loves himself' can only take the role reading, it seems, for 'John loves himself, and so does Paul' does not seem to be ambiguous. It cannot mean ' . . . and Paul too loves John'. (I will not attempt to account for that fact, nor, more generally, for the behaviour of reflexives.)

In the framework I am sketching, the anaphoric pronoun contributes a role when the role it indexes is not ascribed a particular value in the antecedent sentence, but in the other cases it may contribute either the role or the value of the role. What about substitution instances? Shall we say, with Evans, that the anaphoric pronoun is referential in substitution instances and contributes the value of the role, i.e. the entity which the referential antecedent refers to? We might, but I see no reason to do so. In evaluating a statement like (6), we look down to substitution instances in which a referring expression substitutes for the quantified phrase, but *everything else remains the same*. In particular, the pronoun which we find in a given substitution instance is the same pronoun we find in the quantified statement, and there is no reason why it should not carry the same semantic content. Since, in the quantified statement, that content is a role, I will assume that it is a role also in the substitution instances. This creates no difficulty whatsoever. In evaluating (6), we look for substitution instances of the form 'β loves his mother', where 'β' names a man and the pronoun contributes the role of LOVER. To evaluate that instance we check whether the value of the role in the situation which the substitution instance describes, i.e. the man β who fills the role of LOVER, has the relevant property, i.e. is an x such that x loves the mother of x. This is very straightforward. On this analysis the logical form of an arbitrary substitution instance (6*) is (6*/D), while for Evans it is (6*/R):

(6*) β_i loves his$_i$ mother

(6*/D) $[\exists e]$ (State_of_love (e) & Experiencer (β, e)
        & Theme $(\iota z$: Mother of $(z, \iota y$: Experiencer(y, e) $), e)$).

(6*/R) $[\exists e]$ (State_of_love (e) & Experiencer (β, e)
        & Theme $(\iota z$: Mother of $(z, \beta), e)$)

For Evans, the content of the pronoun in substitution instances is referential. In my analysis that content is descriptive.

In Section 2, I claimed that Evans's argument goes through only if we opt for the referential analysis: if we choose the descriptive analysis, we may escape Evans's conclusion by arguing that the *content* of the pronoun is determined by context even though its *reference* (its extension) is not. But the framework set up in Section 3 enables us to escape Evans's conclusion *even if we opt for the referential analysis*. In that framework, we draw a distinction not only between content and reference (extension), but also between content and index. It follows that, even if we equate the content of a pronoun to its reference, we can resist Evans's conclusion that anaphoric uses are not free uses. Let us assume that the pronoun in substitution instances is referential, in accordance with (6*/R). What determines the reference of the pronoun, on this view, is not the context but the rule that the pronoun refers to the value of the indexed role. This is a new version of the 'rule of anaphora'. Even if the reference of the pronoun is determined by this rule, however, we can maintain that the indexed role itself is determined by context. *The context of the quantified statement determines the role that is indexed in the quantified statement and in each of its substitution instances.* The fact that the reference of the pronoun depends upon a contextually determined index in this way is arguably sufficient to justify treating the pronoun as free.

The Context-Sensitivity of Anaphora

In the theory I have sketched anaphoric pronouns are like demonstratives and other indexicals. Interpreting such an expression in context is a two-step procedure which requires, first, identifying the index, then identifying the content in terms of the index.

Some indexicals have their index and their content determined in a rule-governed manner. Thus 'tomorrow' systematically indexes the day of utterance and refers to the following day. In other cases (e.g. demonstratives) the index and/or the content heavily depend upon the intentions of the speaker. Anaphoric pronouns belong to this last category. Within certain constraints of accessibility, the indexed argument position is up to the speaker. That much is obvious. What is less obvious is that the content of the pronoun also depends upon the speaker's intentions, even after the index has been fixed.

As we have seen, the content of a pronoun anaphoric on a referential expression can be either the role articulated at the indexed position, or the value of the role. But that is not the only dimension of contextual variation for the content of anaphoric pronouns. I said that the indexed position uniquely determines a role in the situation described by the antecedent sentence. This should be qualified; for, in certain cases at least, more than one role can be associated with a given position. This generates a second dimension of variation for the content of an anaphoric pronoun.

Consider sentence (4) again:

(4) Bill gave the book to Mary.

I said that there are three argument positions here:

$$(\ \ )_i \, \text{gave} \, (\ \ )_j \, \text{to} \, (\ \ )_k.$$

That is true if we disregard the noun phrases which occupy the argument slots and which come to be associated with the thematic roles articulated at those positions. However, if we take the noun phrases themselves into account, we see that there is at least one additional argument position, namely that which corresponds to the predicate 'book' in the noun phrase 'the book'. Each predicate, whether verbal or nominal, comes with one or several argument positions. What makes the argument position corresponding to the noun 'book' hardly noticeable in (4) is the fact that the noun phrase 'the book' itself occupies the second argument position of the verb, in such a way that the role articulated at that position (the GIFT role) and the role corresponding to the noun 'book' (the BOOK role) are co-instantiated in the event described by (4). It is as if a single complex role was articulated at the relevant position: the role of a book that is given. This superimposition of roles at a single position in (4) I represent as follows:

$$(\ \ )_i \, \text{gave} \, (\ \ )_j^{\text{book}} \, \text{to} \, (\ \ )_k.$$

The complex role BOOK_&_GIFT articulated at position j in this example I call the 'S-role', because it results from the joint contributions of the verb and the noun phrase as they combine in the complete sentence. This is distinct both from the 'V-role'—the GIFT role—which the verb itself articulates at the relevant position, and from the 'N-role'—the BOOK role—corresponding to the noun.

The coexistence of the three types of role generates a second dimension of contextual variation for the content of an anaphoric pronoun. In a two-sentence discourse like 'Three students came. They . . . ', where the pronoun 'they' in the second sentence is understood as anaphoric, the pronoun can pick up either the S-role, or the V-role, or the N-role, thus giving rise to three distinct interpretations. On the S-role interpretation, 'they' means something like *the students who came*. On the N-role interpretation, it means *the students*. On the V-role interpretation, it means *the persons who came*.

At this point obvious objections and counterexamples spring to mind. First, it may be objected that the three readings I have just mentioned are simply not available. Sentence (8) seems to have only one anaphoric reading, and it is the E-type reading, corresponding to what I have called the S-role interpretation:

(8) Three students came. They were accompanied by their girlfriends.

The second sentence of (8) says that *the students who came* were accompanied by their girlfriends. If the V-role interpretation was available, (8) would entail that no one came unaccompanied (since the second sentence, on that interpretation, would say that *the comers* were accompanied by their girlfriends). But the truth of (8) is clearly compatible with a situation in which many people came by themselves, unaccompanied.

Second objection: which interpretation is available is not a pragmatic matter (as I have suggested) but, to a large extent, a syntactic matter. Thus if we change the syntax of the example we make the V-role interpretation possible:

(9) Three students came with their girlfriends.

Like the pronoun 'they' in (8), the pronoun 'their' in (9) indexes the argument position occupied by 'three students'. But in (9) the anaphoric pronoun picks up the V-role (the role of agent of the action of coming, or COMER) rather than the S-role. The sentence says that '*x* came with *x*'s girlfriend' is true of three students. The property it ascribes to the three students is the property of being a comer accompanied by *the comer's* girlfriend.

I grant the second point: the syntax obviously affects the possibilities of interpretation for the anaphoric pronoun. In (9) the quantified noun phrase 'three students' binds the pronoun in such a way that the anaphoric relation between the pronoun and its antecedent is confined to the formula on which the quantifier 'three students' operates (a formula which does *not* contain the noun 'student'). The N-role interpretation and the S-role interpretation are therefore ruled out. But in (8) the anaphoric pronoun 'they' is not in the scope of the quantifier 'three students', hence there is no such restriction: the anaphoric pronoun can point, from outside, to the S-role jointly contributed by the verb and the noun phrase. This is the standard E-type reading: the pronoun 'they' contributes the S-role STUDENT_&_COMER rather than merely the V-role of COMER.

This leaves us with the first objection. Can the pronoun 'they' in (8) really contribute the N-role or the V-role, as I have claimed, or can it only contribute the S-role, as theorists of E-type anaphora claim? Can the second sentence of (8) mean that *the persons who came* (whether or not they were students) were accompanied by their girlfriends, or that *the students* (whether or not they came) were accompanied? I tend to think that both interpretations are indeed available, even though I agree that they are not very salient. To make them visible, let me change the example while retaining its overall structure:

(10) Three students came. Actually they were not students, but school-children.

(11) (Only/at most) three students came. They were too scared.

I claim that in (10) the anaphoric pronoun 'they' contributes the role of COMER: the second sentence of (10) says that *the persons who came* were not students but school-children. This is the V-role interpretation.[15] I also claim that, in one possible interpretation for (11), the anaphoric pronoun 'they' picks out the role of STUDENT carried by the noun in the antecedent sentence: the second sentence says that *the students* were too scared to come.[16] This is the N-role interpretation.

I have to admit that these examples are not fully convincing—more detailed investigations are obviously required. Yet I wish to maintain, tentatively, the general conclusion: even after a given argument position has been pragmatically selected as index in interpreting an anaphoric pronoun, the content of the pronoun can still vary according to the intentions of the speaker. The pronoun may contribute a role or the value of the role, and the role itself may vary to some extent.[17]

---

[15] As one reader pointed out, the second sentence could equally have continued (without sounding unacceptable) 'and they never came, they just pretended to come'. This creates an obvious difficulty for my account.

[16] On another possible interpretation for (11), the pronoun 'they' belongs to the associative type and refers to the students who did not come. But I take it that there is also an interpretation in which 'they' means *the students* (rather than *the other students*).

[17] There is a third dimension of contextual variation: the situation used in evaluating a role is not always the situation described by the antecedent sentence. In (10), for example, the situation used in evaluating the role is not the situation described by the antecedent sentence but a distinct situation, namely the 'historic' situation referred to by the speaker. (On the distinction between the situation described by a sentence and the 'historic' situation referred to by the speaker, see Austin 1950; Barwise and Etchemendy 1987; Recanati 2000.) If the situation of evaluation was the situation described by the antecedent sentence, the statement made by the second sentence would be self-contradictory.

Sentences with anaphoric pronouns therefore display a high degree of context-sensitivity, similar to that displayed by sentences with demonstrative pronouns.

4. Conclusion

According to the pragmatic theory of anaphora, anaphoric uses of pronouns are free uses, like deictic uses and associative uses. Evans's argument against the pragmatic theory has been shown to rest on unargued assumptions. In the version of the pragmatic theory I have outlined, anaphoric uses of pronouns turn out to be very similar to deictic uses. Like deictic uses, anaphoric uses are 'indexical' in the rather strict sense discussed by Nunberg: their content is contextually determined in terms of some feature of the situation of utterance (the index). For demonstratives the index is a position in space; for anaphoric pronouns, it is a position in 'discourse space', i.e. an argument position articulated in the surrounding discourse. (Not all free uses of pronouns possess that property of indexicality. In associative uses a content is contextually assigned to the pronoun directly, rather than via a two-step procedure involving an index. See Nunberg 1993: 36–8.)

Besides indexicality, another thing that is arguably common to deixis and anaphora is what I call *the context-dependence of character*. The character of 'pure indexicals' such as 'I' or 'tomorrow' is fixed by the linguistic meaning of the expression type. Thus the character of 'tomorrow' is the rule that a token of that expression (directly) refers to the day following the day of utterance. According to Kaplan, a demonstrative *qua* expression type does not possess a character. It is semantically incomplete and acquires a full-fledged character only when it is indexed to a contextual demonstration or, more simply, to a 'directing intention' which may or may not be externalized. On my view, the same thing holds for anaphoric pronouns. An anaphoric pronoun acquires a character only when its index, and possibly (some of) the additional parameters necessary to determine its content, have been contextually fixed.[18] This point, which I can only mention in passing, is of some significance given its potential consequences for the structure of the theory of meaning, and especially for the division of labour between semantics and pragmatics.

A third important feature of the theory outlined in this chapter is the subdivision of anaphoric uses into two sub-categories: referential anaphora and

---

[18] Again, I leave reflexives and their cognates aside in this discussion.

descriptive anaphora, with bound uses turning out to be nothing but a special case of descriptive anaphora. We wind up with the following classification, which summarizes the chapter:

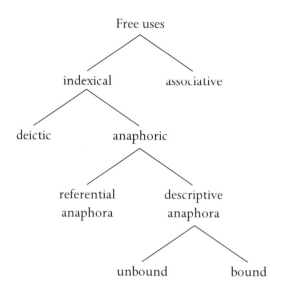

REFERENCES

Ariel, M. (2001), 'Accessibility Theory: An Overview', in T. Sanders, J. Schilperoord, and W. Spooren (eds.), *Text Representation: Linguistic and Psycholinguistic Aspects* (Amsterdam: John Benjamins), 39–87.

Austin, J. (1950), 'Truth', repr. in Austin, *Philosophical Papers* (Oxford: Clarendon Press, 1970), 117–33.

Barwise, J., and J. Etchemendy (1987), *The Liar: An Essay on Truth and Circularity* (New York: Oxford University Press).

Bühler, K. (1934), *Theory of Language*, trans. D. F. Goodwin (Amsterdam: John Benjamins, 1990).

Chafe, W. L. (1974), 'Language and Consciousness', *Language*, 50: 111–33.

Chomsky, N. (1976), 'Conditions on Rules of Grammar', *Linguistic Analysis*, 2: 303–51.

Clark, A. (2000), *A Theory of Sentience* (Oxford: Oxford University Press).

Clark, H. (1992), *Arenas of Language Use* (Chicago: University of Chicago Press and CSLI).

Evans, G. (1977), 'Pronouns, Quantifiers, and Relative Clauses (I)', repr. in Evans, *Collected Papers* (Oxford: Clarendon Press, 1985), 76–152.

—— (1980), 'Pronouns', repr. in Evans, *Collected Papers* (Oxford: Clarendon Press, 1985), 214–48.

—— (1982), *The Varieties of Reference*, ed. J. McDowell (Oxford: Clarendon Press).

Fauconnier, G. (1985), *Mental Spaces* (Cambridge, Mass.: MIT Press/Bradford Books).

Fillmore, C. (1968), 'The Case for Case', in E. Bach and T. Harm (eds.), *Universals in Linguistic Theory* (New York: Holt, Rinehart & Winston), 1–88.

Heim, I. (1988), *The Semantics of Definite and Indefinite Noun Phrases* (New York: Garland).

—— (1990), 'E-Type Pronouns and Donkey Anaphora', *Linguistics and Philosophy*, 13: 137–77.

—— and A. Kratzer (1998), *Semantics in Generative Grammar* (Oxford: Basil Blackwell).

Kadmon, N. (2001), *Formal Pragmatics* (Oxford: Basil Blackwell).

Kamp, H., and U. Reyle (1993), *From Discourse to Logic* (Dordrecht: Kluwer).

Kaplan, D. (1989*a*), 'Demonstratives', in J. Almog, H. Wettstein, and J. Perry (eds.), *Themes from Kaplan* (New York: Oxford University Press), 481–563.

—— (1989*b*), 'Afterthoughts', in J. Almog, H. Wettstein, and J. Perry (eds.), *Themes from Kaplan* (New York: Oxford University Press), 565–614.

Keenan, D., and D. Westertahl (1997), 'Generalized Quantifiers in Linguistics and Logic', in J. van Benthem and A. ter Meulen (eds.), *Handbook of Language and Logic* (Amsterdam: Elsevier), 837–93.

Lasnik, H. (1976), 'Remarks on Coreference', *Linguistic Analysis*, 2: 1–22.

Leslie, A., Xu Fei, P. D. Tremoulet, and B. J. Scholl (1998), 'Indexing and the Object Concept: Developing "What" and "Where" Systems', *Trends in Cognitive Sciences*, 2/1: 10–18.

Lyons, J. (1975), 'Deixis as the Source of Reference', in E. Keenan (ed.), *Formal Semantics of Natural Language* (Cambridge: Cambridge University Press), 61–83.

Nunberg, G. (1992), 'Two Kinds of Indexicality', in C. Barker and D. Dowty (eds.), *Proceedings from the Second Conference on Semantics and Linguistic Theory* (Columbus: Ohio State University Press), 283–301.

—— (1993), 'Indexicality and Deixis', *Linguistics and Philosophy*, 16: 1–43.

Parsons, T. (1990), *Events in the Semantics of English* (Cambridge, Mass.: MIT Press).

Pylyshyn, Z. (1989), 'The Role of Location Indexes in Spatial Perception', *Cognition*, 32: 65–97.

—— (2000), 'Situating Vision in the World', *Trends in Cognitive Sciences*, 4/5: 197–207.

—— (2001), 'Visual Indexes, Preconceptual Objecthood, and Situated Vision', *Cognition*, 80: 127–58.

Recanati, F. (1993), *Direct Reference: From Language to Thought* (Oxford: Basil Blackwell).

—— (2000), *Oratio Obliqua, Oratio Recta: An Essay on Metarepresentation* (Cambridge, Mass.: MIT Press/Bradford Books).

Strawson, P. (1961), 'Singular Terms and Predication', repr. in Strawson, *Logico-Linguistic Papers* (London: Methuen, 1971), 53–74.

Treisman, A. (1988), 'Features and Objects: The 14th Bartlett Memorial Lecture', *Quarterly Journal of Experimental Psychology*, 40: 201–37.

—— and G. Gelade (1980), 'A Feature Integration Theory of Attention', *Cognitive Psychology*, 12: 97–136.

7

Two Conceptions of Semantics

Nathan Salmon

Ever since Charles W. Morris distinguished among syntax, semantics, and pragmatics, those of us who attempt to teach philosophy of language to undergraduates have agonized over the boundary between the latter two. The distinction is typically explained in terms of the concept of *use*: pragmatics is the study of the way signs or symbols are used in context, whereas semantics concerns the meaning of a symbol in abstraction from its use. But this is more of a slogan than a clarification or explanation. How are we supposed to understand the difference between semantics and pragmatics when the meaning of an expression is so closely bound to the manner in which that expression is used? An expression is used a certain way because of its meaning, and yet the expression came to have the meaning it does through usage. Each of meaning and use seems to be a direct product of the other. Wittgenstein went so far as to identify the meaning of a word in a large proper class of cases with its use (*Philosophical Investigations*, §43). Many regard this identification as one of the deepest philosophical insights of the twentieth century.[1]

Anguish over the semantic–pragmatic distinction has become especially acute since it emerged in the work of such writers as David Kaplan that even the *pure* semantics of some expressions—like 'here', 'this', and other indexicals— necessarily involves "indexing", or relativizing, standard semantic attributes, like truth value, content, and designation (reference, denotation), to contexts

I thank the editor and a referee for their comments.

[1] It is significant that Wittgenstein did not go so far in §43 as to identify the meaning of a sentence or phrase with its use.

of use.[2] Some writers have mistaken this as demonstrating that semantics (at least the semantics of indexicals) includes some pragmatics, or even is wholly contained within the latter. The various roles played in semantics by a speaker's use of an expression, and also the highly systematic, rule-governed interaction between meaning and use—these have made the correct characterization of pragmatics, as distinct from semantics, into a particularly thorny problem. This difficulty, however, is no excuse for blurring the distinction. However deep and pervasive are the interconnections between meaning and use, the fundamental character of the relationship between the two has been greatly overstated by some of Wittgenstein's admirers.

Michael Dummett presents the following argument:

The meaning of a mathematical statement determines and is exhaustively determined by its *use*. The meaning of such a statement cannot be, or cannot contain as an ingredient, anything which is not manifest in the use to be made of it, lying solely in the mind of the individual who apprehends that meaning: if two individuals agree completely about the use to be made of the statement, then they agree about its meaning. The reason is that the meaning of a statement consists solely in its rôle as an instrument of communication between individuals, just as the powers of a chess-piece consist solely in its rôle in the game according to the rules. An individual cannot communicate what he cannot be observed to communicate: if one individual associated with a mathematical symbol or formula some mental content, where the association did not lie in the use he made of the symbol or formula, then he could not convey that content by means of the symbol or formula, for his audience would be unaware of the association and would have no means of becoming aware of it . . . there must be an observable difference between the behaviour or capacities of someone who is said to have [implicit knowledge constituting understanding of the language of mathematics] and someone who is said to lack it. Hence it follows, once more, that a grasp of the meaning of a mathematical statement must, in general, consist of a capacity to use that statement in a certain way, or to respond in a certain way to its use by others.[3]

Dummett's argument, if it is correct about mathematical statements, is equally applicable to statements made in non-mathematical language. Dummett's observation that only an observable act by a speaker can succeed in communicating, even

---

[2] D. Kaplan, 'Demonstratives', in J. Almog, J. Perry, and H. Wettstein (eds.), *Themes from Kaplan* (Oxford: Oxford University Press, 1989), 481–563. In unpublished material Kaplan has argued in connection with expressions like 'hello' and 'ouch' for an even broader assimilation between meaning and use.

[3] M. Dummett, 'The Philosophical Basis of Intuitionistic Logic', in H. E. Rose and J. C. Shepherdson (eds.), *Logic Colloquium '73* (Amsterdam: North-Holland, 1975), 5–40; repr. in Dummett, *Truth and Other Enigmas* (Cambridge, Mass.: Harvard University Press, 1978), 215–47.

if correct, in no way yields the conclusion that an expression's meaning is secured by, or understood by observing, the use of the expression—whether actual or potential uses.[4] The meanings of most sentences of natural language, in fact, *cannot* lie in their actual use. This is a simple logical consequence of the fact that at any given time, only finitely many sentences have actually been used, whereas natural language includes infinitely many meaningful sentences. And indeed, very many, probably nearly all, of the sentences that are actually used are immediately understood by both the speaker and the audience despite the fact that the sentence has not been used in their presence before, and even its potential use has not been contemplated.[5] We typically and routinely understand sentences on hearing or reading them for the first time. (Consider, for

---

[4] Though this is at least close to Dummett's conclusion, it is unclear exactly what Dummett means in speaking of the use *to be made* of a sentence. Is this the use that has actually been made of the sentence? Is it the actual (immediate) future use? Is it the union of the actual past, the actual present, and the actual future use? Is it a possible future use? Is it perhaps the *semantically correct* use, a use that accords with the literal meaning (a use by the speaker to express the content that the expression itself semantically expresses with respect to the speaker's context)? Among the various conclusions that result by substituting one of these more explicit phrases for Dummett's 'the use to be made', none follows from the observation that communication requires observation.

Dummett's view expressed elsewhere (cf. *The Logical Basis of Metaphysics* (Cambridge, Mass.: Harvard University Press, 1991), 223–5) is that the meaning of a typical sentence is determined compositionally, whereas the meaning of the ultimate sentence components is determined by past use of special sentences—the lexical meaning givers—whose meanings are themselves determined by their own actual past use, rather than compositionally. The meaning of 'fragile', for example, is supposed to be gotten by observing the use of particular "simple predications" (the meaning givers) like 'That plate is fragile'. It is difficult to reconcile this view with Dummett's argument quoted in the text, which is not restricted to the allegedly meaning-giver sentences and instead covers every mathematical sentence. The meaning of any typical mathematical sentence (e.g. '$e^{\pi i} + 1 = 0$', etc.) is secured and understood compositionally. For this very reason, one need not observe a use of the sentence in order to understand it. Indeed, in the absence of a prior understanding of its component expressions ('e', 'i', '$+$', exponentiation, etc.), observation of a particular use of the sentence will typically leave the observer clueless as to the meaning.

Some of the considerations to be made shortly apply straightforwardly to the allegedly meaning-giver sentences. We do not understand what 'That plate is fragile' expresses in a given use simply by observing the utterance. A non-French-speaker, for example, does not observe what Pierre expresses by 'Cette assiette là est fragile' when the plate that Pierre is demonstrating remains entirely intact. Rather, we understand what is expressed (namely, that a particular plate is easily broken) in the standard way, by a kind of compositional computation on the basis of a prior understanding of each of the words.

[5] This generalization may not extend to sentences of a purely mathematical language. Nevertheless, the manner in which such sentences are understood is essentially the same compositional–computational manner as in the case of non-mathematical language.

example, the sequence of sentences that make up this very essay.) Even on hearing or reading a previously used sentence, we do not understand it by remembering how it was used in the past. The fact that we understand sentences independently of any previous use, and we do this routinely, is not particularly mysterious. For we have observed actual uses of the individual words that make up the sentences of novel utterances, and have also learned (presumably at least partly through observation) how these words are composed to form sentences, and also how to understand a sentence on the basis of the meanings and the mode of composition of the words themselves. Observation of use undoubtedly plays a very significant role in understanding. But the conclusion that we understand an expression only through observation of actual uses of that very expression is incorrect. We definitely do not understand the sentences that give expression to the thoughts that fill our lives on the basis of previous uses of those sentences.

The point is not merely that the meaning of a sentence or phrase is not determined by its actual past uses. It should be even more obvious that the meaning of an expression is also not determined by its actual future uses, let alone by its possible future uses. Many expressions will actually come to be used to express contents that those expressions do not presently express. And *any* expression *might* yet come to be so used. There is no backward road from future use to present meaning, much less is there a trans-modal road from possible use to actual meaning. The meaning of a sentence or phrase is in fact determined *independently* of its actual or potential use, but by its semantic composition, by the meanings of the words and the manner in which the words are combined to form the sentence or phrase.

Even the converse thesis that the meaning of an expression determines its use is significantly overstated. Many sentences are commonly used only to convey something other than their literal content, or would be so used if they were used at all. Such uses deviate from the meaning, but they are uses all the same. The connection between meaning and use is not a matter of historical anthropology. It is a normative matter, not merely descriptive but also prescriptive. Perhaps it may be said that the meaning of a sentence (or other type of expression) determines its *correct* use. But even this formulation requires due caution. Many sentences are sufficiently unnatural, inappropriate, insulting, offensive, or bizarre, etc., that they would essentially never be used to convey the information they literally contain. In any normal sense, it would be *incorrect* to use some sentences to assert what the sentence literally expresses. There are sentences such that to use them with their literal meaning—to assert what the sentence literally expresses (and not as part of a parody, or in an attempt at offensive humor, etc.)—would violate every condition on civilized human society as we know it. There is indeed a dimension of evaluation on which the use of an expression may be deemed correct if and only if the expression is used with its literal meaning. But this does not provide for an illuminating identification or assimilation of meaning with use in any philosophically significant manner (e.g. a conceptual reduction of meaning to use). For the dimension of evaluation in question is peculiarly within the realm of semantics proper: an expression is used correctly *from the point of view of pure semantics* if and only if it is used with its literal meaning. Along any genuinely distinct, non-semantic dimension of evaluation, some expressions, if they are used with their literal meaning, are counter-recommended in even a minimally civilized society, if not outright prohibited by the dictates of common human decency, i.e. they are not used correctly in the relevant non-semantic way. (The publisher prefers that specific examples of outlandishly offensive sentences be left to the reader's imagination.) The claim that meaning determines correct use is true only if it is vacuous.

The problem of correctly characterizing the semantic–pragmatic distinction remains open. It is accompanied by competing conceptions of the very enterprise known as *semantics*. Some writers conceive of semantics as concerned with what a speaker *says* or *asserts* in uttering a declarative sentence, as contrasted with what the speaker *means* or *accomplishes* by means of the utterance, and/or with how the audience interprets, or how the audience correctly interprets, the utterance (these being matters of pragmatics). I believe these distinctions are properly seen as distinctions wholly *within* pragmatics, distinctions that do not so much as touch on semantics properly so-called (except in so far as semantics provides one source, among many, for what the speaker asserts in the utterance). To conceive of semantics as concerned with speaker assertion (i.e. with what the speaker who uses the sentence thereby asserts) is not merely to blur the distinction between semantics and pragmatics. It is to *misidentify* semantics altogether, and to do so sufficiently badly that those who conceive semantics in this way, when using semantic expressions like 'denote', 'content', or 'true', are often fruitfully interpreted as not speaking about the notions of denotation, content, or (semantic) truth at all, but about other notions entirely—specifically various pragmatic notions.

To clarify this point, I want to distinguish here between two radically opposing conceptions of semantics. The rivalry between these conceptions has seriously exacerbated the problem of maintaining the conceptual integrity of the semantic–pragmatic distinction. One or the other of these competing conceptions of semantics seems to be presupposed by virtually everyone who has worked in the philosophy of language. The gulf that separates the two conceptions came forcefully before my mind while reflecting on the current debate among such writers as Keith Donnellan, Saul Kripke, Howard Wettstein, myself, and others, concerning the alleged semantic significance of Donnellan's *referential–attributive* distinction—although numerous contemporary controversies in the philosophy of language equally illustrate the fundamental difference between the two rival ways of conceptualizing semantics. A definite description, "the *such-and-such*", is *used referentially* for a particular object *x* if the use in question is relevantly connected to *x* in the right way—paradigmatically, the speaker has that particular object in mind and believes of the object that it uniquely answers to the description (i.e. that it is a unique *such-and-such*)—and the speaker uses the description as a name or label for that object. By contrast, a definite description is *used attributively* if no object is relevantly connected to the use and instead the speaker means something to the effect that whoever or whatever is uniquely *such-and-such* is . . . The central controversy concerns whether a referential use of a definite description results in a different semantic content from an attributive use. The *thesis of semantic significance*, which Donnellan holds, is that a referential use, unlike an attributive use, results in a proposition directly about the relevantly connected object—typically, the object that the speaker has in mind.

On the *speech-act centered conception* of semantics, semantic attributes of expressions—like a singular term's designating an object, or a sentence's containing or expressing a proposition—somehow reduce to, are to be understood by means of, are derived from, or at least are directly determined by, the illocutionary acts performed by speakers in using those expressions, or perhaps the illocutionary acts that would normally be performed in using those expressions. Theorists who embrace the speech-act centered conception typically ascribe semantic attributes to such things as expression tokens or utterances, or to possible utterances.

The speech-act centered conception yields a serious misconceptualization of the semantic–pragmatic distinction. That distinction is properly understood by recognizing signs or expression-types (not tokens) as genuine *symbols*. Symbols symbolize; i.e. they represent. Speakers, of course, also represent. We represent things, we represent ways for things to be, and we represent things as being one way rather than another. We routinely do these things, and we routinely do these things by producing symbols *which also do these same sorts of things*. The symbols we use, or at least many of them, represent in the way they do by means of, or in accordance with, a highly systematic assignment of representations to symbols. This systematic assignment of representations is semantics. And it is aptly representable by means of inductive (recursive) definitions for concepts like *designation*, *truth*, and *content*. This is how, and why, semantics is a formal discipline employing mathematical methodologies, rather than, say, psychological methodologies or anthropological methodologies—even though the semantics of a natural language is an a posteriori discipline. However deep the influence of actual usage on the representational nature of our symbols may be, it remains that the symbols themselves (including complex symbols like sentences) have specific representations systematically assigned to them, some of these assignments being a function of context.

As we have seen, our understanding of certain complex symbols is not, as it were, on a case-by-case basis, by one-at-a-time learning and rote memory. Instead we achieve an understanding of the atomic symbols, perhaps in a case-by-case one-at-a-time way, and we learn the system through which we are enabled to work out for ourselves on a case-by-case basis exactly what any given molecular symbol represents or means. What we represent with the symbols we produce need not be the very same as what the symbols themselves represent. We are constrained by the symbols' system of representation—by their semantics—but we are not enslaved by it. Frequently, routinely in fact, what we represent by means of a symbol deviates from the symbol's semantics. Most obviously this occurs with the sentences we utter, whereby we routinely assert something beyond what the sentence itself semantically expresses. Irony, sarcasm, and figurative language may be cases in point. Even in non-figurative discourse, we routinely use sentences to assert more than they semantically express. One such phenomenon that is frequently misunderstood is instanced by the following sort of case: The words 'My daughter is 12 years old' express with respect to my present context something tantamount to my having a 12-year-old daughter (more accurately, following Russell, that someone or other is both uniquely my daughter and 12 years old), whereas in uttering those same words I thereby assert something more directly about my daughter: that *she* is 12 years old. What I additionally assert—not merely that I have some 12-year-old daughter or other but specifically that *she (that very girl)* is 12 years old—is not semantically expressed by my words. This is exactly the sort of phenomenon that the speech-act centered conception does not adequately characterize.[6]

[6] The phenomenon in question lies at the heart of what David Kaplan has misnamed the *pseudo de re* in 'Demonstratives', 555–6 n. 71. Cf. my 'The Good, the Bad, and the Ugly', in A. Bezuidenhout and M. Reimer (eds.), *On Descriptions* (forthcoming).

The principal rival to the speech-act centered conception of semantics is what I call *the expression centered conception*. According to this alternative conception, the semantic attributes of expressions are not conceptually derivative of the speech acts performed by their utterers, and are thought of instead as intrinsic to the expressions themselves, or to the expressions *as* expressions of a particular language (and as occurring in a particular context). The expression centered conception takes seriously the idea that expressions are symbols, and that, as such, they have a semantic life of their own. The expression centered conception need not deny that semantics, at least for a natural language, may be ultimately a result or product of speech acts, rather than (or more likely, in addition to) the other way around. But the expression centered conception marks a definite separation between semantics and pragmatics, allowing for at least the possibility of extreme, pervasive, and even highly systematic deviation. The speech-act centered conception is more reductionist in spirit.

The expression centered conception is the received conception of semantics in the tradition of Frege and Russell. With their emphasis on artificial or idealized languages, it is they more than anyone else who deserve credit for cultivating the expression centered conception among contemporary philosophers of language. Wittgenstein focused, in contrast, on spoken natural language in his impenetrable but seemingly penetrating diatribe against the expression centered conception. Whether or not he himself subscribed to the speech-act centered conception, he is largely responsible for the preeminence of that rival conception in contemporary philosophy of language. I fear that the speech-act centered conception may currently be the dominant conception of semantics—especially among philosophers with a propensity toward nominalism, physicalism, functionalism, anti-realism, or various other philosophically timid doctrines, and also among those who trace their scholarly lineage to Wittgenstein.

Anyone whose lineage traces to Wittgenstein can trace it a step further to Russell. Elements of both traditions are clearly manifest in Donnellan's thought on reference and related matters. Still, his commitment to the speech-act centered conception might explain Donnellan's unwavering endorsement of a particularly strong version of the semantic-significance thesis according to which a referentially used description semantically designates the speaker's intended designatum regardless of whether the description actually fits. The speech-act centered conception cannot distinguish correctly between the semantic content of a sentence with respect to a given context and the content of the assertion, or assertions (statements, utterances), normally made by a speaker in uttering the sentence in that context. If this interpretation (which is somewhat speculative) is correct, then Donnellan conceives of *speaker reference* (i.e. a speaker designating an object through the use of an expression) as, at least implicitly, a semantic, rather than a pragmatic, notion. Furthermore, he then conceives of Russell's notion of denotation for definite descriptions as a *non-semantic* notion, since it does not concern (at least not directly) acts of speakers' reference normally performed with descriptions.[7] This interpretation seems to be confirmed by Donnellan's subsequent discussion in 'Speaker Reference, Descriptions, and Anaphora'.[8] There he adopts Kripke's terminology of 'speaker reference' and 'semantic reference', but he does not equate what he means by the latter with Russellian denotation, vigorously arguing instead that "semantic reference" depends on, and is determined by, speaker reference, which may be other than the Russellian denotation.[9]

It is the expression centered conception of semantics, and the general Frege–Russell tradition, that is the natural habitat of the distinction between

[7] For present purposes, Russell's notion of *denotation* for definite descriptions may be defined by saying that a definite description ⌜the α: φ_α⌝ *R-denotes* (with respect to semantic parameters, such as context) the individual that uniquely satisfies its matrix φ_α (with respect to those same parameters), if there is such an individual; and otherwise, it *R*-denotes nothing. Though it may be obvious that the relation of *R*-denotation between a definite description and the object that uniquely answers to it is fundamentally a semantic relation, Russell's use of John Stuart Mill's term 'denotation' is highly misleading. As is well known, Russell regarded definite descriptions as complex quantificational phrases that have neither semantic content ("no meaning in isolation") nor semantic designation (reference). The description's relation to the object uniquely answering to it *simulates* semantic designation on his theory. Russell should have called the notion 'quasi-denotation', or even 'simulated denotation'. Cf. my 'On Designating', *Mind* (forthcoming in an issue celebrating the centennial of the original publication of 'On Denoting', ed. Stephen Neale).

[8] In P. French, T. Uehling, and H. Wettstein (eds.), *Contemporary Perspectives in the Philosophy of Language* (Minneapolis: University of Minnesota Press, 1979), 28–44.

[9] Donnellan sometimes appears to allow for semantic designation in the absence of speaker designation. On the one hand, he says in 'Speaker Reference, Descriptions, and Anaphora' (pp. 30, 32) that in using a definite description attributively, the speaker does not designate anything even if the description happens to be proper, in the Russellian sense. But he also seems to say (on the same p. 32, and in the same paragraph) that an attributively used description itself designates its Russellian denotation. This leads to the curious position that when a speaker uses a proper description attributively, the description designates but the speaker does not. And this does not fit well the speech-act centered conception of semantics. But coupled with Donnellan's more central position that when a description is used referentially for something x, both the description and the speaker designate x even if x is not the Russellian denotation, neither does this curious position exactly fit the expression centered conception—or any other conception that I can think of.

Though I am uncertain what to make of Donnellan's assertions here, I believe that a careful reading reveals that appearances are deceptive, and that Donnellan (through a carefully placed occurrence of the subjunctive 'would') deliberately avoids any commitment to the claim that an attributively used proper description has semantic designation. I may be wrong.

speaker designation and semantic designation (as well as such other Gricean distinctions as that between speaker meaning and sentence meaning). Donnellan originally characterized the referential–attributive distinction in terms of speaker reference and denotation. It would be dangerous, however, to take Donnellan's characterization at face value. My own view—well within the Frege–Russell tradition—is that Donnellan's apparent cataloging of speaker reference as semantic and of Russellian denotation as non-semantic obviously gets matters exactly reversed. It is just one piece of evidence of the extent to which the speech-act centered conception presents a seriously distorted picture of what semantics is, enough so that I am tempted to say that those in the grip of that conception, when using such semantic terms as 'designate' and 'express'— especially when applying such terms to such things as utterances rather than expressions—are not talking about anything semantic at all.[10]

Confronted with the two rival conceptions of semantics, those in the grip of the speech-act centered conception will typically protest that the distinction merely reflects a purely terminological difference, superimposed on a biased preference for one sort of theoretical investigation over another. Indeed, I have offered these arguments in favor of the expression centered conception over the speech-act centered conception in several venues, invariably invoking the response that the issue is merely terminological. This response misjudges the extent of disagreement that has been registered in numerous controversies in the philosophy of language during the past several decades. Again, the debate over the alleged semantic significance of the referential use is illustrative of the general point. Proponents of the semantic-significance thesis have not claimed merely that referential use issues in a *de re* assertion by the speaker. They have claimed furthermore that the resulting *de re* assertion reflects the semantics— the content and truth value—that the sentence uttered takes on when the description therein is given such a use. I have argued elsewhere against the semantic-significance thesis.[11] It is not to my present purpose to rehearse those arguments. It is sufficient here to note that the two rival conceptions of semantics differ sharply over substantive issues: the question of the designation of particular definite descriptions and the question of the truth values of partic- ular sentences. No less significant is the current controversy concerning whether co-designative names are inter-substitutable in attributions of belief or

---

[10] See my 'Being of Two Minds: Belief with Doubt', *Noûs*, 29/1 (1995), esp. 18–19 n. 27.

[11] See 'Assertion and Incomplete Definite Descriptions', *Philosophical Studies*, 42/1 (July 1982), 37–45; 'The Pragmatic Fallacy', *Philosophical Studies*, 63 (1991), 83–97; 'The Good, the Bad, and the Ugly'.

other propositional attitudes. It is doubtful that those (perhaps the vast majority) who insist that such substitutions fail, on the basis of what is imparted by uttering the result of such a substitution, would be prepared to grant that, nevertheless, such substitutions preserve truth value in every admissible model in which the names co-designate. While the debate over substitution might be fueled to some extent by terminological confusion or equivocation, the two competing conceptions of semantics tend to support competing judgments concerning the truth values of certain sentences, as they do also in the semantic-significance controversy. The different choices of terminology are accompanied, at least sometimes, by different verdicts concerning the truth values of particular sentences.

The battle cry "It's all just terminology" is the last refuge of the speech-act centered conception. To be sure, there is a legitimate enterprise of investigating and cataloging the systematic correlation of speakers' utterances or other speech acts with, say, the propositions thereby asserted or the objects to which the speaker thereby refers. Such an enterprise raises issues and questions of a philosophical nature. What are the conditions on which a speaker makes a *de re* (or *relational*) assertion? Must the speaker, for instance, use a directly referential, logically proper name? Are these conditions systematically related to the conditions on which a speaker forms or harbors a *de re* belief? Can a speaker inadvertently refer to distinct objects in a single utterance? If so, is one of the referents the primary referent, to which all other referents are subordinate? If so, in what sense is it primary, and how is it determined which referent is the speech act's primary referent? Can a speaker make two statements in a single utterance? Several? When a speaker makes a statement, is the proposition semantically expressed by the uttered sentence *ipso facto* at least one of the propositions asserted in the speech act? Is it the primary assertion? Can a speaker assert a proposition that he or she does not grasp or understand? Do we learn the meaning of a word from its usage even when the meaning determines an infinite extension and we have only observed a finite number of applications? If so, how do we do this? What kind of fact is it about me that I mean a particular concept with an infinite extension, rather than some other concept with a different extension, one that overlaps with the one I do mean on those applications that I have observed?

These questions and more like them cry out for exploration. Their answers may reveal deep insights into the nature of cognition and the human mind. They are notoriously difficult. Some may be intractable. They are philosophically legitimate, even important questions. They are questions in the philosophy of language, broadly construed. But they do not belong to the philosophy of logic and semantics. They do not address, for example, whether the semantic content of a demonstrative is the object demonstrated or something more perceptual or conceptual. Their answers do not specify the logical form of a belief attribution. They do not say whether quantification into a non-extensional context is semantically coherent. They do not say whether definite descriptions are indexicals. The attempt to derive properly semantic conclusions from pragmatic observations in any simple, straightforward manner is doomed to failure. It is at best misleading and confusing to use semantic jargon when talking about utterances or speech acts—to characterize utterances using terms like 'semantic content' and 'semantically express', 'true with respect to context' and 'true under an assignment of values to variables'. It is perfectly legitimate and instructive to observe that a speaker would typically assert or convey or impart p in uttering sentence S in a context c. It is at best misleading to put this observation by saying that an utterance of S in c "expresses" p. Such formulations invite a construal as an observation—immediate, straightforward, obvious—that S semantically contains p with respect to c. It is perforce wrong to suppose that the observation has any direct bearing whatsoever on the issues concerning S's truth value. Observing that we typically use descriptions in conveying or imparting different propositions from those Russell assigns as semantic content cannot refute Russell's semantic theory of descriptions.[12] It only confuses the issue to formulate the observation in terms of what propositions various *utterances* "express". Nor can the question of logical validity for a proposed inference be settled by appeal to a general willingness or readiness to draw the inference, or conversely to a general unwillingness or reluctance.[13] For the very same reason, neither can Frege's semantic theory of proper names be supported by observing that we have general, non-singular thoughts in mind when we use names. Here again reformulating the irrelevant observation, focusing on an utterance of a sentence using a proper name and looking for the thought thereby "expressed" (i.e. pragmatically imparted), engenders no genuine support, only confusion. Semantic issues may be obfuscated, but cannot even be addressed, let alone settled, by making non-semantic observations using a semantic-sounding formulation. Calling a sow's ear a *silk purse* is not a way to make it so.

---

[12] Cf. my 'The Pragmatic Fallacy'.

[13] This would include substitutivity arguments in the logic of propositional attribution like $\lceil O(\text{that } \varphi_\alpha). \alpha = \beta \therefore O(\text{that } \varphi_\beta) \rceil$, where α and β are logically simple constants. (Let O represent 'it is necessary' or, more controversially, 'Jones believes'.)

8

Presupposition and Relevance

Mandy Simons

1. Two Types of Relevance Implicature

Recall Grice's well-worn example from *Logic and Conversation* about Smith, his girlfriend, and his trips to New York:

(1) A: Smith doesn't seem to have a girlfriend these days.
    B: He has been paying a lot of visits to New York recently.

Grice says that in this dialogue, B implicates that Smith has, or may have, a girl-friend in New York. But in saying this, Grice under-describes his own example. For this proposition alone does not suffice to satisfy the requirements of Relation, the maxim presumed to be operative in this case.

Grice says that '[B] implicates that which he must be assumed to believe in order to preserve the assumption that he is observing the maxim of Relation' (Grice 1989: 32). But the assumption that B thinks that Smith might have a girl-friend in New York is not in itself sufficient to render B's utterance relevant. An additional assumption is required, one which explicitly links the issue of having girlfriends to the issue of travel to New York: perhaps, the proposition that a person who has a girlfriend somewhere travels there frequently; or that many people have long-distance relationships, and these involve frequent trips to the same place. If A can work out that B is making *this* supposition, then she can immediately see the relevance of B's response to her remark. Without it, relevance cannot be established. So this general background assumption must be implicated by the utterance.[1]

Now, this background assumption is not enough by *itself* to guarantee relevance. Suppose that B believes the background assumption, but does not believe that Smith might be traveling to New York to visit a girlfriend. Then his utterance is still in violation of Relation. B should invoke the background assumption only if it is relevant itself, that is, only if he believes that it might provide an explanation for Smith's trips to New York. So (at least) two propositions are implicated: some 'background' proposition connecting girlfriends and travel; and the 'foreground' proposition that Smith might have a girlfriend in New York. The 'background' implicature is in some sense prior to the 'foreground' implicature; the calculation of the latter requires the prior calculation of the former. The difference between these two types of implicature is made explicit in Sperber and Wilson's (1986) distinction between *implicated assumptions* and *implicated conclusions*. This chapter will be concerned with implicated assumptions, and with the possibility that this notion has a central role in explicating the nature of presupposition.

2. Implicated Assumptions and Presuppositions

Using the ordinary, non-technical sense of the term, we might be inclined to say that B, in saying what he says in the dialogue above, is presupposing a particular relation between girlfriends and travel. Moreover, this implicated assumption has certain properties in common with the kinds of things which, in technical parlance, are often called presuppositions. The implicated assumption might come as new information to A, but probably not: probably she shares this assumption with B. Presuppositions, of course, may constitute new information but frequently don't. If A does not share B's assumption about the relation between travel and girlfriends, or doesn't think it applicable to Smith, then an appropriate response on her part to B's assertion would be to deny that assumption—to say *Smith only travels for business* or some such thing. Similarly, faced with a presupposing utterance the presupposition of which one does not accept, the appropriate response is to deny the presupposition. Also, of course, the implicated assumption is in some sense backgrounded; it is not the main point of B's

---

[1] Zoltán Szabó points out (personal communication) that Grice may be reluctant to call this background proposition an implicature because the speaker does not really intend to convey this proposition to the addressee. But there are cases where the speaker may intend the background proposition as part of, or even as the main point of, what is communicated. See example (2) below.

utterance. However, an implicated assumption *may* be a main point. Consider the dialogue below:

(2) Ann: Did George get into a top university?
     Bud: His father is a very wealthy man.

Bud here implicates that a place at a top university can be bought. From this implicated assumption and the content of his assertion can be derived the implicated conclusion that George did get into a top university. Although this is the ostensible main point, being the answer to Ann's question, it is plausible that Bud's real point has to do with the privileges of wealth. Similarly, the presuppositions of utterances are normally backgrounded, but may in some cases provide the real point of an utterance.

These observations raise a tantalizing possibility: perhaps the things which we call 'presuppositions' are a kind of relevance implicature: propositions which a hearer must assume in order to find the utterance relevant. This is the thesis which I will pursue here. This proposal builds on that of Wilson and Sperber (1979), in which focal presuppositions are argued to be propositions necessary for establishing the relevance of the main point of the utterance. It also draws on Blakemore (1987), where it is argued that certain lexical items function to guide the addressee's process of establishing the relevance of an utterance. I will attempt here to extend these ideas into a broad characterization of presupposition.

3. Desiderata for a Theory of Presupposition

I want to begin by clarifying the goals of this discussion. My proposal will constitute (a preliminary formulation of) a theory of presupposition. So let me say what I think a theory of presupposition is supposed to do. It is supposed to do two things: first, it is supposed to provide a relevant *description* of the phenomenon as a whole; second, it should provide an *explanation* for why things are as described. This chapter aims to accomplish only the first of these two tasks. But the importance of this task, of getting the description right, should not be underestimated. The task of giving an explanation is enormously simplified when we have an appropriate characterization of the phenomenon we are trying to explain. It is not impossible that we would arrive at the correct explanation in the absence of a correct description, but it is not very likely.

Both the traditional semantic account of presupposition and the now widely accepted pragmatic view proposed by Stalnaker offer *descriptive characterizations* of the phenomenon of presupposition.[2] (For a recent formulation and detailed discussion of the semantic account, see Burton-Roberts 1989; for Stalnaker's account, see in particular Stalnaker 1974, 1998, and 2002.) Stalnaker (2002) makes very clear that his goal, in formulating his account of presupposition, was to offer a redescription or reinterpretation of the familiar data concerning presupposition, and not to offer a predictive or explanatory theory. The attempt to formulate a pre-theoretical description of presupposition is problematic in (at least) one respect, which is that there is disagreement about the cases which constitute the phenomenon. However, there is a reasonably well-established set of central cases on which the descriptive characterization can be based. The descriptive characterization will, in turn, serve to delimit the scope of the phenomenon for which we seek an explanation (see Section 4.3.2 below). And the plausibility of the limits set by the description will, in turn, provide a criterion for evaluating it.

To reiterate: the importance of the descriptive characterization is that it tells us just what it is that we need to explain. According to the description offered by the semantic view, the presuppositions of a sentence are those propositions which must be true in order for the sentence to have a truth value. This description turned out to be problematic in a variety of ways. But if this were the correct description of presupposition, it is clear what an explanation of the phenomenon would have to look like: it would have to explain, for each of the variety of cases, why (presuppositional) sentence S, or an utterance thereof, would lack a truth value if proposition p were false. Strawson offers such an explanation for the existential presuppositions of expressions used to refer. Strawson suggests in 'On Referring' that 'one of the main purposes for which we use language is the purpose of stating facts about things and persons and events' (Strawson 1990: 228). The achievement of this purpose involves two tasks: identifying what you are talking about (the referring task), and then saying something about it (the predication task). But if the expression used to refer does not in fact do so—if the existential presupposition fails—then the second task cannot be undertaken. In Strawson's view, the truth or falsity of an assertion of this kind depends on what happens in performing this second task. Hence, where the existential presupposition fails, no statement evaluable for truth is made.

Stalnaker's view takes the presuppositions of a sentence to be those propositions which must be presupposed by the *speaker* of the sentence in order for the sentence to be appropriately used. Again, this is not offered as an *explanation* of

---

[2] The same is true of the various accounts of presupposition in the dynamic semantic literature. See e.g. Heim (1983); Van der Sandt (1992).

presuppositional phenomena. Rather, it is offered as the description which our further research should be oriented towards explaining. An explanatory theory of presupposition would have to tell us why utterance of particular sentences would turn out to be inappropriate unless some proposition *p* were presupposed by the speaker. Stalnaker offers one such explanation, for the presuppositionality of *know*. He suggests that a speaker who asserts 'x knows that P' in a situation in which P is in doubt or dispute 'would be saying in one breath something that could be challenged in two different ways' (Stalnaker 1974: 206). The speaker would thus leave his communicative intention unclear: is his main point to make a claim about the truth of P, or about the epistemic state of *x*? Stalnaker suggests that as speakers normally aim to communicate effectively, it would normally be unreasonable to assert 'x knows that P' in such a context. So a speaker can reasonably make this assertion only if he presupposes P, that is, believes P to be commonly accepted by the group of interlocutors.

Note that in both of these examples, the descriptive account of presupposition is highly general, intended to cover all presuppositional phenomena; but the explanations given are highly specific, and tell us for only a limited set of cases why presuppositionality arises.

Stalnaker's account points towards another measure of adequacy of a description of the phenomenon, namely, that explanations for some of the phenomena in question fall out from the description. Thus, Stalnaker's description of presupposition provides an explanation for certain projection facts, even prior to a specific explanation of why the atomic sentences in question meet the description given. Ultimately, the adequacy of any proposed description is measured by the adequacy of explanations which depend upon it.

My goal in this chapter, then, is to offer a new description of the phenomenon of presupposition. I will not attempt here to argue against existing descriptions. Instead, I will focus on the arguments in favor of the redescription I offer, in particular, its potential to provide the foundation for an explanatory theory of presupposition.

4. The Thesis and Some Initial Support

4.1. The Thesis

The redescription I propose is this: the presuppositions of an utterance are the propositions which the hearer must accept in order for the utterance to be relevant for her. I use the term *accept* in the sense of Stalnaker (1984), who characterizes acceptance as 'a category of propositional attitudes and methodo-logical stances toward a proposition, a category that includes belief, but also some attitudes (presumption, assumption, acceptance for the purposes of argu-ment or an inquiry) that contrast with belief and with each other. To accept a proposition is to treat it as true for some reason.'[3] The first consequence of my proposal: on this view, it is utterances, rather than sentences or speakers, which are the primary bearers of presupposition. Sentences bear presuppositions in the following derivative sense: for a sentence S to have a presupposition p is for the relevance of an utterance of S usually to require the hearer to accept p. (The vagueness of this formulation accommodates the fact that it is almost imposs-ible to find a sentence—even among the classic cases of presupposition—whose utterance invariably induces a presupposition.) Speakers also have presupposi-tions in a derivative sense: for a speaker to presuppose p in uttering S is for the speaker to intend the addressee to accept p for the purpose of establishing the relevance of the utterance. Or we can perhaps say more simply that for a speaker to presuppose p in uttering S is for the speaker to intend p to be a relevance establisher for her utterance. The questions we must now ask are: What is it for an utterance to be relevant, and what is it for a proposition to be a relevance establisher for an utterance? To answer these questions, I will appeal to the con-strual of relevance within Relevance Theory (Sperber and Wilson 1986; Wilson and Sperber 2003).[4]

For Sperber and Wilson, relevance is a matter of how well and productively some input interacts with existing salient assumptions of the interpreter. An utterance is *relevant in a context* just in case it has some contextual effects in that context. A *context* is here construed as a set of propositions, a subset of an indi-vidual's assumptions. This notion of context concerns an individual's epistemic state, not the common beliefs (or commonly accepted propositions) of a group of individuals. *Contextual effects* are any changes to the context, in particular, addi-tion or elimination of propositions, or strengthening of the degree of belief in the proposition. Such effects are derived by deductions involving (*a*) the proposi-tion expressed and (*b*) any *contextual assumptions*, i.e. propositions in the context.

---

[3] Stalnaker also takes acceptance to be the propositional attitude relevant to presupposition. See Stalnaker (2002).

[4] There is a second major thread in Sperber and Wilson's work, which is the argument that the truth conditional content of utterances is not determined solely by compositional semantic inter-pretation and linguistically mediated references to context, but includes information derived via relevance driven inference. By invoking Sperber and Wilson's notion of relevance in the explication of presupposition, I do not intend to commit myself to this other aspect of their view.

An utterance is *relevant for an individual* at a given time just in case it is relevant in one or more of the contexts accessible to that individual at that time.[5] Finally, an utterance is *optimally relevant* for an individual just in case it produces adequate contextual effects for the processing effort required. Processing effort is presumed to be affected by the complexity of the utterance being processed; by the size of the context required to derive contextual effects; by the complexity of the deductions required to derive them; and by the relative accessibility of the required assumptions. What determines whether the contextual effects are *adequate* for the effort required? While there is no definitive answer to this question, it is clear that the adequacy of contextual effects is a matter not just of their number, but of their current usefulness. Sperber and Wilson (1995) suggest that the worth of a contextual effect is determined by its contribution to the individual's cognitive goals.[6]

The basic picture we have, then, is this: In interpreting an utterance, an addressee must select a context—a set of propositions—relative to which to interpret it. She will seek a set of propositions which interacts productively with the content of the utterance, allowing her to derive further inferences which are of interest to her. The harder she has to work to find such a context, or to derive interesting inferences, the less relevant the utterance will be for her.

This picture of interpretation corresponds nicely to some basic intuitions about relevance. If we are preparing to cook pasta sauce, and you tell me *We're out of garlic*, the utterance is intuitively relevant. And it is plausible that in such a situation, I have readily available a context—a set of propositions—with which the content of your utterance will interact productively. On the other hand, if you were to say the same thing while we are at the movies and planning to go out for dinner afterwards, I would be likely to find your utterance quite *irrelevant*. And this seems to correspond to the fact that in this situation, there is no set of assumptions currently salient to me which, in conjunction with your utterance, allows me to derive inferences which serve my current cognitive goals.

However, the technical notion of relevance defined above does not always correspond to the intuitive one. Nor is it intended to. Sperber and Wilson make explicit that the notion of relevance defined in terms of contextual effects is not

---

[5] All of these notions are elaborated on in Sperber and Wilson (1986).

[6] Sperber and Wilson (1995) introduce the term *positive cognitive effects* for those contextual effects which contribute to the achievement of cognitive goals. Since 1986 they have in general used the term *cognitive effects* for any contextual effects occurring in a cognitive system (e.g. a human interpreter).

intended as a definition or characterization of the ordinary notion. Rather, it is intended to provide a foundation for a cognitive theory of utterance interpretation. It will be important to keep in mind in what follows that I use the term relevance in this technical sense. We will have occasion below to consider cases where a prediction of relevance failure in the technical sense does not correspond to irrelevance in the ordinary, intuitive sense.

We want now to see how the machinery of Relevance Theory might be used to explicate the notion of a proposition being a relevance requirement for an utterance. However, there are clearly many, many different ways for an utterance to be relevant, and many, many different ways for an utterance to fail to be relevant. So in different cases, there will be different reasons why a certain proposition is required for the relevance of a particular utterance. I cannot attempt here anything like a complete investigation of this topic. But let me offer a couple of possibilities, as indications of the sort of requirements that we might find.

The simplest way for a proposition to serve to establish the relevance of an utterance is for it to be a contextual assumption which, in conjunction with the utterance content, leads to the derivation of a (useful) contextual effect, an effect which justifies the required processing effort. In the Gricean example with which I opened the chapter, the background proposition connecting girl-friends and travel serves to establish the relevance of B's utterance about Smith's trips to New York. If A accesses a context containing this proposition, she will be able to infer that B believes that Smith might have a girlfriend in New York, and this is a useful contextual effect in the situation. Indeed, A *needs* to access such a context in order to derive a useful contextual effect. So we can think of this proposition as being a relevance *requirement* for the utterance: A must be willing to accept this proposition and to treat it as a contextual assumption in order for B's utterance to be relevant for her.[7]

We do not, of course, say that the sentence uttered by B—*He's been paying a lot of visits to New York recently*—itself presupposes anything about girlfriends and travel. It is its utterance in that particular dialogue which bears the presupposition. To apply this notion of relevance requirement to the familiar cases of presupposition, we need to be able to say for particular sentences, or classes of sentences, that their utterance will in almost every case be relevant to an addressee only if she is able and willing to interpret the utterance relative to a

---

[7] Here, I'm ignoring other possible interpretations of B's utterance, such as that Smith has been too busy with his business trips to form any romantic attachments. Deriving this implicature (contextual effect) would require a different background assumption.

context containing a particular (kind of) proposition. I think that the existential presuppositions associated with referring expressions may be explicable in this way, and perhaps for reasons not dissimilar to those suggested by Strawson (see Section 3 above). The relevance of an utterance in which a speaker attributes some property to someone or something depends on what further inferences the addressee can derive from the fact that the individual in question has the property named. The derivation of such inferences cannot get off the ground unless the addressee is willing to accept the existence of the relevant individual in the first place, i.e. is willing to interpret the utterance relative to a context containing the proposition that the individual in question exists.

Now, it is true that the addressee of an utterance with a failed existential presupposition would not necessarily find the utterance irrelevant, in the ordinary intuitive sense of the word. Suppose, for example, that I tell you:

(3) I met Jill's husband yesterday.

Suppose further that you know that Jill has no husband. So my utterance has a relevance requirement that you do not accept, and thus, by the characterization of relevance adopted here, it fails to be relevant. Nonetheless, you might find my utterance interesting in a number of ways: the fact that I produced it allows you to deduce that I believe that Jill has a husband; maybe it makes you wonder whether Jill might have a partner who could be mistaken for her husband; and so on. Moreover, if we are currently talking about Jill, or about what I did yesterday, then you are unlikely to judge my utterance irrelevant in the ordinary sense.

To address the second point first: you can certainly deduce from my utterance that I met someone who I believed to be Jill's husband. And this proposition is likely to produce effects in whatever context has been made salient by our conversation so far. Hence, the utterance does not completely fail to be relevant, even in the technical sense.

But it is also useful here to distinguish between what I would call *intended relevance* and *non-intended relevance*. In making my utterance, I presumably intended you to derive contextual effects from the proposition that I met Jill's husband yesterday. But as a matter of fact, you don't. At best, you derive contextual effects from the proposition that I met someone who I *believed* to be Jill's husband. Most probably, the principal contextual effect you derive is that I mistakenly believe Jill to be married. In other words, my utterance turns out to be relevant to you in ways in which I did not intend: it achieves non-intended relevance. I suspect that in many cases, perhaps even most, an interpreter faced with a presupposing utterance whose presupposition she rejects will derive some unintended relevance from it, because the utterance provides information about the beliefs of the speaker.[8] The situation is similar to cases discussed by Sperber and Wilson (1986: 121) where a hearer makes inferences from the fact that an utterance with a particular content was made, rather than from the content itself.

We might then refine the proposed characterization of presupposition thus: the presuppositions of an utterance are the propositions which the addressee must accept in order for the utterance to be relevant for her in the way intended by the speaker.

We have now seen one way in which a proposition may be a relevance requirement for an utterance: it must be part of the context relative to which the utterance is interpreted in order for the utterance to be relevant in the way intended by the speaker. If we assume that an interpreter will include in a context only propositions which she accepts, then any propositions so required must be accepted.[9]

There is a second kind of consideration which may force an addressee to accept a proposition if she is to find an utterance relevant, and which may be the source of some presuppositional intuitions. This consideration stems from the principle of relevance itself, so we must begin by taking a closer look at the formulation of this principle.[10]

(4) *Communicative principle of relevance*
    Every utterance conveys a presumption of its own optimal relevance.

(5) *Optimal relevance*
    An utterance is optimally relevant to an audience iff:

---

[8] Given the possibility of unintended relevance, we can imagine cases where a speaker intentionally produces a presupposing sentence, knowing that the interpreter will reject the presupposition but knowing also that she will find it relevant that the speaker apparently believes the presupposition. This is a typical kind of case of exploiting the processes of interpretation to get someone to acquire a belief in a less than transparent way.

[9] Sperber and Wilson require that propositions in the context be *manifest* to the addressee, where a proposition is manifest to an individual just in case she is capable of accepting its representation as true or probably true. I am not sure that this is a strong enough notion. However, what this notion shares with the notion of acceptance is that neither requires the propositions in question to be ones which the addressee believes true, but only propositions which she is willing to treat as true (at least for the purposes of the discourse) once they are raised for consideration.

[10] The following definitions are taken from the postface to the second edition of Sperber and Wilson (1996). I have modified them slightly to eliminate some terminology not introduced here.

(*a*) It produces adequate contextual effects to be worth the audience's processing effort.

(*b*) It is the most relevant utterance, compatible with the communicator's abilities and preferences, for the production of those contextual effects.

What is crucial here is clause (*b*) of the definition of optimal relevance. Let us look at its effects in the interpretation of an utterance of the following sentence:

(6) Jane knows that Louise is in love.

An interpreter faced with this utterance might well proceed in the following way. She extracts from the utterance the proposition that Jane knows that Louise is in love, and proceeds to derive inferences—contextual effects—from it. One of those inferences may well be the proposition that Louise is in love—a legitimate inference from the proposition expressed—and this proposition may in turn give rise to further contextual effects. But the interpreter will also look to derive further contextual effects from the proposition expressed by the speaker: perhaps that Jane will be displeased, or that the speaker thinks that Jane is a busybody. Now, if the speaker considers that the relevance of her utterance of (6) resides in the (subordinate) proposition that Louise is in love, and contextual effects derivable from it, then she should choose a form from which the interpreter will infer only this proposition and its further contextual effects (or at least as little as possible beyond this). Otherwise, she imposes on the interpreter a good deal of worthless processing effort. If the principal contextual effects of an utterance of (6) are expected to arise from the proposition that Louise is in love, then the utterance used is not the most relevant utterance for the production of these effects. But, by the principle of relevance, the very utterance of (6) conveys a presumption that it *is* optimally relevant. So the hearer of (6) would, under normal circumstances, assume that the proposition that Louise is in love is *not* the source of the principal contextual effects she is intended to derive. This assumption will lead the hearer to treat this proposition as 'background' or 'non-main-point', and to foreground the maximal proposition expressed, and contextual effects derivable from it.

This feature of the principle of relevance leads to the expectation that in general, the strongest proposition communicated will be considered the main point of an utterance, that is, the primary source of its relevance. Non-maximal entailments of this proposition would generally be treated as secondary, or backgrounded. This seems plausible, at least for simple sentence structures. But it is also to be expected that various pragmatic considerations may override this expectation. One such case will be discussed below, where we consider cases in which a presupposition acquires main-point status.[11]

Now, note further that if the addressee of (6) is not prepared to accept the back-grounded proposition, then she also cannot accept the proposition which *is* supposed to carry the relevance of the utterance, i.e. the maximal entailment. So an utterance of (6) will have (the intended) relevance for an addressee only if she accepts the backgrounded proposition. Roughly speaking, then, I suggest that some presuppositions arise when propositions inferable from an utterance are, by virtue of the assumption of relevance, treated as background, but are such that their acceptance is a prerequisite for the acceptance of the maximal entailment.[12]

I have framed this suggestion somewhat tentatively, as it is certainly in need of refinement. The logic of the discussion so far would lead to the conclusion that all (obvious) non-maximal entailments of the content of an utterance should have presuppositional status, and this is clearly incorrect. For example, from an utterance of (7) a hearer can easily infer (8) and (9):

(7) Jane washed the windows.
(8) Someone washed the windows.
(9) Jane washed something.

Moreover, if the hearer were unwilling to accept (8) or (9), she would also be unwilling to accept the content of (7) itself. However, (7) does not intuitively presuppose either of these entailments.[13] Similarly, utterances of conjunctions do not intuitively presuppose their conjuncts. So, if the account of the presup-positionality of sentence (6) above is on the right track, then some way is needed of differentiating between the inference from a *know* sentence to its complement, and these other non-presupposition-inducing inferences.

In my discussion of this case, talk of identifying the locus of relevance led naturally into talk about main-point and non-main-point content. Abbott (2000)

---

[11] In addition, there may be conventional means for indicating that a non-maximal entailment is the primary bearer of relevance.

[12] It is instructive to compare the *know* case with, for example, *believe*. Why does an utterance of:

(i) Jane believes that Louise is in love

not require that the addressee accept the content of the complement clause in order to achieve relevance? The answer is that the interpreter is not licensed to derive the content of the complement clause as an inference from (i), or to derive further contextual effects from this content. So there is no inference to this content to be backgrounded. (Thanks to Chris Gauker, personal communication, for insisting on the need for a way to distinguish these two cases.)

[13] As an anonymous OUP reader points out, focus structure might be taken to give rise to a pre-suppositional relation between an utterance of (7) and one or more of the entailments in (8)–(9). Indeed, this is the position taken in Wilson and Sperber (1979).

argues that presuppositions are non-asserted propositions conveyed by the utterance, propositions which are of necessity conveyed but which are not intended by the speaker to be part of the main point. Presuppositions arise, she argues, by virtue of two facts: first, that there is a preference for utterances to have, roughly, a single 'main point'; and second, that the expression of any thought will involve expression of many atomic propositions. As a consequence, any utterance involves the expression of propositions which are not part of the main point. My suggestion here is very close to her position. However, I derive the requirement for a single main point from general considerations of relevance. And I suggest that this is only one of the ways in which a proposition may acquire the status of a relevance requirement, and hence of a presupposition.

I opened this section with a formulation of my thesis: that the presuppositions of an utterance are the propositions which the addressee must accept in order for the utterance to be relevant for her. (Recall that to accept a proposition is not necessarily to believe it, but only to treat it as true for current purposes.[14]) Given the possibility of non-intended relevance, I added that these are propositions which the addressee must accept in order for the utterance to be relevant in the way intended by the speaker. I have made here two suggestions as to why acceptance of a particular proposition may be required in order for an utterance to achieve relevance for an addressee. I reiterate that it is to be expected that there are multiple sources of relevance requirements. The explication of particular cases of presupposition will require an explanation of how and why utterances of the presupposing sentence require acceptance of the presupposition in order to achieve relevance. This work remains to be done. But I hope that the thesis is clear enough for me to move to the next step: to show that some of the standard properties of presuppositions follow straightforwardly if we conceive of presuppositions as relevance requirements.

4.2. Initial Consequences of the Thesis

4.2.1. *Backgrounding*

The proposed characterization of presuppositions explains the intuition that presuppositions are 'backgrounded', or 'non-main-point'. Indeed, it points the way towards a clarification of that notion. To be backgrounded is to be a relevance requirement: either a component of the intended interpretative context, or a communicated proposition which is not the locus of relevance.

---

[14] This becomes particularly important in complex cases involving pretense on the part of speaker or hearer or both.

Sometimes, a relevance requirement—a presupposition—can have main point status, as in the familiar example:[15]

>(10) Ann: The new guy is very attractive.
>   Bud: Yes, and his wife is lovely too.

In the imagined context, the main point of Bud's utterance is to inform Ann that the new guy has a wife. Nonetheless, we have the intuition that this proposition is a presupposition, and that Bud, by conveying the information in this way, is engaging in indirection. And of course he is. For he has produced an utterance which, by the principle of relevance, *should* have as its main point the proposition that the guy's wife is lovely. But it happens to be the case that another of the communicated propositions, namely that the new guy has a wife, is more relevant for Ann than the fact that the wife is lovely. And moreover, in the situation envisaged, Ann will recognize that Bud believes that this proposition is more relevant for her. Hence, she will take his main point to be that the new guy has a wife.[16] But identification of this proposition as the intended main point is a secondary process, which is in some sense dependent on the primary, automatic process of interpretation. In this process, the proposition that the new guy has a wife functions as a relevance requirement.

4.2.2. *Noncontroversiality*

Under the proposed thesis, presuppositions are not required to have common-ground status, to be presumed to be shared information at the time of utterance. However, the thesis provides a straightforward explanation of why there would be a tendency on the part of speakers to produce utterances whose presuppositions are in fact shared information, or are at least highly non-controversial: Speakers want their utterances to be relevant to their addressees. An utterance judged non-relevant by an addressee is in danger of being ignored. At the very least, the utterance will not have the intended effect on the cognitive state of the addressee, and may well result in a derailment of the speaker's communicative intentions. Production of an utterance whose presuppositions are not accepted by the addressee inevitably leads to a judgment of non-relevance; so this is something which a speaker will try to avoid.

---

[15] Thanks to my student Jessi Berkelhammer for raising the issue of these cases.

[16] Note that Bud could produce his utterance quite innocently, not imagining that Ann has any interest in the new guy. Then his intended main point—what he believes to constitute the locus of relevance of his utterance—is the strongest proposition expressed. Ann may nonetheless pay more attention to the existential entailment, by virtue of her own interests.

The consequences of non-relevance may be worse for the speaker than the consequences of simply being wrong. Suppose that I tell you:

(11) Classes have been cancelled.

Presumably, I would say this in order to convey the information to you, and I do so because I think it is relevant for you in one way or another. It is probably also the case that it serves my interests in some way to get this information to you. Now, suppose you think that I am wrong. The consequence is likely to be a conversation about whether or not classes have been cancelled. Whatever the outcome, my communicative intention has in some sense been realized: we have communicated on the topic of the cancellation of classes.

Now suppose that I tell you:

(12) I'm glad that classes have been cancelled.

In this case, what I intend to communicate is something about my mental state. Presumably, it is from this information that I intend you to derive contextual effects. Now, suppose again that you believe that classes have not been cancelled. It is again likely that what will ensue is a conversation about whether or not classes have been cancelled. But in this case, my conversational aims will have gone awry: we are not likely to be talking about my feelings concerning the cancellation of classes any more.

As far as presuppositionality is concerned, then, the safest choice for a speaker hoping to avoid non-relevance is to produce utterances whose presuppositions are clearly already accepted by the addressee. But it is also safe to produce utterances whose presuppositions can be assumed to be non-controversial for the addressee. On the other hand, to produce an utterance whose presuppositions are controversial is to invite a judgment of non-relevance.

To reiterate the original point: although the current account predicts that utterance presuppositions should be non-controversial, it does not predict that presuppositions are required to be common ground, or to be believed by the speaker to be so. Thus, under the view presented here, cases of informative presuppositions, which on the Stalnakerian account must be treated by accommodation, raise no special issues.

In example (10) above we saw a case where a relevance requirement is also the intended main point of the utterance. This, I suggested, involves a secondary, pragmatically driven re-evaluation of the intended relevance of the utterance. A further complication arises where a main-point relevance requirement is also controversial, as in an example from Von Fintel (2000), where a daughter informs her father that she is engaged by saying:

> (13) Oh Dad, I forgot to tell you that my fiancé and I are moving to Seattle next week.

The speaker here has produced an utterance whose relevance requires the addressee to accept (without discussion) the proposition that she has a fiancé. This is not something that, under the circumstances, can be expected to go through without challenge. But of course, the speaker in this case would not normally expect the utterance to go through without challenge. The choice to convey such momentous information as a presupposition has various stylistic effects. But the presuppositional status of the information is still attributable to the fact that the presumption of relevance requires that information to be given non-main-point status, and thus to be accepted by the addressee in order to establish the relevance of the utterance as a whole.

The proposed analysis allows for a nice distinction between ordinary cases of informative presupposition, and cases that have the feel of exploitation (in the Gricean sense) of a conversational principle. In the ordinary cases, such as my telling a colleague:

> (14) I can't come to the meeting. I have to take my cat to the vet,

new information is introduced as a presupposition, i.e. as a relevance requirement. But in these cases, the intended status of this information matches its ostensible status: it not only appears to be (merely) relevance establishing, but is intended to be so. In examples (10) and (13), however, the intended status is different from the ostensible status: in these cases, what appears to be merely relevance establishing information is intended as a main point.

4.2.3. *Defeasibilty*

Another well-known property of presuppositions is that they are often (although not always) defeasible.[17] There are three fairly familiar sorts of situations in which this occurs.

- When presuppositions are explicitly denied.

   Example. The king of France isn't bald—there *is* no king of France!

- When a (normally) presupposing clause is embedded in certain linguistic environments.[18]
   Example. Either there is no king of France, or the king of France is bald.

---

[17] See Simons (2000) for an argument that whether or not presuppositions are defeasible depends on whether they are conversationally or conventionally generated.

[18] I return to this case in Sect. 5 below.

- When the normal presupposition of a clause or sentence is incompatible with conversational implicatures or other contextual assumptions.

    Example. [Context: speaker and hearer both know that speaker does not know Maud's whereabouts, but knows that Harold is looking for her.]

    If Harold discovers that Maud is in New York, he'll be furious.

All of these types of cancellation are compatible with the view of presuppositions as relevance requirements. The basic idea in each case would be that the relevance of the utterance as a whole is incompatible with the potential presupposition. In the first case, the explicit denial makes clear that the addressee is not to assume a context containing the proposition that there is a king of France. In .the second case, the addressee cannot assume that the intended context contains the proposition that there is a king of France, as relative to such a context the disjunction would be equivalent to its second disjunct, and there would thus be no justification for the additional processing effort involved in processing the more complex utterance. In the third case, extra-linguistic factors—the addressee's knowledge about the speaker's background knowledge and about the goals of the discourse—override considerations of optimizing relevance. (And clearly the utterance is adequately relevant evaluated in the context which is available.)

In addition to these three familiar cases of cancellation, there is an additional type which has received somewhat less attention, and which is in fact predicted by the proposed view. Presuppositions may fail to arise in situations in which the relevance of the utterance does *not* depend on the assumption of the expected presupposition. Consider the following case: A researcher is conducting a study on the effects of quitting smoking. She needs subjects who have undergone this change of state. A subject comes to take part in the study. But while the criteria for participation are being explained, the subject turns to the researcher and says: 'I'm sorry, I'm no use to you for this study. I haven't stopped smoking.' The utterance, in these circumstances is, I think, neutral as to whether the speaker has never smoked or is an unrepentant smoker. The situation ensures the relevance of the utterance in either case.

4.2.4. *Variety of Strength of Presuppositions*

Many authors, probably beginning with Stalnaker (1974: 205), have observed that presuppositionality seems to come in different degrees. As Stalnaker observes: 'Sometimes no sense at all can be made of a statement unless one assumes that the speaker is making a certain presupposition. In other cases, it is mildly suggested by a speech act that the speaker is taking a certain assumption for granted, but the suggestion is easily defeated by countervailing evidence.'

Stalnaker claims for his pragmatic account the advantage that it predicts such variation. The pragmatic account suggested here has the same advantage. For an utterance can fail to achieve relevance for a variety of reasons, and to different degrees. Some types of relevance failure will be worse than others. The worse the consequences of the relevance failure, the stronger will be the assumption on the part of the interpreter that the speaker intends her to assume whatever proposition is required to avoid that failure.

Probably the most egregious failure of relevance occurs when an utterance fails to have propositional content, or has propositional content which is not truth-evaluable, as in the case of reference failure. Consider utterances of (15) or (16):

(15) Do you like the big red one? [Said when nothing is indicated and no red object is visible.]

(16) If France's current king abdicates, the French will be in disarray.

There is a variety of views as to the consequences of reference failure, but whichever of these views one adopts, it is clear that something goes very badly wrong in such utterances. The absence of a referent for the relevant NPs leads to a radical failure of relevance, a failure so bad that there is really nothing—no contextual effect—that the addressee can derive. (The addressee might find the utterance relevant in ways not intended by the speaker, in the way discussed above.) Because the consequences of relevance failure in this case are so severe, there is a robust assumption that one is expected to assume the existence of a referent.

Now, compare this case with the following example, due to Van der Sandt (1992):

(17) If someone at the conference solved the problem, it was Smith who solved it.[19]

An utterance of this sentence might be understood presuppositionally, i.e. an interpreter might infer that she is supposed to assume that the problem has been solved. (The antecedent then reflects uncertainty as to whether the problem was solved by someone at the conference, or someone else.) But this is only

---

[19] The crucial property of this example is its logical structure: the antecedent entails the potential presupposition of the consequent, but not vice versa. Such examples contrast with conditionals in which there is mutual entailment between the antecedent and the potential presupposition of the consequent, as in (i). Such sentences have no presuppositional reading:

(i) If someone solved the problem, it was Smith who solved it.

a weak inference: a non-presuppositional interpretation is also available. By adopting the presuppositional interpretation, the addressee might gain additional contextual effects deducible from the new assumption that the problem has been solved. However, the non-presuppositional reading is also likely to be adequately relevant. On any actual occasion of utterance, salient contextual assumptions might well lead an interpreter to prefer one interpretation over the other. (Intonation also may serve to disambiguate: focal stress on *conference* tends to favor the presuppositional reading.) But considerations of relevance do not rule out the non-presuppositional reading, and thus the presupposition is relatively weak.

4.3. Further Consequences

4.3.1. *Dedicated Triggers*

So far, I have looked at properties of presupposition that are accounted for to some degree in other accounts of presupposition, in particular in the Stalnakerian account. Here, I want to consider a question which, I believe, the Stalnakerian account does not answer. The question arises with respect to what I will call *dedicated presupposition triggers*: lexical items whose sole function appears to be the triggering of a presupposition. These items can be omitted without affecting the assertoric content of the utterance. Examples of such triggers are the words *even*, *yet*, *again*, and *too*. Triggers of this kind differ from, say, factive or change-of-state verbs. In the latter cases, the presupposition is non-detachable from the content expressed by the verbs. For example, any close paraphrase of the presupposition-inducing (18a), such as the sentences given in (18b), bears the same presupposition, given in (18c).

(18a) Jane didn't leave the house.
(18b) Jane didn't exit/go out of/depart from/quit the house.
(18c) Jane was in the house immediately before the reference time.

A speaker who wishes to express the content of (18a) really cannot do so without triggering the presupposition, unless she takes some additional steps to suppress or cancel it. So in these cases, the question of why the speaker has used a presupposition-inducing expression does not arise. But in the case of sentences like (19)–(21), the presupposition-inducing expression clearly could have been omitted without (on standard views) changing the content of what has been said.

(19) Even Bush has admitted that global warming is real.

(20) Jane has failed her driver's test again.

(21) Harold failed his driver's test too.

The question then arises: Why should a speaker bother to include a presupposition trigger? The Stalnakerian account gives an answer to this question for the (supposedly 'exploitative') cases where the presupposition is not in fact common ground. In these cases, according to that account, the presupposition is accommodated, and becomes common ground. So inclusion of the presupposition trigger allows the speaker to convey more information. But of course a speaker can include a presupposition trigger also when the presupposition *is* in the common ground; indeed, this is supposed to be the standard case. In this case, then, what function do presupposition triggers serve? Why should a speaker include them when the presupposition is already in the common ground? For then, presumably, the triggered presupposition will not provide the addressee with any new information.[20]

On the proposal being made here, the answer is straightforward: the presupposition trigger is a conventional marker of a proposition which the hearer is supposed to take as contributing to the relevance of the utterance. The relative strength and undefeasibility of presuppositions triggered in this way is also to be expected on this account. In the case of cancellation, the addressee infers that the speaker cannot after all intend her to presuppose the potential presupposition, given a conflict between the presupposition and other contextual or discourse information. But when a speaker uses a dedicated presupposition trigger, she thereby makes her intentions explicit.

This treatment of dedicated presupposition triggers is a natural extension of the proposals made in Blakemore (1987). Blakemore considers the function of a variety of expressions which have standardly been thought *not* to contribute to truth conditional content: expressions like *therefore, so, moreover,* and *after all.* She argues that the role of these expressions is to guide interpretation by indicating the intended inferential relations between two or more propositions expressed in a discourse. But her general claim is that the semantic contribution of certain expressions is to constrain, in one way or another, the contexts (in the relevance theoretic sense) in which utterances are interpreted. Blakemore mentions the

---

[20] Sperber and Wilson (1986, ch. 4 n. 21) make a similar point, noting that the Stalnakerian framework provides no reason to expect the occurrence of conventional markers of presupposition. They also suggest that Blakemore's work (see below) offers a promising treatment of the phenomenon.

possibility that standard presuppositional phenomena might be treated along these lines, but does not pursue the idea. My argument here is that Blakemore is right: that the function of dedicated presupposition triggers is to indicate that the speaker intends the (truth conditional content of) her utterance to be interpreted relative to a context which contains the 'presupposition'. By indicating this intention, the speaker indicates that she believes that interpretation of the utterance in such a context will guarantee its relevance for the addressee.

Let me try to clarify this claim with respect to *even*. Consider sentence (19) above. My claim is that the speaker of this sentence asserts that Bush has admitted that global warming is real, but also indicates to the addressee that the reason this is of current relevance is that Bush is a particularly unlikely person to do so. To support this idea, consider the differences between situations in which one might utter (19) and in which one might utter the sentence without *even*, given in (22).

(22) Bush has admitted that global warming is real.

Suppose that Bush has just made his admission during a public appearance. To tell you about it, I would most naturally (I think) say (22). Sentence (19) would be odd. In the situation just described, Bush's admission is relevant because it is brand new information. (Presumably, it is only relevant to people who care about Bush's environmental policy, but let's assume that we have such an audience.) The Stalnakerian common-ground story doesn't provide any explanation for why (19) would be somewhat peculiar in the circumstances just described. But the relevance story does. In the situation described, the fact that Bush is a particularly unlikely person to admit the reality of global warming isn't the primary provider of relevance for the utterance: it's the fact that he just did it. So the *even* would somehow lead the hearer astray.

On the other hand, suppose some time has passed since Bush's admission, and we are discussing continued obstacles to environmental progress. You mention the fact that there are still global-warming-deniers, to which I reply:

(23) How much longer can they hold out? Even Bush has admitted that global warming is real.

One important point about this case is that *neither* the information that Bush was unlikely to make this admission *nor* the fact that he has done so is supposed to be new information. But the fact that Bush has made this admission is a relevant observation at this point in the conversation in light of the fact that he has been, let's say, one of the staunchest warming-deniers.

This discussion brings out two points: First, that some explanation is needed for the function of presupposition triggers in situations in which the presupposition *is* in the common ground. The common-ground view tells us why they are allowed in these circumstances, but not what they *do*. The second point is that the common-ground story doesn't tell us why certain presupposition triggers are disallowed in some situations even where the licensing conditions are supposedly met, e.g. when announcing something.

The claim seems equally plausible with respect to examples with *again* and *too*. Consider the following examples, repeated from above:

(24) Jane has failed her driving test again.
(25) George failed his driving test too.

It seems quite plausible in each case to say that the proposition 'invoked' by the presence of the presupposition trigger is what provides the utterance with maximal relevance.[21] The significance of Jane failing her driving test having failed it before is different—perhaps greater—than the significance of her having failed it without consideration of her prior attempts. (To announce dejectedly *Jane failed her driving test* is to consider this failure in isolation from other failures; to say (24), on the other hand, is to consider the sequence of failures and to invite conclusions based on the sequence.) The same seems true of the presupposition generated by *too* in (25): George's failure has a different significance in conjunction with (let's say) Jane's, than it would have alone.

4.3.2. *A Broad Notion of Presupposition*

One further consequence of the characterization of presuppositions as relevance requirements is that the notion of presupposition is broadened beyond the range of linguistically triggered presuppositions. Any given utterance may require all kinds of propositions to establish its relevance; and any given sentence will require different propositions to establish its relevance on different occasions of utterance. Consider, for example, an utterance of the sentence:

(26) It's 8.01.

For an utterance of this sentence to be relevant, something must follow from it. On one occasion of use the relevance establisher might be the proposition that the bus comes at 8.03 (and so we should hurry). On another, the relevance

---

[21] Clearly, these propositions are calculated, presumably compositionally, on the basis of the content of the trigger plus the rest of the content expressed. One aspect of the semantics of the presupposition trigger must be to trigger a second process of meaning composition whereby the presuppositional proposition is derived.

establisher might be the proposition that the meeting was supposed to start at 8.00 (and so we should proceed). And so on. On the account proposed here, all of these relevance establishers would be considered presuppositions, on a par with the linguistically triggered presuppositions considered above. This may seem a defect of the account, if our goal is to give an account of the phenomenon of linguistically triggered presupposition.

However, there is no particular reason to decide a priori that linguistically triggered presupposition is a distinct phenomenon from the broader notion conjured by the ordinary use of the term. On the view presented here, linguistically triggered presupposition would be a sub-case of the broader phenomenon. If there is in fact some common property shared by the class of cases normally included under the title of presupposition, a property not shared by other cases, then it will be possible to delineate this class in some way. The obvious candidate is, of course, the linguistic triggering itself.

This point, like others noted above, does not distinguish the proposal made here from the Stalnakerian treatment of presupposition. For Stalnaker, presuppositions are properties of speakers, not of sentences.[22] A speaker's utterances may reveal her presuppositions. But given Stalnaker's assumptions, I believe he would agree that a speaker who utters *It's 8.01* with the intention of getting the chairperson to start the meeting is presupposing (i.e. taking it to be part of the common ground) that the meeting was supposed to start at 8.00.

5. Projection

One very daunting problem for any fully pragmatic account of presupposition is the issue of presupposition projection. Various researchers, particularly those working in dynamic semantic frameworks, have shown that projection behavior is highly complex, in particular where presuppositions involve quantification or interaction with modals.[23] Researchers in those frameworks have also been very successful in providing formally elegant and descriptively adequate algorithmic accounts of projection. This work certainly makes a convincing case that there

[22] Indeed, Stalnaker contends that no contentful notion of sentence presupposition can be defined. For him, sentence presuppositions are artifacts of the interaction of general conversational principles and properties of particular sentences. See e.g. comments in the introduction to *Context and Content* (Stalnaker 1999: 8).

[23] There is an enormous literature in this area. For some of the foundational proposals, see Heim (1982); Van der Sandt (1992); Zeevat (1992); Beaver (1995).

is an algorithmic component to the behavior of projection. However, what this work does not do is explain why particular presuppositions attach to particular atomic propositions or sentences in the first place.

On the algorithmic view of presupposition projection, it is claimed that presuppositions attach to atomic clauses and are then passed up to complex sentences which embed them through some mechanism of projection. To fully incorporate projection facts into the framework suggested here, one would have to argue that the appearance of projection of presuppositions from lower to higher clauses is in fact the result of a *sharing* of presuppositions among 'families' of sentences. A family of sentences shares a presupposition just in case that presupposition is required to establish the relevance of utterances of any member of the family.

Can it be demonstrated that sentences share presuppositions in this way? Some initial support for the idea comes from an observation due to McLaughlin (2001). What McLaughlin observes is that very standard cases of relevance implicature sometimes show behavior analogous to the projection behavior of standard cases of presupposition. Consider first the following dialogue:

(27) Ann: Are we going on a picnic?
     Bud: It's raining.

Recall from Section 1 that Bud's utterance introduces both an implicated assumption and an implicated conclusion. The implicated assumption is that there is a connection between rain and picnics: probably, that if it rains, one does not picnic. The implicated conclusion is that there will be no picnic.

Now, consider the following similar discourse:

(28) Ann: Are we going on a picnic?
     Bud: It's not raining.

For Bud's response to be relevant, Ann must still attribute to Bud the assumption that there is some connection between rain and picnics. With the right intonational clues from Bud, Ann might well retrieve a slightly strengthened version of the same implicated assumption: that if it rains, one doesn't picnic, but if it doesn't rain, one can picnic. Then the implicated conclusion would be along the lines of: There's nothing to stop us from going on a picnic.

Now, suppose Bud had replied with either (29) or (30):

(29) It might be raining.
(30) Is it raining?

Again, these responses would be in compliance with Relation only if Bud assumed a connection between rain and picnics, and assumed that Ann could work out that he did. The same would seem to be true of the following conditional response:

(31) If it rains, maybe we'll go to the movies.

In none of these cases, I think, would we want to say that the implicature projects from the embedded clause. Rather, we would want to say that each utterance gives rise to the same implicated assumption: one and the same background assumption serves in each case to relate Ann's question to Bud's indirect response. Of course, on my view this implicated premise, which is required to establish the relevance of the utterance, simply is a presupposition. McLaughlin's observation thus provides at least prima facie support for the claim that, given a particular conversational context, families of sentences might require the same background assumptions in order to satisfy the requirements of relevance.

6. Conclusion

In this initial presentation I have touted what I see as the potential strengths of this proposed account of the phenomenon of presupposition. But what I have offered here is no more than a sketch of a full account. The idea of propositions serving as relevance establishers must be given more substance—enough substance that it will be possible to determine the predictions made by the account about the expected presuppositions of particular utterances.[24] This is clearly a difficult task. It requires at the very least some more rigorous understanding of

---

[24] Here again, I am not much worse off than the competition. Stalnaker has never attempted to construct a theory of presupposition capable of making predictions about the presuppositions of particular sentences or utterances. In the various frameworks of dynamic semantics which have provided formal accounts of presupposition based (in some cases loosely) on Stalnaker's framework, precise predictions are made about the presuppositions of complex sentences, based on the assumption that certain atomic constituent clauses have a given presupposition. But these frameworks do not offer any predictions about which presuppositions will be associated with atomic sentences, or why. In contrast, those who attempt to explain presupposition in terms of conversational implicature (see e.g. Kempson 1975; Wilson 1975; Atlas and Levinson 1981) do attempt such predictions, but generally are able to deal with only a limited set of cases, and do not deal with complex projection examples. Clearly, it is an enormously difficult task to accomplish both descriptive and explanatory adequacy through the full range of cases.

the notion of relevance itself, and some quantitative measure of relevance. Relevance Theory provides some machinery to begin to address this task. Computational approaches to the representation of inference in interpretation also seem promising frameworks in which to pursue these questions. The questions are undoubtedly hard. But they may nonetheless be the right ones to ask.

REFERENCES

Abbott, Barbara (2000), 'Presuppositions as Nonassertions', *Journal of Pragmatics*, 32: 1419–37.

Atlas, Jay D., and Stephen C. Levinson (1981), 'It-Clefts, Informativeness and Logical Form: Radical Pragmatics (Revised Standard Version)', in P. Cole (ed.), *Radical Pragmatics* (New York: Academic Press).

Beaver, David (1995), 'Presupposition and Assertion in Dynamic Semantics', Ph.D. diss. (University of Edinburgh).

Blakemore, Diane (1987), *Semantic Constraints on Relevance* (New York: Blackwell).

Burton-Roberts, Noel (1989), *The Limits to Debate: A Revised Theory of Semantic Presuppositions* (New York: Cambridge University Press).

Grice, Paul (1989), *Studies in the Way of Words* (Cambridge, Mass.: Harvard University Press).

Heim, I. (1982), 'The Semantics of Definite and Indefinite Noun Phrases', Ph.D. diss. (University of Massachusetts at Amherst) (pub. New York: Garland, 1988).

—— (1983), 'On the Projection Problem for Presuppositions', *WCCFL*, 2: 114–26; repr. in Steven Davis (ed.), *Pragmatics: A Reader* (New York: Oxford University Press, 1991).

Kempson, R. (1975), *Presupposition and the Delimitation of Semantics* (Cambridge: Cambridge University Press).

McLaughlin, Daniel (2001), 'Presuppositions as Conversational Implicatures', MS, Carnegie Mellon University.

Simons, Mandy (2000), 'On the Conversational Basis of Some Presuppositions', *SALT* 11: 431–48.

Sperber, Dan, and Deirdre Wilson (1986), *Relevance: Communication and Cognition* (Cambridge, Mass.: Basil Blackwell; 2nd edn. 1995).

—— —— (1995), Postface to the 2nd edn. of Sperber and Wilson (1986: 255–79).

Stalnaker, Robert (1974), 'Pragmatic Presuppositions', in Milton K. Munitz and Peter K. Unger (eds.), *Semantics and Philosophy* (New York: New York University Press), repr. in Stalnaker (1999: 47–62).

—— (1984), *Inquiry* (Cambridge, Mass.: MIT Press).

—— (1998), 'On the Representation of Context', *Journal of Logic, Language and Information*, 7: 3–19; repr. in Stalnaker (1999 :78–95).

—— (1999), *Context and Content* (New York: Oxford University Press).

—— (2002), 'Common Ground', *Linguistics and Philosophy*, 255–6: 701–21.

Strawson, Peter (1990), 'On Referring', in A. Flew (ed.), *Essays in Conceptual Analysis* (London: Macmillan, 1956); repr. in A. P. Martinich, *The Philosophy of Language* (New York: Oxford University Press, 1990), 219–34.

Van der Sandt, Robert (1992), 'Presupposition Projection as Anaphora Resolution', *Journal of Semantics*, 9: 333–77.

Von Fintel, Kai (2000), 'What is Presupposition Accommodation?', MS, Massachusetts Institute of Technology.

Wilson, Deirdre (1975), *Presuppositions and Non-Truth-Conditional Semantics* (London: Academic Press).

—— and Dan Sperber (1979), 'Ordered Entailment: An Alternative to Presuppositional Theories', in C.-K. Oh and D. A. Dinneen (eds.), *Syntax and Semantics*, xi: *Presupposition* (New York: Academic Press).

—— —— (2003), 'Relevance Theory', in L. Horn and G. Ward (eds.), *Handbook of Pragmatics* (Oxford: Basil Blackwell).

Zeevat, Henk (1992), 'Presupposition and Accommodation in Update Semantics', *Journal of Semantics*, 9: 379–412.

9

Naming and Asserting

Scott Soames

Many essays in semantics and the philosophy of language seem to proceed on the assumption that—special circumstances involving ironic, metaphorical, or other non-literal uses of language aside—the proposition asserted by an utterance of a sentence in a context is the proposition semantically expressed by the sentence in that context. At some level, of course, we all know that this is a fiction, since sometimes a single utterance may involve the assertion of more than one proposition. For example, the assertion of a conjunction involves the assertion of the conjuncts, too. Nevertheless, the fiction is often thought to be harmless, since it is standardly taken for granted that even in those cases that falsify it, the proposition p semantically expressed by a sentence that is assertively uttered is the **primary** proposition asserted, with other propositions counted as asserted only when they are particularly obvious, and relevant, consequences of p. In my book *Beyond Rigidity* I argued that this comfortable, but complacent, view is false.[1] In many cases in which one speaks literally (i) the primary proposition q asserted by an utterance of S in a context C is **not** the proposition semantically expressed by S in C, and (ii) the proposition that is semantically expressed by S in C counts as asserted only because it is an obvious and relevant consequence of q. In the book I argued that these points are important, in part, because of the role they play in explaining how substitution of coreferential names in simple sentences may change the propositions asserted by utterances of those sentences, even if they don't change the propositions semantically expressed. Once this

---

[1] Scott Soames, *Beyond Rigidity: The Unfinished Semantic Agenda of Naming and Necessity* (New York: Oxford University Press, 2002).

lesson is learned, it can be applied to sentences that ascribe beliefs and assertions to others, as well. Sometimes substitution of coreferential names in these sentences changes the truth values of the propositions the sentences are used to assert, even if the propositions they semantically express remain the same. In short, I tried to show how a more sophisticated conception of the relationship between the semantic contents of sentences and the propositions they are used to assert can make an important contribution to solving Frege's puzzle.

But *Beyond Rigidity* was only the first step. The real relationship between the semantic contents of sentences and the propositions they are used to assert is even more indirect than indicated there. For one thing, semantic contents of grammatically complete sentences (relative to contexts) are not always complete propositions; sometimes they are incomplete propositional matrices, together with partial constraints on how contextual information may be used to complete them. Moreover, even when the semantic content of S (relative to a context) is— or, at any rate, fully determines—a complete proposition, this proposition is not always among those asserted by competent speakers who use S with its normal, literal meaning. For these reasons, the semantic content of a sentence in a context is often not something asserted by an utterance of the sentence in that context. Instead, its function is to constrain the candidates for assertion in certain ways, while allowing speakers and hearers a degree of freedom to operate within these constraints. In what follows, I will fill out this conception of the relationship between semantic content and assertion in more detail. First, I will review, and then pose certain problems for, the version of the conception presented in *Beyond Rigidity*. Next, I will indicate how those problems can be solved by making the conception more sophisticated in certain ways. Finally, I will illustrate the generality of the new conception of the relationship between semantic content and assertion by citing a few of the vast range of further examples that support it.

The View from *Beyond Rigidity*

We utter sentences to convey information. Some of this information is asserted, some is conversationally implicated, and some is merely suggested by virtue of idiosyncratic features of speakers and hearers in particular contexts. Because of this, the information carried by an assertive utterance of one and the same (unambiguous) indexical-free sentence S varies greatly from one context to another. Not all of this information is part of the meaning of S in the language in which it is being used. Suppose, as is usual, that the meaning of S is the proposition it semantically expresses. It is natural to think that this proposition should consist of information that a competent speaker who assertively utters S asserts and intends to convey in any normal context in which S is used with its literal meaning (without irony, sarcasm, defeating conversational implicatures, and the like).[2]

With this in mind, consider the example:

(1) Carl Hempel lived on Lake Lane in Princeton.

Suppose I were to assertively utter this sentence to a graduate student in the philosophy department at Princeton University. In this situation I would expect the student to have heard the name *Carl Hempel* before, to know that it refers to a well-known philosopher, to know that I know this, and to know that I expect all this of him. Because of this presumed common ground between us, I would intend my utterance to be understood as committing me to the claim that the well-known philosopher Carl Hempel lived on Lake Lane in Princeton. I would intend my utterance to convey this information, and, depending on the situation, I might even intend to assert it.[3] Of course, it is clear that an utterance of this sentence wouldn't assert or convey the same information to every competent speaker of English. One doesn't have to know that Carl Hempel was a philosopher in order to understand and be a competent user of his name. So if I uttered the sentence to a boyhood friend of his in a conversation in which it was understood that the friend had known the young Carl Hempel by name, but lost touch with him at an early age before he went into philosophy, then I would convey, and perhaps even assert, different information.

What information would be asserted and conveyed to competent speakers by nearly all assertive utterances of (1) (interpreted as containing a name of the man to whom I here use it to refer)? Surely it would include little or no substantive descriptive information about Mr Hempel. Many speakers would know something about his philosophy, but others would not. Some would know what he looked like at a certain age, but not everyone would. Some would have knowledge of his family background, but many would not. Although most speakers who had enough familiarity with the name to be able to use it could be expected to possess some descriptive information about Mr Hempel, virtually none of it would be common to all such users.[4] What would be common is that

---

[2] Normality is not a matter of statistical regularity. For more on normal contexts, see ibid. 58–60.

[3] The distinction between asserting (or intending to assert) p and merely conveying (or intending to convey) p is discussed in ibid. 72–86.

[4] In order to keep matters simple, I here ignore the possibility that some extremely general sortal might be predicated of Mr Hempel in all these situations.

the property of having lived on Lake Lane in Princeton would be ascribed to one and the same individual by utterances of the sentence by competent speakers in normal contexts. In light of this it is natural to take the singular proposition assertion of which predicates this property of Mr Hempel as the proposition semantically expressed by (1).

In *Beyond Rigidity* I used considerations like these to develop a model of the semantics and pragmatics of proper names, and sentences containing them. According to the view developed there, proper names come in two main types— linguistically simple names like *Saul Kripke* and *Carl Hempel*, and linguistically complex, partially descriptive names like *Princeton University* and *Mount Washington*. The meaning, or semantic content, of a linguistically simple name is its referent; the meaning, or content, of a linguistically complex name is its referent together with a partial description of it.[5] For example, the content of *Mount Washington* is a complex consisting of the property of being a mountain, together with the mountain itself. Though for present purposes the details don't matter much, we may think of its content as being given by the description *the x: [x is a mountain and x = y]*, relative to an assignment of the referent of the name to the variable y—where the range of the variables includes all individuals, past, present, and future, plus individuals that exist in other possible worlds, as well as those that exist in the actual world.[6]

In order to be a competent user of a linguistically simple name n of an object o two requirements must be met: (i) one must have acquired a referential intention that determines o as the referent of n. This may be done by picking up n and intending to use it with the standard meaning–reference it has already acquired in the language due to the baptisms, authoritative stipulations, and referential uses of others. (ii) One must realize that to assertively utter a simple sentence *n is F* (in a normal context) is to say of the referent of n that it "is F".[7] Analogous

---

[5] Here, and throughout this chapter, I put aside any consideration of proper names without referents. See *Beyond Rigidity*, ch. 3, app., for some relevant considerations.

[6] Possible worlds are really possible states of the world—ways the world could have been. To say that an individual o exists "in" another possible world w is to say that had w obtained (i.e. had the world been in state w), o would have existed. The actual world is the possible state that the world is actually in.

[7] I use bold face italics to play the role of corner quotes. Thus, (ii) in the text is to be understood as saying that for any linguistically simple name n and predicate F, one must realize that to assertively utter a simple sentence consisting of n followed by 'is' followed by F (in a normal context) is to say of the referent of n that it "is F". The scare quotes are used to call attention to what I hope is a bit of comprehensible sloppiness. A more precise way of putting the point would be to substitute 'to predicate the property expressed by F of the referent of n' for *to say of the referent of n that it "is F"*. Here, *say of* is a variant of *say*, which, throughout, I use only in its indirect discourse sense. As I understand that sense, *x says that S* is roughly equivalent to *x asserts that S*.

conditions hold for linguistically complex, partially descriptive names. Here, I assume that to say of an object o that it "is F" is to assert the singular proposition that predicates F-hood of o. Hence, these competence conditions ensure that this singular proposition will be among the propositions asserted whenever a competent speaker assertively utters **n is F** in a normal context.

Putting all this together, we get a unified picture of the meanings of sentences containing names, plus the propositions those sentences are used to assert and convey in different contexts of utterance. The idea, roughly put, is (i) that assertive utterances of sentences containing names often result in the assertion of several propositions, (ii) that which propositions are asserted by utterances of such a sentence varies significantly from context to context, and (iii) that the meaning of an indexical-free sentence, the proposition it semantically expresses, is something which remains invariant from one context to another—i.e. it is a proposition that is asserted in all normal contexts in which the sentence is used by competent speakers with its literal meaning (without irony, sarcasm, defeating conversational implicatures, and the like).

One interesting feature of this model is the explanation it provides of how the sentences

(2a) Peter Hempel is Carl Hempel
(2b) Carl Hempel is Carl Hempel

can mean the same thing, even though assertive utterances of the former virtually always involve the assertion of propositions different from those asserted by utterances of the latter.[8] This result is extended to cases in which the two sentences are embedded under attitudes verbs like *believe* and *assert*. In these cases, the attitude ascriptions have the same semantic content, even though assertive utterances of them may well involve the assertion of propositions with different truth values.

Problems of Extending the *Beyond Rigidity* Model

My aim here is to build on this semantic–pragmatic model by extending and revising it to handle problematic cases in the hope of producing a more widely applicable and acceptable framework. Two principles of the model that require

---

[8] *Beyond Rigidity*, 67–72.

scrutiny are:

(P1) In order to be a competent user of a name n for an object o, one must realize that to assertively utter **n is F** in a normal context (without irony, sarcasm, defeating conversational implicatures, and the like) is to say of the referent of n that it "is F".

(P2) The semantic content of an indexical-free sentence S is a proposition p which is asserted and conveyed by utterances of S in any normal context involving competent speakers in which S is used with its literal meaning (without irony, sarcasm, defeating conversational implicatures, and the like).

P1 is true as stated, where **n is F** is a simple, operator-free sentence. Although it remains true if it is generalized in limited ways, it appears to fail in some cases in which n is partially descriptive and **n is F** is replaced by a complex sentence ... **n** ... containing the name. P1 also seems to fail (though perhaps not as obviously) in these environments when n is linguistically simple. Because of this, it appears that P1 cannot be fully generalized. If this is so even when n is linguistically simple, we face an immediate problem with P2. If competent speakers may assertively utter ... **n** ... (in a normal context) without saying of its referent o that it "is an x such that ... **x** ... ", then it may very well be that they may do so without asserting the singular proposition expressed by ... x ... with respect to an assignment of o to 'x'. Since this proposition is the proposition semantically expressed by ... **n** ..., we have a violation of P2. Something has to give.

Proposal for Revising P2

P2 is a prime suspect. Though the principle approximates the truth, we may be able to improve it and make it more plausible by revising it so that it no longer presupposes that the semantic content of a sentence is always a complete proposition, or at any rate one that is asserted and conveyed by normal utterances in every normal context. Instead, the semantic content of a sentence S may be viewed as something that constrains—but does not always completely determine—the propositions asserted and conveyed by utterances of S in normal contexts involving competent speakers.

For example, the semantic content of

(3a) Peter Hempel isn't Carl Hempel

may be seen as constraining normal assertive utterances of it in such a way that they are counted as assertions of propositions built around that content, without always counting as assertions of the content itself.[9] One way of thinking of this is to view the semantic content of (3a) as the potentially gappy propositional matrix (4).[10]

(4) $<$Neg $<$Identity $<<$___, Mr Hempel$>$, $<$___, Mr Hempel$>>>>$

When (3a) is assertively uttered in a particular context, the gaps in the matrix may be filled with salient descriptive information associated with the corresponding names by speaker–hearers in the context. (If there is no such contextually salient information, then the proposition asserted is one that simply denies that Mr Hempel is Mr Hempel.) In a context in which (3a) is used to assert that the man, Peter Hempel, standing over there isn't the famous philosopher Carl Hempel, the gaps in (4) are filled in so as to produce (5a)—which may also be represented as the proposition expressed by (5b), relative to an assignment of Mr Hempel to 'z' and 'w'.

(5a) $<$Neg $<$Identity $<<$Man standing over there, Mr Hempel$>$, $<$Famous philosopher, Mr Hempel$>>>>$

(5b) $\sim([\text{the x: (x is a man standing over there \& x} = z)] = [\text{the y: y is a famous philosopher \& y} = w])$.

Whereas someone who asserts (5a) asserts the proposition expressed by (5b) relative to an assignment of Mr Hempel to 'z' and 'w', it may not be a foregone conclusion that he thereby asserts the absurd proposition semantically expressed by

(3b) Carl Hempel isn't Carl Hempel.

If it turns out that this proposition is not asserted, then we have a potential violation of P2; more precisely, we have a violation of the conjunction of P2 with a principle, P3, identifying the proposition semantically expressed by (3a) and (3b) with one that arises from propositional-matrix (4) by eliminating the gaps.

---

[9] In discussing this and related examples, I ignore tense.

[10] A different, perfectly acceptable, way of thinking of it would be to retain the view that the semantic content of (3a) is the singular proposition $<$Neg $<$Identity $<$Mr Hempel, Mr Hempel $>>>$, but to allow the propositions asserted by utterances of (3a) to be enrichments of this proposition obtained by adding descriptively salient properties to the arguments of the identity relation. I adopt the description in the text primarily to highlight the process of contextual supplementation. The gaps in (4) aren't intended to have any special metaphysical status.

(P3) If the semantic content of S (relative to a context C and assignment f of values to variables) is a prepositional matrix like (4) (in which the constituents corresponding to names in S are pairs consisting of the referent of a name and a gap), then the proposition semantically expressed by S (relative to C and f) is the proposition that arises from the matrix by eliminating the gaps.

The point of the principle is to abstract away from the effects of contextual supplementation, thereby identifying a proposition entirely determined by the meaning of the sentence.

In what follows, I will argue that more complex examples in which sentences containing names are embedded under certain propositional attitude verbs provide serious challenges both to P2 (when conjoined with P3) and to unrestricted versions of P1. Particularly troubling are assertive utterances of examples like

(6a) Mary doesn't know that Peter Hempel is Carl Hempel.

in contexts in which the speaker's primary intention is to assert and convey the information that Mary doesn't know that the man, Peter Hempel, standing over there is the famous philosopher Carl Hempel. In such a case, it would seem that the speaker may **truly** assert that Mary doesn't stand in the knowledge relation to the proposition

(6b) <Identity <<Man standing over there, Mr Hempel>, < Famous philosopher, Mr Hempel>>>

without **falsely** asserting that Mary doesn't stand in the knowledge relation to the trivial proposition

(6c) <Identity < Mr Hempel, Mr Hempel >>

which is the proposition semantically expressed by the complement clause of (6a) (according both to *Beyond Rigidity* and to P3). Suppose, as I now believe, that this is right—i.e. (i) that the speaker does assert that Mary doesn't stand in the knowledge relation to proposition (6b), without asserting that she doesn't stand in the knowledge relation to proposition (6c), (ii) that proposition (6c) is the proposition semantically expressed by the complement clause of (6a), and (iii) that the proposition semantically expressed by (6a) characterizes Mary as not standing in the knowledge relation to the proposition expressed by its complement clause. It will then follow that the speaker does **not** assert the proposition semantically expressed by (6a) in the context in which that sentence is assertively uttered. This is a challenge to P2. Unless the context can be shown to be one in which there is a conversational implicature canceling what would otherwise be the normal presumption that the proposition semantically expressed is asserted, we will have to reject P2 and find a replacement.

This is the path I will explore. In so doing, I will put aside the possibility of resolving the problem by finding a canceling implicature. I do this despite the fact that this alternative is not entirely without plausibility.[11] After all, the claim that Mary does not know, of Mr Hempel, that he is who he is is an obvious falsehood that everyone in the conversation could be expected to recognize, if brought to their attention in the proper way. Moreover, in cases in which it appears to conversational participants that a speaker may have asserted something the falsity of which is utterly obvious, familiar Gricean principles motivate the search for an alternative interpretation of the speaker's remark. In such cases, the normal presumption that the speaker has asserted p (where p is the proposition semantically expressed by the sentence assertively uttered) is often conversationally canceled, and the speaker is taken to have asserted something else.[12]

However, there is a serious problem in applying this model to the present case: namely, that it would **not** appear to conversational participants in our imagined scenario that the speaker has said anything obviously false in assertively uttering (6a). Let us suppose that everyone in the conversation already knows, and is taken to know, that *Carl Hempel* and *Peter Hempel* are different names for the same man. Even then, they cannot be expected to recognize that the proposition semantically expressed by (6a) is an obvious falsehood. Since it would never occur to them that there is any presumption that the speaker should be taken to have expressed anything false, Gricean principles would **not** motivate them to search for an alternative interpretation. Thus, if there is a canceling conversational implicature, it can only be an implicature of some other sort—one that is quite distant from the (conscious or unconscious) thought processes of conversational participants. Since I am not sure precisely how genuine implicatures relate to the actual thought processes of agents, I do not wish to rule out the possibility that some basis for such a canceling implicature

---

[11] I am indebted to my student Mike McGlone for helping me appreciate the force of this point.

[12] See *Beyond Rigidity*, 343–4, n. 7, for a discussion of how this works in other cases in which an utterance of a propositional attitude ascription does not result in the assertion of the proposition semantically expressed, because of a canceling conversational implicature.

might, ultimately, be found.[13] However, neither do I wish to rely on this abstract possibility. Instead, I will sketch a different strategy for solving the problem.

In what follows I will propose a modification P2* of P2, based on the idea that the semantic content of a sentence (its meaning if it is indexical-free) is **not** always what is said (i.e. asserted) by normal utterances of it; rather, it is the skeleton of what is said—the inner structure around which speakers construct their assertions.

> (P2*) The meaning, or semantic content, of an indexical-free sentence S is a prepositional matrix pm, which is such that for any normal context involving competent speaker–hearers in which S is assertively uttered with its literal meaning (without irony, sarcasm, defeating conversational implicatures, and the like), the assertive utterance of S in the context is to be counted as an assertion of a proposition p which is an acceptable completion of pm. (When S contains linguistically simple names the bare singular proposition arising from pm by eliminating gaps corresponding to the names counts as an acceptable completion in contexts in which no descriptive enrichment takes place.)

Having argued for this revision of P2, I will indicate how the model might be extended to indexicals—which often can be regarded as constraining, rather than determining, contents in given contexts of utterance—and to sentences containing the possessive construction, the semantic contents of which are naturally seen not as complete propositions, but as propositional matrices including partially specified relations between possessor and possessed that require contextual supplementation.[14]

The end result is a conception of semantics and pragmatics in which the relationship between the semantic content of a sentence and what the sentence is

---

[13] See ibid. 59–60 for a brief discussion of one natural way of understanding Gricean conversational implicatures that does not require the actual conscious or unconscious reasoning of speaker–hearers to match the idealized Gricean reasoning that explains the implicature. McGlone is exploring ways to develop this idea that would allow one to generate a canceling implicature in the case involving (6a).

[14] Following the thinking in n. 10, one could maintain the substance of this view while treating sentences containing linguistically simple names as expressing non-gappy propositions, provided one allowed for their enrichment by contextually salient properties. For example, one might define propositional matrices to include both explicitly gappy structures and ordinary singular propositions, while conceiving of enrichment (completion) as encompassing both filling in gaps and adding properties to individuals that occur as constituents of singular propositions. I leave it open which way of formulating the view is to be preferred.

used to say, or assert, is looser than commonly thought. The former constrains and influences the latter, without always determining it, even when the sentence is used with its normal literal meaning, without canceling implicatures. The semantic contents of expressions provide the building blocks for assertions, and constrain how these blocks are assembled in normal contexts of use. But the rules of the language provide one with only a minimum common denominator. They facilitate communication and coordinate our linguistic activities, while allowing speakers considerable freedom to exploit the features of particular contexts to shape the information asserted and conveyed by their utterances.[15]

Apparent Failures of P1 to Fully Generalize: Partially Descriptive Names

In this section I will show that in a certain range of cases in which n is a partially descriptive name and S(n) is a sentence containing n, a speaker who assertively utters S(n), and thereby asserts the proposition semantically expressed by S(n), may nevertheless **not** assert the singular proposition expressed by S(v) relative to an assignment of the referent of n to the variable v (where S(v) arises from S(n) by replacing one or more occurrences of n by free occurrences of v). This result is based on an elementary observation: standardly, the fact that a particular utterance counts as the assertion of a certain proposition p in a conversational context C will, in and of itself, guarantee that the utterance also counts as the assertion of another proposition q only if q is both a necessary and a priori consequence of p (together with other obvious and salient shared background assumptions in C).[16] For example, the fact that an utterance of a conjunctive

---

[15] Important aspects of this general conception of the relationship between semantics and pragmatics can be found in a number of places in the recent literature. See in particular Kent Bach, 'You Don't Say', *Synthese*, 128 (2001), 15–44, for useful discussion and examples supporting the theses (i) that the semantic contents of non-indexical sentences are not always complete propositions, and (ii) that the (primary) propositions asserted by utterances of sentences are often contextual enrichments and completions of the semantic contents of the sentences uttered (even in some cases in which those contents themselves determine complete propositions). Other relevant literature includes id., 'Conversational Impliciture', *Mind and Language*, 9 (1994), 124–62; Robyn Carston, 'Implicature, Explicature, and Truth-Theoretic Semantics', in R. M. Kempson (ed.), *Mental Representations: The Interface between Language and Reality* (Cambridge: Cambridge University Press, 1988), 375–409; François Recanati, 'The Pragmatics of What Is Said', *Mind and Language*, 4 (1989), 294–328; and id., 'What Is Said', *Synthese*, 128 (2001), 15–44.

[16] Note, I here give only a necessary, not a sufficient, condition for when the assertion of p guarantees the assertion of q. It is not to be assumed that assertion is closed under the relation of necessary, a priori consequence.

sentence counts as an assertion of the proposition that A and B guarantees that it also counts as an assertion of both the proposition that A and the proposition that B, each of which is a necessary and a priori consequence of the conjunctive proposition. Similarly, the fact that assertive utterances of (7a) and (8a) count as assertions of the propositions semantically expressed by (7b) and (8b) (relative to an assignment of the referent of the name to 'y'), guarantees that these utterances also count as assertions of the associated propositions expressed by (7c) and (8c) (relative to the same assignment).

(7a) Senator Clinton represents New York.
(7b) [the x: x is a senator & x = y] represents New York.
(7c) y represents New York.
(8a) Ralph knows that Senator Clinton represents New York.
(8b) Ralph knows that [the x: x is a senator & x = y] represents New York.
(8c) Ralph knows that y represents New York.

To assert the proposition expressed by (7b) is, in effect, to assert of Hillary Clinton that she both is a senator and represents New York, which includes asserting that she represents New York. To assert the proposition expressed by (8b) is, in effect, to assert of Hillary that Ralph knows that she both is a senator and represents New York, which includes asserting that Ralph knows that she represents New York. In each of these cases, the proposition q (expressed by (7c) or (8c)) asserted as a result of asserting the proposition p (expressed by (7b) or (8b)) is a trivial, necessary, and a priori consequence of p.

In order for this pattern of reasoning to be universally applicable to assertive utterances of sentences containing partially descriptive names, it would have to be the case that for any sentence S(n) containing such a name n of an object o, if S(v) resulted from S(n) by replacing one or more occurrences of n with the variable v, then the proposition expressed by S(v) relative to an assignment of o to v would be a necessary and a priori consequence of the proposition semantically expressed by S(n). Of course, this is not so. Three illustrative classes for which this generalization fails are those in (9):

(9a) negations of simple sentences containing n (within the scope of negation)
(9b) negations of attitude ascriptions α *says/believes/knows that . . . n . . .*
(9c) attitude ascriptions α *just learned/realized that . . . n . . .*

Sentences of these types raise the possibility of exportation failure—i.e. of there being sentences S(n) and contexts involving competent speaker–hearers in which one who assertively utters S(n) asserts the proposition it semantically expresses **without** asserting the proposition expressed by S(v), relative to an assignment of the referent o of n to v. Any sentences that do allow this constitute instances in which P1 fails to generalize. Our next task will be to examine sentences of the types (9a), (9b), and (9c) to determine whether assertive utterances of them do give rise to exportation failure, and hence whether P1 really does fail to generalize in these cases.

Negations of Simple Sentences: Examples of Type (9a)

We consider the case of Ralph, who has heard and seen pictures of Hillary Rodham Clinton, when she was First Lady, and who has read about Senator Clinton from New York, but who does not know that Senator Clinton is the former First Lady, or that Senator Clinton's name is *Hillary Rodham Clinton.* Ralph understands, accepts, and assertively utters sentence (10a), which semantically expresses the proposition indicated by (10b), and may roughly be paraphrased as (10c).[17]

(10a) Hillary Rodham Clinton is not Senator Clinton.

(10b) Hillary Rodham Clinton $\neq$ [the z: z is a senator & z = y] (relative to an assignment of H.R.C. to 'y').

(10c) It is not the case that there is a unique person who is both a senator and identical with H.R.C., and who is identical with H.R.C.

The corresponding proposition (11b), semantically expressed by (11a),

(11a) Hillary Rodham Clinton $\neq$ Hillary Rodham Clinton

(11b) $<$ Neg $<$ Identity, $<$ HRC, HRC$>>>$

is neither a necessary nor an a priori consequence of the proposition semantically expressed by (10a) (since the former is true in any circumstance in which Hillary Clinton is not a senator, whereas the latter is not). The question to be answered is whether in asserting, and expressing his belief in, the former

---

[17] As before, I represent the partially descriptive name as a description, which I let occupy an argument place for an n-adic predicate. Although I leave open the possibility that these descriptions are generalized quantifiers, I do not presuppose this or any other particular analysis. The one thing I insist on in discussing (10), and the later examples built upon it, is that however the descriptions corresponding to partially descriptive names are analyzed, occurrences of them in the negative identity sentences that appear below are to be understood as within the scope of the negation operator in the clause. Take this to be part of the stipulation of the cases.

(contingently false) proposition, Ralph asserts, and expresses a belief in, the latter (necessarily false) proposition.

The details of the case are roughly as follows: When Ralph assertively utters (10a), he asserts the proposition it semantically expresses, which is necessarily equivalent to the singular proposition that Hillary is not a senator. It is because Ralph accepts the sentence *Hillary Rodham Clinton is not a senator*, and thereby believes this singular proposition, that he assertively utters (10a).[18] However, he also believes of Hillary that she is a senator, since this is part of what is involved in his accepting the sentence *Senator Clinton exists* and believing the proposition it expresses. These facts, together with Ralph's assertive utterance of (10a), may make it clear to everyone in the conversation that he would accept (12) (when the first occurrence of *Clinton* is taken by him to be a linguistically simple name for the senator).

(12) Clinton is a senator, but she is not Hillary Rodham Clinton.

If it is clear that Ralph would accept (12) while taking its second conjunct to express the singular proposition (11b), then he may very well believe, and be taken by conversation participants to believe, that proposition. Since all of this is pretty obvious, that proposition may even count as having been asserted by Ralph, in which case P1 **can** be generalized to include this example. On this account, the reason the singular proposition (11b) is asserted is not that it is an obvious consequence of the proposition the speaker was primarily interested in asserting (which in this case is also the proposition semantically expressed by the sentence uttered); rather, it counts as asserted because it is an obvious consequence of this together with everything else that is both relevant and obvious in the context of utterance. As is so often the case, there may be quibbles about what is both relevant and obvious enough to be included in what has been asserted by the speaker. For this reason, some might resist the conclusion that proposition (11b) is asserted in this case. Still, since neither view is entirely obvious, the most we can say is that this example does **not** provide a clear, uncontroversial instance of the failure of P1 to generalize. The same may be said of other sentences of type (9a).

---

[18] In this and other sections where I examine whether sentences containing partially descriptive names provide cases of failure of P1 to generalize, I ignore possible descriptive enrichments corresponding to linguistically simple names in a sentence. The issue of whether such enrichments give rise to failures of P1 to generalize is taken up later.

Negations of Certain Attitude Ascriptions: Examples of Type (9*b*)

Next, we continue the story of the previous section by considering the examples (13) and (14).

(13*a*) Ralph doesn't know/believe that Senator Clinton is a former First Lady.

(13*b*) Ralph doesn't know/believe that [the z: z is a senator & z = y] is a former First Lady (relative to an assignment of H.R.C. to the variable 'y').

(14*a*) Ralph doesn't know/believe that Hillary Rodham Clinton is a former First Lady.

(14*b*) $<$Neg $<$ knowledge/belief, $<$ Ralph, $<$Being a former First Lady, HRC$>>>>$.

The proposition (14*b*), semantically expressed by (14*a*), is neither a necessary nor an a priori consequence of the proposition indicated by (13*b*), which is semantically expressed by (13*a*). Since Ralph doesn't accept any sentence that characterizes someone as being both a senator and a former First Lady, he does not believe, and so does not know, the proposition semantically expressed by (15*a*).

(15*a*) Senator Clinton is a former First Lady.

(15*b*) Hillary Rodham Clinton is a former First Lady.

However, since he does understand and accept (15*b*), he believes—and may even know—the proposition semantically expressed by (15*b*). Hence (13*a, b*) are true even though (14*a, b*) are false. Ralph does, of course, believe, of Hillary (i) that she is a former First Lady (in virtue of understanding and accepting (15*b*)), and (ii) that she is a senator (in virtue of understanding and accepting *Senator Clinton exists*). However, he does not believe that she has the property P expressed by (16), or even that anyone does, which is, in effect, something he would have to believe if he were to believe the proposition semantically expressed by (15*a*).[19]

(16) λx [x is a senator and x is a former First Lady].

Since (13*a, b*) are true, while (14*a, b*) are false, it would be quite surprising if asserting the **true** proposition semantically expressed by (13*a, b*) invariably involved

[19] If we treat *Senator Clinton* as a generalized quantifier, then (on one familiar analysis) (15*a*) will semantically express the proposition that predicates the property of being a property of a unique individual who is both a senator and H.R.C. of the property of being a former First Lady. We may take it that believing this proposition involves believing that someone (in fact H.R.C.) is both a senator and a former First Lady. Although I don't presuppose any specific analysis of partially descriptive names, I do presuppose that any adequate analysis will give this result.

also asserting the **false** proposition (14*b*). However, I see no reason why it should. On the contrary, if Mary were to assertively utter (13*a*) she might say something true without thereby saying anything false, and in particular, without asserting the false (14*b*).

This result constitutes a failure of P1 to fully generalize, since Mary, who assertively utters (13*a*), does not assert the singular proposition expressed by

(17) Ralph doesn't know/believe that y is a former First Lady

relative to an assignment of the referent, H.R.C., of the partially descriptive name *Senator Clinton* to 'y', and so does not say of H.R.C. that Ralph doesn't know or believe that she is a former First Lady.[20] Of course this "failure" is not a bad thing; it simply means that we must be careful in formulating our theory to restrict P1 to the cases in which it is correct.

Related Attitude Ascriptions: Examples of Type (9*c*)

Our final example involving partially descriptive names is a simple extension of the example in the previous section. (It is included to show that the sentences we are interested in do not all contain the negation operator, or other overtly negative expressions.) Imagine that after long being ignorant about the matter, Ralph finally discovers that Senator Clinton is the former First Lady, Hillary Rodham Clinton. Learning of this, Mary reports Ralph's discovery by assertively uttering (18*a*), thereby asserting the true proposition semantically expressed by (18*b*), relative to an assignment of H.R.C. to 'y', without asserting the false proposition expressed by (18*c*), relative to an assignment of H.R.C. to 'y'.

(18*a*) Ralph just learned that Senator Clinton is the former First Lady.
(18*b*) Ralph just learned that [the z: z is a senator & z = y] is a former First Lady.
(18*c*) Ralph just learned that y is a former First Lady.

Here, I assume that the proposition semantically expressed by *Ralph just learned that S* is true with respect to a context of utterance C (and assignment A of values to variables free in S) if and only if (i) until just prior to the time of C, Ralph did not believe the proposition semantically expressed by S (with respect

---

[20] Here I assume without argument that the reason she doesn't assert this is not that there is a conversational implicature which defeats some presumption that it is asserted.

to C and A), but (ii) at t Ralph has come to believe that proposition. In the scenario imagined, (18a) satisfies this condition, and so is true. By contrast, (18c) is false (relative to an assignment of H.R.C. to 'y'), since Ralph has long believed of H.R.C. that she is a former First Lady. Again, this constitutes a failure of P1 to fully generalize when partially descriptive names are involved. As before, however, there is nothing wrong with this result. Surely, someone who assertively utters (18a) in the sort of case we have imagined may say something true without thereby saying anything false. Since we want a theory to be consistent with this fact, we want our theory to limit the range of P1.

Lessons for Linguistically Simple Names: Apparent Failures of P1 to Fully Generalize, and Counterexamples to P2

In this section I will explain how the results of the previous section may be extended to cases involving linguistically simple names. In particular, I will argue that in a certain range of examples in which a sentence S(n) contains a linguistically simple name n, a speaker who assertively utters S(n) with the primary intention of asserting a descriptively enriched proposition p—which results from filling in the gaps accompanying occurrences of the referent of n in the propositional matrix semantically associated with S(n)—may succeed in asserting p **without** asserting the singular proposition q expressed by S(v) relative to an assignment of the referent of n to the variable v. Since q is also the (unenriched) proposition semantically expressed by S(n) (according to P3), these cases constitute not only failures of P1 to fully generalize, and but also counterexamples to P2.

These results are obtained in cases in which the unenriched proposition q semantically expressed by S(n) is **not** a necessary and a priori consequence of either (i) the descriptively enriched proposition p which it is the speaker's primary intention to assert, or (ii) p together with other obvious and relevant shared background assumptions at the time of utterance. In these cases, the successful assertion of p does not guarantee that q has also been asserted. Absent an antecedent commitment to the idea that in normal contexts (without defeating conversational implicatures, and the like) the proposition semantically expressed by the sentence uttered is always asserted, we have no reason to think that anything else guarantees that q has been asserted. Since, as we shall see, it would be counterintuitive to suppose that q has been asserted in the cases in question, we have positive reason to reject P2 in favor of P2*.

As with partially descriptive names, I will discuss examples of assertive utterances of sentences of the linguistic types indicated in (9b) and (9c), only this time the names will be linguistically simple. However, I will not discuss examples involving assertive utterances of sentences of type (9a)—negations of simple sentences containing an occurrence of a name n within the scope of negation. As we have already seen, when n is partially descriptive, sentences of this type do not provide clear instances of the failure of P1 to generalize. The same is true when n is linguistically simple; hence, these sentences don't provide clear counterexamples to P2, either. For this reason, we will concentrate on the interaction of propositional attitude constructions and linguistically simple names. In each case, it will be assumed that the speaker's primary intention in assertively uttering the attitude ascription (or its negation) is to assert a descriptively enriched proposition obtained by adding contextually salient descriptive information associated with the names to the propositional matrix semantically expressed by the sentence uttered.

Counterexamples to P2 Involving Linguistically Simple Names

First, an example of type (9b). The scene is the annual newcomers' party at the Princeton philosophy department, where Mary has been introduced to a distinguished white-haired gentleman called 'Peter Hempel'. Not knowing who he is, she responds a few minutes later to another newcomer's question "Is he Carl Hempel?", by assertively uttering, *No, Peter Hempel isn't Carl Hempel*. The context of utterance is such that in assertively uttering

(3a) Peter Hempel isn't Carl Hempel

Mary asserts that the man, Peter Hempel, standing over there, isn't the famous philosopher Carl Hempel. This proposition, which we may take to be represented by (5a), is semantically expressed by (5b), relative to an assignment of Mr Hempel to 'z' and 'w'.

(5a) $<$Neg $<$Identity, $<<$Man standing over there, Mr Hempel$>$, $<$ Famous philosopher, Mr Hempel$>>>>$.

(5b) $\sim([\text{the x}: (\text{x is a man standing over there} \& \text{x} = \text{z})] = [\text{the y}: \text{y is a famous philosopher} \& \text{y} = \text{w}]).$

This is the information that Mary primarily intends to get across; however, it is not the proposition (3c) semantically expressed by the sentence she uttered.

(3c) $<$Neg $<$Identity, $<$ Mr Hempel, Mr Hempel $>>>$.

Although Mary believes the trivially true proposition

(6c) $<$Identity $<$ Mr Hempel, Mr Hempel $>>$

of which (3c) is the negation, she does not believe the true, but non-trivial proposition

(6b) $<$Identity, $<<$Man standing over there, Mr Hempel$>$, $<$ Famous philosopher, Mr Hempel$>>>$

of which (5a) is the negation.

Suppose, next, that someone else at the party who is in the know about Mr Hempel reports Mary's ignorance by assertively uttering

(6a) Mary doesn't know that Peter Hempel is Carl Hempel

with the primary intention of asserting and conveying the information that Mary doesn't know that the man, Peter Hempel, standing over there, is the famous philosopher Carl Hempel. This speaker **truly** asserts that Mary doesn't stand in the knowledge relation to (6b). He does not also **falsely** assert that Mary doesn't stand in the knowledge relation to (6c); no ordinary conversational participant—not even those fully apprised of Peter Hempel's identity—would dream of accusing the speaker of **falsely** asserting that Mary doesn't know of the pair consisting of Mr Hempel and Mr Hempel that the former is the latter. But if the speaker doesn't assert that Mary doesn't know (6c), then the speaker doesn't assert the proposition **semantically** expressed by the sentence (6a) that he assertively utters.

Here, the proposition (6e), which is semantically expressed by (6a), is neither a necessary nor an a priori consequence of the descriptively enriched proposition (6d), which the speaker intended, successfully, to assert and convey.

(6d) $<$ Neg $<$ Knowledge, $<$ Mary, 6b $>>>$.
(6e) $<$ Neg $<$ Knowledge, $<$ Mary, 6c $>>>$.

As a result, the speaker's assertion of (6d) provides no reason, in and of itself, to suppose that (6e) has also been asserted. This means that one can retain principle P2 only if one can establish that there is a conversational implicature which defeats what would otherwise be a presumption that (6e) is asserted. Since I have already indicated the difficulty inherent in such a strategy, I take this example to provide evidence of the failure of P1 to fully generalize, the falsity of P2, and the truth of P2*.

Our final example, of type (9c), is a simple extension of this case. Upon learning of Mary's ignorance, Paul sets her straight by assertively uttering (2a), *Peter Hempel is Carl Hempel*, thereby asserting and conveying the information that the man, Peter Hempel, standing over there is the famous philosopher Carl Hempel. Gil, overhearing the conversation, reports Mary's new-found knowledge by assertively uttering (19a) with the intention of asserting and conveying the descriptively enriched, **true** proposition (19c) expressed by (19b), relative to an assignment of Mr Hempel to the variables 'z' and 'w'.

(19a) Mary just learned that Peter Hempel is Carl Hempel.
(19b) Mary just learned that [the x: (x is a man standing over there & x $=$ z)] $=$ [the y: y is a famous philosopher & y $=$ w].
(19c) $<$ Just learned, $<$ Mary, 6b $>>$.

It was no part of Gil's intention to assert or convey the **false** proposition (19d), which characterizes Mary as having just learned, as opposed to having long known, that Mr Hempel is Mr Hempel.

(19d) $<$ Just learned, $<$ Mary, 6c $>>$.

Nor do his hearers, who know that (19d) is false, take him to have asserted it. Since this proposition is the semantic content of the sentence (19a), which Gil assertively uttered, we have another strongly intuitive counterexample to P2 that is fully consistent with the revised principle P2*. More precisely, we have this, absent the ability to establish what seems to me to be the questionable claim that there is a conversational implicature that cancels what would otherwise be the presumption that one who assertively utters (19a) should be taken as asserting (19d). In light of this, shouldn't we reject P2 in favor of P2*?

Well, yes, but I didn't always think so. Although I was aware of these problems with P2 when writing *Beyond Rigidity*, I was reluctant to abandon it. I was convinced that there must be some reasonably close relationship between the semantic content of a sentence and that which is asserted and conveyed by utterances of it in normal contexts. Since I hadn't yet formulated P2*, I couldn't see what that relationship might be, if it weren't the one expressed by P2. Now that a reasonable alternative has been put on the table, this consideration no longer has force, and our pre-theoretic intuitions about what is asserted and conveyed by utterances of sentences like (6a) and (19a) can be given their proper weight. Hence, I now believe that P2 should be rejected in favor of P2*.

However, before resting with this conclusion, it is necessary to address one further argument. In *Beyond Rigidity* I was not content merely to insist on P2 despite apparent counterexamples like (19a). In addition, I offered an independent argument that in assertively uttering (19a) the speaker **must** assert the proposition (19d) that it semantically expresses, in addition to the descriptively enriched proposition that is the primary assertion made by the utterance. This argument must be disarmed before we can replace P2 with P2*.

The Argument from *Beyond Rigidity*

The argument from *Beyond Rigidity* is based on an example almost exactly like the one built around (19). In giving the argument I will use the formulation and the numbering from the book. In the example, Gil assertively utters (38) with the intention of asserting and conveying the descriptively enriched proposition expressed by (40).

(38) Mary just learned that Peter Hempel is Carl Hempel.

(40) Mary just learned that our colleague Peter Hempel, standing over there, is the famous philosopher Carl Hempel.

In *Beyond Rigidity* I argued that although Gil succeeds in asserting the true proposition (40), his utterance also counts as the assertion of a false proposition. Here is the argument for that point:

For example, suppose that shortly after his assertive utterance of (38) we were to ask "*Is there some man such that Gil asserted that Mary has just learned that he is Carl Hempel?*" I think that if Gil and his audience were confronted with this question, they would be inclined to agree with the following answer: "*Yes, there is a man, Peter Hempel (standing right over there), such that Gil asserted that Mary just learned that he is Carl Hempel.*" In this way, conversational participants could be brought to recognize the truth of (49).

(49) $\exists x$ (x = Peter Hempel & Gil asserted that Mary just learned that x = Carl Hempel)

Next we might ask, "*But isn't it true that Mary has known for a long time that Carl Hempel is Carl Hempel?*" Surely, the answer to this would be "*Yes*" We might follow this up with: "*Isn't it therefore also true that there is a certain man, Carl Hempel, such that Mary has long believed that he is Carl*

Hempel?" Here again, I think that if ordinary speakers and hearers were to reflect on the matter, they would be inclined to agree that Carl Hempel is such that Mary has long believed that he is Carl Hempel. In this way they could be brought to recognize the truth of (50).

(50) $\exists x\,(x = $ Carl Hempel & Mary has long believed that $x = $ Carl Hempel)

Finally, we remind them of the truth of (51).

(51) Peter Hempel is Carl Hempel

But surely, we would point out, (52) is a logical consequence of (49)–(51); therefore since they are true, it is true as well.

(52) $\exists x\,[x = $ Peter Hempel & $x = $ Carl Hempel & (Gil asserted that Mary just learned that $x = $ Carl Hempel) & (Mary has long believed that $x = $ Carl Hempel)]

This means that there is a certain man such that Gil asserted that Mary just learned that he is Carl Hempel even though, in fact, Mary has long believed that he is Carl Hempel. But then, since Gil asserted that Mary has just learned that so and so, when in fact Mary has long believed (and even known) that so and so, it follows that at least one thing that Gil asserted is false.[21]

This argument can easily be extended, since if it is correct, then surely (53*a*) and (53*b*) must also be correct. (I here continue the sequence of numbering of the *Beyond Rigidity* examples.)

(53*a*) $\exists x\,\exists y\,[x = $ Peter Hempel & $y = $ Carl Hempel & (Gil asserted that Mary just learned that $x = y$)].

(53*b*) $\exists x\,[x = $ Peter Hempel & $x = $ Carl Hempel & (Gil asserted that Mary just learned that $x = x$)].

But then, if the propositions semantically expressed by these sentences are true, Gil must have asserted the false proposition that is semantically expressed by the sentence he uttered. That is how I previously sought to defuse the objection to P2.

Although the argument can appear compelling, I no longer believe that it is successful. The natural response to it is, I think, to grant the force of each step, while retaining one's conviction that the conclusion cannot be correct. Gil

---

[21] *Beyond Rigidity*, 233–5.

simply didn't say anything false when he assertively uttered (38). If this is right, then we should look for subtle confusions along the way that may lend one or more of the steps an initial, but misleading, appearance of validity. I now think that we can find two such confusions.

The first significant problem involves the move to (49). In order to assess this move, we have to determine what (49) is to be inferred from. The argument presupposes that conversational participants will grant the truth of the proposition expressed by what I will here number as (38a).

(38a) Gil asserted that Mary just learned that Peter Hempel is Carl Hempel.

But which proposition is that? Are the conversational participants implicitly asked to endorse the proposition **semantically** expressed by (38a), or are they asked to endorse the descriptively enriched proposition

(38b) Gil asserted that Mary just learned that our colleague Peter Hempel, standing over there, is the famous philosopher Carl Hempel

that they would primarily intend to assert were they to use (38a) to report Gil's remark? Although the argument fails to address this question, the answer to it is crucial.

Even though the truth of (49) follows from the truth of the proposition semantically expressed by (38a), it **does not** follow from the truth of (38b). Because of this, one bad, but nevertheless initially persuasive, reason for acquiescing in the move to (49) may be a failure to distinguish the austere proposition that sentence (38a) semantically expresses from the descriptively enriched proposition (38b) it would naturally be used to assert. A person who fails to make this distinction may focus on the latter proposition when judging Gil to have asserted a truth, while focusing on the former proposition when making the inference to (49)—wrongly concluding, thereby, that (49) is validly inferred from a true premise.

A second source of potential confusion involves (49) itself, or its English equivalent, (49a).

(49a) There is a man, Peter Hempel, such that Gil asserted that Mary just learned that he is Carl Hempel.

In the previous paragraph I assumed that the proposition corresponding to these sentences in the argument from *Beyond Rigidity* is the proposition they semantically express. However, it is conceivable that these sentences might themselves be used to assert the further, descriptively enhanced, proposition indicated by (49b).

(49*b*) There is a man, Peter Hempel, such that Gil asserted that he, our colleague standing over there, is the famous philosopher Carl Hempel.

This proposition is clearly true, while being an obvious consequence of the descriptively enriched proposition (38*b*) that conversational participants would assert if they used (38*a*) to report Gil's remark.[22] Since the conversational context is one in which participants are invited to endorse (49*a*) on the basis of an implicit inference from their characterization of what Gil asserted, it is conceivable that they might use the sentence (49*a*) to assert the proposition (49*b*). On this understanding, the move from (38*b*) to (49) is fully acceptable, as is an analogous move to (50). However, on this way of understanding sentences (49) and (50)—namely as sentences used to assert one or more descriptively enriched propositions—the false proposition semantically expressed by (52) does **not** follow from (49–51).[23] That being so, we have no argument that in assertively uttering (38) Gil asserted anything false, let alone the false proposition semantically expressed by (38).

   This completes my response to the argument from *Beyond Rigidity*. Although the example is a difficult one, I have come to believe that the account just presented is the best that can be given. Its virtues are: (i) that it preserves our strong pre-theoretic intuition that in assertively uttering (38) Gil did not say anything false, (ii) that it explains the plausibility of the individual steps in the argument by indicating the senses in which each is valid, and (iii) that it vindicates our sense that there is nevertheless something wrong with the argument as a whole by indicating why there is no single interpretation on which its premises are true and each of its steps are truth-preserving. I therefore reject the argument quoted from *Beyond Rigidity*, and I accept the conclusion that this example, and the others discussed in the previous section, provide evidence that P1 fails to fully generalize, that P2 is false, and that P2* should be adopted as a replacement of P2. I will close with a brief discussion of ways in which the idea behind the new principle might profitably be extended and applied to a broader range of cases.

---

[22] Think of proposition (49*b*) as expressed by a sentence that comes from *Gil asserted that Mary just learned that [the x: x is our colleague standing over there & x = z] = [the y: y is a famous philosopher & y = w]* by existentially generalizing on 'z'.

[23] Perhaps (52), or an English equivalent, could itself be used to assert a true descriptively enriched proposition in which different descriptive enrichments accompany the final two occurrences of the variable. That would be rather unnatural, but even if it is possible, it doesn't help the argument, since from such an understanding of (52) we don't get the conclusion that Gil has asserted anything false.

Semantic Incompleteness and Pragmatic Enrichment

As stated, P2* applies only to indexical-free sentences. There was no principled reason for this restriction; it was adopted solely to simplify the discussion. The idea of contextually determined, descriptive enrichment of singular propositions—involving either the mechanism of gappy propositional matrices or its equivalent mentioned in footnotes 10 and 14—can easily be extended to familiar treatments of indexicals, such as that of David Kaplan.[24] More important than any such mechanical extension of P2*, however, is the way in which the guiding idea behind it meshes with certain kinds of indexicality.

The guiding idea is that the meaning of an expression constrains its contributions to the assertions made by normal, literal utterances of sentences containing it, without always fully determining those contributions. This is just what we find when we consider demonstratives like *he, she, that, then, there, we,* and *now*. A natural way of understanding these expressions is to see their meanings as constraining, but not fully determining, their referents in different contexts. Oversimplifying, and idealizing a bit, the referent of *he* is constrained to be male, the referent of *she* is constrained to be female, the referent of *that* may be any salient non-animate thing, the referent of *then* must be a time, the referent of *there* must be a place, the referent of *we* is a group that contains the agent (the speaker in cases in which *we* is uttered), and the referent of *now* is some stretch of time including the present moment.[25] To know the meanings of these terms is, roughly, to know these constraints, and to know that when one uses the terms in simple sentences one says of their referents that they are so and so. Everything else used to determine the referents of the expressions in different contexts, and to fill out the assertions made by utterances of sentences containing them, is non-semantic, extra-linguistic, pragmatic information.

These demonstratives differ from proper names in two significant ways. First, there is a significant contrast between proper names and all indexicals—including both pure indexicals, like the first-person singular pronoun and certain temporal

---

[24] D. Kaplan, 'Demonstratives', in J. Almog, J. Perry, and H. Wettstein (eds.), *Themes from Kaplan* (New York: Oxford University Press, 1989).

[25] There are, of course, extended uses of some of these demonstratives, as when one refers to a ship as *she* even though the ship is not female, or says of one's favorite team *We won the game* even though one is not really a member of the group that won the game. In addition, one may say, while listening to a piece of music "Here is where the tubas come in, and there is where the trumpets come in" without, arguably, referring to a spatial location. As for 'now', uses of it in narratives invoking the specious present need not refer to the time at which the narrative is given. I leave aside the question of how one accommodates such uses. (Thanks to the referees for bringing some of this material to my attention.)

indexicals like *today*, and the kinds of demonstratives we have just been discussing. Whereas there is a natural sense in which the semantics of a (disambiguated) sentence **n is F** by itself determines a complete proposition, independent of any contextual contribution (in the manner of P3 above), the semantics of *i is F* is never sufficient to determine a proposition without some contextual contribution to the content of the indexical i. Second, there is a contrast between the demonstratives mentioned above, on the one hand, and both proper names and pure indexicals, on the other, involving the greater extent and variety of contextual supplementation with demonstratives. With names and pure indexicals, reference is secured without pragmatic supplementation. In the case of (linguistically simple) names, their referents are their meanings. In the case of pure indexicals, their meanings together with fixed parameters of the context in which they are used—e.g. the agent, plus the time and place of the utterance—fully determine their referents, which may be taken to be their semantic contents relative to the contexts. In both cases, descriptive enrichment (based on speaker intentions and salient assumptions in the conversational background) may associate extra, pragmatic information with the referents that have already been determined semantically—thereby contributing to the propositions asserted by utterances of sentences containing names or pure indexicals. However, the referents themselves are fixed prior to any such pragmatic supplementation. This is not so in the case of demonstratives, where any descriptive enrichment of the sort that occurs with names and pure indexicals comes on top of a prior **pragmatic** completion that is needed to provide the referents of demonstratives in the first place.[26] The lesson here is that the conception of meaning, and its relation to assertion, that stands behind P2*, and the analyses I have given of examples containing proper names, is part of a much broader and more pervasive picture of language and language use.

My final illustration of this picture involves possessive noun phrases. A striking feature of these noun phrases is the staggering variety of interpretations they may receive. Here is a sample: one may use *Sam's sibling* to talk about a person with the same parents as Sam; one may use *Sam's leg* to talk about a part of Sam, *Mary's wish* to talk about something she wishes for, *Susie's property* to talk about property she owns, *Martin's watch* to talk about a watch he owns, or a watch he wears; one may use *Barbara's book* to talk about a book she wrote, a book she

---

[26] For this reason it is natural to deny that sentences containing these demonstratives semantically determine complete propositions, even relative to contexts. See Bach, 'You Don't Say', sect. 5.1, and Kenneth Taylor, 'Sex, Breakfast, and Descriptus Interruptus', *Synthese*, 128 (2001), 45–61, for discussions of this issue.

wants to write, a book she is reading, a book she owns, or a book she has requested from the reference desk; one may use *Martha's party* to talk about a party for Martha or a party she is giving; one may use *Gopal's language* to talk about a language he speaks, a language he has decided to study, or a language he invented; one may use *Tuesday's meeting* to talk about a meeting that will occur on Tuesday; one may use *the argument's premises* to talk about the starting points of the argument, and *the argument's conclusion* to talk about the proposition to be inferred from the premises of the argument; and one can use *John's car* to talk about a car he owns, a car he is driving, a car he has rented, a car he is riding in, the car he arrived in, or a car he wagered on in the Indianapolis 500.

This is not ambiguity; it is pragmatic contextual supplementation. Call it indexicality, if you like, but if so, recognize that it is of the demonstrative sort, with relatively few semantic constraints on the relationship between the nominal possessor and the nominally possessed.[27] To know the meaning of the construction *NP's N* is, at a first approximation, to know that the referent of the possessor noun phrase is characterized as standing in some not too heavily constrained relation to something to which N applies. Which relation this is in any given case is not something for semantics to decide; it is determined by pragmatic features of the context of utterance. Accordingly, we should **not** view the semantic content of a sentence like *John's car is a Corvette* as being a complete proposition, let alone one that is asserted in all normal contexts in which the sentence is assertively uttered. Rather, the semantic content of this sentence is something more like a propositional matrix with a gap in it to be filled by a contextually determined relation (meeting relatively minimal semantic constraints) that the speaker is claiming to hold between John and a certain car. Thus, what is asserted by an utterance of this sentence is not the proposition the sentence semantically expresses, but a proposition that arises from the semantic content of the sentence by adding features of the right sort that are obvious and salient in the conversational background.

I have argued that essentially this process of contextual supplementation is also the key to understanding the relationship between the semantic content of sentences containing proper names and the propositions that those sentences are used to assert. If I am right, this process, relating semantic content to assertion, is a ubiquitous one in language. This, in my view, is the thing we most need to better understand, if we are to continue to make progress in natural language semantics, pragmatics, and the relationship between the two.

---

[27] For a discussion of some constraints that do appear to be imposed by the possessive construction, see Chris Baker, *Possessive Descriptions* (Stanford, Calif.: CSLI, 1995).

In Defense of Non-Sentential Assertion

Robert J. Stainton

In what follows, I introduce a pragmatics-oriented approach to non-sentential speech, and defend it against two recent attacks. Among other things, I will rehearse and elaborate a defense against the idea that much, or even all, of such speech is actually syntactically elliptical—and hence should be treated semantically, rather than pragmatically. The chapter is structured as follows. In Section 1 I introduce the phenomenon, contrast semantic versus pragmatic approaches to it, and explain some of what hinges on which approach is taken. In Section 2 I present Jason Stanley's objections to the pragmatics-oriented approach, and his counterproposal that all truth-conditional effects of context on what is asserted can be traced to elements of underlying structure. In Section 3 I canvass numerous varieties of ellipsis. The focus in Section 3 will be on what kind of "ellipsis" is required if the pragmatics-oriented approach is actually to be rejected rather than being recast in other terms. In Section 4 I respond to

Work on this chapter was supported by a grant from the Social Sciences and Humanities Research Council of Canada, held jointly by myself and Ray Elugardo of the University of Oklahoma, and covering the years 1999–2002. I would like here to express my great debt to Professor Elugardo for many useful discussions, and of numerous issues, surrounding non-sentential speech. I'm also grateful, in particular, for his help on the present chapter. Thanks also to Ash Asudeh, Alex Barber, Ellen Barton, Emma Borg, Lenny Clapp, Steven Davis, Corinne Iten, Dave Matheson, Jason Merchant, Ljiljana Progovac, Aryn Pyke, Zoltán Szabó, and Catherine Wearing for very useful comments on a previous draft. This chapter is dedicated to my daughters, Moonisah and Saima—both because they speak sub-sententially all the time, and because they unknowingly encourage me to maintain a healthy perspective on debates about semantics versus pragmatics.

Stanley, and show that the two known varieties of ellipsis which would turn the trick for the semantics-oriented approach are not empirically plausible when applied to the cases in question. In further defense of this conclusion, in Section 5 I present a family of syntactic arguments, from Peter Ludlow and others, in favor of ellipsis (and a concomitant semantics-based approach), and I give replies to these latter arguments. In Section 6, the final section, I return explicitly to issues of the semantics–pragmatics boundary, and I draw some larger lessons about what sub-sentential speech does and does not entail— including in particular what it does not entail vis à vis the distinctiveness of linguistic communication, and the viability of truth-conditional semantics.

1. Introduction: Non-Sentences and the Semantics–Pragmatics Boundary

Let me begin with the phenomenon to be explained, whether semantically or pragmatically. It seems that agents can produce ordinary words and phrases (more precisely, lexically headed phrases, though I'll abbreviate to the shorter term in what follows) and thereby perform speech acts. In particular, what will be the focus of this chapter, they apparently can make assertions while speaking sub-sententially. Spelling this out a little, speakers seemingly can and do utter maximal projections of lexical items: noun phrases, verb phrases, prepositional phrases, etc. (This includes, of course, cases where the phrase consists of a single word.) And the things they utter can be of semantic type $<e>$, $<e,t>$, $<<e,t>, t>$ and so on. Hence speakers need not, and do not, only utter inflectional phrases (i.e. maximal projections of inflectional elements like tense and subject agreement), which projections are more commonly known as sentences in the syntactic sense, when performing speech acts. Nor do they only utter things of type $<t>$, also known as sentences in the semantic sense, when performing genuine speech acts.[1]

Here is an attested case in point. Meera was spooning out strawberry jam onto her toast, and produced (or, more safely, appeared to produce) the phrase 'Chunks of strawberries'. Anita nodded, and (seemingly) added 'Rob's mom'. It appears that Meera asserted something like *This jam contains chunks of strawberries*, while Anita asserted something like *Rob's mom made it*. In both cases, they appear to have made true statements while using something sub-sentential. Or again, to take a case I have discussed elsewhere (Stainton 1997a: 61), it seems that

---

[1] I discuss various senses of 'sentence' in Stainton (2000).

someone could hold up a letter and say 'From Spain', thereby claiming, about the displayed letter, that it comes from Spain.

Now, it's crucial that in the above description of the phenomenon there was regular reference to what *seemed* or *appeared* to be the case. It's important to speak in this manner because there are two quite different ways to react to such appearances. One may take the appearances at face value, and conclude that speakers really do utter plain old words or phrases, and thereby perform speech acts. Or one may treat the appearances as illusory—saying that where a speech act really is performed, the thing produced isn't really a word or phrase after all. Of particular interest here, these two ways of reacting assign different weights to semantics and pragmatics. The pragmatics-oriented approach takes the appearances at face value, and concludes that pragmatics does rather more, even in literal conversation, than is sometimes allowed—in particular, pragmatics provides the missing real-world object (or property or whatever) which joins with the linguistic content of the word or phrase to yield what is asserted, stated, or claimed. The semantics-oriented approach denies the appearances, and maintains that syntax, and with it semantics, are doing more than what meets the eye.

Let me spell out the two competing approaches a bit, before turning briefly to the question of why it matters which one is correct. Starting with the pragmatics-oriented approach, the view would be roughly this: Speakers really do utter unembedded lexical projections (including single words), with both the syntax and semantics of such items. Applied to the above examples, the view would be that the speaker tokened, and the hearer recovered, the very things which occur embedded in (1) through (3)—though on the occasion in question they appeared *un*embedded in any larger linguistic structure:

(1) [Chunks of strawberries] are expensive.
(2) [Rob's mom] lives in Toronto.
(3) I flew here [from Spain].

According to the pragmatic story, in order to treat the speaker as genuinely communicating, in a relevant way, the hearer must look for a proposition which the speaker meant to convey. After all, Meera could not have intended to convey only what the ordinary phrase 'chunks of strawberries' literally encodes in English, since what it encodes is not a proposition; nor could the speaker of 'From Spain' have meant the property λx[from Spain (x)], which is more or less what that prepositional phrase expresses. The hearer, therefore, must not only recover the semantic content of the word or phrase, but must also draw on linguistic and non-linguistic information, from context, to supply the missing property (as in the former example) or the missing object (as in the latter example). (I stress: on the pragmatics-oriented view, what is intended by the speaker and recovered by the hearer is a missing *property* or *object*, not a missing predicate or referring term. This contrast will loom large in what follows.) The sub-sentential speaker intends the hearer to do all of this; and said speaker's intentions play a key role in determining both the content and the illocutionary force of the utterance. Thus it is that the utterance can be an assertion of a complete proposition, even though the word or phrase uttered and recovered does not itself encode a proposition, even relative to a context. In short, on this approach, pragmatics fills the major gap between (*a*) linguistically encoded content and (*b*) what is conveyed by the speaker.

There are, in the literature, two competing views on how pragmatics fills this gap. Barton (1989 and elsewhere) maintains that there are pragmatic sub-modules that do the job. Specifically, though speaking roughly, she postulates (i) a sub-module of linguistic context, that operates exclusively on the sub-sentence uttered plus prior explicit discourse, and (ii) a sub-module of conversational context, that takes the output of the first sub-module as input, and uses non-linguistic context (provided by vision, olfaction, background knowledge, short-term memory, etc.) to derive what the speaker meant to convey. For Barton, both modules perform non-deductive, context-sensitive inferences, which—as typically happens with inductive and abductive inferences—do not necessarily and determinately yield a single result. Still, in general, the first sub-module is more automatic and rule-driven than the second—applying, for example, to discourse sequences (e.g. non-sentential answers to wh-questions). The alternative approach, pursued in Stainton (1993, 1994, and elsewhere), is to agree with Barton that the "filling in" occurs via non-deductive inference rather than "decoding", but to deny that there are pragmatics *modules* at work—appealing instead to central system processes, inferential processes not specific to language, to bridge the gap.[2] (In contrast, as both Barton and Stainton agree, the language system proper, which is a distinct module for both of them, is conceived as performing purely formal derivations, rather than inferences—which derivations are context-free and determinately yield one or more meanings for the string.) I put aside this in-house dispute here, defending the pragmatics-oriented

---

[2] The pragmatics-oriented theorist obviously owes a concrete story of how the bridging occurs: a general outline is not enough. Within the "pragmatics module" camp, see Barton (1990) for a carefully worked out attempt. Within the non-modular camp, see Stainton (1993, 1994) and (at least with respect to fairly simple cases in which a predicate is used and an object is visually salient) Elugardo and Stainton (2003). This latter paper also addresses in much greater detail the issues surrounding integration of information from non-linguistic modes during speech comprehension.

approach construed broadly to include both sub-varieties. What is worth stressing is that, on either approach, it is pragmatics and not syntax–semantics per se which also triggers the hearer's attempt to fill the gap. Not only is the search carried out by a pragmatic process, it is begun by one. This is clear because sometimes words and phrases are used to do something other than communicate a proposition: e.g. in labels, book titles, lists, and so on. (Or so it seems.) Hence merely producing a word or phrase in isolation cannot trigger the quest for a proposition-meant. Instead, producing them in a situation in which only a proposition would be pragmatically appropriate is key.

Importantly, the pragmatics-oriented theorist need not treat the proposition communicated as merely a variety of implicature, or anything of the sort. For example, it seems perfectly plausible that someone who utters 'From Spain', while demonstrating a letter, does not merely implicate the proposition, about the displayed letter, to the effect that it is from Spain; she actually asserts this. Thus, the pragmatics-oriented approach can be committed to non-sentential *assertions*, not just to non-sentential (but fully propositional) communication.[3]

---

[3] For further discussion of non-sentential speech, including extended discussion of its philosophical implications, the reader is directed to Elugardo and Stainton (2004) and to my earlier papers. Here is a brief synopsis of the latter. In Stainton (1997*a*) I argue, on the basis of non-sentential assertions, that Michael Dummett's (1973) analysis of assertion—according to which, put roughly, an assertion just is the utterance of a declarative sentence under conventionally specified circumstances—cannot be correct. I therefore propose, instead, that the utterer's complex mental state plays a central role in determining that something is an assertion. (A useful and insightful discussion of my critique can be found in Kenyon 1999.) In Stainton (1997*b*) I point out that to arrive at utterance-meaning from expression-meaning it is not sufficient to disambiguate and assign reference to indexicals. This is a point I will try to drive home in the present chapter. I also argue that, assuming the existence of genuine syntactic ellipsis, it is not necessary, for finding literal utterance-meaning, to discover precisely what expression was uttered. In particular, the hearer doesn't need to know whether the speaker uttered an (elliptical) sentence or just a lexical projection to find what was literally asserted—since the correct interpretation could be the same either way. In Stainton (1998*a*), reprinted in Davis and Gillon (forthcoming), I contend that the meaning of quantifier phrases should not be given by a metalinguistic rule which describes the meaning of potential whole sentences containing such phrases; I urge instead that, quantifier phrases being usable without any sentence frame whatever, the appropriate semantics would have them denoting generalized quantifiers. In Stainton (1998*b*), I draw a similar lesson for definite descriptions. In Stainton (2000) I show that the familiar doctrines (*a*) that "only sentences can be used in isolation", and (*b*) that "only sentences have meaning in isolation", each have three quite distinct readings, two of which readings are interesting (but not well supported), and the third of which is well supported (but not interesting). Finally, in Elugardo and Stainton (2001), Ray Elugardo and I argue, this time on the basis of the ability to make less than sentential *arguments*, that there are things other than natural language expressions which have logical forms; and not only that, but said things have their logical forms non-derivatively. For an overview article, see Stainton (2004).

It is, of course, often quite tricky to sort out what is asserted from what is merely conveyed. We have intuitions about such things, including especially intuitions about whether an utterance is lie-prone, and hence truly assertoric. But it's hard to give necessary and sufficient conditions on "assertion-hood" which honor all of those intuitions. (And it's also sometimes hard to know how seriously to take the intuitions, independently of practical reasons for distinguishing assertion from mere communication—a point I return to later in the chapter.) This is equally true when sub-sentential speech is at issue. But a natural first pass at a generalization about sub-sentence cases—which, for the most part, captures the intuitions correctly—goes like this. Sub-sentential expressions are sub-propositional—in the sense that, to arrive at a proposition, they must be supplied with an argument, or they must modify a certain kind of content, or what-have-you. Thus the expression 'From Spain' doesn't express a proposition, and neither does 'Chunks of strawberries', etc. Leaving details aside, what is asserted when a sub-sentence is used communicatively is that proposition which results from minimally saturating the content of the bare phrase actually uttered. Non-asserted content is inferentially arrived at content which goes beyond the minimal proposition, such that the enrichment is forced not by the sub-propositional nature of the thing uttered, but solely by considerations of the *conversational* inadequacies of the propositional result of "saturating".[4] An example may help to illustrate this way of contrasting what is asserted and what is merely conveyed, as applied to sub-sentence use. Consider the following dialogue from *The Presidential Transcripts*, as reported in Barton (1989: 8):

(4) **President Nixon**: Somebody is after him [Maurice Stans] about Vesco. I first read the story briefly in the *Post*. I read, naturally, the first page and turned to the *Times* to read it. The *Times* had in the second paragraph that [Vesco's] money had been returned, but the *Post* didn't have it.

---

[4] I should stress that I take no stand here on the larger issue of whether there is, in every case, only one "minimal proposition" so arrived at. Nor do I intend to claim that the first proposition arrived at is, in every case, the only one literally asserted. For one thing, arguably in sentential speech the "minimal proposition" sometimes isn't asserted, or isn't the only one asserted. Thus what I say here is intended to be consistent with an utterance of 'I've had breakfast' being a literal statement to the effect that "I've had breakfast already today", even if the latter isn't the first proposition accessed. (See Bach (1994*b*) for discussion of such "expansion" cases.) Being a "first pass", I also leave aside the difficult detail of how 'breakfast'-type cases might arise with sub-sentential speech. Presumably, a Sperber and Wilson (1986) style story applies in this case, just as it does in sentential speech: a propositional form which is a "development" of the minimal one is asserted; a propositional form which is produced by something more robust than Sperber and Wilson's "development" is implicated only. That said, laying out a detailed proposal would take me too far a field. (See Stainton 1994 for a bit more.)

John Dean: That is correct.

H. R. Haldeman: The *Post* didn't have it until after you continued to the back section. It is the (adjective omitted) thing I ever saw.

John Dean: Typical.

Here, Dean non-sententially asserts, of the salient event described by Nixon and Haldeman, that it was typical. This is asserted, on the proposed account, rather than merely being implicated, because the content of 'Typical', being an adjective that must apply to some thing or event, would otherwise remain sub-propositional. That content becomes fully propositional, however, as soon as the contextually salient event—i.e. so publishing the Vesco story—is conjoined with this content. So this, and only this, is asserted. Now suppose, as might well have been the case, that Dean in so speaking also conveyed the information that he disapproves of the fact that such events are typical for the *Post*. On the proposed account, this extra content would not be asserted; it would merely be implicated. The reason is that this content goes well beyond the minimal proposition one gets by finding an appropriate content for 'Typical' to combine with. Crucially, what makes the former filling-in-to-arrive-at-what-is-asserted pragmatic is that the saturation is not a matter of linguistic derivation, but is instead a matter of all-purpose inference triggered by the pragmatic unfitness of the sub-propositional content—where, moreover, the inference is based on both linguistic context and other kinds of knowledge.[5] (Indeed, if Elugardo and Stainton 2003 are on the right track, it couldn't be linguistic derivation, because what is arrived at is not an item of natural language syntax—it is a *content*, rather than a syntactic form, that is sought; and it is sought by the agent as a whole.)

Thus ends this brief overview of the pragmatics-oriented approach. Let's turn to the more semantics-heavy approach. It will hold that, in cases of apparent sub-sentential assertion, the expression type which the speaker actually tokened does not simply encode an object, property, or what-have-you. Despite the sound heard, the expression type uttered will be said to encode a proposition—or, more exactly, the type will be said to encode a propositional character. How exactly this is done will be one focus of what follows. But, put roughly for

---

[5] What the search process does resemble is finding an appropriate referent for a demonstrative: both kinds of search are triggered (albeit in quite different ways) by the "incomplete", sub-propositional, semantics of the expression uttered, and both involve context-sensitive, non-deductive inference. However, as will emerge below, the pragmatics-oriented theorist denies, on empirical grounds, that there are "covert" demonstratives being filled in, in sub-sentential speech. Thus, on the pragmatics-oriented view, sub-sentential speech cannot be reduced to reference assignment to "slots".

now, there are two possibilities. First, it might be that there is ordinary syntactic material present at some level, such that this material is elided, i.e. "deleted" somehow, so that it goes unpronounced. Second, it might be that the expression produced contains special indexical items of a sort which are never pronounced. Notice that on both versions, the sound produced maps onto a more complex syntactic structure than what the sound pattern initially suggests, with that syntactic structure then mapping onto semantic content in a normal way. Thus, on both stories, there is a somewhat unorthodox, non-obvious, mapping from sound pattern to syntax, but a perfectly normal mapping from syntax to semantics.[6] I take this to be the heart of syntactic ellipsis. (See Stainton 2004 for discussion.) How does this help the semantics-oriented approach? Well, on either syntactic ellipsis story, returning to Meera's utterance, the syntactic item that Meera used, and that her interlocutor recovered—the type that is—will be claimed to have the same context-invariant semantics as the sentence type 'This has chunks of strawberries'. (Or something like that.) Thus the syntactic structure uttered is of semantic type $<t>$ after all, despite the sound produced. Context is required to get a particular true or false proposition—there are still gaps to be filled, and they must be filled by pragmatics—but this is the usual state of affairs. In particular, on the semantics-oriented approach, only something quite familiar needs to be done: in the first variant, pragmatics helps determine which expression type was uttered (the sound produced, taken alone, leaves the nature of the unpronounced material underdetermined), and in both variants pragmatics helps supply the non-linguistic input for the propositional character encoded by the expression type uttered, so that this character can output a proposition-meant. But, says the proponent of the semantics-oriented approach, this is no different than when a speaker produces an ambiguous expression, and/or one containing a context-sensitive item.[7]

---

[6] Actually, there is still another way to save the semantics-oriented approach. One might propose that the sound is mapped to the syntactic structure that one would expect, but that this structure has a special context-invariant meaning when it occurs unembedded. This would be what I've elsewhere called "semantic ellipsis". The parallel here is with "one-word sentences", and special uses of words like 'Out' as said by a baseball umpire, or 'Attention' as said by a sergeant. I mostly ignore this option here. Detailed discussion of this idea may be found in Stainton (1995) and, under the rubric of "shorthand", in (Elugardo and Stainton 2004b).

[7] In fact, there are at least two other theories of syntactic ellipsis familiar from the literature. Dalrymple et al. (1991) treat ellipsis as trying to find not an unpronounced syntactic structure, but something more like a *semantic content* having certain properties. (Similar ideas may be found in Crouch 1995, and also in Schachter 1977.) I discuss this kind of view in Section 3, pointing out that it does not provide any solace to semantics-oriented approaches to sub-sentential speech. See also n. 14. A different account is due to Williams (1977), who posits an empty element, Δ, that works like

Having introduced the phenomenon and the pragmatics versus semantics-oriented approaches to it, I'd like to briefly canvass here why it matters who is right. (I'll return to the issue of implications at length in the final section of the chapter.) Most obviously, the (apparent) phenomenon of sub-sentential speech raises a subtle question about where to draw the semantics–pragmatics boundary in such cases: Is the job of pragmatics in these cases merely to disambiguate and/or find appropriate contents for (unpronounced) indexicals, with the semantics providing a "slot" (where "slots" include indexicals, tense markers, demonstratives, covert variables, etc.) that needs to be filled? Or does pragmatics do rather more, and semantics rather less?[8]

The debate about where to draw the boundary in these cases has become important for a narrower reason as well. In the last twenty-five years or so, numerous theorists have challenged the (purportedly) Gricean view that pragmatics plays only two roles:

(5) The "Gricean picture" of the two roles for pragmatics
   (a) Disambiguating and finding items to fill linguistically provided "slots", thereby contributing to what is asserted, stated, or said;
   (b) Determining non-literal content which goes beyond "what is said" (e.g. determining conversational implicatures).

Carston (1988), Récanati (1989), Searle (1978, 1980), Sperber and Wilson (1986), and Travis (1985, 1996, 1997) have all argued, contra the (purportedly) Gricean line, that there are pragmatic determinants of what is literally stated, asserted, or said which cannot be traced to elements of linguistic structure.[9] This has become known as the thesis of *pragmatic determinants of what is said*. (This thesis is closely related to the idea

an anaphor: Δ gets co-indexed with prior appropriate linguistic material which was actually pronounced, and takes over its content from that overt material. This contrasts with the second view to be addressed in the body of the text, which will have ellipsis being a matter of a context-sensitive item *deictically* picking out a non-linguistic object or property. (Roughly speaking, the postulated empty element that I will discuss in this chapter is more like 'that' and PRO, while Williams's Δ is closer to 'himself' and NP-trace.) It would take me too far afield to treat Williams's view here. Put in a nutshell, however, my view is that in so far as Williams's view is different from Dalrymple *et al.*, when read as a proposal for (apparent) sub-sentential speech, it is subject to the same objections that will be raised against deletion-type views.

[8] Equally, but now with respect to the illocutionary force of the speech act, rather than its propositional content: can speaker's intentions (pragmatics) determine that something is an assertion, or must this be done by the "linguistic conventions" (semantics)? For discussion, see Stainton (1997a).

[9] In my view, Kent Bach belongs in this list as well. This may surprise some readers, because Bach (1994a, b, and elsewhere) has repeatedly argued that there are no pragmatic determinants of what is said. However, what Bach means by 'what is said' is something rather narrower than what his (supposed) opponents have in mind. Whereas the authors listed here mean something illocutionary and of

that there exist what Perry 1986: 138 calls 'unarticulated constituents': a constituent of the propositional content of the speech act for which there is no corresponding constituent in the expression uttered.) Now, as first noted in Stainton (1997*b*), sub-sentential speech provides another example of pragmatic determinants of what is stated, asserted, or claimed—at least if the pragmatics-oriented approach sketched above is the right one. To see this, consider again the 'From Spain' example. On the pragmatics-oriented approach, this phrase is not ambiguous, and contains no "slots" needing to be filled. What was uttered was simply the ordinary phrase 'From Spain', which is a prepositional phrase of semantic type $<e,t>$. Thus the result of process (5*a*) will remain something of semantic type $<e,t>$, since disambiguation and slot-filling will contribute nothing. It is the fact that this content is not pragmatically fit—it being non-propositional—that triggers further "saturation". And yet, the case was claimed to be one of *assertion*: the person holding the envelope literally stated, of the letter, that it was from Spain. The speaker did not merely con-versationally implicate a proposition, while stating nothing propositional at all—she made a literal claim. Thus the content *asserted* is of semantic type $<t>$, not $<e,t>$. In which case, pragmatics is playing a role in determining the truth conditions of what is stated, asserted, or said that goes well beyond what the (purportedly) Gricean view allows.

The issue of where to draw the semantics–pragmatics boundary in such cases also ties in with a topic that has been central to cognitive science of late. That topic is informational integration, specifically how information that comes from linguistic processing gets integrated with information that comes from other modes—memory, vision, inference, etc. The role of semantics and prag-matics in sub-sentential speech provides a nice case study of just this debate: the semantics-oriented approach has the integration happening via the encoding of non-linguistic kinds of information into a natural language format, with that non-linguistic material making it into communicated content either by the reconstruction of bits of descriptively contentful syntax (variant one of "syntactic

necessity propositional when they speak of 'what is said', i.e. *what is asserted, stated,* or *claimed,* Bach seems to mean, by definition, the merely locutionary result of disambiguation and slot-filling. Putting the terminological confusion aside, Bach would emphatically agree that pragmatics plays a role in deter-mining what is asserted, stated, or claimed. Indeed, his implic-*i*-tures (in contrast to implic-*a*-tures) help bridge the "gap" between what disambiguation and slot-filling yield (*his* notion of 'what is said') and what is asserted/stated/claimed. But Bach's (1994*b*) implicitures are patently pragmatically deter-mined. Speaking of Bach, it's also worth noting that he denies that *Grice* meant anything illocutionary by the phrase 'what is said'. If this is right, then maybe even Grice himself allowed that what is asserted is pragmatically determined. To avoid exegetical complications, I usually speak of the "purportedly Gricean view" of the determinants of what is asserted, stated, or claimed.

ellipsis"), or by becoming the non-linguistic referent of linguistically provided "slots" (ordinary ones like 'this' in variant one, special pronunciation-free ones in variant two). A consequence of the pragmatics-oriented approach, in contrast, seems to be that integration of information from other sources during speech understanding can happen without additional natural language encoding of the information coming from other sources. Put another way, the idea is that environmental and other information need not be translated into descriptive natural language, or even be made the referent of natural language items, in order to be understood by a hearer as part of speech content. Instead, putting things very roughly, the output of the language faculty is presumably combined with other kinds of information in a neutral code of some sort, say Mentalese. (This debate leads quickly to even larger questions about the relationship between thought and talk. But those issues must be left for another day.)

In a series of papers I have repeatedly defended the pragmatics-oriented approach to (apparently) non-sentential assertions. I have also defended the two consequences of that approach noted above: the idea that integration in such cases occurs in something other than natural language, and the idea that there are pragmatic determinants of what is asserted, stated, or said. The latter conclusion has been explicitly rejected by Jason Stanley in his admirably bold paper 'Context and Logical Form' (Stanley 2000). He there argues that all truth-conditional effects of context trace to elements in the (possibly covert) structure of the item spoken. The former position is threatened as well by novel arguments presented by Peter Ludlow and others, drawing on work in theoretical syntax. As noted at the outset, my aim in this chapter is to rebut these arguments, thereby defending the pragmatics-oriented approach. By way of reply, I will shortly introduce numerous "varieties of ellipsis". Having narrowed down the kind of ellipsis which must be in play, if the pragmatics-oriented view is to be genuinely rejected, I will (among other things) rebut Stanley and Ludlow's arguments for ellipsis. I will end by discussing in greater detail the implications of the pragmatics-oriented approach here defended. The first step, however, is to explain Stanley's critiques.

2. Stanley's Challenge to the Pragmatics-Oriented Approach

As sketched briefly above, one way to resist the genuineness of sub-sentential assertion is by appealing to syntactic ellipsis. Another way is to argue that speakers aren't really performing speech acts in so speaking. Finally, one could say that it's "semantic ellipsis": crudely, that speakers are using "one-word sentences" (and "one-phrase sentences"), with the syntax of words or phrases, but the semantics of complete sentences. I have argued (Stainton 1997*b*) that syntactic ellipsis, whether in the reconstruction variant or the empty element variant, cannot account adequately for the appearances. I have also argued (Stainton 1995, 1997*a*) that "semantic ellipsis" cannot turn the trick either. Having also rebutted the claim that what is being done is something less than assertion, this seemed enough to show that the phenomenon ought to be treated pragmatically, rather than semantically. Jason Stanley pointed out, correctly, that this is not enough. Stanley's fundamental insight is that, even granting that none of these strategies taken alone can work, a "divide and conquer" strategy might allow one to combine these various gambits, thereby rejecting the genuineness of non-sentential assertion after all. He writes:

The persuasiveness of Stainton's arguments is due in part to the tacit assumption that all alleged examples of non-sentential assertion must be treated by the same general strategy. However, there is no reason to accept this assumption. I do not believe that there is a uniform phenomenon underlying all apparent examples of non-sentential assertion. (Stanley 2000: 403)

Stanley then goes on to argue that some cases might be syntactic ellipsis, for all I have said; and that some cases might not be assertions; and that some cases might be "semantically elliptical" (he calls it "shorthand") in some sense. I will address these one at a time.

It is exceedingly tempting, upon first reflecting on the use of things like 'Chunks of strawberries' and 'From Spain' to perform speech acts, to suppose that these are actually not less-than-sentential. Instead, goes this tempting idea, these and related cases involve the utterance of elliptical sentences. One natural comparison is with what B says in examples like (6)–(9):

    (6) A: Will Juan move to Madrid?
           B: Yes, he will.
    (7) A: Juan already lives in Madrid.
           B: No, he doesn't.
    (8) A: Who lives in Madrid?
           B: Juan doesn't.
    (9) A: Juan will soon move to Madrid.
           B: I wonder why.

It's very natural to say, about these four examples, that in each case B uttered a complete sentence, containing, for instance, not only a subject and an auxiliary, but also a main verb, a complement, and so on—this despite the fact that what B *pronounced* does not sound complete. A standard view is that the expression produced is a whole sentence nevertheless, at one level of representation, but that material which usually receives some pronunciation is deleted, or otherwise omitted, in these cases. (As explained above, there is another way to treat these cases, namely with empty elements that are never pronounced. I will address that option in Section 5.) Specifically, one might say that at some level the sentences uttered by B were:

(10) Yes, he will [move to Madrid].
(11) No, he doesn't [already live in Madrid].
(12) Juan [doesn't live in Madrid].
(13) I wonder why [Juan will soon move to Madrid].

Let's agree that B's utterances in examples (6)–(9) are paradigm cases of syntactic ellipsis. The aim, then, is to explain away apparent examples of non-sentential speech by assimilating them to the broad phenomenon illustrated by (6)–(9).

As I say, this is a very tempting thought. However, as Nancy Yanofsky (1978) and Ellen Barton (1989, 1990) first stressed, this assimilation seems unlikely to succeed, because there are several key differences between the paradigm cases of ellipsis in (6)–(9) and (apparent) examples of less-than-sentential speech, of the sort exemplified by uttering 'From Spain' in isolation. One such difference is this: whereas B's utterances demand a linguistic context, 'From Spain' can occur discourse initially. Thus consider an utterance of 'No, he doesn't' in discourse initial position. It would be exceedingly awkward. Similarly for 'I wonder why'. So, one reason for rejecting the "tempting idea" is this: whereas non-sentence cases can occur discourse initially, familiar cases of syntactic ellipsis cannot. Hence the former cannot be assimilated to the latter.

I have frequently used this appeal to occurrence in discourse initial position. In particular, I've used it to derail attempts to reduce apparently sub-sentential speech to fully sentential, but elliptical, speech. The objection Stanley makes against me here is that, while some cases of non-sentential speech genuinely are discourse initial, and hence are not plausibly treated as genuine syntactic ellipsis, many other examples are not truly discourse initial. More precisely, Stanley charges that the notion of "discourse initial" that I invoke is overly restrictive. Once the notion is broadened, so that no gestures or other means of making sentences salient are allowed, says Stanley, it turns out that many speech acts which appear to be discourse initial really are not. Here is his own example

(I have altered the numbering):

Now consider the following context. Suppose Bill walks into a room in which a woman in the corner is attracting an undue amount of attention. Turning quizzically to John, he arches his eyebrow and gestures towards the woman. John replies:

(S5) a world famous topologist. (Stanley 2000: 404)

What Stanley says about this example is that John's utterance of (S5) should not count as discourse initial in any interesting sense. Rather, the quizzical glance, the arched eyebrow, the pointing gesture, and all the rest raise a question[10] to salience, namely: 'Who is she?' (Stanley 2000: 406). So the utterance isn't discourse initial after all. Given that this "implicit prior discourse" exists, elliptical expressions are licensed—and it is precisely this implicit prior discourse that permits the use of (S5). Hence, he concludes, this is simply the use of an elliptical sentence *with prior discourse*. Stanley goes on to consider a use of (S5) with absolutely no background context, that is, with no linguistic items either explicitly spoken or otherwise made salient. This is a "discourse initial situation" in a broader sense. He suggests that 'A world famous topologist' cannot be felicitously used in such a context. Hence, it is fallacious to conclude that 'A world famous topologist' is truly non-sentential, on the grounds that it "can occur discourse initially"—because, in fact, it can do no such thing. (The same critique would presumably apply, *mutatis mutandis*, to my 'From Spain' example, and to many others.)

As noted, Stanley conjectures that by combining several strategies, one can explain away all apparent cases of sub-sentential speech. By dodging the "discourse initial" test, Stanley seemingly extends the compass of the syntactic ellipsis strategy, as just seen. The next sub-category into which he will put some cases are utterances which are truly sub-sentential, but which are not really assertoric. It certainly seems that speakers really can use a plain old word or phrase in discourse initial position—in the broad sense in which no linguistic material has been made previously salient at all, either by being explicitly spoken, or by pointing gestures, eyebrow arching, or what-have-you. Stanley considers in particular the example of a thirsty man who staggers up to a street vendor and utters 'Water'. He grants that this utterance occurs discourse initially in the broader sense. Hence, he concedes, it cannot plausibly be treated

[10] In Elugardo and Stainton (2004*b*) we point out that what Stanley really needs is for an *interrogative* to be salient. It isn't sufficient, to avoid pragmatic determinants of what is asserted, for a question (i.e. issue or topic) to be salient. Rather, what is required is a uniquely salient linguistic expression. We then argue that in very many cases no unique interrogative will be salient.

as a syntactically elliptical sentence. However, Stanley says, one should not conclude on this basis that there are genuine non-sentential *assertions*, because "I doubt that the thirsty man has made a linguistic speech act" (2000: 407). He gives two reasons for this. The first is that the utterance of 'Water', in the example in question, was not performed with a determinate force—in particular, it is not at all obvious that the thirsty man uttered 'Water' with determinate *assertoric* force. It could with equal right (i.e. not much right) be treated as a request, or a command. The second reason for denying that a genuine speech act was performed is that, according to Stanley, genuine linguistic acts must have determinate propositional contents. But, plausibly, the thirsty man's utterance of 'Water' cannot be assigned such a determinate content. Stanley concludes: "The available facts simply do not determine a determinate propositional content for the alleged assertion. And when a communicative act lacks a determinate content, it is not a linguistic speech act" (2000: 408). Now, if many of the cases of alleged non-sentential assertion can be placed in this category (i.e. genuinely non-sentential, but not genuinely assertoric), then further progress can be made towards his desired (immediate) conclusion, namely that all alleged cases can be explained away by assigning them to the appropriate sub-category.

The final category into which the alleged cases are to be placed are utterances of apparent words or phrases which (*a*) really do have a determinate force and a determinate propositional content but, (*b*) occur discourse initially in the broader sense, with no gestures or what-have-you, and hence are not elliptical. To illustrate this sub-category, imagine someone utters 'Nice dress' to a woman passing by in the street. Here, it is agreed on both sides, an assertion has been made, about the dress, to the effect that it is a nice dress. There is no indeterminacy of force: this is clearly not a question, and it is equally clearly not an order. Instead, the speaker is in every sense making a statement. And yet there is neither prior spoken discourse, nor implicit linguistic expressions made salient by gestures and such. What Stanley says about this example is that "it is intuitively plausible to suppose, in this case, that the speaker simply intended her utterance to be shorthand for 'that is a nice dress'" (2000: 409).[11]

Stanley summarizes his overall objection as follows:

Each and every alleged example of non-sentential assertion can be classified in one of the three ways I have described [i.e. as elliptical, not genuinely linguistic, or "shorthand"]. The illusion that each strategy is unsatisfactory stems from the tacit assumption that, to

---

[11] For detailed discussion of the "shorthand" gambit, see Elugardo and Stainton (2004*b*).

be satisfactory, a strategy must work for each case of an alleged non-sentential assertion. The assumption presupposes that the "phenomenon" of non-sentential assertion constitutes a natural kind. Once this presupposition has been abandoned, it is far less clear that there are any actual everyday examples of non-sentential assertion. (Stanley 2000: 409)

3. Varieties of Ellipsis

In Section 1 I noted two possible consequences of taking a pragmatics-oriented approach to the phenomenon at hand. The first consequence was that non-sentential assertions provided genuine—indeed glaring—examples of pragmatic determinants of what is asserted, stated, or said. The second consequence was that the integration of linguistically derived information with other sorts, in speech comprehension, might not happen in the medium of natural language. Specifically, it might not simply be a matter either of recovering extra syntactic material, or of simply filling in a referent for a linguistically provided "slot". Rather, on the pragmatics story, a representation from vision, olfaction, or what-have-you, without "translation", gets combined with a representation (but not of type $<t>$) coming from the language faculty. (For detailed, albeit uncomfortably speculative, discussion, see Elugardo and Stainton 2003.)

Stanley wants to say that the first consequence does not hold, because (*a*) in many purported cases, nothing is asserted and (*b*) in the remaining purported cases, what is asserted is not pragmatically determined (in the sense required), because the case is either one of "shorthand" or of syntactic ellipsis, hence really of "slot-filling" after all (albeit of an unpronounced "slot"). This strategy would also mean that integration of non-linguistic content, in understanding supposedly sub-sentential speech, actually *does* happen by somehow getting non-linguistic things represented by items of natural language.

Before addressing Stanley's arguments head on, it will be important to distinguish several varieties of ellipsis.[12] In particular, if his line of response is to

---

[12] In what follows I speak of "varieties of ellipsis" and the like. This is actually loose talk, in the sense that not all of the things described are sub-*varieties* of one single phenomenon. Sometimes what are presented are conflicting theories about one single phenomenon, not different varieties of that thing. And sometimes what are presented are not varieties of one natural kind, but are rather quite different phenomena that have nevertheless had the label "ellipsis" applied to them. I believe this loose talk is harmless in this context.

avoid the two consequences just noted, the Constraint below must hold:

(14) *The Not-Just-Recasting Constraint.* If the speech act is syntactically elliptical, then it's not a case of pragmatics determining what is asserted, and it's not a case of integration occurring outside the medium of spoken language.

In fact, this Constraint—which makes ellipsis a way of *rejecting* the pragmatics-oriented approach, rather than a way of *recasting* it in other terms—is non-trivial. Whether it is met depends enormously on which variety of ellipsis is at play, and on how one takes each variety of ellipsis to work.

Let me first introduce and put aside a "loose" version of ellipsis that would not satisfy the Constraint. Some philosophers, as well as some ordinary folk, speak of "ellipsis" whenever context (linguistic or otherwise) has to play an important role in filling in what the speaker said—whenever, put colloquially, the utterer "spoke elliptically" by leaving something implicit or unspoken. Sub-sentential speech clearly *is* "elliptical" in this very loose sense, since context is undoubtedly helping to determine a proposition which was not explicitly articulated. However, saying this is not to reject the pragmatics-oriented approach; it is, rather, to put a different label on things, while granting the general soundness of the pragmatics-oriented approach. This loose sense of 'ellipsis' would include, for example, Sellars's (1954) notion,[13] and what Neale (2000) calls "the explicit approach to quantifier incompleteness". On that kind of approach, the expression type which the speaker appeared to utter is precisely what she did utter. At best what one can say, taking Neale's "explicit" approach, is that the speaker *could have* used something more complete, while performing the same speech act. But, patently, if S produced u, though S could have produced u', it's

---

[13] Sellars writes, about uttering 'Seven is' in a dialogue, that "utterances of 'Seven is' are as such not complete and are only made complete by the context in which they are uttered . . . Let us call this type of ambiguity *ellipsis* and say that in ellipsis the context completes the utterance and enables it to say something which it otherwise would not, different contexts enabling it to say different things" (1954: 200). Sellars goes on to chastise Strawson for the latter's failure to distinguish completion of this "elliptical" variety from the kind one finds when sentences contain what I have called "slots" (i.e. indexicals, tense markers, etc.). Sellars equally distinguishes his "ellipsis" variety of ambiguity from the more familiar kind in which one has to figure out what expression has really been uttered (e.g. which of the different words pronounced /baenk/ was used). Clearly, then, Sellars does not think of "ellipsis" either as the presence of "hidden variables" that need to be filled in by context, or as a matter of figuring out what completed expression was "really" uttered. It seems clear, to the contrary, that his notion of "ellipsis" involves the context functioning directly to change the statement made, without doing so via elements of syntax. Thus ellipsis in *his* sense, far from rejecting pragmatic determinants of what is asserted, stated, or said, is fully committed to their existence.

nevertheless the case that S did produce *u*. Applied to a sub-sentence example, notice that if the speaker really did utter 'From Spain' in making an assertion then—even if context somehow completes her act, indeed even if she could have uttered some full sentence instead, so that the speech act counts as "elliptical" in the sense at work in the explicit approach—what she *actually did* was to make an assertion using a non-sentence. In what follows, then, I will never use 'ellipsis' in this loose sense.

Another move that is no real help to the semantics-oriented story is to use 'ellipsis' in some avowedly technical sense, all the while stressing that the kind of ellipsis at play, whatever it is, must be very unlike the familiar forms that occur within sentences. Until a detailed positive account is given, this amounts, once again, to simply adopting a comforting label. I think this move is especially problematic, in the present context, because in speaking this way it remains wholly unclear whether the Constraint would be satisfied or not, since it gets left open what "syntactic ellipsis" amounts to. Yet one rests content dismissing the phenomenon as "just ellipsis" anyway. It is for good reason, then, that when Stanley, Ludlow, and others endorse syntactic ellipsis and thereby reject the pragmatics-oriented approach to (apparently) sub-sentential speech, I read them not only as having *some* quite technical sense of 'ellipsis' in mind, but also as intending to assimilate, at least in broad strokes, (apparently) sub-sentential speech to VP-ellipsis, sluicing or some other kind of ellipsis familiar from sentence grammar. Where my opponents resist being so read, one must conclude that they have yet to offer a version of syntactic ellipsis that truly satisfies the Constraint.

I have already introduced two "varieties of ellipsis" that won't help the semantics-oriented theorist. I now want to introduce a third. One might think that sub-sentential talk is like VP ellipsis (and such) in that, in both kinds of cases, some *non-linguistic stuff*, or some *semantic content*, is supplied contextually but without accompanying hidden syntactic structure. If that is one's view of so-called "syntactic ellipsis" generally—and, very roughly, it is the view of Crouch (1995), Dalrymple (2004), Dalrymple *et al.* (1991), and Schachter (1977), among others—then the Constraint is simply not met.[14] Indeed, if *all* "syntactic ellipsis" works like

---

[14] For example, on the Higher-Order Unification approach of Dalrymple and her colleagues, resolution of ellipsis is a matter of trying to solve an equation that relates the meaning of the ellipsis antecedent to the meaning of the elliptical expression. Thus, in 'Samir likes Kirit. Sanjay does too', the meaning of the antecedent, 'Samir likes Kirit', can be represented as *likes(samir)(kirit)*, while the meaning of the elliptical expression 'Sanjay does too' is simply *P(sanjay)*—where, simplifying, *P* can be thought of as something like the property of DOING. Clearly, "that Sanjay *does*" is not what is

that, then pragmatic determinants of what is asserted, stated, and said end up being absolutely ubiquitous: even elliptical speech acts of the most familiar kinds (e.g. B's utterances in (6) through (9)) would provide examples of pragmatics helping to supply a *property* (symbolized in Crouch, Dalrymple, and such by the recovery of a lambda-abstract) directly, without any mediation by underlying morphosyntactic structure. Clearly then, whatever its plausibility, this version of ellipsis is not what semantics-oriented theorists need either.

Given the foregoing, the broad sense of 'syntactic ellipsis' which is required for Stanley's critique (and with it the semantics-oriented project) to succeed is surely this: sub-sentential speech must be like the kind of ellipsis one sees within sentences (e.g. VP ellipsis and sluicing), in that there is hidden syntactic structure in both cases. There are, as noted above, two versions of ellipsis which fit that description, both of which would help the semantics-oriented theorist—if only they were truly applicable to such cases. First, it might be that there is unpronounced "ordinary syntactic material": nouns, tense markers, and the like which ordinarily have a pronunciation, but which somehow fail to be pronounced in this situation. Second, it might be that there are elements of syntax which never have a pronunciation, but which are syntactically present nonetheless. Taking the first road, sub-sentential speech is explained away as being rather like VP ellipsis ('Maria likes milk, but Jaime doesn't') as this was understood by, say, Sag (1976). That is, the speaker intends what is at one level a complete (ordinary) sentence, and this is what the hearer recovers; but what the speaker pronounces, and what the hearer hears, has been abbreviated by some kind of grammar-driven deletion process. To take an example, the idea would be that the speaker who appeared to utter the phrase 'From Spain' in fact uttered a sentence whose syntax is $[_{IP}[_{DP} \text{This letter}][_{I'} \text{is} [_{PP} \text{from Spain}]]]$, but that all that was pronounced was /frəm speɪn/. Taking this first road, ordinary syntactic material must be recovered in order for the hearer to find the expression actually produced. The second alternative is to explain away apparent

---

asserted. To determine what *is* asserted, the hearer must reason roughly as follows. Given that 'Samir' and 'Sanjay' are syntactically parallel expressions, whatever (more specific) property goes in for *P* should render true the equation $P(sanjay) = likes(samir)(kirit)$. The salient solution is clearly $P = \lambda x.likes(x, kirit)$. Taking this, rather than DOING itself, as the value for *P* in the meaning of the elliptical expression, we get $likes(sanjay)(kirit)$. This is what is asserted. Notice that, putting things roughly, it is the unhelpful meaning of 'does too', rather than some hidden syntax, which causes the hearer to embark on this search; and what she looks for is not a natural language predicate, but a suitable property. Thus ellipsis in the sense of Higher-Order Unification does not avoid the consequences of the pragmatics-oriented view, presented at the outset; it just arrives at the same consequences by a somewhat different route.

sub-sentential speech as the production of elements vaguely similar to "big PRO", as posited in Government and Binding Theory. (The postulated element couldn't actually *be* PRO as classically construed, for reasons that will emerge below.) The hypothesis here would be that the speaker uttered a sentence whose syntax was, say, [IP [DP PRO][I' (light-verb) [PP from Spain]]]. Again, this is pronounced /frəm spein/. On the second version, the task is not to recover unpronounced ordinary syntactic material; it is to find a contextually salient non-linguistic referent for the empty element PRO and for the unpronounced light-verb.

The versions of "ellipsis" presented above may be summarized with the following tree:

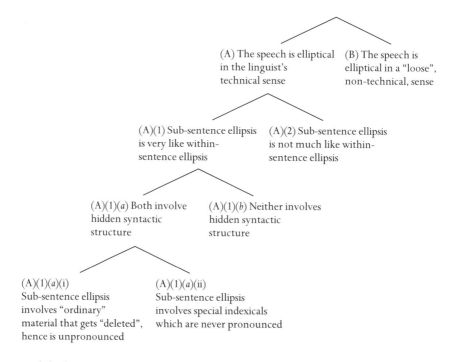

(A) The speech is elliptical in the linguist's technical sense

(B) The speech is elliptical in a "loose", non-technical, sense

(A)(1) Sub-sentence ellipsis is very like within-sentence ellipsis

(A)(2) Sub-sentence ellipsis is not much like within-sentence ellipsis

(A)(1)(*a*) Both involve hidden syntactic structure

(A)(1)(*b*) Neither involves hidden syntactic structure

(A)(1)(*a*)(i) Sub-sentence ellipsis involves "ordinary" material that gets "deleted", hence is unpronounced

(A)(1)(*a*)(ii) Sub-sentence ellipsis involves special indexicals which are never pronounced

And the key conclusion can be put this way: what Stanley *et al.* need is for one of (A)(1)(*a*)(i) or (A)(1)(*a*)(ii) to be true. Discussing these two proposals is thus sufficient, for my purposes, because none of the other versions of ellipsis meets (14), repeated below:

(14) *The Not-Just-Recasting Constraint.* If the speech act is syntactically elliptical, then it's not a case of pragmatics determining what is asserted, and it's not a case of integration occurring outside the medium of spoken language.

The remaining question is: When 'syntactic ellipsis' is read in the ways required, is it plausible that syntactic ellipsis really is occurring? This question will be a central focus of the rest of my discussion. I will address it in two steps. First, I will consider (A)(1)(*a*)(i) above, "the deletion story", and explain why it is not plausible that anything like what (the deletion theorists maintain) occurs in VP ellipsis and sluicing is occurring when speakers (appear to) speak sub-sententially. Second, I consider whether it's plausible that (A)(1)(*a*)(ii), "the empty element story", is responsible for the appearances. My overall conclusion is that no version of ellipsis meeting the Constraint can plausibly be extended to non-sentential speech.

4. Replies to Stanley

Before turning to my replies, it will be useful to briefly recap. In Section 1 I introduced two broad approaches to sub-sentential speech. The pragmatics-oriented approach treated the phenomenon as genuine, and had pragmatic processes of varying sorts bridging the gap between what the sub-sentential expression-uttered means (i.e. something sub-propositional) and what the speaker meant (indeed, *stated*) in so speaking (i.e. something fully propositional). The semantics-oriented approach, in contrast, treated the appearances as illusory, claiming that covert syntax of some kind made it the case that the expression-uttered was, despite appearances, fully propositional after all—at least once all syntactically provided "slots" were filled. Having distinguished the two approaches, I highlighted two reasons why it matters who is right. First, there are consequences for where to draw the semantics–pragmatics boundary—in particular, consequences about whether there really are pragmatic determinants of what is said. Second, there are consequences for cognitive science, having to do with how information gets integrated during speech comprehension. In Section 2 I briefly surveyed some of my earlier arguments against the semantics-oriented approach, and introduced a multifaceted reply that Jason Stanley offered to defend the semantics-oriented approach. In particular, Stanley suggested that a "divide and conquer" strategy—treating some cases as not genuinely assertoric, some as syntactic ellipsis, and some as shorthand—would allow the semantics-oriented theorist to explain away all apparent cases of sub-sentential speech acts. In Section 3, as a preliminary to my reply to Stanley (and to Ludlow), I canvassed a variety of things that one might mean by 'ellipsis'. I argued that only two of those would actually rescue the semantics-oriented approach: the others are either mere promissory notes, or else, in one fashion or another, they grant the consequences of the pragmatics-oriented approach. What remains is (*a*) to respond to Stanley's "divide and conquer" objection, including (*b*) critically discussing in detail the two familiar senses of 'ellipsis' that really would help the semantics-oriented theorist; and (*c*) to revisit at length the implications of taking sub-sentential assertion to be a genuine phenomenon. I turn to those issues now.

I think Stanley is unquestionably wrong that there aren't any examples left of genuine non-sentential speech acts, once his "divide and conquer" strategy has been applied. For instance, I believe that all three examples introduced at the outset—'Chunks of strawberries' as said by Meera, 'Rob's mom' as said by Anita, and 'From Spain' as said by the person holding the letter—are immune to this three-pronged strategy. They aren't shorthand, in any sense that would save the semantics-oriented approach. They aren't ellipsis—again, not in any familiar sense that doesn't just recast the pragmatics-oriented view. And they are genuine speech acts. I will defend this view by discussing each sub-strategy in detail. I discuss Stanley's three "prongs" in reverse order. Section 4.1 will deal with both the appeal to "shorthand" and the claim that much of non-sentential speech is somehow not properly linguistic. Section 4.2 will address at length the deletion-type variant of syntactic ellipsis. Section 5 will focus on the empty element variant of syntactic ellipsis, as recently defended by Peter Ludlow.

4.1. Shorthand and Not-an-Assertion

The appeal to "shorthand" can be put aside quickly here. First, Stanley does not say nearly enough to make this a genuine proposal. Second, all of the ways of spelling out the proposal either merely recast the pragmatics-oriented view in other terms, or are subject to very serious problems. (See Elugardo and Stainton 2004*b* for detailed discussion.) Third, Stanley himself (personal communication), in light of these considerations, has now given up the idea that "shorthand" can be usefully appealed to.

As for the second prong, we saw that Stanley suggests that many alleged cases of non-sentential assertion lack determinate propositional content, and determinate illocutionary force, and hence are not genuine assertions after all. His example, recall, is 'Water', as spoken by the thirsty man. The first thing I want to say is that, precisely in so far as there really is an indeterminacy, this is an unhelpful example. It would have been better to address directly the sort of cases I have always presented, where the idea that there is no determinate propositional content is highly implausible. In those cases, the content conveyed is just as determinate as in the vast majority of wholly sentential speech. Thus suppose the thirsty man had said 'A nice tall glass of water with three cubes of ice and a slice of lemon'. It is simply absurd to suppose that such an utterance is not "genuinely linguistic"—to suppose that, content-wise, this communicative act is more akin to a kick under the table than to an utterance of a complete sentence. But this phrase could easily be used when approaching the street vendor, with no special signals or prior discourse, just as easily, in fact, as 'Water' itself was imagined to be used.

By way of rubbing this in, consider some features of non-sentential speech—even in discourse initial position, and without gestures or other actions that might make a linguistic string salient:

(a) speakers can produce, and hearers can understand, an unlimited number of words or phrases, including absolutely novel ones like 'Another healthy dollop of that fruity whipped cream from Switzerland';

(b) the meaning of the expression is recursively compositionally determined;

(c) the thoughts communicated can be terrifically complex and subtle, indeed just as complex and subtle as the thoughts communicated by complete sentences;

(d) systematic changes in the words used yield systematic (and very fine-grained) changes in the meaning communicated;

(e) someone not wholly competent in the language in question often cannot understand these sorts of speech acts, precisely because they lack this competence;

(f) the things used exhibit features like structural ambiguity, logical relations, etc., as well as exhibiting degrees of grammatically, speech-specific errors, and other hallmarks of syntactic items;

(g) a person who suffers from an aphasia will (typically) have not just their sentential speech, but also their non-sentential speech, altered in quite specific and systematic ways. (For example, if a patient lost her ability to understand fruit-words, she would cease to understand both the sentence 'Give me three red apples' and the unembedded phrase 'Three red apples'.)[15]

---

[15] Speaking of aphasias, there appear to be lesions and genetic abnormalities that specifically attack the ability to use and process syntactically complete sentences, but which leave the use and comprehension of sub-sentential speech (and especially single-word speech, whether containing free and bound morphemes or otherwise) more or less intact. Elugardo and Stainton (2003) argue, tentatively, that in such cases it is far less plausible that speakers and hearers are covertly processing sentences; and that, if this is not happening in the abnormal case, there is less reason to believe that sentential processing happens in the normal case either. Some relevant clinical cases and theoretical discussion of different sub-varieties of aphasics manifesting this and related symptoms may be found in Breedin and Saffran (1990), Chatterjee *et al.* (1995), Jarema (1998), Nespoulous *et al.* (1988), Sirigu (1998), and Varley (1998).

This list could go on. Indeed, think of just about any feature which distinguishes human speech from other types of communication. That feature is very likely to be exhibited by communication that is less-than-sentential—essentially because, from the point of view of the "language module", the only difference between non-sentential speech and sentential speech is that the former involves the use of projections from lexical categories, of semantic type $<e>$, $<e,t>$, $<<e,t>,t>$, etc., while the latter involves the use of a projection from an inflectional element, assumed to be of semantic type $<t>$. This surely is not akin to the difference between language use on the one hand, and under-the-table-kicks on the other. Moreover, to classify cases of non-sentential speech as "not genuinely contentful" would be to set a truly ubiquitous (and, as Barton 1990 notes, a highly grammatically constrained) speech phenomenon outside the bounds of language proper. Pick up any novel, listen to the radio or TV, read magazine or subway ads—and sub-sentential speech will jump out at you. Thus, all of the following appeared in a recent advertising flier (for a pharmacy), in the *Ottawa Citizen*:

(15) Recommended for ages 6 and older.
(16) Effective medicine for pain.
(17) Nicorette plus. Stop smoking aid. 4 mg. For smokers of over 25 cigarettes per day.
(18) 2nd set of prints. Everyday. $1.99 for 36 exposures.
(19) For temporary relief of minor aches and pains.

As I will continue to argue in Section 5, these are no less bearers of semantic content than maximal projections of INFL, i.e. sentences in the syntactic sense. (Nor will it do to say that these are ungrammatical slips of the tongue, since they exemplify "edited language use", in particular a published form thereof!)

Nevertheless, I can imagine an argument that sub-sentential utterances do not amount to authentic assertions—not in terms of lacking *both* propositional content *and* force, but solely in terms of lacking force. (It is not an argument to be found in Stanley; but it's worthy of discussion nonetheless.) In particular, an opponent of my positive view could argue as follows:

The illocutionary force of an expression token is inherited from the illocutionary force assigned to its type. (Call this the "force-inheritance principle".) But sub-sentences (the types, that is), including syntactically quite complex ones like (15)–(19), do not have illocutionary force. (For example, they do not have, as part of their expression-meaning, any kind of standard use—e.g. used-to-ask.) In which case, tokens of these cannot have illocutionary force either. Therefore, lacking determinate force, they are not genuine linguistic acts.

In response to this line of argument, note that whether the force-inheritance principle is true is not something that one simply stipulates; rather, we must look at speech instances, assess whether they have illocutionary force, and on this basis either verify or falsify the principle. To my mind, non-sentence cases falsify it.

But simply saying this would seem to leave my opponent and me at an impasse. For, what he or she may want to say is that, to the contrary, one can employ the force-inheritance principle to evaluate whether an utterance genuinely exhibits illocutionary force. Intuitions that run counter to this principle should be overruled on theoretical grounds. Applying the principle, my opponent could then conclude that non-sentential speech acts do not exhibit force.[16] And hence that there are no non-sentential *assertions*.

One way out of this apparent impasse is to ask "Why does it matter whether something really is an assertion?" Reflecting on this question may give us a (rough and ready) test, a way of telling whether something has illocutionary force—independently of brute intuitions about whether something like 'From Spain', said of the letter, is an assertion. Now, I think assertion matters for comparatively practical reasons. Which isn't to say, of course, that non-assertions (e.g. mere implicatures) lack practical consequences—assertions just have *different* practical consequences. In particular, one can justifiably be accused of lying, and not merely misleading, only if one has asserted something false—which can leave one open to (easier) libel suits, stricter contractual obligations, perjury convictions, and so forth.[17] One reasonable test, then, for whether an utterance is an assertion or not might have to do with its special practical (including legal and moral) consequences. Suppose that's right. (If it's not right,

---

[16] An exception might be made for word or phrase types that carry special intonation. For instance, one might think that the *type* 'From Spain?', with rising intonation, has illocutionary force. But if these are exceptions, they are ones which work against Stanley. I'll ignore the issue here.

[17] As Stanley pointed out to me in conversation, it is by no means true that assertion is the only kind of communication which can get one in legal or moral hot water. Merely conveying, in a way that isn't lie-prone, can also have legal and moral implications. For instance, to develop an example of Stanley's, suppose I am an alleged gangster on trial, who catches a juror's eye. First, I give a thumbs up, followed by rubbing my thumb and index finger; then, I give a thumbs down, followed by mimicking the firing of a gun with my hand, in the juror's direction. Here I may convey some kind of

I begin to lose a grip on why one should *care* about the determinants of what is asserted, stated, or said—since it would then appear that 'what is asserted' is used in some special sense, divorced from its ordinary implications.) Now, imagine a used car salesman who says, of a car whose odometer reads 10,000 kilometers, 'Driven only 10,000 kilometers. Like new.' Suppose further that, as the salesman well knows, the odometer reads thus because the car has been driven 1,010,000 km, so that the meter returned to zero some months before, and then climbed up to 10,000 again. Has the salesman lied in this case? Or did he merely mislead? Clearly, say I, he lied. If the prospective buyer foolishly pays cash and doesn't get the details written down, can the verbal contract later be overthrown, on the grounds that it was framed on the basis of a lie? Or can the salesman say: "I didn't tell him that it had only been driven 10,000 kilometers. In fact, I didn't make any kind of statement at all, because I spoke sub-sententially. In particular, I made no claim about how worn-in the car was. The buyer just drew his own conclusions." Clearly, I think, the contract *is* vitiated by the lie, despite the sub-sentential nature of the speech act—just as it would have been if the salesman had instead uttered the complete sentence 'That car has only been driven 10,000 kilometers'. Now, despite certain uses of it sharing in the legal and other practical consequences specific to assertion, no force attaches to the *expression type* 'Driven only 10,000 kilometers'. Hence, as cases like this show, the force-inheritance principle is doubtful. But then one cannot use it to argue that non-sentential utterances lack illocutionary force.

Summing up so far, non-sentential speech typically exhibits determinate propositional content. The content may be vague, of course. But much of the time, it is not *so* vague as to make it "indeterminate" in the sense in question, i.e. such that it is robbed of being a genuine speech act. One need only glance at a magazine, or listen to the radio, or attend to casual speech, to find very large numbers of examples of sub-sentential speech with determinate propositional content.[18] Moreover, putting aside a few quite special examples (e.g. 'Water' as said by the thirsty man), no reason has been given to think that sub-sentential

message, about a reward versus a punishment—sufficiently so that I may be convicted of attempting to tamper with the jury. But, it seems, I made no assertion. Be that as it may, my point remains: assertion, and saying what could be an actual lie, do play a central and *distinctive* role in some kinds of legal or moral disputes.

[18] The proportion of sub-sentential speech in a corpus of interactive conversation among 10- to 12-year-olds turned out to be nearly a third, not including the ungrammatical stops and starts. Assuming this particular corpus was even somewhat representative, we may conclude that sub-sentential speech really is ubiquitous. (Parts of the corpus appear in Stainton and Hillier 1990.)

utterances only *appear* to have illocutionary force.[19] Certainly uttering one—i.e. speaking sub-sententially—can make it the case that one has lied, committed perjury, or incurred a highly specific contractual obligation.

And besides, it's not as if all genuine *sentential* speech acts have to exhibit "determinate illocutionary force". Surely an immigration official may utter 'Foreigners must present their passports before boarding', this act sitting somewhere between an assertion and an order—without her utterance ceasing to be a speech act. Or suppose a professor produces an utterance of 'I will give you a B on that paper', such that it's unclear from context whether it is a statement, a promise, or a threat. Does it simply have to be exactly one of these, if it is to qualify as *a speech act* at all? Surely not. In these and many other cases it seems to me possible to have "genuinely linguistic" activity, but not a unique and determinate illocutionary force. But then the same lesson should apply to less-than-sentential speech: even when there isn't one determinate force, there may still be a speech act. (If that's right, then even the utterance of 'Water' by the thirsty man might, when all is said and done, provide an example of a genuine sub-sentential speech act—even if it isn't determinately an assertion, a request, or a command.) In sum, at best a few examples of (allegedly) non-sentential assertion can be explained away by the "not genuinely linguistic gambit". So, there remain a whole host of examples of less-than-sentential speech that cannot be explained away. Except maybe by syntactic ellipsis. That will be the central focus of the remainder of the chapter, starting with the deletion-type theory.

4.2. Syntactic Ellipsis, 1: Reconstruction of "Ordinary" Syntactic Material

A key step in settling the issue of whether the first "syntactic ellipsis gambit" can really help avoid pragmatic determinants of what is literally asserted is to recall the notion of a discourse initial utterance. There is, as Stanley notes, both a broad and a narrow sense of this notion. On the narrow sense, an utterance is discourse initial if it is the first explicitly spoken utterance. Thus, in this narrow sense, Stanley's example of 'A world famous topologist' was discourse initial.

---

[19] In fact, even 'Water' can be used to make an assertion. Suppose someone with a very poor sense of smell is looking for water to put into her car's near-empty radiator. I help her out by sniffing at some substance that we find sitting by the side of the road, in a large plastic tank. I discover, from the smell, that it is probably alcohol, or some other highly flammable substance. Nevertheless, being poorly disposed to the woman with the deficient nose, I say 'Water'. This clearly was neither a question, nor an order. Rather, it was a (false) assertion.

In contrast, on the broad sense, an utterance is discourse initial only if there is neither any previously spoken expression, nor any expression which is otherwise made salient by the speaker. Obviously then an utterance could be discourse initial in the narrow sense, because nothing has yet been said, but not discourse initial in the broad sense—because of, for example, pointing gestures, arching of the eyebrows, etc. Indeed, this is precisely what Stanley says about the utterance of 'A world famous topologist'.

The question now is, Which of these (if either) tests for syntactic ellipsis? Or more precisely, which tests for ellipsis of kind (A)(1)(*a*)(i), in which it is ordinary syntactic material that somehow goes unpronounced? Stanley argues that being discourse initial in the broad sense is not a useful test. In fact, I agree. As will emerge when I discuss Hankamer and Sag type cases, being able to so appear doesn't prove that something is non-elliptical. What's more, lots of things which I take to be non-elliptical (e.g. an unembedded use of 'From Spain') often *cannot* occur without a significant amount of background preparation: both constructions involving syntactic ellipsis and most apparent examples of non-sentential speech cannot occur discourse initially, in the broad sense, because context must supply something to arrive at a complete proposition.[20] Indeed, just to drive the point home, notice that infinitely many complete sentences are incapable of occurring felicitously without a large amount of background context. Here is one example. Though (20) can be felicitously used at the beginning of a discourse in the broad sense, the closely related and non-elliptical sentence (21) cannot so occur.

(20) A man was walking through New York City.
(21) He was walking there.

Thus *this* "test" fails in both directions. Therefore, I will not here take discourse initial position in this broad sense to be the appropriate diagnostic: it tells one almost nothing about the syntactic structure of the item under consideration.

---

[20] Moreover, the pragmatics-oriented proposal explains why sub-sentences (generally speaking) cannot so occur: in general, context must supply a talked-about object, property, or what-have-you, to combine with the meaning of the word or phrase uttered. Typically, that is, using a bare word or phrase demands a "pragmatic controller": an extra-linguistic something referred to by the speaker. (More on this term below.) No background context, no salient object or property. No salient object or property, no felicitous use. Importantly, though, in this respect the use of an unembedded word or phrase is akin to the use of a non-elliptical, perfectly ordinary sentence that happens to contain explicit indexicals. (By the way, noting the need for a pragmatic controller in much sub-sentential speech shouldn't lead one to conclude that the things used, in such speech, actually contain pragmatically controlled *indexicals*, even covertly. See Sect. 5 for the reasons.)

However, there is the other sense of "discourse initial". And that is the one which, I maintain, should be appealed to when evaluating this variant on the syntactic ellipsis theme.

That is, the appropriate sense of "discourse initial" is the narrow one— precisely the one that I have employed in my previous writings on this topic. But there is a complication. The diagnostic is a bit more complex than "If it can occur in discourse initial position in the narrow sense, then it isn't elliptical." To get a grip on the complexities, and to see why this second "diagnostic" never- theless ultimately works for this postulated variety of syntactic ellipsis, let me introduce some distinctions due to Hankamer and Sag (1976), who write within the "ellipsis-as-deletion" framework. I'll begin by quoting at length from their own "summary of conclusions":

1. Anaphoric processes divide into two classes: *deep anaphora*, in which the anaphor is not derived transformationally but is present in underlying representations; and *surface anaphora*, in which the anaphor is derived transformationally by deletion.
2. Some anaphoric processes accept pragmatic control and others do not. (All anaphoric processes accept syntactic control.)
3. The pragmatically controllable anaphors are just the deep anaphors. . . .
5. Surface anaphora requires superficial syntactic identity of structure between the antecedent segment and the segment to be anaphorized; it does not require that the anaphor represent a coherent semantic unit.
6. Deep anaphora does not require that the anaphor be related to a superficially coherent syntactic unit, but it does require that it represent a coherent semantic unit. (Hankamer and Sag 1976: 421–2)

The terminology employed in this passage will be unfamiliar to many, so let me give some rough-and-ready glosses. "Pragmatic control" is essentially a matter of a deixis, i.e. a matter of a context-sensitive element taking on a semantic value by picking out some pragmatically salient non-linguistic element in the con- text. For instance, if I point at a woman and say 'She is a professor', this is prag- matic control. In other words, in pragmatic control, the pronominal expression can refer directly to something in the extra-linguistic context, rather than hav- ing to be explicitly tied to prior spoken discourse. "Syntactic control", in con- trast, precisely involves some kind of "link" between a pronoun (or anything else which is appropriately context-sensitive) and a previous expression, so that the pronoun (or whatever) takes on the content of the linguistic item to which it is linked. Next, the link between the two kinds of control and "deep" versus "surface" anaphors. Hankamer and Sag take surface anaphors to be (something like) derived "gaps" in an expression, brought about by (something like) deletion—such that the "gap" in the resulting form is linked to a prior complete expression, the gap getting its content from the latter.[21] Deep anaphors, in contrast, are context-sensitive pronouns (or whatever) that are base-generated. (This would include explicit pronouns or demonstratives, e.g. 'she', 'it', and 'that', as well as elements that remain unpronounced at the surface, like Government and Binding Theory's "big PRO".) Now, Hankamer and Sag's central conclusion is that *"deep anaphors" can be pragmatically controlled, but "surface anaphors" cannot be*. The latter must be controlled syntactically. What's crucial for present purposes is that syntactic ellipsis—of the sort exemplified by VP ellipsis (e.g. 'She doesn't', 'No, John will') and sluicing ('I wonder who')—counts as surface anaphora. Elliptical sentence fragments are, in these cases, supposed to be derived by the deletion of redundant material. In which case, elliptical expressions require that the material omitted be explicitly spoken in prior discourse. Otherwise, the structures cannot be linked up appropriately. In contrast, expressions which contain indexical elements inserted in the base, such as 'She is a professor', can be "pragmatically controlled": they can get their content not only parasitically, by linking up with prior linguistic material, but also directly, by linking up with the environment. Suppose this is right. Given this, the absence of a syntactic controller *is* diagnostic for syntactic ellipsis of the kind familiar from VP ellipsis and sluicing: if there is no syntactic controller, then it isn't truly syntactic ellipsis in this sense.[22]

It is true that some theorists are now suspicious of this contrast. Some think that, in all cases, there isn't hidden syntactic material at all—whether linked to prior overt linguistic material, or linked to non-linguistic stuff. Ellipsis, for such theorists, is *neither* surface anaphora nor deep anaphora, in the sense of Hankamer and Sag, because ellipsis isn't anaphora at all. This is the sort of view shared by Dalrymple *et al.* Taking this line will likely force one to give up the diagnostic, because both (apparently) sub-sentential speech and familiar kinds

---

[21] What syntacticians call "gapping", e.g. 'Sue loves chocolate ice cream and Phil cookies', is at best a sub-variety of this. So the word 'gap' may carry unwelcome (because so specific) connotations for some readers. The connotation is not intended. I should also issue the following warning: the relation between the "gap" and the item "linked to" need not be precisely that now assumed to obtain between an anaphor and its binder. For instance, the "linked to" item may merely provide, at some later derivational stage, the material that gets reinserted at the gap site. This would equally count as syntactic control, in the intended sense.

[22] As they put it elsewhere (Hankamer and Sag 1976: 406), "It is just those anaphoric processes that involve syntactic deletion at a superficial level of structure that require syntactic control." Or again, "It is just those anaphoric processes which consist in syntactic deletion, leaving no pro-form in place of the deleted structure, that require syntactic control" (Sag and Hankamer 1977: 122).

of ellipsis (e.g. VP ellipsis and sluicing) will be subject only to "pragmatic control". But, as noted, taking this line will *ipso facto* yield many cases of pragmatic determinants of what is asserted, stated, or said, and many cases of integration of non-linguistic content which does not involve translation into natural language syntax. So, taking this route, Stanley and the semantics-oriented theorists would win a battle (i.e. over tests for syntactic ellipsis) only by losing the war. Others think that VP ellipsis and such always involve a covert deictic element, so that it's not a matter of surface anaphora after all. This view would save the semantics-oriented approach, as noted: this just is version (A)(1)(*b*)(ii) of syntactic ellipsis, introduced in the last section, but put in other terms. It will be discussed below. But, in so far as the framework for syntactic ellipsis remains that of Sag and the like, this contrast ought to be accepted, and so should the concomitant diagnostic.

The idea then, by way of summary, goes like this:

(P1) Surface anaphora requires a syntactic controller.
(P2) Syntactic ellipsis, understood as deletion, is a sub-variety of surface anaphora (precisely because it arises from deletion, or some such).
(C1) Syntactic ellipsis, understood as deletion, requires a syntactic controller. (From P1 and P2)
(P3) In discourse initial situation in the narrow sense there is no prior linguistic material at all, hence no syntactic controller.
(C2) In discourse initial situation in the narrow sense, syntactic ellipsis, in the sense of deletion, is not possible. (From P3 and C1)

If C2 were true, it could be used to show that what appears to be non-sentential speech really is non-sentential, when there is no actually spoken prior linguistic material. (Assuming, that is, that the other variant of syntactic ellipsis is equally implausible.) For, in discourse initial position in the narrow sense, there can be no prior material for any supposed "gap" to link to, precisely because nothing has yet been said. Unfortunately, as I've said, things are empirically a bit more complicated than this. The fact is that even "surface anaphors", the kind which *do* ordinarily require syntactic control, can (under very special circumstances) occur without the appropriate material—though when they do so appear, they sound rather awkward. Thus, borrowing still from Hankamer and Sag (1976: 408), suppose that nothing has yet been said as two people (say Jorge and Ivan) walk onto an empty stage. Jorge, without speaking a word, produces a gun, points it into the distance, and fires. This is followed immediately by an agonized scream somewhere off in the distance. In this quite extraordinary circumstance, Ivan can say 'I wonder who', and be understood as meaning 'I wonder who screamed'. Crucially, however, his utterance has a highly marked flavor. (Many theorists even label it ungrammatical. See, for example, Tanenhaus and Carlson 1990.) So the caveat to C2 is this: it holds unless circumstances are quite exceptional; and when it doesn't hold, i.e. when such exceptional circumstances obtain, the utterance is highly marked, or even ungrammatical.

In light of this, one can reconstruct the following test from Hankamer and Sag's discussion.

(22) *H&S-inspired diagnostic.* If an expression can be used in discourse initial situation in the narrow sense when circumstances are not especially exceptional, then that is evidence that it is not syntactically elliptical in the sense countenanced by deletion-type theories. Moreover, if a use of the expression in discourse initial situation in the narrow sense does not sound especially marked, then that too is evidence that the expression is not syntactically elliptical in this sense.

Now, let's apply this to utterances of plain old words and phrases. They can occur as freely in discourse initial position, in the narrow sense, as indexical-containing complete sentences. Indeed, they routinely so occur. And, unlike speech errors and false starts, they routinely occur in discourse initial situation, even in carefully edited published documents. Moreover, discourse initial uses of words/phrase do not sound the least bit awkward to the unbiased ear.[23] Hence there remains a real difference between syntactic ellipsis in sense (A)(1)(*a*)(i)—a variety of "surface anaphora"—and (what I call) the use of ordinary words and phrases.

Hankamer and Sag's distinctions being on the table, it should be clear that while occurring discourse initially in the narrow sense is sufficient for there being no syntactic controller, so occurring is not necessary for there being no syntactic controller. Sometimes there won't be a syntactic controller, in their sense, even when a discourse is ongoing. Hence the real issue isn't "Can (apparent)

---

[23] Granted, sub-sentential speech might, during explicit reflection on its use, distress individuals whose intuitions have been shaped (dare I say "warped"?) by lessons in "proper grammar". Such speakers may find—or may claim to find—the use of words and phrases in isolation to be highly marked. Given the constant and utterly unnoticed use of sub-sentences, however, even by such speakers, I put such conscious reflections aside as misleading and irrelevant to descriptive linguistics. (Compare claims that it is awkward to begin a sentence with 'and', or ungrammatical to end an English sentence with a preposition. At best, sub-sentential speech is "awkward", "marked", or "ungrammatical" in only this strained, prescriptive, sense.)

non-sentences occur discourse initially?" Rather, the real issue is "Can (apparent) non-sentences occur without a syntactic controller?" Before addressing that question head-on, I propose a not-so-brief interlude, to spell out in greater detail what a syntactic controller is supposed to be within this kind of framework, and to explore why syntactic ellipsis, in sense (A)(1)(a)(i), really does require one. This will allow me to greatly sharpen the question of whether ellipsis in sense (A)(1)(a)(i) is plausibly going on in (apparent) cases of sub-sentential speech, and to give that question a pretty definitive (negative) answer.

Consider two general features of syntactic ellipsis. First, whenever syntactic ellipsis-understood-as-deletion occurs, it must be possible for the hearer to recover the material omitted. Otherwise, such ellipsis would get in the way of the hearer's comprehension of what was said. Second, syntactic ellipsis, if it is to help Stanley resist pragmatic determinants of what is said, must be a grammatical rule, a rule of syntax. It must operate, to use the familiar jargon, "within the language faculty". Thus, though ellipsis in this sense is subject to the constraint that the hearer can understand what the speaker meant, in speaking elliptically, it is also subject to additional, specifically syntactic, constraints. (Thus familiar issues of grammaticality will arise, above and beyond any issues of interpretability.) More than that, ellipsis, at least the kind exemplified by deletion-type treatments of VP ellipsis, sluicing, and such, is a matter of syntactic derivation, not a matter of "guesstimating" (using abduction or some such) what expression the speaker probably uttered. It is fast and automatic . . . essentially algorithmic. It is also, like syntactic operations generally, very likely to be informationally encapsulated, in Fodor's (1983) sense: *qua* rule of syntax, ellipsis does not have access to all of the information available to the agent. In particular, rules of syntactic ellipsis, as captured by (A)(1)(a)(i), do not make use of: knowledge of beliefs shared by the speaker and hearer; general information about the world, stored in long-term general-purpose memory; knowledge about the topic of conversation, its general direction, or its specific aims; etc. Nor, I would hazard, can rules of syntactic ellipsis so understood make use of information from other perceptual modes. In which case, rules of syntactic ellipsis in this sense do not interact with information about the current physical context.

Consider now an important implication of these two features, namely, the requirement of recoverability and the autonomously grammatical nature of the process. If reconstruction of the elided material is to be properly syntactic, then there must be sufficient *linguistic* material for the reconstruction rules to operate on. This will allow the hearer, on linguistic grounds alone, to reconstruct the unique and precise sentence uttered by the speaker.[24] Call this the Constraint of Syntactic Recoverability. Syntactic ellipsis, given this constraint, cannot happen freely: an entry condition for the rule's application is that the Constraint of Syntactic Recoverability be met. To see how a deletion-type account of syntactic ellipsis meets this constraint, let me give a rough sketch of such an account. (What follows abstracts away from many details. But I hope it gets the key points across.) Syntactic ellipsis, so conceived, involves two sentences, and some sort of operation. The first sentence, sometimes called the "*trigger* sentence", is actually spoken, and hence available "in the hearer's language module". There is also a "*target* sentence", the one to which the operation applies. It is not spoken, at least not in its entirety. Rather, only a fragment of it, call it the "*remnant*", is actually pronounced by the speaker. For example, in (8) the trigger is 'Who lives in Madrid', the target is 'Juan lives in Madrid', and the remnant is 'Juan does'.

(8) A: Who lives in Madrid?
    2B: Juan does.

Crucially, to repeat, the target is not pronounced. The fundamental problem for a theory of ellipsis of this kind is then to explain, in a precise and explicit way, how something which doesn't sound like the target sentence—here, 'Juan does'—nevertheless shares the interpretation of the target sentence, 'Juan lives in Madrid'. The usual answer is this: the meaning of the pronounced bit comes from the target sentence itself, the thing that the remnant—the thing actually pronounced—is derived *from*. Given this, the hearer's job is to reconstruct the target sentence, on the basis of the trigger and the part of the target which is actually pronounced. Recovering the target, which is what endows the

---

[24] It has generally been assumed that syntactic identity (or near identity) is required between the antecedent and the material to be elided. Indeed, this requirement of "syntactic parallelism" has been experimentally supported: see Tanenhaus and Carlson (1990 and elsewhere). As they note, the requirement accounts for the experimentally robust difference between (the parallel) 'It always annoys Sally when anyone mentions her sister's name. However, Tom did anyway out of spite' and (the non-parallel) 'The mention of her sister's name always annoys Sally. However, Tom did anyway out of spite'. (Interestingly, Tanenhaus and Carlson 1990 not only found that syntactic parallelism has an impact on "make sense judgments" when subjects are processing surface anaphors, they also found that syntactic parallelism or lack thereof *does not* make a significant difference to "make sense judgments" when subjects are processing deep anaphors. They take this to be evidence of the psychological reality of Hankamer and Sag's contrast between deep and surface anaphors.) The requirement of *syntactic* identity (or parallelism) is not universally accepted, however. In particular, Jason Merchant (2001) has persuasively argued that what matters is something more like identity of semantic content.

utterance with its meaning, allows the hearer to understand what was literally said.

That's the general picture. Here, in a bit more detail, is how this is supposed to be achieved. Within the trigger and within the target there are elements which, at some level (usually thought to be LF), are qualitatively identical. Taking another example, the trigger might be 'Juan lives in Spain', and the target 'He doesn't live in Spain'. It's hypothesized that, corresponding to 'lives in Spain' (the element in the trigger) and 'live in Spain' (the element in the target), there is (again, at some level) a structure shared by both. For instance, the LF [live in Spain] might be thought to be the "identical material" in question. When the trigger and the target share this "identical material" at LF, a highly constrained syntactic operation applies, which leaves the (straightforward) remnant of the target sentence. On one variant, due to Sag (1976), the rule deletes from the target sentence the surface material corresponding to the "identical material". In the example at hand, the input to the rule is the target sentence's surface structure, 'He doesn't already live in Spain', and the output is the surface remnant, 'He doesn't'—again, under the condition that 'already live in Spain' has an LF exactly identical to the LF of the corresponding element in the trigger, namely 'already lives in Spain'. Looked at from the hearer's perspective, she hears the remnant as well as the trigger sentence, and uses them—applying the operation in reverse, as it were—to rebuild the target sentence. The recovered target sentence then supplies the interpretation of the utterance.

Now, the trigger sentence, in this picture, is a specific example of what Hankamer and Sag termed a "syntactic controller". And it should now be clear *why* syntactic ellipsis, on this kind of story, requires such a thing: without it, the Syntactic Recoverability Constraint would likely be violated.

At last I return to the question at hand: "Can (apparent) non-sentences occur without a syntactic controller?" Given the foregoing, this question can be sharpened, since it is now pretty clear what features a syntactic controller for syntactic ellipsis must have, on this kind of story. Those features are summarized in (23):

(23) *A syntactic controller for syntactic ellipsis, in the sense of (A)(1)(a)(i).* An explicitly occurring sentence containing (at some level) material identical with the material deleted from the target sentence. This sentence must be such that, together with a straightforward remnant of the target, it permits a deterministic and highly grammatically constrained, syntax-based, recovery of the precise target sentence—without the use of general purpose inference, or information not available to the "language module".

Is it the case that, in most instances of less-than-sentential speech, there is a syntactic controller, so described? Absolutely not. In particular, in none of the examples given in my writings on this topic was there a syntactic controller for the alleged examples of less-than-sentential speech. Moreover, the examples I considered aside, even in cases where there is an item that would fit the bill, it clearly isn't *required*. In contrast, genuine syntactic ellipsis, on this kind of account, demands a syntactic controller, in this highly technical sense— because without one, the Syntactic Recoverability Constraint will not be met. So, the use of sub-sentences cannot be reclassified as syntactic ellipsis *in this sense*.

It's worth the effort to introduce an example of speech which is not discourse initial, but such that there is still no syntactic controller in the requisite sense. Doing so will help make the point that this, and not discourse initial position per se, is the real issue. The following is a slightly modified[25] variant of an example that is discussed at length by Ellen Barton. In it, B explains the White House staff's behavior in terms of their old grudge against O'Neill. The example is this:

A: The White House staff doesn't visit Tip O'Neill in his Congressional office.
B: An old grudge.

And here is what Barton says about this example,

[An ellipsis analysis cannot generate this NP, 'An old grudge', in this context] because the NP is not a demonstrably straightforward remnant of some previous sentence or question in the linguistic context, and any deletion rules generating such a structure would violate the Condition of Recoverability on Deletion. (Barton 1990, p. xiv)

Quite so. B's utterance cannot be treated as an elliptical sentence on familiar deletion-type accounts, because there isn't any target sentence from which it could have been straightforwardly derived, such that the target sentence would share "identical material" with the (supposed) trigger, the sentence uttered by A. So here we have a case of non-sentential speech, but not in discourse initial position in either the broad sense (which, as I've said, is not typically relevant to syntax), or the narrow sense (which at least seems to be highly relevant to syntax). It should be identified as non-sentential, and non-elliptical, because there is no syntactic controller in sense (23). And too, it clearly is a genuine speech act,

---

[25] Barton's original (attested) example has B saying not 'An old grudge' but simply 'Old grudge'. The latter variant complicates matters, because it appears to be not an NP, but an N-bar constituent. Barton (1990) argues that appearances are misleading in this case, and that 'Old grudge', so used, really is a maximal projection. I remain unconvinced. In order to sidestep that debate, however, which is largely irrelevant to present purposes, I here insert the determiner 'An'.

and it's not "shorthand". Thus we here have an example that cannot be reclassified in any of the three ways Stanley mentions.

Having said all this, it's worth returning to that earlier dispute, about whether it is the narrow or the broad sense of discourse initial that is wanted. Specifically, it's worth reflecting on why (22), repeated below, succeeds as a diagnostic where the broad sense of 'discourse initial' fails. Doing so will also bring out, still more clearly, the respects in which non-sentential speech is not syntactically elliptical in the sense here being discussed.

(22) *H&S-inspired diagnostic*. If an expression can be used in discourse initial situation in the narrow sense when circumstances are not especially exceptional, then that is evidence that it is not syntactically elliptical in the sense countenanced by deletion-type theories. Moreover, if a use of the expression in discourse initial situation in the narrow sense does not sound especially marked, then that too is evidence that the expression is not syntactically elliptical in this sense.

First, an obvious point. As I've just explained, true ellipsis, on this kind of account, involves deleting certain material under (quite complex) "conditions of identity" with material spoken in prior discourse.[26] There is always a "trigger" and a "target", with some portion of the target being deleted (or otherwise rendered unpronounced) because of the presence, within the trigger, of the very same material (again, at some level, usually considered to be LF).[27] Obviously, however, you can't have identity (of an element's underlying structure) with *nothing*. The trigger must exist. That is why discourse initial position in the narrow sense is a good diagnostic after all, at least if one adopts this theory of ellipsis: in that position, there is no trigger, no syntactic item containing material supposedly also found in some "target".

[26] Actually, deletion accounts are just one sub-class of theories which treat ellipsis as a syntactic process. As already noted, Williams (1977) offers a copying theory, according to which null elements ("deltas") are base-generated, such that material from prior discourse is linked to these null elements. Interpretation then involves copying the linked material into the site of the "delta". Here too, though, there can be no linking-and-copying in syntax if there is nothing appropriate, within the language module, for the "gap" to link to. So, albeit for different reasons, Williams's account also requires a syntactic controller for genuine ellipsis.

[27] Why "at some level"? Because, to take one example, the trigger can be 'Mary bought a gun', with the target 'She didn't buy a gun', and the resulting remnant being 'No, she didn't'. What is deleted from the target, notice, is not 'bought a gun', but 'buy a gun'—despite the fact that this latter does not appear, on the surface anyway, in the trigger sentence. The thought, however, is that at *some* level, probably LF, the trigger and the target share the same material, [buy a gun], and this licenses deletion.

Now a less obvious point. It's reasonable to ask why gestures, arched eyebrows, and so forth cannot raise an expression to salience, so that the made-salient expression can then serve as the trigger, even without being explicitly uttered. Why not allow identity of underlying syntactic structure with some sentence which merely manages somehow to be *pragmatically* salient? A very good question. Here is the answer: following Barton (1990), I have proposed that true syntactic ellipsis in the sense at hand, like anaphora in the sense of contemporary Binding Theory, is a process that is resolved purely linguistically. Put in Fodor's terms, it is resolved within the language module: recovery of the unuttered material is a specifically linguistic process, not a pragmatic process; that is, ellipsis is not resolved in an all-things-considered sort of way, in the "central system"; in particular, apart from the highly marked cases discussed by Hankamer and Sag, it cannot involve the pragmatic process of the hearer "guesstimating" what the trigger sentence was. But then, to have a non-marked use, actual prior discourse of the right sort is crucial—because that is what allows the whole process to take place within the language module. In brief, if it's the whole agent who, holistically and all-things-considered, figures out as best she can what sentence was (supposedly) produced, rather than this process occurring in some special-purpose language module, then it isn't ellipsis in the sense familiar from the literature on VP ellipsis and sluicing. (Besides, it will very seldom be the case that a specific and determinate linguistic something is made salient in this way anyway. And true syntactic ellipsis in this sense patently requires *that*.[28])

To illustrate the difference between pragmatic "guesstimating" of a full sentence versus genuine syntactic ellipsis, recall the example of the commander who purportedly cabled 'peccavi' to his superiors. As the story is told, the commander wanted the recipients of the cable to translate this Latin sentence into the English equivalent 'I have sinned'. He further intended them to move from that English sentence to the homophonous English sentence 'I have Sind', thereby coming to understand that he had conquered the province in question.

---

[28] Curiously, Stanley and Szabó (2000) make just this point against a syntactic-ellipsis analysis of quantifier domain restriction. Roughly speaking they say, about an attempt to explain the domain restriction of 'Every bottle is empty' to just those bottles recently purchased by the speaker, that this sentence cannot be treated as an elliptical version of, for example, 'Every bottle I just purchased is empty', because "In cases of syntactic ellipsis, there is a unique phrase recoverable from context" (Stanley and Szabó 2000: 25). Quite right, say I. But I would have thought that precisely the same condition would apply to an ellipsis analysis of (apparently) sub-sentential speech. For an argument against deletion-type approaches to ellipsis on the basis of the "indeterminacy" of the supposed convert material, see Clapp (2001). See also Elugardo and Stainton (2001, 2004b).

Patently, however, the mere fact that the speaker intended, and the hearers recovered, the sentence 'I have Sind' does not show that 'peccavi' is *syntactically elliptical* for 'I have Sind'. What makes this not a case of syntactic ellipsis is precisely that the "recovery" was not wholly linguistic, but instead drew on lots of background information—e.g. that the commander would not mean only that he had committed a sin, and that the commander was in the general neighborhood of Sind. Similarly, say I, if the "recovery" of the full sentence, in a case of sub-sentential speech, is not a grammatical derivation, but is instead just an informed guesstimate based on everything known by the agent, then the process is not syntactic ellipsis as this is standardly understood.

The results of this section on syntactic ellipsis can be summed up as follows. I first pointed out that if pragmatic determinants of what is said are to be resisted, the Constraint below must hold:

(14) *Constraint.* If the speech is syntactically elliptical, then it's not a case of pragmatics determining what is asserted, and it's not a case of integration occurring outside the medium of spoken language.

This, in turn, requires that syntactic ellipsis in a quite specific sense should be going on. In particular, there must be hidden syntactic material being processed. I then argued that one variant of ellipsis, of the requisite sort, is not occurring in non-sentential speech. Here I appealed to the fact that unembedded words and phrases occur without an explicitly spoken "syntactic controller" as freely as complete sentences do, and they so occur without awkwardness. In contrast, prototypical syntactically elliptical sentences can only occur without a syntactic controller in quite exceptional circumstances; and when they do so occur, they are highly marked—some would say ungrammatical. It is this feature that distinguishes genuine syntactic ellipsis from non-sentence use. What's more, I tried to make clear *why* genuinely elliptical constructions would require a syntactic controller on a deletion-type view: genuine syntactic ellipsis, on this view, would require that the hearer be able to recover, by a process of syntactic derivation, the complete sentential "source" of the fragment actually pronounced. But then elliptical constructions, if they are derived this way, cannot occur without adequate *linguistic material* as input to the derivation. To repeat, syntactic ellipsis in this sense—in sharp contrast with the 'peccavi' example—is not a matter of "guesstimating", on the basis of an all-things-considered inference, more or less what the speaker had in mind. (Besides, if it were a matter of drawing inferences in that way, wouldn't there once again be pragmatic determinants of what is asserted, stated, or said?) The job of the syntactic controller is precisely to supply (part of) the necessary input to this derivation. In contrast, words and phrases can occur without a syntactic controller precisely because there is no syntactic process of reconstruction. This is why, on this sort of account, non-sentences are predicted to behave so differently.

4.3. Syntactic Ellipsis, 2: Empty Elements

Given the last section, let us grant that non-sentential speech doesn't look at all like VP or CP deletion (a kind of "surface anaphora") as classically conceived, because the latter, if it exists at all, would require a syntactic controller. As a result, appeal to this variety of ellipsis will not save the semantics-oriented approach, because it is not empirically plausible that sub-sentence use requires a syntactic controller in the same way.

It also emerged in the last section, however, that sub-sentential speech does make extensive use of non-linguistic context. And precisely this observation may inspire another, quite different, variant of the ellipsis gambit. Maybe (apparently) isolated words and phrases are really syntactically more complex expressions that contain base-generated, phonologically null, context-sensitive elements. This is version (A)(1)(a)(ii) of ellipsis, the other version which actually would help the semantics-oriented theorist.[29] To give the idea, let me lay out a specific proposal. Peter Ludlow (2004) suggests that many (possibly all) cases of apparent sub-sentential speech are really cases in which the expression uttered, at some level of representation, contains some subset of:

PRO in subject position;
an unpronounced "light verb" (e.g., 'have', 'do', etc.) in V;
OBJ in object position;
DET in determiner position.

He maintains, for example, that (24) is a possible syntactic structure.

(24) $[_S$ PRO (give) OBJ [DET brick]]

This structure would be pronounced /brIk/, because none of the other syntactic items receive pronunciation. But, despite how it is pronounced, it is sentential nonetheless.

---

[29] I say "the" other version of ellipsis which would help the semantics-oriented theorist, but I should stress again that there could be novel accounts of syntactic ellipsis waiting in the wings, which would also do the job. Indeed, Jason Merchant, in empirically rich and inventive work in progress, is attempting to construct just such a novel account. Discussion of Merchant's very recent work on non-sentences, however, must wait for another day.

Let's first be clear about how positing (24) and related structures would bear on the semantic versus pragmatic approaches to apparently sub-sentential speech. Imagine a case in which Alice, taking advantage of a very rich background context, seems to utter the word 'brick', and thereby manages to assert that Bruce gave Cammi the brick. This looks like a case in which there are pragmatic determinants of what is asserted. It equally looks like a case in which the hearer understands Alice without integrating contextual clues into a natural language expression of type $<t>$. But suppose that what Alice really uttered, and what her interlocutor recovered, was (24). This syntactic structure *is* of semantic type $<t>$. Roughly, its character is a function from three contextually supplied items—two individuals x and y (i.e. one each for PRO and OBJ) plus one determiner meaning for DET—to the proposition that x gave y some quantity of brick. Thus if Alice actually produced (24), rather than the noun [N brick], then Alice did not utter a sub-sentence after all. And the role of pragmatics was merely to find real-world referents for PRO, OBJ, and DET—which is just another kind of slot-filling. Hence there aren't pragmatic determinants of what is asserted after all. And informational integration in this case, within the hearer, *is* occurring in natural language: by assigning referents to the empty elements.

That is the idea. Here is what I find problematic about it. My first objection is that the proposal leaves too much under-described. In particular, nothing has been said about where these empty elements can and cannot occur. Before taking this conjecture wholly seriously, we must be told, for example, what blocks 'PRO broke OBJ', from being well-formed in English, and meaning, in the right context, that Fiona broke the pot. Equally, Ludlow must explain why 'Loves baseball' is fine as a sub-sentence. In its familiar incarnations, PRO is only supposed to be the subject of non-finite verbs; so what occurs as the subject of 'Loves baseball' cannot be PRO. (See Chomsky 1981 on the "PRO theorem" and finite verbs.) But the subject cannot be pro either, which is the empty element that appears as subject of finite clauses, since English is not a pro-drop language. Since this suggest that the structure here isn't 'PRO loves baseball' or 'pro loves baseball', what is it? It must be some third, wholly unfamiliar, empty element. Again, Ludlow needs to provide the licensing conditions for this new empty element.

The next objection runs rather deeper. When one posits empty elements in a given structure, a key methodological constraint must be met: reasons must be given for positing the element. In particular, the empty elements should explain things that otherwise go unexplained. This is not to say that empty elements are per se promiscuous. (Though many contemporary syntactic frameworks do, in fact, disallow "inaudibilia" in their entirety.) But to accept inaudibilia in some cases should not lead one to open the floodgates: in each new case, the explanatory burden must be met. The problem here is, no compelling syntactic evidence has been given for positing PRO, OBJ, and DET in *these* structures. (More on this in the next section.) No psycholinguistic or other evidence has been offered either. Indeed, no evidence in favor of them has been given at all. As things stand, the only reason for positing these empty elements, in these cases, is merely to account for what the sound *was used to say*. Methodologically, I think it rather rash to move quickly from type meaning to syntax. (Positing covert syntax solely on the basis of semantic content was, I seem to recall, a cardinal sin of Generative Semantics.) It is equally rash to move quickly from literal utterance meaning, "what was asserted or stated", to context-invariant type meaning.[30] The inference required here is thus doubly rash: we are asked to posit hidden syntax merely on the basis of what the *speaker asserted and the hearer understood* on a particular occasion. Moreover, there is no need to posit these items even on such feeble grounds: a pragmatic story—which is required anyway, to determine the referent of the alleged empty elements— can capture the observed usage without positing any extra syntactic structure.

Here is a way of making the point that these elements really are explanatorily otiose—until, anyway, specifically syntactic arguments can be provided for their existence. Taking a leaf from Kripke (1977), imagine a language, Lingesh, which sounds exactly like English, and has the same meanings assigned to all "ordinary" words, phrases, and sentences. By stipulation, however, empty elements of the kind proposed above do not exist. What looks like a word in Lingesh just is a word. Let's further stipulate that speakers of this language have, as a matter of fact, never once uttered anything but a maximal projection of INFL, i.e. a sentence in the syntactic sense. Now, consider what would happen if someone, say Angelika, chose to utter an unembedded phrase, while holding up some mail. Say she utters the plain old phrase 'From Spain'—where, as in English, this phrase is assigned as its semantic value that property shared by all and only things from Spain. Could Angelika be understood to have communicated the proposition that the displayed letter was from Spain? My very strong intuition is that she could be so understood. What this suggests is that even without introducing empty elements, sub-sentential communication is predictable. I concede that it's not clear, even to me, whether Angelika, our bold Lingesh speaker, would thereby also make an *assertion* the first time she used a plain old phrase not embedded in any sentence. But I don't think it really matters. For suppose her fellow Lingesh speakers follow suit, and many of them

---

[30] I am here in agreement with Cappelen and Lepore (1997).

start using sub-sentences—not, I stress again, sentential structures containing phonologically null elements, but genuine sub-sentences. In such an imagined situation, where the general practice of less-than-sentential speech becomes established, it seems clear, at least to my (admittedly biased) ears, that nothing bars them from making legally binding, "lie-prone", assertions. So, a language *without* these otherwise unfamiliar empty elements, a simpler language, could be used to make non-sentential assertions. Hence there is no need, at least on grounds of communicative capacity, to posit them.

Before leaving this topic, it's worth stressing just how much hidden material would need to be introduced, so far without independent grounds. For instance, the empty elements will not only appear in the spots Ludlow considers. There will be empty prepositions, empty complementizers, empty negations, etc. And there will be lots and lots of these empty elements. Take Barton's 'An old grudge'. The empty elements in this case would have to contribute the content of 'The White House staff doesn't visit Tip O'Neill in his Congressional office because of———'. To achieve that, even simplifying greatly, the tree for the thing uttered would be as complex as (25), containing empty I, P, C, and Neg nodes:

(25)

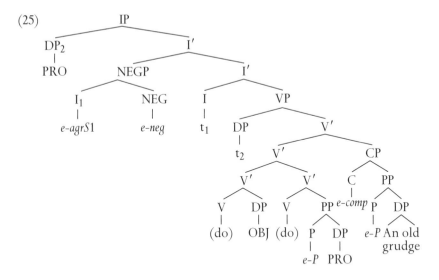

Is it plausible that there is *so much* hidden structure in this case? And so many different kinds of hidden element?

When considering the answer, notice that no independent evidence has been given for these items, and that it will frequently be indeterminate precisely which sentence-frame is in play. Here is a further example. Suppose that Lucas is rabidly anti-Brazilian, and he wants to convince his friend that Brazil is the cause of many social ills. Lucas points at two young men, obviously drunk, and says (or appears to say): 'Two bottles of Brazilian gin and vodka'.[31] Here, Lucas might assert something like *what caused those two boys to be so drunk was two bottles of Brazilian gin and vodka*. Then again, an equally good paraphrase would be *those boys got drunk on two bottles of Brazilian gin and vodka*. One could dream up several other sentential paraphrases. On the empty element view, precisely one exceedingly complex sentential structure was used by Lucas. We just don't know yet which one it was. (Similar remarks apply to the 'Chunks of strawberries' and 'Rob's mom' examples, and many others.) Rather than saddle ourselves with a puzzling unknown here, it would be preferable to take the appearances at face value, and grant that the speaker uttered precisely the phrase he appears to have uttered.

Now, these methodological arguments aren't knockdown. But they surely make this second special and technical notion of syntactic ellipsis quite implausible, if no evidence is provided for the empty elements. It thus seems that the only *plausible* variants of ellipsis, applicable to the cases in question, are ones which recast, rather than reject, a pragmatics-oriented story. Or so one must conclude, barring independent reasons for positing syntactic ellipsis in one of the helpful senses. Which leads to my final topic: recent syntactic arguments for such an ellipsis account.

5. Ludlow's Challenge: Other Arguments for Syntactic Ellipsis

Early on in this chapter, I noted two consequences of sub-sentential speech, assuming one takes the appearances at face value: first, that there would be pragmatic determinants of what is said, asserted, or claimed, and second, informational integration, even during speech comprehension, could and would happen in a medium other than spoken language. In Section 3 I contrasted numerous variants on the ellipsis theme, and noted that most of them are unhelpful in avoiding these two consequences. This held both for some commonsense takes on "ellipsis", and for some technical variants as well, e.g. Dalrymple-type accounts. Much of the rest of the chapter has considered

---

[31] Notice that this phrase exhibits a scope ambiguity. It is thus extremely implausible that it is not "genuinely linguistic", as Stanley might have it.

whether the two varieties of ellipsis that really would let one reject non-sentential assertion are plausible. The first variant, which sees ellipsis as like the deletion of redundant material in VP ellipsis and sluicing, was found to entail the requirement of a syntactic controller, except in highly marked situations. But syntactic controllers are not at all required for sub-sentence use. The second variant, which sees syntactic ellipsis as a matter of phonologically null elements getting assigned real-world referents from context, was methodologically suspect: it posited lots of hidden structure, whose nature remains largely mysterious, without any explanatory gain at all. Or so I said.

What remains is to make good on this claim that there aren't solid and independent reasons for positing hidden syntactic structure. To do this, I need to address directly some arguments which purport to provide such reasons. That is the task of this section. I will structure my replies around an argument that seems to me to run through Ludlow (2004). The argument, as I reconstruct it, goes like this:

> *Premise 1.* The grammar of English does not generate expressions of the kind required by the pragmatics-oriented approach, except within sentences. Nor does the semantics of English assign meanings to expressions of the kind required, except within sentences.
> *Premise 2.* Apparently sub-sentential speech is grammatical.[32]
> *Premise 3.* If P1 and P2 are true, then speakers who appear to utter bare words and phrases must really be uttering sentences.
> *Conclusion.* Speakers who appear to utter bare words and phrases must really be uttering sentences.

Ludlow puts his conclusion this way:

The view that I am defending is that in more cases than not (and perhaps all cases) if we utter something that is well-formed and meaningful then at least at one level of representation [it] is a fully inflected clause.[33]

---

[32] Were it not for this premise, one might say: "It doesn't matter whether the grammar generates words or phrases, since people use ungrammatical expressions all the time to perform speech acts. For instance, non-native speakers frequently make assertions using fractured grammar. Thus the only question is whether words or phrases are used assertorically, not whether they are *grammatically* so used." Premise 2 is important precisely because it allows Ludlow to block the complaint that grammaticality is irrelevant to the debate at hand.

[33] Ludlow (2004: 96). The kind of exception that Ludlow does allow for are cases in which a special code has been pre-established, so that the use of a single word is understood as communicating a full proposition. He gives the example of stipulating beforehand that saying 'apple' means that someone in the crowd has a gun. He rightly sets aside such cases as uninteresting. I gather that these are the only

Ludlow gives a series of examples to support P1. He also offers a more general reason for accepting P1, based on theoretical principles in Chomsky's Minimalist Program. I will discuss these two kinds of argument in turn.

There are surface constructions which have long been considered to be created via transformation. For instance, passive sentences have been thought to work this way. To give an example, and putting things roughly, the idea is that the active voice sentence 'A missile sank that ship' is transformed into 'That ship was sunk by a missile'. Similarly, notes Ludlow, 'The children are all in the garden' is derived by applying a transformation, Q-float, to 'All the children are in the garden'.[34] Crucially, these sorts of transformations only apply to sentences. Ludlow infers that the grammar does not generate things like the *bare* phrase 'Sunk by a missile', or the *bare* phrase 'All in the garden'. It only generates sentences that contain these phrases. Thus P1.

Here is another set of examples, equally designed to support P1. There are morphosyntactic phenomena which are only licensed by specific surrounding syntactic material. One example is case-markings on noun phrases. Case-markings on an NP are taken to require an appropriate expression standing in the right syntactic relation to the NP, such that the case in question gets *assigned* to the noun phrase by that expression, in that relation. For instance, accusative case is supposed to be assigned by object-agreement features on the verb, where that verb must govern the noun phrase.[35] Given this, it is reasonable to infer

exceptions he is willing to countenance, and that, in every other case, he will predict that alleged examples of non-sentential speech, where grammatical and meaningful, are in fact uses of structures that are sentential at some level of representation.

[34] It might be thought that a well-known alternative theory of "Q-float", argued for in Sportiche (1988), would pose problems for Ludlow, and thus might support my story. On this view, it is not the quantifier word (e.g. 'all') which floats "down" from the subject position into the VP. Rather, sentential subjects originate inside the VP, and in "Q-float" it is the rest of the complex quantified NP (e.g. 'the children') which moves up from within the VP to subject position, without "pied piping" the quantifier word (e.g. 'all'). Applied to the example at hand, and simplifying, the base form would be $[_{IP}$—— $[_{VP}$ are all the children in the garden]], the segment [the children] raises to subject of IP position, and the result becomes $[_{IP}$ the children $[_{VP}$ are all——in the garden]]. Whatever the merits of this account, however, and whatever complications it poses for Ludlow's positive story, I suspect that it does not especially favor the pragmatics-oriented view any more than more traditional accounts of Q-float. That is because the Sportiche account, like its traditional rivals, equally requires that 'all in the garden' be derived by a *sentence*-level operation, rather than being base-generated.

[35] In Minimalism, case assignment is achieved by "feature checking". The core idea, roughly speaking, is that case-markings on nominals get "checked off" against corresponding features on verbs—though only when the nominal and the verb stand in the right structural relation. Once a case-feature has been "checked", it ceases to be visible at Conceptual Structure. This has the same

that when accusative case is present, there must be a verb assigning the right sort of agreement features; and that verb must be in the proper syntactic relation to the noun phrase. This kind of phenomenon shows up even more clearly in heavily case-marked languages like German, Russian, and Korean. Importantly for present purposes, that seemingly implies that the grammar of these languages cannot generate *bare* noun phrases—which are marked for case, yet are completely outside a sentence—for there would then be neither the case-assigning features nor the structural relation in which case gets assigned. Or again, reflexive anaphors like 'himself' must, it seems, be licensed by an appropriate co-indexed NP that stands in the right structural relation (e.g. c-command) to the reflexive. That is why 'Jim's mother likes himself' is ungrammatical: the only appropriate NP is 'Jim', and it does not c-command 'himself'. Again, this seemingly shows that the grammar of English (and of languages generally) cannot generate bare phrases containing reflexive anaphors (e.g. 'From himself'). Instead, the grammar can only generate sentences containing such phrases. Ludlow gives other examples, all of which seem to support P1. But these are sufficient to give the flavor of his first kind of argument.[36]

Insisting that these kinds of phrases cannot be generated outside sentences, Ludlow then observes that phrases of this kind *appear* to be used in isolation. He infers that the appearances must be misleading: what speakers must really be using, in these cases, are sentences containing unpronounced material. That is how Ludlow's examples support an ellipsis story. (Note too that the *syntactic* material must be present, in the right structural relationship. It's not just that the content is clear from the "pragmatic" context. So the variety of ellipsis supported is, in fact, the kind that would help the semantics-oriented theorist.)

The second kind of argument that Ludlow offers for P1 is less tied to specific examples. (It also has less of a "retro" flavor.) Before introducing it, it is worth

effect as the old "case filter" of Government and Binding Theory because, crucially, case-marking features are taken to be uninterpretable, and a key principle of Minimalism is that anything still visible at Conceptual Structure must be interpretable. So, if a nominal's case-markings *don't* get checked—put in GB-talk, if nothing is in the right position to assign case—the case-markings will be both visible *and* uninterpretable at this interface, and the derivation will "crash".

[36] Some of the examples that Ludlow discusses strike me as beside the point, at least with respect to the present debate. The issue before us, after all, is the semantics–pragmatics boundary, and in particular whether speakers can perform speech acts using things that do not, even in context, encode something propositional. Thus uses of syntactically non-sentential expressions that are nevertheless semantically of type <e> are not in dispute. Hence I put aside as irrelevant Ludlow's examples 'All were' and '*Hood* sunk', since I grant that they are "semantically sentential".

noting why Ludlow needs this broader kind of argument. It is important for his purposes because, without it, the consequent of P3 would have to read "then speakers who appear to utter bare words and phrases *of the kind derived in sentence-level transformations* must really be uttering sentences". At best, as he himself acknowledges, Ludlow's specific examples show only that *some* speech which looks like the use of sub-sentences might actually be better treated as the use of elliptical sentences. And this is something that believers in genuine non-sentential speech have never denied.[37] Indeed, I myself have been quite happy to grant this in the past, in part because I do not think it saves the semantics-oriented approach: as long as some cases aren't ellipsis, in the sense required, the pragmatics-oriented approach is vindicated. Realizing this, Ludlow wants to support the stronger view that, some scattered and uninteresting cases of stipulated special uses for bare words aside, *all* grammatical speech is sentential speech. Towards this end, he describes the fundamental principle behind Chomsky's Minimalist Program as requiring "that grammatical elements must be combined and moved (under economy constraints) until a successful deriva-tion is computed" (Ludlow 2004: 106). In particular, a fundamental principle of Minimalism is the restriction that uninterpretable features must get "erased" ("checked off") before arriving at the end-of-derivation interface: this restric-tion yields the same effects as the many "filters" in prior frameworks; and, since this checking off sometimes requires that an element move, the demand of full interpretability also yields the same effects as the movement rules of prior frameworks. Ludlow is correct to say that, within Minimalism, the grammar would over-generate wildly if this restriction were removed. Ludlow then sug-gests that in order for the grammar to generate non-sentences—like 'From Spain', 'Rob's mom', 'An old grudge', and 'Chunks of strawberries'—outside of sentences, this principle would have to be rejected. He writes: "If success could

---

[37] Indeed, having noted, following Morgan (1973, 1989), both that there are "fragments" that appear to arise from sentence-level transformations like *tough*-movement and passive, and that case-marking in fragments is typically a reflection of the fragments' position in the corresponding full sentence, I myself concluded in an earlier paper that "In my view, such cases strongly suggest that the interpretation of *some* fragments involves reconstruction of elided material" (Stainton 1997b: 71). Barton (1998) makes a similar concession. That said, as will emerge below, I am now less convinced that these kinds of examples should, on these grounds anyway, be treated as elliptical *in the sense required to save the semantics-oriented approach.* To anticipate, I now think that whether they are derived via a sentence-level process—which is what Morgan argues for, and what Barton and I concede—is actually neither here nor there, with respect to whether the things uttered are really phrases rather than elliptical sentences. (Compare: that a butterfly passes through a stage in which it is a caterpil-lar surely does not show that the thing fluttering outside my window actually *isn't* a butterfly after all.)

be won for any arbitrary subsentential element, then the theory would be incapable of blocking anything" (Ludlow 2004: 106). Thus, suggests Ludlow, we must either reject Minimalism or we must reject the genuineness of sub-sentential speech.

Interestingly, this broader objection brings together the two parts of P1 above: namely, not being generated by the grammar, and not being assigned a meaning. A central idea underlying the Minimalist Program is that what arrives at the end of a derivation, and remains "visible", must be fully *interpretable*—if it isn't, the derivation is unsuccessful, and it "crashes". But if no meaning is assigned to bare phrases, then they aren't interpretable; and if they aren't interpretable, then bare phrases can't be left over at the end of a derivation. Hence they cannot be generated by a Minimalist grammar.

Before addressing Ludlow's objections in detail, let me explain why I think that P1 of my reconstruction, to the effect that the grammar does not generate or assign meanings to words or phrases outside sentences, simply cannot be correct. It is one thing to insist, as Stanley does, that words and phrases are perfectly well-formed but that they cannot be used to perform a genuine speech act, e.g. an assertion. It is quite another to say that words and phrases, if not embedded in a sentence, are just plain ungrammatical, and/or cannot be interpreted at all. A natural reaction to the latter idea is an uncomprehending stare. True, the claim isn't logically incoherent; but it strikes me as up there with the suggestions that all apparent dogs are really robots, or that all sentences underlyingly have the word 'Jehovah' in them. Not to put too fine a point on it, it is *immensely* implausible that every book title, dictionary entry, label, bank check, etc. is riddled with ungrammaticality and nonsense. Equally implausible is the idea that book titles and such actually aren't phrases, and that trucks, currency, store fronts, and license plates never *really* have words and phrases on them. This implausibility derives, in part, from the hard-to-fathom consequence that, if these things aren't really words or phrases, then we (whether professional linguists or ordinary folk) don't really know what they are—since we can't (yet) tell what specific sentence underlies the apparent word or phrase. Sometimes this will be because multiple sentences would be equally fine paraphrases. Sometimes it will be because no sentential paraphrase comes to mind at all: for example, when I call out 'Oh Sweet thing' as a vocative, merely to get my spouse's attention, what *sentence* can I have meant which simply gets her attention, without saying anything about her? Taking another example, I have before me a business card which *appears* to say 'McMaster University' at the top, followed by the personal name 'Anita Kothari', affiliations 'Health Research Methodology Program', 'Centre for Health Economics and Policy Analysis', and ending with a street address. But if Ludlow's argument is sound, and only sentences can be used, this business card, assuming its contents are grammatical, cannot really say any of these things. That's peculiar enough. Worse, this business card must contain a slew of sentences whose nature is at the moment outside human ken, in part because no ordinary declarative fits the bill. (Each ordinary sentence would, I take it, incorrectly have the business card containing multiple articulated assertions: "The bearer works at McMaster University", "The bearer is named Anita Kothari", etc. And, while I grant that *the act of handing over the card* may convey such things, it seems quite wrong to add that such things are implicitly or covertly contained on the card itself.)

Well, but implausible views are rife in philosophy, and in science too. And some quite implausible theses have proven to be correct.[38] So, let me move beyond the uncomprehending stare, and raise three problems for P1.

First, and related to the point about not yet knowing what the things are, one can't simply stop with the claim that appearances radically mislead: there is the heavy burden of explaining away street signs, maps, chapter headings, product labels, business cards, names on boats, vocative uses of titles, addressed envelopes, shopping lists, CD covers, dictionary entries, phone books, TV guides, bank checks, book and movie titles, menus, etc.[39] To cite three specific

---

[38] In fact, Ludlow has been known to reply that this is just another example of a very successful scientific theory conflicting with commonsense appearances, as when chemistry arrived at the surprising conclusion that rusting and burning are very similar processes. I'm willing to let this go, for the sake of argument. But I will say this: I think drawing such a comparison quite seriously misrepresents the present situation. First, as Chomsky (1995) himself regularly insists, inquiry in formal syntax remains in the very beginning stages. Indeed, it is suggestive that he calls his latest attempts a "Program": Minimalism, even more than the Extended Standard Theory or Government and Binding Theory, is genuinely a program of research, just starting to yield its first fruits. What's more, as Chomsky also freely admits, the Minimalist Program can claim far less descriptive adequacy than many of its predecessors. Thus, not to put too fine a point on it, if the Minimalist Program really did have the consequence that every grocery list and business card is either rife with ungrammaticality and nonsense, or covertly filled with undiscoverable sentences, then that really ought to strike one as a quite good reason for rejecting it. (Happily, as I will argue below, I do not think Minimalism entails any such thing.)

[39] A great variety of attested cases of (what I would call) sub-sentential speech—produced under a huge array of circumstances, in many linguistic registers and within widely differing media (e.g. everyday conversation, commercial advertisements, recipes, sports commentary, personal ads, literature)—may be found in Wilson (2000). He also offers a useful overview of the scope and range of things sometimes labeled 'ellipsis'.

examples essentially at random, I have before me a water bottle which (appears) to contain:

> Pure Refreshment
> DASANI
> REMINERALIZED WATER
> REVERSE OSMOSIS—NON-CARBONATED
> 591 ML
> WATER, MAGNESIUM SULPHATE, POTASSIUM CHLORIDE, SALT,
>   OZONE
> REGISTERED TRADE MARK OF THE COCA-COLA COMPANY, USED
>   UNDER LICENCE. IMPORTED BY COCA-COLA BOTTLING
>   COMPANY
> Return for refund where applicable
> —Recyclable—

And, on my orange juice bottle I read (or so it seems):

> PROVIDES 53% OF THE RECOMMENDED DAILY INTAKE OF CALCIUM
> NEW   Minute Maid
> 100% PURE
> ORANGE JUICE
> FROM CONCENTRATE WITH ADDED CALCIUM
> 473 ML   CALCIUM RICH
> SPECIALLY DESIGNED AS A SOURCE OF CALCIUM FOR PEOPLE WHO
>   DO NOT DRINK MILK

Finally, opening my *Oxford Canadian Dictionary* I find (or seem to find):

marrow. n. **1** = BONE MARROW. **2** the essential part. **3** (in full **vegetable marrow**) **a** a large usually white-fleshed gourd used as food. **b** the plant, *Cucurbita pepo*, yielding this.

In all these cases, one seems to find mere words or phrases being used grammatically, and with a genuine content. If Ludlow is right, however, these and other cases must be explained away as *mere* appearance: either each apparent word or phrase on the bottles and in the dictionary must be ungrammatical and/or contentless, or each must be underlyingly sentential. The problem is, absolutely none of this explaining away has yet been done.

Second, notice that there are *two* kinds of appearances being denied. The first is that our linguistic competence generates words or phrases, so that these very things can get regularly used in grammatical speech. That we are misled about this is easier to swallow: our supposed "error" here might be explained by some kind of performance error, and by the general point that people have a quite shaky grasp on their own competence. But the second kind of appearance we have to deny is about what we *do* with these expressions. It has to do with errors about our own performance, not merely about our competence. Specifically, we think we often mean something sub-propositional when we produce what appears to be a word or phrase. However, if all such things are underlyingly sentential, and if what determines speech act content is just disambiguation and slot-filling (as per the view being defended), we are presumably regularly wrong about what speech acts we perform in using these items. We are asserting, though we think we are only vocatively calling out a name or title. We are asserting, though we think we are only labeling. And so on. (There is, of course, an implicit assumption behind my present critique: that if pragmatic enrichment can't add content or force to a speech act proper, then it can't take content or force away either. Crudely, if pragmatics won't let you assert with a referring or predicative expression, it equally won't let you refer with an assertoric expression.) To put the point in terms of causes and effects, one can think of linguistic competence as one causal force among others, giving rise to the effect of performance. For instance, grammaticality is one causal factor that contributes to the effect of whether a sentence "sounds right"; but grammaticality is not the only factor, since memory limitations and so forth contribute to the observed effect as well. It's then natural to say that ordinary people are often wrong about the causes: they find that a sentence doesn't "sound right", and they incorrectly conclude that ungrammaticality, a matter of the linguistic competence, is the cause. Thus is speaker error explained away. The problem, put in terms of cause and effect, is that Ludlow appears committed not only to our being wrong about the causes of what appears to be sub-sentence use, but also to our being very frequently wrong about the effect of such speech. We think the effect is to label, or draw attention, but we are mistaken: in fact, we must have asserted.

Putting aside our ordinary talk exchanges, there is a more artificial situation which seems to demonstrate our competence with bare words or phrases. This third problem for P1 has to do with native speakers' contrastive judgments about bare words and phrases, in response to investigator queries. With respect to the "content" side of P1, if we ask a reliable subject whether 'Big cats and dogs' is ambiguous—without offering up any sort of sentence-frame, or any discourse context—they can (rightly) say that it is. The same holds for the bare word 'can': ordinary folks seemingly know that it, the word, is ambiguous. Or again, turning to the "grammatical" side of P1, if we ask a reliable subject whether 'The if second at' is just as grammatical as 'The man who lives next door'—again, without offering any sentential frame or context whatever—she can easily report that it is not. This presumably should not be possible, if the grammar does not generate phrases outside sentences, and does not assign a meaning to them. To come at basically the same point another way, one can give a group of subjects a piece of paper with bare words and phrases on the left, and corresponding drawings on the right, and indicate by example that one is to connect the words phrases with the corresponding picture. Having tried this out, let me report the wholly unsurprising result that people can do this task without the least difficulty. Let me add, too, that informants can make judgments, and perform tasks, that require knowledge of the content and syntactic form of 'all in the garden', 'sunk by a missile', and 'from himself'. Someone who endorses P1 needs to find a way to explain how this is possible, despite the fact that the subjects' competence says nothing whatever about words phrases outside sentences.

In sum, whatever Ludlow's two kinds of argument show, I believe they simply *cannot* show that English words and phrases are all (or mostly all) both ungrammatical and gibberish, unless embedded in a sentence. Since P1 can't be right, and his arguments seem to support it, it behoves me to explain where his arguments in support of P1 might have gone wrong. I'll begin with his specific difficult cases, and then turn to the broader point about Minimalism.

In discussing constructions such as passive, it is important to distinguish *whether* the grammar generates something, from *how* the grammar generates it. Ludlow claims, for example, that passive phrases such as 'sunk by a missile' are created by sentence-level processes. Similarly for Q-float phrases like 'all in the garden'. But, I want to ask, even if true, how exactly would this show that 'sunk by a missile' and 'all in the garden' are not generated at all, except within sentences? At best the argument would demonstrate that in deriving such phrases, the derivation must pass through some stage at which the phrase is embedded in a sentence-frame. But even if that were true, crucially, the result of such a process would still be the plain old phrase. It would not *be* a sentence. Thus even if the derivation worked like that, it would still be the case that speakers were producing words or phrases, not sentences.[40] This offers one means of resisting

---

[40] It is worth mentioning here another kind of case that Ludlow (2004) considers. He notes that there are idiom chunks that must occur in the presence of a special verb, giving the example of 'close tabs'. This idiom chunk must be generated with the verb 'keep', in the right structural relation. (To 'keep close tabs on something', for those who don't know the dialect, means to monitor that something closely.) Given this, it once again seems that the grammar cannot generate the bare

P1—which, I insist, just cannot be right—while taking into account some of the examples which Ludlow provides.[41]

Of course another possibility for the generation of unembedded phrases exhibiting passive and Q-float is that these sort of phrases are not created by a transformation at all, but are instead base-generated. Given the decreasing importance of surface-level transformations nowadays, and given how under-developed the alternative Minimalist Program remains with respect to specific constructions like these, this could very well be what is going on. Either way, it's early days to conclude that, extremely implausible as it may seem, such expressions simply cannot be generated at all.

The argument from licensing, applied above to both case and reflexive anaphors, is different from the argument from sentence-level processes. In the latter sort of examples, the licensing material has to be present not just at some stage, but always. Hence the reply "It's not how, it's whether they're generated" will not work for these examples. Some other explanation must be given of how, though these examples seem to entail P1, they don't really do so. I will address case and reflexives in turn.

With respect to case, the most obvious view is that espoused by Barton and Progovac (2004), who write that "nonsententials differ from sententials in one basic property: they are not required to check Case features" (p. 85). One might wonder, of course, why there is this difference. A natural answer goes like this. Many languages have a default, or unmarked, case. A simple example is provided by contrasting unembedded personal pronouns in English and Spanish. In English one puts up a hand and says 'Me, me', in accusative. In Spanish one uses not accusative but nominative: one puts up a hand and says 'I, I'. This illustrates

expression 'close tabs'. It can only generate sentences containing this expression together with 'keep'. So, argues Ludlow, when it appears that people utter 'Close tabs!' unembedded, they really must be uttering a sentence. In response, I would apply the same reasoning offered in the text: it may be that the "how" of 'close tabs' being generated will involve a sentential frame (including 'keep'); but it doesn't follow that this phrase is neither grammatical nor contentful outside the context of a sentence. So idiom chunks don't support P1 after all.

[41] Morgan (1989: 240) makes a similar point, contrasting (a) fragments being generated deriva-tively of sentences with (b) individual spoken fragments being derived from sentences. Spelling out this idea, Morgan notes that we could make a technical refinement to the notion of 'generates'— such that "G generates a string X, with structural description SD, just in case X is analyzable as SD in the surface structure of some S generated by G" (Morgan 1989: 230). This would then make it the case that idiom chunks, case-marked phrases, passivized phrases, etc., are all generated *because the grammar generates sentences containing them*. Yet it would not be the case that the speaker of such an item, in isolation, had "really" uttered a sentence. Rather, they uttered a mere phrase—which phrase is licensed by the grammar in virtue of its being a constituent of some sentence(s).

their different default (unmarked) cases. Spelling out Barton and Progovac's idea, it is reasonable to add that no licensor is required for unembedded phrases exhibiting the default case, whatever it happens to be. Put in Minimalist terms, default case does not need to get "checked" on non-sententials. (Maybe that's what it means to call it "default".) An external licensor is also not required for N-bar fragments, like 'Nice car' and 'Flat tire', because these occur not as arguments, but as predicates.[42] So, this captures two instances where case doesn't get checked. There is a third rather different kind of example, however: there are certain examples where non-default case shows up on an NP that is functioning as the "argument" with respect to the proposition asserted. Here, though, the case-marking *plays a semantic role*, e.g. when the presence of nominative versus accusative indicates whether the denotation of the NP is agent, patient, etc. In this circumstance, case doesn't need to get checked because it is interpretable— and in Minimalism, what is interpretable can remain visible at Conceptual Structure. Applying this to an example, we see why a German speaker will identify a substance with 'Ein Kaffee' [NOM] in isolation, while she will request the same substance with 'Einen Kaffee' [ACC] in isolation. The former exhibits nominative marking because that is the default case in German, while the latter exhibits the accusative marking because of the content of the speech act. Thus case is allowed to be visible in this special circumstance, because the case-markings are getting interpreted at Conceptual Structure.

An alternative sentialist story, of course, is that a case-bearing "fragment" is derived, by deletion say, from a sentential source—this hypothesis being supported on the grounds that the case of the fragment always reflects the case which the phrase exhibits in the corresponding sentence. This is frequently taken as evidence that ellipsis is taking place. Morgan (1989: 232), for example, notes the following contrast in Korean. Where the questions at issue is "Who did you see?", the accusative-marked name (26) is well-formed as an assertion, but the nominative-marked name (27) is not. In contrast, when the question at

---

[42] Barton and Progovac (2004) treat these cases somewhat differently. They adopt Abney's (1987) DP hypothesis, treating these sort of expressions not as N-bars, but rather as NPs that do not project to DP. They then suggest that it is the presence of D which demands case-checking. Not being DPs, hence lacking D, these examples thus do not need to undergo case-checking. As they note, this explains why 'Car broken down' is fine, as a way of communicating that the car is broken down, whereas 'The car broken down' is bad. 'The car broken down' cannot be so used because 'the car' here is a DP functioning as an argument, hence it would need to have its case features checked. (Of course 'The car broken down' can be used, e.g. when pointing at a picture of the car in its unfortunate state; but this usage is not predicating BROKEN DOWN of the argument THE CAR.)

issue is "Who bought this book?", just the reverse is true: the answering phrase must be marked nominative, as in (27), not accusative, as in (26).

(26) Yongsu-ka
Yongsu (acc.)

(27) Yongsu-rul
Yongsu (nom.).

A natural explanation for this pattern is that what the speaker must utter, to convey the answer "Yongsu" to the question "Who did you see?", is (underlyingly) the sentence (28). And this sentential structure demands accusative marking on the name. In contrast, what the speaker must utter, in conveying the answer "Yongsu" to the question "Who bought this book?", is (underlyingly) the sentence (29). This sentence demands nominative on the name.

(28) Yongsu-rul   po-ass-ta
Yongsu (acc.) saw
"I saw Yongsu"

(29) Yongsu-ka   sa-ass-ta
Yongsu (nom.) bought
"Yongsu bought it"

But this deletion-based story ought to be rejected, at least as a general account, because it simplifies matters far too much. For instance, suppose Hans and Frank are speaking German, discussing things which reminds them of various people. They part, and meet up again a few days later. The first thing Hans says, in German, is 'My father', pointing at an old beer-stained table. The corresponding sentence would have to be (30), with 'my' in accusative. (The context 'reminds me of ——' demands this case in German.) But the sub-sentence that one uses in this scenario, in German, actually exhibits the nominative case, as in (31).[43]

(30) Das   erinnert   mich   an meinen   Vater
That   reminds   me   of my-ACC   father

(31) Mein   Vater
My-NOM   father.

In this example, then, it is simply not true that the Case of the phrase in isolation corresponds to what it would have been in a sentence. The ellipsis story

---

[43] I am indebted to Corinne Iten for the example, and for discussion of the German facts.

makes the wrong prediction. (Notice, in contrast, that the positive non-sententialist account of case, sketched above, applies straightforwardly: the phrase takes on nominative case, the default, because using accusative case would carry the (unwanted) semantic information that the denotation was the theme (patient).) Nor is German the only language where case markings ultimately point away from an ellipsis analysis. Thus Morgan (1989: 236–8) himself notes that Korean has both case-marked noun forms and case-less forms, each apparently occurring unembedded.[44] Morgan argues that the case-marked forms are derived from sentences, but that the case-less forms are not: they are bare phrases, even generated as such, which may be used to make assertions and other speech acts. This must be the case because, when embedded in a sentence, they are ill-formed. Consider, finally, the case of pronouns in English. If ellipsis were occurring, one would expect the case of the pronoun to be that which shows up in the corresponding sentence. But, in many situations, even though the isolated English pronoun is marked accusative, the case on the corresponding embedded pronoun must be nominative. Recall, for example, how in English one puts up a hand and says 'Me, me' not 'I, I'. Spelling out the example, if the question in the air has to do with who likes Elvis best, the fans will shout 'Me, me!', even though the corresponding sentence would be 'I like Elvis best!' So again, the ellipsis story makes the wrong prediction about what case will show up on the unembedded phrase.

Given that an alternative story can explain the facts, while allowing words and phrases to be generated, and given that certain examples in English, German, and Korean actually cut against the case-is-only-licensed-within-sentences story, we should conclude that appeals to case-marking do not come close to establishing P1 after all. Which is just as well, as I've said, since P1, though logically possible, is wildly implausible.

Ludlow also argued, as noted above, that English grammar cannot freely generate anaphor-containing phrases outside of sentences, because anaphors require a c-commanding antecedent. This again suggests that what speakers really utter, when they seem to utter bare anaphor-containing phrases, aren't really bare phrases after all. For example, Alex could look through Betty's photo

---

[44] Interestingly, the Korean case-less forms require no linguistic context, though they are also permitted to occur within a discourse context; in contrast, the case-marked forms require overt linguistic context, e.g. a question asked. To give an example from Morgan, 'nae cha!' ["my car" (no case)] can be used by a person returning to a parking lot and finding her car stolen. But both 'nae cha-ka' ["my car" (nom.)] and 'nae cha-rul' ["my car" (acc.)] are ill-formed in that discourse initial circumstance.

album, and finding a picture of Betty on nearly every page, he could turn the page once more and (appear to) say:

(32) Another picture of herself!

On Ludlow's view, what Alex really must have produced is a complete sentence that contains the phrase 'another picture of herself' as a proper part. Otherwise, Alex's ability to speak this way would falsify Principle A of the Binding Theory, since we would here have the grammatical appearance of an anaphor without a c-commanding antecedent.

In reply, I think one must simply conclude that it is not universally true that reflexive anaphors must be licensed by a c-commanding co-indexed NP. But this conclusion is not really that hard to accept. First, there are independent reasons having nothing to do with sub-sentential speech for thinking that there are "exempt anaphors" that are not subject to Binding Theory's Condition A, as the latter is classically construed. Indeed, "picture noun reflexives" like the one in (32) are among the most familiar candidates for being exempt. Building on work by Postal (1971), Kuno (1987), and Zribi-Hertz (1989) among others, Pollard and Sag (1992) argue that exempt anaphors may be licensed by "discourse", in the broad sense of point of view and content, rather than being licensed by a c-commanding syntactic item which is a co-argument. So the appearance of unbound reflexive anaphors is not something peculiar to sub-sentential speech.[45] Indeed, to drive home the point that (apparently) unbound reflexive pronouns do not per se point towards an ellipsis analysis, note that the complete sentence 'Here's yet another picture of herself!', which lacks an antecedent for the reflexive is fine—and surely *it* isn't elliptical for anything. Second, as noted in Stainton (1993), such reflexives can occur without any prior discourse whatever. (I would now add, in light of Stanley's criticisms, that they can occur with no eyebrow raisings, etc., either.) Given this, at least some

---

[45] Nor are these the only kind of exception. Reinhart and Reuland (1993 and elsewhere) discuss examples like 'There were five tourists in the room apart from myself' and 'She gave both Brenda and myself a dirty look'. In neither case is the reflexive pronoun 'myself' c-commanded by an antecedent NP. As Reinhart and Reuland point out, however, in these and related cases there is not a "reflexive-marked predicate" in play—i.e. there is no predicate with the same argument appearing twice. Since they further contend that Condition A, properly construed, is actually about reflexivization in this sense, rather than being about co-indexing under a structural relation (e.g. c-command) per se, such cases are not, in their view, ultimately violations of (their variant on) Condition A. That, they maintain, is why these sentences are well-formed, despite the lack of a c-commanding antecedent for the reflexive pronoun. For further complications, see Keller and Asudeh (2001).

theories of ellipsis will have to say that these cases are not elliptical, in the sense required to preserve the semantics-oriented approach. Also, there are expressions which are clearly not elliptical sentences, but which may contain reflexives, and without a syntactic antecedent. I have in mind 'ditto'-phrases. Thus Luke may non-linguistically convey that the barber shaves Bill, and John may reply:

(33) Ditto for himself.

Since there is evidently no sentence that (33) could be elliptical *for*, this provides another, independent, case of 'himself' occurring without a syntactic binder.

Having rebutted a number of specific examples that Ludlow offers, which initially seemed to support P1, let me briefly turn to his broader objection. Ludlow worries that a Minimalist grammar would over-generate massively if sub-sentences could be derived without "crashing". But, frankly, I do not see why Minimalism is, or needs to be, committed to having only IPs interface with Conceptual Structure. Indeed, as Barton and Progovac (2004) point out, it seems rather that Minimalism in particular should *not* be committed to a special status for sentences. They write:

Since both phrases and clauses are derived bottom-up through merger, to say that generation must start with a sentence would be problematic in [the Minimalist] framework for two reasons. First, it would be contrary to the minimalist considerations of structure building. Second, it would be pure stipulation, given that there is nothing special about sentence/clause in this framework. (2004: 74)

[The generation of non-IPs] via merger is supported and reinforced within the framework of Minimalism by two of its basic properties: (i) the bottom-up strategy of phrase creation based on merger of words, rather than a top-down strategy which would start with an arbitrary top category, such as sentence; and (ii) by the general requirement in Minimalism for economy, which prohibits any superfluous and unmotivated pieces of structure. (2004: 75)

Nor, *pace* Ludlow, is it the case that generating non-IPs would leave no constraints at all: the key constraint remains that any material which has not been "checked" has to be interpretable by the Conceptual System. (This general constraint would explain, as noted, why non-default case-markings are allowed on sub-sentential utterances when, but only when, case has a semantic role to play—e.g. indicating whether the item mentioned is agent, theme, or what-have-you. As explained above, case doesn't get checked off in such cases, but that's acceptable because case here actually gets interpreted.) So, Minimalism does not need to privilege IPs.

Unless, of course, only IPs are interpretable. If nothing else can be interpreted, then nothing else can be allowed to arrive at Conceptual Structure without crashing. Thus the key issue remains the one flagged above: within Minimalism, sub-sentences can be allowed to be generated only if they are interpretable. But, since we surely can interpret words or phrases without any linguistic or other context—noticing their entailment patterns, ambiguities, anomalies, etc.—then surely they are interpretable. (To claim this is not, let me stress again, immediately to make the stronger claim that they can be used to perform speech acts. I hold that too, but that claim needs defending in a way that the bare interpretability of words or phrases does not.) Given that such things can be *interpreted*, there is, *pace* Ludlow, no reason to think that Minimalism rules them out.

Once we grant that words or phrases are generated, and assigned a meaning—i.e. once we reject P1—there remains no positive reason, from Minimalism or elsewhere, for thinking that syntactic ellipsis is going on in such cases. I have also argued that the specific examples which Ludlow gives, which seem to support P1, do not actually do so. Given this, the central criticism of the empty element view is sustained: there is simply no need to posit an unfamiliar kind of syntactic ellipsis here, since pragmatics is required anyway, and can easily enough fill the gap.

6. Concluding Remarks on Implications (and Genuineness Again): Six Theses

My defense of non-sentential assertion is now complete. Before moving on to implications, let me very briefly review the results of that complex defense.

I responded to Stanley in three ways: I set aside "shorthand" as under-described; I argued that, *pace* Stanley, sub-sentential speech often achieves the level of a genuine speech act, the key point here being the deep formal, functional, and informational similarities between sub-sentential speech and fully sentential speech; and, having canvassed in Section 3 several things one might mean by "ellipsis", I argued that the only two variants of "ellipsis" that are at all worked out, and that would really avoid the consequences Stanley wishes to avoid—i.e. the Sag-style deletion variant and the Ludlow-style empty element variant—cannot plausibly be applied to sub-sentential speech in very, very many cases. Thus, once "shorthand" is set aside, there are a host of examples of (apparently) sub-sentential speech that (*a*) cannot be reduced to any familiar (and helpful) notion of "ellipsis" and yet (*b*) clearly are genuine speech acts. Hence Stanley's "divide and conquer" strategy will not cover all cases.

I responded to Ludlow by making four key points. First, it just cannot be true that our competence assigns an asterisk equally to all unembedded sub-sentential expressions, and that it assigns no meaning whatever to them. It is somewhat controversial that speakers can use bare words and phrases to perform speech acts; but it stretches credulity too far to maintain that words and phrases are simply never understood or used grammatically. Second, it's crucial to distinguish *whether* non-sentences are generated from *how* they are generated. It might be that (some) non-sentences—e.g. passivized phrases, idiom chunks, etc.—are derived by a process that involves embedding them in a sentence-frame at some stage. But, even if true, this wouldn't show that such bare phrases aren't really generated at all, so that the only thing one can use are sentences. Third, it's not at all clear that Minimalism is in conflict with the existence of bare words and phrases. To the contrary, some authors have argued that Minimalism predicts their existence straightforwardly. (However, *if* Minimalism is in conflict with the production and comprehension of bare words and phrases, the right conclusion is surely "So much the worse for Minimalism"—since, to repeat, it's patent that words and phrases are used on business cards, street signs, maps, etc.) And if Minimalism is consistent with words or phrases being generated, it is presumably also consistent with them being used assertorically, on the grounds that Minimalist syntax simply makes no commitments one way or the other vis-à-vis what speech acts can be made with things generated by the grammar. Finally, I considered two constructions that seemed particularly worrisome: phrases that bear case and phrases that contain reflexive anaphors. I argued that the facts about case are actually more complicated than a syntactic ellipsis account allows (recall the German and Korean data), and proposed that case might be appearing on bare phrases in some instances as a bearer of information about thematic role and such, in other instances as default. With respect to reflexive anaphors, I gave reasons independent of non-sentential speech for thinking that they actually can occur without a c-commanding binder.

I want to end the chapter by returning to the implications of non-sentential assertion. Such implications are important in their own right, of course. But considering the implications carefully is also important because if certain things *aren't* implied by the reality of non-sentential assertion, it can be easier to accept the genuineness of the phenomenon. The game plan for this final section is as follows. First, I rehearse six theses, four of which have appeared above—though not necessarily in so many words—and two of which make their first appearance below. The theses in question are:

(T1) Truth-conditional semantics is justified.

(T2) Truth-conditional interpretation is fundamentally different from other kinds of interpretation (e.g. the kind involved in interpreting kicks under the table and taps on the shoulder).

(T3) All truth-conditional effects of context are traceable to logical form. Put otherwise, all truth-conditional context dependence results from fixing the values of contextually sensitive elements in the real structure of natural language sentences.

(T4) All effects of extra-linguistic context on the truth conditions of an assertion are traceable to logical form.

(T5) There are no genuine examples of non-sentential assertions.

(T6) All apparent cases of non-sentential assertions are merely apparent, falling into one of three categories: they are either (*a*) not genuine linguistic acts, (*b*) not genuinely sub-sentential, because (plausibly) syntactically elliptical, or (*c*) shorthand.

Second I revisit how the four familiar theses relate to one another. This initial discussion will serve to highlight again some of the previously discussed implications of non-sentential assertion: in particular, I hope to clarify still further the sense in which the pair T3–T4 entails the pair T5–T6. That's the bit about "implications which are important in their own right". In addition, I consider the relationship between the two theses that have not been discussed explicitly until now (T1–T2) and the other four. What will emerge, among other things, is that the pair T1–T2 *does not* entail T5. Indeed, I think one can endorse T1–T2 and reject all of the other theses. That's the bit about "if certain things *aren't* implied, it can be easier to accept the genuineness of the phenomenon".

Let me begin with what the theses say. Thesis T1 endorses semantics built around truth-conditions. There are various flavors of truth conditional semantics, of course. There is truth-theoretic semantics, as pursued by Tarski, Davidson, and their followers. There is truth-centered semantics of the Fregean variety, which has the meaning of a sentence going together with how the world is, to determine a truth value as referent. There is the possible worlds variation on the latter. And so on. T1 is meant to be silent on which variety is correct: it says only that the general approach is on the right track.

Thesis T2 rejects the idea that all interpretation is of a piece. In particular, interpreting language, which is truth-conditional interpretation, is special and different. Differences that come immediately to mind are: that linguistic interpretation is compositional and recursive; that a special encapsulated knowledge base is at play; that such interpretation is algorithmic rather than abductive; and so on. Some will add, as motivation for T2, that linguistic interpretation being different is crucial to the ultimate success of truth-conditional semantics, since the kind of interpretation at work in figuring out why so-and-so kicked me might appear intractable, especially using the kinds of formal means at the disposal of formal semanticists. Thus T1 may well bring T2 in its wake, in some loose sense, because for truth-conditional semantics to be tractable—hence "justified"—there must be a part of linguistic interpretation that is distinctive, thereby making it more tractable than the understanding of kicks and taps.

Thesis T4 showed up early on, in the form of the issue of pragmatic determinants of what is asserted, stated, or claimed: cases in which "pragmatic processes" (e.g. general-purpose inference, on the basis of all available information) supposedly play a role in the determination of what is asserted. (Well, more precisely, such processes play this role in a way that goes beyond disambiguation and "slot-filling".) As explained at the outset, the view that truth conditions are affected by pragmatics in this additional way—a view defended by Robyn Carston (1988), François Recanati (1989), Dan Sperber and Deirdre Wilson (1986), and Charles Travis (1985) among others—contrasts with the purportedly Gricean (1975) idea that what is asserted is exhaustively determined by disambiguation and reference assignment to explicitly indexical elements. That is, as many people read Grice, it is only "what the speaker meant", and not "what the speaker literally stated", that is calculated pragmatically. To take one example, Recanati (1989) believes that what is strictly and literally *asserted* by an utterance of 'I've had breakfast', in reply to the question whether one is hungry, can be that the speaker has had breakfast on the day in question. (The speaker may also thereby implicates that she is not hungry. But that's another matter.) According to this view, the speaker would not, in this instance, simply assert that at some time in his life he had eaten breakfast, while merely communicating that he had eaten breakfast on the day of the speaking. That is, this latter proposition is not just implicated, it is "said".[46] On the other hand, arriving at this proposition requires

---

[46] As noted above, Kent Bach (1994*a* and elsewhere) has argued that one should restrict the term 'what is said' to the result of disambiguation and reference assignment. Thus "what is said" by a non-sentential utterance, in Bach's minimal sense, is not a proposition. He also insists, however, that "what is said" in his sense falls quite far short of what is asserted, asked, or demanded. (Thus on his view, "what is said" by an utterance of 'I've had breakfast' is precisely *that the speaker has, at some time in his life, eaten breakfast*. Bach would add, however, that this is not necessarily what is asserted.) As I have

appeal to salient real-world information—for instance, the information that eating breakfast is an exceedingly common practice, so that it's very unlikely that the speaker would never have eaten breakfast in his life, and hence quite unlikely that he is communicating the obvious proposition that he has done so. (Compare, 'I've had lizard'.) So "what is said" in this case is partially determined by information provided only pragmatically.

As for thesis T3, it encompasses not only assertion, but speech acts generally. T3 requires that the truth-conditional effects on *all* speech acts—questions, promises, commands, and so forth—be traceable to items in logical form: if there are pragmatic determinants of what is asked or commanded or promised (again, that go beyond some role in "slot-filling" and disambiguation), T3 is false.

T5 baldly denies the genuineness of non-sentential assertions. Not much need be said to explain it. T6 makes good on the claim that speakers only appear to perform non-sentential assertion, by drawing on Stanley's "divide and conquer" maneuver. Having discussed these issues at *great* length, I won't say more about them right here.

So much for what the six theses say. Let me turn, first, to how the latter four theses relate. P4 is a special case of P3: P3 says that there are no pragmatic determinants of truth conditions at all; P4 says that there aren't any in the special case of assertion. Instead, what determines truth conditions is just disambiguated logical form, plus reference assigned to any indexicals. (Notice, by the way, that T3 could still be false, even if T4 is true—if there are pragmatic determinants of what is promised, or asked, or commanded.) T5, in essence, is forced upon one by T4: if there are no pragmatic determinants of what is asserted, then there can't be any in the particular case of sub-sentential speech. Returning to the earlier example, it seems that the hearer of 'From Spain' must consult the extra-linguistic context to find the thing which the speaker who utters 'From Spain' most likely had in mind. (Here, the displayed letter.) This is a role for context which is not built into the logical form of the expression used—though there is, of course, a sense in which the sub-propositional content of the expression helps along the relevance-driven search for something to "saturate" the property, so as to yield a proposition-meant. Since sub-sentence use seems to provide counterexamples to T4, the only way to save T4 is if non-sentential assertions are not genuine: they either aren't genuinely assertions, or they aren't genuinely sub-sentential. Thus T5. The problem is, simply asserting T5 seems to fly in the

suggested, given his usage of 'what is said', I do not think there is ultimately much substantive disagreement between my view and his, since Bach will not deny that there are sub-sentential, albeit fully propositional, assertions.

face of experience. To make T5 plausible, these appearances must be explained away. That is the job of T6: to explain away every apparent example by assigning it to one of three categories. (Notice that Ludlow's arguments come in precisely here, since they seem to provide further reasons for favoring a syntactic ellipsis account in many cases.) So we have:

(T3) (no pragmatic determinants of truth conditions) → (T4) (no pragmatic determinants of what is asserted).

(T4) (no pragmatic determinants of what is asserted) → T5 (no genuine non-sentential assertions).

(T5) (no genuine non-sentential assertions) → (T6) (all apparent cases fall into three categories).

I should stress that the arrows above need not amount to "logically entails". Since T4 is a special case of T3, it's arguable that there is genuine entailment here. But T4 requires T5 in the sense that the latter sets aside one variety of purported counterexample as not genuine. And T5 requires T6 only in the sense that T6 affords *one* way to explain away the appearances that initially make T5 look implausible.

Two notes are in order about further relations between these four. First, I pointed out above that T3 can be false because of pragmatic determinants of what is promised, or asked, or what-have-you. In particular, let me now add, T3 could be falsified by *sub-sentential* promises, questions, or orders. So non-sentence use remains apposite to T3 even if T5 is true. Second, and to anticipate a point that will re-emerge at the very end, it's worth stressing *how* T5 might be used to support T4 (the thesis about assertion) and T3 (the more general claim). T5 plays this supporting role in the sense that if there isn't any good evidence for pragmatic effects on truth conditions, then it might (I stress: *might*) be safe to assume, as the simplest hypothesis, that the only effects on truth conditions come from (*a*) the structure of the expression and (*b*) the denotations of the elements of that structure—some of these denotations being extra-linguistically determined, via the appearance of indexicals. The idea here is that the burden of proof may rest with those who would *deny* T4 and T3: they need to provide counterexamples. Thus, Stanley and Ludlow both try to argue that all the alleged counterexamples from non-sentence use are unconvincing. Therefore, T3 and T4 are sustained, in so far as they are the default assumptions. (Whether this move from the truth of T5 to the truth of T3–T4 is actually warranted is, of course, a more complex matter. Elugardo and Stainton 2004*b* address such "burden of proof" issues at some length.)

Now that the six theses have been explained, and the relations between the latter four of them have been noted, we can turn to the question of how the pair T1–T2 relate to T3 *et al*. If all truth-conditional effects of context are traceable to logical form, then there is a very clear difference between natural language communication and other sorts of communicative behavior: specifically, natural language utterances have their (literal) content determined solely by semantic operations on their logical forms, where those logical forms can at most be context-dependent in the sense of containing explicit "slots" to be filled in. In short, T3 supports T2. (As does T4, for the special case of assertion.) T3 also supports T1, because the former thesis establishes a tight connection between something patently linguistic (i.e. logical form) and truth conditions, which, in turn, makes it plausible that one will be able to generate truth conditions for linguistic expressions—as justifying truth-conditional semantics requires. Specifically, truth-conditional semantics can remain, as always, the theory of how the truth conditions of whole sentences get compositionally determined from the structure of the expression (i.e. its logical form) plus the meaning assignments of its parts—where some of those parts have constant meanings, and some of them (i.e. the indexicals) have their meaning fixed by context.

In short:

(T3) (no pragmatic determinants of truth conditions) → (T1) (truth-conditional semantics is justified).

(T3) (no pragmatic determinants of truth conditions) → (T2) (truth conditional interpretation is different).

What remains to consider is how T1–T2 relate to T5–T6. I'll get to that very shortly. But first, having them laid out this way, let me now clarify even more explicitly my own views on the last four theses. I have argued, here and elsewhere, that T6 isn't true. But then there are lots of non-sentential assertions which cannot be explained away. I can thus run several iterations of *modus tollens* on the argument from the previous page, concluding first that T5 isn't true because T6 isn't; concluding further that since non-sentential assertion is a genuine phenomenon, and not merely apparent, this means that neither of T4 or T3 is true either: neither of them is consistent with the existence of non-sentential assertions. So, there are pragmatic determinants of what is asserted in particular, and of speech act content in general. And informational integration, even during speech understanding, presumably is not, then, a matter of building up linguistic structures and assigning extra-linguistic referents to those natural language structures. I also believe, though I have not argued the point here, that even if T5 is true, so that there aren't any convincing examples of non-sentential *assertions*, there are still, in other cases of non-sentential speech, truth-conditional effects of pragmatic processes. That is, non-sentential speech can be used to call T3 into question even if there aren't any clear cases of non-sentential assertions—specifically because there are non-sentential questionings, and other speech acts. For instance, one can ask whether a demonstrated letter is from Spain by saying, with rising intonation, 'From Spain?' (And, I insist, rising intonation does not make something a sentence, either syntactically or semantically speaking. See Stainton 2000 for why.) This speech act has the illocutionary force and the truth conditions—maybe better, the satisfaction conditions—of an utterance of 'Is that from Spain?' But it does not get those satisfaction conditions merely by the assignment of reference to elements in its logical form, because what is uttered is simply a prepositional phrase. It is not an elliptical sentence and it is not "shorthand", at least not in any sense that would allow one to save T3. Thus, I believe, T3 would still not be credible, even if Stanley and Ludlow were right about T5 and T6. (Which, as I argued at length, they aren't.)

At last, let me get to the punch line about what *isn't* implied, and how this bears on accepting the genuineness of the phenomenon. I'm willing to grant that T3 somehow supports T1 and T2. But, I insist, it is not true that T1 and T2, either individually or together, entail T3. Nor do they entail its sub-case, T4. It is thus not necessary, to rescue T1–T2, that one reject pragmatic determinants of speech act content, whether assertions or other kinds. In particular, and this is crucial, T1–T2 are compatible with pragmatic determinants of speech act content *in the case of sub-sentence use*. That is, T1–T2 do not entail T5.[47]

To defend this result, I will sketch a model of linguistic communication which attracts me, and which is consistent with T1 and T2. (I do not say that all

---

[47] Jason Stanley seems to worry that one can run a long *modus tollens* argument, of roughly the following form:

T1 → T2
T2 → T3
T3 → T4
T4 → T5
¬ T5

Therefore

¬ T1.

Indeed, this imagined sort of argument seems to be Stanley's prime motivation for endorsing T6. But, say I, T2 (truth-conditional interpretation is different) definitely does not entail T3 (all truth-conditional effects of context come in via elements of logical form). So, the feared iterated *modus tollens* is, at a minimum, blocked at that point.

of the model's proponents *endorse* T1 and T2, especially not in this form; just that the model is consistent with them.) I will also explain along the way how that model permits one to reject T5. So, there is a way to make T1–T2 consistent with the denial of T5. Here is the idea. Following Sperber and Wilson (1986), I maintain that understanding a linguistic act involves two sorts of processes. First, there is the decoding process, a specifically linguistic process presumably carried out by a separate "language module". Decoding an expression requires knowing the language in question—knowing both its syntax and its semantics, among other things. That is why, though I can decode expressions in English, I cannot decode expressions in Japanese: I simply do not have the right knowledge base for that, stored in my "language faculty". As noted briefly in Section 1, in addition to the decoding process, I also take understanding a linguistic act to involve a general-purpose inferential process, which makes use of all available information to arrive at all-things-considered judgments. (This isn't to say that all things *have* been considered, of course. It rather means that all things could, in principle, end up being relevant.) In my view, this latter process is likely not confined to a special module or series of modules, precisely because it draws on information from vision and the other senses, memory, face recognition, as well as speech, and numerous other things as well. It appears, therefore, to be a non-algorithmic process within what Fodor (1983) labels the "central system". (As should be clear, this kind of picture lends itself very naturally to the model of not-language-based informational integration, which I also take to be supported by sub-sentential speech.) That's the model of linguistic communication. On the other hand, still following Sperber and Wilson (1986), I do not believe there to be any special, task-specific, decoding process for kicks under the table, or taps on the shoulder. There is no special-purpose faculty of the mind–brain dedicated to this. Communicative acts of these sorts are understood using only the general-purpose inferential system, on the basis of commonsense knowledge. (Which is why, for instance, someone who does not speak a word of Japanese can fully understand the intent of a Japanese person who kicked them.)

Suppose the model is even broadly correct. Then T2 can easily be true: there would be an obvious and a fundamental difference between the two sorts of interpretation. Specifically, whereas one sort (the truth-conditional linguistic sort) involves two quite distinct processes, drawing on two quite distinct bodies of information, one of which is language-specific, the other sort (the kick/tap sort) involves a single process, and no special-purpose body of information, let alone one trained upon language. True enough, it is not the case that the difference between spoken communication and other sorts ends up being a matter of one single mental faculty in the truth-conditional case, and a wholly disjoint faculty in the non-linguistic case: there is, instead, some significant overlap. In particular, the second kind of "central system" process plays a part in each, because integration of the information coming from the language system happens there. But this doesn't make the difference between linguistic interpretation and non-linguistic interpretation somehow less than fundamental. (As any hapless unilingual world-traveler will tell you.)

On a Sperber and Wilson type account, then, linguistic interpretation remains fundamentally different from other kinds of communication. And that is the account I endorse. (I won't try to defend it here.) Now consider how non-sentential speech fits into this model. It quite clearly involves both of the two aforementioned processes. Returning to our first example, to understand 'Chunks of strawberries', a hearer must know (at least) the syntax and semantics of this English construction—which information is surely stored in the very same module which would allow them to understand 'Steven made jam containing chunks of strawberries'. Put otherwise, to understand 'Chunks of strawberries', used on its own, the hearer must *decode* this expression. Only once she has done so can general-purpose inference play its part, in determining for instance what object the speaker had in mind. Integration, then, happens separately from decoding. That non-sentential speech does in fact draw on special-purpose knowledge of language should be absolutely evident, at least to anyone in the broadly Chomskian tradition. From the point of view of the "language module", the only difference between non-sentential speech and sentential speech, as noted above, is that the former involves the use of projections from lexical categories, of semantic type $<e>$, $<e,t>$, $<<e,t>,t>$, etc., while the latter involves the use of a projection from an inflectional element, assumed to be of semantic type $<t>$. This surely is not akin to the difference between language use on the one hand, and under-the-table-kicks on the other.

In sum: T2 can be true in this general model of linguistic communication; and even if T2 is added to the general model as a hypothesis, that is *not* sufficient for T3 to be true as well. Moreover, the resulting bipartite picture (i.e. a two-process view of linguistic communication, plus a truth-centered story about type semantics) allows one to grant the genuineness of non-sentential assertion. Hence T2 doesn't entail ¬T5.

I hope the foregoing at least begins to hint at why, on one reading of T1 anyway, this thesis need be no more threatened by non-sentential speech than T2 is. T1, recall, says that truth-conditional semantics is justified. True enough, on *one* way of understanding this preservationist goal, and on one of the ways Jason Stanley intends, it is the job of semantics—read the process of compositionally determining whole-meanings on the basis of part-meanings plus structure, where part-meanings can include indexically determined denotations—to *all on its own* yield the truth conditions of an utterance. On this reading, T1 essentially reiterates T3, and hence on this reading T1 *is* in conflict with the existence of genuine non-sentential assertions. But another thing one can understand by "justifying truth-conditional semantics"—something which seems to me much more important—is justifying the idea that meaning and truth are very intimately related, an idea closely associated with Frege, Tarski, and such. If one understands T1 as saying that truth-*centered* semantics is justified, then non-sentential speech does not, so far as I can see, conflict with T1. For it can still be the case, at least according to one positive proposal, that linguistic expressions (types and tokens) get assigned, as extensions, things like functions from objects to truth values, or functions from such functions to truth values, etc. Indeed, on the bipartite proposal given just above—which departs from the letter of Sperber and Wilson (1986), but is consistent with the overall model of linguistic communication—truth remains absolutely central to semantics. The fact is, if one adopts my broadly pragmatic approach to the issue, while sticking to a truth-centered semantics, one might not need to make a single change to that truth-centered theory, i.e. at the level of expression types, to account for less-than-sentential speech.[48] So, not only is non-sentential speech consistent with the general orientation of truth-centered semantics, it's consistent with existing detailed proposals about how truth relates to meaning.

Put another way, because of non-sentential speech, pragmatics plays a part in determining the content of what is asserted; but this doesn't mean that pragmatics plays a role in determining the reference and/or satisfaction conditions of expressions. These remain untouched. In which case, it's hard to see how non-sentential speech can pose a threat to "truth-conditional semantics" in this broad sense. In particular, non-sentential speech doesn't seem to me to raise any immediate concern for Fregean semantics, or its contemporary heirs—as long as these refrain from making claims about the determinants of speech act contents,

---

[48] Actually, I'm not sure that every imaginable truth-centered semantic theory will be able to accommodate less-than-sentential communication this easily. For instance, a theory which said that the only things hearers have provided to them by their semantic knowledge are T-sentences might be left with an explanatory gap—since it's not clear how knowing T-sentences alone would allow one to interpret 'From Spain' or 'A healthy dollop of whipped cream'. Truth be told, however, I take this to be a good prima facie reason for not adopting such theories.

and stick to describing the content of expression types.[49] The same kind of lesson holds for syntax, not least because my key claims are not about the grammar itself, but about how its products can be deployed in speech acts.

Finally, let me remind you why all this matters to the issue of genuineness. T1 and T2 are very widely endorsed in philosophy and formal linguistics: a great deal of evidence would be required to make the language theory community give them up. Now suppose, contrary to what I've just argued, that T5 *were* entailed by T1–T2. Then there would be a very heavy burden of proof on any theorist (myself included) who argues against T5—a burden as heavy as that required on one who would deny T1 and T2 themselves. But that burden vanishes if T1 and T2 are silent on T5. Which they are. Let me also add this. If T3 and T4 *aren't* supported by T1–T2—and given the availability of Sperber and Wilson's general model, there's little reason to think they are—then I can see no reason to take the former theses to be initially plausible. The default hypotheses, say. At best, one could say that T3–T4 are neutral, with the burden of proof lying equally with those who deny them and those who endorse them. If that's right, then even if T5 and T6 were true, one couldn't conclude that T3 and T4 were *true*. One could only conclude that the issue with respect to the latter theses remained wholly open, since they had not been proven false, but have also not been positively supported. This, I think, is the most that Stanley and Ludlow's arguments could show.

In fact, however, I have given lots of reasons for thinking that T5 and T6 are out-and-out false. These are equally reasons for thinking that there are pragmatic determinants of what is asserted, and for thinking that informational integration, even during speech comprehension, doesn't always happen via natural language. Moreover, and of most pressing concern here, they are also reasons for adopting a pragmatics-oriented approach to non-sentential speech acts.

---

[49] Speaking of Frege, it might be thought that non-sentential speech calls into question his notorious "context principle". My own view is that there are very many ways of reading the context principle, only some of which are threatened by the existence of non-sentential speech acts. Specifically, as I explain in Stainton (2000), I ultimately do not think that non-sentential speech acts call into question Frege's key methodological idea, namely, that when asking for the meaning of some expression, one should ask how it alters truth conditions. And, given that it is *this* methodological principle which allows Frege to avoid psychologism—after all, what numerals contribute to truth conditions are not images or anything mental—it may be that this methodological reading is the only reading of the context principle that Frege himself should have cared about. As a result, non-sentential speech acts might pose no real problem for Frege's larger philosophy after all.

REFERENCES

Abney, Stephen (1987), 'The English Noun Phrase in its Sentential Aspect', Ph.D. diss. (Massachusetts Institute of Technology).

Bach, Kent (1994a), 'Semantic Slack: What Is Said and More', in S. L. Tsohatzidis (ed.), *Foundations of Speech Act Theory* (London: Routledge), 267–91.

—— (1994b), 'Conversational Impliciture', *Mind and Language*, 9: 124–62.

Barton, Ellen (1989), 'Autonomy and Modularity in a Pragmatic Model', in B. Music, R. Graczyk, and C. Wiltshire (eds.), *Papers from the 25th Annual Regional Meeting of the Chicago Linguistic Society, Part Two: Parasession on Language in Context* (Chicago: Chicago Linguistic Society), 1–14.

—— (1990), *Nonsentential Constituents: A Theory of Grammatical Structure and Pragmatic Interpretation* (Philadelphia: John Benjamins).

—— (1998), 'The Grammar of Telegraphic Structures: Sentential and Nonsentential Derivation', *Journal of English Linguistics*, 26: 37–67.

—— and Ljiljana Progovac (2004), 'Nonsententials in Minimalism', in Elugardo and Stainton (2004a, 71–93).

Breedin, Sarah D., and Eleanor M. Saffran (1999), 'Sentence Processing in the Face of Semantic Loss', *Journal of Experimental Psychology: General*, 128 4: 547–62.

Cappelen, Herman, and Ernest Lepore (1997), 'On an Alleged Connection between Indirect Quotation and Semantic Theory', *Mind and Language*, 12: 278–96.

Carston, Robyn (1988), 'Implicature, Explicature, and Truth-Theoretic Semantics', in R. M. Kempson (ed.), *Mental Representations* (Cambridge: Cambridge University Press), 155–81; repr. in Davis (1991: 33–51).

Chatterjee, Anjan, *et al.* (1995), 'Asyntactic Thematic Role Assignment: The Use of a Temporal-Spatial Strategy', *Brain and Language*, 49: 125–39.

Chomsky, Noam (1981), *Lectures on Government and Binding* (Dordrecht: Foris).

—— (1995), *The Minimalist Program* (Cambridge, Mass.: MIT Press).

Clapp, Lenny (2001), 'What Unarticulated Constituents Could Not Be', in J. C. Campbell, M. O'Rourke, and D. Shier (eds.), *Meaning and Truth: Investigations in Philosophical Semantics* (New York: Seven Bridges Press), 231–56.

Crouch, Richard (1995), 'Ellipsis and Quantification: A Substitutional Approach', *Proceedings of the Seventh European Association for Computational Linguistics*, 7: 229–36.

Dalrymple, Mary (2004), 'Against Reconstruction in Ellipsis', in Elugardo and Stainton (2004a, 31–55).

—— Stuart M. Shierber, and Fernando C. N. Pereira (1991), 'Ellipsis and Higher-Order Unification', *Linguistics and Philosophy*, 14: 399–452.

Davis, Steven (1991), *Pragmatics: A Reader* (Oxford: Oxford University Press).

—— and Brandon Gillon (forthcoming) (eds.), *Semantics: A Reader* (Oxford: Oxford University Press).

Dummett, Michael (1973), *Frege: Philosophy of Language* (Cambridge, Mass.: Harvard University Press).

Elugardo, Reinaldo, and Robert J. Stainton (2001), 'Logical Form and the Vernacular', *Mind and Language*, 16 4: 393–424.

————— (2003), 'Grasping Objects and Contents', in A. Barber (ed.), *The Epistemology of Language* (Oxford: Oxford University Press), 257–302.

————— (2004*a*), *Ellipsis and Nonsentential Speech* (Dordrecht: Kluwer).

————— (2004*b*), 'Shorthand, Syntactic Ellipsis and the Pragmatic Determinants of What Is Said', *Mind and Language*, 19(4): 442–71.

Fodor, Jerry A. (1983), *The Modularity of Mind* (Cambridge, Mass.: MIT Press).

Grice, H. Paul (1975), 'Logic and Conversation', in P. Cole and J. Morgan (eds.), *Syntax and Semantics, iii: Speech Acts* (New York: Academic Press), 41–58.

Hankamer, Jorge, and Ivan Sag (1976), 'Deep and Surface Anaphora', *Linguistic Inquiry*, 7 3: 391–428.

Jarema, Gonia (1998), 'The Breakdown of Morphology in Aphasia', in B. Stemmer and H. A. Whitaker (eds.), *Handbook of Neurolinguistics* (San Diego: Academic Press), 221–34.

Keller, Frank, and Ash Asudeh (2001), 'Constraints on Linguistic Coreference: Structural vs. Pragmatic Factors', in Johanna D. Moore and Keith Stenning (eds.), *Proceedings of the 23rd Annual Conference of the Cognitive Science Society* (Mahwah, NJ: Lawrence Erlbaum), 483–8.

Kenyon, Tim (1999), 'Non-Sentential Assertions and the Dependence Thesis of Word Meaning', *Mind and Language*, 14 4: 424–40.

Kripke, Saul (1977), 'Speaker's Reference and Semantic Reference', in P. A. French, T. E. Uehling, and H. K. Wettstein (eds.), *Contemporary Perspectives in the Philosophy of Language* (Minneapolis: University of Minnesota Press).

Kuno, Susumu (1987), *Functional Syntax* (Chicago: University of Chicago Press).

Ludlow, Peter (2004), 'A Note on Alleged Cases of Nonsentential Assertion', in Elugardo and Stainton (2004*a*, 95–108).

Merchant, Jason (2001), *The Syntax of Silence* (Oxford: Oxford University Press).

Morgan, Jerry (1973), 'Sentence Fragments and the Notion "Sentence", ' in B. Kachru *et al.* (eds.), *Issues in Linguistics: Papers in Honor of Henry and Renee Kahane* (Urbana: University of Illinois Press), 719–51.

————— (1989), 'Sentence Fragments Revisited', in B. Music, R. Graczyk, and C. Wiltshire (eds.), *Papers from the 25th Annual Regional Meeting of the Chicago Linguistic Society, Part Two: Parasession on Language in Context* (Chicago: Chicago Linguistic Society), 228–41.

Neale, Stephen (2000), 'On Being Explicit: Comments on Stanley and Szabó, and on Bach', *Mind and Language*, 15: 284–94.

Nespoulous, Jean-Luc, *et al.* (1988), 'Agrammatism in Sentence Production without Comprehension Deficits', *Brain and Language*, 33: 273–95.

Perry, John (1986), 'Thought without Representation', *Proceedings of the Aristotelian Society*, suppl. vol. 60: 137–51.

Pollard, Carl, and Ivan Sag (1992), 'Anaphors in English and the Scope of Binding Theory', *Linguistic Inquiry*, 23 2: 261–303.

Postal, Paul (1971), *Crossover Phenomena* (New York: Holt, Rinehart & Winston).

Recanati, François (1989), 'The Pragmatics of What Is Said', *Mind and Language*, 4: 294–328.

Reinhart, Tanya, and Eric Reuland (1993), 'Reflexivity', *Linguistic Inquiry*, 24 4: 657–720.

Sag, Ivan (1976), 'Deletion and Logical Form', Ph.D. diss. (Massachusetts Institute of Technology).

—— and Jorge Hankamer (1977), 'Syntactically vs. Pragmatically Controlled Anaphora', in R. W. Fasold and R. W. Shuy (eds.), *Studies in Language Variation* (Washington: Georgetown University Press).

Schachter, Paul (1977), 'Does She or Doesn't She?', *Linguistic Inquiry*, 8: 763–7.

Searle, John R. (1978), 'Literal Meaning', *Erkenntnis*, 13: 207–24.

—— (1980), 'The Background of Meaning', in J. Searle, F. Kiefer, and M. Bierwisch (eds.), *Speech Act Theory and Pragmatics* (Dordrecht: Reidel), 221–32.

Sellars, Wilfrid (1954), 'Presupposing', *Philosophical Review*, 63: 197–215.

Sirigu, Angela (1998), 'Distinct Frontal Regions for Processing Sentence Syntax and Story Grammar', *Cortex*, 34: 771–8.

Sperber, Dan, and Deirdre Wilson (1986), *Relevance* (Cambridge, Mass.: Harvard University Press).

Sportiche, Dominique (1988), 'A Theory of Floating Quantifiers and its Corollaries for Constituent Structure', *Linguistic Inquiry*, 19 3: 425–49.

Stainton, Robert J. (1993), 'Non-Sentential Assertions', Ph.D. diss. (Massachusetts Institute of Technology).

—— (1994), 'Using Non-Sentences: An Application of Relevance Theory', *Pragmatics and Cognition*, 22: 269–84.

—— (1995), 'Non-Sentential Assertions and Semantic Ellipsis', *Linguistics and Philosophy*, 18 3: 281–96.

—— (1997a), 'What Assertion Is Not', *Philosophical Studies*, 85 1: 57–73.

—— (1997b). 'Utterance Meaning and Syntactic Ellipsis', *Pragmatics and Cognition*, 5 1: 49–76.

—— (1998a), 'Quantifier Phrases, Meaningfulness "in Isolation", and Ellipsis', *Linguistics and Philosophy*, 21: 311–40; repr. in Davis and Gillon (forthcoming).

—— (1998b), 'Unembedded Definite Descriptions and Relevance', *Revista Alicantina de Estudios Ingleses*, special issue: *Relevance Theory*, 11: 231–9.

—— (2000), 'The Meaning of "Sentences" ', *Nous*, 34 3: 441–54.

—— (2004), 'The Pragmatics of Non-Sentences', in L. Horn and G. Ward (eds.), *The Handbook of Pragmatics* (Oxford: Basil Blackwell), 266–87.

—— and Alisa Hillier (1990) (eds.), *A Le Camp Sourcebook* (Toronto: Applied Linguistics Research Working Group, Glendon College of York University).

Stanley, Jason (2000), 'Context and Logical Form', *Linguistics and Philosophy*, 23 4: 391–434.

—— and Zoltán G. Szabó (2000), 'On Quantifier Domain Restriction', *Mind and Language*, 15: 219–61.

Tanenhaus, Michael K., and Greg N. Carlson (1990), 'Comprehension of Deep and Surface Verb Phrase Anaphors', *Language and Cognitive Processes*, 5 4: 257–80.

Travis, Charles (1985), 'On What is Strictly Speaking True', *Canadian Journal of Philosophy*, 15 2: 187–229.

—— (1996), 'Meaning's Role in Truth', *Mind*, 100: 451–66.

—— (1997), 'Pragmatics', in B. Hale and C. Wright (eds.), *A Companion to the Philosophy of Language* (Oxford: Basil Blackwell), 87–107.

Varley, Rosemary (1998), 'Aphasic Language, Aphasic Thought: An Investigation of Propositional Thinking in A-Propositional Aphasic', in P. Carruthers and J. Boucher (eds.), *Language and Thought: Interdisciplinary Themes* (Cambridge: Cambridge University Press), 128–45.

Williams, Edwin (1977), 'Discourse and Logical Form', *Linguistic Inquiry*, 8 1: 101–39.

Wilson, Peter (2000), *Mind the Gap* (Harlow: Pearson Education).

Yanofsky, Nancy (1978), 'NP Utterances', in D. Farkas, W. Jacobsen, and K. Todrys (eds.), *Papers from the Fourteenth Regional Meeting: Chicago Linguistics Society* (Chicago: Chicago Linguistics Society), 491–502.

Zribi-Hertz, Anne (1989), 'Anaphor Binding and Narrative Point of View: English Reflexive Pronouns in Sentence and Discourse', *Language*, 65: 695–727.

INDEX